THE COMPLETE ROMAN DRAMA

THE RANDOM HOUSE
Lifetime Library

THE
Complete Roman Drama

ALL THE EXTANT COMEDIES OF PLAUTUS AND

TERENCE, AND THE TRAGEDIES OF SENECA,

IN A VARIETY OF TRANSLATIONS

EDITED, AND WITH AN INTRODUCTION, BY

GEORGE E. DUCKWORTH

Associate Professor of Classics, Princeton University

IN TWO VOLUMES

VOLUME ONE

RANDOM HOUSE . NEW YORK

ACKNOWLEDGMENTS

FOR PERMISSION to reprint copyrighted translations in these volumes, the editor wishes to make the following acknowledgments:

To Samuel French for Barrett H. Clark's translation of the *Phormio*, copyright, 1915, by Samuel French.

To Hamilton College and Cleveland K. Chase for the translation of *The Rope*.

PREFACE

THE PURPOSE of the present publication is to give in English translation all the extant plays of ancient Rome, plays which are extremely important not only for their intrinsic value as comedies and tragedies, but also for the wide influence that they have exerted upon European drama and particularly the drama of the sixteenth and seventeenth centuries. The book is thus a companion volume to *The Complete Greek Drama*, edited by Whitney J. Oates and Eugene O'Neill, Jr., and the two works together present all the plays which have survived from classical antiquity.

I have endeavoured to select translations that are both accurate and readable. It proved impossible, however, to find satisfactory versions of many of Plautus' plays, for the only complete modern translation of his comedies, that by Paul Nixon in the Loeb Classical Library, was not available. The nineteenth century rendering by H. T. Riley was unsuitable on every count: it was based upon an antiquated text, was filled with archaisms, and was too closely transliterated to be read as drama. Good versions were therefore at my disposal for only seven of Plautus' comedies. New translations of the remaining thirteen plays have been made expressly for *The Complete Roman Drama* and are now published for the first time. I have undertaken eight of these translations, three were prepared by Dr. Charles T. Murphy, one by John R. Workman, and one by Edward C. Weist and Richard W. Hyde, who made a new version of *The Twin Menaechmi* to replace their 1930 rendering of the same play. The new translations, with the exception of that of the *Epidicus*, were made from the Oxford text edited by W. M. Lindsay, the most accessible of the complete editions of Plautus. For the *Epidicus* I have used the more recent text of my own edition. Corrections and revisions in the other versions have been based upon Lindsay's edition. The translations by Sir Robert Allison and by Edward H. Sugden are metrical; those by Sugden attempt to reproduce the changing meters of the Latin original as closely as is possible in English verse. All other translations of Plautus are in prose, with the exception of *The Twin Menaechmi* which in its mixture of prose and verse seeks to give the effect of the lyrical songs, or *cantica*, of the original.

The translations of the comedies of Terence are in prose. I have cor-

vii

rected and revised the anonymous version of 1900, using for this purpose the Oxford text of Terence, edited by R. Kauer and W. M. Lindsay. A few passages, omitted by the translator, have been added to Barrett H. Clark's version of Terence's *Phormio*. The nature and content of Seneca's tragedies are such that for this dramatist verse translations seemed far more suitable. Only minor modifications (based upon the Latin text by R. Peiper and G. Richter) have been introduced into these versions, and reference is made to such corrections in the notes. The *Querolus*, a late Roman comedy which I have translated and added in an Appendix, appears here for the first time in English.

In the editing of the plays a certain degree of uniformity has seemed desirable. The conventional divisions into Acts and Scenes have been followed, although the Latin manuscripts indicate only the scene divisions. The manuscripts contain no stage directions, but a few have been added to clarify the action. In most instances such directions may reasonably be inferred from the text itself.

The General Introduction presents a brief account of the origins and development of Roman drama, as an aid to understanding the comedies of Plautus and Terence and the tragedies of Seneca, and indicates the main lines of their later influence. Accompanying each play is a brief introduction, which considers the outstanding features of the play and its relation to other works by the same dramatist. Each play is followed by notes, which are designed to explain historical and mythological references and to indicate certain structural or textual difficulties. The Glossary, it is hoped, will be of particular value in connection with Seneca's tragedies which abound in mythological allusions.

I wish to thank Professors A. C. Johnson, F. R. B. Godolphin, W. J. Oates, K. M. Abbott, N. T. Pratt, Jr., S. D. Atkins, E. L. Hubler, E. B. O. Borgerhoff, and Dr. C. T. Murphy for their valuable assistance in the preparation of this book. I owe an especial debt of thanks to Professor Oates, who kindly read and criticised the General Introduction and the special introductions to the plays, and to Dr. Murphy, who translated Plautus' *The Merchant, The Girl from Persia,* and the *Pseudolus,* and also wrote the notes to these three plays. Thanks are due also to Mr. Workman for his rendering of the *Stichus,* and to Messrs. Weist and Hyde for their new version of *The Twin Menaechmi.*

I am deeply indebted to Random House and particularly to Mr. Saxe Commins for their kind and helpful cooperation in making available to English readers the comedies and tragedies of ancient Rome.

G. E. D.

Princeton University
March 1, 1942

CONTENTS · VOLUME I

COMEDIES

CONTENTS · VOLUME II

COMEDIES

TRAGEDIES

APPENDIX

GENERAL INTRODUCTION

DRAMA is one of the most universal forms of human expression. Each age has its own stage conventions, its own theories of dramatic technique, but the basic themes of great tragedy and great comedy remain unchanged, for they deal with human nature and with life. A modern theatre-goer finds amusement in plots of mistaken identity and comic misunderstandings, in trickery and deception, in the laughable and ridiculous plight of young lovers. Such themes gave equal enjoyment to spectators in Elizabethan England, in republican Rome, in ancient Athens. Or again, when a modern dramatist portrays conflicts between persons or principles, conflicts which often can be brought to an end only by murder or suicide, he is presenting in new guise the basic material of tragedy that was so effective in the hands of Shakespeare or Sophocles. Such plots are ever new and yet are as old as drama itself.

The comedies and tragedies of Rome occupy an intermediate position in the long tradition of the stage. Later than the Greek drama and strongly influenced by it, Roman drama served as a direct model for European drama of the sixteenth and seventeenth centuries. Molière, Corneille and Racine, Marlowe, Ben Jonson and Shakespeare—the lordliest names in the dramatic history of France and England—take their place among the many playwrights who owe a great debt to the Romans. To give an adequate understanding of the nature of this indebtedness, it will be necessary to evaluate the achievements of Plautus and Terence in comedy and of Seneca in tragedy. Each dramatist composed plays which were adapted from Greek originals, but each stamped his work with his own originality and genius. It would be misleading to isolate Plautus and Terence from the dramatic activity of which they were a part, and many features of Plautus' comedies are best explained by the influence of earlier Italian forms of popular farce. For this reason the Introduction presents a brief survey of the origins and development of drama at Rome before giving an analysis of the nature and content of Roman comedy. Seneca, writing in the first century A.D., falls outside the main period of Roman drama. Since the works of the earlier, and perhaps greater, writers of tragedy did not survive, it was to him that dramatists of the Renaissance turned for inspiration. Seneca's greatness, which was largely thrust upon him by circumstance, as F. L. Lucas aptly states, will be treated in the closing section of the Introduction.

I

ROME had no real literature in the early centuries of its existence, for the Romans were busily engaged in consolidating their position as the ruling people of the Italian peninsula and had little time for the development of literary forms. In the third century B.C. they came into closer contact with the Greeks of southern Italy and Sicily and realised how inadequate had been their own cultural growth. At the close of the First Punic War there came a demand for better education and amusement; this provided the necessary stimulus to literature, and it was but natural that the Romans turned to the fully developed Greek epic and drama as models. Roman literature traditionally begins in the year 240 B.C., when Livius Andronicus, said to be a Greek slave, but more probably a Greek actor and tutor in the family of Marcus Livius Salinator, adapted both a Greek tragedy and a Greek comedy for production in Latin. It was Livius also who translated Homer's *Odyssey* into Latin for use as a textbook in schools.

Little is known about Roman literary endeavours prior to 240 B.C., but there is considerable evidence that various rudimentary forms of drama had existed for more than a century in and about Rome. The most complete account of these early forms is given by the historian Livy,[1] who describes the various stages of the development as follows: (1) An Etruscan dance to the music of the flute was introduced at Rome during a plague in 364 B.C. as one means of appeasing the wrath of the gods. (2) This dance was taken over by young citizens who added gesticulation and rough dialogue. The name *histriones* was given to the actors, since the Etruscan word for dancer was *ister*. These productions, containing repartee and impromptu verse, are said by Livy to be similar to the Fescennine verses. (3) A more elaborate performance followed, a kind of musical medley, to which Livy applies the term *satura*, although it is exceedingly doubtful if the word was ever so used in the earlier period. This medley of song, dance, and dialogue had no real plot and was easily displaced by (4) plays with a plot (*argumentum*) which were introduced by Livius Andronicus. Livy fails to mention that these were Greek plays that were translated and adapted for the Roman stage. (5) The production of such plays was left to professional actors, while the Roman amateurs returned to the more primitive songs and improvised jests, which they presented as *exodia,* or afterpieces, accom-

[1] VII, 2; cf. Valerius Maximus, II, 4, 4; Horace, *Epistles*, II, 1, 139-163.

panying the *fabula Atellana,* a type of comedy that had been developed by the Oscans in Campania.

There has been considerable criticism of Livy's account by scholars who believe that it combines guesswork with knowledge and that it parallels too closely Aristotle's statements concerning the origin of Greek comedy. To Livy and his contemporaries of the Augustan Age there may well have been a dearth of available material on the early history of the drama at Rome. There seems little doubt, however, that Livy presents in broad outline a fairly true picture of the early period. We may safely assume that native Italian dramatic forms existed before 240 B.C., and that these were characterised by song, dance, gesticulation, and crude and obscene jokes. They were far inferior to the imported Greek plays, but did not die out. Our information concerning these early productions is slight and is derived in part by inference from the later, more literary plays of the same type, of which scattered fragments have survived. It is probable that their essential nature remained unchanged, but that the earlier types were far cruder.

The Fescennine verses, probably named for a town in Etruria, were improvised, responsive, and jesting; they were associated particularly with rural festivals and weddings. If accompanied by dramatic gestures, as seems most probable, they may well have contained a germ of real drama. The development of such a form into a more elaborate medley of song and dance would be a natural step for the Romans to take. The two more important forms of early popular drama were the *fabula Atellana* and the mime; these had a long literary history far down into the Roman Empire and retained their popularity long after the more artistic Roman comedy had died out. The *Atellana,* named for Atella, a town in Campania, was originally an Oscan production and was taken over by the Latins at an early date. The plays were short, probably about three hundred verses, and were acted by stock characters who wore masks. The characters, whose roles were predetermined, were Maccus, the stupid clown, Bucco, the glutton or braggart, Pappus, the foolish old man, and Dossennus, the hunchback and trickster.[2] The scene was usually the country or small town, and the plays dealt with farcical situations which included trickery and obscenity. They have often been likened to the Italian Pulcinello comedy and to Punch and Judy shows. The Latin mime (if we can judge from the titles of the plays in the later, more literary period) was not unlike the *Atellana* in

---

[2] Cf. however W. Beare, "The Italian Origins of Latin Drama," *Hermathena,* LIV (1939), pp. 46 ff. Beare expresses grave doubts concerning the usual description of Dossennus.

subject matter. There were, however, no fixed characters, no masks, and far more music and dancing. These plays were at first chiefly monologues, with one or more subordinate characters; they presented a simple farcical situation and were characterised especially by impersonation and lively gesticulation.

Even these early dramatic forms could not be called purely Italian, for Greek popular farces and mimes had long existed in Sicily and southern Italy. There can be little doubt that the Italian mime was strongly influenced by the older and more artistic Greek mime. Another type of Greek farce, the *phlyax,* had been developed by Rhinthon of Tarentum in the early third century and may well have had some degree of influence upon the *fabula Atellana.* All these forms of popular drama had much in common: they dealt with broadly humorous situations, preferred a slap-stick plot, and were noted for their liveliness, irrelevance, and indecency.[3] The elements of song and dance were prominent.

When Livius Andronicus in 240 B.C. adapted to the Roman stage both a Greek comedy and a Greek tragedy, he brought to the Romans a more highly polished drama than anything that they had known up to that time. Both tragedy and comedy in Greece had reached a peak of excellence in the fifth century B.C. The tragedies of Aeschylus, Sophocles, and Euripides, which had presented in powerful dramatic form the great legends of Greek mythology, were translated or adapted by Livius and his successors. Euripides was in general preferred as a model, doubtless because of his greater simplicity, his freedom in handling plot, and his interest in human psychology. In the realm of comedy, however, the Roman playwrights did not go back to the fifth century. The plays of Aristophanes, for all their brilliant fantasy and sparkling humour, were far less suitable than fifth century tragedy for purposes of imitation. The political, literary, and philosophical satire of Aristophanes would have had little appeal to a Roman audience. The Latin dramatists chose as their models the Greek New Comedy; these plays of the late fourth and early third century were the current Greek drama of the time, and because of their cosmopolitan nature could be easily reworked. Dealing with universal human relations, they required comparatively few alterations to be made intelligible to the Roman spectators. Thus it was that the *fabula crepidata,* or tragedy based on Greek themes, went back for its inspiration to the great tragic dramatists of the fifth century, while the *fabula palliata,* or comedy in Greek dress, was based on the later plays of Diphilus, Philemon, Menander, and their contemporaries.

---

[3] For a fuller treatment of the subject, the reader may be referred to A. M. G. Little, "Plautus and Popular Drama," *Harvard Studies in Classical Philology,* XLIX (1938), pp. 209 ff.

The hundred years which follow the introduction of Greek plays may well be called the Golden Age of Roman Drama. Not only did numerous writers rework the Greek masterpieces, but they composed plays that were thoroughly Roman in content. Although in most instances the plays are known only by title or at best by a few scattered fragments, occasionally passages have survived of sufficient length to give a more adequate idea of the language and style of the different poets.

Among the tragedies written by Livius Andronicus were several on the story of the Trojan cycle: *Achilles, Ajax, The Trojan Horse, Aegisthus.* Other well-attested titles are *Danae, Ino, Tereus.* Unfortunately, little is known about his comedies. Cicero considered his plays as hardly worth a second reading,[4] but Cicero was doubtless judging him by the standard of later attainment in drama. In any case, Livius deserves great credit as a pioneer, as the first to present in Latin the types of Greek drama which were destined to flourish on the Roman stage for more than a century.

Gnaeus Naevius (*c.*270-*c.*201 B.C.), like his predecessor, wrote both tragedy and comedy, and composed an epic on the First Punic War, in which he himself had taken part. Many of his tragedies dealt with the Trojan War, e.g. *The Departure of Hector, Iphigenia, The Trojan Horse.* Naevius was apparently far more interested in comedy than tragedy, for the titles of thirty-four comedies are known, as against seven tragedies. Among the comic titles are *The Soothsayer, The Charcoal-Woman, The Flatterer, The Quadruplets, The Demented Ones, The Girl from Tarentum.* A fragment in trochaics from the last-named play reveals a certain liveliness and charm, in spite of its prosaic quality:

"Like a dancer in a chorus, she gives herself to each in turn,
  Nodding here and winking there, embracing this one, loving that one,
  Giving now her hand to one while touching another with her foot,
  Giving a ring for one to gaze on, enticing others with her lips,
  Singing with one, and at the moment beckoning coyly to another."

The scene of *The Soothsayer* was evidently laid in Italy, and this implies that Naevius originated the *fabula togata,* a type of comedy in which the characters and scenes were Latin. In the *fabula palliata,* both the Greek setting and the Greek characters were retained. Naevius' originality and his strong national feeling led him also to compose Roman historical plays. *The Nurture of Romulus and Remus* dealt with

---

[4] *Brutus,* 71. Horace (*Epistles* II, 1, 69 ff.) states that the poetry of Livius was taught in school in his own day. This doubtless refers to Livius' translation of the *Odyssey.*

the legendary beginnings of Rome, and the *Clastidium* described the
victory of Marcellus, consul in 222 B.C., over the Insubrian chief
Virdumarus. To Naevius therefore must be ascribed the invention of
the Roman historical drama, the *fabula praetexta*.[5] Naevius was a writer
of ability, and in both poetic expression and dramatic power advanced
far beyond his predecessor. He introduced political allusions into his
plays, and his outspoken criticism of men in high position led to his
imprisonment and eventual exile.

After Naevius the Roman dramatists devoted themselves either to
tragedy or to comedy, seldom to both. The next, and perhaps the greatest, tragic poet of this period was Quintus Ennius (239-169 B.C.). His
tragedies are represented by fragments of twenty plays, totalling about
four hundred lines. Among his plays were *Achilles, Ajax, Alexander,
Andromache Captive, Andromeda, The Ransoming of Hector, Iphigenia,
Medea, Telamon,* and *Thyestes*. Again it will be noted that many of the
titles refer to famous characters of the Trojan cycle. The interest of the
Romans in the legend of Aeneas which linked together the Trojans and
the Latins at an early date undoubtedly accounts for the emphasis upon
Troy in the tragedy of this period. An innovator in both metre and
language, Ennius displayed an ease of style and a literary power which
Livius and Naevius had never attained. He was the most versatile of
the early Latin poets; although few comedies appear under his name,
he wrote not only tragedies, but also historical drama, satires, epigrams,
and, most important of all, a great national epic, the *Annals*. For this
he used the dactylic hexameter, the traditional metre of Greek epic
poetry, instead of the primitive Saturnian metre, which had been employed by Livius and Naevius. In tragedy also his use of Greek metres
established the forms which later dramatists followed. Ennius' influence
upon all fields of Latin poetry was enormous. In the realm of epic poetry
he was a precursor of Vergil. The value of his tragedies has been well
summarised by J. W. Duff: "His immediate influence contributed to
civilise the nation. It was his to introduce a flood of Greek ideas—the
wide humanity and critical attitude of Euripides, so appropriate to a
people whose destiny now called them from circumscribed views to a
tolerant cosmopolitanism."

Marcus Pacuvius (*c.*220-*c.*130 B.C.), the nephew of Ennius, was a
painter as well as a tragic poet, and in spite of a long life wrote comparatively few dramas. The titles of only fourteen plays are known, one
of which, *Paulus,* was an historical drama. The other tragedies were
modelled upon Greek originals, mostly by Sophocles and Euripides, and

---

[5] Of the Roman historical drama only one play has survived, the *Octavia*, composed in the first century A.D. and ascribed to Seneca.

many of them dealt with more recondite mythological stories, e.g. *Chryses, Antiopa, Periboea, Iliona, Atalanta.* One of his longer fragments, describing in trochaics a storm at sea, is translated by Duff as follows:

"Happy when their fleet left harbour, they could watch the fish at play,
  They were never weary watching, though they watched the livelong day.
  Meanwhile when it turned to sundown, rough and rougher grew the
    main,
  Darkness doubled, blinding blackness came with night and clouds of
    rain,
  Flame flashed out athwart the welkin, thunder made the heavens rock,
  Hail, with plenteous sleet commingled, sudden fell with headlong
    shock.
  Everywhere the gales broke prison, cruel whirling winds arose,
  And the ocean boiled in fury. . . ."

Among ancient critics Pacuvius had a reputation for learning and was noted for his careful versification and tragic diction, although the latter was marred by occasional awkwardness and obscurity.

Lucius Accius (170-*c*.86 B.C.), although a grammarian and a literary critic, was much more prolific as a writer of tragedy than Pacuvius. Fragments of more than forty plays reveal an amazing versatility. Titles such as *Philoctetes, Hecuba, The Trojan Women, Astyanax, Atreus, Aegisthus, Clytemnestra, Antigona, The Phoenissae, Alcestis, The Bacchae, Prometheus,* and *Medea* recall the great tragedies of fifth century Athens dealing with the Trojan War, the House of Atreus, the Theban cycle, and other familiar legends. He wrote also two *fabulae praetextae, Brutus,* and *Decius* or *Aeneadae.* As a dramatist Accius was famed for his elevated tone and for his rhetorical skill.

Ancient critics disagreed in their estimates of the early Roman writers of tragedy. Velleius Paterculus[6] apparently considered Accius to be Rome's greatest tragic poet, while Cicero[7] gave the palm to Pacuvius. Although both poets undoubtedly were superior to Ennius in tragic diction and style, an examination of the fragments of the three playwrights reveals that in sheer poetic power Ennius surpassed both his successors. Of all the tragic writers of the period, the loss of his plays is perhaps most to be regretted. That all three dramatists gave to their adaptations from the Greek a strong Roman flavour is evident from the fragments, which, as W. Y. Sellar has pointed out, "are expressed not with the subtlety and reflective genius of Greece, but in the plain and

---

[6] I, xvii, 1.
[7] *De optimo genere oratorum,* 1.

straightforward tones of the Roman Republic." Early Roman tragedy, like Roman oratory, was characterised by great moral weight and dignity, and by deep and impassioned feeling.

With Accius, the first period of tragedy comes to an end. The plays of these dramatists continued to be performed to the end of the Republic, and new tragedies were written, such as Varius' *Thyestes* and Ovid's *Medea* in the Augustan Age. But after Accius there are no great names in tragedy until we come to Seneca, whose plays will be considered later.

Just as Roman tragedy is represented in the early period by three great dramatists, Ennius, Pacuvius, and Accius, so Roman comedy after Naevius flourished in the hands of a trio of playwrights, Plautus, Caecilius, and Terence, who devoted themselves entirely to the writing of *fabulae palliatae*, plays that were based upon the Greek New Comedy. Titus Maccius Plautus (*c.*254-*c.*184 B.C.), an Umbrian from Sarsina, and a contemporary of Naevius and Ennius, was the most famous of the writers of Roman comedy. Tradition recounts numerous picturesque details of his life—how he made money by theatrical work, invested it in foreign trade, lost it and returned to Rome penniless where he began to write plays while working in a mill. Although the story has been rejected as fiction, at least in part, by modern students of ancient biographical method, Plautus' consummate knowledge of stagecraft and his obvious understanding of the different types of popular farce make it very likely that he had a long connection with the stage, possibly as an actor in Atellan farces,[8] before he turned to the writing of plays.

More than a hundred comedies were ascribed to Plautus in antiquity, and of this number twenty-one were accepted as genuine by all critics. Varro, the great scholar of the first century B.C., compiled the list of the twenty-one authentic plays and chose nineteen more which on the basis of style he considered Plautine. There are extant the twenty-one plays of the first list, or, to be more exact, twenty, for *The Travelling Bag* (*Vidularia*), the twenty-first play, has survived only in fragmentary form.

Plautus' successor in comedy was Caecilius Statius (*c.*219-*c.*166 B.C.), an Insubrian Gaul who was brought to Rome as a slave and later freed. Of his *palliatae* about forty titles and three hundred lines of fragments are in existence; several of the titles, e.g. *The Man from Ephesus, Hymnis, The Imbrians, The Shipmaster, The Necklace,* correspond to

---

[8] It is believed by many that he acted the part of Maccus, the clown. Named Titus Plautus, he was called also Maccus, which was adopted as a *nomen* under the form Maccius.

the titles of comedies by Menander. Caecilius is believed to have followed the plots of his originals with far greater fidelity than did
Plautus. But he did not always translate closely, as is shown by Aulus
Gellius,[9] a writer of the second century A.D., who quotes parallel passages from Menander's *The Necklace* and Caecilius' adaptation in order
to illustrate the inferiority of the Latin playwright. Caecilius was rated
above both Plautus and Terence by ancient critics. Theodor Mommsen
suggests that the reason for this may be "simply because he was more
regular than Plautus and more vigorous than Terence; notwithstanding
which he may very well have been far inferior to both." To what extent
Caecilius exerted an influence upon his younger contemporary, Terence,
is difficult to determine. The theory has recently been advanced that
Terence in his rather unusual handling of suspense was following in the
footsteps of Caecilius, but this can neither be proved nor disproved.

Publius Terentius Afer (*c.*195-159 B.C.) was born in Carthage, brought
to Rome at an early age, and manumitted. An intimate friend of Scipio
and his learned circle, Terence shared the interest of his friends in the
improvement and refinement of the Latin language. His six comedies,
based upon originals by Menander and Apollodorus, are all extant,
and breathe a spirit very different from that of Plautus' plays. Though
he lacks the vigour and robust humour of his great predecessor, his
plays are on a higher literary plane and reveal a more careful handling
of plot and character.

With Terence the important writers of the *palliata* come to an end.
Other playwrights of the century, such as Trabea, Atilius, Luscius
Lanuvinus, and Turpilius, are little more than names. The very perfection and refinement of Terence's comedies have been cited as a reason for
the decline in popularity of the comedy in Greek dress. The fact that
after Terence's death there was a revival of Plautine plays[10] would tend
to support this view. Another reason may lie in the desire of the Roman
audience for a more national comedy. Playwrights now turned to the
fabula togata, the comedy of Latin scenes and characters. This type of
drama, more national and realistic, had been developed by Naevius, but
did not become really popular until after Terence's death. The three
writers of the *togata* were Titinius, Quinctius Atta, and—the most
famous of the three—Afranius. The scene of the plays was laid in
country towns and the characters were taken from the middle or lower
class. In the latter case, the term tavern play (*fabula tabernaria*) was
sometimes given to the comedies. Little is known about their plots; the

---

[9] *Noctes Atticae,* II, xxiii.
[10] See the post-Plautine prologue of the *Casina.*

ancient commentator Donatus[11] states that in the *togata* the slave was
seldom portrayed as cleverer than his master. This is in striking contrast
to the usual situation in the *palliata,* and is probably to be explained by
the desire to maintain Roman *dignitas* and *gravitas.* More emphasis
was given to family roles and particularly to feminine characters. Among
the extant titles are *The Girl of Setium, The Ladies of Brundisium, The
Lady Lawyer, The Divorce, The Departure of the Recruit, The Blind
Man, Hot Springs, The Feast of the Crossroads.*

From the *togata,* which was probably far coarser than had been the
palliata in the hands of Caecilius and Terence, it was but a step to the
Atellana which rose to popularity in the early part of the first century
B.C. This old Atellan farce now received a more literary form in the
hands of two dramatists, Pomponius and Novius. The usual stock characters appear in many of the titles, e.g. *Pappus as a Farmer, Pappus'
Bride, Maccus as a Soldier, Maccus as a Maiden, Bucco the Adopted
Son, The Two Dossenni.* Other titles reveal an emphasis on country
life and humble circumstances: *The Yokel, The Vine-dressers, The
Fullers' Holiday, The Doctor, The Pregnant Girl.* Such titles recall those
of the *togata,* while some (*Andromacha, The Award of Arms*) indicate
that parodies of tragedy were occasionally written.

By the time of Julius Caesar the literary Atellan farces had lost their
popularity and been supplanted by the mime. As developed by writers
like Decimus Laberius and Publilius Syrus, the mime was more artistic
and respectable, and many of the titles (e.g. *The Pot of Gold, The
Flatterer, The Ghost, The Twins, The Fullers, Hot Springs*) sound like
plays of the *palliata* or the *togata.* But much of the appeal of the mime
doubtless resided in its unsavoury jokes and immoral situations. Female
parts, which in the more respectable comedy had been acted by men,
were now taken by women. The plays often dealt with intrigues in which
the stupid husband was regularly deceived by a faithless wife and her
lover. Although there was a temporary revival of the *Atellana* in the first
century A.D., it was the mime that persisted in the Roman theatre down
through the Empire, gradually developing more and more into a
pantomimus, or dumb-show—an inglorious ending for Roman comedy
which had reached so high a degree of artistic development in the days
of Plautus and Terence. The elements of the mimes and Atellan farces
survived through the Middle Ages and appeared again in the *commedia
dell' arte,* which, as Richard Garnett points out, "has pervaded the
theatres of Europe in the costume of harlequin, columbine, and panta-
loon."

---

[11] On Terence, *The Eunuch,* 12.

II

A MODERN READER of the comedies of Plautus and Terence must guard against thinking of the plays in terms of modern stage productions. Methods of staging plays in Rome were very unlike those of the theatre today and differed also, in many respects, from the way in which the great dramas of fifth century Athens were produced. To recreate imaginatively the Roman comedies as actual plays produced before an audience, it is necessary to understand both the nature of the theatre of the day and the stage conventions which the dramatist accepted as normal.

In the second century B.C. dramatic performances were given in connection with the Roman games, or *ludi*. These *ludi* were of several different kinds and consisted not only of the regular games given each year by the aediles but also of special games to celebrate a great victory, the dedication of a temple, or the funeral of a famous Roman.[12] The regular games, celebrated annually, combined both circus games (*ludi circenses*) and theatrical productions (*ludi scaenici*). Several days were devoted to *ludi scaenici* at the two festivals of Jupiter, the *ludi Romani* in September, and the *ludi plebeii* in November. Plays were presented also in July at the *ludi Apollinares* in honour of Apollo (first celebrated in 212 B.C.) and in April at the *ludi Megalenses* in honour of the Great Mother (from 194 B.C. on). Estimates concerning the number of days available for stage productions in 200 B.C. vary from five to eleven, but the number was gradually increased until in the Augustan Age more than forty days were devoted to *ludi scaenici*. Much of this increase undoubtedly occurred in the second century during the great period of drama. The historian Livy refers frequently to the *ludi Romani* and the *ludi plebeii* in his account of the Second Punic War, and makes numerous allusions to *instaurationes,* or repetitions of the games. The normal reason for such a repetition was a religious one, some impropriety in the observance of the festival that made it inacceptable to the god. The frequency of the repetitions—approximately two-thirds of the time—can hardly be explained entirely on religious grounds, and it is entirely possible that the popularity of the games may have been responsible for the number of repetitions. The festivals were often repeated three or four times, and in one instance, in 205 B.C., the *ludi plebeii* were performed an additional seven times. C. H. Buck, Jr. suggests that the popularity of one of

---

[12] The reader may be referred to Lily Ross Taylor, "The Opportunities for Dramatic Performances in the Time of Plautus and Terence," *Transactions American Philological Association*, LXVIII (1937), pp. 284-304. See also C. H. Buck, Jr., *A Chronology of the Plays of Plautus* (Baltimore, 1940), pp. 10-18.

Plautus' most amusing comedies, *The Braggart Warrior,* caused the unprecedented number of *instaurationes* on that occasion.

The numerous annual festivals with their repeated performances, and the additional games—funeral games, victory games, and the like—provided the Roman theatre-goer with a large number of occasions on which he could view stage productions—a far larger number, incidentally, than was available to an Athenian audience in the days of Aeschylus, Sophocles, Euripides, and Aristophanes. Yet there were, surprisingly enough, no permanent theatres at Rome in the second century B.C.[13] Stone theatres with stone seats had long existed in the Greek world, but the Roman audiences in the time of Plautus and Terence watched plays that were acted on a long wooden stage constructed outdoors merely for the occasion. It was the theory of nineteenth century scholars that no seats were available and that the spectators stood around the stage in a noisy jostling throng. All references in Plautus' plays to seated audiences were rejected as post-Plautine additions. Many recent critics regard this procedure as too arbitrary, and conclude that the plays of Plautus were written for presentation before a seated audience.[14] Such benches or scaffolding as were erected for the spectators would also be temporary structures of wood.

The stage was very long and narrow, and was regularly looked upon as a city street. The stage buildings in the background represented two or three city houses, with doors opening on the street. Occasionally only one house was needed. The one exception to the usual setting among the extant comedies is Plautus' *The Rope,* where the stage represents a strip of seacoast with a cottage and a temple in the background. It is usually believed that a narrow street, or *angiportum,* sometimes ran back between the two houses at right angles to the main street. Such an opening would provide a convenient place from which a character could overhear an important conversation, and would also afford an extra way to enter or leave the stage. The extent to which the *angiportum* was used for these purposes cannot be clearly determined; the usual means of entrance and exit were the side-entrances at the two ends of the stage and the doors of the houses opening on the stage. The exit to the left of the spectators led to the harbour and foreign parts, that on the spectators' right to the forum or the country. If the *angiportum* was

---

[13] It was not until 55 B.C. that the first permanent stone theatre was built in Rome, the theatre of Pompey. Many smaller towns in Italy, however, had permanent theatres at an earlier date.

[14] See W. Beare, "Seats in the Greek and Roman Theatres," *Classical Review,* LIII (1939), pp. 51-55.

used, it afforded an additional means of departure to the forum or to the country.[15]

Unfortunately, our information is very slight concerning the garb of the actors who presented the comedies of Plautus and Terence on the stage. To scattered allusions in the plays themselves have been added statements by Roman writers of a later date and the evidence of the illustrated manuscripts of Terence, also dated centuries after the time of the dramatist.[16] The resultant picture is far from clear, although there can be no doubt that the actors wore Greek dress. The *pallium* was the usual outer garment, as is implied by the term *fabula palliata,* and was worn over a close-fitting, long-sleeved tunic by both young and old men. The *pallium* of the old men was white, that of the younger men dark-red or purple. Slaves wore merely tunics, and in the Terentian miniatures are portrayed as having a scarf around their neck, which they frequently grasp with the left hand. This scarf was apparently a conventionalised form of the *pallium collectum,* the cloak gathered up to make it possible for the slave to hurry with his errands or to run across the stage, as he so often does in the plays of Plautus. The female roles were played by male actors who wore long, flowing robes over long-sleeved undergarments. Black wigs were worn by the youthful characters, white by the aged, while the slaves usually, if not always, had red wigs.

It is difficult to determine if the actors of the *palliata* had masks in the days of Plautus and Terence. The use of masks would facilitate the doubling of roles and make more plausible the presence on the stage of twin brothers, as in Plautus' *The Twin Menaechmi,* or of two pairs of doubles, as in his *Amphitryon.* The ancient references to the use of masks in early Roman times are confusing and ambiguous. There is no doubt that masks were worn in the Roman theatre in the first century B.C., and the Greek comedies on which the *palliatae* were modelled were performed by masked actors. Yet the orthodox view has long been that the actors of the comedies of Plautus and Terence wore no masks, and that masks were first introduced shortly after Terence's death. The weaknesses of this theory have been pointed out by recent writers[17] who

[15] These are the conclusions of Eleanor F. Rambo, "The Significance of the Wing-Entrances in Roman Comedy," *Classical Philology,* X (1915), pp. 411-431. Mary Johnston, *Exits and Entrances in Roman Comedy* (Geneva, N. Y., 1933) believes that the side-entrance on the spectators' left was used not only by characters coming from abroad but also by those from the country.

[16] The material is presented fully by Catharine Saunders, *Costume in Roman Comedy* (New York, 1909), to whom I am indebted for many points.

[17] A. S. F. Gow, "On the Use of Masks in Roman Comedy," *Journal of Roman Studies,* II (1912), pp. 65-77; W. Beare, "Masks on the Roman Stage," *Classical Quarterly,* XXXIII (1939), pp. 139-146.

conclude that the evidence favours the early use of masks and believe it very possible that the Romans took over masks as well as costumes directly from the Greek models.

As the stage setting remained unchanged throughout the play, it seems highly probable that the action was for the most part continuous. There were no divisions into acts,[18] but short pauses in the action may have been filled by simple music provided by a flute player. In Greek comedy the elaborate choruses of Aristophanes had been given up; the plays of the Greek New Comedy contained choral interludes which were un-related to the action of the plays. Roman comedy dispensed with these choruses entirely, although traces of the Greek chorus are believed to exist in such a song as that of the Fishermen in Plautus' *The Rope*.

In spite of the omission of the choral song, the comic playwrights made great use of lyrical metres. Roman comedies may be divided metrically into two parts—*diverbia,* spoken scenes written in a six-foot iambic line and used for soliloquy or dialogue without musical accompaniment, and *cantica,* scenes in more elaborate and melodious measures which were recited or sung to the accompaniment of music. The recited scenes were the *cantica* proper and were written in longer iambic or trochaic lines; the lyrical *cantica* were sung, either by a single person (e.g. Philolaches' monody in Plautus' *The Haunted House,* Act One, Scene II) or by two or more persons (as in Act One, Scene IV of the same play). The songs were often accompanied by dancing, as in the closing scenes of the *Stichus*.

The element of song and dance, which is especially prominent in the plays of Plautus, does not appear in the Roman comedies in the form of interludes, but is an integral part of the action. In many instances there appears to be little difference between *diverbia* and *cantica* except the metrical form in which the dialogue is composed. The metrical struc-ture of many of Plautus' comedies is exceedingly intricate, and in general there seems to be a steady progression from more simple metres in the plays believed to be his earliest (*The Comedy of Asses, The Braggart Warrior*) to the latest plays (*Casina* and *The Girl from Persia*), where more complicated lyric rhythms are employed. The relative frequency of lyric has been used to some extent as a means of determining the approximate chronological order of the comedies, for it is believed that

---

[18] The act-divisions in modern editions of Plautus were introduced into the text in the Renaissance in an attempt to apply to Roman comedy the five-act rule which Horace later assumed to be normal. These divisions were made, wherever possible, at points in the plays where pauses in the action were accompanied by empty stages. Such pauses may often represent the places where in the Greek originals choral interludes had appeared. The divisions into scenes are ancient and regularly appear in the Mss. of Plautus and Terence.

Plautus at first followed the simple metrical structure of his Greek models, and then, as he began to adapt plays with ever increasing facility and freedom, composed more numerous lyrical portions to be sung by his actors. The fact that Terence, who brought to comedy a more Hellenic polish and refinement, failed to use the variety of metres found in Plautus and but rarely availed himself of lyric song strengthens the supposition that one of Plautus' original contributions to Roman comedy was the frequent introduction of song and dance into his plays.

The extent to which Plautus was indebted to earlier playwrights for his metrical form cannot be clearly established. We know little about the hundreds of Greek plays written in the time of Menander and his contemporaries, and it is entirely possible that many Greek playwrights may have employed a greater variety of metres than can be found in the fragmentary plays of Menander. It has been suggested also that Plautus may have been influenced by contemporary Greek songs of a less dramatic nature. The important problem, however, as Eduard Fraenkel points out, is not the source of the lyric element, but the reason which induced Plautus to replace the dialogue of the original by song. He suggests that both Livius and Naevius in their tragedies and comedies had introduced such *cantica* and that Plautus in comedy and Ennius in tragedy followed their predecessors. This explanation seems far from satisfactory, for it merely pushes back the problem to the very beginnings of formal Roman drama. The weaving together of song and dialogue into an unbroken unity may well have been an inheritance from the pre-literary Italian farces, which had combined song and dance and dialogue. These popular farces, as I have already shown, were not free from Greek influence at an early date, and may well go back ultimately to the beginnings of comedy in Greece. In one sense, therefore, the polymetry of Aristophanes is not entirely unrelated to the lyrical structure of Plautus. Although the later Greek comedy simplified the metres as it lessened the importance of the choral element, Plautus reversed the process and, by adding to his Greek models the feature of song and dance which he may have found in the earlier Italian popular plays, he brought to the Roman audiences a combination of comedy and musical farce. The great popularity that Plautus attained in his own day is undoubtedly due in part to the musical element which is so firmly embedded in the structure of his later plays.

Many of the stage conventions of Roman comedy, conventions which at first seem strange to the modern reader, are the direct outcome of ancient methods of staging. When the scenery represents a street and remains unchanged throughout the play, the action must necessarily take place in front of the homes of the main characters. Great ingenuity was demanded of the playwright to make the entrances and exits of the characters plausible. For this reason, characters usually tell where they are going when they leave the stage, and, similarly, their entering speeches regularly inform the audience of the reason for their appearance. When a character departs to the forum or to the harbour, he must return from the same place. A character who has gone to the forum on business, for instance, should not appear suddenly in one of the house-doors on the stage unless he makes clear the reason for his presence there; that is, he may have returned from the forum and entered the house through a rear door. In plays where there are two characters of like appearance, special pains must be taken by the playwright to avoid confusion on the part of the spectators. Plautus' *The Twin Menaechmi* is an excellent illustration of the manner in which the ancient dramatist could keep the identity of two similar characters clear by the careful motivation of their entrances and exits.

The spectators had no program and did not know the identity of the characters when they first appeared. Many of the actors introduce themselves on their first entrance. The length of the stage made it possible to see an approaching actor before he was within speaking distance. Frequently a person says: "Look, there he comes up the street, the very man I'm looking for"—and the identity of the newcomer is immediately established. A similar way of introducing a character is the frequent remark: "Hush! The door of my neighbour's house is creaking. There he comes out now." Such references to the door, the *ostium*, which Gilbert Norwood rather facetiously considers "a leading Plautine character," are perhaps awkward, but they result from the playwright's desire for clarity, and are found in Menander and Terence as well as in Plautus. Such devices are a part of ancient comic technique.

Asides and soliloquies are numerous. Soliloquies often give the thoughts and sentiments which are appropriate to the occasion and may be dramatically justifiable. Others, introduced primarily for the purpose of giving information to the spectators, exceed the bounds of dramatic probability. Frequently the opening scene is a monologue in which either the prologue or one of the characters gives the expository material necessary for the understanding of the situation. To avoid the unreality of long undramatic monologues, the playwright sometimes avails himself of protatic characters, who are brought on the stage for the express purpose of making exposition by dialogue possible, and who disappear from the action when they have served their purpose. If the protatic character is introduced merely to provide a listener, as usually in Terence, the effect is more artificial than in such plays as Plautus' *The Braggart Warrior* and *The Haunted House,* where Artotrogus and

Grumio make admirable foils for the leading personages. The best form of exposition is the normal dialogue between two main characters in which the pertinent facts are revealed in a natural way (e.g. Plautus' *Curculio* and *Pseudolus,* Terence's *The Self-Tormentor*).

A special type of soliloquy is often uttered by a slave who hurries on the stage breathless with important news. He delivers a long monologue which is strikingly inconsistent with his haste, and frequently bustles about, failing to see the very person he is so eager to meet. Such "running slaves" provide considerable amusement, and even when they meet the desired character there is often much buffoonery and delay before the important message is finally delivered. The length of the Roman stage makes possible the combination of haste and volubility that is characteristic of these scenes, and it has been suggested also that the slave acted his part in a burlesque fashion, pretending to run but getting nowhere, in treadmill style.

Soliloquies on important matters are sometimes delivered by an actor when other characters are on the stage to overhear it. This seems dramatically unsound, as does the planning of trickery by characters who fail to take precautions against being overheard. These features of comic technique are sometimes called "evasions of dramatic method," but are rather conventions imposed by ancient theatrical conditions. The lack of verisimilitude, furthermore, is perhaps less than many modern critics maintain. Although the characters of the plays calmly discuss their most private affairs upon the public street, it must be remembered that men in Athens and in Rome spent much of their time out of doors, and that, in some respects, the street offered them more privacy for discussion than was afforded by their houses, where a remark in any room could be heard in almost any other room.[19] The length of the stage rendered possible conversations by two pairs of characters, with one pair oblivious of the presence of the other (e.g. *The Carthaginian,* Act One, Scene II). Likewise, a single character frequently listens to a conversation without being seen and comments on what he has heard in humorous asides to the audience (cf. *The Haunted House,* Act One, Scene III).

The ancient playwright was limited by the nature of the stage to the presentation of outdoor scenes. He could solve the difficulty by two means: by presenting on the stage scenes that would more naturally take place indoors, and by describing what had taken place off stage. The Roman comic writers used both methods. Banquet scenes and dressing scenes were enacted in front of the houses, but there was apparently no attempt to use mechanical devices such as a platform on wheels (the *eccyclema*) which had been employed in Athens in the fifth century B.C.

[19] Cf. Johnston, *op. cit.,* p. 17.

Care was taken to make the off-stage action clear to the spectators; where the characters had been and what they had done were set forth in detail by means of soliloquy or dialogue. Sometimes important features of the plot, such as the planning of a deception or a recognition scene between several main characters, take place indoors and are described later.

Any consideration of the content of Roman comedy must begin by stressing the fact that Plautus and Terence used both the plots and characters of Greek comedies. The degree of their dependence upon their models must remain a matter for scholarly conjecture, inasmuch as none of the originals has survived. We cannot assume, however, that the differences between Plautine and Terentian comedy are to be explained merely by the nature of the different Greek plays which each adapted. On the contrary, each playwright had his own conception of the nature of comedy and used the Greek material as a framework which could be moulded to suit his purposes. It is probable that Terence in the structure of his plots followed the Greek plays more closely. Yet he himself admits that he "contaminated" many Greek plays to produce a few Latin plays. *Contaminatio* is usually defined as the process of combining two or more Greek plays, or parts of plays, into one Latin play. Whether the original significance of the word was "spoiling" or "interweaving," the procedure implies considerable independence in the treatment of the Greek originals. Terence states that Naevius, Plautus, and Ennius had indulged in the same practice. Numerous attempts have been made to explain occasional inconsistencies and structural flaws in some of Plautus' plays (e.g. *The Braggart Warrior* and *The Carthaginian*) on the assumption that he worked together two Greek plays. These theories are impossible of proof and have been abandoned by many modern scholars. Some of the characteristics which are considered typically Plautine perhaps existed to some degree in the Greek originals; others he doubtless added from his own knowledge of what would provide the most effective comedy.

The plots of New Comedy on which Plautus and Terence drew for their material were somewhat stereotyped, but admitted of countless possibilities for variety of detail. An analysis of the extant Roman plays reveals that one of the most common themes is that of love and the unhappy complications that confront the youthful lover. Often a young Athenian is thwarted in his love affair because the object of his affection is in the power of a pimp (*leno*) who is about to sell her to a more wealthy rival, usually a soldier. The difficulty may be solved by a slave who aids his master by devising some ruse that will either raise the necessary money to purchase the girl, or will free the girl from the *leno* in some other manner. Or the girl may be discovered to be of Athenian birth, having been lost or kidnapped as a child. If the young man is in love with a respectable girl of humble circumstances, the course of his love may be blocked by his father's desire to have him marry a more wealthy and socially prominent maiden. Again the discovery of the real identity of the loved one will bring about a happy solution. If the youth is in love with a professional courtesan (*meretrix*), money is needed to procure her favours and some sort of trickery to raise the money becomes necessary. Often the young man's father is the butt of the deception. If we can judge from the fragmentary plays of Menander, the Greek poet worked especially with themes of mistaken identity and recognition and was less interested in plots of trickery. Terence seems to have followed him in this respect, whereas Plautus, drawing his material from a wider range of sources, reveals far greater variety in his plots. Amusing deceptions of every kind form a large part of his stock in trade. Often in plays in which mistaken identity and recognition appear, the main interest resides in the working out of some intrigue and in the amusing results which inevitably follow. When the deception is directed at a pimp or a soldier, it is invariably successful. If the slave aims his darts at his young master's father, he is found out sooner or later and is then in danger of serious punishment, unless the intercession of his young master or a friend saves him from disaster.

Lane Cooper says of the Greek New Comedy that it "must have been full of incidents turning upon both innocent mistakes and guileful deceptions with regard to identity." This well summarises the plots of Plautus and Terence, for most of the comedies may be classified as plays of mistaken identity (e.g. Plautus' *The Twin Menaechmi, The Rope,* Terence's *The Woman of Andros, The Mother-in-law*) or plays of guileful deception (e.g. Plautus' *The Comedy of Asses, The Braggart Warrior, Pseudolus*). In comedies of the first group the characters are primarily the sport of a waggish fortune, for it is the working of coincidence that is responsible for their difficulties; the complications in the plays of the second group result directly from the trickery and ingenuity of one or more characters. Sometimes the confusion of identity may be the outcome of deliberate intention, as in Plautus' *Amphitryon* and *The Captives.* In many plays deception and mistaken identity go hand in hand, and the recognition of the identity either supplements the trickery and helps to bring it to a successful conclusion (as in Plautus' *Curculio* and *The Carthaginian*) or it creates a dilemma and complicates the action still more (as in Terence's *The Self-Tormentor* and *Phormio*).

The analysis given above over-simplifies the subject-matter of Roman comedy. By no means can all the plays be classified as plays of mistaken identity, plays of deception, or a combination of the two. In several comedies the portrayal of characters or customs seems to be the main theme, and there is a direct relation between plot and character. In these plays the action is motivated by character rather than by coincidence or trickery. Chief among plays of this type are Plautus' *The Pot of Gold, Truculentus,* and Terence's *The Brothers.* Even in a play of deception such as *The Braggart Warrior* the plot hinges largely on the character of Pyrgopolinices, for his traits make it possible for the trickery to be effective. It should be stressed that, for all their basic similarities, there is an amazing variety to be found in the plots of the plays. This is especially true of Plautus, as will be evident from reading several of his better-known plays.[20]

The characters which appear most frequently in both Plautus and Terence are male roles—young men (*adulescentes*), old men (*senes*), and slaves (*servi*). The female parts, which were acted by men, include married women (*matronae*), maid servants (*ancillae*) and courtesans (*meretrices*). The seclusion of unmarried girls in Greek society accounts for the absence of young maidens from the action. Although they often have a prominent part in the plot, they are represented as being indoors. Girls who have been kidnapped in infancy and are rescued from shame by the timely discovery of their free birth frequently take part in the action, since they appear as courtesans in the power of a pimp. Other roles which are less numerous but equally important to the plot are soldiers, parasites, pimps, cooks, and bankers. It would be a mistake to consider the characters of Roman comedy as merely stock characters, for there is a great diversity among the characters in each class, and many instances of excellent character drawing may be found in both Plautus and Terence. Plautus often presents his characters in a ridiculous and grotesque manner; in spite of this, however, his gallery is extensive, and there is a wide gulf between characters of the same general type; Philematium has little in common with a gold-seeker like Phronesium, Stratophanes has few of the characteristics of the conceited Pyrgopolinices, and devoted servants like Tyndarus and Messenio are the very opposite of the deceitful slave as represented by Chrysalus, Epidicus, or Pseudolus. J. W. Duff correctly states that "those who read Plautus oftenest will find least sameness in him." Terence makes his characters more humane and more subtle. He portrays the same society, but in a far more amiable and sympathetic light. The old men are more reasonable, the slaves less deceitful, the courtesans more refined. The Terentian

---

[20] E.g. *Amphitryon, The Captives, The Pot of Gold, The Braggart Warrior, The Haunted House, The Rope.*

characters are perhaps truer to life, but lack the vigour and colour of Plautus' creations.

An attempt has been made in the foregoing paragraphs to describe the conventions of the *palliata* and the plots and characters which are found in the plays as a whole. That Plautus and Terence, working in the same general field, differed in their interests and their achievements has already been apparent. Plautus' work, characterised by a greater use of song and dance, presents a wider range of plot and character and at the same time places more stress on the grotesque and the ridiculous than does Terence. Several other differences in the dramatic qualities of the two playwrights must now be considered as a further aid to the understanding of their comedies.

In the structure of his plots Plautus was not infrequently guilty of careless workmanship. Many of his plays are loosely jointed and he is often indifferent whether all the threads of the action are carefully tied together at the end. He worked with the carelessness and spontaneity of a master of comic effect and introduced laughter-raising scenes wherever possible, even if they interfered with the action of the plot. The contradictions and irrelevancies in many of his plays, which have often been attributed to the process of joining together parts of several different Greek plays, are probably the outcome of the many changes he made to produce greater humour in plot, character, and dialogue. Terence, less interested in scenes of broad humour, devoted more attention to the structure of his plots. The result is greater mechanical perfection, but the better workmanship is secured at the price of energy and strength. The plots move more slowly and the action is in general far more serious. One of the most interesting features of Terentian workmanship is his use of the double plot; he weaves together the stories of two young men and their respective love affairs, and more or less successfully makes the solution of the two difficulties depend upon each other. Since the double plot appears in all Terence's comedies except *The Mother-in-law* but is scarcely ever used by Plautus, and since Terence handles the two plots with greater skill in his later plays, it seems highly probable that he himself developed this feature and in many cases altered the Greek originals to make his own comedies more intricate.

Both playwrights are successful in maintaining dramatic tension, but they do this by different methods. Terence used his prologues for literary purposes, for the defence of his position as a dramatist and for a criticism of his rivals, and could not set forth the expository material that Plautus presented in many of his prologues. As a result of this innovation, many of the pertinent facts of the Terentian plot were not revealed to the spectator until late in the action. To this extent the elements of suspense and surprise are vital factors in his comedies. Whether Terence's desire to keep the audience uncertain of the outcome was the main reason for his elimination of the expository prologue, as has been suggested, or merely a chance result of his treatment of the prologue cannot be determined. The statement is sometimes erroneously made that Plautus had no regard for suspense and that the prologue regularly disclosed the outcome of the plot to the audience. The prologues of Plautus, especially in plays of mistaken identity, reveal the basic facts of the situation; they give the audience the clue to the recognition, but very seldom do they give any real information about the action of the plot. Moreover, when the plot is concerned primarily with deception, there is either no prologue, or the prologue deals only with a secondary phase of the action. In almost no instance can the opening of a Plautine comedy be said to destroy suspense by revealing the details of the plot. In plays of trickery, the deception may be discussed or rehearsed before being carried out. But there are several devices which the playwright uses to heighten the tension and arouse the suspense of the audience. The intriguing slave is often portrayed as helpless in the face of difficulties and uncertain of his method of procedure; the slave may state that he has a plan in mind, but the nature of the trick is not divulged to the audience; again he may state that he has important information, but the news is not revealed to the audience until after considerable time has passed. This means of arousing suspense is particularly characteristic of the "running slave" in Plautus, where the ignorance and uncertainty of the spectators are intensified by the various comic devices which delay the slave's announcement.[21] Even when a trick is being carried out, there is often uncertainty as to the outcome, as in *The Braggart Warrior,* where the soldier's suspicions are almost aroused. Plautus thus combines a generous amount of exposition with scenes which deliberately create tension. The effect on the spectators is a combination of anticipation and uncertainty; in no case does he arouse such perplexity as does Terence in *The Mother-in-law,* where the secret is not revealed until late in the play.

The language of both playwrights is the colloquial, every-day speech of the early Romans. Terence writes with a lightness and a grace that are almost Greek and which reflect the linguistic interests of his friends in the Scipionic circle; Plautus writes with an exuberance and a freedom that reveal his knowledge of the theatre and his audience. While Terence

[21] In Terence the running slave seldom heightens the tension, for the information which he brings is already known to the spectators.

expresses his thoughts in neat and polished maxims (*sententiae*), Plautus abounds in puns, word-play, verbal jests, and comic words coined for the occasion.[22] Laughable names such as *Thensaurochrysonicochrysides,* "Gold-treasure-surpassing-gold-son," and *Bumbomachides Clutomestoridysarchides,* "Roaring-battle-son Mighty-adviser-of-wretched-strategy-son," roll from his pen. Most of his puns are untranslatable, many are indecent, but all are amusing. His language is copious to the point of redundancy, filled with assonance and alliteration, and rich in grotesque compounds. It is Latin in its raciness and illustrates how free from Graecisms the language of the early reproducers of Greek literature could be. Ancient writers quote the statement of Aelius Stilo, an early critic, that if the Muses had chosen to speak in Latin, they would have spoken in the language of Plautus. Equally glowing tributes are paid to his language by modern critics. W. A. Oldfather, for instance, writes, "The style that he produced was capable of expressing almost any shade and variety of emotion. . . . He was a fertile and vivacious master and maker of language who deserves to be named with Aristophanes and Shakespeare."

The New Greek Comedy as a whole was undoubtedly less serious than the fragmentary works of Menander imply. As Eugene O'Neill, Jr., points out,[23] there is nothing really funny about Menander's plays; "the characters find themselves in a complicated and unpleasant situation which for a while seems destined to grow steadily worse, but the story is so manipulated that everything works out well in the end and everyone is left happy and contented. . . . We do not laugh at the temporary misfortunes of the characters; they elicit too much of our sympathy for that." Other Greek dramatists, such as Diphilus and Philemon, several of whose works were adapted by Plautus, may well have presented more farcical situations in more humorous language. Terence, modelling his plays chiefly upon those of Menander, displays the characteristics of his great predecessor. A genial sympathy pervades his work and he awakens the same "thoughtful laughter" that George Meredith finds so typical of Menander and Molière. There is much delightful comedy, however, in *The Brothers,* and *The Eunuch* and *Phormio* are far more amusing than Plautus' serious plays, such as *The Casket* and *The Three Penny Day.*

Often Terence achieves amusing effects by unexpected turns in the action and by sudden departures from the usually accepted conventions. In this respect he perhaps went far beyond Menander, for, evidently conscious of the limitations of the ancient stage and the tendency to deal

---

[22] See especially C. J. Mendelsohn, *Studies in the Word-Play in Plautus* (Philadelphia, 1907).

[23] *The Complete Greek Drama* (New York, 1938), Vol. I, pp. xlviii f.

with stereotyped plots and characters, he sought to handle the usual themes in new ways. In his deceptions the slave is sometimes tricked, or the slave tells the truth and other characters, refusing to believe him, deceive themselves. Or the slave, who in Plautus produces laughter by his impudence, his buffoonery, and his comic antics, is pushed off the stage and prevented from being funny. It was an accepted convention that a character, entering the stage from a house-door, could talk to a person inside the house. Terence quietly pokes fun at this procedure when another person views the conversation with suspicion and considers it faked for his benefit. Again the recognition instead of bringing a happy solution may complicate the action still further and create a new set of problems. All such innovations would be amusing to spectators well acquainted with the normal comic technique.

There is little in Terence, however, that can match the gaiety and exuberance of Plautus, who has at his command all the devices of comic technique—incongruity and exaggeration of plot and character, sarcasm, satire, and parody. He ranges from plays that are serious in thought and treatment to outright slapstick and farce, from a play like *The Captives* with its ennobling theme of self-sacrifice to one like the *Casina* with a coarse plot and a vulgar but laughable conclusion. There are obscene allusions in Plautus, particularly in the puns and jests, but such allusions usually have the saving grace of humour. If Plautus gradually increased the quantity and vigour of his vulgarity during his dramatic career, as has recently been suggested,[24] we may safely assume that much of the coarseness in his plays was his own addition to the Greek originals, as a concession to the demands of his audience. He may have been influenced in this respect also by the earlier Italian farces. But the plays contain far less coarseness and indecency than is often supposed, and in no way can their effect be considered harmful. Vice is made repulsive, depravity is ridiculed, and virtue is seldom unrewarded. Another source of comic effect which Plautus often uses is the breaking of the dramatic illusion. The actor for the moment steps out of his part, speaks directly to the audience, and calls attention to the fact that he is an actor in a play. This shattering of the dramatic effect for the sake of humour is a characteristic device of lower forms of comedy and is often found today in vaudeville skits and comic programs on the radio. Occasional allusions to Roman places and persons, and references to historical events give a Roman flavour to Plautus' plays and make them as much a truly native comedy as was possible in a framework based on Greek plots and characters.

[24] J. N. Hough, "Miscellanea Plautina," *Transactions American Philological Association*, LXXI (1940), pp. 186 ff.

To say with Gilbert Norwood that the work of Terence is high comedy, that of Plautus mostly farce, is misleading. Both worked from the social drama of the New Comedy, Terence in the direction of subtlety and elegance, Plautus toward bustling vivacity and boisterous humour. Both were limited by the forms and conventions of their originals, but both deserve great credit as independent and creative dramatists. Terence remoulded the Greek plays so as to reveal his interest in human character and his perfect control of dramatic structure. Plautus transformed the more serious works of the Greeks and produced laughable comedies to delight the audiences of his day. His versatility is well described by J. W. Duff: "As a master of stage-craft, he plays a whole gamut of comic effects, and manipulates to his liking the elements of comedy, farce, burlesque, operetta, pantomime, and extravaganza."

The comedies of Plautus and Terence were read and studied until the end of the Roman Empire. Sidonius, a prominent Roman of the fifth century A.D., refers to both Plautus and Terence, and relates the pleasure with which he and his son read together Terence's *The Mother-in-law* and compared it with Menander's *The Arbitration*. During the Middle Ages Terence was admired for his style and his maxims, but was little understood as a dramatist. In the tenth century the nun Hrotswitha composed pious comedies that were inspired by a desire to imitate in a moral manner the "immoral" plays of Terence. Her six plays, written in prose and bearing little resemblance to Terence, fill a gap between the Roman classical drama and the beginnings of drama in the Renaissance. With the development of Italian, French, and English comedy in the sixteenth century the Roman playwrights were considered norms of excellence. Their plays were translated and acted on the stage, and new comedies were composed, which were indebted to the Roman works for their plot, characters, and treatment. The youthful lover, the swaggering and conceited soldier, the intriguing servant, and other roles of European comedy were directly modelled upon the creations of Plautus and Terence. Acts and scenes from different Latin plays were joined in new combinations, and the same Plautine or Terentian comedy appeared in various forms in different parts of Europe. Berrardo, Machiavelli, Ariosto, Trissino, Aretino, Dolce, and Cecchi in Italy, Baif, Larivey, Rotrou, Scarron, Molière, Regnard, and Destouches in France, Shakespeare, Heywood, Dryden, Shadwell, Fielding, and others in England all fall, either directly or indirectly, under the Roman influence, and the list of their imitations and adaptations is long.[25]

[25] The most thorough treatment of Plautus' influence on later drama is K. von Reinhardstoettner, *Plautus. Spätere Bearbeitungen plautinischer Lustspiele* (Leipzig, 1886). The Introduction (pp. 1-111) treats also of the influence of Terence.

The influence of the various comedies of Plautus and Terence is indicated briefly in the Introductions to the plays and need not be repeated here. Suffice it to say that in each country the classical influence appeared in a somewhat different form and was moulded both by national characteristics and by the qualities of the individual dramatist. In Italy complicated plots of trickery and mistaken identity were favoured and the characters tended to be types. The French dramatists placed less stress on double plots and mistaken identity and preferred themes in which human weakness provided the mainspring of the action. The development from comedies of pure plot to comedies of character is seen in the dramatic output of Molière whose finest qualities are his insight into human motives and his marvellous skill in revealing character. In England, comedy grew from a combination of Latin comedy and mediaeval drama, and placed more emphasis on the foibles of mankind and the follies of the time. Varied as was the course of European comedy, its roots are to be sought in Roman soil, and it is as impossible to ignore the indebtedness of the later comic dramatists to Plautus and Terence as it is to discuss the nature of European tragedy without an understanding of Seneca and his contributions.

III

LUCIUS ANNAEUS SENECA was born in Spain about 4 B.C. and was brought to Rome at an early age. He had a thorough training in rhetoric under various teachers—his father was famed as the author of the *Controversiae* and the *Suasoriae,* collections of arguments used in rhetorical training—and for a time had a brilliant career as a lawyer. The story is told that his eloquence aroused the jealousy of the emperor Caligula who would have put him to death but for the rumour that the orator was in bad health and would soon die a natural death. By degrees Seneca's interests gradually turned to literature and philosophy. He remained prominent in court circles until 41 A.D., when he was charged with an intrigue with Julia, niece of Claudius, who had now become emperor. The accusation may have been invented by Messalina, wife of Claudius, but it was believed by the emperor who exiled Seneca to the island of Corsica.

In 49 A.D. Seneca was recalled to Rome by Agrippina, who had now become empress, and was made tutor of her son, the youthful Nero. With the death of Claudius in 54 A.D. Nero became emperor. Much of the decency and moderation of the first five years of Nero's reign—the so-called *quinquennium*—is attributed to the sane guidance of his two mentors, Seneca and Burrus, prefect of the guard. In 59 A.D. occurred the murder of Agrippina, followed three years later by the divorce and exile of Octavia, Nero's wife. It was now obvious to Seneca that he could no longer influence or restrain the emperor; he retired as much as possible from public affairs and devoted himself to the study of philosophy. Many of his important treatises were written in this period. In 65 A.D. he was accused of complicity in the conspiracy of Piso and committed suicide by imperial order.

The life of Seneca was one of contradictions. His position in the court of Nero made it difficult to maintain his principles, and the great wealth he amassed in a short period seemed to his critics definitely inconsistent with his philosophical teachings. He met his death with true Stoic calm, and the numerous prose works—*Natural Problems, Moral Letters, On Clemency, On Benefits,* and other treatises—which he left behind him make him one of Rome's outstanding Stoic philosophers. His interest was chiefly in ethics, and his beliefs were both more spiritual and more human than those of the earlier Stoics. Christian writers of the later Empire found in him many of the qualities of a Christian saint.

Ten tragedies have come down under Seneca's name. All are believed to be genuine, with the exception of the *Octavia,* a *fabula praetexta,* which is usually considered the product of a later hand. The other nine tragedies deal with Greek characters and legends, and all but one (*Thyestes*) have themes which are treated in extant tragedies of Aeschylus, Sophocles, and Euripides. There is little reason to doubt that Seneca is the author of the plays ascribed to him, for they resemble his extant prose treatises both in their philosophic content and in their epigrammatic and pointed style. When the tragedies were composed is not known; many critics favour the period of his exile, or earlier, while others believe they were written after the accession of Nero in 54 A.D.

A more important problem involves the purpose of the plays. Theatrical productions were given in the time of Nero, but we have no evidence that the tragedies of Seneca were ever presented on the stage. Some scholars maintain that the very nature of the plays is such that they could not possibly be acted. In a recent book about Seneca, C. W. Mendell, writing of *The Trojan Women,* gives a typical argument: "The failure to motivate entrances and exits or properly to introduce characters is quite sufficient evidence that the play was never intended for acting. It was for recitation solely." Other adherents of this view stress various aspects of the plays—long descriptive speeches, an overabundance of rhetoric, a lack of clarity in handling characters, and scenes of horror, such as the killing of Medea's children on the stage, or the references to the mangled remains of Hippolytus. Yet there is no proof that the tragedies were written merely to be read or recited before small literary gatherings. Some of the very features which impress the modern

critic as undramatic, particularly the rhetorical passages and the gruesome scenes, would undoubtedly have appealed to the hardened audiences of the first century A.D. It was an age of rhetoric and an age of
gruesome spectacles. We must remember also that in the Renaissance
Seneca's plays were acted. It seems far more satisfactory to adopt the
theory of many modern critics, which may be stated briefly as follows:
whether or not the plays were actually presented on the stage, they were
written for the stage in such a way as to make effective presentation possible, and they conformed to the technical requirements of production
on a stage.[26]

Like Ennius and other early writers of tragedy, Seneca was attracted
most to Euripides. The Greek poet's blend of romance and realism, his
interest in human psychology, and his rhetorical tendencies held a strong
appeal for the Roman playwright, and it is not surprising that Seneca's
most successful plays were those modelled upon Euripides' tragedies.
Seneca treated his originals with great freedom. Keeping the basic
themes of the Greek plays, he gave new direction to the tragedies by
omitting scenes and characters, adding new scenes, and presenting characters and situations in a different light. It is possible that many of his
alterations may have been suggested by tragedies on the same theme
written by earlier Roman dramatists, but it is even more probable that
Seneca composed his plays with a far greater degree of originality than
Roman tragedy had hitherto attained. The fragments of Ennius' *Medea*
reveal a fidelity to the Euripidean model that is very unlike the freedom
of Seneca's treatment. In certain scenes the influence of Vergil is apparent. Theseus' description of his trip to the Underworld in the *Mad
Hercules* recalls Aeneas' descent in *Aeneid* VI, and Andromache's account of the vision of the dead Hector in *The Trojan Women* echoes
Hector's appearance to Aeneas in *Aeneid* II. Yet it is primarily to
Seneca himself that both the strength and the weaknesses of his plays
must be attributed.

Many of the principles by which he reworked the Greek tragedies
were in themselves admirable. He sought to unify the plot by subordi-
nating minor incidents and crises, and by concentrating his interest on
the main characters at the expense of minor personages. He endeavoured to give psychological motivation to actions which seemed to him
weakly or illogically motivated in the originals, and he attempted to
reduce to a human level many problems which in the Greek tragedies
involved matters of religion and theology, themes of divine retribution

---

[26] This is the conclusion of L. Herrmann after an exhaustive survey of the various aspects of the problem in *Le Théâtre de Sénèque* (Paris, 1924), pp. 153-232.

and the workings of Fate. In this respect he was carrying further the tendency of Euripides to portray the complex problems of human life on a human plane. Less admirable was his desire to give rhetorical fullness to his plays, for the rhetorical element often appears as an end in itself. His desire for theatrical effects led him to stress the supernatural; ghost scenes and scenes of divination, when uncontrolled by the religious tones of the Greek tragedies, tended to produce horror instead of terror. His desire to emphasise the gruesome aspects of his themes may be best seen in the *Thyestes* and in the conclusion of the *Phaedra*. The religious and philosophical depths of the Greek tragedies become philosophical moralising by the chorus and brilliant and epigrammatic utterances by the characters. The Stoic fortitude with which the personages meet disaster and death is definitely Senecan and Roman.

Structurally, the tragedies reveal a striking uniformity. The episodes of dialogue (or monologue) are written in iambic trimeter, a six-foot iambic line far more akin to that of Greek tragedy than to the rugged senarius of older Roman drama, and are separated by choral passages, many of which are but loosely connected to the action of the plays. Since there are usually four such lyric passages, the play is divided into the five parts or acts, to which Horace had referred in his *Ars Poetica* a half century earlier. The lyric metres of the choruses, Sapphics, Asclepiadeans, and Glyconics, are reminiscent of Horace, but usually lack strophic arrangement. Some choruses are dull and wearisome, while others contain real poetic beauty in theme and execution. The praise of Sleep in the *Mad Hercules*, the doctrine of annihilation, and the farewell to Troy, both in *The Trojan Women*, are among Seneca's most successful choral odes. Many of the songs express Seneca's own Stoic doctrines, e.g. the nature of true kingship in the *Thyestes*, but Epicurean themes are occasionally found. Although the chorus takes no real part in the action, it is often sympathetic with certain of the main characters and indicates the playwright's attitude toward his subject. The hostility of the chorus toward Medea, for instance, is of definite value in Seneca's delineation of her character and that of Jason.

The prologue of a Senecan tragedy is technically the First Act and usually is spoken by one character, either superhuman (Juno, the ghost of Thyestes, the ghost of Tantalus) or human (Hecuba, Medea, Oedipus, etc.). These opening speeches often contain a wealth of allusion to the later action, but this does not mean that the plays are without suspense. The standard versions of the Greek myths had become firmly established by the time of Nero; the educated Roman, versed in Greek and Latin literature, would be well acquainted with the main outlines of the story of Agamemnon, Oedipus, Phaedra, or Medea. Seneca assumed such preknowledge on the part of his hearers, and was able to play on it again and again by means of veiled allusions and subtle references to the later course of the drama. In this respect his procedure was very unlike that of the Greek dramatists, in whose tragedies preknowledge was restricted and uncertainty and surprise played a more prominent part.[27] Seneca's foreshadowing arouses keen anticipation which is all the more effective when the characters themselves have no foreknowledge of the future. In the prologue of the *Medea* the heroine has as yet no definite idea of her subsequent actions, but her words are filled with ambiguity and give to the hearers many hints of the ultimate form of her vengeance. Prologues delivered by superhuman personages may reveal the denouement more clearly, but it is not that the prologues are in themselves too explicit; their contents are rendered significant only by the knowledge which the hearers are assumed to have. The suspense which Seneca creates is thus largely anticipative, but it is developed throughout the plays with cleverness and subtlety.

As a dramatist Seneca is inferior to Aeschylus, Sophocles, and Euripides. The grandeur and lofty conceptions of the originals, their great characterisations, and their beautiful choral lyrics are missing. His plots, treated on a human level, are chiefly those of love, hatred, and revenge. The characters at times become too rhetorical in their utterances to be realistic. The epigrammatic, line by line dialogues (*stichomythia*), in which the personages speak in *sententiae,* are artificial in their cleverness, and yet they are often successful in delineating the characters of the two speakers. The dialogue between Pyrrhus and Agamemnon in *The Trojan Women* is an excellent case in point. To say with H. E. Butler that Seneca's "recipe consists in the employment of three ingredients—description, declamation, and philosophic aphorism" and that "in Seneca there is little else" betrays a lamentable failure to grasp both the dramatist's intent and his achievement. It must be emphasised that Seneca was interested not merely in themes of horror, philosophical commonplaces, and an abundance of rhetoric, but also in rationalising his material, in stressing the psychological aspects of his characters, and in giving to his tragedies a cosmopolitan and universal quality. The material of his plays is essentially the material of great tragedy. The plays present powerful emotions and tragic occurrences, and are successful in arousing pity and sympathy and fear. Seneca portrays human life as dignified and meaningful. Superhuman forces may be at work,

[27] See N. T. Pratt, Jr., *Dramatic Suspense in Seneca and in his Greek Precursors* (Princeton, 1939).

but the Senecan characters, perhaps even more than those of Greek tragedy, have freedom of will and are responsible for their own deeds.[28] Like Hercules, they rise triumphant over disaster and defeat, or, like Astyanax and Polyxena, they meet death with calmness and fortitude. If the tragedies have less significance than their Greek originals, the fault lies not with the subject-matter of the tragedies, but with the form in which Seneca presents his tragic themes. He was the product of the age in which he lived, and description and declamation were characteristic of the literature of the period.[29] Curiously enough, it was Seneca's weakness as a dramatist as much as his strength that made him so suitable as a model for playwrights of a later age.

The true memorial of Seneca, as F. L. Lucas states, is the tragic stage of England, France, and Italy. The writers of the Renaissance were charmed by Seneca's ornate and lofty style, his regularity of form, and the Stoic fatalism of his characters. He was to them the most modern of the ancient dramatists; although rhetorical and fond of sensational themes, he was also reflective and introspective. The lofty themes and the tragic power of Greek drama did not appeal to the Renaissance playwrights, but Seneca they were able to understand and appreciate. It was thus inevitable that he should eclipse the Greek poets and become the greatest force in the moulding of Renaissance tragedy. To an even greater degree than was the case with Roman comedy, the nature of the influence varied with the country. The individuality of each nation brought about a modification of the Senecan type, and as a result Italian tragedy based upon Seneca differed strikingly from Senecan drama in France, while in England the union of popular and classical drama produced tragedy which in its early stages resembled the Italian but developed far beyond it. It is a brilliant testimony to the richness and variety of Seneca's tragedies that their influence could be so widespread and could appear in such different forms.[30]

Italian tragedy became almost purely Senecan after the failure of Trissino's attempt to introduce tragedies based on Greek originals. Cinthio in 1543 proclaimed the superiority of Roman over Greek tragedy

[28] For the basic assumptions of tragedy, the dignity of man, the freedom of his will, and the existence of a superhuman factor, see W. J. Oates, *The Complete Greek Drama* (New York, 1938), Vol. I, pp. xxvii f.

[29] See Moses Hadas, "The Roman Stamp of Seneca's Tragedies," *American Journal of Philology*, LX (1939), pp. 220-231.

[30] See L. E. Kastner and H. B. Charlton, *The Poetical Works of Sir William Alexander, Earl of Stirling*, Vol. I (Edinburgh, 1921). The Introduction (pp. xvii-clxxxvi), to which I am indebted for many points, gives a detailed account of the nature of Seneca's influence upon Italian, French, and English tragedy.

and stated that Seneca excelled the Greeks in gravity, decorum, majesty, and sententious maxims. His *Orbecche,* produced in 1541, contained the vengeance motive, Furies and ghosts at the opening, narrated horrors, long speeches, a chorus uttering platitudes, death on the stage. Although Cinthio conceived of tragedy as theatrical melodrama, he was the first to modernise classical tragedy and adapt it to the stage. Cinthio and his followers, Speroni, Dolce, Mondella, and others, emphasised the element of horror and sought for gruesome effects. The subjects of their plays were taken from Ovid, from Oriental stories, or from fictions of their own creation. Plays with a happy ending were grafted on the Senecan tradition, and plays were written with a double plot, which permitted two main threads of interest with divergent fates. Although Aristotle was studied and admired, his theories of drama were twisted to apply to tragedy written under the Senecan influence. The Italian dramatists of the sixteenth century did not rigidly uphold the three unities of time, place, and action and were chiefly interested in marvels and spectacular effects. The three unities were formulated by Castelvetro in 1570 after most Italian tragedy of the Renaissance had been written. Many of the earlier plays had conformed to the unities, but the playwrights had not been bound by a pseudo-classical regularity and had been able to give a free rein to their impulse toward the romantic and the striking.

In France tragedy from the first was more scholarly and academic. Plays were written for schools and there was little consideration given to the needs of a living theatre. Buchanan, Muret, Jodelle, and others modelled their plays upon Seneca; they were, in the words of Kastner and Charlton, "theoretic reformers seeking to establish a new dramatic form on ancient models in utter contempt of popular drama. . . . The French from the outset are crusading against the public taste." In French tragedy the ghost was usually omitted, scenes of violence and death were banned, and there was little interest in the gruesome and the marvellous. The plots were simple, with very little action. Neither Greek nor Roman drama had known such restrictions. The French even went so far as to criticise Seneca for not transforming more action into narrative. Many of the writers, with a complete lack of dramatic sense, turned their plays into rhetorical declamation. While the Italians had been interested in deeds of violence and tales of horror, the French stressed the elegiac lamentation resulting from the tragic situation. The three unities, formulated by Castelvetro, were rigidly imposed upon French drama.

Garnier, the most Senecan of the French playwrights, combined scenes from various Senecan dramas in his *Porcie* (1568) and *Hippolyte* (1573). His *Troade* (1579) contained scenes from both Euripides and Seneca. In his attempt to complicate the action and in his use of more romantic themes, which is best seen in his *Bradamente* (1582), he laid the foundations for a more popular and more successful form of tragedy. With Alexandre Hardy, drama became something to be acted, not merely to be read. He did for French tragedy what Cinthio had done for Italian. Although he used ghosts and messengers and retained the five acts, he banished the chorus as undramatic and observed the unities of time and place only if they did not interfere with the dramatic qualities of his work. He was far more interested in portraying action and believed that events and characters should react upon each other. In Corneille's plays (*Le Cid, Horace, Cinna, Polyeucte*) the interest was centred on the characters and on the indomitable will which enabled them to overcome all obstacles. His tragedies resembled the earlier French drama in that the appeal was primarily to the ear and not to the eye. Scenes of exposition were still presented in the form of narration. Unity of action was carefully observed, because only in this way could the sequence of cause and effect be maintained. As a result of the acceptance of the unity of action, the other unities were usually kept. Although Corneille's plots were exceedingly intricate, the psychology of his characters was far from complex. Racine, working with simpler plots, complicated the psychology of his characters, making them vacillate in a human and more dramatic manner. In his interest in psychology he was much closer to Seneca than had been his predecessors. Seneca's prestige in France was now declining, but Racine was probably far more indebted to the Roman dramatist, either directly or indirectly (through Garnier and Hardy), than he himself realised or was willing to admit.

Racine marked the high point in the French treatment of classical tragedy. Later dramatists felt that tragedy suffered from simplicity of plot and lack of stirring events. Crébillon stressed again the melodramatic and the horrible, while the psychological element practically disappeared. In his *Atrée et Thyeste* he presented the same gruesome theme that Seneca had treated so effectively in his *Thyestes*. Voltaire, believing that French tragedy tended to be conversation rather than representation of events, was convinced that more action and spectacle should be introduced into drama. Influenced by the Senecan characteristics of Elizabethan tragedy, Voltaire in his *Eriphyle* (1732) brought back on the stage the ghost, which had long before been discarded by the French. Many of his plays were spectacular melodramas with frequent *coups de théâtre*. Classical tragedy in France had now become more like the

Italian drama of the Renaissance, but the moral content and psychological depth that had made Racine the greatest of the neo-classical dramatists were lacking.

In England many features of Senecan tragedy were blended with native forces to produce a far greater drama than the Italians or the French achieved. Seneca's influence was first felt in the schools and universities and by 1560 his plays were being presented on the stage in English translation. Sackville and Norton's *Gorboduc,* produced in 1561, was Senecan in its revenge motive, its choruses, its messengers, and its five acts. It was spectacular, used new dramatic material, and had no regard for the unities. Its characteristics were thus unlike those of the French Seneca and similar to those of the Italian. Gascoigne's *Jocasta* (1566) and *Gismond of Salerno* (1567) were produced by students of the Inns of Court, but were ultimately passed on to the people, who in this way became more and more familiar with plays that were popular in form but classical in story. *Horestes, Appius Claudius, Cambyses,* and *Damon and Pythias* aided in the popularisation of classical drama, and in 1588 the students of Gray's Inn produced *The Misfortunes of Arthur,* considered the most slavishly Senecan of all English plays. The year 1581 was a landmark in the growth of the Senecan influence, for in this year Newton collected and published the earlier translations of individual plays under the title *Seneca His Tenne Tragedies Translated into Englysh.* The translators took some liberty with their material; many choruses were shortened and others were lengthened to make room for more commonplaces, the style was made more declamatory, and new matter was added to increase the element of melodrama. In his translation of *The Trojan Women,* for instance, Jasper Heywood brought the ghost of Achilles on the stage and made it shriek for blood and vengeance. In the words of Kastner and Charlton, "Thus, fully equipped in manner, speech, and dramatic function, the Senecan ghost first enters Elizabethan drama—and he is by law, at all events, Heywood's ghost, not Seneca's at all!"

By 1580 the Senecan influence began to diverge into two separate courses. More purely Senecan plays were written for academic circles. Between 1590 and 1607 a group of writers—the Countess of Pembroke, Daniel, Brandon, Greville, and Sir William Alexander—presented the Seneca of argument and description in a rigorous classical form. Their plays were book-dramas and unsuited for the stage. These writers were strongly influenced by French classical tragedy, and the Senecan features of their plays were the features that had appealed to the French dramatists of the sixteenth century.

The second and far more significant course of Seneca's influence was in the living drama of the theatre. Here Seneca and the popular tradition were fused. With Kyd's *The Spanish Tragedy* (*c.*1586) and Marlowe's *Tamburlaine* (*c.*1588) both the revenge-play and the conqueror-play were firmly established on the English stage. The former was both the more important and the more Senecan.[31] Furthermore, early Elizabethan tragedy was definitely influenced by the drama of Italy, and it was the Italian Seneca of blood and revenge and spectacle that entered the main stream of English drama at this time, not the more regular and more colourless Seneca of the French writers, whose influence, as we have seen, was limited to an isolated group of playwrights of little importance. The Elizabethans, like the Italians, did not consider themselves bound by the fixed form and structure of classical tragedy. They went even further in their disregard of the unities and in the portrayal of scenes of horror and violence on the stage.

The period from 1590 to 1610 is the period in which English tragedy reached its greatest heights. Throughout these years and well into the seventeenth century the dramatists reveal, to a varying degree, the effect of the Senecan influence. Kyd, Marlowe, Peele, Greene, Shakespeare, Chapman, Marston (the most Senecan of them all), Jonson (who in his *Catiline* and *Sejanus* attempted to reform the Senecan tradition in England and make it more purely classical), Webster, Tourneur, Ford, Massinger—all are indebted to Seneca directly or indirectly for rhetoric, horror, themes of murder and revenge, ghosts, *stichomythia,* reflective utterances, and Stoic fatalism. To quote parallel passages or to discuss the features of Seneca which each playwright stressed is unnecessary, as the material is available elsewhere.[32] But there can be no doubt that Seneca, either in the original Latin or in English translation or in the modernised manner of the Italians, was a great storehouse of tragic material. The extent of his influence has been well summarised by Kastner and Charlton:

"He provided the most tragic motive, revenge exacted on the closest consanguinity. He provided the most tragic theme, the inevitability of Fate's decrees. He provided the most tragic appeal, horror piling itself on horror. He provided the most tragic machinery, ghosts, supernatural forces, and foreboding dreams; the most tragic incidents, murder inflicted in the most cruel and most bloodthirsty way. He provided the most tragic characters, superhuman villains dominated with one abnormal consuming passion.

[31] See the Introduction to Seneca's *Thyestes* in Volume Two.
[32] See especially J. W. Cunliffe, *The Influence of Seneca on Elizabethan Tragedy* (London, 1893), F. L. Lucas, *Seneca and Elizabethan Tragedy* (Cambridge, 1922), and T. S. Eliot, "Seneca in Elizabethan Translation" and "Shakespeare and the Stoicism of Seneca," in *Selected Essays 1917-1932* (New York, 1932), pp. 51-88, 107-120.

He provided the most tragic sentiment, morbid introspective self-pity and self-reliance. He provided the superlative tragic style, whether for the utterance of passion, picture, or sentence. Above all, he warranted the use of all these elements extravagantly and without restraint. . . . He gave example of dramatic technique and even of devices of stagecraft for enhancing the marvel of it all; and he furnished an unmatchable model of the fence of words in stichomythic dialogue and of their sparkle in crystalled proverb."

The Senecan influence remained very strong in English tragedy until the eighteenth century. Many a critic has commented upon the difficulty of imagining what Elizabethan tragedy would have been without the Roman playwright. The development from the miracle play would undoubtedly have been slow, and English drama might well have taken a very different course. If the Elizabethans exaggerated Seneca's faults, they also emphasised his virtues, and they found in him what they did not find elsewhere. T. S. Eliot says of Elizabethan tragedy, "If we reflect, not on the more grotesque exaggerations, but on the dramatic poetry of the first half of the period, as a whole, we see that Seneca had as much to do with its merits and its progress as with its faults and its delays. Certainly it is all 'rhetorical,' but if it had not been rhetorical, would it have been anything?" The importance of the influence of Seneca cannot be questioned. Through him the Elizabethan playwrights absorbed a greater drama in a form they could understand and use, and with his aid they created a drama far greater than their model. Seneca thus provides the link between two great periods of tragedy, and stands out in literature as one of the most important figures in the history and development of tragic drama.

GEORGE E. DUCKWORTH

THE PLAYS OF
PLAUTUS

I

AMPHITRYON

CHARACTERS IN THE PLAY

MERCURY, *a god, disguised as* SOSIA
SOSIA, *slave of* AMPHITRYON
JUPITER, *a god, disguised as* AMPHITRYON
ALCMENA, *wife of* AMPHITRYON
AMPHITRYON, *general of the Theban army*
BLEPHARO, *a pilot*
BROMIA, *maid-servant of* ALCMENA

ARGUMENT I[1]

Great Jupiter assumes Amphitryon's shape
While he is fighting with the Teloboans,
And so secures admission to Alcmena;
And Mercury takes the form of Sosia,
An absent slave; Alcmena's thus deceived.
The true Amphitryon and Sosia come,
And both are most amazingly beguiled.
Hence quarrels rise and strife 'twixt wife and husband,
Until with voice of thunder from the sky
Great Jupiter confesses he's the sinner.

ARGUMENT II (ACROSTIC)

A lcmena's charms enslaving Jupiter,
M ake him assume her husband's outward form,
P oor fellow, while he fights his country's foes.
H is slave is Mercury in Sosia's shape.
I n turn he fools them both when they arrive.
T roubles arise between the man and wife,
R ecriminations too. Then Blepharo
U mpire is chosen, but he can't decide
O n it. All's cleared at last, and twins are born.

INTRODUCTION

THE *Amphitryon* is one of Plautus' most successful comedies and is unique among his plays; it is the only example of a mythological travesty that has survived from Roman comedy. Jupiter and Mercury are characters and appear in human form disguised as Amphitryon and his slave Sosia. Jupiter has spent the night with Alcmena, Amphitryon's wife, and the play opens before dawn with the return from war of the real Amphitryon and his slave. The existence of two pairs of doublets produces great confusion. The result is brilliant farce in the case of the two slaves, especially when Sosia is convinced that he has lost his real identity—a scene as amusing as any to be found in Roman comedy. The outcome of the confusion is far more tragic for Alcmena, since Amphitryon, not realising that both he and his wife are the victims of a divine deception, suspects her of unfaithfulness. The play is thus not merely a farce, but is composed of both comic and tragic elements; it is a tragicomedy, as Mercury states in the prologue.

The *Amphitryon* resembles many other comedies by Plautus in that it is primarily a play of mistaken identity; it is a comedy of errors, but unlike *The Twin Menaechmi,* the mistaken identity is here the direct result of divine motivation. Jupiter in human form is not a noble character; he takes delight in the deception and finds enjoyment in increasing Amphitryon's bewilderment; he redeems himself to some extent by his endeavours at the end to clear Alcmena of all reproach. The most interesting character in the play is Alcmena; she is a devoted wife, a woman of dignity and honour; she is unable to understand Amphitryon's accusations and is deeply grieved by them. Plautus has created in Alcmena his noblest woman character, "his sweetest and purest woman," as J. W. Duff says.

The Greek original of the Roman play is not known. Many conjectures have been made, e.g. *The Night* by Philemon, or *The Long Night* by Plato, the comic writer, but such suggestions are at best only guesswork. The fact that the play has a mythological theme has led some scholars to assume that the original was a play of Greek Middle Comedy or a parody of tragic themes such as was composed by Rhinthon of Tarentum. Such views seem unnecessary, as in all other respects the

Amphitryon is typical of the technique of New Comedy. Friedrich Leo suggested that two Greek plays had been combined by Plautus into one: one original concerned the long night of Jupiter's visit to Alcmena, during which Hercules was conceived; the other was a play which dealt primarily with the birth of Hercules. This view has not been generally accepted. The Roman play ends with the miraculous births of Hercules and Iphicles and includes the incident of the two serpents killed by the infant Hercules. Plautus, and doubtless the author of the Greek original, considered that for the purposes of the plot it would be best to have Amphitryon return shortly before the birth of the two children. To make possible the comic confusion, it was necessary for Jupiter's visit to Alcmena to take place at the time of Amphitryon's return. The long night of Jupiter's visit was not, in this case, the night of conception, but a night of love-making. In this way the action of the play was unified. Similarly, the story of the two serpents was placed immediately after the birth instead of some months later.

The date of the production of the Roman play is not definitely known. The presence in the play of numerous lyrical passages has been used as an argument for a late date. C. H. Buck, Jr., in his recent work on the chronology of the plays of Plautus, believes that the *Amphitryon* was produced in 186 B.C., the same year in which Ennius produced his *Ambracia,* the historical tragedy honouring the capture by M. Fulvius Nobilior of Ambracia, an important city in Epirus. Buck further suggests that Sosia's amusing description of the battle may be in reality a travesty on a battle scene described by Ennius in his tragedy.

The *Amphitryon* has in modern times exerted an extensive influence upon writers of comedy in Italy, Spain, France, Germany, and England. There have been numerous translations, adaptations, and imitations; among the most important should be mentioned those by Rotrou (1638) under the title *les Sosies,* by Molière (1668), Dryden (1690), and von Kleist (1807). Arthur Palmer, in the introduction to his edition of the *Amphitryon* of Plautus, writes as follows: "It is sufficient to contrast it with Molière's *Amphitryon* to show the immeasurable superiority of Plautus; it would be an insult to Plautus to compare it with Dryden's. Whatever Molière has added to Plautus has been a detriment; wherever he has departed from the treatment of Plautus he has lowered his conception. . . . Neither Molière nor Dryden for one instant arrived at the conception of the loving husband and faithful wife which Plautus places before us. The play is the most simple, dignified, and tender of all the plays of Plautus." It should be added here that Shakespeare's *The Comedy of Errors,* while based primarily upon Plautus' *The Twin Menaechmi,* is probably indebted to the *Amphitryon* for the idea of the two sets of twins and for the theme of master and slave excluded from their own home. Even in very recent times the story of Alcmena and Amphitryon has had a striking appeal, as was shown by the success of the New York production of Jean Giraudoux' *Amphitryon 38*, adapted by S. N. Behrman, in which Lynn Fontanne and Alfred Lunt played the leading roles.

AMPHITRYON

(SCENE:—*A street in Thebes in front of the house of* AMPHITRYON.)

Prologue

MERCURY (*disguised as* SOSIA): As you in all your merchandisings wish,
    Whether you buy or sell, that I should help
    And render aid in everything you do,
    And see that all your businesses and plans
    Should turn out well, whether they be at home
    Or else abroad, and bless you with a rich
    And full reward in all you are engaged,
    Or will engage in, still to you and yours
    Bring tidings of success, and still report
    Of all that may be for your common good;
    For you already know the gods have given
    And granted me a preference as to news
    And trade; and, as you wish, I still should try
    To bless, and bring to you perpetual gain;
    Listen in silence to this comedy,
    As fair, impartial arbiters should do.
    Now I will tell at whose command I come,
    And wherefore, and will give my name as well.
    Jove is my master; Mercury my name;
    He sent me here as his ambassador;
    Although he knew his word would be for you
    As good as a command, and that you fear
    And reverence his name, as well you should;
    But still he bid me now to come to you,
    Entreatingly, with kind and gentle words.
    For sure this Jove as much as any one
    Of you, dreads ill mischance; born as he is
    Like you of mortal mother, mortal sire,
    'Tis nothing strange, if he fears for himself.
    And I too, I who am the son of Jove
    Infected am with this same dread of ill.
    Therefore with kindly feeling 'tis I come

8

And bring the same to you; from you I ask
But what is just and feasible; as one
Who justice does, justice he asks from you.
To ask unfairness from the fair were wrong;
And to ask fair play from the unfair were but
To lose one's time; they know not what is right
Nor try to do it. Now attend to me.
You ought to wish the same as we; for we,
I and my father, have deserved well
Of you and of your State. Why needs recall
How I in plays have seen the other gods,
Neptune and Virtue, Victory and Mars,
Aye, and Bellona, tell the good that they
Have done to you, while of that very good
My sire, who reigns in Heaven, was architect.
But sure, it never was my father's way
To throw the good he's done in people's teeth;
He thinks you're grateful for his services;
And ne'er regrets what he has done for you.
Now first I'll tell you what I come to say;
And then explain the plot, which underlies
This tragedy; but why contract your brows,
When I say tragedy? For I'm a god
And soon can change it; if you like I'll make
These selfsame verses be a comedy.
Shall I or not? But sure I am a fool,
Being a god, and yet not knowing what you wish.
Ah, yes! I know your mind; and I will make it
A tragicomedy; for it is not right
To make a play where kings and gods do speak
All comedy. But since a slave takes part
I'll make it for you tragicomedy.
Now Jupiter desires I ask of you
That the detectives look the seats all through,
And if they find there men who are suborned
To clap the actors, that they take their cloaks
To be security to meet the charge.
And so those actors who have sought to arrange,
Whether by letter written, or themselves,
Or intermediaries, to have the palm,
Or that the magistrates should act unfairly,
Then Jove has granted that the law apply
The same as if they had conspired to get

An office for themselves, or some one else.
You victors, he has said, must fairly win,
And not by canvassing and treachery.
Why should not that be law to actors too
As is to greatest men? By merit we
Should seek to win, and not by hired applause.
Virtue's its own reward to well-doers,
If those who are in power act fairly by them.
And he has further given a command,
That there shall be detectives, who shall see
If any actor has arranged for men
To applaud himself, or to prevent some other
Receiving his applause, that they shall flay
His dress and hide in pieces with a scourge.
I would not ye should wonder that Jove cares
For the actor's welfare; he'll be one himself.
Why be amazed, as though 'twere something new
For Jove to turn an actor? Even last year
When the actors did invoke him on the stage
He came and helped them out; in tragedy
He certainly appears. And so today
He'll act in this and I will do the same.
And now attend: I will relate the plot.
This city's Thebes; and in that house there dwells
Amphitryon, of Argive blood, and born
At Argos; he is wedded to a wife,
Alcmena, daughter of Electryon.
He was the leader of the army when
The Thebans and the Teloboans fought.
But ere he joined the army in the field,
He left Alcmena pregnant; now you know,
I think, by this time that my father is
In these same matters somewhat free, and when
The fancy takes him, loves with all his strength;
Thus he began to love Alcmena, and
Borrowed her, as it were, all unbeknown,
And left her pregnant too. So, as you see,
Alcmena has a double progeny.
My father now is in the house with her;
And for that reason this night has been made
Longer than usual, that he may take
His pleasure with her as he will. And then
He has disguised himself, so that he's like

Amphitryon. And do not wonder at
This dress of mine, and that I've come today
In likeness of a slave; believe me 'tis
A novel rendering of an ancient theme;
And therefore I come dressed in novel garb.
My father is within, in likeness of
Amphitryon; all the servants think 'tis he;
So clever is he to transform himself,
Just as he chooses. I have taken the form
Of Sosia, who went with him to the war.
In this way I can serve my father; and
The servants do not ask me who I am,
When thus they see me passing to and fro.
For when they think I am their fellow-slave
No one will ask my name, or why I came.
My father now within enjoys himself
Just as he will, with her he loveth most;
He tells her what has happened at the war;
She thinks it is her husband. So he tells
What forces of the foe he's put to rout,
What costly gifts he has received from them.
The things thus given to Amphitryon
We carried off; an easy task for him
Who can do as he likes. But now today
Amphitryon will return, and he whose form
I've taken as a slave; and that you may
Distinguish 'tween us I will wear a plume
Upon my hat; while with the same intent
My father wears a tassel under his;
Amphitryon will not have one; but these marks
No one will see, but only you alone.
But see, here's Sosia, Amphitryon's slave,
Fresh from the port,[2] his lantern in his hand.
I'll keep him from the house—and see, he's there.
'Twill be worth while, I think, to the spectators here
As actors to see Jove and Mercury appear.

Act One.   Scene I

(Enter SOSIA *from the harbour, holding a lantern.)*

SOSIA *(to himself)*: Is there a bolder or more valiant man
Than I, who know the habits of our youth,
Yet walk abroad by night and all alone?
And what if the night-watchmen in their rounds
Put me in jail, and from the prison's cell
Tomorrow I was handed over to
The whipping-post, no one to take my part,
And no help from my master; none to think
Me worthy; eight strong fellows then would flay
My back as 'twere an anvil; such would be
The public welcome that I should receive,
On thus returning from a foreign shore.
My master's haste has this to answer for,
Who for no purpose forces me by night
To leave the harbour; was it not as well
To let me go by day? Hard, hard, it is
To serve a wealthy man; and this is why
A rich man's slave more miserable is;
By night and day enough and more to do,
And something still which must be said or done
To rob you of your rest; your lord himself
Rolling in wealth, and all unused to toil,
Thinks everything that comes into his head
Can easily be done; he thinks it fair,
And never reckons what the cost may be,
Nor thinks if what he wants be just or no.
We then have much to suffer, we poor slaves;
The burden must be borne whate'er the toil.

MERCURY *(aside)*: I have more reason to complain today;
For I was free, his father was a slave;
And yet this fellow, who was born a slave,
Thinks he may grumble. I a slave in name
Have just as much to suffer.

SOSIA: Now it comes
Into my head to pay my grateful thanks
On landing to the gods for what they've done;

Amphitryon

> For, if they treated me as I deserve,
> They'd send some fellow who would smash my face,
> Because for all the good that they have done
> I ne'er have thanked them.

MERCURY (*aside*):   Well, this fellow does
> What is not common; his deserts he knows.

SOSIA: What I, nor any ever thought would happen,
> That we should reach our homes all safe and sound,
> Has come to pass; we are the conquerors,
> The enemy have lost; our legions come;
> The war's all over; what a war it was,
> With hosts of slain; the town, which bitter trouble
> Has wrought the Theban people, is destroyed
> Under Amphitryon's happy leadership.
> With booty rich, and land, and great renown,
> He has repaid his soldiers; and secured
> The crown to Creon. From the harbour he
> Sent me straight home to tell his wife the news,
> How under him as guide the State has fared.
> And I must think how best to tell it her.
> If I tell lies, I'm doing as I'm wont;
> For when they fought the most, I furthest fled;
> Yet still I must pretend that I was there,
> And tell what I have heard; yet in what words,
> And how I am to tell it, I must think.
> I'll begin thus: when first we did arrive,
> First touched the land, Amphitryon did choose
> His leaders out, and sent them to the foe,
> To announce his terms; if they, without being forced,
> Their booty and its captors would restore,
> If they returned what they had carried off,
> He would withdraw his army home again,
> The Argives would have the land, and peace be theirs.
> But if they're otherwise disposed, nor grant
> What he demands, then he with all his force
> Will straight besiege their town. And when they heard
> From those whom thus Amphitryon had sent
> What were his terms, these proud and mighty men,
> Strong in their valour, and their sense of power,
> Fiercely attack our envoys; say that they
> Can well defend themselves and theirs in war;
> And that the army must at once withdraw.

And when our envoys told Amphitryon
What had been said, he leads his army out;
The Teloboans in their turn come forth,
And range their legions, clad in armour bright.
Then was there marshalling on either side;
Leaders and regiments each set in their place,
We in our wonted fashion, they in theirs.
Then comes a leader out on either side;
They hold a parley there, and then agree
Whichever loses in the fight, should give
His land and city, hearths and altars up;
That done, the trumpets sound on either side;
The earth responsive rings, the armies shout,
The leaders, both on this side and on that,
Make prayer to Jove, and call upon their troops;
Each soldier to his utmost strength and power
Strikes with his sword; the lances splinter then,
And heaven rings with mingled shouts of men.
The breath of men, the panting of the steeds,
Rises in clouds; the while on every side
Stricken with wounds they fall; at length our troops
Prove themselves better; we have conquered them;
On every side they fall; our men rush on;
Yet no one turns to flight, and no one leaves
The place appointed to him; rather they
Would lose their lives than stir from where they stand.
So each lies where he stood, and keeps his rank.
This when Amphitryon, my master, saw,
He straightway bids his cavalry to charge
On the right wing; immediately they go,
And fall with shouts and clamour on the foe,
Still urging onwards, while beneath their feet
They tread and trample on the impious men.

MERCURY (*aside*): So far at least this man's said nothing wrong;
For I was there, when this great fight was fought,
I and my father too.

SOSIA: At last they take
To flight; this gives fresh courage to our men,
And as they fly their backs are filled with darts.
With his own hand Amphitryon slew their king.
And so the fight went on from morn till eve.
I know it was so, for I went undined.

Night stayed the battle by its coming on.
On the day after, to our camp there came
Their princes all in tears, with clasped hands,
Beseeching us to pardon their offense,
And promising to give themselves, their children,
Their city, all things human and divine,
Into the keeping of the Theban people.
And then was given to Amphitryon
In token of his valour, the gold cup
Which Pterela had used. This will I tell
My mistress. Now, as bidden by my master,
I will go home, and do as he has said.

MERCURY (*aside*): Ah, he is coming! But I'll go before him;
Nor shall this man approach this house today.
Since I am masquerading in his form
'Tis certain I can cheat him; and, besides,
If I have ta'en his form I also take
His manner and his actions; I must be
A rascal, sly, astute; with his own arms
Of roguery I'll keep him from the house.
But what is that? He's gazing at the sky;
I will observe him.

SOSIA: If there's anything
One may believe or know, I am quite sure
The God of night has drunk too much tonight;
For neither Charles's Wain moves in the sky,
Nor does the Moon, who is just where she rose;
Nor do Orion, Venus, or the Pleiads set;
The constellations keep their stated posts;
And night no longer gives place to the day.

MERCURY (*aside*): Proceed, Night, as you have begun; obey
My sire's command; great favour you have done,
And great will be the reward you shall receive.

SOSIA: I never saw a longer night than this,
Save that when I was scourged and hung by the heels;
And this I think is longer ev'n than that.
The Sun 'twould seem is sleeping, and has drunk
Too much; 'tis strange, if he's not been too free
At dinner-time.

MERCURY (*aside*):   And say you so, you wretch?
                    D'ye think the gods are somewhat like yourself?
                    I'll hold you to account for what you say;
                    Come here, you rascal; you'll not find it pleasant.

SOSIA: Where's that vile herd that cannot sleep alone?
                    This night will bring some gain to those they hire.

MERCURY (*aside*): Then if this fellow's right my father has
                    Been wise to stay within Alcmena's bed,
                    Following his own sweet will.

SOSIA: And now I'll go
                    And tell Alcmena as my master bade. (*He sees* MERCURY)
                    But who's this man I see before the house?
                    I do not like it.

MERCURY (*aside*):   There is not, I'm sure,
                    A greater coward than he.

SOSIA: It seems to me
                    This man intends perhaps to steal my cloak.

MERCURY (*aside*): He's in a fright; I'll cheat him.

SOSIA: I'm undone.
                    My teeth all chatter; this man surely will
                    Receive me in a most pugnacious way.
                    Yet he has pity; and because my master
                    Has made me stay up all the night out here,
                    His fist will lull me into sleep again.
                    I am quite ruined; see how strong is he!

MERCURY (*aside*): I'll speak out clearly; he'll hear what I say;
                    And so will be the more afraid. (*Aloud*) Now, fists,
                    Bestir yourselves; for long you've had no food;
                    'Tis ages since you sent four men to rest
                    And stole their clothes.

SOSIA (*aside*):   I'm terribly afraid
                    He'll change my name, and make of me the fifth,
                    And Quintus in the future I'll be called.
                    Four men already he has sent to rest,
                    I fear that I shall to their number add.

MERCURY: Ha! there! I'm ready for him.

SOSIA (*aside*):   He's prepared.
        He's making haste.

MERCURY: He shan't escape a beating.

SOSIA (*aside*): Who shan't?

MERCURY: Whoever comes here eats my fists.

SOSIA (*aside*): I do not eat at night; and I have dined;
        Pray give your supper unto those who starve.

MERCURY: This is a weighty fist.

SOSIA (*aside*):   I am undone.
        He weighs his fist.

MERCURY: What if I stroke him gently
        That he may sleep.

SOSIA (*aside*):   You've hit upon the thing;
        For three long nights I have been watching now.

MERCURY: But this won't do! My fist, you must not learn
        To strike him feebly. Whom you even graze,
        Must have himself all changed, and take again
        Another form.

SOSIA (*aside*):   That man will touch me up
        And make my face quite different.

MERCURY: If you hit
        Him fair and square, I'm sorry for his bones.

SOSIA (*aside*): Strange if he does not bone me like an eel.
        Away with one who bones his fellow-men!
        I'm done for, if he sees me.

MERCURY: There's a smell,
        I think, of man—which bodes no good to him.

SOSIA (*aside*): What have I done?

MERCURY: He cannot be far off;
        Though he was far enough just now.

SOSIA (*aside*):   This man
        Is sure a wizard and a sorcerer.

MERCURY: And now my fists are itching to begin.

SOSIA (*aside*): If you are going to use them upon me,
Try the wall first.

MERCURY: A voice has reached my ear,
Flying on wings.

SOSIA (*aside*): Unhappy that I am,
Not to have clipped the wings; I seem to have
A birdlike voice.

MERCURY: He evidently wants
A thrashing for his beast.

SOSIA (*aside*): I have no beast.

MERCURY: He must be loaded with my fists.

SOSIA (*aside*): Nay, sir,
I am weary of my voyage on the sea,
And still am sick; even without a load,
I scarce can walk; and with one I believe
I should not walk at all.

MERCURY: Some one, I think,
Is talking here.

SOSIA (*aside*): So I am safe at last;
He sees me not; some one, he says, is talking;
But I am Sosia.

MERCURY: Somewhere on the right
This voice would seem to strike my ear.

SOSIA (*aside*): I fear
'Tis not my voice that strikes his ear that will
Be struck, but I myself.

MERCURY: He is advancing.

SOSIA: I'm stiff with fright; if any ask, I know
Not where I am; nor can I move from fear;
Now all is over; and my master's mission
And Sosia himself go down together.
Howe'er, I'll try to speak as bold as may be,
And then perhaps he'll keep his hands off me.

MERCURY: And whither, carrying Vulcan in your lamp
Of horn?

SOSIA: And who made you inquisitor,
           Who say you knock men's teeth out with your fists?

MERCURY: Are you a slave or free?

SOSIA: Both if I choose.

MERCURY: Aye, say you so?

SOSIA: Why, yes, I do indeed.

MERCURY: You lie; I'll make you learn to speak the truth.

SOSIA: What need of that?

MERCURY: Now I must know at once
           Whither you go, as well as whose you are
           And why you came.

SOSIA: Well, then, I'm coming here;
           I am my master's slave. Is that enough?

MERCURY: I'll stop that wretched tongue of yours today.

SOSIA: You cannot; 'tis as good and clean as yours.

MERCURY: And do you quibble? What have you to do
           Here at this house?

SOSIA: Why, what is that to you?

MERCURY: King Creon stations separate sentinels
           To watch by night.

SOSIA: So doing he does well;
           While we're abroad our house is safe and sound.
           But go and say the servants have arrived.

MERCURY: Well, I know nought of that; unless you go
           At once, I will arrange that your reception
           Is not the sort that family servants get.

SOSIA: But I live here, and am these people's slave.

MERCURY: Dost thou know how? I'll have you carried out
           Upon a litter, in your pride of state.

SOSIA: How, pray?

MERCURY: You will not need to walk, but will
           Be carried off if once I take my stick.

SOSIA: But I assert, I am this family's slave.

MERCURY: Look to't—you'll soon be ready for a beating,
            Unless you go at once.

SOSIA: Do you pretend
            To stop me coming home who've been abroad?

MERCURY: Is this your home?

SOSIA: Why, yes, it is indeed.

MERCURY: And who's your master?

SOSIA: 'Tis Amphitryon,
            The general of the Theban army, he
            Who's married to Alcmena.

MERCURY: What's your name?

SOSIA: They call me Sosia, the son of Davus.

MERCURY: Then you have come today with made-up tales
            And patched-up lies, thou height of impudence!

SOSIA: Nay, if you like, with patched-up clothes, not lies.

MERCURY: And now you lie again; upon your feet
            You came, not on your clothes.

SOSIA: Yes, very true!

MERCURY: Then take that for your lies. (*Striking him.*)

SOSIA: That will I not.

MERCURY: Whether you will or no; for this is sure;
            It is no matter of opinion.

SOSIA: Be civil, please.

MERCURY: And dare you say that you
            Are Sosia, when I myself am he. (*Still striking him.*)

SOSIA: I'm killed entirely.

MERCURY: That is but a small
            Instalment of what will be. Whose are you now?

SOSIA: Why yours; your fists have marked me for your own—
            Your help, ye citizens of Thebes!

MERCURY: Do you
          Call out, you rascal? Say for what you came.

SOSIA: To be a target for your fists, good sir.

MERCURY: Whose are you then?

SOSIA: Amphitryon's slave.

MERCURY: Therefore, the more you shall be beaten for
          Your idle talk; 'tis I am Sosia.

SOSIA: I wish you were, and I was beating you.

MERCURY: And are you murmuring?

SOSIA: I will be quiet.

MERCURY: Who is your master?

SOSIA: Any one you like.

MERCURY: What then? How are you called?

SOSIA: As you may bid.

MERCURY: You said you were Amphitryon's slave,
          And Sosia called.

SOSIA: 'Twas a mistake I made.
          I meant Amphitryon's associate.

MERCURY: I knew that none but I was Sosia.
          You made a slip.

SOSIA: Would that your fists had, too.

MERCURY: I am that Sosia that you said you were.

SOSIA: I pray you let us have a truce between us
          And no more blows.

MERCURY: An armistice be it,
          If you have aught to say.

SOSIA: I will not speak
          Unless there be a peace; for you are stronger.

MERCURY: Then call it what you like; I will not hurt you.

SOSIA: But can I trust you?

MERCURY: Me?

SOSIA: What if you fail?

MERCURY: Then Mercury will revenge himself on Sosia.

SOSIA: Now, sir, observe, since I may freely speak,
              I'm really Sosia, Amphitryon's slave.

MERCURY: Do you repeat that?

SOSIA: Yes, I made a truce,
              The peace is signed, I speak the very truth.

MERCURY: Take that then. (*Striking him again.*)

SOSIA: Do just as you please to me,
              Your fists are stronger; but whate'er you do
              On this I'll not be silent.

MERCURY: While you live
              You will not make me any one today
              But Sosia.

SOSIA: And you will never make
              Me other than myself. Nor is there here
              A slave save Sosia, who went from hence
              To join the army with Amphitryon.

MERCURY: The man is mad.

SOSIA: Nay, that disease is yours.
              What the plague, am I not Sosia the slave,
              Amphitryon my master; did not the ship
              Which came to port tonight bring me with it?
              Did not my master send me? Did I stand
              Before the house, a lantern in my hand?
              Do I not speak? Not watch? Did not this man
              Attack me with his fists? He did indeed;
              And even now my cheeks smart with his blows.
              How can I doubt all this? And why not go
              Into our house?

MERCURY: Your house?

SOSIA: 'Tis so, indeed.

MERCURY: In what you said just now, you lied, you know.
              I am Amphitryon's Sosia; our ship
              This night returned home from foreign lands;
              And where King Pterela reigned, we took the town,

Destroyed by force the Teloboan troops;
Amphitryon himself in savage flight
Cut off King Pterela's head.

SOSIA (*aside*):   I scarce believe
Myself when thus I hear this fellow talk.
He knows by heart the deeds that were done there.
(*Aloud*) But say; what was the Teloboans' gift
To King Amphitryon?

MERCURY: The golden cup
King Pterela used.

SOSIA (*aside*):   He's right. (*Aloud*) Where is the
                                                    cup?

MERCURY: It's in a chest, stamped with Amphitryon's seal.

SOSIA: What's on the seal?

MERCURY: The sun arising, with
Four horses in his car. Why do you try
To trip me up?

SOSIA (*aside*):   He wins in argument;
And I must seek another name myself;
How has he seen these things? Now I will catch
Him nicely; what I did within my tent,
Alone, when no one else was there to see,
That, anyhow, he cannot say. (*Aloud*) If you
Are Sosia, tell me what took place the while
The battle was going on, within my tent.
If you can say, you win.

MERCURY: There was a cask
Of wine from whence I filled myself a jug—

SOSIA (*aside*): On the right road!

MERCURY: And that I drained it pure,
As it came from the grape.

SOSIA (*aside*):   A wondrous tale,
Unless himself was hid within the cask;
'Tis true I drank it pure, without a drop
Of water in it.

MERCURY: Now is't true that you
          Are not our Sosia?

SOSIA: You deny I am?

MERCURY: What else to do when I am he myself?

SOSIA: I swear by Jove I'm he, and that's no lie.

MERCURY: And I by Mercury declare that Jove
             Does not believe you. He would rather trust
             To me unsworn, than you upon your oath.

SOSIA: Then if not Sosia, who the deuce am I?

MERCURY: When I'm not Sosia, you, of course, are he;
             Now when I am, unless you go, you wretch,
             You will be beaten.

SOSIA (*aside*):   When I see this man
             And contemplate my own appearance too
             (I've often done it in a glass), I see
             How like he is to me. He has on him
             A hat and coat like mine; as like to me
             He is indeed as I am to myself.
             His calf, his foot, his stature, beard and eyes,
             His nose, his cheeks, the way he wears his hair,
             His neck, the whole—what need of further words?
             If but his back is scarred, then nothing can
             Be more alike than he; yet when I think
             I really am just what I always was.
             I know my master; know our house; can think
             And feel; I won't mind what he says; I'll knock
             Upon the door.

MERCURY: Where are you off to now?

SOSIA: To home.

MERCURY: Ev'n if you take Jove's car itself
             And fly from hence, you shan't escape from ill.

SOSIA: May I not tell my mistress what my master
             Bids me to say?

MERCURY: Your own tell what you like,
             But not to mine; if you provoke me further,
             You'll take a broken back from hence today.

SOSIA: I'll off. (*Aside*) Ye gods immortal, give me help!
Where did I lose myself? Where was I changed?
Where did I lose my shape? Did I forget
Myself when going to the war abroad
And leave myself at home? For sure this man
Has all the appearance that I did possess.
I'll to the port, and tell my master all.
Ev'n he, perhaps, won't know me; grant he mayn't,
That I today with head all shorn and bare
The glorious cap of liberty may wear.
(SOSIA *departs to the harbour.*)

Act One. Scene II

MERCURY (*to himself*): With all good luck this day has passed for me;
This piece of work's proceeded splendidly;
I have removed the greatest obstacle
That could prevent my sire's illicit joys.
For when this fellow comes before his master,
He'll tell how Sosia drove him from the door;
His master straightway will believe he lies,
And that he never went as he was bid.
I'll fill them both with error and mistake
And all Amphitryon's family beside,
Until my sire has tasted to the full
The joys he wishes; after, all will know
What's taken place; and Jove himself will bring
Alcmena into favour with her lord.
For sure Amphitryon will have a row
With her, accusing her of doing wrong;
And then my sire will end the strife between them
And bring back peace. (*To audience*) Now, as I left
    unsaid
A while ago, Alcmena will bring forth
Today two sons, the one a ten months' child,
The other seven: one Amphitryon's,
The other Jove's; the greater father to
The younger boy, the lesser to the other,
You understand. My sire has taken care
That for Alcmena's sake both should be born
Together, so to hide the secret wrong.

Yet, as I said, in the end Amphitryon
Will know the truth. What then? Does any think
The worse of poor Alcmena? The god will not
Allow his sin and fault to fall upon
A mortal's head. And now I'll end my speech,
The door has creaked; the false Amphitryon
Comes out, and with him comes his borrowed spouse.

Act One. Scene III

(*Enter* JUPITER *and* ALCMENA *from the house.*)

JUPITER: Good-bye, Alcmena, look well to the house,
As you are wont, and of yourself take care;
I must go hence; do you bring up the child.

ALCMENA: What is't, my husband, that you haste away
So soon?

JUPITER: 'Tis not because you weary me.
But when the general is not with the force,
What should not be, comes quicker than what should.

MERCURY (*aside*): He is a clever rogue, and 'tis no wonder,
Since he's my father;[3] watch how he will coax
The woman.

ALCMENA: Now I clearly see how much
You value me.

JUPITER: Is't not enough there is
No other lady that I love so much?

MERCURY (*aside*): But if your wife should hear of these proceedings,
You'd rather be Amphitryon than Jove.

ALCMENA: I'd rather taste your love than hear of it.
You've hardly come; you came at mid of night,
And now you go; pray, is it kindly done?

MERCURY (*aside*): I'll go and talk to her and back him up.
(*To* ALCMENA). I do not think that any man e'er loved
His wife to such distraction as he does.

JUPITER: Do I not know you, wretch? Out of my sight!
               What care of yours to interfere with me,
               Or even mutter? With this staff of mine—

MERCURY: Oh, don't!

JUPITER: One word and—

MERCURY (*aside*):   So my first appearance
               As flatterer has turned out rather poorly.

JUPITER: As to your words, dear wife, you must not be
               Angry with me; I left upon the sly;
               I stole these moments for you, so that you
               Might learn the progress of affairs; I've told
               You all; unless I loved you very much
               I could not do it.

MERCURY (*aside*):   Just as I did say:
               He soothes her fears and pets her.

JUPITER: Lest the troops
               Perceive my absence I must now return.
               Let them not say that I preferred my wife
               To state affairs.

ALCMENA: Your going leaves your wife
               In tears.

JUPITER: Nay, nay, don't spoil your eyes, my dear,
               I'll come again, and soon.

ALCMENA: That soon is long.

JUPITER: I do not leave you gladly.

ALCMENA: So it seems,
               For the same night sees you both come and go.

JUPITER: Why keep me thus? I wish to leave the city
               Before the dawn. And now this cup which they
               Have given me for my valour, which the king
               Did use himself, the king my hand has slain,
               I give it to you.

ALCMENA: You do as you're wont.
               In truth a noble gift, like him who gave it.

MERCURY: Indeed a noble gift, worthy of her
To whom 'tis given.

JUPITER: Will you not depart,
You wretch? And can I not escape you yet?

ALCMENA: And don't, my dear Amphitryon, be vexed
With Sosia for my sake.

JUPITER: That as you like.

MERCURY (*aside*): Though he's in love, he can be pretty cross.

JUPITER: Hast aught you wish?

ALCMENA: Yes, that you love me well,
Ev'n when I am away.

MERCURY: Amphitryon,
'Tis time to go. The day begins to dawn.

JUPITER: Sosia, go first; and I will follow thee.
(MERCURY *departs*)
Want you aught more?

ALCMENA: Yes, that you soon return.

JUPITER: I'll come before you've time to think of it.
Be of good cheer. (*As* ALCMENA *goes into her house*)
Now, Night, who stayed your course
To speed my plans, depart; give place to day,
That men may have its bright and shining light;
And by how much this night was longer than
The last, by so much shall the day that dawns
Be shorter; so there'll be equality,
And night succeed to day even as it's wont.
Now I will go and follow Mercury.
(JUPITER *departs*.)

Act Two.   Scene I

(*Enter* AMPHITRYON *and* SOSIA *from the harbour; attendants follow
with luggage.*)

AMPHITRYON: Go you behind.

SOSIA: I follow close to you.

Amphitryon

AMPHITRYON: You are the greatest rascal I have known.

SOSIA: And why?

AMPHITRYON: Because what you tell me is not,
Nor was, nor will be.

SOSIA: Sure, a pretty state!
You won't believe your servants when they speak.

AMPHITRYON: What is't? I will cut off that wretched tongue
Of yours!

SOSIA: I am your slave, and I suppose
That you will do exactly as you choose.
Yet you shall not deter me; I will tell
Things as they are.

AMPHITRYON: You rascal, do you dare
To say you are at home, who'rt here with me.

SOSIA: I speak the truth.

AMPHITRYON: The gods will punish you
For this: and I will do the same today.

SOSIA: That's in your hand; for me, I am your slave.

AMPHITRYON: And do you dare to mock your master thus?
You dare to say what no man ever saw,
Nor yet can be, that at the selfsame time
A man may in two places be at once?

SOSIA: It was as I have said.

AMPHITRYON: The gods destroy you!

SOSIA: What harm through me has happened your affairs?

AMPHITRYON: D'ye ask that even when you're mocking me?

SOSIA: Blame, if you like, if matters are not so;
I do not lie; I speak things as they are.

AMPHITRYON: The man is drunk.

SOSIA: I only wish I were.

AMPHITRYON: You need not wish; you are.

SOSIA: What, I?

AMPHITRYON: Yes, you.
        Where did you get it?

SOSIA: I've had none at all.

AMPHITRYON: What can I do with him?

SOSIA: A dozen times
I've said I am at home; d'ye hear me now?
And also I am here, the selfsame man.
Now is that clear, and have I spoken plain?

AMPHITRYON: Off with you!

SOSIA: What's the matter?

AMPHITRYON: You've the plague.

SOSIA: Why say you that? I am alive and well.

AMPHITRYON: But I, today, will give you your deserts;
Make you less well, more full of misery,
If I return home safe. Now follow me,
Who mock your master with such idle tales.
You have neglected my express commands,
And now have come to laugh at me besides.
Things which could never be, and which no one
Has ever heard of, these you now put forward.
You wretch, your back shall pay for these your lies.

SOSIA: Amphitryon, the greatest trouble that befalls
An honest servant when he speaks the truth
Is, sure, to find that truth rammed down his throat
And disbelieved.

AMPHITRYON: How can it be, you wretch,
That you're both here and yet at home as well?
Argue it out, I want you to explain it.

SOSIA: I am both here and there. It may seem strange
And 'tis as strange to me as any one.

AMPHITRYON: But how?

SOSIA: 'Tis not a jot more wonderful
To you than to myself; nor by the gods
Did I, this Sosia, believe the tale
Until that other Sosia made me do so.
In proper order all that happened when

We met the enemy he did disclose;
And took my very shape, my name as well.
Milk's not more like to milk than he to me.
For when before the dawn you sent me home—

AMPHITRYON: What then?

SOSIA: Why long before I ever came,
I stood before the house.

AMPHITRYON: What silly nonsense!
Say, are you sane?

SOSIA: Just as you see me here.

AMPHITRYON: Some wizard has bewitched this wretched man
After he left me.

SOSIA: That is true enough;
I'm bruised all over.

AMPHITRYON: Who has beaten you?

SOSIA: Why I myself, the one that's now at home.

AMPHITRYON: Just answer what I ask. And first of all
Who is this Sosia?

SOSIA: He is your slave.

AMPHITRYON: It seems I have more Sosias than I need;
Yet since my birth I never had but you.

SOSIA: And yet, Amphitryon, I warrant you
Will find another Sosia waiting there
When you arrive; born of the selfsame father,
Same form and age as I. Need I say more?
There is a double Sosia born to you.

AMPHITRYON: These things are strange. But did you see my wife?

SOSIA: I was not even allowed to come within.

AMPHITRYON: Who stopped you?

SOSIA: Why, this other Sosia,
Who used his fists upon me.

AMPHITRYON: Who is he?

SOSIA: 'Tis I, I say. How often have I told you!

AMPHITRYON: How can it be? Pray did you go to sleep?

SOSIA: No, never in the world.

AMPHITRYON: I thought perhaps
That you had seen this Sosia in your dreams.

SOSIA: I never sleep when following your behests;
I was quite wide awake as I am now
And as I speak to you; and wide awake
I was when he attacked me with his fists.

AMPHITRYON: Who did?

SOSIA: This other Sosia, can't you hear?

AMPHITRYON: How can one when you prate such silly tales?

SOSIA: Well, soon you'll know.

AMPHITRYON: Know whom, d'ye mean?

SOSIA: That other Sosia.

AMPHITRYON: Then follow me, for first
I must enquire. Let all be disembarked.

SOSIA: I will take care that all you wish is done.
I have not swallowed your commands
As they were wine.

AMPHITRYON: May the gods grant to me
That nought of what you say has come to pass.

Act Two. Scene II

(Enter ALCMENA *from the house, not seeing them.)*

ALCMENA *(to herself)*: How little pleasure there remains in life
When placed beside the sorrows we endure;
Such is the lot of man, the will of gods
That pain should still accompany pleasure here,
And that the more we have of good, the more
Of ill will follow. I find this at home,
And in my own experience, to whom
But little pleasure's come; a single night

Was all my husband could remain with me.
And suddenly before the dawn he went.
Now I am here alone; and he is gone
Whom most I love; more sorrow do I find
Now he has gone than pleasure when he came.
But this is well that he has won the fight
And comes back full of honour to his home.
'Tis that consoles me, that with glory won
He now returns; with courage and in faith
I'll bear his absence to the very end;
If only this reward be given to me
That he is hailed the conqueror in war,
That is enough; it is the best reward;
And valour comes before all other things.
Our liberty, our health, our life and wealth,
Our country and our friends are safe and sound
When there is valour; it possesseth all things.
And he who valour has, has all things else.

AMPHITRYON (*to* SOSIA): Yes, I believe my wife is longing for
My quick return; she loves me well, I know,
And I love her. And now that all's gone well
And far beyond our expectation, we
Have routed all our foes; in the first encounter,
Under my leadership, we won the day.
And so I'm sure she will be glad to see me.

SOSIA: And don't you think my spouse will be as much so?

ALCMENA (*aside*): It is my husband.

AMPHITRYON: Now keep close to me.

ALCMENA (*aside*): But why does he return who said just now
He must depart? Was't but a trial of me?
If that was it, to see if I deplored
His absence, I rejoice at his return.

SOSIA: We'd best return to the ship, Amphitryon.

AMPHITRYON: And why?

SOSIA: Because there's nothing here to eat.

AMPHITRYON: And how comes that into your mind, I pray?

SOSIA: Because we come so late.

AMPHITRYON: And how is that?

SOSIA: I see Alcmena has already dined.

AMPHITRYON: She was with child when last I went away.

SOSIA: Oh! What a nuisance!

AMPHITRYON: What is it to you?

SOSIA: I've just come home in time to carry water
For the child's bath according to your reckoning.

AMPHITRYON: Be of good cheer!

SOSIA: D'ye know how brave I am?
If once I take. the bucket, ne'er believe
Aught that I say in any sacred matter,
If I don't draw the well to the very bottom.

AMPHITRYON: Now follow me: I'll find another slave
To do that work. Don't fear.

ALCMENA (*aside*): I think that I
Will better do my duty if I go
To meet him now.

AMPHITRYON (*to* ALCMENA): Amphitryon salutes
His darling wife, the best, her husband says,
That ever was in Thebes, and whom as well
The citizens of Thebes most highly think of.
How are you? Are you glad to see me·back?

SOSIA (*aside*): Not much of that, I think; she would receive
A dog as well.

AMPHITRYON: I'm glad to see you thus
With such a goodly bulk spread out as this.

ALCMENA: I pray you don't salute and speak me thus,
In way of mockery, as if you had
Not lately seen me; and for the first time
After the war were now returning home,
And talk as if it was a long time past
Since you had seen me.

AMPHITRYON: Till this moment I
Have never seen you anywhere today.

ALCMENA: But why deny it?

AMPHITRYON: 'Tis the truth I say.
I've learned to speak the truth.

ALCMENA: He does not well
Who what he's learned unlearns. D'ye wish to know
What mind I'm of? But why so soon returned?
Was it some omen that delayed your start,
Or does the weather stay you, and prevent
Your going to the army, as you said
You must just now?

AMPHITRYON: Just now? And how was that?

ALCMENA: Art trying me? Why, just a moment since—

AMPHITRYON: I ask you how it's possible?

ALCMENA: D'ye think that I
In turn should try to fool you, who declare
That you've just come, when you've just gone away?

AMPHITRYON: She's talking nonsense.

SOSIA: Wait a little while,
Until she sleeps her sleep out.

AMPHITRYON: Aye, she dreams,
While waking.

ALCMENA: I am wide awake, and tell
All that has taken place; how long ago
Before the dawn I saw both him and you.

AMPHITRYON: And in what place?

ALCMENA: Of course the house you live in.

AMPHITRYON: Never; it never was.

SOSIA: What if the ship
Brought us to shore asleep?

AMPHITRYON: Do you assist her?

SOSIA: What can one do? For don't you know that if
You wish to cross a raving maenad you
Will make her worse; and sometimes they will strike;
But if you humour them you will escape
With a single blow.

AMPHITRYON: But I'm determined now
To rate her well, because she did omit
To welcome me again on my return.

SOSIA: You'll raise a nest of hornets.

AMPHITRYON: Do be quiet!
Alcmena, I would ask one question of you.

ALCMENA: Ask what you will.

AMPHITRYON: Is't folly or is't pride
That overmasters you?

ALCMENA: Why ask the question?

AMPHITRYON: Because at coming you were wont to greet me,
To speak to me as modest wives are wont;
But now I came upon you, nor did find
The usual welcome.

ALCMENA: Yesterday, my lord,
I certainly did greet you when you came,
Inquired most carefully how you had been,
And took you by the hand and gave a kiss.

AMPHITRYON: You greeted me?

ALCMENA: I did, and Sosia too.

SOSIA: Amphitryon, I thought that she would have
A boy; I was mistaken.

AMPHITRYON: What then is't?

SOSIA: 'Tis folly she produces.

ALCMENA: I'm quite sane,
And pray the gods that I may have a boy.
But you will have a thrashing if he does
What is his duty; from your prophecy
You'll get, my prophet, what you well deserve.

SOSIA: A pregnant woman in her day should have
An apple given to gnaw, if she feel sick.

AMPHITRYON: You saw me yesterday?

ALCMENA: I did indeed;
I can repeat it ten times if you like.

AMPHITRYON: Perhaps in dreams?

ALCMENA: No, I was wide awake.

AMPHITRYON: Alas!

SOSIA: Why, what's the matter?

AMPHITRYON: She is mad.

SOSIA: 'Tis bile she has; naught makes men mad so soon.

AMPHITRYON: When first were you affected by it, wife?

ALCMENA: I am quite well and sound.

AMPHITRYON: Then why d'ye say
You saw me yesterday, who only came
This night to port; and there I dined and slept
The whole night in the ship, nor ever put
My foot into the house since first I went
Against the Teloboans and subdued them.

ALCMENA: You supped with me, and slept with me as well.

AMPHITRYON: How's that?

ALCMENA: 'Tis true.

AMPHITRYON: Not certainly, in this;
The rest I know not.

ALCMENA: At first blush of dawn
You left me for the army.

AMPHITRYON: How was that?

SOSIA: She says what she remembers; she relates
Her dreams. But surely, ma'am, when you awaked,
You should have given a salted cake or incense
To Jove, who wards off omens such as these.

ALCMENA: May you be hanged!

SOSIA: 'Tis for your interest
To see it done.

ALCMENA: This man, for the second time,
Is rude, and yet receives no punishment.

AMPHITRYON (*to* SOSIA): Be still! (*To* ALCMENA) You say I went from
         here at dawn?

ALCMENA: Who but yourself has told me that there was
         A battle?

AMPHITRYON: You know that?

ALCMENA: And how you'd stormed
         A mighty town and slain King Pterela.

AMPHITRYON: I told you this?

ALCMENA: With Sosia standing by.

AMPHITRYON (*to* SOSIA): Did you hear this?

SOSIA: Where was I when I heard?

AMPHITRYON: Ask her.

SOSIA: No such event took place when I
         Was present.

ALCMENA: 'Tis a wonder if he does
         Not contradict his master.

AMPHITRYON: Sosia,
         Look here!

SOSIA: I do.

AMPHITRYON: And please to speak the truth,
         Not merely to agree with me; did you
         Hear me say these things which she says I did?

SOSIA: And are you mad as well to ask me this?
         I who now see her here for the first time.

AMPHITRYON: Now hear him, wife.

ALCMENA: I do, and hear him lie.

AMPHITRYON: You don't believe your husband, nor yet him?

ALCMENA: Because I do believe and know these things
         Were as I say.

AMPHITRYON: I came here yesterday?

ALCMENA: Do you deny you went from here today?

AMPHITRYON: Most certainly; this is my first visit.

ALCMENA: And will you say you have not given me
             A golden cup today, which you declared
             Was given you there?

AMPHITRYON: I neither gave't nor said so;
             But still I did intend, and do so still,
             To give it you. But who was it who said so?

ALCMENA: 'Twas your own lips, and from your hand I took it.

AMPHITRYON: Stay, stay, I do beseech you! Yet I wonder,
             Sosia, who told her that I had received
             The golden cup, unless yourself did so?

SOSIA: I told her not, nor have I seen her save
             With you.

AMPHITRYON: What sort of man is this?

ALCMENA: Would you
             That I produce the cup?

AMPHITRYON: I wish it so.

ALCMENA: It shall be done. (*Calling inside*) Now, Thessala, bring
                  the cup
             My husband gave today.

AMPHITRYON: Sosia, come here,
             For this will be the strangest thing on earth
             If she should have this cup.

SOSIA: Can you believe it?
             I have it in this box, sealed with your seal.

AMPHITRYON: And is the seal untouched?

SOSIA: Why, look at it.

AMPHITRYON: 'Tis right; just as I made the seal myself.

SOSIA: Why not command that she be purified
             As being a lunatic?

AMPHITRYON: It must be done.
             Her head is full of fancies; she's bewitched.
                  (*Enter* THESSALA *with cup.*)

ALCMENA: What need of further words? See, there's your cup.

AMPHITRYON: Pray hand it here.

ALCMENA: Yes, look at it, you who
Deny what's taken place; I will convince
You openly 'tis so. Is that the cup?

AMPHITRYON: What do I see, great Jupiter? It is
The cup. Ah, Sosia, I am quite undone!

SOSIA: Either this woman is the greatest witch
Or else the cup's in here.

AMPHITRYON: Open the box.

SOSIA: Why open it? The box is firmly sealed
And all is going well. You have brought forth
Amphitryon the second, I in turn
A second Sosia, and if the cup
Has done the like, we all are doubled now.

AMPHITRYON: It must be opened and inspected then.

SOSIA: Look at the seal lest you should blame me after.

AMPHITRYON: Just open it; this woman by her words
Does make one mad.

ALCMENA: Whence comes this cup, I pray,
Unless by you 'twas given?

AMPHITRYON: I must enquire.

SOSIA: By Jupiter!

AMPHITRYON: What is't?

SOSIA: There is no cup.

AMPHITRYON: What do I hear?

SOSIA: You hear what's true enough.

AMPHITRYON: If 'tis not found you will be crucified.

ALCMENA: 'Tis found and here.

AMPHITRYON: Who gave it to you, then?

ALCMENA: The man who asks.

SOSIA (*to* AMPHITRYON):   You're trying to catch me;
You ran before me from the ship by stealth
Some other way, you took the cup from hence,
Then gave it to her and replaced the seal.

AMPHITRYON: Alas, her madness you encourage too.
(*To* ALCMENA) D'ye say we came here yesterday?

ALCMENA: I do.
And coming you saluted me, I you,
And kissed you.

SOSIA: That kiss does not quite please.

AMPHITRYON: I will pursue my enquiries.

ALCMENA: Then you bathed.

AMPHITRYON: What then?

ALCMENA: You came to supper.

SOSIA: Excellent!
Enquire about that.

AMPHITRYON: Don't interrupt. (*To* ALCMENA) Go on.

ALCMENA: Dinner was served; we sat together there.

AMPHITRYON: On the same couch?

ALCMENA: The same.

SOSIA: He does not like
The dinner.

AMPHITRYON: Let her state her arguments.
What after we had dined?

ALCMENA: You said that you
Were sleepy; so the table was removed.
We went to bed.

AMPHITRYON: Where did you sleep, I pray?

ALCMENA: In the same bed with you.

AMPHITRYON: O God!

SOSIA: How now?

AMPHITRYON: She's good as killed me.

ALCMENA: Why, what is it, dear?

AMPHITRYON: Don't speak to me!

SOSIA: What is it?

AMPHITRYON: I'm undone!
To all the troubles of my absence this
Is added that the honour of my wife
Is lost.

ALCMENA: And why, my lord, do I hear you say so?

AMPHITRYON: What! I your lord? Nay, do not use that name!

SOSIA: The matter is at a deadlock indeed
If she has changed him now from lord to lady.

ALCMENA: What have I done you should address me so?

AMPHITRYON: You tell the tale, yet ask how you have sinned?

ALCMENA: I was with you I married, where's the sin?

AMPHITRYON: You were with me? A more audacious lie
Was never told; and even if you have
No modesty, you might assume a little.

ALCMENA: Such conduct as you hint does not become
My race; and if you try to prove a charge
Against me of immodesty you'll fail.

AMPHITRYON: Now, Sosia, by the gods, at least you know me!

SOSIA: Why, rather!

AMPHITRYON: Yesterday I dined on board?

SOSIA: We've many witnesses to speak to that.
I know not what to say unless there be
Amphitryon the second who looks after
Your business in your absence, and can fill
Your place; to have another Sosia
Was strange; but it was stranger still to find
A new Amphitryon standing in your shoes.

AMPHITRYON: Some witch, I think, this lady does befool.

ALCMENA: By the high heaven, by Juno too, herself,
Whom most of all I reverence and regard,

I swear that no one else has ever come
Near me to wreck my modesty.

AMPHITRYON: I wish
Indeed 'twere so.

ALCMENA: I speak the truth, but you
Will not believe.

AMPHITRYON: You are a woman still,
And swear audaciously.

ALCMENA: Who has not sinned
Must needs be bold, and speak with confidence,
Aye, ev'n and forwardness, in her defence.

AMPHITRYON: Boldly enough, I grant.

ALCMENA: As one who is
Quite innocent.

AMPHITRYON: Yes, you are so in word.

ALCMENA: A dowry, sir, is not what people deem;
But love and modesty, and all desires
Controlled in fitting bounds, the fear of Heaven,
Respect of parents, good will to my friends,
Conforming in my likings to your own,
Bounteous in kindly service for your good,
These things I had, and these my dowry were.

SOSIA: If she speaks true she's innocence itself.

AMPHITRYON: I am bewitched; I know not who I am.

SOSIA: You are Amphitryon surely; see that you
Don't let another man your name usurp
And take it to himself (men change so much),
Now that we have at last arrived at home.

AMPHITRYON: I'll probe this matter to the very bottom.

ALCMENA: That as you choose.

AMPHITRYON: What say you? Answer me.
What if I bring your kinsman Naucrates,
Who sailed on board with me, and he denies
That what you say is true, what would be fair?
Can you say aught why I should not divorce you?

ALCMENA: Naught if I so have sinned.

AMPHITRYON: 'Tis settled then.
You, Sosia, bring these in; and I will fetch
This Naucrates from off the ship with me.
(AMPHITRYON *departs towards the harbour.*)

SOSIA: We are alone; now tell me seriously,
Is there another Sosia still inside?

ALCMENA: Leave me, thou slave, who such a master fits.

SOSIA: I go if so you will. (*Goes into the house.*)

ALCMENA (*to herself*): It is too strange
That to my husband it should now occur
To charge me falsely with this grievous sin;
But still my kinsman Naucrates will tell us all.
(ALCMENA *goes inside.*)

Act Three. Scene I

(*Enter* JUPITER.)

JUPITER (*to the audience*): Friends, I am still Amphitryon whose slave
Is Sosia now, but when occasion serves
Is Mercury again; I live above
In the top attic; when it pleases me
I Jupiter become. At other times
When I come here I am Amphitryon,
And change my dress. Now for your sake I come,
Lest I should leave the comedy unfinished;
I also come to give Alcmena help
Who by her husband is accused of sin,
Being innocent herself; for 'tis my blame
If all the trouble I have caused should fall
On innocent Alcmena's head. And now
I will pretend to be Amphitryon
And in this family will introduce
The greatest mischief; then at length again
I'll make all clear, and to Alcmena bring
Assistance, and secure that she bring forth
Two children, mine and his, at a single birth.

I ordered Mercury to attend me close
If I should want him; now I'll speak to her.

Act Three.   Scene II

(*Enter* ALCMENA *from the house.*)

ALCMENA (*to herself*): I cannot rest within the house, accused
                     Of wrong, adultery, and foul disgrace,
                     By my own husband; he declares these things
                     Which happened are not so; what never was,
                     Which I have ne'er admitted, does affirm;
                     And thinks that under this I will sit down,
                     Nor care at all, but that's impossible.
                     I'll not endure to be thus falsely charged.
                     Either I'll leave him, or he makes it clear
                     And swears as well that he is sorry for
                     The charge which he has made against me thus.

JUPITER (*aside*): I certainly must do as she demands
                     If I would bring this mad woman to herself.
                     Since what I did annoyed Amphitryon,
                     And this poor lady's come in grievous trouble
                     By reason of my love, I must expect
                     His anger and ill feeling against her
                     Will turn on me.

ALCMENA (*aside*):   Ah, there he is, the man
                     Who accuses me of immodesty and shame.

JUPITER: I wish to speak with you. Why turn you from me?

ALCMENA: It is my nature; I have always loathed
                     To look upon my foes.

JUPITER: Your foes!

ALCMENA: Yes, so it is—
                     Unless you argue that is false as well.

JUPITER: You are too angry.

ALCMENA: Nay, keep off your hands.
                     For surely if you're wise or know at all
                     The woman whom you say and think immodest,

With her you'd have no conversation, or
In joke or earnest, unless indeed you are
The greatest fool that lives.

JUPITER: And if I did
Say so, it surely does not make you so
A whit the more, nor do I think you such.
And I returned to clear myself of this;
For nothing ever did annoy me more
Than when I heard that you were vexed with me.
"Why said you so?" you ask. I will explain.
I did not think that you were e'er immodest;
I tried your disposition, how you'd bear it;
I said those things in joke for a little fun.

ALCMENA: But why not bring my kinsman Naucrates,
As you did promise me, to prove you were
Not here?

JUPITER: If aught were said by way of joke,
It is not fair to treat it seriously.

ALCMENA: I know how much those words have grieved my heart.

JUPITER: By your right hand I pray, Alcmena dear,
Forgive me—pardon; be not vexed with me.

ALCMENA: My virtue makes your words of none effect;
And now, since I abstained from unchaste deeds,
I wish to avoid all unchaste words as well.
Farewell; keep all you have; return me mine;
And bid these women to accompany me.

JUPITER: But are you mad?

ALCMENA: I'll go, at any rate;
My chastity shall bear me company.

JUPITER: Oh, stay! At your discretion I'll propose
This oath: that I do not believe my wife
To be immodest; if I fail in that,
Then, mighty Jupiter, I pray that you
Will on Amphitryon let your anger fall.

ALCMENA: Propitious rather may he be!

JUPITER: I trust he will.
           For I have sworn a sincere oath to you.
           You are not angry now?

ALCMENA: I'm not.

JUPITER: 'Tis well;
           For in the life of man there often happen
           Things of this sort; they meet with pleasure first,
           And then with pain; quarrels occur ofttime
           And reconciliation takes their place;
           And if perchance angry disputes occur,
           There comes return of kindly feeling; so
           They're greater friends than e'er they were before.

ALCMENA: 'Tis well at first to avoid such words at all;
           But if you so apologise for them
           Then I must be content.

JUPITER: Now bid, I pray,
           The sacred vessels here to be prepared
           To celebrate with fitting rites the vows
           Which I when with the army vowed to pay,
           If I returned home safe; I'd pay them now!

ALCMENA: I'll see to it.

JUPITER: Call Sosia hither now.
           And let him summon Blepharo the pilot,
           Who was on board with me, to dine today;
           (*Aside*) But he himself, undined, shall be befooled,
           And I will take Amphitryon by the neck
           And put him out.

ALCMENA (*aside*):   'Tis strange he speaks apart.
           But the door opens; Sosia arrives.

                    Act Three.   Scene III.

                    (*Enter* SOSIA.)

SOSIA: Amphitryon, I'm here; and, if you will,
           Command me what you want.

JUPITER: I'm glad to see you.

SOSIA: And peace, I hope, is now restored to you?
I'm glad to see you happy and rejoice.
It is a servant's place to conform himself
To what his master is, to arrange his face
According to his master's; is he sad,
Let him be sad as well, and is he merry,
Let him rejoice. But come now, answer me,
Are you once more in amity again?

JUPITER: You laugh; you know I only spoke in joke.

SOSIA: A joke was it? I thought, indeed, you were
In sober earnest.

JUPITER: I've apologised,
And peace is made.

SOSIA: That is the best of news.

JUPITER: I'll make an offering within, as I
Have promised.

SOSIA: Yes, I think you should at once.

JUPITER: And call the pilot Blepharo from the ship,
That, service over, he may dine with me.

SOSIA: I will be there before you think me gone.

JUPITER: Return at once. (SOSIA *departs*.)

ALCMENA: Should I not go within
In the first place, and see that all is ready?

JUPITER: By all means, go and bid them be prepared.

ALCMENA: Come when you wish inside; I'll see to it
That there is no delay.   (ALCMENA *goes into the house*.)

JUPITER (*calling after her*):   Rightly you speak,
And as a good and careful housewife should.
(*To himself*) These two, both slave and mistress, are
     mistaken
In that they think that I'm Amphitryon.
(*To the absent* MERCURY) But thou, my Sosia in godlike
     form,
Be here; hear what I say though you're not present;
And, when Amphitryon comes, see that you keep

Him from the house, whatever way you can.
I wish him to be mocked, while I amuse
Myself a little with this borrowed wife.
Have all things done according to my wish,
And help me while I offer to myself.
        (JUPITER *goes into the house.*)

Act Three.   Scene IV

(*Enter* MERCURY *running.*)

MERCURY (*to imaginary passers-by*): Out of the way, out of the way,
        all you good people, out of the way!
He's a bold man who'd venture to stay
When I bid him to go; I'm a god, and can threaten
The people as much as a slave who is beaten,
In comedies often; they come in and tell
That the ship has arrived in port safe and well;
Or some angry old gentleman is come on the scene.[4]
I am the servant of Jove, and so long have been;
I obey his behests, so why shouldn't I make
All you people depart to make room for my sake.
The father, he summons, I come at his call,
As good son should do, I obey him in all;
I flatter and fawn, assist, humour his whim,
Give advice and joy with him; what's pleasant to him
Is always the greatest of pleasures to me.
Does he love? He is wise and as right as can be;
And wherever he follows his own inclination,
As all men should do if within moderation,
He does well; he would like this Amphitryon to gull,
And gulled he shall be, in your sight to the full.
A wreath now I'll wear on my head, and pretend
That I am quite drunk; and then I will wend
Upstairs, and will watch him and see what I see.
I'll make him as drunk as a lord although he
Has not tasted a drop; and, if Sosia appear,
Most certainly he will the penalty bear
Of all that I've done; and he'll say it was he
Who has done all the mischief that rested with me.
What matters to me? I must always obey

My master's commands, and fall in with his way.
And, look here, here's Amphitryon; now for the fun,
If you'll only wait here, you'll see how it's done.
And now I'll go in, dress myself as I should,
And forbid him to enter his house if he would.

(*He goes into the house.*)

Act Four. Scene I

(*Enter* AMPHITRYON.)

AMPHITRYON (*to himself*): This Naucrates I wished was not on board;
Nor in the city could I find a man
Who'd seen him, nor within the house; I've scoured
The squares, gymnasiums, the barbers' shops,
The mart, the shambles, and the wrestling school,
The forum, and the street where doctors dwell,
The perfume-sellers, all the sacred shrines,
I'm wearied with the quest, but Naucrates
I cannot find. Now I'll go home and try
To find out from my wife who it has been
Who has dishonoured her; I'd rather die
Than not pursue this matter to the end.
The doors are closed; 'tis just like all the rest.
I'll knock. Pray open! Open now the door.

Act Four. Scene II

(MERCURY *appears on the roof.*)

MERCURY: Who's there?

AMPHITRYON: Why, I.

MERCURY: What I?

AMPHITRYON: Well, I who speak!

MERCURY: Well, Jupiter and all the gods are vexed with you
For breaking thus the door!

AMPHITRYON: Pray tell me, how?

MERCURY: That all your life you'll be a wretched man.

AMPHITRYON: Now, Sosia!

MERCURY: Yes, I am he, unless
You think that I've forgot my name.
What do you want?

AMPHITRYON: You villain, do you ask
Me what I want?

MERCURY: I do indeed; almost
You've broken off the hinges of the doors.
D'ye think we get them at the public charge?
Why look at me, fool! Tell me who you are,
And what you want!

AMPHITRYON: You ask me what I want,
You scoundrel, you who have destroyed more rods
Than Acheron souls; and for those words of yours
This very day I'll warm you with the scourge.

MERCURY: Ah, yes, in your young days you must have been
A prodigal.

AMPHITRYON: How's that?

MERCURY: Because ev'n now
In your old age you ask a thrashing from me.

AMPHITRYON: These words you pour so glibly forth will bring
A heavy punishment on you today.

MERCURY: I'll pay my sacrifices to you.

AMPHITRYON: Why?

MERCURY: Because I've cursed you with bad luck today.

(*At this point there is a gap in the manuscripts. The gap may be filled
somewhat as follows: The present scene concludes with* MERCURY
emptying a pail of water over AMPHITRYON. ALCMENA *comes out
and has a dispute with her husband; she returns to the house, convinced that he is mad.* SOSIA *appears with* BLEPHARO. JUPITER *enters, and husband and lover abuse each other.* BLEPHARO *is completely puzzled and is unable to decide which is the real*
AMPHITRYON. *Here the play resumes.*)

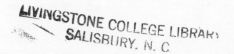

Act Four. Scene III

(BLEPHARO, AMPHITRYON, *and* JUPITER *are on the stage.*)

BLEPHARO: And now arrange yourself in parties as
You choose; I go; my business is done.
Nor have I ever seen such strange things happen.

AMPHITRYON: Nay, Blepharo, do not go; assist me now;
And be my advocate.

BLEPHARO: What use of me,
Who do not even know which side I'm on!
(BLEPHARO *departs.*)

JUPITER: I go within; Alcmena's taken ill.
(JUPITER *goes inside.*)

AMPHITRYON (*to himself*): Ah! Woe for me, when all my advocates
And friends desert me; never sure will I
Be mocked by this man, and be unavenged.
I'll go direct before the king, and tell him
All that has taken place; yes, I will punish
This sorcerer of Thessaly, who has
Unstrung the mind of all my family.
But where is he? He went in to my wife;
Was ever there more wretched man at Thebes,
Whom every one at will ignores and laughs at?
I'll burst into the house, and there straightway
Whoe'er I see, or maid, or slave, or wife,
Sire, or grandsire, or this adulterer,
I will destroy; nor Jupiter nor all
The gods ev'n if they will will hinder me
In what I am resolved. And now I go! (*As he rushes to
the door, there is a peal of thunder;* AMPHITRYON
falls motionless.)

Act Five. Scene I

(*Enter* BROMIA *from the house.*)

BROMIA (*to herself*): Now all my hopes and means of life lie wrecked
And gone; my heart has failed; nor does remain
One spark of courage; all things, sea and land,

And heaven itself, do wish to drag me down
And slay me; what to do I cannot tell.
Such wondrous things have happened in the house.
I'm faint! Oh, for a little water now!
I am exhausted and my strength is gone!
My head is sick! I neither see nor hear!
Nor is there one who is or does appear
More wretched than myself! Such things have chanced
My lady here today; her hour has come;
She straight invokes the gods. What voices come,
What noise, what flashes, how the thunder pealed,
How frequently! And every one fell flat
Just where he was; then with a mighty voice
Some one exclaimed: "Alcmena, help is nigh,
Be not afraid; for he who dwells on high,
Comes both to you and yours with kindly aid.
Rise up," he says, "who've fallen to the ground
In terror and alarm." Then where I lay
I rose; I thought the house was all on fire
Such flashes were there; then Alcmena cries
For me to come; and that brings fresh alarm.
Fear for my mistress is my first concern.
I go to see what she may wish, and there
I see two sons are born, nor any know
When they came forth, or did suspect their birth.
But what is this? And who is this old man,
Who lies before our door? Has he been struck
By Jupiter? 'Twould seem as if he had,
He lies as still as if he were quite dead.
I'll go and search out who he is; it is
My master; 'tis Amphitryon himself.
Amphitryon!

AMPHITRYON: I'm dead!

BROMIA: I pray thee rise!

AMPHITRYON: Nay, all is over.

BROMIA: See, take now my hand.

AMPHITRYON: Who holds me?

BROMIA: 'Tis your maid, 'tis Bromia!

AMPHITRYON: I'm full of fear; for Jove has thundered so!
Nor is it otherwise than just as if
I was in Hell. But why have you come out?

BROMIA: Why, the same things that filled your heart with dread
Alarmed us too; I never saw such sights;
Alas! Amphitryon, my mind gives way!

AMPHITRYON: Be quick; art sure I am Amphitryon?

BROMIA: I am.

AMPHITRYON: Quite sure? Look once again!

BROMIA: I am.

AMPHITRYON: Alone of all my household she retains
Her senses.

BROMIA: Nay, my lord, we all are sane.

AMPHITRYON: And yet my wife has made me to be mad
By her foul deeds.

BROMIA: But I will make you tell
Another tale, Amphitryon; you shall know
Your wife is good and faithful; in few words
The reasons and the arguments for that I'll tell.
And first of all Alcmena's borne two sons.

AMPHITRYON: Two sons?

BROMIA: Yes, two.

AMPHITRYON: The gods preserve me now!

BROMIA: Permit me now to speak that you may know
The gods are all propitious to your wife and you.

AMPHITRYON: Speak then.

BROMIA: Well, when her labour first began,
She invoked the immortal gods to give her aid
With washen hands and covered head. There came
A sudden thunderclap with constant crashing.
We thought the house was coming to the ground.
The whole house flashed as if 'twere made of gold.

AMPHITRYON: I pray you let me go, you've fooled enough.
What happened then?

BROMIA: While this proceeded, none
Of us did hear her either groan or cry;
It passed without a pain.

AMPHITRYON: Of that I'm glad,
Whatever her deserts towards me.

BROMIA: Pass on,
And hear my words. When she had brought forth boys,
She bade us wash them; we began to do so;
But the boy I washed, how large and strong
He was; we could not bind him in his cot.

AMPHITRYON: Too strange your tale! And if these things are true,
I do not doubt that help came from on high.

BROMIA: Still greater things remain, as you will say.
For after he was put into his cot
Two crested snakes of awful size come down
Into the tank for rain; and straightway both
Upraised their heads.

AMPHITRYON: Alas! Alas!

BROMIA: Fear not!
The snakes looked all around, and when they saw
The boys, they fly towards the cot. I then,
Retreating backward, draw them back as well,
Fearing for them, and for myself the while.
But when that one of whom I spoke saw them,
Immediately he jumped out of the cot
And made straight for the snakes; each with one hand
He seizes in a fatal grasp of death.

AMPHITRYON: Strange is your tale; too terrible to hear,
And horror seizes on me as you speak.
And say, what happened next?

BROMIA: The boy killed both;
And while this passes, one with clear loud voice
Calls out your wife's name.

AMPHITRYON: Tell me who was that?

BROMIA: The king of gods and men, the mighty Jove.
He said he was the consort of Alcmena,
And that the son who slew the snakes was his;
The other yours.

AMPHITRYON: Indeed, then, I'm content,
To divide this happiness with Jove. Go home,
And bid your vessels to be straight made fit,
That I with many offerings may seek
The kindly will of Jove. (*To himself, as* BROMIA *goes
      inside*) Meanwhile I'll ask
Counsel and help from seer Tiresias.
But what is this? How loud the thunder rolls!
Gods, I beseech your help.

Act Five.   Scene II.

(JUPITER *appears above.*)

JUPITER: Be of good cheer. Amphitryon, I am
The friend of you and yours; dismiss, I pray,
Your seers and soothsayers; the future I
Will tell you better far than they can do.
And, first of all, I borrowed for a time
Your wife, Alcmena, and so had a son;
You too had got one when you left to join
The army; both were born together at one birth.
That which is mine shall bring immortal fame
To you by his achievements; so return
Into your ancient friendship with your wife.
She has done nothing to deserve your blame,
She was compelled by me. I go to Heaven.
(JUPITER *disappears.*)

Act Five.   Scene III.

AMPHITRYON: It shall be as you wish; and see that you
Your promises perform. I'll go within
To see my wife, and leave Tiresias.
(*To the audience*) And now, spectators, clap for mighty
      Jove,
And give applause for him that reigns above.

1. Acrostic arguments are regularly prefixed to the plays of Plautus, and occasionally, as here, non-acrostic arguments are also found. The dates of these arguments are not known but are usually considered to be two or three centuries after the time of Plautus. The verse translation of the two arguments of the *Amphitryon* is by E. H. Sugden.

2. Plautus disregards geography here and places Thebes near the sea coast.

3. Mercury was the patron god of rogues and thieves.

4. Mercury here satirises the typical running slave of Roman comedy; cf. e.g. *The Comedy of Asses,* Act Two, Scene II; *The Captives,* Act Four, Scene I; *Curculio,* Act Two, Scene III; *The Merchant,* Act One, Scene II.

II
THE COMEDY OF ASSES

CHARACTERS IN THE PLAY

LIBANUS, *slave of* DEMAENETUS
DEMAENETUS, *an aged Athenian*
ARGYRIPPUS, *his son, in love with* PHILAENIUM
CLEARETA, *a procuress*
LEONIDA, *slave of* DEMAENETUS
A DEALER *in asses*
PHILAENIUM, *a courtesan, daughter of* CLEARETA
DIABOLUS, *a young Athenian*
A PARASITE
ARTEMONA, *wife of* DEMAENETUS

ACROSTIC ARGUMENT

A good old man, whose lady is his lord,
S eeks money for his son who's fallen in love.
I n doing it, pay is given for some asses,
N ot to the steward, but to Leonida,
A slave of his; and so the lover gets it.
R ival affection drives Diabolus mad;
I n wrath he tells the whole thing to the wife,
A nd she runs in and drags her husband off.

INTRODUCTION

The Comedy of Asses (the *Asinaria*) was adapted by Plautus from a Greek comedy by Demophilus, *The Ass-Driver*. The play takes its name from the asses, the sale of which provides the money that enables the two intriguing slaves to help their master. The comedy is primarily one of deception, and the situation at the beginning of the play is one frequently found in Roman comedy: a young man (Argyrippus) in love with a courtesan (Philaenium) needs money to secure the girl's favours and to satisfy the demands of the procuress (Cleareta, the girl's mother). The necessary amount is procured by two slaves, one of whom impersonates the steward and collects the money for the asses under false pretences.

The date of the Roman production is not known, but possible allusions to contemporary events, lack of lyrical passages, and flaws in the structure of the plot, have made most scholars agree that the play is one of the earliest of Plautus' extant comedies. The late and unexpected entrance of Diabolus, the rival for the affections of the courtesan, has been severely criticised, and many editors and critics solve the difficulty by assigning the speeches of the young man in Act One, Scenes II and III, to Diabolus instead of to Argyrippus. This seems unlikely, however, for, as J. N. Hough has pointed out, no rival in Roman comedy would be so impecunious as the youth who is portrayed in the first Act. Louis Havet's theory that the author of the play was not Plautus but a certain Maccus, who lived after the time of Terence, has not been accepted, and there seems no reason to doubt that the comedy should be assigned to the earlier years of Plautus' dramatic activity.

Several of the characters are of unusual interest. Argyrippus, like Mnesilochus in *The Two Bacchides* and Alcesimarchus in *The Casket*, is a violent lover; he swears vengeance on Cleareta and threatens suicide if he is unable to gain the favours of his sweetheart. Philaenium is portrayed as deeply in love with him, but obedient to her mother's wishes; her characterisation is marred in the final scene where she plays the part of a pert and wanton courtesan. Demaenetus, unlike many fathers in comedy, is easygoing and tolerant, eager to assist his son in his love affair even if it involves cheating his own wife. He becomes still more disreputable in the closing scenes of the play, where he demands as his reward a share in the affections of his son's sweetheart. He proposes to steal a dress from his wife for the girl, as Menaechmus actually does in *The Twin Menaechmi,* and just as Menaechmus is betrayed by an angry parasite, so here too it is a parasite who informs Demaenetus' wife of his actions. Artemona, the angry wife, who drags her husband home at the end, is an amusing character, and has provided Molière with material for the portrayal of Madame Jourdain in *Le Bourgeois Gentilhomme.*

The Comedy of Asses has been both praised and condemned. It is not one of Plautus' most successful comedies, but it is witty and swift-moving and has few dull scenes. It is broad farce varied by sentimental scenes. The play has been damned for its low moral tone; Gilbert Norwood cites the conclusion to illustrate how "Plautus carries bad taste to the pitch of infamy"; this same scene to others appears "irresistibly comic," "one of the best in ancient drama." Paul Lejay considers the comedy as a whole "a play of youth, love, and joy," and points out three scenes that are particularly successful: Cleareta's discussion with Argyrippus about the life of a courtesan, the tricking of the dealer by the two slaves, and the scene in which the same two slaves tease Argyrippus and Philaenium and make them ridiculous. Two other scenes should be added to this list: the one in which Diabolus and the parasite discuss the contract, and the conclusion when Artemona finds her husband banqueting with his son and Philaenium.

THE COMEDY OF ASSES

(SCENE:—*A street in Athens in front of the houses of* DEMAENETUS *and* CLEARETA.)

Prologue

Pray, gentlemen and ladies, pay attention,
And may good fortune wait on me and you,
Our company, our poets, our lessees.
Come, crier, kindly make the crowd all ears!
There, now, sit down; and mind you charge for that.
Now why I'm on the stage, and what I want,
I'll tell you. 'Tis that you may know the name
Of this our play. The plot's extremely simple.
Now I will tell you what I said I would;
Onagos[1] is the name o' the play in Greek;
Demophilus wrote, Maccius translated it;
He calls it *Asinaria,* by your leave.
The comedy is full of wit and mirth.
It's sure to make you laugh; so listen kindly,
And now and always Mars be your defence!

Act One. Scene I

(*Enter* LIBANUS *and* DEMAENETUS *from the latter's house.*)

LIBANUS: As you would wish your only son to live
And close your eyes in health and happiness,
So I beseech you by your hoary hairs,
By her, whom most you fear, your wife, I mean;
If you don't speak the truth to me today,
Then may your wife outlive you many a year,
And while she lives may you find speedy death.

DEMAENETUS: By all the gods, I'll swear it as you wish.
I see that I must tell you what you ask.

63

So hard you press me, that I really daren't
Refuse to tell you anything you want;
So speak out quickly what you fain would know,
And if I know it, you shall know it too.

LIBANUS: Answer me seriously what I shall ask.
Don't tell me any lies!

DEMAENETUS: What *do* you ask?

LIBANUS: Then are you taking me where stone rubs stone?[2]

DEMAENETUS: What do you say? Where in the world is that?

LIBANUS: Where sinners weep, who feed on barley meal.
In the cudgel-thumping, fetter-clanking isles,
Where living men are set on by dead oxen.[3]

DEMAENETUS: Ah, now I see, by Pollux, where it is!
Where barley-meal is ground, you mean to say.

LIBANUS: I neither say nor want to hear it said!
Oh, I beseech you, spit out that foul word!

DEMAENETUS (*spitting*): All right; I'll humour you!

LIBANUS: Come, hawk away!

DEMAENETUS (*spitting again*): Will *that* do?

LIBANUS: Nay, from the bottom of your throat!
Away!

DEMAENETUS: How far away?

LIBANUS: Even to the death!

DEMAENETUS: Take care, sir!

LIBANUS: Oh, your wife's, I mean, not yours!

DEMAENETUS: For that good jest I pardon all your faults!

LIBANUS: The gods fulfil your wishes!

DEMAENETUS: Listen here!
Why should I ask you this, or threaten you,
Because you didn't tell it me before?
Or why should I be angry with my son,
As other fathers are?

LIBANUS (*aside*):   Hallo, what's this?
                    What can he mean? I fear what's coming next.

DEMAENETUS: I'm certain sure, my son has fallen in love
                    With that Philaenium, the girl next door.
                    Am I right, Libanus?

LIBANUS: You're on the track.
                    The thing is so; but he is very ill.

DEMAENETUS: What's his complaint?

LIBANUS: His gifts don't match his words.

DEMAENETUS: Then you are backing up my love-sick son?

LIBANUS: Indeed I am, and so's Leonida.

DEMAENETUS: You do quite right, and you shan't lose by it.
                    But, Libanus, you do not know my wife!

LIBANUS: You know her best; but we have got a notion.

DEMAENETUS: Believe me, she's a fearful trial to me!

LIBANUS: Oh, I believe you, long before you speak.

DEMAENETUS: All parents, Libanus, who'll be ruled by me,
                    Will treat their children with indulgent care,
                    And so they'll make their son their truest friend.
                    That is my aim; I want my sons to love me.
                    I'll be like my own father; for my sake
                    In sailor's dress he stole away the girl
                    I loved, by trickery, from her mother's house.
                    Old as he was, he counted it no shame
                    To lay the plot, and win his son by kindness.
                    I'm quite resolved to follow in his steps.
                    Well, Argyrippus, my son, asked me today
                    To let him have some money for his sweetheart;
                    In this I long to gratify my son,
                    To indulge his passion, and so win his love.
                    His mother keeps him tied up and confined
                    As fathers often do: so I will not.
                    And since he's thought me worthy of his trust,
                    I ought to honour his good disposition.
                    As he's approached me like a dutiful son,
                    I want the gold for him to give the girl.

LIBANUS: You want what I'm afraid you'll want in vain.
Your wife brought her slave, Saurea, with her dowry,
And he's more money in his hands than you.

DEMAENETUS: Ah, yes, I sold my empire for that dowry!
But now I'll briefly tell you what I wish.
What my son wants just now is twenty minae.
You get it for him!

LIBANUS: Where am I to get it?

DEMAENETUS: Steal it from me.

LIBANUS: What nonsense you do talk!
You send me to steal clothes from nakedness.
Steal it from you! Yes, fly with ne'er a wing!
Steal it from you! You've nothing left to steal,
Unless you first can steal it from your wife.

DEMAENETUS: Swindle myself, my wife, and Saurea
By any means you can, and get the money.
I swear you shall not suffer if you do.

LIBANUS: Yes, bid me go a-fishing in the air,
A-hunting in the middle of the sea!

DEMAENETUS: Well, take Leonida to be your second.
Devise some plan, contrive some clever trick,
And get the money for my son today
To give the girl.

LIBANUS: Look here, Demaenetus!
Supposing I should land myself in trouble,
Will you redeem me if the enemy catch me?

DEMAENETUS: I will.

LIBANUS: All right then; leave it all to me.
I'll to the market-place.

DEMAENETUS: Good; off you go!
Yet stay!

LIBANUS: Well, what?

DEMAENETUS: Supposing I should want you,
Where shall you be?

LIBANUS: Exactly where I please.
          (*Aside*) I'll ne'er again fear any mortal man.
          No one can hurt me, since in your discourse
          You've shown me all the secrets of your soul.
          At *you* I'll snap my fingers, if successful.
          (*Aloud*) Now I'll be off and get my plot in train.

DEMAENETUS: And please observe, you'll find me at the banker's.

LIBANUS: In the market?

DEMAENETUS: If you want me.

LIBANUS: I'll remember. (*Departs to the forum.*)

DEMAENETUS (*to himself*): No slave could be a bigger scamp than this,
          Or craftier, or more difficult to dodge.
          Yet, if you want a thing exactly done,
          Tell *him:* he'll rather die a thousand deaths
          Than fail to do what he has undertaken.
          He'll get the money for my son, I know,
          As surely as this is my walking-stick!
          But I'll be off to the market, as I purposed;
          There at the banker's I'll await events. (*Departs.*)

                    Act One.   Scene II

(*Enter* ARGYRIPPUS *hastily from the house of* CLEARETA.)

ARGYRIPPUS (*angrily, to those within*): Oh, has it come to this? Kicked
               out of doors by her!
          This is the prize for my gifts that she stores by her!
          Foe to your friend, and a friend to your foe, you are.
          Curse you! I'll soon let the magistrates know you are
          Swindler and thief, of young fellows the slaughterer!
          Oh, I'll bring ruin on you and your daughter there!
          Sea's no more sea when compared with your treachery!
          There I got gain, which I lost by your witchery.
          All my kind gifts I've bestowed so effusively
          Only provoke you to treat me abusively.
          Now, I'll do you all the mischief in my power, and serve
               you right!

Back to poverty I'll drive you, out of decent people's
sight.
Yes, by Jove, I'll make you know, ma'am, what you are,
and what you were
In the days before I came and gave my loving heart
to her.
Dry bread was a dainty to you in your rags and poverty;
If you got e'en that, you blessed the gods above on
bended knee.
Now, you wretch, when things are better, you forget
who gave good cheer.
Ah, you savage beast! With hunger will I tame you.
Never fear!
I've no reason to be angry with the girl; she's not to
blame;
She's compelled to do your bidding, tyrant with a
mother's name!
You I'll be revenged on! *You* to utter ruin I'll send!
Ah! The wretch! Why, don't you see, she doesn't even
condescend
Now to come and talk with me, my grace and pardon
to implore!
There! Behold, the witch is coming! Here at last, out-
side the door,
I shall speak my mind. I couldn't there, inside the house,
before.

Act One.   Scene III

(*Enter* CLEARETA *from her house.*)

CLEARETA: Not a single word of yours should anybody buy of me,
Though he tried to strike a bargain with a pound apiece
for fee.
All the insults you have uttered are just so much sterling
gold;
For your heart is nailed and fastened here in Cupid's
grip and hold.
Ply the oar and hoist the sail and hasten from this loved
resort.
Seek the ocean as you may, the storm will drive you
back to port.

ARGYRIPPUS: Not another cent of duty to your custom-house I'll pay!
              No! I'll treat you as your actions merit from this very
                   day,
              Though you don't do so to me! I've not deserved to be
                   turned out!

CLEARETA: Yes, your tongue can chatter finely, and you'll do it!
                   Oh, no doubt!

ARGYRIPPUS: I alone have rescued you from loneliness and poverty;
              I alone should wed the maiden, and that's less than due
                   to me.

CLEARETA: You alone shall wed her, if alone you give me what I ask.
              Keep your presents up, and you shall always in her
                   favour bask.

ARGYRIPPUS: There's no limit to this giving! You are never satisfied.
              After all that I have given you, you want something
                   else beside.

CLEARETA: There's no limit to your loving! There's no satisfying
                   you!
              You've just left her; yet you beg to have another
                   interview.

ARGYRIPPUS: Well, I gave you what you bargained.

CLEARETA: And I let you see your dear.
              You have had your money's worth; "no credit" is our
                   motto here.

ARGYRIPPUS: You're unkind!

CLEARETA: How can you blame me, if I play a
                   mother's part?
              Never sculptor, painter, poet left on record in his art
              That a mother helped her daughter's lover, when he
                   couldn't pay.

ARGYRIPPUS: It'll pay you to be gentle; else you'll drive me clean
                   away.

CLEARETA: No, sir! She who spares a lover is unkind to her own
                   flesh.
              For a lover's like a fish; no good at all unless he's fresh!
              Then he's full of juice and tender; you can cook him
                   any way;

Stew him, fry him, take your choice; it doesn't matter
    which you say.
So your lover longs to give: "Do ask for something;
    I'm no churl!"
Doesn't care how much he loses, thinks of nothing but
    the girl.
Wants to please her, wants to please me, wants to please
    my little page,
Wants to please my men and maidens, yes, extends his
    patronage,
Your fresh lover, to my lap-dog, so to be a welcome
    guest.
That's the truth. And every one must look to his own
    interest.

ARGYRIPPUS: Yes, it's true. I've learnt the lesson and I've had to
    pay the price.

CLEARETA: If you'd anything to give me now, you'd talk as nice
    as nice.
But because you haven't, you demand with threats my
    daughter's hand.

ARGYRIPPUS: No, I don't.

CLEARETA: Nor I don't either let you have her, under-
    stand!
Still in pity of your youth and gentle blood, I'll offer
    this:—
As you've cared more for our profits than for your own
    dignities—
If you'll get for me two talents,[4] pay it down upon the
    nail,
For the great respect I bear you, you shall have her
    without fail.

ARGYRIPPUS: If I can't?

CLEARETA: Oh, I shan't trust you. Someone else shall
    have her then.

ARGYRIPPUS: Where's the money I have given you?

CLEARETA: Spent; it can't be used again.
If your cash would last for ever, I'd not ask a penny
    more.

True, for day and night and water we've not got to pay
    a score;
But for other necessaries we are forced to pay cash
    down;
That's the custom with the bakers and the vintners in
    the town;
"Pay your cash and take your purchase!" Well, it's
    just the same with me.
Day and night my hands have eyes, and only trust what
    they can see.
Quoth the proverb "There's no getting"—you know
    what!—I'll say no more.

ARGYRIPPUS: Oh yes! Now you've picked my pockets, you can turn
    me out o' door.
This is not the way you used me, when I had the cash
    to spend,
When you used to flatter me and pay me compliments
    no end.
Then your house was wreathed in smiles to welcome
    me whene'er I came,
And you never tired of telling how you loved me still
    the same.
When I'd given you a present you were like two turtle
    doves,
Hanging on my lips and cooing of your deep and tender
    loves.
How you clung to me and ran to carry out my least
    desire!
Everything that didn't suit or please me, that you
    shunned like fire!
Wouldn't dare attempt to do it; my least wish was
    made your law.
Now for my desires or wishes you don't seem to care
    a straw.

CLEARETA: O my boy, there's no such fowler as a match-making
    mamma!
When your fowler sets his traps, he scatters grain both
    near and far,
So the birds grow tame; thus money must be spent if
    profit's sought.
True, the birds get many a meal; but he is paid, when
    once they're caught.

So it is with me, my house here is the trap, the fowler I;
My sweet daughter is the bait; her lovers are the birds
    so shy.
They grow tame by kindly greetings, by her soft and
    warm embrace,
By her kisses and her speeches full of sportiveness and
    grace;
If one steals his arm around her, that just helps the
    fowler's game;
If he takes a kiss, why, let him; I shall catch him all
    the same.
Surely you have not forgotten, who have been at school
    so long!

ARGYRIPPUS: Well, then, don't dismiss your scholar half instructed!
    'Twould be wrong!

CLEARETA: Come back bravely, when you've got the money; for
    the present, go!

ARGYRIPPUS: Stay! Stay! Listen! Tell me truly, for your answer I
    must know;
What's the least you'll take to give me her?

CLEARETA: Well, twenty minae will do.
But if any other suitor brings it first, good-bye to you.

ARGYRIPPUS: Oh, I'll bring it. But there's one thing more before
    you go.

CLEARETA: Say on.

ARGYRIPPUS: I'm not altogether ruined; some resources have not
    gone.
I can give you what you ask me; but before I go away,
Give her to me for a whole year, if I bring the cash
    today.

CLEARETA: Certainly, and if you wish it, have a settlement prepared
Wherein all the terms of union may be legally declared.
Only bring the money with you; that's the only thing
    I mind.
For our door is very like a custom's office, as I find.
If you bring the cash, it opens; if you don't, it's closed
    to you.
    (CLEARETA *goes into her house.*)

ARGYRIPPUS (*to himself*): I must find those twenty minae. If I can't,
  what shall I do?

  I must either lose the money or be lost myself, that's
   plain!

  Now to the market! There I'll see what can be done
   with might and main.

  I'll entreat and supplicate my friends, whoe'er comes
   in my way;

  Good and bad, I'll try them all and get some answer,
   yea or nay.

  If no friend will lend it me, the interest I'll have to pay.
  (ARGYRIPPUS *departs to the forum.*)

Act Two.   Scene I

(*Enter* LIBANUS *from the forum.*)

LIBANUS (*to himself*): Come now, Libanus, wake up and give attention
  to this case!

  Hours ago you left your lord and went down to the market-place.

  Did you think you could discover how to come across the
   money,

  Snoring till this time of day in idleness? No, no, my
   sonny!

  Nay, cast off this sluggishness, or you'll be in a pretty
   fix!

  Come, awake, recall to memory some of your old clever
   tricks!

  Guard your master; don't you do, as other servants
   often will,

  Who employ, to cheat their masters, all their cunning,
   craft, and skill.

  Where to get it? Whom to swindle? Whither shall I
   steer my bark?

  Ah! The omens favour me; the birds permit it! Pray
   you, mark!

  Left, a crow and wood-pecker, and right, a screech-owl
   and a raven

  Give me luck; I must succeed! Come, Libanus, don't be
   a craven!

Ha, the wood-pecker's a-tapping on an elm! What does
  that mean?
Yes, from master wood-pecker as much as this I surely
  glean;
Elm rods are in store for me—or for the steward
  Saurea!
But what's this? Leonida is running breathlessly this
  way!
Oh, I fear he's spoiled the omens for the tricks I mean
  to play.

Act Two. Scene II

(Enter LEONIDA *running; he does not at first see* LIBANUS.*)*

LEONIDA (*to himself*): Where on earth am I to find them, Libanus or
  my master's son?
  Joyfuller than Joy herself I'll make them if this job
  gets done.
  Yes, the greatest spoil and triumph will my advent bring
  to them.
  Since they've shared their drinks with me and joined
  in many a stratagem,
  When I get this spoil I'm after, I will share it with
  them too!

LIBANUS (*aside*): Oh, he's been a-burgling, has he? Just the sort of
  thing he'd do!
  Well, I'm sorry for the man that kept the door! Unlucky
  cuss!

LEONIDA: All my life I'd be a slave if I could but meet Libanus.

LIBANUS (*aside*): Oh, if that depends on me, you'll be a slave until
  the close!

LEONIDA: Might I see him, from my back I'd give two hundred
  swelling blows!

LIBANUS (*aside*): See, he offers all he has! His treasure's all upon
  his back.

LEONIDA: If he lets this chance get past him, he may follow on
  its track,

Horse and chariot, but he'll never catch it, once it gets
    away;
In despair he'll leave his master, fill his foes with joy
    today!
But if we can bravely seize the chance that now presents
    itself,
We'll enrich our noble masters with illimitable pelf,
Full of endless joy and gladness both to father and to
    son;
They'll be under obligation all their lives for what we've
    done,
Fettered to us by our kindness.

LIBANUS (*aside*):   He said "fettered," 'pon my troth!
    I don't like it; I'm afraid he's making mischief for us
    both.

LEONIDA: I'm undone if I can't find that Libanus. What *is* he
    doing?

LIBANUS (*aside*): Now he's seeking a companion who will go with him
    to ruin!
    I don't like it; it's a bad sign first to sweat and then
    to shiver!

LEONIDA: Fool I am, to tie my feet and let my tongue run on for
    ever!
    I must bind her down to silence, cutting up this precious
    day!

LIBANUS (*aside*): Oh, the wretch! To bind his best protectress in this
    shameful way!
    For whene'er he gets in mischief, she is perjured for his
    blunder!

LEONIDA: I must hurry off or I shall be too late to get the plunder.

LIBANUS (*aside*): Eh, what plunder? I'll accost him! I won't go with-
    out my share.
    (*Aloud*) Hey! Good morning! How d'ye do? Come,
    don't you hear me shouting, there?

LEONIDA: Ah, you training ground for scourges!

LIBANUS: What are you doing, prison bird?

LEONIDA: Good old lodging-house for fetters!

LIBANUS: Switches' sweetheart, how've you fared?

LEONIDA: How much do you think you weigh now, with your
            clothes off?

LIBANUS: I don't know.

LEONIDA: No, I rather thought you didn't; so I weighed you long
            ago.
            Bound and naked, hanging by your feet you weigh a
            hundred pounds.

LIBANUS: How d'ye prove it?

LEONIDA: Oh, I'll tell you on the most convincing grounds.
            When a hundred pounds exactly hung suspended from
            your feet,
            And your hands were shackled up and fastened to the
            beam so neat,
            You weighed neither less nor more, but were—the same
            old scoundrel still!

LIBANUS: Damn you!

LEONIDA: No, sir! Slavery has left *you* that by his
                last will.

LIBANUS: Come, I say, let's stop this chaffing! Come to business
            speedily!
            What's this matter that's turned up? Nay, you can
            safely trust in me.

LEONIDA: If you want to lend a hand to help our master's amor-
            ous son,
            Such a chance presents itself. But there'll be risk be-
            fore it's done!
            Oh, the executioners will have a regular festival!
            Now for cheek and craftiness, my Libanus! We need
            it all.
            I've invented such a piece of villainy that you and I
            Shall have torments heaped upon us, and deserve them
            thoroughly.

LIBANUS: Ah, I wondered what my shoulder-blades were itching
            for today;
            Now I see they were foretelling trouble that was on
            the way.
            Tell me what it is, however.

LEONIDA: Great the risk, but great the plunder.

LIBANUS: Then let all the world together pile their tortures on,
            by thunder!
            I've a back, I guess, can bear 'em; yes, I'll give 'em all
            the bluff!

LEONIDA: Only keep that courage up, my boy, and we are safe
            enough.

LIBANUS: Nay, if backs can pay the piper, I would rob the Rev-
            enue;
            Then deny it, and stick to it, and be perjured through
            and through.

LEONIDA: That's true valour which, if need be, is in suffering
            evils bold.
            If you suffer evils bravely, you will stuff your purse
            with gold.

LIBANUS: Oh, get on and tell me quickly; I just long for misery.

LEONIDA: Easy then with all your questions; let me rest. Why,
            don't you see
            That I still am out of breath with running?

LIBANUS: All right, I can stay
            Till you're ready; if you like, until you die.

LEONIDA: Where's master, eh?

LIBANUS: At the market-place; his son is in that house—
            (LIBANUS *points to the house of* CLEARETA.)

LEONIDA: I've got enough!

LIBANUS: Oh, then, you've been made a millionaire!

LEONIDA: Come, stop your silly stuff!

LIBANUS: Right you are! My ears are itching till your precious
            news you mention.

LEONIDA: Listen then, and you shall know as much as I.

LIBANUS: I'm all attention!

LEONIDA: Good! Do you remember some Arcadian asses that were
            sold
            By our steward to a trader come from Pella?

LIBANUS: Yes; that's old.

LEONIDA: Well, then, he's sent on the money to be paid to Saurea
            For those asses; and the fellow with the money's come
                today.

LIBANUS: Where's the man?

LEONIDA: Why, would you eat him, if you got
                him in your sight?

LIBANUS: Wouldn't I? But stay a bit—you mean the asses—am I
                right?
            Old and lame, whose hoofs were worn off right away up
                to their thighs?

LEONIDA: Yes; and when you wanted elm rods, they would bring
                the fresh supplies.

LIBANUS: Aye, and take you to the farm in fetters!

LEONIDA: What a memory!
            Well, as I was at the barber's, in he comes, and asks
                of me,
            If I knew Demaenetus, the son of Strato. "Yes, I have
            That distinguished honour," says I, "and, in fact, I am
                his slave."
            Then I showed him where our house is.

LIBANUS: Get on! What's the next thing, eh?

LEONIDA: Well, he says he's brought the money for our steward,
                Saurea,
            Twenty minae for those asses; but he doesn't know the
                man,
            Though he knows Demaenetus as well as anybody can.
            When he's done his yarn—

LIBANUS: What then?

LEONIDA: Well, listen! Ain't I telling you?
            Straight I turn myself into a splendid fellow, spick-span
                new!
            And I tell him *I'm* the steward! Then replied my coun-
                try tyke:
            "But, by Pollux, I don't know your Saurea, nor what
                he's like.

Oh, you needn't get so savage; kindly fetch your master
here;

I know him; and then I'll pay the money over, never
fear!"

Well, I said I'd fetch the master, and then wait for him
at home.

He'll be going to have a bath; and when that's over,
here he'll come.

Now, what trick shall we be up to? Tell me quickly.

LIBANUS: Well, dear sonny,

We've to swindle our friend Saurea and the stranger of
that money.

Come, we've got to rough it out! Suppose the stranger
gets here first,

Bringing that same money with him, then our bubble
will be burst.

For today the old man took me, drew me quietly aside;

Threatened that both you and I should feel the elms
upon our hide,

If this day for Argyrippus twenty minae were not found.

Then he gave us full permission, if we could, to get
around

Both the steward and his wife; and promised he would
help us too.

Go now to the market-place, and tell him what we're
going to do.

You, Leonida, are going to be the steward Saurea,

When the dealer brings the money for the asses.

LEONIDA: As you say!

LIBANUS: Meanwhile I'll just keep him quiet, if he happens to
come here.

LEONIDA: Oh, I say!

LIBANUS: What's that?

LEONIDA: Supposing I should soundly box your ear

When I'm shamming to be Saurea, don't you let your
temper rise.

LIBANUS: See, my friend, you'd best be careful not to touch me,
if you're wise.

You'll be sorry that you changed your name, if you
begin to whack.

LEONIDA:　Suffer it with patience.

LIBANUS:　　　　　　　　Nay, you'll suffer, when I hit you back.

LEONIDA:　But I tell you, it's his custom.

LIBANUS:　　　　　　　　　　And I tell you what I'll do.

LEONIDA:　Don't refuse me!

LIBANUS:　　　　　　　Oh, I promise I can hit as hard as you.

LEONIDA:　Well, I'm off! I know you'll bear it like a man. What's
　　　　　this? Hallo!
　　　　　Here he is! I'll cut and run! Meanwhile, you keep him
　　　　　here in tow.
　　　　　I must tell the master of it.

LIBANUS:　　　　　　　　　Quick! About your business go.
　　　　(LEONIDA *hurries off toward the forum.*)

Act. Two.　Scene III

(*Enter the* DEALER *in asses, with a slave.*)

DEALER (*to his slave*): Unless I've been directed wrong, this is the
　　　　　house, I'm sure,
　　　　　Where dwells Demaenetus. Go, boy, and knock upon the
　　　　　door,
　　　　　And if the steward Saurea's in, just ask him to come
　　　　　here.

LIBANUS (*stepping forward*): Who's smashing down our door like this?
　　　　　Hallo there! Do you hear?

DEALER:　Why, no one touched it! Are you mad?

LIBANUS:　　　　　　　　Ah, well, I thought you'd knocked,
　　　　　Because I saw you coming here. Indeed, I should be
　　　　　shocked
　　　　　To see our door get thrashed by you; I love my fellow-
　　　　　slaves.

DEALER:　Your door will ne'er be broken down, if every one who
　　　　　craves
　　　　　An entrance has so short a time to wait; it can't be
　　　　　shorter.

LIBANUS: Ah, that's a way our door has got; it always calls the porter,
    Whene'er it sees a fellow come who looks too vigorous
    At kicking! But who is't you seek?

DEALER: I want Demaenetus.

LIBANUS: He's not at home or you should know.

DEALER: Well, is his steward in?

LIBANUS: He's not.

DEALER: Where is he?

LIBANUS: Oh, he's at the barber's with his chin.

DEALER: I met him. Hasn't he come back?

LIBANUS: He's not. What is there more?

DEALER: If he were here, I'd pay him twenty minae now.

LIBANUS: What for?

DEALER: He sold some asses at the fair to an ass-dealer from Pella.

LIBANUS: I know; ah, well, he'll be not long, or I'm no fortune-teller.

DEALER: But tell me, what's your Saurea like? (*Aside*) I'll see if it's the same.

LIBANUS: He's pot-bellied, with lantern jaws, and hair as red as flame,
    With savage eyes, of medium height, a frown upon his brow.

DEALER (*aside*): No painter could have pictured him more faithfully, I vow!

LIBANUS: By Hercules, he's coming now! See how he shakes his head!
    If any one should cross his rage, I guess he'll strike him dead!

DEALER: Well, if he comes with Hectoring threats and eyes with fury flashing,
    And lays an angry hand on me, he'll get an angry thrashing!

Act Two. Scene IV

(*Enter* LEONIDA *as* SAUREA.)

LEONIDA (*to himself*): There's no one pays the slightest heed to any-
                    thing I say!
            I ordered Libanus to come to the barber's shop today;
            He never came; his legs and back shall pay the penalty.

DEALER (*to* LIBANUS): How arrogant the fellow is!

LIBANUS: Oh, wretched, wretched me!

LEONIDA (*to* LIBANUS): You've been set free, no doubt, today!

LIBANUS: Have mercy, I beseech!

LEONIDA: Oh, you'll be feeling sorry that you've come within my
                    reach.
            Why weren't you at the barber's as I bade?

LIBANUS (*pointing to* DEALER):   He kept me here.

LEONIDA: By Hercules, and if you said that it was Jupiter,
            And he himself should plead your cause, I'd flog you,
                    never doubt.
            You'll disobey me, will you, hound?

LIBANUS: Kind stranger, help me out!

DEALER: I beg you not to punish him for my sake, Saurea!

LEONIDA: I only wish I had a goad—

DEALER: Oh, do be quiet, pray!

I.EONIDA: To stick it in your idle ribs, too tough to feel a blow.
            Depart and let me flog this wretch, who irritates me so!
            An order only given once he swears he never heard;
            So you must yell a hundred times, until, upon my word,
            I really haven't strength enough to scold and objurgate.
            I bade you, villain, shift away that filth from our front
                    gate;
            I bade you clear the spiders' webs that clothe these pil-
                    lars o'er;
            I bade you polish, till it shone, the handle of the door.

It's all no use; I might be lame, I have to walk with
    sticks.

Because three days I've been from home, and trying
    hard to fix

On some one who would take a loan, you slumber like
    a bear,

And so I find when I come back a pigsty, I declare!

Take that! (*Striking him.*)

LIBANUS: Kind stranger, help me, do!

DEALER: Good Saurea, I pray,
For my sake please to let him off.

LEONIDA (*to* LIBANUS):   Did anybody pay
The carriage of that oil?

LIBANUS: Oh, yes!

LEONIDA: To whom?

LIBANUS: Your deputy,
Good Stichus.

LEONIDA: Bah, you're flattering! My deputy is he,
Nor have I got in all the house a more trustworthy slave.
But what about the wine that I let Exaerambus have?
Has he paid Stichus?

LIBANUS: So I think; on this my faith I anchor;
I saw that Exaerambus coming hither with his banker.

LEONIDA: That's right; last time I trusted him he took a year to
    pay;
He's frightened now; so brings him[5] home and writes
    the cheque straightway.
Has Dromo brought his wages in?

LIBANUS: But half of it, he said.

LEONIDA: What of the rest?

LIBANUS: He'll pay it you, as soon as he gets paid.
They're keeping it until he's done the job that was
    agreed.

LEONIDA: The cups lent Philodamus, has he brought them back
    d'ye heed?

LIBANUS: No.

LEONIDA: Better give a thing away than lend it to a friend!

DEALER (*annoyed*): Oh, damn his temper! I'll be off!

LIBANUS (*aside to* LEONIDA):   Come, bring this to an end.
     D'ye hear him?

LEONIDA (*aside to* LIBANUS): Yes; I'll hold my tongue!

DEALER (*aside*):   At last he's ceased his jangle.
     I'd better speak to him before he starts again to wrangle.
     (*Aloud*) How soon can you attend to me?

LEONIDA: Have you been waiting long?
     By Hercules, I didn't see you; pray don't take it wrong!
     My anger so obstructs my sight.

DEALER: I've not the slightest doubt!
     I've called to see Demaenetus.

LEONIDA: This slave still says he's out.
     But never mind; that money you can pay me just the
         same;
     I'll give you a receipt in full in my good master's name.

DEALER: I think I'd rather pay you when Demaenetus is by.

LIBANUS (*to* DEALER): My master trusts him!

DEALER: Him I'll pay, but not upon the sly.

LIBANUS: Oh, give it him; I'll take the risk; I'll make the thing
         all square.
     For if the old man finds you would not trust his steward
         there,
     He will be mad; he trusts to him all things to regulate.

LEONIDA: He needn't pay unless he likes; 'gad, let the fellow wait!

LIBANUS: Pay it, I say; or else I fear he'll think that I have said
     Something to make you doubt his word; come, pay,
         don't be afraid.
     It's right enough.

DEALER: I think it is, as long as I stick to it;
     I don't know Saurea.

LIBANUS: This is he; I thought, of course, you knew it.

DEALER: He may or mayn't be; I can't tell; if he is, it must be so.
                 But I shan't pay the money to a man I do not know.

LEONIDA: May all the gods confound him then! (*To* LIBANUS)
                 And don't you say a word!
                 The rascal proudly keeps my twenty minae! It's absurd!
                 (*To* DEALER) Come, get away! Be off from here! Don't
                 vex me more, you pup!

DEALER: Oh, what a temper! For a slave you're rather too stuck
                 up!

LEONIDA (*to* LIBANUS): By Hercules, I'll flog you if you don't abuse
                 him too.

LIBANUS (*obeying*): You filthy villain! (*Aside to* DEALER) Don't you
                 see he's angry?

LEONIDA (*to* LIBANUS):   That will do.

LIBANUS (*aloud to* DEALER): You dirty rascal! (*In an undertone*) Pay
                 him, do, or you'll get such a slanging!

DEALER: Oh, you'll be sorry for all this!

LEONIDA (*to* LIBANUS):   I'll give your legs a banging
                 If you don't curse that shameless rogue!

LIBANUS (*to* DEALER):   Alas! You shameless villain,
                 You wretch! (*In an undertone*) To help poor wretched
                 me, I pray you will be willing!

LEONIDA: You dare entreat that scoundrel's help?

DEALER: What's that? You slave, you dare
                 Speak of a gentleman like that?

LEONIDA: Be thrashed!

DEALER: No, you'll be there;
                 If once I see Demaenetus, you'll not have one sound
                 member.
                 I'll summons you!

LEONIDA: I'll not appear.

DEALER: You'll not appear? Remember!

LEONIDA: All right.

DEALER: I'll see I get revenged upon your back.

LEONIDA: Be hanged!
Don't think, you hangman, that by you we're going to
be banged.

DEALER: Ah, well, for all your slanderous words the penalty
you'll pay.

LEONIDA: What, you whipped cur! You gallows-bird! Don't think
I'll run away.
Go to my master, whom you call and want so much to
see.

DEALER: At last! But you will never get the money out of me
Until Demaenetus commands.

LEONIDA: All right; come, walk away.
If you insult your fellow man, you must expect rough
play.
I'm just a good a man as you.

DEALER: Quite so.

LEONIDA: Then follow me.
Without offense I now may say there's no one that
would be
So bold as to impugn my faith; there's not another man
In Athens whom they trust so much.

DEALER: Maybe! But nothing can
Persuade me to transfer the cash to you whom I don't
know.
A man you don't know is a wolf; the proverb tells us so.

LEONIDA: Ah, now you're coming round a bit; I knew you'd make
amends
For all the wrong you've done to me. Although my dress
offends,
For all that I'm a careful man, my savings can't be
counted.

DEALER: Maybe!

LEONIDA: Periphanes brought from Rhodes a sum that
just amounted
To a whole talent's worth; although my master was
away,
He counted it and paid it, nor did I his trust betray.

DEALER: Maybe!

LEONIDA: And if you'd only made inquiry on the quiet,
You would have trusted me with all you've got.

DEALER (*dryly*): I don't deny it.
(LEONIDA, LIBANUS, *and the* DEALER *depart to the forum.*)

Act Three. Scene I

(*Enter* CLEARETA *and* PHILAENIUM *from their house.*)

CLEARETA: Can I never hinder you from doing things that I forbid?
If you had your way, you minx, you'd soon be of your
mother rid.
Is it right to disobey me? Come, what have you got to
say?

PHILAENIUM: How could I do right, dear mother, if I acted in the way
You prescribe, and tried to please, doing as you order
me?

CLEARETA: Right, indeed! D'you call it right to sneer at my authority?

PHILAENIUM: Mothers who do right I blame not, love them not when
wrong they do.

CLEARETA: You can chatter well enough, miss!

PHILAENIUM: Mother, 'tis my nature to!
What I think I'm bound to utter, when I've opportunity.

CLEARETA: Why, I brought you here to scold you; don't begin to
lecture me!

PHILAENIUM: Lecture you? I couldn't, mother, for I shouldn't think
it right—
Only I lament the fate which keeps my sweetheart from
my sight.

CLEARETA: Won't you let me have a chance of speaking all this
live-long day?

PHILAENIUM: Take my share and yours as well; dear mother, gladly I
give way.

You shall give me sailing orders, you shall urge me on or check;

Though if I laid down my oar and fell asleep upon the deck,

All the ship would stop, I fancy, you and all your household too.

CLEARETA: Listen! You're the sauciest girl with whom I ever had to do.

How much oftener must I tell you, you're to let that fellow go,

Argyrippus, son of old Demaenetus. Oh, yes! You know! What's he given us? What's he sent us? Oh, his love is growing cold.

You think witty words are presents, tender speeches good as gold.

So you love him and pursue him and invite him to the house;

Mock your generous suitors, dote on one who's impecunious.

For we can't afford to wait, although it's true he promises

He will make you roll in riches, when his good old mother dies.

Can't you see that all our household is with deadly peril cursed?

While we're waiting for her death, we'll die ourselves of hunger first.

If he can't bring twenty minae, as I told to him before,

Never shall your lavish giver of his tears come in this door.

For the last time I have listened to his plea of poverty.

PHILAENIUM: Mother, stint me of my food and I will bear it patiently.

CLEARETA: Love the men that give you presents that they may be loved by you.

PHILAENIUM: But I've lost my heart! Oh, mother, tell me what I ought to do.

CLEARETA: Look at my grey hairs, my dear, and think of your own interest.

PHILAENIUM: Many a shepherd, who is feeding other's sheep, himself is blessed

With just one ewe lamb, the earnest of the flock he
        hopes to own;
Let me love my Argyrippus, darling of my heart alone!

CLEARETA: Get you in! I've heard enough of your impertinence
        today.

PHILAENIUM: Mother, you have trained me well, and so to hear is
        to obey.

        (PHILAENIUM *and* CLEARETA *go inside.*)

Act Three.   Scene II

(*Enter* LIBANUS *and* LEONIDA *from the forum.*)

LIBANUS: Great laud and praise we ought to pay to thee, great god
        of swindling,
For certainly our knavishness has shown no signs of
        dwindling.
Despising all the elm rod's might, and trusting to our
        shoulders,
We've bravely stood against hot-plates and crosses and
        shin-holders,
And stocks and chains and prison-cells, and shackles,
        bonds, and fetters,
And those infernal dogs who live by scourging of their
        betters.
Alas, they know our backs too well by many an ancient
        scarring.
Now all their regiments and troops and soldiers armed
        for warring,
By force of fight and lying hard, we've put to dreadful
        slaughter.
All this was done by my address, and this my brave
        supporter.
I'll suffer stripes with any man, although it's true they
        hurt you.

LEONIDA: By Pollux, I can tell you this, you cannot praise your
        virtue
As well as I your villainies, though I should not have
        said it;

In countless numbers they abound, and greatly to your
    credit.
You've cheated those who trusted you, you've used your
    master badly,
And with a fabricated tale you've perjured yourself
    gladly.
You've broken into houses, you've been often caught in
    thieving,
And hanging by your feet maintained your cause past
    all believing
Against eight strong and sturdy men, who plied their
    rods upon you.

LIBANUS: I must confess, Leonida, that all you say is quite true.
But yours are just as plentiful. Oh, yes, I will be just
    too
And tell them all; you always prove a rogue to those
    who trust you;
You've been discovered in a theft, red-handed, and got
    beaten;
You've sworn to lies, you've robbed a shrine, your words
    you've often eaten;
You've always proved a loss, disgrace, and nuisance to
    your masters;
If anybody trusted you, you collared the piastres!
Your mistress you have always more than any friend
    befriended;
And often by your toughness you've successfully con-
    tended
With strongest lictors' elm rods till their vigour was
    expended.
And now I think we're even, so your praises shall be
    ended.

LEONIDA: Your catalogue adds lustre to our well-known ingenuity.

LIBANUS: Come, drop it now and tell me this.

LEONIDA: Ask on with perspicuity.

LIBANUS: Well, have you got that twenty minae?

LEONIDA: You've the right afflatus!
How nobly did Demaenetus his best to vindicate us!
How cleverly the old man shammed I was his faithful
    factor!

I almost burst out laughing, as he ranted like an actor,
Because the stranger wouldn't trust me with that precious money.
To hear him call me, "Saurea, my steward!" Oh, 'twas
funny!

LIBANUS: Hold on!

LEONIDA: What's up?

LIBANUS: Why, isn't that Philaenium appearing
And Argyrippus?

LEONIDA: Hold your tongue; let's give attentive hearing.

LIBANUS: They're crying, and she's grasping at his cloak! What
can it be now?
Be still! Let's listen!

LEONIDA: Out alas! It just occurs to me, how
I wish to heaven I had a stick.

LIBANUS: What for?

LEONIDA: Why, just to knock it
About those asses,[6] if they start to bray inside my
pocket.

Act Three.   Scene III

(*Enter* ARGYRIPPUS *and* PHILAENIUM *from the house of* CLEARETA; *they
do not at first see the two slaves.*)[7]

ARGYRIPPUS: Why do you hold me back?

PHILAENIUM: Because I'm sad when you're away.

ARGYRIPPUS: Farewell!

PHILAENIUM: I'd fare much better, love, if only you would stay.

ARGYRIPPUS: Good-bye!

PHILAENIUM: When you are gone, no good remains, but bitter woe.

ARGYRIPPUS: Your mother's sung my funeral dirge and ordered me
to go.

PHILAENIUM: Her daughter she may bury next, if she sends you away.

LIBANUS (*to* LEONIDA): By Jove, he's been turned out!

LEONIDA (*to* LIBANUS): He has!

ARGYRIPPUS: Come, let me go, I pray!

PHILAENIUM: Where are you going? Why not stop?

ARGYRIPPUS: I'll come again tonight.

LIBANUS (*aside to* LEONIDA): The evening's all that he can spare. Oh,
isn't he polite?
Of course, he's busy all the day, a second Solon he!
A-making laws to regulate the people's manners. See?
If he had power to make the laws, and folks had to obey,
They'd squander all their property, and drink both
night and day.

LEONIDA (*to* LIBANUS): By Jove, he'd never move a step, if he had any
choice.
In spite of all his hurry and his threats, he won't rejoice.

LIBANUS (*to* LEONIDA): Oh, stop your talking; it is his I want to hear.
Now then!

ARGYRIPPUS: Farewell!

PHILAENIUM: Where goest thou?

ARGYRIPPUS: Fare thee well! In heaven we'll meet again.
For as for me I am resolved from this vile life to fly.

PHILAENIUM: Ah, why should you condemn me thus, an innocent, to
die?

ARGYRIPPUS: Condemn you? I? Why, if I thought that you were
dying, love,
I'd give my life instead of yours my faithfulness to
prove.

PHILAENIUM: Then don't you threaten any more to die by suicide.
For what d'you think that I should do, supposing you
had died?
I'm quite resolved that I should do the same as you
had done.

ARGYRIPPUS: O sweeter than sweet honey!

PHILAENIUM: O my life, my darling one!
          Embrace me, love!

ARGYRIPPUS (*doing so*): Aye, that I will.

PHILAENIUM: Oh, that we so might die!

LEONIDA (*aside to* LIBANUS): O Libanus, how wretched is a man in love!

LIBANUS (*to* LEONIDA):   Aye, aye!
          But one who's flogged is wretcheder.

LEONIDA (*to* LIBANUS):   I know it, for I've tried.
          Come, let's accost them; I on this and you on t'other
          side.
          (*To* ARGYRIPPUS) Hail master! Is this woman smoke
          that in your arms is lying?

ARGYRIPPUS: What's that?

LEONIDA: I see she's got into your eyes and set them crying.

ARGYRIPPUS: You've lost a man who would have been your patron
          and no bad one.

LEONIDA: Oh, no, I haven't lost him, sir—because I never had one.

LIBANUS: Philaenium, hail!

PHILAENIUM: May heaven grant you all your heart is craving!

LIBANUS: I'll have a cask of wine and kiss from you, if wishing's
          having.

ARGYRIPPUS: You scoundrel, take care what you say!

LIBANUS: My wishes were for you, sir.

ARGYRIPPUS: Oh, well, say what you like.

LIBANUS: Then let me beat him (*indicating* LEONIDA)
          black and blue, sir.

LEONIDA: What, you flog me, you foolish fop, you scented Syb-
          arite!
          Why, flogging suits your back as well as food your ap-
          petite!

ARGYRIPPUS: Ah, Libanus, though you're a slave, you're better off
          than I.
          Before this evening's shadows fall, I shall be dead.

LIBANUS:	Pray why?
ARGYRIPPUS:	Why, I love her and she loves me; I've nothing left to give;
	And as her mother's turned me out, why should I longer live?
	Yes, I am driven to my death, unless that money's found,
	Which young Diabolus has sworn to give to bring her round,
	That she may give her daughter to him on this very night.
	To think that twenty minae'd have such wondrous power and might!
	He who can spend them saves himself, while I am lost who can't.
LIBANUS:	But has he paid the cash?
ARGYRIPPUS:	Not yet.
LIBANUS:	Cheer up, then! Fear, avaunt!
LEONIDA:	Here, Libanus, a word with you.
LIBANUS:	All right. (*They whisper together.*)
ARGYRIPPUS:	Look here, I say,
	You might as well embrace outright; it's much the nicer way.
LIBANUS:	Tastes differ, sir; and what suits you may not so well suit me.
	You lovers like embracing well enough, as we can see.
	I wouldn't mind embracing her, but she's too coy and nice;
	So go ahead yourself, dear sir, and take your own advice.
ARGYRIPPUS:	Aye, that I will, and gladly too; you too withdraw meanwhile.
LEONIDA (*aside to* LIBANUS):	Well, shall we make a fool of him?
LIBANUS (*to* LEONIDA):	We will, boy! That's the style!
LEONIDA:	Suppose I make Philaenium kiss me before his eyes?
LIBANUS:	The very thing!
LEONIDA:	Then come along! (*They rejoin the others.*)

ARGYRIPPUS: Now what is your device?

LEONIDA: Come listen and attend to me; devour the words I say.
                  Well, first of all, we don't deny that we're your slaves
                      this day.
                  But if we find you twenty minae to take to that old
                      matron's,
                  By what name would you call us then?

ARGYRIPPUS: Oh, freedmen!

LEONIDA: Why not patrons?

ARGYRIPPUS: Most certainly!

LEONIDA (*displaying the bag of money*): This bag will prove the right
                                    amount's been found;
                  And if you like I'll give it you.

ARGYRIPPUS: May heaven's best gifts abound
                  To you, your master's saviour, you hoard of treasure
                      trove,
                  Salvation of my inmost soul and emperor of love!
                  Come, hang your bag around my neck all fair and square
                      and level.

LEONIDA: For you to carry such a load would be the very devil!

ARGYRIPPUS: But why not free yourself from toil and put it on to me?

LEONIDA: I'll be your porter, you go on in front; so should it be.

ARGYRIPPUS: Come, come; what's this? Why don't you give the bag
                      to your poor master?

LEONIDA: Then bid your sweetheart beg of me to save you from
                      disaster;
                  For that's a steepish slope whereon you bade me place
                      it level.

PHILAENIUM: Thou apple of mine eye, my rose, my soul, in whom I
                      revel,
                  Leonida, O give it me; let lovers' prayers prevail.

LEONIDA: Well, call me then your sparrow, and your chicken, and
                      your quail;
                  Your lambkin, and your kidling, and your calf that
                      gaily skips;
                  And then catch hold of my two ears and kiss me on the
                      lips.

ARGYRIPPUS: Must she kiss you, you worthless scamp?

LEONIDA: Pray why not, if you please?
(PHILAENIUM *kisses him.*)
(*To* ARGYRIPPUS) By Pollux, you shan't have it, if you
don't embrace my knees.

ARGYRIPPUS: My need compels me; I'll embrace your knees; now
hand it over.

PHILAENIUM: Come, my Leonida, I pray, bring help to my dear lover.
Buy both your freedom and his love by giving him the
money.

LEONIDA: What a sweet pretty girl you are! If it were mine, my
honey,
I'd give it you without a word; but he's the man to dun;
He only gave it me to keep. Gently, my gentle one!
Here, Libanus, catch hold of this.
(*Gives him the money.*)

ARGYRIPPUS: D'you mock me to my face?

LEONIDA: I wouldn't, but you clasped my knees with such a sorry
grace.
(*Aside to* LIBANUS) Now take your turn, and bubble
him, and kiss her, if you can.

LIBANUS (*to* LEONIDA): Say nought, but watch me!

ARGYRIPPUS (*to* PHILAENIUM): Come, my love, let us approach this man,
For he's a very decent sort, not like that treacherous
thief.

LIBANUS (*aside*): I'll strut about; and in my turn they'll ask me for
relief.

ARGYRIPPUS: Oh, save your master, Libanus, and hear him humbly
plead.
Give me the money now; you see my love and my sore
need.

LIBANUS: I'll see; I'd like to do it; come again tomorrow early.
Now let the lady beg and pray; she will not find me
surly.

PHILAENIUM: Shall I prevail by loving you or giving you a kiss?

LIBANUS: Why, both.

PHILAENIUM: Then I beseech of you, save us from this abyss!

ARGYRIPPUS: Oh, Libanus, my patron, give it me; 'twould be more meet;
A freedman, not his patron, should bear burdens in the street.

PHILAENIUM: My Libanus, my eye of gold so precious, and my honey,
My darling, I'll do aught you like; but do give us the money.

LIBANUS: Well, call me then your ducky, and your puppy, and your dovey,
Your swallow, and your jackdaw, and your sparrow, and your lovey!
Transform me to a serpent, let me have a double tongue!
And throw your arms around my neck and hug me! Come along!

ARGYRIPPUS: Shall she embrace you, hangman?

LIBANUS: Why, don't I deserve it, eh?
(PHILAENIUM *embraces him*)
(*To* ARGYRIPPUS) And now as you've insulted me, I'll have to make you pay.
If you would have this money, you must just give me a ride.

ARGYRIPPUS: What, carry you?

LIBANUS: Why, certainly! There is no way beside.

ARGYRIPPUS: Oh, hang it! If you think it's right that I should carry you,
Mount up!

LIBANUS: This is a noble way proud spirits to subdue!
Stand up then as you used to, when once a boy at play.
Yes, so! That's it! You are the smartest horse I've seen today.

ARGYRIPPUS: Mount up!

LIBANUS: I will. (*Gets on* ARGYRIPPUS' *back*) Hallo, what's this? You are a lazy lot!
I'll take away your corn, by Jove, unless you go full trot.

ARGYRIPPUS: Sweet Libanus, come, that's enough—

LIBANUS: I want a bit more still.
For now I'm going to spur you on to gallop up the hill.
Then to the mill I'll send you where they'll flog you
     till you go.
Whoa up! I'll get down at this hill; you don't deserve
     it, though.
(LIBANUS *gets off* ARGYRIPPUS' *back*.)

ARGYRIPPUS: Well, now you've fooled us both, I hope you'll not prove
     a defaulter.
Pay up the cash!

LIBANUS: First put me up a statue and an altar,
And sacrifice a bull to me; for I am your Salvation.

LEONIDA: Here, master, shunt that fellow off, and hear my appli-
     cation.
You'll pray to me and offer me the same things as he
     wishes?

ARGYRIPPUS: And what, pray, is your godhead's name?

LEONIDA: 'Tis Fortune and propitious.

ARGYRIPPUS: So much the better.

LIBANUS: Why, what can be better than Salvation?

ARGYRIPPUS: I do no wrong to her when I pay Fortune adoration.

PHILAENIUM: They both are good!

ARGYRIPPUS: Yes, when they give me good, then I'll believe it.

LEONIDA: Now pray to me for what you want.

ARGYRIPPUS: What then?

LEONIDA: You shall receive it.

ARGYRIPPUS: I want to marry this dear girl.

LEONIDA: And so you shall, say I!

ARGYRIPPUS: Do you say true?

LEONIDA: Of course I do.

LIBANUS: Now come to me and try;
Desire of me what most you wish to happen; and it's
     done.

ARGYRIPPUS: What could I wish for more than that, of which, alas,
              I've none;
              Those twenty minae now to give to my dear sweet-
              heart's mother.

LIBANUS: They shall be yours; cheer up, my boy, you're rid of all
              your bother.

ARGYRIPPUS: As usual, Fortune and Salvation make a mock of men.

LEONIDA: I was the head today when we the money did obtain.

LIBANUS: And I the tail.

ARGYRIPPUS: I can't make either head or tail of you.
              Your speeches and your fooleries, I own, I can't see
              through.

LIBANUS: We've fooled enough, I think; so now we'll tell you
              everything.
              Hear, Argyrippus, what I say: your father bade us bring
              This money to you.

ARGYRIPPUS: Oh, you've come just in the nick of time!

LIBANUS: Well, here are twenty minae true, gained by a naughty
              crime;
              On certain terms he gives them you.

ARGYRIPPUS: What are the terms, I pray?

LIBANUS: That you should share the banquet night.

ARGYRIPPUS (*taking the bag of money*): Go, bid him come away![8]

LEONIDA: Oh, Argyrippus, will you let your father have a share
              Of your sweet maiden?

ARGYRIPPUS: Well, his kindness makes it but seem fair.
              We never can repay him who has joined our severed
              lives.
              Go, run, Leonida; for I'm on pins till he arrives.

LEONIDA: He's in the house. (*Indicating* CLEARETA'S *house*.)

ARGYRIPPUS: He didn't come this way.

LEONIDA: No, he went round
              And got in by the garden gate, for fear he should be
              found

By any of the slaves; he doesn't want his wife to know,
For if your mother knew how we had got the cash—

ARGYRIPPUS: Hallo,
Good words!

LIBANUS: Go quickly in.

ARGYRIPPUS: Good-bye.

LEONIDA: And may your love still grow!
(ARGYRIPPUS *and* PHILAENIUM *go into the house of* CLEARETA; LIBANUS
and LEONIDA *into* DEMAENETUS' *house.*)

Act Four.   Scene I

(*Enter* DIABOLUS *and the* PARASITE.)

DIABOLUS: Come, show me that agreement you've drawn up
              Between me and my darling. Read the terms,
              For you're a perfect artist in this kind.

PARASITE: 'Twill make the mother tremble when she reads.

DIABOLUS: Well, read it to me.

PARASITE: Are you listening?

DIABOLUS: Yes.

PARASITE (*reading*): "Diabolus, the son of Glaucus, gives
              Cleareta the sum of twenty minae,
              That he may have Philaenium, her daughter,
              And keep her night and day for one whole year." [9]

DIABOLUS: She mustn't ever see another man.

PARASITE: Must that be in?

DIABOLUS: It must, and write it plain!

PARASITE: "She shall not ever see another man,
              Though she should say he is her friend or patron,
              Or feign that he's the sweetheart of her friend;
              Her doors must be fast closed to all but you,
              And she must always say she's not at home.

Then, though she say it's come from foreign parts,
No letter shall be found in all the house,
Nor a waxed tablet; also any picture
From which wax might be got for writing letters,
She now shall sell; and if they are not sold
Within four days from when she gets the money,
They shall be yours, to burn them, if you like,
That she may have no wax wherewith to write.
She shall invite no guest; you shall do that.
If she catch sight of any other man,
She instantly shall look the other way.
She shall not drink from any one but you;
Shall take the cup from you and hand it back;
Nor drink a single drop without your knowledge."

DIABOLUS: That's well.

PARASITE: "To turn suspicion from herself,
She shall not tread on anybody's foot
When she gets up or crosses the next couch.
Nor in descending shall she give a hand.
She shall not give her ring to anyone
To look at, nor shall ask his in return,
Nor shall she challenge anyone but you
To play at dice; and she shall name your name,
And not say, "Thee," when challenging to throw.
And only goddesses shall she invoke,
And no male god; but if she must do so,
She shall tell you, and you shall do it for her.
She shall not nod, or wink her eye, or beckon
To any man; and if the light goes out,
She shall not move a limb until it's lit." [10]

DIABOLUS: First-rate! But in her room, I'd rather have
Her move her limbs a bit. Cut out that clause;
For she shan't say the contract does forbid.

PARASITE: I know; you fear a catch.

DIABOLUS: True!

PARASITE: I'll remove
The clause. Now hear the rest.

DIABOLUS: All right; read on.

PARASITE: "She shall not utter an ambiguous word,
                 Or speak in any language but her own.
                 If she perchance must cough, she shall not cough
                 So as to put her tongue out when she coughs.
                 If she pretends she wants to clean her lips,
                 She shall not do it so; it would be better
                 For you to wipe her lips yourself than suffer
                 That she should show her open mouth to men.
                 Her mother never shall drop in to dinner,
                 Nor start to make complaints; and if she does,
                 Her punishment shall be to have no wine
                 For twenty days."

DIABOLUS: Bravo! A clever bond!

PARASITE: "Then, if she bids her maidens take to Venus
                 Or Cupid garlands, wreaths, or precious ointments,
                 Your slave shall see that Venus gets them all,
                 And not some man to whom she's sending tokens."
                 These are not trifles, nor mere funeral songs.

DIABOLUS: I'm satisfied. Let's enter!

PARASITE: After you!
(*They go into the house of* CLEARETA, *where they find* ARGYRIPPUS *and*
DEMAENETUS *with* PHILAENIUM.)

Act Four. Scene II

(*Enter* DIABOLUS *in anger, followed by the* PARASITE.)

DIABOLUS: Come on! Oh, shall I suffer this in silence?
                 I'll die but I'll go tell the villain's wife.
                 (*To* DEMAENETUS *within*) Shall you sit there, kissing
                     that lovely girl,
                 And tell your wife 'twas only fatherly?
                 Where did you get the money for her mother?
                 Didn't you steal it from your wife at home?
                 I'm hanged if I'll keep silence one more minute,
                 I'll go at once and tell her that I know
                 You'll quickly strip her bare, unless she stops you,
                 To furnish means for your extravagance.

PARASITE: It should be done; but don't you think that I
               Had better tell her, lest she should suppose
               That you have done it more for your own passion
               Than for her sake?

DIABOLUS: By Jove! I think you're right.
               You go and stir her up and make a row;
               Tell her he's drinking with her darling son,
               And with his sweetheart, and she's robbing him.

PARASITE: I'll see to it.

DIABOLUS: And I'll go wait at home.
(DIABOLUS *departs, and the* PARASITE *goes into the house of* DEMAENE-
TUS.)

Act Five.   Scene I

(*Enter* DEMAENETUS, ARGYRIPPUS, *and* PHILAENIUM *from the house of*
CLEARETA; *slaves prepare the banquet in front of the house.*)[11]

ARGYRIPPUS: Come, father, let us take our places, please.

DEMAENETUS: Just as you say, my son.

ARGYRIPPUS: Slaves, set the table!

DEMAENETUS: I hope that you don't mind, my boy, that I am sitting
               by your girl.

ARGYRIPPUS: I honour you too much for that, although with love I'm
               in a whirl;
               And so I do not mind a bit, dear father, that she sits
               by you.

DEMAENETUS: A youth, my Argyrippus, should be modest.

ARGYRIPPUS: Father, you say true;
               I only do as you deserve.

DEMAENETUS: Then let us fall to this good cheer,
               With draughts of wine and pleasant talk. I want your
               love and not your fear,
               My dearest son.

ARGYRIPPUS: By Pollux! I would give you both, like a good lad.

DEMAENETUS: I should believe it if I saw you jolly.

ARGYRIPPUS: Do you think I'm sad?

DEMAENETUS: I don't *think* so; I *see* you are, as if your neck were in the noose.

ARGYRIPPUS: Oh, don't say so!

DEMAENETUS: Then don't be so, and I'll not say it. What's the use?

ARGYRIPPUS: Why, see, I'm smiling!

DEMAENETUS: May my foes be always blessed with such a smile!

ARGYRIPPUS: Well, I'll confess that what you say is true. I'm angry all this while,
Because she's sitting by your side. For, father, the plain truth to say,
It does annoy me; not because I don't want you to have your way,
But I love her; and I should like another girl to sit by you.

DEMAENETUS: But I want *her*!

ARGYRIPPUS: You have your wish, but I should like to have mine too.

DEMAENETUS: You needn't grudge me this one hour, since I have found the means for you
To pay the money, and to have her for your own this whole year through.

ARGYRIPPUS: Ah! You are right; I see my folly.

DEMAENETUS: Then fire away, and let's be jolly.

Act Five. Scene II

(*Enter* ARTEMONA *and the* PARASITE *from the house of* DEMAENETUS; *they do not at first see the banqueters.*)

ARTEMONA: Do you say you saw my son and my old husband drinking here?
That he's stolen twenty minae to give to his sweetheart dear?
That my son knew all about it, while his father did the deed?

PARASITE: Ne'er again believe my statements, though you find them
in the creed,
Artemona, if deception in my present words you find.

ARTEMONA: Out, alas! I thought my husband was the noblest of
mankind—
Sober, temperate, and saving, and devoted to his wife.

PARASITE: Now you see that he has been a worthless rascal all his
life—
Drunken, reprobate, intemperate, hating his poor wife
like mad.

ARTEMONA: If it were not so, he'd never do as he does. Oh, he's bad!

PARASITE: Well, you know, I always took him for a decent, sober
man.
But his present actions show he's built upon another
plan.

ARTEMONA: This is what he meant by saying he was off, so serious,
Just to dine with Archidemus, Chaerea, Chaerestratus,
Clinias, Chremes, Cratinus, Dinias, Demosthenes;
All the time, no doubt, the scamp's been carrying on
such games as these.

PARASITE: Why, then, don't you bid your maidens pick him up and
take him home?

ARTEMONA: You be quiet; he shall suffer!

PARASITE: Ah, I knew that this would come,
From the day when you were married.

ARTEMONA: Oh, dear me, I always thought
He was busy in the senate or with clients, as he ought;
That exhausting toil in business made him snore the
livelong night.
He was toiling at a business of a different nature quite;
Going to other people's houses, while poor I sat all
alone;
Bad himself, he's not contented till he's taught it to
his son.

PARASITE: Follow me then; you shall catch him at it in the neatest
way.

ARTEMONA: There is nothing I'd like better.

PARASITE: Stay a minute!

ARTEMONA: What d'you say?

PARASITE: Could you recognise your husband, if you saw him at a
              feast,
              With a garland on his head and sitting by a girl, the
              beast?

ARTEMONA: Yes, I could!

PARASITE: Well, there you see him! (*Pointing out the ban-
              queters.*)

ARTEMONA: Oh, the wretch!

PARASITE: Here, wait a bit!
              Let's observe them from our ambush, while they're not
              suspecting it.

ARGYRIPPUS (*to* DEMAENETUS): When will you stop all this hugging?

DEMAENETUS: Well, I must confess, my son—

ARGYRIPPUS: What?

DEMAENETUS: Your girl's the nicest wench that ever I set eyes
              upon.

PARASITE (*aside to* ARTEMONA): Do you hear him?

ARTEMONA (*to* PARASITE):   Yes, I hear him.

DEMAENETUS (*to* PHILAENIUM):   Now I'll tell you what I'll do;
              I'll just steal my wife's best mantle as a little gift for
              you.
              I would do it, even though it cost my spouse a year of
              life.

PARASITE (*aside*): Ah, I fear it's not the first time he has robbed his
              wretched wife!

ARTEMONA (*aside*): Yes, no doubt he was the robber, when I thought
              it was my maids;
              Those poor innocents have suffered for their master's
              escapades.

ARGYRIPPUS: Father, set the wine a-going; my next drink is overdue.

DEMAENETUS: Waiter, take the wine to him; meanwhile I'll have a
              kiss from you. (*Kisses* PHILAENIUM.)

ARTEMONA (*aside*): Wretched me! He's kissing her—a man with one
foot in the grave!

DEMAENETUS: Ah! Your kisses are much nicer than my lady ever gave.

PHILAENIUM: Don't you like to kiss your wife, then?

DEMAENETUS: Bless you, no! I'd much prefer
If I must, to drink bilge-water, rather than be kissed
by her.

ARTEMONA (*aside*): Just come home to me! I'll show you there are
risks in speaking ill
Of the woman whom you married for her money, that
I will!

PHILAENIUM: How I pity you!

ARTEMONA (*aside*):   He'll need it!

ARGYRIPPUS: Hallo, father, what d'you say?
Don't you love my mother?

DEMAENETUS: Love her? Certainly, when she's away!

ARGYRIPPUS: When she's there?

DEMAENETUS: I wish her dead!

PARASITE (*aside to* ARTEMONA):   You see how much he loves you,
ma'am.

ARTEMONA (*aside*): Oh, I'll make him pay for this with interest, when
I get him home!
Yes, I'll kiss him with a vengeance, as he seems so fond
of it.
Would you slander me, you villain? All right, only wait
a bit.

ARGYRIPPUS: Now then, father, throw the dice and we'll throw next.

DEMAENETUS: All right. No tricks!
Here's to you, Philaenium, and my wife's death!—Ah,
double six![12]
Cheer me, boys, and pass a goblet full of wine for that
good throw.

ARTEMONA (*aside*): I can't bear it any longer.

PARASITE (*to* ARTEMONA):   Well, you haven't learnt, you know,
How to be a porter. Come on, let's go for him; now's your chance.

(ARTEMONA *and the* PARASITE *confront the banqueters.*)

ARTEMONA: I won't die; and for that wish, sir, I'll lead you a pretty dance.

PARASITE: Please, will someone run and quickly bring an undertaker here?

ARGYRIPPUS: Mother, hail!

ARTEMONA: A truce to greetings!

PARASITE (*aside*):   Poor old man! He's dead with fear!
Now it's time for me to toddle; ah, this quarrel's looking well.
I'll go to Diabolus and tell him how it all befel;
And I hope he'll stand a dinner for me, while they fight it out.
Then tomorrow I'll devise some dodge to get the girl, no doubt.
If I don't, I've lost my patron, for he's all on fire with love.

(PARASITE *departs.*)

ARTEMONA (*to* PHILAENIUM): What's your business with my husband? Tell me that, miss!

PHILAENIUM: Why, by Jove,
He's half killed me, he's a nuisance!

ARTEMONA: Get up, gallant, come on home!

DEMAENETUS: Oh! I'm nothing!

ARTEMONA: Yes, you are, for you're a scoundrel! Back you come!
See, the cuckoo still keeps sitting! Get up, gallant, come on home!

DEMAENETUS: Woe is me!

ARTEMONA: O truthful prophet! Get up, gallant, come on home!

DEMAENETUS: Go away! I'll come directly.

ARTEMONA: Get up, gallant, come on home!

DEMAENETUS: Pray you, wife—

ARTEMONA: Oh, wife, indeed! I am your wife, then, you allow! I believe I was your pet aversion, not your wife, just now.

DEMAENETUS: Oh, I'm done for!

ARTEMONA: Tell me, have you learnt to like my kisses yet?

DEMAENETUS: Yes, they smell of myrrh.

ARTEMONA: And did you steal my mantle for your pet?

PHILAENIUM: No, by Castor! Ma'am, he only promised he *would* steal me one.

DEMAENETUS (*to* PHILAENIUM): You be quiet!

ARGYRIPPUS: But I tried to hinder him.

ARTEMONA: A pretty son! That's the way you think a father ought to teach his child to do? Don't you feel ashamed?

DEMAENETUS: I do, love! Very much ashamed—of you!

ARTEMONA: Hoary-headed cuckoo, I will drag you from your haunts. Proceed!

DEMAENETUS: Mayn't I stay—the dinner's ready—just until I've had my feed?

ARTEMONA: You shall have a dinner such as you deserve when you get home.

DEMAENETUS: I shall have a poorish night; I see my wife's pronounced my doom.

ARGYRIPPUS: If you plotted 'gainst my mother, didn't I a row foretell?

PHILAENIUM: Don't forget the cloak!

DEMAENETUS (*to* ARTEMONA): I wish you'd silence in this jade compel.

ARTEMONA (*dragging* DEMAENETUS *home*): Come on!

PHILAENIUM: Give me one more kiss before we part.

DEMAENETUS: Oh, go the hell!

PHILAENIUM: No, inside! (*To* ARGYRIPPUS) And you, my darling,
    follow me.

ARGYRIPPUS (*accompanying her inside*):   And all is well.

Epilogue

If the old man did deceive his wife and have a little game,
That is nothing new or wondrous; other people do the same;
No one has so strict a conscience or so resolute a breast
That, if once the chance is given, he won't do just like the rest.
Now if you would save the old man from a beating, plead his cause,
And he cannot fail to win it, if you give him your applause.

NOTES

SUGDEN'S TRANSLATION has been altered in the following verses: 89, 193, 230, 243, 341, 348, 364, 396, 468, 500, 532, 579, 633, 636, 651, 653, 684, 725, 734, 752-753, 830-831, 852. Most of these changes were made in order to preserve the monetary system of the original. Sugden believed certain passages "too gross for modern taste" and occasionally deleted one or more verses; these verses have been translated by the editor; cf. below, notes 8, 9, 10.

1. The Greek title means "The Ass-Driver."

2. A reference to the mill where slaves were often punished. Libanus avoids the word, since it is an evil omen.

3. The "dead oxen" are whips of ox-hide.

4. Cleareta here mentions an impossibly large sum. Since the talent was equal to sixty minae, the price here demanded is six times the amount requested later, twenty minae. Cleareta is obviously trying to provoke Argyrippus and amuse herself at his expense.

5. This refers to the banker.

6. He means the money which has been paid for them. The *as* was a small Roman coin.

7. Plautus fails to explain how Argyrippus happens to be in Cleareta's house, after his departure to the forum at the end of Act One, Scene III. This is a violation of the usual technique of Roman comedy.

8. The following two verses were omitted by Sugden.

9. This verse was omitted by Sugden.

10. The four verses which follow were omitted by Sugden.

11. Many editors and translators consider that Act Five took place inside the house of Cleareta, and that the actors were visible through the open door. Sugden suggests that the front of the house was removed. It is far more likely that the banquet scene was presented in front of the house, as is the regular procedure in Roman comedy. The first two verses of Act Five, Scene I, and the final verse of Act Five, Scene II, support this interpretation. Sugden omitted all three verses.

12. Literally, the Venus, the highest throw, in which the four dice all came up different.

III
THE POT OF GOLD

CHARACTERS IN THE PLAY

HOUSEHOLD GOD
EUCLIO, *an aged Athenian*
STAPHYLA, *an old woman, slave of* EUCLIO
EUNOMIA, *a lady of Athens*
MEGADORUS, *brother of* EUNOMIA
STROBILUS, *his slave*
CONGRIO, *a cook*
ANTHRAX, *another cook*
PYTHODICUS, *a slave*
LYCONIDES, *a young man, son of* EUNOMIA
SLAVE *of* LYCONIDES
PHAEDRIA, *daughter of* EUCLIO
MUSIC GIRLS

ARGUMENT I[1]

A miserly old man called Euclio,
Who hardly dares to trust himself, has found
Buried within his house, a pot of gold.
This pot he hides again, and pale with fear
Keeps guard on it. A youth, Lyconides,
Has violated Euclio's only daughter.
Meanwhile, one Megadorus, an old man,
Persuaded by his sister to get married,
Demands the miser's daughter for his wife.
The hard old man reluctantly consents,
And, fearing for his pot, takes it away.
And hides it, first in one place, then another.
The servant of that same Lyconides
Who wronged the girl, lays plots against the miser.
The youth himself beseeches Megadorus,
Who is his uncle, to give up the girl.
When Euclio's been tricked out of his pot,
He unexpectedly receives it back,
And gladly gives Lyconides his daughter.

ARGUMENT II (ACROSTIC)

A pot of gold old Euclio preserves
U nsleepingly with anxious vigilance.
L yconides has wronged his only daughter.
U ndowered, Megadorus seeks her hand.
L iking the match, he sends both cooks and meat.
A nxious about his gold, old Euclio hides it.
R ight soon the lover's slave finds out and steals it.
I t is restored to Euclio by the lover,
A nd for his pains he gets both wife and gold.

INTRODUCTION

The Pot of Gold (the *Aulularia*) is one of the most famous of Plautus' comedies, and one of the best. Unlike many of his plays which have plots based on trickery or mistaken identity, the central interest here is the character of Euclio. He is a poor man who has carried thrift to the point of stinginess. When he discovers a pot of gold in his house (with the assistance of his household god), he finds it impossible to adjust himself to his changed circumstances, and he is even more miserable in his attempts to keep the existence of the gold from being known. He suspects everyone—his own maid, his neighbours, the cooks who come to prepare the wedding feast. When the gold is finally stolen, his anguish and despair know no bounds; he is both a laughable and a pathetic figure. While Euclio is often called a miser, he can be considered one only with reservations. His meanness, so amusingly described by the slaves, is the result of his former impoverished circumstances; it does not come from an innate and insatiable greed. Harpagon in Molière's *L'Avare*, the most famous of the adaptations of this play, is a true miser, a man whose avarice ruins not only his own life but the lives of those who come in contact with him. Molière's delineation of the character of Harpagon far surpasses Plautus' portrayal of Euclio, but the purposes of the two dramatists were very different, and Molière's play is a far more serious comedy. The conclusion of *The Pot of Gold* is unfortunately lost, but we infer from the argument and a short fragment of the ending that Euclio, after regaining his gold, gave it to his daughter for her dowry. Such an act would have been impossible for Harpagon.

The plot of the Plautine comedy is double, in a sense; it deals not only with Euclio and his amusing attempts to keep his gold secure, but is concerned also with the story of Euclio's daughter who has been seduced by Lyconides, the nephew of Megadorus. The two themes are cleverly interwoven; it is Megadorus' desire to marry Euclio's daughter that leads to the presence of the cooks in Euclio's house; this in turn is the reason why Euclio transfers the gold to an outside hiding place, where it is stolen by a slave of Lyconides. The two difficulties reach their solution at the same time when Lyconides, in the lost ending of the play, returned the gold and received permission from Euclio to marry his daughter.

The play moves rapidly and is amusing throughout. Euclio's constant suspicions, his frantic rushing to and fro to assure himself that his gold is safe, his fruitless attempts to find a secure hiding place—all these provide delightful comedy. The high point of the play occurs after his discovery of the theft; Lyconides enters to confess that he has wronged Euclio's daughter, and they talk at cross purposes; Lyconides thinks Euclio is heartbroken because of his daughter's condition, and Euclio believes Lyconides is confessing to the theft. The fact that the Latin word for pot is feminine in gender contributes not a little to the amusing misunderstanding.

Characters representing different types of the "miser" appeared frequently in Greek New Comedy, and Menander wrote three or four plays, any one of which may have been the original of Plautus' play. To make a more exact identification seems impossible, and some scholars even deny the Menandrian authorship of the original. The Roman adaptation is usually dated in the middle of Plautus' career. If the reference in lines 794 ff. to the rape of Euclio's daughter nine months before at the festival of Ceres (in early August) implies that the play was produced in April at the Megalensian games, the date of the production must be 194 B.C. or later, as the Megalensian games were first presented in 194.

The influence of the comedy, as in the case of the *Amphitryon*, has been considerable. The extant *Querolus*, written in the late Roman empire, is an amusing play about a pot of gold. The playwright knew and alluded to the Plautine comedy; he introduced a household god into his play as one of the characters, and gave the name Euclio to the man who had buried the gold in his house without his son's knowledge. These are the only points of similarity, however, and the plot of the play has nothing in common with the one written by Plautus almost six hundred years earlier. The influence of the Plautine play was greatest on comedies of the sixteenth and seventeenth centuries. Among the plays to be mentioned in this connection are *La Sporta* by Gelli (1543), *The Case is Altered* by Jonson (1597; this play has two plots, both from Plautus: one based on *The Pot of Gold*, the other on *The Captives*), and *Warenar* by Hooft (1617). But the most famous adaptation is Molière's *L'Avare* (1668), and the popularity of his play was such that later versions were indebted directly to Molière and only indirectly to Plautus; this is true of *The Miser* by Shadwell (1672) and Fielding's play of the same name (1732). *Die Aussteuer* was an adaptation of Plautus' comedy for the German stage by Lenz (1774).

THE POT OF GOLD

(SCENE:—*A street in Athens on which are the houses of* EUCLIO *and* MEGADORUS *and the temple of Faith.*)

Prologue

HOUSEHOLD GOD: Lest any wonder who in the world I am,
I'll tell you shortly. I'm the household God
Of this house, which you see me leaving now;
These many years I have it in my care;
Grandfather, father, son who has it now,
Have all been friends; the grandfather himself
Intrusted to me secretly a hoard
Of gold, which he within the hearth had buried,
Beseeching me to keep it safe for him.
He died, and was of such a greedy soul
He never would reveal it to his son,
But wished to leave him poor and penniless
Rather than show him where the treasure was.
He left him just a bit of ground, on which
With pain and labour he could make his living.
And when he died, who gave the trust to me,
I watched with care whether his son would show
More reverence to me than his father had.
But he, it seemed, spent less and less upon me,
And paid me less of honour. So he died;
And I revenged myself. And next in line
Is he who has it now, like-mannered too
With those who went before. He has a child,
A daughter, who with incense or with wine
Pays daily worship to me, crowning me
With wreaths. And for the sake of her it was
That I to Euclio disclosed the treasure,
That he more easily might marry her;
A youth of high position had led her
Astray; he knew her who she was, but she
Did not know him; nor did the father know

119

What had taken place. Today I will arrange
That an old man, a neighbour, shall demand
Her for his wife; more gladly will I do it,
That the young man, who was the first to love her
(He met her on the night of Ceres' festival),
May marry her more easily. The old man
Who wants to do so is the young man's uncle.
But Euclio's calling out, as is his wont;
He's turned the old woman out of doors, lest she
Should know where the treasure is; he wants to see
That the hoard of gold has not been carried off.

(*The* HOUSEHOLD GOD *departs.*)

Act One. Scene I

(*Enter* EUCLIO *from his house, pushing* STAPHYLA *in front of him.*)

EUCLIO: Go out; go out, I say, and get you gone,
           You that are looking round with prying eyes!

STAPHYLA: Why beat a miserable wretch like me?

EUCLIO: That you may be more miserable still,
           And lead the wretched life you well deserve.

STAPHYLA: Pray, why have you thus thrust me from the house?

EUCLIO: Am I to argue with a wretch like you,
           Whose back is scored with stripes; go from the door,
           Be off, I say; how leisurely she goes!
           See to yourself, for if I take in hand
           A stick or goad, I will increase the pace
           Of that old tortoise.

STAPHYLA: Would the gods would bring
           Me to the gallows than to serve you thus!

EUCLIO: How the old wretch is murmuring to herself!
           I'll dig your eyes out that you may not see
           What I am doing; now away, away,
           And further yet; stand there; if from that place
           You stir by the width of a finger or the breadth
           Of a nail, or if you look back till such time
           I give you leave, I'll hand you over straight

To torture. (*Aside*) Never surely did I see
A wickeder old woman; much I fear
Lest she may gather from some words of mine
Too rashly said, where the gold is hidden away.
Wretch, she has eyes, too, in the back of her head.
Now I will go and see if the gold is there,
Just as I hid it, gold which has become
A constant source of trouble to myself.
    (EUCLIO *goes into his house.*)

STAPHYLA (*to herself*): I can't think what has happened to my master,
Nor why he is so mad; he beats me so,
And thrusts me out of doors ten times a day.
I don't know what has put him out of tune;
He wakens all the night, and then by day,
Like a lame cobbler, sits for hours at home.
Nor can I tell how best I can conceal
His daughter's state; and nothing more remains
Than to make one long letter of myself—
The letter I—and hang myself full length.

Act One.   Scene II

(*Re-enter* EUCLIO *from the house.*)

EUCLIO (*aside*):   And now with mind at ease I leave the house,
As soon as I have seen all's safe within.
    (*To* STAPHYLA) Return now to your work.

STAPHYLA: Why should I go?
Is some one going to take the house away?
There is nothing here for thieves; nor aught indeed
But emptiness and spider webs.

EUCLIO: D'ye think
That for your sake the gods would make me rich,
As Philip or Darius, sorceress?
I like to keep those cobwebs; I am poor,
I do admit; and bear it. I'm content
With what the gods may give. Go in and close
The door; I'll come again; let no one enter.
If any ask a light, see that the fire

Is quite put out; that none may ask for it;
If it is not, you'll be put out yourself.
Say that the pump is dry, if any seek
For water. If a spade, an axe, a mortar,
Or a pestle, things which neighbours always borrow,
Say that the thieves have come and stolen them.
No one's to enter, while I am away.
These are my orders; if Good Fortune comes,
Please say I am not at home.

STAPHYLA: No fear of that;
That never comes, however near it be.

EUCLIO: Be quiet and go within.

STAPHYLA: I'll go at once.

EUCLIO: Draw both the bolts. I will be back anon.
            (*To himself, as* STAPHYLA *goes into the house*)
            I'm vexed because I have to leave the house;
            I go unwillingly; yet what to do
            I know not; for the master of our guild
            Has said he will divide the funds amongst us.
            If I don't go and take my share, they'll think
            That I have gold at home; for 'tis not likely
            A poor man would despise a dole, though small.
            For now, although I keep the secret to myself,
            All seem to know it, and pay greater court
            Than they used to do before; they come, they stay,
            They give me their right hands; ask how I am,
            And what I'm doing, what my business.
            Now I'll be off where I was going; and
            Return as soon as possible again. (EUCLIO *departs.*)

Act Two.   Scene I

(*Enter* EUNOMIA *and* MEGADORUS *from the house of the latter.*)

EUNOMIA: I wish, my brother, you would think that I
             Am acting in your interest, for your sake,
             As well becomes a sister; though I know
             We women are not held in much esteem.
             We all are told we talk by far too much,
             And never in the world they say was found

A silent woman. But remember, brother,
How near you are to me, and I to you.
'Tis right that we should one another help.
You should advise and counsel me, I you;
Nor keep it secret, nor be afraid to speak,
Make me your confidant, and I the same.
So now I brought you out of doors to speak
In private, as to your and mine concerns.

MEGADORUS: Your hand, my best of women!

EUNOMIA: Who is she?
Where is such woman?

MEGADORUS: You!

EUNOMIA: Do you say so?

MEGADORUS: If you deny it, I will do the same.

EUNOMIA: Well, one must speak the truth. There is no best;
For one, I fear, is only worse than other.

MEGADORUS: I think the same; it needs no argument.

EUNOMIA: Lend me your ear.

MEGADORUS: 'Tis yours! Do as you like.

EUNOMIA: I come to advise—what is the best for you.

MEGADORUS: You do as you have always done to me.

EUNOMIA: I wish—

MEGADORUS: What, sister?

EUNOMIA: What will be to you
An everlasting blessing, that you may
Have many children.

MEGADORUS: May the gods forfend!

EUNOMIA: I would that you should marry.

MEGADORUS: I'm undone!

EUNOMIA: How so?

MEGADORUS: Your speech nigh splits my head in two!
Poniards you speak, and every word's a stab.[2]

EUNOMIA: Do as your sister wishes.

MEGADORUS: If you wish, I will.

EUNOMIA: It is for your advantage.

MEGADORUS: May I die
Before I marry, or on this condition,
That she I marry, on the morrow may,
Or the day after that, be carried out
To burial. This being settled, get the bride,
Prepare the marriage.

EUNOMIA: I will get for you
The largest fortune that I can; but she
Is older, of the middle age, and if
You like, I'll ask her hand.

MEGADORUS: One question first.

EUNOMIA: Ask what you will!

MEGADORUS: You see when one has passed
Mid-life, and marries one who's passed it too,
If there should be a child, his name would be,
What could it be but Posthumus? Now I,
Dear sister, will relieve you of this care.
I by the goodness of the gods, and our forbears,
Am rich; great family, high spirit, wealth,
Applause, position, splendid equipage,
Dresses and purple, these which oft reduce
A man to slavery, do not appeal
At all to me.

EUNOMIA: Then who d'ye wish to marry?

MEGADORUS: Know you poor Euclio who lives next door?

EUNOMIA: I know him; he is quite a decent man.

MEGADORUS: I wish his daughter for my wife. I know
What you are going to say; that she is poor.
Don't say a word; I like her poverty.

EUNOMIA: The gods direct things well!

MEGADORUS: I hope so too.
Farewell. (EUNOMIA *departs*.) I'll see if Euclio is at
    home.
Ah! There he is! I do not know from whence he
    comes.

Act Two.   Scene II

(*Enter* EUCLIO.)

EUCLIO (*to himself*): I thought 'twas all in vain when I went out
And so I went unwillingly; for none
Belonging to the guild has ever come;
Nor yet the master, who should give to us
Our share of the funds; so now I hasten home,
For though I'm here myself, my heart is there.

MEGADORUS: Good morning, Euclio, good luck to you!

EUCLIO: The blessing of the gods!

MEGADORUS: And are you well?
And as you wish?

EUCLIO (*aside*):   It is not without cause,
When a rich man addresses thus the poor.
He knows I've gold; and hence his kindly words.

MEGADORUS: You say you're well?

EUCLIO: I am, but not too well
In point of money.

MEGADORUS: If you are content,
You have enough for life and all its needs.

EUCLIO (*aside*):   The old woman's told him of the gold; that's clear.
I will cut out her tongue, and gouge out too
Her eyes, when I get home.

MEGADORUS: What say you now,
Thus muttering to yourself?

EUCLIO: I do bemoan
My poverty; I have a grown-up daughter
Without a dowry whom I cannot wed,
Nor give to any.

MEGADORUS: Pray be still. Take courage!
I'll help you, you shall have enough and more.
What do you want?

EUCLIO (*aside*):   His promises are fair;
But still there's something that he wants himself.
He gapes for gold to swallow it; he brings
Bread in one hand, a stone within the other.
I never trust the man who shows himself
So generous to the poor; he gives his hand
So kindly, but behind there is some hurt.
I know those polyps, with their tentacles,
Clinging to all they touch.

MEGADORUS: Euclio, a word
Respecting what concerns yourself and me.

EUCLIO (*aside*): Alas! My gold is stolen; he wants, I know,
To come to some arrangement. I will have
A look at home.

MEGADORUS: Where are you going, Euclio?

EUCLIO: I will return; there's something that I want
To see about at home. (*Hurries into house.*)

MEGADORUS (*to himself*):   I do believe
When I make mention of his daughter that
I wish to marry her, that he will think
I'm laughing at him; nor is any one
More niggardly in poverty than he.
(*Re-enter* EUCLIO.)

EUCLIO (*aside*): All, all is safe! Nothing at all is gone.
I was too much afraid before I went,
Half mad with fear. (*To* MEGADORUS) Now, Mega-
dorus, I
Return to thee, if there is aught you want.

MEGADORUS: Thanks. Now please answer what I ask of you.

EUCLIO: So be it you ask not what I cannot grant.

MEGADORUS: What think you of my family?

EUCLIO: 'Tis good!

MEGADORUS: My reputation?

EUCLIO: Good!

MEGADORUS: My conduct, then?

EUCLIO: Why, that I think is neither bad nor good.

MEGADORUS: You know my age?

EUCLIO: I know it is advanced,
As great as is your fortune.

MEGADORUS: As to you
I've always thought, and think you are a man
Quite without guile.

EUCLIO (*aside*):   Alas! He smells my gold.
(*Aloud*) What want you now?

MEGADORUS: Well, as we know each other,
That all may turn out well for me and you,
And for your daughter, I do ask for her
In marriage. Promise me her hand.

EUCLIO: Alas!
That which you do is unworthy of your acts;
To mock at one who's poor, and has never given
Offence to you or yours; in word or deed
I have done naught, that you should treat me so.

MEGADORUS: I do not come to mock, nor do I so;
I would not think it fitting.

EUCLIO: Then why ask
My daughter's hand?

MEGADORUS: That you, through me,
May be the better off, and I through you.

EUCLIO: But I do bear in mind that you are rich,
Eager for power; while I am very poor;
So poor, and if I give my daughter's hand
To you, you are a mighty ox, and I
A humble ass; and when I'm joined with you,
Unequal to the load that you can bear,
I, the poor ass, shall founder in the mire;
While you, proud ox, will not acknowledge me.
I'll find you worse than heretofore you were,
While those of my own order will deride;
If we should separate, there'll be no stall
Left for me; while the asses with their teeth
Are rending me, the oxen will proceed
To butt me with their horns. This is the danger
Of climbing from one class into another,
And being an ass, to try to be an ox.

MEGADORUS: The main thing is still to ally yourself
With honest men. Hear me; accept my terms,
And give your daughter to me.

EUCLIO: But I have
No dowry.

MEGADORUS: Give her none; as long as she
Is well conducted, that's enough for me.

EUCLIO: I name it, lest you think I've found a treasure.

MEGADORUS: I know; don't tell me; only give her hand.

EUCLIO: Well, be it so. But stay, by Jove, I'm ruined!

MEGADORUS: What is it?

EUCLIO: I heard some iron weapon strike.
(*He runs into his house.*)

MEGADORUS: It was my gardener digging. Where's the man?
He's gone without an answer; he scorns me,
Because he sees I seek his friendship, just
As men often do; for if a rich man seeks
A favour from a poor one, he's afraid
To grant it, and, through fear, misses his chance;
And when the occasion's past, he's sorry for it.
(*Re-enter* EUCLIO.)

EUCLIO (*to* STAPHYLA *within*): If I don't have your tongue taken out
by the roots,
You may have me mauled and damaged as you like.

MEGADORUS: I see you think that I'm an old man now,
Who may be mocked, although I don't deserve it.

EUCLIO: It is not so, nor could I, if I would.

MEGADORUS: Then do you give me your daughter?

EUCLIO: Yes, I do;
Upon the terms I said, without a dowry.

MEGADORUS: You promise?

EUCLIO: Yes.

MEGADORUS: And may the gods bless it!

EUCLIO: I wish they may. Only remember this:
               My daughter brings no dowry.

MEGADORUS: I remember.

EUCLIO: I know that sometimes men mislike a bargain;
               The bargain's on or off, just as they please.

MEGADORUS: There shall be no dispute. Now, can we have
               The marriage for today?

EUCLIO: Most certainly.

MEGADORUS: I'll go and get me ready. Want you aught?

EUCLIO: No, only that!

MEGADORUS: 'Tis done. Farewell. (*Calling at his
                     door*) Now, slave,
               Follow me to the market; now, at once.
               (MEGADORUS *departs*.)

EUCLIO (*to himself*): He's gone. Ye gods immortal, what can gold
               Achieve! He must have heard I think there is
               Some treasure here; he's gaping for it now,
               And that is the reason he persists in this proposal.

Act Two.   Scene III

EUCLIO (*calling at his door*): Where are you, who has blabbed to all
                     our neighbours,
               Gone chitter-chattering to all the town,
               That I would give a dowry to my daughter?
               Hi! Staphyla! I call! D'ye hear? Bring in
               The sacred dishes; wash them well. Today
               I have betrothed my daughter; she will wed
               Today.

STAPHYLA (*as she enters*): The gods direct it well; but stay,
               It cannot be; it is too sudden, sure.

EUCLIO: Begone! Be quiet! See these things are done
               When I return; shut to the door at once;
               I will be here anon.   (EUCLIO *departs*.)

STAPHYLA (*to herself*):   What must I do?
　　　　Destruction waits me and my master's daughter.
　　　　Her state must now be known; I'll go within
　　　　And see my master's orders carried out.
　　　　I fear some evil; and of such a kind
　　　　That I must drink the poison to the dregs.
　　　　(STAPHYLA *goes into the house*.)

Act Two.　Scene IV

(*Enter* STROBILUS *bringing the cooks,* ANTHRAX *and* CONGRIO, *and music girls; attendants follow with provisions.*)

STROBILUS:　　After my master had laid in his stores,
　　　　And hired his cooks and flute players at the market,
　　　　He bid, that I divide the feast in two.

ANTHRAX:　　Most certainly you shall not divide me;
　　　　But if you wish the whole of me, I'll help.[3]

CONGRIO:　　You lovely boy, the people's little dear!
　　　　If one should wish, you scarcely would refuse.

STROBILUS:　　Anthrax, I meant the word quite differently.
　　　　My master weds today.

ANTHRAX:　　　　　　　　　　　Whose daughter is it?

STROBILUS:　　Our neighbour Euclio's here; he bid me give
　　　　Him half the dinner, and a cook as well,
　　　　And one flute player.

ANTHRAX:　　　　　　　　　　Half that is for here,
　　　　And half for the other house.

STROBILUS:　　　　　　　　　　　　Just as you say.

ANTHRAX:　　Could this old man not find his own provisions
　　　　To grace his daughter's wedding?

STROBILUS:　　　　　　　　　　　　　Bosh!

ANTHRAX:　　　　　　　　　　　　　　　What is't?

STROBILUS:　　What is't you ask? A pumice-stone is not
　　　　So hard and dry, as is this old man's heart.

ANTHRAX: Is't so indeed?

STROBILUS: Why, judge him for yourself.
He's always calling upon gods and men
To witness that he's ruined and undone,
If but a puff of smoke come from his chimney.
Why, when he sleeps, he binds the bellows to his
        throat—

ANTHRAX: Why that?

STROBILUS: For fear in sleep he'll lose his breath.

ANTHRAX: And does he close the lower outlet too,
Lest he lose wind?

STROBILUS: You might believe my tale,
As I do yours.

ANTHRAX: I do indeed believe.

STROBILUS: And when he washes, he bewails the waste
Of water.

ANTHRAX: Do you think there could be begged
A good round sum from this man for to buy
Our liberty?

STROBILUS: By Jove! He would not give
Starvation, if you asked him. The other day
The barber cut his nails; he gathered all
The parings up, and carried them away.

ANTHRAX: He is indeed a stingy soul you tell of.

STROBILUS: And can you think indeed he lives so sparely?
A hawk, it seems, once carried off his dinner.
So, full of tears, he goes before the judge;
Howling and plaining there, begins to ask
That the hawk should be bound over to appear.
If I had time I'd tell a thousand tales.
But which of you is nimblest?

ANTHRAX: I, by far.

STROBILUS: A cook I want, and not a thief.

ANTHRAX: I am one.

STROBILUS: And what say you?

CONGRIO: I am as you can see.

ANTHRAX: He's only fit to cook a funeral feast;
                That's all he does.

CONGRIO: Five letters would describe
                What you are; you're a thief.

ANTHRAX: Trebly a thief.

                        Act Two.   Scene V

STROBILUS: Be still! Which is the fatter lamb of these?

ANTHRAX: This. (*Departs to house of* MEGADORUS *with lamb.*)

STROBILUS: You, Congrio, take this one straight within.
                (*To some of the attendants*) You follow him; the
                    rest will come with me.

CONGRIO: It is not fair, they have the fatter lamb.

STROBILUS: But you shall have the fatter music girl.
                Go with him, Phrygia; you, Eleusium,
                You come with us. (ELEUSIUM *and attendants go into
                    house of* MEGADORUS.)

CONGRIO: O clever Strobilus!
                You've put me off upon a mean old man,
                From whom ev'n if I cried myself all hoarse
                I should not get a shilling.

STROBILUS: You're a fool,
                And most ungrateful.

CONGRIO: How is that?

STROBILUS: D'ye ask?
                Why first there'll be no crowd of servants there.
                If you want aught, you get it for yourself,
                Lest you should waste your time in asking for it;
                With us there'll be a large establishment,
                A crowd of servants, gold and silver plate,
                Dresses and furniture; if any one
                Should something lose (and you I know could not,
                If none were by, prevent yourself from theft),
                They say at once: "The cooks have taken it;

Catch him and bind him, put him in the well,
And beat him!" None of these will happen there,
For there is naught to steal. Come, follow me.
(*They approach the house of* EUCLIO.)

Act Two.   Scene VI

STROBILUS (*knocking*): Hi! Staphyla, come out, open the door!

STAPHYLA (*opening the door cautiously*): Who calls?

STROBILUS: 'Tis Strobilus.

STAPHYLA: And what d'ye want?

STROBILUS: Here, take these cooks, this music girl, the food
To serve the wedding. Megadorus sends
All these for Euclio.

STAPHYLA: I suppose it is
For Ceres' marriage?

STROBILUS: Why?

STAPHYLA: Because I see
You bring no wine.

STROBILUS: That will be brought anon
When he comes from the market.

STAPHYLA: We've no wood.

CONGRIO: Are there no doors?

STAPHYLA: There are.

CONGRIO: Then you have wood.
You need not go outside.

STAPHYLA: What, wretch, although
Vulcan you serve, are we, to cook your dinner
That you may get your wage, are we to burn
Our dwelling to the ground?

CONGRIO: I don't ask that.

STROBILUS: Then take them in at once. (*Goes into house of*
MEGADORUS.)

STAPHYLA (*opening wide the door*): Come, follow me! (CONGRIO *and others go inside.*)

Act Two. Scene VII

(*Enter* PYTHODICUS *from the house of* MEGADORUS.)[4]

PYTHODICUS (*to himself*): Well now, I'll see to what the cooks are
      doing;
      And that today's a pretty heavy job.
      They ought to do it in the cellar; thence
      To take it up in baskets; if they eat
      Below what they have cooked, then those above
      Will go without their dinner, those below
      Will get it. I am talking just as if
      I had no business; when there's in the house
      Such a crowd of harpies as is here today. (*Goes into
      the house.*)

Act Two. Scene VIII

(*Enter* EUCLIO *from the forum with some flowers and a small package.*)

EUCLIO (*to himself*): I wished today to brace myself a little,
      To make a show at this my daughter's wedding;
      I go to market; ask the price of fish;
      They say they're dear, the lamb and beef are dear;
      The veal, the dogfish, and the pork are dear;
      And all the dearer, that I had no money.
      Full vexed I come away; there's nought to buy;
      To all this unclean herd I said adieu.
      Then as I walked I thought thus to myself;
      If, on a festal day like this, you spend
      Your money freely, nothing spare, then you
      Will want tomorrow; and this reasoning
      My stomach and my heart approved, so I
      Intend to celebrate this wedding here
      At the smallest possible expense I can.
      So I have bought a little frankincense,

And a few flowers; these shall now be placed
Around our household god, that he may grant
A happy issue. But do I really see
My house-door open? Such a noise within!
What, am I robbed?

CONGRIO (*within*):   Go fetch a larger pot
If you can get one; this is far too small.

EUCLIO (*in great alarm*): I am undone; and all my gold is taken!
The pot is sought; unless I run within
At once I'm good as dead. Oh! Help me now,
Apollo! Help, and with your arrows slay
These treasure-laden thieves, as you have done
Before. Here must I rush and see what's taking place.
(EUCLIO *runs into his house.*)

Act II.   Scene IX

(*Enter* ANTHRAX *from the house of* MEGADORUS.)

ANTHRAX (*to servants within*): Here, Dromo, clean the fish; Machaerio,
            you
Bone if you can the lamprey and the eel,
That all may be prepared when I return.
I go to seek a bread pan; see that cock
Is plucked e'en smoother than a player's chin.
But what's this noise next door? It is the cooks
At work. I'll go within and try to stop
Them making like confusion in this house.
(*He returns to the house of* MEGADORUS.)

Act Three.   Scene I

(CONGRIO *and his assistants rush in haste from the house of* EUCLIO.)

CONGRIO: Dear citizens, and fellow-countrymen,
Dwellers or strangers, whosoe'er ye be,
Make room for me to fly; let the whole street
Be open to my path. I never came

Before today to cook at such a place;
'Tis like a Bacchic orgy; they have beaten
My pupils and myself with sticks and staves.
I'm sore all over, and indeed quite dead!
That old boy took me for a boxing school;
I never saw posts come in handier
Than these; he beat us all and turned us out.
Alas! I am undone! Here comes again
The Bacchanalian orgy; he is here;
He follows. I know what to do; I'll go
The way my master went before today.[5]
I never saw a place more generous
With sticks and cudgels for us all to bear.

Act Three.   Scene II

(*Enter* EUCLIO *from his house, stick in hand.*)

EUCLIO: Hallo! Why fly? Return, return, I say!

CONGRIO: Why are you shouting, fool?

EUCLIO: I'll lay your name
Before the magistrates.

CONGRIO: I pray you why?

EUCLIO: Because you wear a knife.

CONGRIO: As well becomes
A cook.

EUCLIO: Ay, and because you threatened me.

CONGRIO: The wrong was that I did not sheath it in you.

EUCLIO: There's not a man more wicked than you are,
Nor one I'd rather do an injury to.

CONGRIO: No need to say so; it is clear enough;
You've made me supple as a dancer is,
Wretch that I am! Why did you touch me thus,
And for what reason?

EUCLIO: Do you ask me why?
Have I done something less than was your due?

CONGRIO: You'll suffer for it, if my head can feel.

EUCLIO: I don't know what may come; but yours feels now.
            But pray what business had you in my house
            When I was absent, without my commands?
            I wish to know.

CONGRIO: Be quiet, then; we came
            To cook your wedding-feast.

EUCLIO: What matters it
            To you if I eat meat that's cooked or raw?
            Are you my master?

CONGRIO: Well, I want to know
            Whether you wish the dinner cooked or not.

EUCLIO: And I whether my things are safe with you
            Or not.

CONGRIO: I only hope that I may take
            The things away, that I have brought with me
            All safe and sound. The rest it matters not,
            For I want none of yours.

EUCLIO: I know, I know.

CONGRIO: But why prevent us cook your dinner here?
            What have we done or said you do not like?

EUCLIO: D'ye ask, you wretch, who thus have made your way
            Through all the corners of my house and rooms?
            If you had stopped beside the hearth, which is
            Your proper place, your head had not been split.
            You well deserved it. Now that you may know
            My sentiments, if you come nearer to
            My door than I shall order, you shall be
            The most unhappy man that is. D'ye hear?
            (EUCLIO *goes into his house*.)

CONGRIO: Art going? Pray come back! And may Laverna,
            Who watches over thieves, be kind to me!
            If you don't order all my cooking things
            To be returned to me, I'll make a row
            Before the house. What am I now to do?
            An evil day it was that brought me here;
            The money that I got won't pay the doctor.

Act Three.   Scene III

(*Re-enter* EUCLIO *from the house, with the pot of gold under his cloak.*)

EUCLIO (*to himself*): Ah! This at all events, where'er I go,
I'll carry with me, as my constant friend,
Nor e'er expose it to like perils again.
(*To* CONGRIO *and others*) Go now within, cooks and
flute-players all,
Bring if you like the whole vile venal herd,
And cook, and act, and bustle as you please.

CONGRIO: Most timely, after you have split our heads.

EUCLIO: Go in! You came to work, and not to talk.

CONGRIO: Old gentleman, for this I'll make you pay;
I was engaged to cook, not to be beaten.

EUCLIO: Don't bother! Go to law! But first to cook,
Or else go and be hanged.

CONGRIO: Pray go yourself.
(CONGRIO *and the assistants go into the house of* EUCLIO.)

Act Three.   Scene IV

EUCLIO (*to himself*): He's gone within. Immortal gods, he who,
Though poor, does business with wealthy men
Needs a brave heart to have. Thus Megadorus
Tries me in every way, pretends to send
His cooks to do me honour; sent this one
To steal this treasure from me. And to match him
Even my cock, that was the special friend
Of that old woman's, nearly ruined me,
And with his claws began to dig a hole
Where this was buried. Further need I say?
My heart was cut to the very quick; I seized
A stick, I kill the cock, in the very act
Of thieving. I believe the cooks themselves
Promised that cock a rich reward if he
Disclosed the treasure. Anyhow, I spoiled
Their little game. No more; the cock is dead.

But see, my neighbour Megadorus comes;
I dare not pass him; I must stop and speak.

Act Three.   Scene V

(*Enter* MEGADORUS *from the forum.*)

MEGADORUS (*to himself, not seeing* EUCLIO): To many friends I've told
                that I propose
        To marry Euclio's daughter; they approve;
        They think it wise and excellently done.
        I would, I think, if others did the same;
        If wealthy people married in this way
        The daughters of the poor, nor asked a dower,
        The state would be more happy than it is,
        With less of jealousy than now we have;
        Our wives would treat us with the more respect,
        And we should live at less expense ourselves.
        'Twould benefit the greater part of men;
        A few old misers would object to it,
        Whose greedy and insatiable souls
        Nor law nor governor can hold in check.
        But some may say, if marriage is for the poor,
        Whom can the wealthy wed? Why, whom they choose,
        If but their fortune has been left behind.
        And in the place of fortune they would bring
        A better disposition; I would make
        Mules, which are dearer now than any horse,
        Cheaper by far than any horse can be.

EUCLIO (*aside*): How gladly here I hearken to this man
        Who speaks such pleasant things of narrow means!

MEGADORUS: No wife could say: "I brought to you a dower
        Much larger than your fortune; therefore I
        Must live in gold and purple, and have maids,
        Pages and lackeys, mules and muleteers,
        And carriages to ride in."

EUCLIO (*aside*):   Ah! How well he knows
        Fine ladies' ways; I wish he was their tutor.

MEGADORUS: But now where'er you go, at your town house
        You'll find more waggons waiting than you will

Ev'n at your country seat. But that's a trifle
To what it is when they present their bills.
There stands the fuller and embroiderer,
The goldsmith and the man who curls your hair,
The tailor and the hosier, and the host
Who dye your bridal veils in red or yellow,
Who sell you muffs, and perfumed slippers too,
Hucksters in linen, showmakers galore,
Clogs, slippers, sandals, all are here to sell,
To dye or mend your garments as you wish;
Sellers of stays and girdles swell the train.
You think them all; three hundred go and come.
Outside the duns are watching in the hall,
The weavers and the men who caskets make;
They've reckoned up; the money paid; 'tis all,
You fancy; when once more these come in view,
Dyers in something else, some wretched thing
That makes still further levies on your purse.

EUCLIO (*aside*): I would address him, but I fear to stop
This nice recital of our ladies' ways.
Let him proceed.

MEGADORUS: And when at length you've paid
For all this female rubbish, comes in view
The taxgatherer, presents his bill; you go
And reckon with your banker, while he waits
Undined, expecting to receive his pay.
When the account is furnished, then you find
You've overdrawn; the tax-man has to wait
Another day. These are the cares that wait,
The inconveniences and vast expense,
On these huge dowries; she who's none at all
Is in her husband's power; and dowered wives
Bring loss and trouble to their husband's lives.
But, see, my neighbour comes. Euclio, good day!

Act Three. Scene VI

EUCLIO: Most gladly have I listened to your words.
MEGADORUS: Didst hear them?
EUCLIO: Ay. I did from the very first.

MEGADORUS: Methinks it would be better still if you
                  Looked rather sprucer for your daughter's wedding.

EUCLIO: According to our means and circumstances,
                  Our wealth and show should still proportioned be.
                  Let those who have, think of their high estate.
                  But I, and such as me, no more of wealth
                  Possess, than public rumour gives to us.

MEGADORUS: Surely you have; may the gods make it more.

EUCLIO (*aside*): I do not like his words: "surely you have;"
                  He knows as well as I do what I have;
                  The old woman's told him.

MEGADORUS: Why d'ye speak apart?

EUCLIO: I thought of making a complaint to you.

MEGADORUS: On what?

EUCLIO: On what, d'ye ask? You who have filled
                  Nigh every corner of my house with thieves;
                  Who've sent into it five hundred cooks at least,
                  With six hands each, like Geryon of old.
                  Argus himself who was all eyes, to whom
                  Jove once entrusted Io, he could not
                  Keep watch upon them, even if he would.
                  A music girl, who by herself could drink
                  The famous fountain of Pirene dry,
                  If bubbling over with wine! And then their food—

MEGADORUS: I've sent as much as would a legion feed;
                  Aye, and a lamb beside.

EUCLIO: I've never seen
                  A more curious beast than that.

MEGADORUS: How curious?

EUCLIO: All bone and skin; so thin with toil and trouble;
                  You can see right through it in the light of day;
                  'Tis as transparent as an ivory lamp.

MEGADORUS: I bought it to be butchered.

EUCLIO: A splendid bargain,
                  For 'tis already dead.

MEGADORUS: Euclio, I wish
            To drink with you today.

EUCLIO: I cannot do so.

MEGADORUS: But I will bid a cask of rich old wine
            To be brought from my cellar.

EUCLIO: I can drink
            But water only.

MEGADORUS: If I live today,
            I'll send you back as drunk as any lord—
            You who drink only water.

EUCLIO (*aside*):   Ah! I see
            What is his aim; to get quit of me with wine,
            That is his plan, and what I have, annex.
            But I'll take care; I'll put it out of doors.
            And he shall lose his wine and trouble too.

MEGADORUS: Unless you want me further, I shall go
            To get me ready for the sacrifice. (*Goes into his
            house.*)

EUCLIO (*to object under cloak*): Ah, little pot, how many foes you have,
            You and the gold entrusted to your care.
            And now the best that I can do is this,
            To take you to the temple of Good Faith
            And hide you there. Good Faith, you know me well,
            And I know you; so take good care to yourself,
            And see you do not change the name you bear,
            If I trust you with this. Relying on
            Your honesty, Good Faith, I come to you.
            (*He goes into the temple of Faith.*)

                    Act Four.   Scene I

                (*Enter the* SLAVE *of* LYCONIDES.)[6]

SLAVE (*to himself*): This is the office of a useful slave
            To do as I do, nor to grumble at
            Nor yet oppose a master's bidding. For
            The slave who wants to serve his master well,
            Does first his master's work and then his own,

And if he sleeps, why let him sleep, as if
He were a slave. Who serves a loving master
Like my own, if he should chance to see
That he's in love, that is the slave's concern:
To bring him back to safety, not to drive
Him further on the path he wants to go.
Just as to boys who learn to swim is given
A raft of rushes to make less their toil,
That they may use their hands more easily;
In the same way a slave should be a raft,
To bear his master up, when he's in love.
His master's will he studies, and his eyes
Note what is on his brow; his least command,
Swifter than courser's flight, he hastes to obey.
Who takes this care, escapes the censuring thong;
Nor keeps his fetters bright by constant wear.
My master is in love with Euclio's daughter;
And now we hear that she is to be married
To Megadorus; he has sent me now
To spy about, and learn what is going on.
Here by this sacred altar I will stand
All unsuspected, and from hence can judge
What here or there is being carried on.

Act Four.   Scene II

(*Enter* EUCLIO *from the temple of Faith.*)

EUCLIO (*not seeing* SLAVE): Take care, Good Faith, you do not indicate
To a single soul that all my gold is there.
I do not fear lest any find the place,
It is so hidden away; still, he would have
A pretty booty who should find the pot
Laden with gold. See to it then, Good Faith.
Now I will wash me for the sacrifice,
And not delay my neighbour when he comes
To take my daughter home. And so, Good Faith,
Again and yet again, I say, that I
May carry off the pot all sound and safe,
To you I so entrust it. In your shrine
And grove it lies securely hidden away.
(*He goes into his house.*)

SLAVE:　　　　Ye gods immortal, what is this I hear
　　　　　　　This man to say, that he has hidden away
　　　　　　　A heavy pot of gold within this shrine?
　　　　　　　Good Faith, see to it that you're not more kind
　　　　　　　To him than me. This man, methinks, is father
　　　　　　　To her my master loves. I will go in
　　　　　　　And spy around the temple; if I find
　　　　　　　The gold, when this man's back is turned; then if
　　　　　　　I do, I'll brew a stoup of wine for you,
　　　　　　　And, when I do it, drink the same myself.
　　　　　　　(*He goes into the temple.*)

Act Four.　Scene III

(EUCLIO *hurries from his house.*)

EUCLIO (*to himself*): 'Twas not for nothing that the raven cried
　　　　　　　At my left hand, and flew close to the ground
　　　　　　　And croaked anon; my heart began to play
　　　　　　　A curious game, and leaped into my throat.
　　　　　　　I am all shaking; I must run and run.
　　　　　　　(*He rushes into the temple.*)

Act Four.　Scene IV

(*Re-enter* EUCLIO, *dragging* SLAVE.)

EUCLIO:　　　Out, out of doors, vile worm, that just has crept
　　　　　　　Out of the ground! But now, you were not here,
　　　　　　　And now you are, you die! You wretched cheat,
　　　　　　　I'll treat you as you well deserve to be.

SLAVE:　　　What demon troubles you? Or what have I
　　　　　　　To do with you? Why do you trouble me?
　　　　　　　Why drag me thus? Why beat me as you do?

EUCLIO:　　　Most worthy of a beating of all men!
　　　　　　　Still asking questions, you, who are a thief,
　　　　　　　Or even more than that, a triple thief.

SLAVE:　　　What have I stolen?

EUCLIO: Bring it back to me.

SLAVE: What should I bring?

EUCLIO: D'ye want to know what 'tis?

SLAVE: I've taken nothing.

EUCLIO: Give it back to me.

SLAVE: What must I do?

EUCLIO: You shall not take it hence.

SLAVE: What do you want?

EUCLIO: Now put it down at once.

SLAVE: I think, old gentleman, you're wont to jest.
              You put it down too often, I believe.[7]

EUCLIO: Be done with jesting; put it down, I say.

SLAVE: And put what down? Pray tell me what it is
              By its own name; I've touched and taken nothing.

EUCLIO: Show me your hands!

SLAVE: Look there!

EUCLIO: And yet again!

SLAVE: See there!

EUCLIO: And show the third hand now, I pray!

SLAVE: Distempered dreams and wild illusions vex
              This old man's soul. D'ye want to do mischief?

EUCLIO: Ay, marry, all I can, not hanging you;
              And that will come if you do not confess.

SLAVE: Confess to what?

EUCLIO: What you have taken away.

SLAVE: The gods destroy me if I have taken aught,
              Or even wished to do so.

EUCLIO: Shake your cloak.

SLAVE: Yes, as you will.

EUCLIO: Lest there be something hidden
              Between the folds.

SLAVE: Try any way you like.

EUCLIO: You wretch, how smooth you speak, that I may not
            Detect you in the theft. I know your dodges.
            Show me your right hand now.

SLAVE: Well, there it is.

EUCLIO: And now your left.

SLAVE: You see, I proffer both.

EUCLIO: I do not care to search. Restore the things.

SLAVE: And what restore?

EUCLIO: You jest, for you must have it.

SLAVE: Have what?

EUCLIO: I need not say, you know full well.
            Restore me what you've had of mine.

SLAVE: You're mad.
            You've searched me as you like, and nothing found.

EUCLIO: Stay, who is that who was inside with you?
            (*Aside*) I am undone; that other is inside.[8]
            If I lose sight of this one, he'll be off.
            Yet I have searched him; he has nothing on him.
            (*Aloud*) Go where you like.

SLAVE: You be completely damned!

EUCLIO: He is not thankful. I will go inside
            And wring the neck of your companion.
            Are you away? Art off? And out of sight?

SLAVE: I am.

EUCLIO: Take care you never see me more.
            (*Goes into the temple.*)

Act Four.   Scene V

SLAVE: I'd rather perish by some foul disease
            Than not contrive to play some nasty trick
            On this old man today. He will not dare

To hide away his gold in this place now.
He'll take it out and change the hiding-place.
I hear the door. And see, he brings the gold!
I'll stand aside behind the door and watch.

Act Four.   Scene VI

(*Enter* EUCLIO *from the temple, with the pot of gold.*)

EUCLIO (*to himself*): I thought Good Faith was fairly to be trusted,
But cruelly she's disappointed me.
But for the raven I had been undone.
I wish to see him once again and make
Some small return—a compliment, not meat.
And now I know a solitary place
Where I may hide this pot; it is the grove
Of our god Silvanus, stretching far beyond
The city wall, with willows planted round.
There I will choose a spot; for I am sure
I had rather trust Silvanus than Good Faith.
(EUCLIO *departs.*)

SLAVE: Good luck! The gods are full of kindness to me.
I'll run before and climb into a tree,
And watch from thence where he may hide the gold.
For, though my master bid me to stay here,
That gain is worth a blow doth still appear.
(*The* SLAVE *departs.*)

Act Four.   Scene VII

(*Enter* LYCONIDES *and* EUNOMIA.)

LYCONIDES: I've told you, mother, and you know the story
Of what has taken place between myself
And Euclio's daughter. Now I pray you tell
My uncle all; once more I do beseech you
As I have done before.

EUNOMIA: Your wish is mine.
And this I hope my brother will consent
To grant; and, if things be as you assert,
Your cause is just. You say it did take place
When you were overcome with use of wine?

LYCONIDES: And think you, mother, I'd impose on you?

PHAEDRIA (*inside* EUCLIO'S *house*): Help me, dear nurse! Juno Lucina, help!

LYCONIDES: The thing is clear enough; she has a child.

EUNOMIA: Then come within with me, and see my brother,
That he at my request may grant your prayer.
(*She goes into the house of* MEGADORUS.)

LYCONIDES: I follow you. (*To himself*) But now I wonder where
My servant Strobilus can be. I bid
Him wait me here. Yet now I think on it,
It were unfair to blame him, as he may
Be helping me elsewhere. I'll come within;
The meeting's one of life or death to me.
(*He goes into the house of* MEGADORUS.)

Act Four. Scene VIII

(*Enter* SLAVE *of* LYCONIDES, *with the pot of gold.*)

SLAVE (*to himself*): Myself I do surpass in stores of wealth
The fabled griffins, who are said to dwell
Upon the golden mountains; mighty kings
I scarce do notice; they are beggars all.
Philip himself I am. Oh! Blessed day,
On which I went from here, and was the first,
And placed myself in hiding on the tree,
And watched from thence where he would place the gold.
When he was gone, I creep along the tree,
And disinter a pot quite full of gold.
I see the old man go; he sees not me;
I leaned aside a little from the road.
But see, he comes. I'll hide the gold at home. (*Departs.*)

Act Four. Scene IX

(*Enter* EUCLIO *frantic.*)

EUCLIO (*to himself*): I'm ruined, slaughtered, quite undone! Oh, where
    Am I to go? Or not to go? Stay! Stop!
    But whom? Or what? I cannot see, I'm blind!
    I cannot say for certain where I go,
    Nor where, nor who I am. (*To audience*) I pray your
      help
    To point me out the man who stole the gold.
    Ay, there they sit in white like honest men.
    What say you? I can trust you; and I know
    An honest man by sight. What is it now?
    Why do you laugh? There are thieves enough, I
      know,
    And many thieves. What, none of these have it?
    You kill me! Don't you know? Say who it is.
    Alas, alas, I am undone! I'm killed!
    A pretty state of things! So much of woe,
    So much of grief has this day brought to me!
    Hunger and poverty, most wretched man!
    What hope of life to one who's lost so much,
    So much that I have guarded? I denied
    Myself all pleasure; others now will joy,
    At my expense, my loss. I cannot bear it!

LYCONIDES (*entering from the house of* MEGADORUS):
    Who is this man who howls before our doors,
    Lamenting loudly? Euclio 'tis, I think.
    Ah, I am ruined! Everything is known.
    He knows what's happened to his daughter now.
    What must I do? Stay here, or go away?
    Approach him, or fly from him? I know not.

Act Four. Scene X

EUCLIO: Who is't who speaks?

LYCONIDES: A most unhappy man!

EUCLIO:
And I not less so, for to me has chanced
Such ills and sorrow.

LYCONIDES:
                                                Nay, be of good heart.

EUCLIO:
How can I?

LYCONIDES:
                        'Cause the deed that troubles you
Is mine. I do admit it.

EUCLIO:
                                        What is this?

LYCONIDES:
The truth.

EUCLIO:
                        What have I done, young man, to you,
That you should ruin me, and leave forlorn
My children and myself?

LYCONIDES:
                                        God was my guide;
'Twas he who led me on.

EUCLIO:
                                        And how was that?

LYCONIDES:
I do admit my sin, and know that I
Deserve your blame. Therefore I come to you
And ask your pardon.

EUCLIO:
                                        But why did you dare
To touch what was not yours?

LYCONIDES:
                                                What do you want?
It cannot be undone. I think the gods
Have willed it, or it never could have been.

EUCLIO:
I think the gods have willed that I should kill you.

LYCONIDES:
Nay, say not so.

EUCLIO:
                                        But why against my will
Have you laid hands on that which was my own?

LYCONIDES:
'Twas wine and love that made me.

EUCLIO:
                                                        Daring man!
To come to me with such a tale as that!
If that is law, then might we just as well
In open daylight take a woman's jewels,
And say when caught that we were drunk, and did it
For the sake of love; too vile are wine and love
If they excuse whate'er we choose to do.

LYCONIDES: I come to ask your pardon for my folly.

EUCLIO: I like not those who first do ill, and then
Excuse themselves. You know it was not yours;
And you should not have touched it.

LYCONIDES: Well, I did it.
And now I will not argue more about it.

EUCLIO: Keep mine against my will?

LYCONIDES: I do not ask
To have it so, but think it should be mine.
And now, O Euclio, I'm sure you'll realise[9]
It should be mine.

EUCLIO: I'll take you to the judge,
And serve a writ, until you bring it back.

LYCONIDES: And bring what back?

EUCLIO: Why, what you stole from
me.

LYCONIDES: I stole? Whence? And what is it?

EUCLIO: May great Jove
Himself so love you in the same degree,
As you are ignorant!

LYCONIDES: Unless you tell me
What 'tis you seek.

EUCLIO: A pot of gold it is
I ask, which you admit that you have stolen.

LYCONIDES: I never said so, and I never did it.

EUCLIO: What, you deny?

LYCONIDES: Most certainly I do.
I know no gold, nor any pot at all.

EUCLIO: Give me the pot you stole from Silvan's grove.
Go, bring it back; I'll give to you a third.
Although a thief, I won't deal hardly with you.

LYCONIDES: You are not sane, in calling me a thief.
I thought that you had spoke of something else,
Which close concerns me. If you have the time,

There is a most important thing I want
To speak of to you.

EUCLIO: Tell me on your word
You have not stolen it.

LYCONIDES: Upon my honour!

EUCLIO: Nor know who did'st so?

LYCONIDES: No, upon my word!

EUCLIO: And if you know, you'll tell me.

LYCONIDES: That I swear.

EUCLIO: And will not ask a share, nor shield the thief?

LYCONIDES: Most certainly.

EUCLIO: And what, if you play false?

LYCONIDES: May Jupiter do with me what he will.

EUCLIO: Enough! Now tell me what you want of me.

LYCONIDES: Well, if you do not know my family,
This Megadorus here, he is my uncle;
Antimachus my father was, and I
Lyconides am called; my mother is
Eunomia.

EUCLIO: The family I know.
But what d'ye want with me?

LYCONIDES: You have a daughter?

EUCLIO: I have, at home.

LYCONIDES: Betrothed to my uncle?

EUCLIO: You know it all.

LYCONIDES: He bid me tell you he
Renounces now her hand.

EUCLIO (*angrily*):   Renounces now
When all is ready and the wedding furnished?
May all the gods and goddesses destroy
This man for whom I've lost so much today.

LYCONIDES: Be of good cheer. May all yet turn out well
For you and for your daughter; pray it be so.

EUCLIO: May the gods do it!

LYCONIDES: And the same to me!
                   Now listen. There's not a man who's sinned,
                   But is ashamed and sorry, if he's worth
                   A straw. Now I beseech you, Euclio,
                   In this misfortune my imprudence caused
                   You and your daughter, you should pardon me
                   And give her me for wife as the law permits.
                   I do confess I did her grievous wrong
                   On Ceres' night, through wine and youthful impulse.

EUCLIO: Alas! Alas! And what is this I hear?

LYCONIDES: Why should you mourn, when at your daughter's
                           wedding
                   You will at once as grandfather appear.
                   She bare a child just ten months after it;
                   Pray reckon for yourself; and therefore 'tis
                   My uncle has renounced her hand for me.
                   Go in, and you will hear that it is so.

EUCLIO: Ah me! I am quite ruined! Evils come
                   One on the top of others, clinging fast.
                   I'll go within and see if this is so.
                           (*Goes into his house.*)

LYCONIDES: And I will follow. (*To himself*) My affairs appear
                   To have reached shoal waters, where my safety lies.
                   But now I cannot find where he should be,
                   My servant Strobilus; I'll wait for him,
                   And then will follow this man; I will give
                   Him time to make enquiries from his daughter
                   And from the nurse; for she at least knows all.

                           Act Five.   Scene I

                   (*Enter* SLAVE *of* LYCONIDES.)

SLAVE (*to himself*): Ye gods immortal, with what joys have you
                   Presented me; how great the sum of them!
                   I have a four pound pot that is full of gold!
                   Who now more rich than me? What man at Athens
                   To whom the gods are kinder?

LYCONIDES (*to himself*): Sure, I thought,
I heard the voice of some one speaking here.

SLAVE (*aside*): Ah! Do I see my master?

LYCONIDES (*aside*): And is it
My servant coming here I see?

SLAVE (*aside*): It is.

LYCONIDES (*aside*): And not another.

SLAVE (*aside*): I'll advance to meet him.

LYCONIDES (*aside*): And I'll draw nearer. I believe that he
Has, as I ordered, seen this lady's nurse.

SLAVE (*aside*): And why not tell him I have found this treasure?
I will that he may set me free. I'll go.
(*To* LYCONIDES) I've found—

LYCONIDES: What have you found?

SLAVE: Why, not that which
Boys look for in a bean and shout with joy,
When they have found it nestling there inside.

LYCONIDES: You're jesting, as you're wont.

SLAVE: Stay, master, hear.

LYCONIDES: Speak then.

SLAVE: Today I found a hoard of wealth,
Too much for me.

LYCONIDES: And where, I pray, was that?

SLAVE: A four pound pot of gold.

LYCONIDES: What crime is this?

SLAVE: I stole it from this old man Euclio.

LYCONIDES: Where is the gold?

SLAVE: Why, in a chest at home.
And now I wish my freedom at your hand.

LYCONIDES: I make you free, most scoundrellest of knaves?

SLAVE: Off with you, master! I know what you want.
                    And cleverly I laid a bait for you.
                    You were prepared to take it. What if I
                    Myself had found it?

LYCONIDES: Now we want no trifling.
                    Bring me the gold.

SLAVE: Must I return the gold?

LYCONIDES: Yes, that it may be given to him.

SLAVE: And whence?

LYCONIDES: Just now you did confess 'twas in your chest.

SLAVE: Yes, I was joking, as I'm wont to do.

LYCONIDES: But how, I pray?

SLAVE: Then kill me if you like;
                    Of this be sure, you shall not take it hence.

*(The remainder of the play is lost. Lyconides apparently returned the
pot of gold to Euclio and received permission to marry his daughter;
Euclio gave the gold to the young couple.)*[10]

1. The verse translations of the two arguments are by E. H. Sugden; these translations have been altered slightly to preserve the tone of the original.

2. Allison compares Shakespeare, *Much Ado About Nothing,* Act Two, Scene I: "She speaks poniards, and every word stabs." A more literal translation of Megadorus' speech is: "Every word's a stone."

3. Allison omitted the next three verses, which have been added by the editor.

4. Many editors assign this speech to Strobilus, who then remains on the stage at the end of Act Two, Scene VI.

5. The following two verses, omitted by Allison, have been added by the editor.

6. This slave is named Strobilus in the Mss., but can hardly be identical with the slave of Megadorus. I follow Lindsay in considering this slave an unnamed character, to whom the name Strobilus has wrongly been assigned.

7. Allison omitted this verse.

8. Euclio suspects that the slave has a partner who is still in the temple searching for the gold.

9. Allison's translation of this verse has been altered for the sake of clarity.

10. Apparently Euclio in this way regained his peace of mind; a fragment of the lost conclusion reads: "I never had any rest day or night; now I shall sleep."

IV
THE TWO BACCHIDES

CHARACTERS IN THE PLAY

PISTOCLERUS, *son of* PHILOXENUS
BACCHIS, *an Athenian courtesan*
BACCHIS, *her sister, from Samos*
LYDUS, *slave of* PHILOXENUS *and tutor of* PISTOCLERUS
CHRYSALUS, *slave of* NICOBULUS *and* MNESILOCHUS
NICOBULUS, *an aged Athenian*
MNESILOCHUS, *his son, in love with* BACCHIS *of Samos*
PHILOXENUS, *an aged Athenian*
A PARASITE
A SLAVE
ARTAMO, *slave overseer of* NICOBULUS
CLEOMACHUS, *a captain*

INTRODUCTION

The Two Bacchides is generally recognised as one of Plautus' better plays. It is a highly amusing comedy, rich in farcical situations and interesting characters. The plot is complex, with unexpected reversals and sudden developments. It is a play of trickery in which the slave Chrysalus plays the leading role. He is one of the best of Plautus' intriguing slaves and deserves to rank with Palaestrio (in *The Braggart Warrior*) or Pseudolus, with Terence's Phormio or Molière's Scapin, in cleverness and ingenuity. The play contains unusual suspense, for the nature of much of the deception is not announced to the audience in advance, as is often done, e.g. in *The Braggart Warrior*. The first part of the play is lost; some foreknowledge of the action may have been given at the beginning, but it is probable that Plautus preferred to have Chrysalus develop his intrigue step by step, as Tranio invents first one lie, then another, in *The Haunted House*.

There is a striking dualism in the construction of *The Two Bacchides*: two young men (Pistoclerus and Mnesilochus), two love affairs, two courtesans (both named Bacchis), two fathers (Philoxenus and Nicobulus). This type of double plot is far more characteristic of Terence than of Plautus. The two sets of characters are closely interwoven, but Pistoclerus' love affair is of secondary importance; the chief interest is in Mnesilochus' difficulty and the attempt of Chrysalus to get money from Nicobulus so that Mnesilochus can free his sweetheart from the soldier. The play is rich in the usual comic types: the youthful lover, the father, the courtesan, the wily slave, the parasite, the professional soldier, and the characters are well delineated. Philoxenus is an easy-going father, Nicobulus gruff and severe. Bacchis of Athens is an expert in the art of seduction, as is shown by the manner in which she wins over the reluctant Pistoclerus and the success which she and her sister have later with the two fathers. The old tutor, Lydus, provides an entertaining discourse on education, disapproving heartily of the lack of discipline in "modern" educational methods. The contrast between the two parents is not unlike that in Terence's *The Brothers,* and had Plautus wished to develop and apply to the action of the play the educational principles enunciated by Lydus, he might have produced something approximating the Terentian play.

The Greek original was Menander's *The Double Deceiver*. Either Menander in this lost play departed from his usual theme of mistaken identity, which led to a recognition scene, or, as some scholars have suggested, Plautus changed the conclusion of the play by omitting the recognition, preferring to end with the farcical and rather immoral situation of the two fathers banqueting with their sons and the courtesans. The ending has been criticised as unsatisfactory on the ground that we are left without any inkling of the fate of the two young men in their love affairs, and without any knowledge of what happened to Chrysalus, the most important character. Such a position seems untenable, for clearly the yielding of the fathers implies that all will be forgiven.

There are two deceptions in the play. The second is made necessary by Mnesilochus' failure to realise that there are two girls named Bacchis. In his anger and resentment at Pistoclerus' apparent faithlessness he returns the money to his father and reveals that Chrysalus' first story is a pack of lies. Nicobulus swears that he'll never believe Chrysalus again, that if Chrysalus said

> "the sun there was the sun,
> He'd believe it was the moon and that the day was really night."

Under these circumstances, far greater ingenuity is required for the second deception. It is wrong to criticise Nicobulus as excessively gullible, as does P. E. Legrand, who finds it hard to believe that Nicobulus would again trust Chrysalus after being once deceived. In the first place, the second trick involves two letters from Mnesilochus, which denounce Chrysalus; second, Nicobulus apparently sees the truth with his own eyes and is, therefore, more easily persuaded that Bacchis is the soldier's wife; third, Chrysalus himself urges Nicobulus not to pay out the money and refuses to take any responsibility in the matter. Few deceptions in Plautine comedy are engineered with more cunning.

The date of the play is uncertain; it is later than the *Epidicus* (cf. 214) and probably is to be assigned to the latter part of Plautus' career, perhaps about 189 B.C. The language of the play is rich and varied, and marked by many mythological allusions. There are numerous lyrical *cantica*, which E. H. Sugden has attempted to reproduce in his verse translation.

The influence of the play on later drama is less noticeable than in the case of the *Amphitryon* and *The Pot of Gold*. Domenichi's *Le Due Cortigiane* (1563) was a prose adaptation of *The Two Bacchides*, while Barbieri's *L'Inavvertito* (1629) and Quinault's *L'Amant Indiscret*

(1654) revealed many points of similarity. Molière's farce, *L'Etourdi*, which deals with Mascarille's attempts to aid his blundering master, was based on Barbieri's play and thus indirectly goes back to Plautus. There are several echoes of *The Two Bacchides* in Cailhava's *Le Mariage Interrompu* (1769).

THE TWO BACCHIDES

(SCENE:—*A street in Athens in front of the houses of* BACCHIS *and* NICOBULUS.)

Act One. Scene I

(*The first part of the comedy is lost, along with the end of* The Pot of Gold. *The missing part may be supplied as follows: Two years before the opening of the play,* NICOBULUS, *a citizen of Athens, had sent his son* MNESILOCHUS *to Ephesus to collect a debt owed to him by* ARCHEMIDES, *a citizen of that place. Calling at Samos on his way,* MNESILOCHUS *fell in love with a girl named* BACCHIS, *who was, however, hired for a year by a certain captain,* CLEOMACHUS, *and taken away by him to Athens.* MNESILOCHUS *writes to* PISTOCLERUS, *a friend of his in Athens, begging him to find the girl, and, if possible, release her from the captain's service. In the first scene of the play,* PISTOCLERUS *is introduced, reading and commenting on his friend's letter.* BACCHIS, *an Athenian courtesan, enters, and informs him that she is expecting a visit that day from her sister, who has come from Samos, and who bears the same name as herself.* PISTOCLERUS *is overjoyed at having found the object of his quest so easily.* BACCHIS *of Samos arrives, and the two sisters greet one another. It is at this point that the play, as we have it, begins.*)

BACCHIS:	Is it best for me to speak, and you be silent?
SISTER:	Yes, that's clear.
BACCHIS:	Well, then, if my memory fails me, you must help me, sister dear.
SISTER:	Nay, love, if I tried to help you, I'd be sure to do it wrong.
BACCHIS:	Sooner would the nightingale forget the way to sing her song. Come with me.

PISTOCLERUS (*aside*):　　　What are they after, these twin sisters
　　　　　with one name?
　　　　　(*Aloud*) What are you discussing?

BACCHIS:　　　　　Something good.

PISTOCLERUS:　　　　　That's not your usual game.

BACCHIS:　Oh, how wretched is poor woman!

PISTOCLERUS:　　　　　As she merits, I aver.

BACCHIS:　This, my sister, begs of me to find someone who'll rescue
　　　　　her
　　　　From that captain, make him send her home when she
　　　　　has served her time.
　　　　Do this, pray!

PISTOCLERUS:　Do what?

BACCHIS:　　　　　Just see that she's sent to native clime,
　　　　So that when her year is ended, he mayn't keep her as
　　　　　his maid.
　　　　If she'd only gold to give him, he'd release her and be
　　　　　glad.

PISTOCLERUS:　Where's the man?

BACCHIS:　　　　　He'll be here shortly. Meanwhile you
　　　　　will serve us best,
　　　　Till he comes, by going indoors and sitting down to take
　　　　　a rest.
　　　　You shall have a glass of wine, and after that a loving
　　　　　kiss!

PISTOCLERUS:　Ah! your flattery's nought but bird-lime!

BACCHIS:　　　　　What do you mean?

PISTOCLERUS:　　　　　Why, I see this,
　　　　You two want to catch a pigeon; if your lime-twig touch
　　　　　his wing,
　　　　I can well foresee, my lady, all the trouble it will bring.

BACCHIS:　How?

PISTOCLERUS:　　　　　Ah, Bacchis, I don't like your Bacchae and your
　　　　Bacchanal.[1]

BACCHIS: What do you fear? To ask you in to take a seat's not criminal.

PISTOCLERUS: Not your seat but your deceit is what I fear, you naughty girl!
I am young, and your attractions set my senses in a whirl.

BACCHIS: Oh, you silly goose, don't fancy I am making love to you.
When the captain comes, I want you to be here and help us through.
You'll protect us from the insults which that fellow may intend;
You'll prevent him; at the same time you will serve your worthy friend.
And the captain, when he comes, will think that I'm engaged to you.
Won't you answer?

PISTOCLERUS: Ah, your words are nice enough to listen to;
But one finds when put in practice they've a sharp point, all the same!
Pierce one's soul, goad through one's goods, and wound one's doings and good fame.

SISTER: Why are you afraid of her?

PISTOCLERUS: Do you ask? What should a lad be doing
With your boudoir for gymnasium, where he'll only sweat to ruin?
For my quoits I shall get losses, and for running shame abhorr'd.

BACCHIS: Hear him talk!

PISTOCLERUS: Within my hands you'll put a dove and not a sword.
When I want my boxing-gloves, I'll get a drinking-cup instead;
For my helm a wine-bowl, for my crest a garland round my head,
For my spear the dice-box, for my breastplate some luxurious weed,
With a girl upon my shield-arm, and a sofa for my steed.
Hence, avaunt!

BACCHIS: Ah, you're too savage!

PISTOCLERUS: Never mind, I know my way.

BACCHIS: I must take in hand and tame you.

PISTOCLERUS: No! There'd be too much to pay.

BACCHIS: Feign to love me!

PISTOCLERUS: Shall I feign in jest, or do it seriously?

BACCHIS: Ah, well, we must get to business. Kindly put your arm
                  round me
                  When the captain comes.

PISTOCLERUS: What for?

BACCHIS: For him to see. I have my plan.

PISTOCLERUS: And, by Pollux! I've my fear! But, here, I say—

BACCHIS: What ails the man?

PISTOCLERUS: What if I drop in upon you when a luncheon or carouse
                  Or a dinner party's on?—You often have them at your
                  house.
                  —Where's my seat?

BACCHIS: By me, my darling! Jolly lad by jolly lass!
                  Come at any time; you'll always find with me a plate
                  and glass.
                  When you want a jolly time, just say to me, "My rose of
                  grace,
                  Make me welcome!" and I'll do it, and find you a jolly
                  place.

PISTOCLERUS: Here's a madly rushing torrent! And it can't be lightly
                  crossed.

BACCHIS (*aside*): And, by Castor! In this torrent something shall by
                  you be lost!
                  (*Aloud*) Take my hand and come along.

PISTOCLERUS: No, no!

BACCHIS: Why not?

PISTOCLERUS: Because, in sooth,
                  Evening hours and wine and ladies are too tempting to
                  a youth.

BACCHIS: Very well! So let it be! It is for you alone I care.
Let the captain take her with him; you can go if you prefer.

PISTOCLERUS: Nay, I'm helpless, for I cannot quell my passion's rising wave!

BACCHIS: What are you afraid of?

PISTOCLERUS: Nothing! Lady, I'm your willing slave!
Yours I am for any service!

BACCHIS: Now you're jolly! Listen here.
I should like to give a feast to welcome home my sister dear.
I will bid them bring you money, then I'll ask you to be pleased
Just to go to market for me and provide a sumptuous feast.

PISTOCLERUS: Nay, I'll pay. It would be shameful that you should find out a way,
For my sake, to do me kindness, and then have the cost to pay.

BACCHIS: But I don't want you to give it.

PISTOCLERUS: Let me!

BACCHIS: All right, if you please.
Be quick, darling!

PISTOCLERUS: I'll be back before my love has time to freeze.
(PISTOCLERUS *departs to the forum.*)

SISTER: So my coming brings you luck, dear sister.

BACCHIS: How is that, I pray?

SISTER: Why, in my opinion, you have made a splendid catch today.

BACCHIS: Oh, he's mine! But we must see about Mnesilochus, my dear;
We must save you from the captain that you may earn money here.

SISTER: It's my wish.

BACCHIS: We'll see to it. Now, let's go in to bathe and dress.
You'll be feeling squeamish from your voyage.

SISTER: Yes, dear, more or less.

BACCHIS: Come along and have a bath, 'twill take away your
weariness.
(*They go into the house of* BACCHIS.)

Act One.   Scene II

(*Enter* PISTOCLERUS, *preceded by slaves carrying food, flowers, etc., for
the feast;* LYDUS *follows.*)

LYDUS: For some time, Pistoclerus, I've been following
In silence at your heels, intent to see
What you are going to do with all this gear.
God bless my soul! Lycurgus' self, I think,
Might well have been debauched by such a show.
Where are you going now, away from home,
With this procession?

PISTOCLERUS: Here. (*Pointing to the house of* BACCHIS.)

LYDUS: Why, who lives there?

PISTOCLERUS: Why, Love, Delight, and Charm and Grace and Joy,
And Jest and Sport and Chat and Kissy-kissy!

LYDUS: What business have you with those cursed gods?

PISTOCLERUS: Cursed is he who curses at the good.
Yea, you blaspheme the gods; it's very wrong.

LYDUS: What, is there any god called Kissy-Kissy?

PISTOCLERUS: Didn't you know? O Lydus, you barbarian!
I used to think you wiser than Thales.
Fie! You've less wits than a Poticius.[2]
So old, and not to know the names of the gods!

LYDUS: I do not like this gear.

PISTOCLERUS: It wasn't meant
For you, but me; I like it well enough.

LYDUS: Oh, you begin to flesh your wit on me!
Had you ten tongues, silence becomes your youth.

PISTOCLERUS:	Come, Lydus, I'm too old to go to school.
	I care for nothing in the world just now
	But that the cook mayn't spoil these luscious viands
LYDUS:	Alas! You've ruined both yourself and me!
	My toil and all my lessons are in vain.
PISTOCLERUS:	I've lost my labour just as much as you;
	Your teaching's been no good to either of us.
LYDUS:	O heart of steel!
PISTOCLERUS:	Come, you're a nuisance, Lydus!
	Be still, and follow me.
LYDUS (*to the spectators*):	Ah, did you hear?
	He doesn't call me "tutor," but plain "Lydus!"
PISTOCLERUS:	Of course! It's quite absurd and out of place,
	When a young fellow goes to see his sweetheart,
	And sits by her, and other guests are present,
	That any "tutor" should be standing by.
LYDUS:	Is that what all this preparation's for?
PISTOCLERUS:	I hope it is; but Heaven determines all.
LYDUS:	Have you a sweetheart?
PISTOCLERUS:	When you see, you'll know.
LYDUS:	You shan't! I won't allow it! Go back home!
PISTOCLERUS:	Drop that, or you'll be whipped!
LYDUS:	What! I be whipped!
PISTOCLERUS:	Yes; I'm too old for you to school me now.
LYDUS:	Find me a gulf wherein to fling myself!
	I've seen more than I ever wished to see.
	Better that I had died than lived for this!
	A pupil utter threats against his master!
	Save me from pupils of such lusty blood!
	His vigorous youth bullies my age and weakness.
PISTOCLERUS:	I shall be Hercules, I guess!—you Linus!
LYDUS:	Nay, but I fear that I shall be your Phoenix,
	To tell your father of your early death!

PISTOCLERUS: Oh, drop your history!

LYDUS: He's lost to shame!—
The gross impertinence that you've assumed
Ill suits your youth.—He's thrown his life away!—
Do you remember that you have a father?

PISTOCLERUS: Am I your slave, or are you mine, good sir?

LYDUS: A viler master taught you this, not I.
More readily you learn his shameful lessons
Than those I taught you with such fruitless toil.
Oh, it was villainously done by you.
To hide these sins from me and from your father!

PISTOCLERUS: So far, good Lydus, I have let you talk;
But that will do. No more! But follow me.
(*They go into the house of* BACCHIS.)

Act Two.   Scene I

(*Enter* CHRYSALUS *from the harbour.*)

CHRYSALUS: Land of my master, hail! I'm glad to see thee
After my two years' stay in Ephesus.
Neighbour Apollo,[3] thee I greet, who dwellest
Next door to us, and beg thee, of thy grace,
Not to permit my master Nicobulus
To come across me, till I first have met
The comrade of Mnesilochus, Pistoclerus,
And given him the letter he has sent
To tell him all about his sweetheart, Bacchis.

Act Two.   Scene II

(*Enter* PISTOCLERUS *from the house of* BACCHIS.)

PISTOCLERUS (*to* BACCHIS *within*): You needn't beg so hard that I'll
                come back,
For I can scarcely tear myself away.
You hold me fast in love's sweet bonds and fetters.

CHRYSALUS: By the immortal gods, it's Pistoclerus!
Hail, Pistoclerus!

PISTOCLERUS: Chrysalus, all hail!

CHRYSALUS: I'll tell you briefly what you want to say:—
You're glad I've come: and I am duly grateful.—
You ask me in to dinner, as you ought
On my return from foreign parts; I'll come.—
I bring you hearty greeting from your friend;
You ask me where he is; he lives.

PISTOCLERUS: How is he?

CHRYSALUS: That's just what I was going to ask of you.

PISTOCLERUS: How can I know?

CHRYSALUS: None better.

PISTOCLERUS: Why, how's that?

CHRYSALUS: He's alive and well, if you have found his sweetheart;
If not, he's ill and very like to die.
His sweetheart is her lover's very soul;
If she's away, he's nought; and if she's there,
She makes his money nought, poor wretched fellow!
But have you executed his commission?

PISTOCLERUS: Rather than he should come and find I've failed
To do what he requested in his message,
I'd go and dwell in the infernal shades!

CHRYSALUS: Then you've found Bacchis?

PISTOCLERUS: Yes, the Samian one.

CHRYSALUS: Take care that no one touch her heedlessly.
You know your Samian ware is precious brittle!

PISTOCLERUS: At your old jests again!

CHRYSALUS: But where is she?

PISTOCLERUS: Here, where you saw me coming out just now.

CHRYSALUS: How jolly! Why, that's just next door to us!
Does she remember her Mnesilochus?

PISTOCLERUS: Nay, he's her only darling!

CHRYSALUS: Oh, indeed!

PISTOCLERUS: Nay, trust her! Oh, she loves to sheer distraction.

CHRYSALUS: That's right.

PISTOCLERUS: Nay, Chrysalus—

CHRYSALUS: Well?

PISTOCLERUS: Not a moment
Passes, but she is mentioning his name.

CHRYSALUS: So much the better she!

PISTOCLERUS: Nay—

CHRYSALUS: Nay, I'm off!

PISTOCLERUS: Why, aren't you pleased to hear of his good luck?

CHRYSALUS: Oh, yes, but I can't stand your wretched acting!
Why, the *Epidicus,* my favourite play,
I can't endure, if Pellio's acting it.
So Bacchis is a fine brave lass?

PISTOCLERUS: She is.
Were mine not Venus, I would call her Juno.[4]

CHRYSALUS: This then is how it stands, Mnesilochus!
You've got your love; now find the wherewithal.
She'll need some gold perhaps.

PISTOCLERUS: Of Philip's coinage.

CHRYSALUS: Perhaps she needs it now.

PISTOCLERUS: Nay, before now.
The captain's coming soon—

CHRYSALUS: A captain too?

PISTOCLERUS: Who wants the gold for setting Bacchis free.

CHRYSALUS: Well, let him come; the sooner 'tis, the better!
I have it with me. I'm afraid of no one,
Nor will I ask for anybody's help,
If but my heart be firm in my design.
Go in; this is my business. And tell Bacchis
Mnesilochus is coming.

PISTOCLERUS: So I will.
                (PISTOCLERUS *goes inside.*)

CHRYSALUS (*to himself*): This business of the gold belongs to me.
                We've brought from Ephesus twelve hundred Philips
                Which our host owed to my old master here.
                Some trick I'll forge today to get the money
                For my young master, him who is in love—
                I hear our door! Who is it coming out?

                        Act Two. Scene III

                (*Enter* NICOBULUS *from his house.*)

NICOBULUS (*to himself*): I'll go to the Piraeus and enquire
                If any ship has come from Ephesus;
                My mind misgives me that my son is taking
                So long a holiday and not returning!

CHRYSALUS (*aside*): Heaven helping me, I'll rob the old man finely.
                I mustn't be caught napping; I want gold;
                Now is the crisis, Chrysalus, my boy!
                I will accost him; he shall prove today
                The ram of Phrixus, and his fleece of gold
                I'll shear to the very quick, or I'm mistaken.
                (*Aloud*) Chrysalus, his slave, salutes good Nicobulus!

NICOBULUS: Good heavens! Why, Chrysalus, where is my son?

CHRYSALUS: I think you might return my greeting first.

NICOBULUS: Well, how d'ye do? But where's Mnesilochus?

CHRYSALUS: Alive and well.

NICOBULUS: He's come?

CHRYSALUS: He has.

NICOBULUS: Bravo!
                Your news is water to a thirsty man.
                And is he well?

CHRYSALUS: Fit as a prize-fighter.

NICOBULUS: And how's the business gone at Ephesus?
                Has he got the gold from Archidemides?

CHRYSALUS: My heart and head are split, good Nicobulus,
To hear the mention of that wretch's name.
Call him not friend: a fiend he's proved to you.

NICOBULUS: Why so, I pray you?

CHRYSALUS: Nay, I'm confident,
Fire, Moon, Sun, Day, four gods of mickle might,
Have never shone upon a greater villain!

NICOBULUS: Than Archidemides?

CHRYSALUS: Than Archidemides.

NICOBULUS: What has he done?

CHRYSALUS: Nay, what has he not done?
First, he began to wrangle with your son,
And said he didn't owe a single penny.
Mnesilochus then summoned to his aid
Pelagon, who's our old and trusty friend.
Then in his presence he produced the seal
Which you had given your son to bring to him.

NICOBULUS: Well, when he'd shown the seal?

CHRYSALUS: He starts to say
That it's forgery, not your seal at all.
What insults on your guiltless son he heaped!
Charged him with forgeries in other cases.

NICOBULUS: Have you the gold? That's what I want to know.

CHRYSALUS: The magistrate appointed arbitrators;
He lost his case and so perforce he paid us
Twelve hundred Philips.

NICOBULUS: Yes, that was the debt.

CHRYSALUS: But hear about the trick he tried to play us!

NICOBULUS: What, is there more?

CHRYSALUS: Yes, this was a kite's swoop.

NICOBULUS: I've been deceived, and trusted all that gold
To an Autolycus.

CHRYSALUS: But, pray you, listen.

NICOBULUS: I didn't penetrate his greedy soul.

CHRYSALUS: After we'd got the gold, we straight embarked,
Longing for home. But sitting on the deck
And looking round, I saw a privateer
Being fitted out for sea.

NICOBULUS: Alas! I'm ruined!
That privateer has pierced me to the heart.

CHRYSALUS: Your friend and certain pirates owned her jointly.

NICOBULUS: Oh, what a dolt I was to trust to him!
The very name of Archidemides
Declares the "damnéd ease" with which he cheats.

CHRYSALUS: The privateer lay waiting for our ship,
And I began to watch what they would do.
Meanwhile our ship sets sail to leave the harbour.
When we had got outside, they followed us
Swifter than birds or winds. When I perceived
What they were doing, we stopped our ship at once.
But when they saw us stop, they set to work
To row about the harbour.

NICOBULUS: Oh, the villains!
What did you do?

CHRYSALUS: Oh, we put back to port.

NICOBULUS: 'Twas wisely done. And what did they do then?

CHRYSALUS: When evening fell, they made for land once more.

NICOBULUS: They meant to steal the gold; that was their aim.

CHRYSALUS: I saw that well enough, and was alarmed.
Well, when we saw them plotting for the gold,
We straightway laid our plans; and the next day
Removed the gold in presence of them all,
Plainly and openly, that they might know it.

NICOBULUS: A clever trick! What's next?

CHRYSALUS: That hipped them sadly.
When they had seen us take the gold away,
They beached the privateer with furious looks.
We placed the gold in Theotimus' care,
Who is Diana's priest at Ephesus.

NICOBULUS: Who's Theotimus?

CHRYSALUS: Megalobulus' son,
And quite the dearest man in Ephesus.

NICOBULUS: By Jove! But he'd be dearer still to me
If he should swindle me of all that gold.

CHRYSALUS: Oh, but it's stored in great Diana's temple,
In public keeping.

NICOBULUS: Oh, you've ruined me!
I'd rather have it in my private care.
But didn't you bring any of it home?

CHRYSALUS: Why, yes, but I don't know how much he brought.

NICOBULUS: What, you don't know?

CHRYSALUS: No, for Mnesilochus
Went secretly by night to Theotimus,
And neither told to me nor anyone
How much he got from him; so I don't know.
But certainly it was not very much.

NICOBULUS: Was it half, do you think?

CHRYSALUS: I really couldn't say;
But I don't think so.

NICOBULUS: Would it be a third?

CHRYSALUS: I don't think so; but really I don't know.
All that I know is that I do not know.
Now you will have to take your passage thither,
To bring the money back from Theotimus.
And, oh, I say—

NICOBULUS: What's that?

CHRYSALUS: You'll not forget
To take your son's ring with you.

NICOBULUS: Why his ring?

CHRYSALUS: Because we gave that sign to Theotimus,
That he who brought the ring should have the gold.

NICOBULUS: I'll not forget, and thanks for your advice.
Is Theotimus rich?

CHRYSALUS: I guess he is;
I tell you, sir, he soles his shoes with gold.

NICOBULUS: Why's he so dainty?

CHRYSALUS: He's so very rich
He don't know what to do with all his gold.

NICOBULUS: I wish he'd give it me! But who was there
When Theotimus had the gold from you?

CHRYSALUS: All Ephesus: there's not a man but knows it.

NICOBULUS: Well, that at least was wisdom in my son,
To give the gold to a rich man to keep;
For he can get it back upon demand.

CHRYSALUS: Nay, he won't keep you waiting for a minute.
You'll have it the same day that you arrive.

NICOBULUS: I thought that I had done with going to sea,
For I am getting old to take a voyage.
But in this case I see I have no choice;
My fine friend Archidemides compels me.
But tell me, where's my son Mnesilochus?

CHRYSALUS: I think he's gone down to the market-place
To greet his friends and the gods on his return.

NICOBULUS: Well, I'll be off and find him if I can.
              (NICOBULUS *goes to the forum.*)

CHRYSALUS (*to himself*): I've put a pretty load upon his back!
My plot I've woven not altogether badly.
It's gained my lovesick master what he wants;
For he can take as much as he requires
Of that same gold, and only give his father
Just what he likes. Now the old gentleman
Will go to Ephesus to fetch his gold.
Meanwhile, we'll pass the time in pleasant fashion,
Unless, indeed, he doesn't leave us here,
But takes Mnesilochus and me with him!
Oh, what a jolly coil it is I'm making!
But what will happen when he finds it out?
When he discovers that he's going for nothing,
And that we've used the gold, alas for me!
I guess when he comes back, he'll change my name
And make me Crossalus, not Chrysalus.

I'll run away, if that should prove the best.
If I am caught, I'll give him trouble yet;
If he has rods in the field, well, I've a back!
But now I'll go and tell my master's son
About the gold and how his sweetheart's found.
(CHRYSALUS *departs to the harbour*.)

Act Three.   Scene I

(*Enter* LYDUS *from the house of* BACCHIS.)

LYDUS (*to himself*): Throw wide open, I beseech you, and unclose this
    door of Hell!
It deserves no better name; it doesn't need a sage to tell
He who enters must abandon every hope of temperance;
Bacchanals,[1] not Bacchides, are ye who lead this fren-
    zied dance.
Hence, avaunt, ye fatal sisters, drinking up the blood
    of men!
Fitted up with costly baits to lure to ruin is your den.
Soon as I had seen them, straightway I betook myself
    to flight.
Shall I keep all this in secret, hiding from your father's
    sight,
Pistoclerus, your excesses, follies, and extravagance?
[Ah, you'll lead me, and your father, and your friends,
    a pretty dance,
Driving us to shame and sorrow, and inextricable ruin!][5]
For you've no regard for me or for yourself in what
    you're doing;
Both your father and myself, your friends and all who
    bear your name,
By your conduct you'll make aiders and abettors of
    your shame.
No, you shan't! I'll tell your father all about this little
    game.
I myself will stop your nonsense, and inform your father
    straight;
Then he'll come and drag you from this swinish feast,
    ere 'tis too late!
(LYDUS *departs to find* PHILOXENUS.)

Act Three. Scene II

(*Enter* MNESILOCHUS *from the harbour, followed by slaves with luggage.*)

MNESILOCHUS (*to himself*): After much consideration, hither my conclusions tend;

Nothing, save the gods, is better than a tried and trusty friend,

One I mean who really is so; and I'll tell you how I know:

When I'd gone to Ephesus, which happened some two years ago,

To my comrade, Pistoclerus, I despatched a messenger,

Begging him to find my sweetheart, Bacchis; now with joy I hear

He has found her, so my servant Chrysalus brings word to me.

Then against my worthy father he's devised some trickery,

To procure me all the money I require. [Why, there's my friend!][6]

Well, by Pollux, in my judgment thanklessness I'd ne'er defend:

Better to let off a foe than slight a man who's done you good;

Yes, extravagance is nobler than such base ingratitude.

Good men praise the one; the other even wicked men will blame.

So that I must watch and labour, lest I injure my good name.

Now your side must be decided, now's the testing time, my lad,

Whether you are what you should be, whether you are good or bad.

Just or unjust, mean or generous, gentlemanly or a clown;

Don't you let your slave surpass you in the kindnesses he's shown.

What you are, you can't conceal.—But who come here? Yes, without doubt,

My friend's father and his tutor! Let me hear what they're about.

Act Three.   Scene III

(*Enter* LYDUS *and* PHILOXENUS.)

LYDUS: Now, I'll see if I can't rouse your indignation, worthy
                   sir!
                Follow me!

PHILOXENUS: Where shall I follow? Where are you taking
                   me?

LYDUS: To her
                Who alone has brought to ruin and destroyed your only
                   son.

PHILOXENUS: Gently, Lydus! Keep your temper, and much folly you
                   will shun.
                At his age we mustn't wonder if he plays a trick or two;
                Greater wonder if he didn't! Why, it's what I used to do.

LYDUS: Out, alas! It's your complaisance ruins him; yes, you're
                   much too kind.
                But for you I should have brought him quickly to a
                   better mind.
                Now by your extreme indulgence you've reduced to utter
                   shame
                Pistoclerus.

MNESILOCHUS (*aside*): Oh, good heavens! Do I hear my comrade's
                   name?
                What has Pistoclerus done to put old Lydus in a rage?

PHILOXENUS: Everybody's swayed by passion for a little at his age;
                Soon he'll loathe himself for doing it. Lydus, treat him
                   tenderly;
                If he doesn't carry matters to extremes, why, let him be!

LYDUS: No, I won't! While I have life, I won't permit it to be
                   done!
                Listen, you, who plead the cause of your abandoned
                   foolish son!
                Had you such indulgence granted, when you were as
                   young as he?
                I'll engage, when you were twenty, you had not the
                   liberty

E'en to stir a finger's breadth, without your tutor, from
your home.

If, before the day had dawned, you weren't at the gymnasium,

You were punished most severely by the trainer of the
youth;

Yea, in such a case, the trouble went still further; for,
in sooth,

On the pupil and his tutor, both alike, the blame would
fall.

Then in racing, wrestling, boxing, hurling spear, and
quoit, and ball,

And in leaping they were practised, not in courting and
in kisses;

There they spent their youth, and not in quiet corners
with the misses.

When from race-course or gymnasium you had got back
home again,

Neatly dressed, upon your stool you sat beside your
tutor then,

Reading in your book, and if you missed a single syllable,

You were striped like any tiger, for your tutor whipped
you well.

MNESILOCHUS (*aside*): How I'm grieved that these reproaches fall upon
him in mistake!

Though he's innocent he suffers this suspicion for my
sake.

PHILOXENUS: Ah, but, Lydus, times are altered.

LYDUS: Yes, I'm well aware of that!

In the good old times a man would oft be made a
magistrate,

Ere he ceased to pay obedience to his tutor's least command;

Now, before a lad is seven, if you touch him with your
hand,

He will seize his slate and with it break his tutor's head
straightway.

If you go and tell his father, this is what you'll hear
him say:

"That's my brave boy! I'm delighted you defend yourself so well."

Then the tutor gets a rating: "You old wretch, incapable,
Don't you punish him for doing it, he's a brave and
merry wag.
Go, sir master, patched up like a lantern with a greasy
rag!"
That's the end of your appeal. I ask how any tutor durst
Exercise authority when he himself is beaten first?

MNESILOCHUS (*aside*): Eh, but his complaint is bitter! After hearing
what he's said,
I should guess that Pistoclerus has been punching Lydus'
head.

PHILOXENUS: Who is this, whom I see standing at the door?

LYDUS: Philoxenus,
Why, not even an apparition of the gods could please
me thus!

PHILOXENUS: Who is it?

LYDUS: Mnesilochus, the friend and comrade of your boy!
But how different! Other things than ladies' love his
thoughts employ.
Happy, happy Nicobulus, to have got a son so dear!

PHILOXENUS: Ah, Mnesilochus, good morning! I'm right glad to see
you here.

MNESILOCHUS: Thanks, Philoxenus! Heaven bless you!

LYDUS: Ah, how is his father blessed!
Here's a son who's crossed the ocean in his father's
interest,
Always thoughtful and attentive to his every wish and
word.
He and Pistoclerus in their boyhood childish friendship
shared.
He's not more than three days older, if you judge them
by their age;
But in sense and wit he's thirty years his senior, I'll
engage.
I would rather trust my troubles than my money to
your son.

PHILOXENUS: Why?

LYDUS: Because, a few days after, all my troubles would
                         be gone!

PHILOXENUS: You'll be whipped, if you don't stop your unjust
                         charges!

LYDUS: You be quiet!
                  You're a fool if you refuse to hear the story of his riot.

MNESILOCHUS: What's my friend been doing, Lydus, that you blame
                         him in this way?

LYDUS: Your friend's ruined.

MNESILOCHUS: Heaven forbid it.

LYDUS: Oh, you'll find it as I say.
                  Nay, I saw him in the act; it's not from hearsay that
                         I'm talking.

MNESILOCHUS: What's he done?

LYDUS: He's fallen in love with a young girl.

MNESILOCHUS: Oh, dear, how shocking!

LYDUS: One who sucks in like a whirlpool everyone she glances
                         on.

MNESILOCHUS: Where's her house?

LYDUS: Why, here. (*Pointing.*)

MNESILOCHUS: And where's she come from?

LYDUS: She's a Samian.

MNESILOCHUS: What's her name?

LYDUS: It's Bacchis.

MNESILOCHUS: You're mistaken, Lydus; I know well
                  All about it; Pistoclerus really isn't culpable.
                  He was only executing a commission, as I'll prove,
                  For his friend with faithful zeal; so don't imagine he's
                         in love.

LYDUS: Must he then, to execute with faithful zeal his friend's
                         commission,
                  Take the lady on his knee and kiss away *sans* intermis-
                         sion?

Couldn't it be executed any other way than this,
With his arm around her waist, with lip to lip in one
    long kiss?
Nay, I'd be ashamed to tell you all I saw him doing
    there,
In my presence, without blushing. But your feelings I
    will spare.
He is ruined, my poor pupil, your companion, and his
    son,
For I say a man is ruined when his modesty is gone.
Why say more? If I'd been willing to remain and see
    his ruin,
I'd have had a better chance of watching what the lad
    was doing;
But I fear I should have seen more than I ought in that
    mad wooing.

MNESILOCHUS (*aside*): Ah, my heart is broken, comrade! Shall I go and
    kill the girl?
If I don't, I'd rather die myself! My brain is in a whirl!
All my confidence is shattered, all my trust in men is
    gone!

LYDUS (*to* PHILOXENUS): See, how bitterly he's grieving at the ruin of
    your son!
How his comrade's bad behaviour robs his soul of all
    her joy!

PHILOXENUS: Come, Mnesilochus, I pray you, try to save my naughty
    boy.
He's my son and your companion; rescue him!

MNESILOCHUS: I hope I may!

LYDUS (*to* PHILOXENUS): Don't you think it will be better, if along with
    him I stay?

PHILOXENUS: No, Mnesilochus will manage.

LYDUS: Well, then, let him have it hot!
For on you and me and all his friends he's put a shame-
    ful blot.

PHILOXENUS: Well, to you I trust this business. Come on, Lydus!

LYDUS: Well, why not?
          (PHILOXENUS *and* LYDUS *depart*.)

Act Three. Scene IV

MNESILOCHUS (*to himself*): I wonder which of them's my deadliest foe,
My comrade, or my Bacchis? I can't tell!
Does she love him the best? Then let her have him.
By Hercules! The curse shall fall on her!
For never be my word again believed,
If I don't in a thousand fashions—love her!
She shall not make a laughing stock of me;
For I'll go home—steal something from my father
And give it her!—Oh, but I'll be revenged!
Yes, though I make—my father beg his bread!
But what a senseless idiot I am
To babble here all I am going to do.
If I know anything, I'm sure I love her.
But I'll take precious care that she shall never
Be a lead filing wealthier for me!
Rather than that I will outbeg a beggar!
She shall not live to mock me! I'm resolved
To pay back all the money to my father.
Then shall she flatter me all penniless
When all her flattery is of no more use
Than to crack jokes with dead men in their graves.
Yes, certainly, I'll take the money back,
And beg my father for my sake to pardon
Poor Chrysalus, and not be angry with him,
Since for my sake it was he hocussed him.
I must look after him, who for my sake
Told him the lie. You slaves, come after me!
(MNESILOCHUS *and the slaves go into the house of* NICOBULUS.)

Act Three. Scene V

(*Enter* PISTOCLERUS *from the house of* BACCHIS.)

PISTOCLERUS (*to* BACCHIS *within*): Everything shall be postponed to
what my Bacchis bids me do.
I'll go seek Mnesilochus and bring him back with me to
you.
But I'm very much astonished, if he's met my messenger,
What he's stopping for. I'll go right to his house. Perhaps he's there.

Act Three. Scene VI

(Enter MNESILOCHUS *from the house of* NICOBULUS.*)*

MNESILOCHUS *(to himself)*: All the gold I've given my father. Now,
    then, I should like to see,
    When I've nothing left to give, the girl who so despises
      me.
    It was hard to get my father to forgive old Chrysalus!
    But at last I did succeed in making him less furious.

PISTOCLERUS *(aside)*: Ah, is that my comrade?

MNESILOCHUS *(aside)*:   Ah, is that my enemy I see?

PISTOCLERUS *(aside)*: Yes, 'tis he!

MNESILOCHUS *(aside)*:   'Tis he!

PISTOCLERUS *(aside)*:   I'll run to meet and greet him lovingly.
    (Aloud) Hail, Mnesilochus!

MNESILOCHUS: Good morning.

PISTOCLERUS: Now you're back from your exile,
    We must have a dinner!

MNESILOCHUS: No, sir! It would only stir my bile.

PISTOCLERUS: Have you caught some illness since returning?

MNESILOCHUS: Yes, pain without end!

PISTOCLERUS: Where've you got it?

MNESILOCHUS: From a man whom up to now I thought my friend.

PISTOCLERUS: Ah, too many of that pattern live amongst us nowadays.
    Friends you think them, but they're shown up traitors
      by their treacherous ways;
    Full of talking, never doing, their honour is a broken
      reed;
    Others' better fortune never fails their envious thoughts
      to feed.
    No one ever envies them, their idleness takes care of
      that!

MNESILOCHUS: Ah, I see you've studied them, and know their practices quite pat.
From their cursed disposition this one curse will still arise;
No one loves them, they may reckon all mankind their enemies.
When they think they're cheating others, it's themselves the fools are cheating!
That's the sort of man he is, whom as a brother I've been treating.
He, as far as in him lay, has done me all the harm he could,
And confounded my resources to my harm and not my good.

PISTOCLERUS: He must be a worthless scoundrel.

MNESILOCHUS: I confess I think so too.

PISTOCLERUS: Tell me who he is, I beg you?

MNESILOCHUS: Softly, he's a friend to you.
If he were not, I would beg you, to the utmost of your power,
To avenge me.

PISTOCLERUS: Tell me who he is, and if that very hour
I don't make him suffer, let me take the prize for laziness.

MNESILOCHUS: He's a worthless wretch, but yet a friend of yours.

PISTOCLERUS: Still, none the less,
Tell me who he is; a worthless villain's friendship I disclaim.

MNESILOCHUS: Well, I see I can't avoid it; I shall have to tell his name.
Pistoclerus, you have ruined me, your comrade, utterly!

PISTOCLERUS: What's that?

MNESILOCHUS: What? Why, didn't a letter come from Ephesus from me
Asking you to find my sweetheart?

PISTOCLERUS: Yes, and I have found her, too.

MNESILOCHUS: Tell me, weren't there girls enough in Athens to suffice
for you

To go courting, but you needs must choose one trusted
to your care;

Lay your wicked plans against me, and go fall in love
with her?

PISTOCLERUS: Are you mad?

MNESILOCHUS: Nay, don't deny it, for your tutor's told me all;
You've betrayed me.

PISTOCLERUS: Do you want to anger me beyond recall?

MNESILOCHUS: You love Bacchis.

PISTOCLERUS: Yes, but there are two girls here who
bear that name.

MNESILOCHUS: Two?

PISTOCLERUS: Yes, sisters.

MNESILOCHUS: Now you know you're talking nonsense; oh, for shame!

PISTOCLERUS: Look you here, if you continue thus my honour to gain-
say,

I shall take you on my back and bear you in.

MNESILOCHUS: Nay, I'll come. Stay!

PISTOCLERUS: No, I won't; you shan't suspect me falsely.

MNESILOCHUS: All right, lead the way.
(*They go into the house of* BACCHIS.)

Act Four.   Scene I

(*Enter* PARASITE *with* SLAVE *of* CLEOMACHUS.)

PARASITE: I am the parasite of that worthless rascal
The captain, him who brought the girl from Samos.
Now he has bid me come to her and ask
Whether she'll pay the gold or go with him.—
You came with her, my boy, not long ago;
You know which house it is; go straight and knock.
(*The* SLAVE *knocks gently at the door of* BACCHIS)

Come back, you scamp! How modestly he knocks!
Though you can eat a good three feet of loaf,
You don't know how to knock!
(*The* PARASITE *knocks furiously*)
                              Ho! Who's within?
Hallo! Who's here? Who'll open me this door?
Come, somebody!

Act Four.   Scene II

(*Enter* PISTOCLERUS *in anger.*)

PISTOCLERUS: What's all this knocking for?
Come, what the deuce do you mean by practising
Your strength in battering other people's doors?
You've nearly smashed the panel! What do you want?

PARASITE: Good day, young sir!

PISTOCLERUS: Good day! But whom do you seek?

PARASITE: Bacchis.

PISTOCLERUS: But which?

PARASITE: Bacchis is all I know.
In brief, Cleomachus, the captain, sent me
To say that she must pay two hundred Philips,
Or go with him to Elatia today.

PISTOCLERUS: Oh, no! Say she won't go! Go back and tell him.
She has a lover here. So you be off!

PARASITE: Don't lose your temper!

PISTOCLERUS: Won't I lose my temper!
By Hercules! Your jaw is near to trouble;
My tooth-crackers are itching to be at it.

PARASITE (*aside*):   I gather from his words that I must mind
He doesn't knock out all my nut-crackers!
(*Aloud*) I'll tell him what you say, but at your peril!
(*The* PARASITE *moves away.*)

PISTOCLERUS: Look here!

PARASITE: I'll tell him what you say.

PISTOCLERUS: But tell me,
            Who are you?

PARASITE: I'm the captain's body-guard.

PISTOCLERUS: He must be a scamp, his body-guard's so vile.

PARASITE: He'll come, swelling with rage.

PISTOCLERUS: I hope he'll burst.

PARASITE: There's nothing else?

PISTOCLERUS: Be off, and quickly too!

PARASITE: Bye-bye, tooth-cracker!

PISTOCLERUS: Bye-bye, body-guard!
            (*The* PARASITE *and the* SLAVE *depart*.)
            (*To himself*) Well, things have got to this, that I don't
                know
            How to advise my friend about his sweetheart.
            The angry fool has given his dad the gold,
            And hasn't got a cent to pay the captain.
            But I'll stand on one side. I hear the door.
            See where Mnesilochus comes sadly forth!

            Act Four.   Scene III

(*Enter* MNESILOCHUS *from the house of* BACCHIS.)

MNESILOCHUS (*to himself*): Pettish, hasty, fool, and nought less!
            Hot, ungovernable, thoughtless!
            Acting without law or measure,
            Scorning right and faith at pleasure!
            Powerless to control my passion,
            Full of hateful, vile suspicion,
            That's my wretched, sad condition.
            Would that someone else were me!
            How can I have done it? Ah, none could be worse,
            Or more richly deserve the gods' bitterest curse!
            To be hated and cut is my fate, I can see.
            Yes, it's foes, not friends, I deserve to have!
            The bad, not the good, must befriend such a knave.
            All the reproaches deserved by the shameless,

I deserve better; my folly is nameless!
Madman! To give back my father the gold
When I had got it! Oh, sorrow untold!
Myself and good Chrysalus too I have sold!

PISTOCLERUS (*aside*): I must comfort him, I'll try it.
(*Aloud*) Mnesilochus, what's up?

MNESILOCHUS: I'm done for!

PISTOCLERUS: Heaven forbid!

MNESILOCHUS: I say I'm done for!

PISTOCLERUS: Be quiet, madman!

MNESILOCHUS: How be quiet?

PISTOCLERUS: Have you lost your wits?

MNESILOCHUS: I'm done for!
Many keen and bitter woes
Rend my heart with piercing throes!
To think that I believed that lie!
I blamed you undeservedly.

PISTOCLERUS: Come, cheer up!

MNESILOCHUS: No use to try!
A corpse is worth far more than I.

PISTOCLERUS: The parasite of the captain bold
Came here just now to get the gold.
I sent him off with a flea in his ear
Away from the door, away from here;
I drove him off.

MNESILOCHUS: That doesn't help me.
What can I do? O misery!
He'll take her away with him, I see.

PISTOCLERUS: Had I the cash, I'd not promise, by Jove!

MNESILOCHUS: You'd give it to me; yes, if you weren't in love
I'd trust your friendship through and through;
But you've enough of your own to do!
How can I look for help from you?
You are helpless.

PISTOCLERUS: Say no more. Some god will sure look after us.

MNESILOCHUS: Nonsense!

PISTOCLERUS: Stay!

MNESILOCHUS: What is it?

PISTOCLERUS: See, here comes your saviour, Chrysalus.

Act Four.   Scene IV

(*Enter* CHRYSALUS *from the harbour.*)

CHRYSALUS (*to himself*): Ah, I'm worth my weight in gold! I ought to
            have a golden image;
        Yes, I've done a double crime, got double plunder from
            this scrimmage!
                Poor old master! How I've paid him!
                What a jolly fool I've made him!
                Clever old man! But my clever plan
        Forced him and drove him to trust all I told to him.
        Now for that bold man, son of the old man,
        My partner in larking, and guzzling, and sparking,
        I have brought royalest treasures of gold to him
        Of his own store, he's not got to fetch it round.
                Not good enough are
        Slaves who can get but some two or three wretched
            pound;
                I'm no such duffer!
        There's nothing worse than a slave without sense,
        With a head that's totally thick and dense,
        Who can't get all he wants from thence.
        For nobody is any good,
        Who cannot rapidly change his mood;
        A villain with villains, a thief among thieves;
                There's not much he leaves!
        If a fellow's worth a pin,
        He can always change his skin;
        With the good or the bad he'll take a hand;
        And always steer as the times demand.
        But I must find out how much money the lad
        Has kept, and how much he's returned to his dad;
        To treat him as Hercules surely was best;

Just pay him a tithe, and then collar the rest!
But see where he's coming of whom I'm in quest.
(*To* MNESILOCHUS) Have you dropped your money,
    master, that you're gazing on the ground?
Well, you are a sad and melancholy couple I have found!
I don't like it; it means mischief. Come, let's have the
    reason told.

MNESILOCHUS: Chrysalus, I'm ruined!

CHRYSALUS: What! Perhaps you took too little gold?

MNESILOCHUS: Curse on it, too little? Nay, but many times much less
    than that!

CHRYSALUS: Why, you fool, when I had gained an opportunity so pat
By my skill, for you to take as much as you could e'er
    desire,
Did you take it with your finger-tips as if it were on
    fire?
Do you think a chance like this would often come to
    you, you muff?

MNESILOCHUS: No, you're wrong.

CHRYSALUS: Nay, you were wrong; you didn't dip in deep enough.

MNESILOCHUS: You'd accuse me far more strongly, if you knew the
    whole affair.

CHRYSALUS: Oh, I'm ruined! By your words you fill me with fore-
    boding care.

MNESILOCHUS: I'm undone!

CHRYSALUS: How so?

MNESILOCHUS: Because I've given my father every cent.

CHRYSALUS: Given it?

MNESILOCHUS: Yes.

CHRYSALUS: What, all?

MNESILOCHUS: Yes, every penny!

CHRYSALUS: Oh, my heart is rent!
What on earth possessed you, man, to do a deed so vil-
    lainous?

MNESILOCHUS: I suspected him and Bacchis on a false charge, Chrysalus,
That they'd laid a plot against me; so, enraged, I gave the gold
To my father.

CHRYSALUS: When you gave it to him, what's the tale you told?

MNESILOCHUS: Oh, I said I'd got the money straight from Archidemides.

CHRYSALUS: If you said so, sorest torments on poor Chrysalus must seize!
When the old man sees me, he will have me bound and flogged straightway.

MNESILOCHUS: I've prevailed upon father—

CHRYSALUS: What, to do just what I say?

MNESILOCHUS: No, to let you off entirely, and his anger to dismiss!
With much trouble I succeeded. Now, you must look after this—

CHRYSALUS: What?

MNESILOCHUS: To find some other way of catching the old gentleman.
Set your wits to work, contrive, concoct, fix up some knowing plan.
Skilfully deceive the old man's skill, and carry off the gold.

CHRYSALUS: Oh, it hardly can be done.

MNESILOCHUS: Yes, easily, if you are bold.

CHRYSALUS: Easily, the deuce! When he's just caught me lying plump and flat.
If I told him I was lying, he'd not dare to credit that.

MNESILOCHUS: Oh, you should have heard him telling me about you!
It was fun!

CHRYSALUS: What did he say?

MNESILOCHUS: That if you told him that the sun there was the sun,
He'd believe it was the moon, and that the day was really night.

CHRYSALUS: He shan't talk like that for nothing; oh, I'll pay him out all right!

PISTOCLERUS: What are we to do?

CHRYSALUS: Oh, nothing; go on loving as you do.
 Tell me how much gold you're wanting; I'll engage to
  give it you.
 As my name is Chrysalus, I'll prove a golden butterfly!
 Come, Mnesilochus, inform me what you want, and
  don't be shy.

MNESILOCHUS: Well, the captain wants two hundred Philips for my
 Bacchis there.

CHRYSALUS: You shall have it!

MNESILOCHUS: And there'll be some more expenses—

CHRYSALUS: Steady, sir!
 One thing at a time! When this is finished, then I'll
  tackle that.
 For two hundred Philips first I'll aim at our old pluto-
  crat.
 If my shot should bring his tower and his outworks
  toppling down,
 I shall straight march through the breach upon his old
  time-honoured town;
 If I take it, you shall carry gold to your girls by baskets
  full,
 As I hope.

PISTOCLERUS: Our hopes are with you, Chrysalus most bountiful!

CHRYSALUS: Pistoclerus, go to Bacchis' house and quickly bring me
 here—

PISTOCLERUS: What?

CHRYSALUS: A pen, some wax, and tablets, and some tape.

PISTOCLERUS: Oh, never fear!
  (PISTOCLERUS *goes into the house of* BACCHIS.)

MNESILOCHUS: What are you going to do?

CHRYSALUS: Just tell me; is your luncheon all prepared?
 There'll be two of you, I reckon, and your sweetheart
  makes the third.

MNESILOCHUS: As you say.

CHRYSALUS: Has Pistoclerus got a sweetheart?

MNESILOCHUS: Never fear!
    He loves one and I the other of two sisters who live here.

CHRYSALUS: What is that you're telling me?

MNESILOCHUS: Our number.

CHRYSALUS: Where's your luncheon set?

MNESILOCHUS: Why do you ask?

CHRYSALUS: Because it's information I desire to get.
    You don't know what I'm intending and am going tc
    begin.

MNESILOCHUS: Take my hand and come up with me to the door.
    (*He takes* CHRYSALUS *to the door of* BACCHIS' *house*)
                                        Now then, look in!

CHRYSALUS: Bravo, that's a splendid place, the very one I would
    desire.
    (*Re-enter* PISTOCLERUS *with the writing materials.*)

PISTOCLERUS: Give a decent fellow orders, and you'll get what you
    require.

CHRYSALUS: What have you got?

PISTOCLERUS: Why, everything that you just asked me to obtain.

CHRYSALUS (*to* MNESILOCHUS): Now, then, quickly take the pen and
    tablets in your hand.

MNESILOCHUS: What then?

CHRYSALUS: Write down there what I shall tell you; you
    must write it, understand?
    So that, when your father reads it, he may recognise the
    hand.
    Write!

MNESILOCHUS: Write what?

CHRYSALUS: Oh, say you hope he's well, just in your usual way.

PISTOCLERUS: Rather write you hope he's dead and buried, if the
    truth you'd say!

CHRYSALUS (*to* PISTOCLERUS): Don't confuse him!

MNESILOCHUS: There, that's written!

CHRYSALUS: Come, then, let's hear what it is.

MNESILOCHUS (*reading*): "I, Mnesilochus, send greetings to my father."

CHRYSALUS: Now add this:—
          "Father, Chrysalus is plying me with taunts and gibes
              untold,
          All because I wouldn't cheat you, but restored you all
              the gold."

PISTOCLERUS: Give him time to write it!

CHRYSALUS: Why, a lover's hand should not be slow!

PISTOCLERUS: Oh, it's not so quick at writing as at spending cash, you
          know.

MNESILOCHUS: Get along; that's written.

CHRYSALUS: "Father, keep an eye upon that man;
          He is laying plots to get the money from you, if he can;
          And he swears and vows he'll get it."—Please take care
              to write it plain.

MNESILOCHUS: Go ahead!

CHRYSALUS: "And then he says he'll give the gold to me again
          To be spent on girls and banquets and on going all the
              pace!
          Mind, dear father, have a care, or he will cheat you to
              your face."

MNESILOCHUS: What's the next?

CHRYSALUS: Oh, write away!

MNESILOCHUS: Well, tell me what I have to write.

CHRYSALUS: "But, dear father, keep the promise that you made me
              in your sight.
          Pray, don't flog him; only bind him and detain him safe
              at home."
          Where's the wax and tape? Just tie and seal the letter.
          Make haste! Come!

MNESILOCHUS: Oh, but tell us why you want a letter written in this way,
          Telling him to bind you fast, and not believe a word you
              say.

CHRYSALUS: It's my whim! So will you kindly look to yourself, and
    don't mind me!
    I've contracted for this job, and at my peril it shall be.

MNESILOCHUS: Right you are!

CHRYSALUS: Give me the tablets.

MNESILOCHUS: Take them!

CHRYSALUS: Now, attention, please.
    You, Mnesilochus, you, Pistoclerus, go, and at your ease
    Sit down and enjoy your banquet, with your sweethearts
    at your side,
    And then drink at the same table where the banquet is
    supplied.

PISTOCLERUS: Is that all?

CHRYSALUS: No, one thing further; when you've once sat
    down, d'you see,
    Don't rise up again from table, till you get the sign
    from me.

PISTOCLERUS: Noble general!

CHRYSALUS: Get along! you should have had two drinks by now.

MNESILOCHUS: Let's be off!

CHRYSALUS: You do your duty. I'll do mine, I dare avow!
  (PISTOCLERUS *and* MNESILOCHUS *go into the house of* BACCHIS.)

Act Four.   Scene V

CHRYSALUS (*to himself*): Ah, it's a mad design I have in hand,
    And like enough it will be overthrown.
    Well, now I want the old man in a fury,
    For it won't suit this trick of mine at all,
    If he's not out of temper when he sees me.
    Oh, if I live today I'll cheat him finely!
    I'll do him browner than a roasted pea.
    I'll walk to the door, and then when he comes out,
    At once I'll place the tablets in his hand.

Act Four.   Scene VI

(*Enter* NICOBULUS *from his house.*)

NICOBULUS (*to himself*): It fills me with vexation when I think
                      How Chrysalus has dodged me all this day.

CHRYSALUS (*aside*): That's right! The old man's angry. Now's my time
                  To go and meet him.

NICOBULUS (*aside*):   Who's that talking there?
                  (*Aloud*) It's Chrysalus, I think.

CHRYSALUS (*aside*):   Now I'll approach him.

NICOBULUS: All hail, good slave! How goes it? Is it time
                  For me to sail for Ephesus and bring
                  My money home again from Theotimus?
                  You're silent? Oh, by all the gods I swear
                  That, if I didn't love my son so well,
                  And wish to grant him all that he desires,
                  I'd have you flayed with rods and put in irons,
                  And sent to spend your life in grinding corn.
                  Mnesilochus has told me all your crimes.

CHRYSALUS: He's charged me, has he! Very fine indeed!
                  Yes, I'm a villain, curséd and abhorred!
                  Well, just take care! That's all I have to say.

NICOBULUS: What, do you threaten me, you scoundrel, you!

CHRYSALUS: You'll find out what he is, before so long.
                  He ordered me to bring these tablets to you,
                  And prayed that you would do what he has written.

NICOBULUS: Give them to me.

CHRYSALUS: Observe the seal!

NICOBULUS: I do.
                  But where's my son?

CHRYSALUS: Oh, I don't know; my duty
                  Is to know nothing, and remember nothing,
                  I know I'm a slave; but what I know, I know not.
                      (NICOBULUS *reads the letter*)
                  (*Aside*) Ah, now, my thrush is getting near the trap,
                  He'll soon be hanging in the noose I've set!

NICOBULUS: Just wait a minute. I'll be back directly.
(NICOBULUS *goes into his house.*)

CHRYSALUS (*to himself*): Hark, how he tries to cheat poor simple me!
I don't know what he's gone for! Not at all!
He's gone to fetch the slaves to bind me fast.
Yon portly galleon's getting finely tossed!
Meanwhile, my little skiff speeds bravely on.
But hush; I hear the door's about to open.

Act Four.   Scene VII

(*Enter* NICOBULUS *with* ARTAMO *and the other slaves.*)

NICOBULUS: Now seize him, Artamo, and bind his hands!

CHRYSALUS: What have I done?

NICOBULUS: Strike him if he but mutters!
(*To* CHRYSALUS) What does this letter say?

CHRYSALUS: How should I know?
I brought it sealed to you, as I received it.

NICOBULUS: So you're the man who with your vile abuse
Annoyed my son for bringing back my gold?
It's you that said you'd get it back again
By trickery!

CHRYSALUS: Did I say so?

NICOBULUS: Yes, you did.

CHRYSALUS: What man is he who says so?

NICOBULUS: Oh, be quiet!
No man says so; this letter proves you guilty,
Which you have brought; yes, bids me bind you.

CHRYSALUS: Ha,
Your son has made me a Bellerophon;
I've brought the letter that condemns me. Right!

NICOBULUS: Besides you've been persuading my weak son
To live a life of riot, you venomous wretch!

CHRYSALUS: Poor fool, you little know you're being sold!
You're on the block, the crier calls your name.

NICOBULUS: Tell me who's selling me?

CHRYSALUS: Whom the gods love
Dies young, whilst yet he's strength and sight and sense.
If any god loved him, (*pointing to* NICOBULUS) ten years
     ago,
Nay, rather, twenty years since, he'd have died.
Too long he walks a burden to the earth;
A senseless, tasteless, worthless, stinking toad-stool!

NICOBULUS: You dare call me a burden to the earth!
Go take him in, and bind him to a pillar.
No, you shall never steal the gold away!

CHRYSALUS: And yet you'll give it me!

NICOBULUS: I give it you!

CHRYSALUS: Yes, and beseech me, too, to kindly take it;
When you find out the danger and the peril
Which threatens him who now accuses me,
Then you'll give liberty to Chrysalus,
But he won't take it.

NICOBULUS: Tell me, prince of rascals,
What danger threatens my Mnesilochus?

CHRYSALUS: Follow me here; I'll show you.

NICOBULUS: But how far?

CHRYSALUS: Only three steps.

NICOBULUS: Ten, if you like.
(CHRYSALUS *leads the way to the door of* BACCHIS' *house.*)

CHRYSALUS: Now then,
Artamo, push this door a little open;
Gently, don't let it creak.—There, that'll do.—
Come here, sir, now! Do you behold this banquet?

NICOBULUS: Bacchis and Pistoclerus I can see.

CHRYSALUS: But who's on t'other side?

NICOBULUS: Oh, you have killed me!

CHRYSALUS: Do you know the man?

NICOBULUS: I do!

CHRYSALUS: But tell me, pray,
             Isn't the girl a beauty?

NICOBULUS: Oh, no doubt!

CHRYSALUS: Surely you don't suspect her?

NICOBULUS: Yes, I do.

CHRYSALUS: You're wrong then.

NICOBULUS: Well, who is she?

CHRYSALUS: Oh, find out!
             For I won't tell you any more about it.

Act Four.   Scene VIII

(*Enter* CLEOMACHUS, *not seeing the others.*)

CLEOMACHUS (*to himself*): And so Mnesilochus, Nicobulus' son,
             Would keep my girl by force. What does he mean?

NICOBULUS: Who's this?

CHRYSALUS (*aside*): In good time has my captain come.

CLEOMACHUS (*to himself*): He thinks I am a woman, not a soldier,
             And can't defend myself and what is mine.
             Mars and Bellona never trust me more,
             If I don't take his life, if once I meet him,
             And disinherit him of vital breath.

NICOBULUS: He threatens my son! Who is he, Chrysalus?

CHRYSALUS: The husband of the girl he's feasting with.

NICOBULUS: Her husband?

CHRYSALUS: Yes, her husband.

NICOBULUS: Is she married?

CHRYSALUS: You'll know ere very long!

NICOBULUS: Oh, I'm undone!

CHRYSALUS: Now then! Is Chrysalus so great a villain?
Yes, listen to your son, and bind me fast!
I told you you'd find out his character.

NICOBULUS: What shall I do?

CHRYSALUS: Tell them to let me go;
For if you don't he'll surely murder him.

CLEOMACHUS (*to himself*): There's nothing I would rather do today,
Than catch him with the girl and kill them both.

CHRYSALUS: D'you hear him speak? Why don't you let me go?

NICOBULUS: Here, loose him! Oh, I'm dead, I'm mad with fear!

CLEOMACHUS (*to himself*): Yes, that bold girl, so lavish of her smiles,
Shall never make a laughingstock of me.

CHRYSALUS: You might be able for a trifling sum
To buy him off.

NICOBULUS: Oh, do it, at any price!
If only he won't kill and murder him.

CLEOMACHUS (*to himself*): Unless I get two hundred Philips down,
I'll drain to the dregs the blood of both of them.

CHRYSALUS: Ah, you can buy him off for that!

NICOBULUS: Do so,
At any cost you like.

CHRYSALUS: I'll go and do it.
(*Crossing to* CLEOMACHUS)
What are you bawling at?

CLEOMACHUS: Where is your master?

CHRYSALUS: Nowhere! I cannot tell. But are you willing,
Upon the promise of two hundred Philips,
To stop your shouting and your quarrelling?

CLEOMACHUS: There's nothing I'd like better, I assure you.

CHRYSALUS: And will you let me curse and blackguard you?

CLEOMACHUS: At your discretion!

NICOBULUS (*aside*):   How the rogue's wheedling him!

CHRYSALUS: Yonder's the father of Mnesilochus.
So come with me and he will give his bond.

You ask for gold; that's all that need be said.
        (*They rejoin* NICOBULUS.)

NICOBULUS: How goes it?

CHRYSALUS: Well, sir, for two hundred Philips
        I've settled it!

NICOBULUS: My saviour, you've preserved me!
        I'm all impatience till I've said, "I'll pay!"

CHRYSALUS (*to* CLEOMACHUS): You ask! (*To* NICOBULUS) You promise!

NICOBULUS: I'll promise; ask away.

CLEOMACHUS: Will you give me two hundred sterling Philips?

CHRYSALUS: "They shall be given," say! Answer him!

NICOBULUS: I'll give them.

CHRYSALUS (*to* CLEOMACHUS): How now, you filthy wretch! Do we owe
            you aught?
        How dare you be a nuisance to my master,
        And threaten him with death? We'll make you suffer!
        If you've a sword, we have a spit at home,
        With which, if you provoke me any more,
        I'll prod you into mouse holes for your pains.
        I long ago have seen the foul suspicion
        That tortures you. You think he's with the girl.

CLEOMACHUS: Nay, but he is.

CHRYSALUS: By Jupiter, Juno, Ceres,
        Minerva, Latona, Spes, Ops, Virtus, Venus,
        Castor and Pollux, Mars and Hercules,
        Mercurius, Summanus, Sol, Saturnus,
        And all the other gods, I vow and swear,
        He's neither sitting with her, no, nor walking,
        Nor kissing her, nor any other thing.

NICOBULUS (*aside*): Hark how he swears! His perjury has saved me!

CLEOMACHUS: Then where's Mnesilochus?

CHRYSALUS: He's in the country;
        His father sent him there. The girl is gone
        To the Acropolis, to see the temple
        Of great Minerva. Go and see yourself
        If she's not there; the doors are open now.

CLEOMACHUS: I'll to the market-place.

CHRYSALUS: Nay, to the gallows!

CLEOMACHUS: I shall demand the money, though, today.

CHRYSALUS: Demand it and be hanged! And don't suppose
We would come begging to a wretch like you.
                    (CLEOMACHUS *departs*)
He's gone! Now, master, by the immortal gods,
I beg you, let me go in to your son.

NICOBULUS: Why go in there?

CHRYSALUS: To castigate him soundly,
For doing such things as this in such a way.

NICOBULUS: Nay, do so, Chrysalus, and, I beseech you,
Don't fail to let him have it.

CHRYSALUS: Don't tell me!
I shall reproach him far more bitterly
Than e'er Demetrius did Clinia.⁷
          (CHRYSALUS *goes into the house of* BACCHIS.)

NICOBULUS (*to himself*): This slave's exactly like a blood-shot eye;
If you've not got one, you're not anxious for it;
But if you have, you can't help rubbing it.
For if he hadn't happened to be here,
The captain would have caught Mnesilochus,
And killed him on the spot, without a doubt.
Now I've redeemed him for two hundred Philips,
Which I have promised I will give the captain.
But I won't pay them till I've seen my son;
I'll never lightly trust that Chrysalus.
But let me read this letter once again;
One ought to trust a letter signed and sealed.
          (NICOBULUS *goes into his house*.)

Act Four.   Scene IX

(*Enter* CHRYSALUS *from the house of* BACCHIS, *with a letter in his hand*.)

CHRYSALUS (*to himself*): The sons of Atreus gained great fame,
When Priam's town they overcame,
And levelled the proud walls of Troy,

Whose building was the god's employ;
With foot and horse, an army stout,
And warriors famed the world about,
And a good thousand ships to boot,
It took them ten full years to do't.
But Priam knew no such disaster
As I've inflicted on my master.
Without a fleet, without an army,
Or host of soldiers to alarm ye,
His father's gold I've stormed and won
To give it to his love-sick son.
Before he comes, my feelings urge
That I should sing the old man's dirge:—

> O Troy, my home! O Pergamum!
> O Priam old! Alack the day!
> Thou hast a fearful fine to pay!
> Four hundred Philips is the sum.

> This letter, which I here present,
> All signed and sealed in proper course,
> Is not a letter, but a horse,
> The horse of wood the Grecians sent.

> Our Epius is Pistoclerus;
> I've left Mnesilochus, our Sinon,
> No hero's barrow to recline on.
> But in the house of Bacchis near us.

> Bacchis, who's with him, is the fire
> For flashing signals; but her kisses
> Burn him instead! I am Ulysses,
> Who formed the plan at their desire.

> The letters written hereupon
> Are soldiers hidden in the horse,
> All clad in arms and full of force;
> So far the thing goes bravely on.

> Not his stronghold but his strong-box
> Shall feel my horse's bold attack;
> Destruction, death, damnation black,
> Shall seize his gold in spite of locks.

The old man's watchfulness remiss is;
I'll call him Ilium suitably;
The captain's Menelaus; I
Am Agamemnon and Ulysses.

Mnesilochus is Alexander,[8]
Who made his ruined country quake;
He ravished Helen, for whose sake
Poor Ilium's wealth I soon shall squander.

Now, as I've heard, Ulysses cherished
A spirit, bold and bad, like mine.
As I was caught in bold design,
So he, caught begging, nearly perished,

Seeking the state of Troy to learn.
My hap was just like his today;
Being bound, by craft I got away;
So he used craft to serve his turn.

At Troy three fatal signs were reckoned
To indicate her coming doom;
The loss of the Palladium;[9]
The death of Troilus, the second.

The third, when at the Scaean gate,
The upper lintel should be riven;
So three like signs to us were given
To show our Ilium's coming fate.

The first one was the monstrous hum,
Which to the poor old man I told,
About the pirates and the gold;
Then stole I the Palladium.

Two signs of fate did still remain;
The city wasn't taken yet.
But when I got that letter writ,
And given him, Troilus was slain.

Then, when he thought Mnesilochus
Was sitting with the captain's wife,
I had a job to save my life;
And with Ulysses it was thus.

For Helen recognised his face,
And told Queen Hecuba his name;
But by the same old wily game
He wrought on her to grant him grace.

So I escaped the pressing throng
Of perils and deceived my lord.
Then with that braggart man o' the sword,
Who captures cities with his tongue,

I next engaged, and won the day;
Then met the old man merrily,
And conquered him with one big lie;
At one blow bore the spoils away.

Two hundred Philips 'twill employ
To satisfy the captain's greed;
Two hundred more we then shall need
To spend when we have taken Troy.

Our soldiers all are thirsty ones,
And wine should always follow war;
Our Priam beats the old one far—
He doesn't stop at fifty sons.

He's got four hundred, all in rows,
Without a flaw, of sterling worth;
But spite of their illustrious birth
I'll kill them all with two strong blows.[10]

If anybody wants our Priam,
I'm quite prepared to knock him down,
As soon as I have stormed the town,
In a job lot, if you will buy him!
(*Enter* NICOBULUS *from his house.*)
But there stands Priam at our door;
I'll go and talk to him some more.

NICOBULUS: Who's that I hear talking near me? Ah! What news
              have you to tell?
              Have you done the work I bade you?

CHRYSALUS: Yes; come nearer.

NICOBULUS: Very well.

CHRYSALUS: I'm a noble orator; my speech begat in him such loathing
Of his crimes, he fairly wept.

NICOBULUS: What did he say?

CHRYSALUS: Oh, he said nothing.
Silently in tears he listened, while I tried to make him better;
Then in silence wrote and sealed, and put into my hands this letter,
Bade me give it to you. But I'm afraid it sings the same old song.
Look at the seal. Is it his?

NICOBULUS: I know it. Let me read it.

CHRYSALUS: Read along.
(*Aside*) Ah, now the upper lintel's riven; and Troy's destruction is at hand.
My wooden horse will make a stir!

NICOBULUS: Stay, till this letter I have scanned.

CHRYSALUS: Why should I stay?

NICOBULUS: I want you to know
What's written here before you go.

CHRYSALUS: I have no wish to hear it, though!

NICOBULUS: Yet stay!

CHRYSALUS: Why should I stay at hand?

NICOBULUS: Be still and do what I command.

CHRYSALUS: Right, I'll stay.

NICOBULUS: The writing's small.

CHRYSALUS: Oh, that's because you cannot see;
If your sight were good, it's big enough.

NICOBULUS: Look here, attend to me.

CHRYSALUS: No, I won't!

NICOBULUS: You shall, I say.

CHRYSALUS: What for?

NICOBULUS: Just do as you are told.

CHRYSALUS: Well, that's fair; for by his master every slave should
             be controlled.

NICOBULUS: Come here, now.

CHRYSALUS: Well, read away, sir; and my ears
             shall wait on you.

NICOBULUS: He didn't spare the wax or pen; but anyhow I'll read
             it through—
             (*Reads*) "Dear father, pray you give two hundred
             Philips
             To Chrysalus, if you would save my life."

CHRYSALUS: Oh, that's a serious loss!—Look here!

NICOBULUS: What is it?

CHRYSALUS: Doesn't he greet you first?

NICOBULUS: No, I don't see it.

CHRYSALUS: Why then, the letter starts with impudence.
             Don't give it, if you're wise; but if you do,
             You'd better get another porter for it;
             For I won't take it, order as you will;
             My innocence has borne enough suspicion.

NICOBULUS: But listen while I read what's written next—
             (*Reads*) "Father, I blush to come into your sight.
             I've heard you know about my monstrous crime,
             How I've been dining with the captain's wife."
             Ah! That's no joke! It cost two hundred Philips
             To save your life, sir, after what you'd done!

CHRYSALUS: Yes; all those points I duly placed before him.

NICOBULUS (*reads*): "I own I've been a fool; but, father dear,
             Do not desert me though I've stooped to folly.
             'Twas my hot passion, my unchastened eyes,
             Persuaded me to what I now regret."
             Better be prudent first than sorry after!

CHRYSALUS: Those are the very words I used myself.

NICOBULUS (*reads*): "Pray you, be satisfied that Chrysalus
             Has plied me with a thousand keen reproaches,

And by his warnings led me to repentance.
It's only right that you should thank him for it."

CHRYSALUS: Does he write that?

NICOBULUS: There, look, see for yourself.

CHRYSALUS: Ah! How a guilty conscience humbles him!

NICOBULUS (*reads*): "Now, if I have a right to ask you, father,
Give me two hundred Philips, I entreat!"

CHRYSALUS: No, not a penny, if you're wise!

NICOBULUS: Be quiet!
(*Reads*) "I've sworn an oath in set and formal terms
To pay it to the woman, ere night falls,
Before she leaves me. Father, save your son
From being forsworn! Oh, rescue me from her,
Through whom I've suffered so much loss and shame.
You needn't let the money worry you.
I promise to pay back six hundred Philips,
Upon my life. Farewell, and help me, father."
Well, Chrysalus, and what is your opinion?

CHRYSALUS: Oh, I'm not going to give you any counsels;
I won't commit myself. If aught goes wrong,
I'll take care you shan't say that I advised it.
But, as I think, if I were in your place,
I'd rather pay the gold than see him ruined.
One of two things must be; so take your choice;
To lose the gold, or let him be forsworn.
But I say nothing, neither yea, nor nay.

NICOBULUS: I pity him.

CHRYSALUS: No wonder! He's your own!
And if you must lose more, that's pleasanter
Than that his shame should be the common talk.

NICOBULUS: I wish the lad had stayed at Ephesus
Where he was safe, and not come home at all.
Well, as it's lost, let's get it quickly over.
I'll go and fetch out twice two hundred Philips;
Two that, alas! I promised to the captain,
And two beside. Stay here: I'll soon be back.
(NICOBULUS *goes into his house.*)

CHRYSALUS (*to himself*): Troy is destroyed, the chiefs are sacking her;
　　　　　　I knew that I should ruin Pergamum.
　　　　　　By Jove! If anybody says that I
　　　　　　Deserve the gallows, I won't contradict him.
　　　　　　I'm making such confusion! Hark! The door!
　　　　　　The spoil's being brought from Troy. I'll hold my peace.
　　　　　　(*Re-enter* NICOBULUS *with the money*.)

NICOBULUS: Here, take the money; bear it to my son.
　　　　　　I'll to the market-place, and pay the captain.

CHRYSALUS: I won't receive it; go find someone else
　　　　　　To take it; I would rather not be trusted.

NICOBULUS: Here, take it; or you'll vex me.

CHRYSALUS: 　　　　　　　　　　　No, not I.

NICOBULUS: But I beseech.

CHRYSALUS: 　　　　　　　I mean just what I say.

NICOBULUS: You're keeping me.

CHRYSALUS: 　　　　　　I will not have that gold
　　　　　　Entrusted to me; or find someone else
　　　　　　To watch me well.

NICOBULUS: 　　　　　　Oh, dear, you are a nuisance!

CHRYSALUS: Well, give it me, if you must.

NICOBULUS: 　　　　　　　　Take care of it!
　　　　　　I'll not be long before I'm back again.
　　　　　　(NICOBULUS *departs to the forum*.)

CHRYSALUS: I've taken care to make you miserable!
　　　　　　This is the way to carry out your plans!
　　　　　　O happy fate! In triumph I retire,
　　　　　　Loaded with spoil. The victory is ours;
　　　　　　The city's taken by my stratagems,
　　　　　　And I lead home my army all complete.
　　　　　　But, gentle hearers, don't you be surprised
　　　　　　That I don't have a triumph; I don't care to;
　　　　　　The thing has grown too common. Nevertheless,
　　　　　　My soldiers shall not go without their wine.
　　　　　　Well, now I'll take our paymaster the spoil.
　　　　　　(CHRYSALUS *goes into the house of* BACCHIS.)

Act Four. Scene X

(*Enter* PHILOXENUS *from the forum.*)

PHILOXENUS (*to himself*): The more I consider the racket and row
 My poor silly son has been making,
The sort of amusement he goes in for now,
 And the rash headlong course he is taking,
The greater my care and anxiety grows
 Lest he should be wrecked by his passion.
I once was his age and did just what he does,
 But in a much modester fashion.
I loved and I courted, I feasted and drank,
 Gave presents, though that was but rarely.
To be overstrict is the mark of a crank;
 Modern fathers don't treat their sons fairly.
So I have determined to give my son rope,
 And permit him to follow his sparking;
I think I've done right; at the same time I hope
 He won't go too far with his larking.
So now I am off to Mnesilochus' house
 To see if he's done my commission.
I hope that his words have been able to rouse
 My son to a lively contrition.
I know he'll do all that occasion allows,
 For that is the lad's disposition.

Act Five. Scene I

(*Enter* NICOBULUS *from the forum.*)

NICOBULUS (*to himself*): Of all the men who ever were, or e'er shall be
  hereafter,
Muddling mules, fat-headed fools, soft, silly subjects for
  laughter,
I freely confess I'm ahead of them all
 In folly and downright stupidity;
A man of my years, too! I blush at my fall!
 Twice choused in my utter stolidity!
The longer I think of the deeds of my son,

The hotter's my just indignation;
I'm ruined, destroyed, and completely undone;
I cannot express my vexation.
   All woes are hastening on my track,
   All misery's piled upon my back.
   Chrysalus stabbed me to death today;
   Chrysalus plundered me as I lay;
   Chrysalus fleeced me of my gold,
   Fool that I was, by his tricks so bold!
Just think! The captain informs me that she
They said was his wife, is his slave; and that he
Had simply engaged her to serve him a year;
In fact, he has made the thing perfectly clear;
The money I promised to pay for my son
Was to compensate him for the months yet to run.
This is the trouble that pierces my heart,
This is the cause of my bitterest smart;
That I at my age should be made a fool,
And sent, by Pollux! again to school;
When my head is white and my beard is grey
Should see my money filched away!
Oh, to think that that worthless slave
Should dare to do it! 'Zounds, I could rave!
I wouldn't have minded losing much more;
It's the way he did it that makes me sore.

PHILOXENUS (*aside*): I certainly thought that I heard someone speak.
   Bless me! It's Mnesilochus' father!

NICOBULUS: A companion in trouble I'll not have to seek;
   Here's someone to share with me, rather!
   Philoxenus, hail!

PHILOXENUS: Same to you! Where've you been?

NICOBULUS: With a wretched, unfortunate fellow!

PHILOXENUS: I'm the wretched, unfortunate fellow you mean!
   For I have been there, I can tell you.

NICOBULUS: It seems we're alike both in fortune and age.

PHILOXENUS: Indeed, that's a fact. But the cause of your rage,
   Tell it me.

NICOBULUS: Certainly; just what makes you so mad!

PHILOXENUS: What! You don't say it's your son that makes you so sad?

NICOBULUS: Yes, it is.

PHILOXENUS: That's the disease that's tormenting me.

NICOBULUS: Chrysalus, sharper, has been circumventing me,
Ruining my son, and myself, and my property.

PHILOXENUS: What's wrong with your son?

NICOBULUS: The truth I'll tell.
He's fallen in love, and your son as well.

PHILOXENUS: Your proof?

NICOBULUS: I saw them.

PHILOXENUS: That ends doubt.

NICOBULUS: Come, then, hesitate no longer, let us knock and bring them out.

PHILOXENUS: Oh, I'm ready.

NICOBULUS (*knocking at the door*): Hallo, Bacchis, bid this door be opened straight!
If you don't, I'll get an axe and smash it open; I won't wait!

Act Five.   Scene II

(*Enter* BACCHIS *and her* SISTER *from the house.*)

BACCHIS: Who's this that is shouting and bawling like thunder,
Stirring up such a dither?

NICOBULUS: It's I and my friend.

BACCHIS: What's their business, I wonder?
Who drove these sheep hither?

NICOBULUS (*to* PHILOXENUS): They're calling us sheep!

SISTER: Sure their shepherd is sleeping,
To let them go wandering away from his keeping.

BACCHIS: But are they not fat and in splendid condition?

SISTER: They both have been close shorn!

PHILOXENUS (*to* NICOBULUS):   I have a suspicion
                 They're mocking us.

NICOBULUS: Let's take no notice, but scorn them.

BACCHIS: I wonder if three times a year they have shorn them.

SISTER: There's one has been twice shorn today, dear, I fancy.

BACCHIS: They're old.

SISTER: But they once have been frisky I can see!

BACCHIS: But look, sister dear, how they're leering and winking!

SISTER: They're meaning no harm by it, sister, I'm thinking.

PHILOXENUS (*to* NICOBULUS): It serves us just right, we were asses to
                 venture.

BACCHIS: Let's drive them indoors.

SISTER: What's the use, if they enter?
                 They've got neither milk nor yet wool. Let them stay
                     there!
                 They've lost all they had; and no fruit can we gather
                 From them. Don't you see how they're aimlessly stray-
                     ing?
                 They're dumb with old age. What's the use of our stay-
                     ing?
                 They don't even bleat for the flock they have left; they
                     seem to be utterly silly.

BACCHIS: Come, let's go in, sister.

NICOBULUS: These sheep are desiring your
                 company; stay with us, will ye?

SISTER: Hark, the sheep like men are talking; miracles will never
                     cease!

PHILOXENUS: Yes, these sheep will pay you back the ill they owe you,
                     if you please.

BACCHIS: I forgive you all you owe us; keep it, I don't want it
                     back.
                 But I'd like to know the reason of your menacing attack.

PHILOXENUS: Why, because two lambs of ours are shut in here; we
know your larks!

NICOBULUS: And beside the lambs, a dog of mine that bites before
he barks.
Now, if you don't bring them forth and send them out
of doors with speed,
We shall turn to savage rams and butt you; so you'd
best take heed.

BACCHIS: Sister dear, just a word with you.

SISTER: Sister, say on.

(They retire.)

NICOBULUS: I'd like to know what they are after.

BACCHIS (*to* SISTER): The further old man I put into your hands
To move him to sweetness and laughter.
This angry old fellow I'll tackle myself.
I think we can get the old boys in.

SISTER: Oh, I'll cheerfully manage the task you have set,
Though I hate the old rascal like poison.

BACCHIS: Take care that you do.

SISTER: You take care of yourself!
As I promised the thing, I shall do it.

NICOBULUS: Those two are concocting some villainy now;
What is it? I wish that I knew it.

PHILOXENUS: Old fellow, I say!

NICOBULUS: Well, what do you want?

PHILOXENUS: I'm afraid what I say will disgust you.

NICOBULUS: Come, why are you blushing?

PHILOXENUS: I know you're my friend,
And so I'm determined to trust you.
I'm an ass!

NICOBULUS: Oh, I knew that a long time ago!
But speak, let me hear your confession.

PHILOXENUS: The bird-lime has got on my feathers, I fear!
I'm pricked to the heart!

NICOBULUS: Oh, a prick in the rear
                    Would better assist your progression!
                    But what are you wanting to tell me? Although
                    I think I can guess pretty fairly.
                    Still, I'd like you to tell me.

PHILOXENUS: You see her? (*Pointing to the* SISTER.)

NICOBULUS: I do.

PHILOXENUS: Well, she's not such a bad sort of girl, eh?

NICOBULUS: She is, though, and you are an ass.

PHILOXENUS: Never mind!
                    I like her.

NICOBULUS: You like—?

PHILOXENUS: *Evidemment!*

NICOBULUS: What! Changing your mind for a girl's pretty face!
                    And at your time of life, too!

PHILOXENUS: Oh, gammon!

NICOBULUS: It's scandalous.

PHILOXENUS: There! There's no need to say more.
                    My wrath with my son is all over—
                    And don't you be angry with yours any more,
                    For no one's so wise as a lover.

BACCHIS: Well, what are we waiting for? Sister, come on!
                    (*They return to the old men.*)

NICOBULUS: See there! They're returning to floor us,
                    Those pestilent girls who can wheedle so well!
                    Come now! Are you going to restore us
                    Our sons and my slave? If you don't, I must try
                    What force can effect.

PHILOXENUS (*to* NICOBULUS):   You be quiet!
                    You're no man, sir, I say, to address a sweet girl
                    So unsweetly; you'd better not try it.

BACCHIS: You darling old man! You're the best in the world!
                    Now surely you'll grant me this favour:—
                    Desist from your savage intemperate wrath
                    And pardon your son's bad behaviour.

NICOBULUS: Be off, or in spite of your sweet, pretty face,
I'll strike you directly.

BACCHIS: No matter!
I don't think you'd strike me so hard as to hurt.

NICOBULUS: Just hark how the lady can flatter!
Oh, dear, I'm afraid!

SISTER: My man's quieter, much!

BACCHIS: Come, lay aside all your suspicion,
And please to walk into the house; when you're there,
You can talk your son into contrition.

NICOBULUS: Go, leave me, you wretch!

BACCHIS: Nay, but, reverend sir,
Be persuaded!

NICOBULUS: Persuaded by you, miss?

SISTER: My man I'll persuade!

PHILOXENUS: Nay, indeed, I entreat
That you'll show me at once where your room is.

NICOBULUS: Well, I've often seen men that were weak, but I ne'er
Saw a weaker than you.

PHILOXENUS: I admit it.

BACCHIS: Oh, come in with me! There are ointments in there,
And in a banquet, and good wine to fit it.

NICOBULUS: Enough of your banquet! It's no little loss
With which you already afflict me;
Out of four hundred Philips, my treacherous son
And Chrysalus, villain, have tricked me.
But I wouldn't accept as much money again
To grant those two wretches remission.

BACCHIS: But, supposing a half of the money's restored,
Won't you come in upon that condition,
And try to persuade yourself, hard as it is,
To grant them forgiveness?

PHILOXENUS: He'll do it.

NICOBULUS: Not a bit of it! No! Not a moment I'll wait!
Let me be! Oh, I'll see that they rue it!

PHILOXENUS: Well, you are an ass, when the gods send you good,
    And you throw it away in your folly!
  She'll give you the half of your gold. Take it, man!
    And come in and let's drink and be jolly.

NICOBULUS: Shall I go in there, where my son has been gulled,
    And drink?

PHILOXENUS: You must drink, that is certain!

NICOBULUS: I'm rather ashamed of my weakness, I own;
    But still, after all, it won't hurt one!
  Oh, how my head itches! I cannot say no.

BACCHIS: And this is a thing should be thought on,
  That though, while you live, you indulge your desires,
    Your life after all is a short one.
  If you pass by the chance that is offered today,
    When you're dead, you will ne'er get another.

NICOBULUS: Oh, what shall I do?

PHILOXENUS: Why, there's no need to ask.

NICOBULUS: I'd like but I fear—

BACCHIS: What's your bother?

NICOBULUS: I can't help being vexed with my son and his slave.

BACCHIS: My honey, my dearest, forgive him!
  He's yours: do you think he would take anything
    Except what he's sure you would give him?
  Come, let me persuade you to pardon them both!

NICOBULUS: Confound her! She won't take an answer!
  What I have refused, she persuades me to do!
  Well, if I do wrong, it's entirely for you.

BACCHIS: Nay, I'd rather it was for your son, sir!
  But can I believe you will stand to your word?

NICOBULUS: When I've once said a thing, I will do it.

BACCHIS: The day is declining; come in now and dine,
  Your sons are expecting you over the wine.

NICOBULUS: Yes, expecting our deaths, if we knew it.

BACCHIS: The evening's at hand; come along.

PHILOXENUS: Lead the way,
        For we are your prisoners ever.

BACCHIS (*aside*): And thus the old men who laid snares for their sons
        Are captured themselves. Ain't I clever?
        (*All go into the house of* BACCHIS.)

                          EPILOGUE

  Had these old men not remembered certain follies of their youth,
  Their sons' escapades would not have gained a pardon here today,
  But the scene we've played before you is a common one, in sooth;
  Sons oft find their fathers kindly, even though their hairs are grey,
  Now farewell, good gentle hearers; lift your hands and clap away!

1. The Bacchic mysteries were introduced at Rome during the time of Plautus and became so infamous that they were declared illegal in 186 B.C.

2. The Poticii had charge of the worship of Hercules; in the time of Appius Claudius they handed over their duty to public slaves, and as a result the family shortly became extinct.

3. The altar of Apollo stood upon the stage.

4. Juno was not the sister of Venus.

5. Lindsay considers these verses a later addition.

6. These words are clearly spurious, as Pistoclerus does not enter at this point.

7. Apparently a reference to characters in some well-known play.

8. Another name for Paris, the son of Priam.

9. A statue of Pallas (Minerva), which was stolen from Troy by Ulysses and Diomedes.

10. The two letters.

V

THE CAPTIVES

Characters in the Play

ERGASILUS, *a parasite*
HEGIO, *an old gentleman of Aetolia*
SLAVE OVERSEER, *belonging to* HEGIO
PHILOCRATES, *a young Elean, now captive in Aetolia*
TYNDARUS, *slave of* PHILOCRATES, *captured with him*
ARISTOPHONTES, *a young Elean captive, friend of* PHILOCRATES
A SLAVE, *belonging to* HEGIO
PHILOPOLEMUS, *son of* HEGIO, *captive in Elis*
STALAGMUS, *slave of* HEGIO

Acrostic Argument

C aptured in fight was one of Hegio's sons,
A nother sold by a slave when four years old.
P risoners from Elis now the father buys,
T o give them in exchange for him who's ta'en;
E nrolled amongst them is the son he'd lost.
I n hope of freedom he's changed with his master
V estments and name; the old man is deceived.
E ager he brings the prisoner and the slave;
I n him the slave points out the long-lost son.

INTRODUCTION

The Captives, in its serious tone and elevated theme, stands alone among the plays of Plautus. The extent to which it differs from the usual Plautine comedy is stated clearly in the prologue:

> "It is not in the hackneyed style, like others.
> There are no filthy verses that one can't
> Repeat; no perjured pimp appears today,
> No infamous abandoned courtesan,
> No braggart soldier."

The epilogue likewise stresses the fact that the play contains nothing improper and indecent and that there are few such comedies written "to make the good still better." Many of the stock characters of Plautine comedy have disappeared; the tyrannical father is replaced by Hegio, an attractive man who wins our respect and sympathy; the wayward son becomes the generous Philocrates; and there is little likeness between the typically cunning slave and Tyndarus, the hero of the drama, who sacrifices himself for his master. As W. M. Lindsay states, "The moving passion of the play is not, as of other plays, the passion of love, generally . . . dishonourable love; it is the chivalrous devotion of a servant to his master, and it is this change of motive which transforms the whole tone of the drama."

Hegio has lost two sons, one long ago when only four years old, the other (Philopolemus) recently. To recover Philopolemus, who has been captured by the Eleans, Hegio buys Elean captives, among them Philocrates and his slave Tyndarus. Tyndarus and his master change roles so that, when the slave is sent to arrange the exchange of prisoners, it is really Philocrates who escapes. Another Elean captive (Aristophontes) convinces Hegio that he has been deceived, and Tyndarus is sent off to the quarry in chains. When Philocrates returns with Philopolemus, he brings along a runaway slave, formerly Hegio's, who reveals that Tyndarus is Hegio's long-lost son.

The play as a whole is serious comedy, not farce. There is excellent irony in the conversations of the pseudo-master and the pseudo-slave with Hegio, especially when Philocrates (as the slave) states that Tyndarus has done as much for him as a slave would have done, and swears that he will always be faithful to Philocrates. Another excellent scene is produced by the arrival of Aristophontes and by Tyndarus' vain attempt to convince Hegio that the newcomer is insane; this scene bears comparison with the famous mad scene in *The Twin Menaechmi*. The one stock character in the play is the parasite Ergasilus; he is not necessary to the plot, and it has been suggested that he was added to the play by Plautus. Whether this be true or not, Ergasilus provides considerable comic relief, but even here, as Lindsay states, "the parasite is toned down to a harmony with the rest of the picture."

This is the comedy which Lessing said was "the finest piece ever put on the stage." More modern scholars admire the play for its unusual features, but do not accord to it such high praise. The uselessness of the substitution of roles, the excessive credulity of Hegio, the failure of Aristophontes to realise the true situation, the unreasonably short absence of Philocrates, the sudden arrival of Stalagmus to make possible the discovery of Tyndarus' real identity—all these have been cited as weaknesses of the play. There is truth in some of these criticisms, e.g. Stalagmus' return is poorly motivated, but many of the points can hardly be termed serious. If Hegio's son could not be found and the proposed exchange of prisoners should prove impossible, the substitution would have achieved its purpose and Philocrates would have been free. Furthermore, Hegio's acceptance of the story of the captives seems justified in view of the cleverness with which they play their parts. *The Captives* may not have so great an appeal today as *The Pot of Gold, The Twin Menaechmi*, or *The Rope*, but it does not lack freshness and originality.

Ariosto's *I Suppositi*, a famous Italian comedy written about 1500, was based largely upon *The Captives*, although it also contained reminiscences from the *Amphitryon, The Twin Menaechmi*, and Terence's *The Eunuch*. Ariosto's play was used by later dramatists, e.g. Gascoigne in *Supposes* (1566) and Massinger in *A New Way to Pay Old Debts* (1625). Other plays based more directly on the Plautine comedy were Calderon's *El Príncipe Constante*, Rotrou's *Les Captifs* (1638), Lenz' lost play, *Die Algierer oder Seeräuber*, and Clerici's *I Prigionieri* (1881). Jonson's *The Case is Altered* (1597) combined the plots of Plautus' *The Captives* and *The Pot of Gold*.

THE CAPTIVES

(SCENE:—*A street in front of the house of* HEGIO, *in a city in Aetolia*.)

Prologue

(PHILOCRATES *and* TYNDARUS *are chained in front of the house of* HEGIO.)
This pair of captives you see standing here,
They do not sit, because they have to stand;
I think you all are witnesses of that.
Hegio, the old man dwelling in this house,
Is father of the one (*pointing to* TYNDARUS); but how
    it is
He is his slave, that's what I'll tell to you.
He had two sons; and one of them was stolen
By a slave, when four years old, who flying hence
Sold him, in Elis, to the father of
This man (*pointing to* PHILOCRATES) that you see
    here; I think you take me;
'Tis good! But there's a man in the back seats
Who says he does not; please, sir, come this way.
If there's no seat, you're free to walk about,
Since thus you force an actor to strain his voice
As if he were a beggar asking alms.
But I'll not break my voice to pleasure you.
To you who can afford to pay your rates
And taxes, and take seats, I'll pay my debts;
I hate to owe to any one at all.
This slave then, as you know already, fled
And sold the young boy he had stolen to
The father of this man (*indicating* PHILOCRATES); who
    when he'd bought him
Gave him to this his son, to be his playmate,
Because their ages were the same. He thus
Becomes the slave of his own father, though
He knows it not. For often thus the gods
Make shuttlecocks of men. And now you know
How he lost one of those his sons that were.

But later, when there was a war between
The Aetolians and the Eleans, as oft happens,
The other son was taken prisoner.
Menarchus, a physician, bought him there.
Then Hegio began to buy up captives,
To see if he could find one to exchange
For his lost son; he knows not even now
He has one safe at home. When yesterday
He heard that there was an Elean knight
Of highest place and family, he spared
No money, if so be that he might win
His son, and bring him back again to home.
Accordingly, he bought these prisoners here
At the quaestor's sale. But they between themselves
Arranged a plot, by which the master (*indicating*
    PHILOCRATES) might
Return to his home, the slave alone remain.
They then proceed to change their dress and name.
He's called Philocrates (*indicating* TYNDARUS), he
    Tyndarus (*indicating* PHILOCRATES);
Today each passes for the other man.
The slave today will carry out this plot,
Will set his master free, and by the same means
Will serve his brother, and return him too
To his own country, to his father's house,
Not knowing what he does, for oftentimes
One does more good by chance than by design.
So by their own wit and unknowingly
They've so arrangèd and prepar'd their plot
That this man should remain his father's slave;
Although, as I have said, he is his son;
And so, in ignorance of the fact, he is.
Ah, when one thinks, what paltry things we are!
This is the subject of the present play
We are about to represent to you,
For you a story only. There's one point
On which I wish to warn you. 'Twill be well
To give your close attention to the play.
It is not in the hackneyed style, like others.
There are no filthy verses that one can't
Repeat; no perjured pimp appears today,
No infamous abandoned courtesan,
No braggart soldier. Don't alarm yourselves,

Because I said there was a war on hand.
The battles will be all fought off the stage;
'Twould be unfair for a comic company
Of a sudden to attempt a tragedy.
Therefore, if any one has set his heart
Upon a battle, he must go to law;
And if he get one stronger than himself
To fight, I promise him a battle he
Won't like, and will not want to see again.
And so good-bye, kind critics, here at home,
Good fighters all if the day of battle come.
(*The* PROLOGUS *and the* CAPTIVES *depart.*)

Act One.   Scene I

(*Enter* ERGASILUS *from the forum.*)

ERGASILUS (*to himself*): Our youth 'bout here have given me the name
                Of "Courtesan," because I come to feasts
                Without an invitation, uninvoked.
                They say't in joke, the wags, but as I think
                Not incorrectly; for we know the lover,
                When throwing dice, does still invoke the name
                Of her he loves. Is she invoked or not?
                Most clearly she is invoked, invited too.
                Just so with us it is, we parasites,
                Whom no one asks, nor ev'n invokes at all.
                Like mice we nibble still at other's food.
                When the vacation comes, and men depart
                Into the country, then our tribe as well
                Have their vacation; just as when it's hot
                Snails crawl into their shells, and live the while
                On their own juice, what time there is no dew.
                So in vacation parasites remain
                In hiding, and live wretched, on themselves,
                While they are retired, on whom we used to feed.
                Yes, in vacation time we parasites
                Are hungry, as a pack of unfed hounds;
                When they return to town, we're watchdogs then,
                And dear hounds, too, and bore hounds if you like.
                Yet here indeed, unless a parasite

Can take a blow, or let them break a pot
Upon his head, he'd better go at once
Outside the Three Arches[2] with a porter's bag.
Indeed, it seems that this will be my fate;
For when my patron fell in with the foe—
The Aetolians and Eleans are at war;
This is Aetolia—he was captured there
In Elis, Philopolemus by name,
The son of Hegio, who is dwelling here;
A house to me that's full of sorrow now;
As often as I see it, I must weep.
Now he began for his son's sake a trade
Distasteful to his feelings, and that none
Approves; he buys up slaves, to see if he
Can find one whom he may exchange, to get
His son; and I intently wish he may.
For if he's not recovered, I myself
Shall be undone. There's no hope in young men;
They love themselves. But he, he is a youth
Of the good old fashion; aye, I never smoothed
The wrinkles of his brow without a fee;
His father is of the same character.
Now I will go to him; but see, the door
Opens, from which I've often sallied forth
Full many a time, drunk with excess of cheer.

Act One.   Scene II

(*Enter* HEGIO *and the* SLAVE OVERSEER *from the house.*)

HEGIO (*to* OVERSEER): Mind what I say; on these two slaves, whom I
Bought yesterday from off the quaestor's hands,
Put lighter chains; the heavy ones knock off
And let them walk within or out of doors;
But see that they be carefully observed.
A captive free is like a wild bird still;
If once you give them but the chance to flee,
You ne'er again can catch them.

OVERSEER: Well, we all
Freedom to slavery would still prefer.

HEGIO: You do not think so, or you'd find the means.

OVERSEER: If I have nought to buy my freedom with,
D'ye wish I'd show you a fair pair of heels?

HEGIO: Well, if you do, there'll be something due from me.

OVERSEER: I'll be a wild bird, as you said just now.

HEGIO: Just so, and I will cage the wild bird then.
But talk no more. Do as I bid, and go.
I'll go and see my brother, he who has
My other slaves, lest there has been a row
In any way this night; and then to home.
(*The* OVERSEER *goes into the house.*)

ERGASILUS (*to himself*): I'm sorry this old gentleman has turned
Slaves' gaoler through the troubles of his son.
But if by any means he could regain him,
For my part he might be a hangman too.

HEGIO: Who speaks?

ERGASILUS: 'Tis I, in mourning for your grief.
I pine, grow old, and dwindle into naught;
I am all skin and bones; and nothing that
I eat at home e'er does me any good.
The very smallest thing I eat elsewhere,
That keeps me up.

HEGIO: Ergasilus, good day!

ERGASILUS (*bursting into tears*): May the gods love you, Hegio!

HEGIO: Don't weep!

ERGASILUS: Must I not weep? Nay, must I not deplore
The loss of such a youth?

HEGIO: I always thought
He was your friend, and you were so to him.

ERGASILUS: We never know the blessings which we have
Till they are gone. And so until your son
Met with the enemy, I never knew
How great his worth; and now I long for him.

HEGIO: If you, a stranger, feel so much for him,
What must I feel? He was my only son.

ERGASILUS: A stranger? And to him? Ah! Never say so,
Nor let your mind believe it! Yes, he was
Your only son, but more than that to me.

HEGIO: You're good to make your friend's distress your own.
But be of good cheer!

ERGASILUS: Oh! What troubles me
Is that the eating army's been disbanded.

HEGIO: Could you not find some one who could bring back
This army, which you led, which is dismissed?

ERGASILUS: Would you believe it? No one wants that office
Since your dear Philopolemus was taken.

HEGIO: It is not strange they do not; you require
So many soldiers with such diverse talents.
First you must have your bakers, and of them
They've many kinds; first those who make our loaves,
And then our cakes, and small confectionery;
Then those who thrushes sell, and becca-ficos.
And then an army's needed from the sea.

ERGASILUS: The world knows nothing of its greatest men!
Ah! What a general was lost to me!

HEGIO: Be of good heart! I trust to bring him back
In a few days; for see this captive youth
Born of a noble family, of great wealth,
From Elis; him I hope I may exchange.

ERGASILUS: May the gods grant it, and the goddesses!

HEGIO: Where are you asked to dine today?

ERGASILUS: Nowhere,
As far as I can tell; but why d'ye ask?

HEGIO: Because it is my birthday and I wish
To ask your company.

ERGASILUS: A happy thought!

HEGIO: If you can be content with frugal fare.

ERGASILUS: Nay, not too frugal; else it will appear
I take my usual meal at home today.

HEGIO: Come on; I'll take a bid!

ERGASILUS: 'Tis sold again,
Unless a better offer comes, which more
May please myself and all my many friends.
As I am selling you my whole estate,
It's only fair that I should make my terms.

HEGIO: 'Tis no estate, but rather a deep pit,
Without a bottom, that you have to sell.
But if you come, come early.

ERGASILUS: Yes, I have
Nought else to do.

HEGIO: Well, go and hunt a hare;
You've only got a weasel now in hand.
My table keeps to hard and stony fare.

ERGASILUS: That does not frighten me; for I will come
With teeth that are well shod.

HEGIO: My fare is rough

ERGASILUS: Brambles do you eat?

HEGIO: My dinner's earthy.

ERGASILUS: A pig is earthy too.

HEGIO: With much green stuff.

ERGASILUS: Then open a sick hospital at home.
Now is that all?

HEGIO: Yes, mind you come in time.

ERGASILUS: I won't forget.
              (ERGASILUS *departs to the forum.*)

HEGIO (*to himself*):   I'll go within and work
A little sum, to see what I have left
In my banker's hands; then to my brother's straight.
              (HEGIO *goes into his house.*)

Act Two. Scene I

(*Enter* OVERSEER *and slaves from the house of* HEGIO, *bringing* PHILOC-
RATES *and* TYNDARUS, *each in the other's clothes.*)

OVERSEER: Well, if the gods have willed this trouble to you,
It must be borne contentedly; and if
You do so, lighter sure will be the load.
At home you were free men; since slavery comes,
'Twere well to accommodate yourselves to that
And by obedience to your master's orders
Render it easy. And whatever wrong
He does, that wrong you must consider right.

CAPTIVES: Oh! Oh!

OVERSEER: No need to shout. You only make
Things worse; in evil days 'tis courage wins.

TYNDARUS: These chains are so disgraceful.

OVERSEER: But my master,
If he should take them off, or let you go,
Would more regret it, since he's bought you both.

TYNDARUS: What does he fear? We know our duty well,
If he would set us free.

OVERSEER: You mean to fly;
I know your little games.

PHILOCRATES: We fly, you say?
And whither?

OVERSEER: To your native land again.

PHILOCRATES: 'Tis not for us to do such things as these.

OVERSEER: But if you can, I've nought to say against it.

TYNDARUS: Just grant us one thing.

OVERSEER: What is that you want?

TYNDARUS: That we may speak without these witnesses,
Alone together.

OVERSEER: Yes, you shall. (*To slaves*) Away!
                    Let us make room. (*To* CAPTIVES) But let your words
                    be few.

TYNDARUS: They shall be. Now come here, Philocrates.

OVERSEER (*to slaves*): Away with you slaves there.

TYNDARUS: We are both
                    Greatly obliged for this, and that you give
                    Us leave to do what greatly we desire.

PHILOCRATES (*to* TYNDARUS): Come here a little on one side, lest they
                    May hear our words, and thus our plan be known.
                    Plots are not plots, if they're not well contrived,
                    But do much mischief, if they are revealed.
                    If you pretend to be my master, I your slave,
                    We must look out, we must be very cautious
                    That it may skilfully be carried out
                    And carefully, without a soul suspecting.
                    'Tis a big job; we have no time for sleep.

TYNDARUS: Pray count on me.

PHILOCRATES: I hope I may.

TYNDARUS: You see,
                    For your dear head I gladly offer mine.

PHILOCRATES: I know you do.

TYNDARUS: And don't forget it, please,
                    When you get what you want. The most of men
                    Are thus-wise; while they're trying to obtain
                    That which they want, they are most courteous.
                    But when they've got it, they become great villains,
                    Men whom you cannot trust.

PHILOCRATES: Now I think well
                    Of you; and what I say in this respect,
                    I would say to my father. If I dared,
                    I would call you my father, for you are
                    A second father to me.

TYNDARUS: You're too good.

PHILOCRATES: And therefore I do press you to remember
                    That I'm not now your master, but your slave,

And that the immortal gods have thus designed
That I who was your master should become
Your fellow-slave, and I who once gave orders
Should humbly ask: by our unhappy fate,
And by my father's kindness to yourself,
By our common lot which is the fate of war,
Pay no more honour to me than I did
To you when slave; forget not to remember
Both what you have been, and who now you are.

TYNDARUS: Oh, yes, I know that I am you and you
Are I.

PHILOCRATES: If you do that, there's hope for us.

Act Two. Scene II

(Enter HEGIO *from his house.)*

HEGIO *(to those within)*: I'll soon return; but first I will inform myself
On certain points. *(To* OVERSEER*)* Where are the men
I asked
You to produce?

PHILOCRATES: You need not ask, I think.
It is sufficiently assured, we are
So hedged about by chains and gaolers.

HEGIO: Who guards against deception does not guard
Enough, if still he's cause to fear; ev'n he
Who thinks that he is safe, is often caught.
Is it not right that I should watch you well,
Who paid so dear for you in ready cash?

PHILOCRATES: It is not fair that we blame you because
You hurt us, nor again should you blame us
If we escape, if but the chance occurs.

HEGIO: As you are here, so in your country is
My son a prisoner.

PHILOCRATES: Then he was captured?

HEGIO: He was.

PHILOCRATES: Then we were not the only laggards.

HEGIO (*to* PHILOCRATES): Come here apart; I have some questions for
you;
I trust you will not answer falsely.

PHILOCRATES: No,
As far as I can tell; what I don't know
I will at once admit.

TYNDARUS (*aside*): The old man now
Is in the barber's hands; the scissors ready;
Not even a napkin will be put upon him
To save his coat. But whether he will crop
Him close, or only take a little off,
I do not know; but if he does what's right,
He'll leave him fully cropped.

HEGIO (*to* PHILOCRATES): Pray tell me now,
Would'st rather be a slave or a free man?

PHILOCRATES: I want the best that I can get, the most
Removed from ill; though as a slave
I was not treated ill, nor otherwise
Than as a son of the house.

TYNDARUS (*aside*): I would not give
A thousand pounds to buy Milesian Thales,
For he was but a trifler to this man.
How cleverly he fitted now his speech
To his position as a slave!

HEGIO: Now tell me
What family Philocrates was of?

PHILOCRATES: The Goldings, multi-millionaires, in Elis
The most respected and most powerful clan.

HEGIO: And he himself, was he much honoured there?

PHILOCRATES: He was, and by the noblest citizens.

HEGIO: Then, since he was so high reputed there,
What of his wealth, a pretty fat lot, eh?

PHILOCRATES: The old man had enough of that and more.

HEGIO: The old man? Does his father live?

PHILOCRATES: He does.
      We left him still alive. But whether now
      He lives or not, that only Plutus knows.

TYNDARUS (*aside*): 'Tis right enough; he's turned philosopher
      As well as liar.

HEGIO: Pray what was his name?

PHILOCRATES: Thesauro-Chrysonico-Chrysides.[3]

HEGIO: I suppose that name was given him for his wealth.

PHILOCRATES: Nay, rather from his avarice and greed.
      His real name is Theodoromedes.

HEGIO: His father then was close?

PHILOCRATES: Most close indeed!
      Why, when he sacrifices to his god,
      He uses nought but Samian earthenware,
      Lest the god should steal them. From that you see
      How much he trusts men.

HEGIO (*to* TYNDARUS):   Now come here aside.
      There's something that I want to ask of you.
      Philocrates, your slave has spoken as
      He should. I know from him how you are born;
      He has confessed it. If you do the same,
      'Twill be to your advantage. I may tell you,
      I know it all already from this man.

TYNDARUS: In telling all he only did what's right.
      Although I greatly wished to hide my birth,
      My race and wealth, now, since I've wholly lost
      My land and liberty, I do not see
      Why he should not respect you more than me.
      The force of war has made our lots the same.
      I can remember when he dare not speak;
      Now he does as he likes. Ah, look you now,
      How fortune moulds and twists us as she will.
      Me, that was free, she made a slave; I fell
      From high to low; who used to give commands,
      I now obey another. Yet even if,
      As I myself was master once, I now
      A master have, I do not fear at all
      That he will rule unfairly or severely.

And this I wished to tell you, Hegio,
If you do not object.

HEGIO: Speak boldly now.

TYNDARUS: I once was free as was your son; from him,
As well as me, the violence of war
Has stolen his liberty; he is a slave
With us, just as I am a slave with you.
There is, you know, a God who hears and sees
All that we do; and as you treat me here,
He'll see your son is likewise treated there.
If you do well, 'twill be to your advantage;
If ill, he'll deal impartially with you.
As you regret your son, so does my father me.

HEGIO: I know all that. Do you admit the truth
Of what your slave has told me?

TYNDARUS: I allow
My father has great wealth at home, that I
Am of illustrious birth. But, Hegio,
I do implore you not to let my wealth
Make you too greedy, lest my father should,
Although I am his only son, think well
To leave me here a slave at your expense,
To feed and clothe, rather than live a beggar
Among my own, where it would be disgrace.

HEGIO: Thanks to the gods, and to my ancestors,
I have enough of wealth. I do not think
That filthy lucre's all that men require.
I know, indeed, that it's made many great.
But there are times when better lose than gain.
For gold I hate; it has caused many crimes.
Now listen, that my meaning you may know.
My son is kept a slave in Elis land;
If you return him to me, I will set
You and your servant free, and take no pay—
No, not a penny; but you cannot go
On any other terms than those I say.

TYNDARUS: You speak both well and justly, best of men!
Is he a private slave, or in the employ
Of the Elean State?

HEGIO: His master is
A doctor, one Menarchus.

PHILOCRATES: He's the client
Of this my master; why, the thing's as plain
As when adown the roof there runs the rain.

HEGIO: Then bring him back.

TYNDARUS: I will; but let me ask—

HEGIO: Ask what you will, provided that you ask
Nought that will hinder this.

TYNDARUS: Hear what I say.
I do not ask to be allowed to go
Until your son returns; but what I want
Is that you set a price upon this man,
That I may send him to my father there,
To be exchanged for him.

HEGIO: Nay, rather I
Will send some other, when the bargain's made,
Who'll carry out your mandates as you wish.

TYNDARUS: But that's no use, to send an unknown man;
You'll only lose your time; but send this man
And he will do it all. You cannot send
A man more faithful, one you can more trust;
Nor one who is a slave more to one's mind,
To whom more gladly he will trust your son.
Fear not! I'll answer for his faithfulness.
I know his character; he knows that I
Am well disposed to him.

HEGIO: Well, then, I'll send him,
When we have fixed his price on your good faith.

TYNDARUS: And may it speedily be carried out
As soon as may be.

HEGIO: And if he comes not,
You'll owe me twenty minae; do you object?

TYNDARUS: Not in the least!

HEGIO (*to* OVERSEER):   Let that one loose at once;
Nay, loose them both.

TYNDARUS: May the gods grant to you
    All good things you can wish; you who treat me
    So nobly, and knock off these wretched chains.
    Indeed, 'tis pleasant to the neck to be
    Without one's collar.

HEGIO: True! The kindness that
    One shows to honest men produces still
    A good return. Now you can send your slave.
    Speak to him, give a message to your father.
    Say, shall I call him here?

TYNDARUS: Call him at once.

Act Two.   Scene III

HEGIO (*turning to* PHILOCRATES): May all this turn out happily for me,
    And for my son and you! Your new master
    Wishes you to obey your old one well
    And faithfully. I've given you to him
    For twenty minae; he'll send you to his father,
    There to redeem my son; that we may make
    A fair exchange between us of our sons.

PHILOCRATES: My conduct shall be suited to you both,
    To you and him; pray use me like a wheel
    Which turns and twirls exactly as you wish.

HEGIO: You bear your burden as it should be borne,
    With excellent intent. Now follow me.
    (*They rejoin* TYNDARUS.) Here is your man.

TYNDARUS: I thank you much indeed
    For all your wealth of kindness, and that I
    May send to my parents by this messenger
    Both what I'm doing here, and what I wish
    That they should do: that he may take the news
    In proper order to my father. We
    Have now agreed, between us, Tyndarus,
    To send you to my father at a price.
    If you do not return, then I will pay
    Him twenty minae.

PHILOCRATES: That will be quite fair.
Your father looks for me, or some one else
To come with news to him.

TYNDARUS: And now attend
To what I wish you to announce to him.

PHILOCRATES: Philocrates, as I have ever done,
So now I'll try to manage your affair
With all success, and bring it to an end
With all my heart and mind and strength and will.

TYNDARUS: You do just as you ought. And now attend:
And first of all bear greeting to my parents,
To my relations, and to all my friends.
Say that I'm well; in service to this man,
Who's always treated and still treats me well.

PHILOCRATES: Nay, do not tell me that; my memory
Knows it so well.

TYNDARUS: Save that I have a guard,
I feel at liberty. Then tell them, too,
The agreement we have made 'bout this man's son.

PHILOCRATES: I know it; to repeat it but wastes time.

TYNDARUS: 'Tis to return the youth and send him hither,
In place of us.

PHILOCRATES: I will remember this.

HEGIO: And no delay, for your sake and for mine.

PHILOCRATES: You do not wish to see your son again,
More than he does to see his own.

HEGIO: I know
That mine to me, as his to him is dear.

PHILOCRATES: Is there aught else you wish me tell your father?

TYNDARUS (*thinking rapidly*): Say I am well; that there has been
            between us
Complete accord, and that our souls were linked
In perfect harmony; you've done no wrong,
Nor've I accused you; you have still behaved
Well to your master, even in distress,

> And never did you fail me even in
> The darkest hour of need; when this he knows,
> How you were minded toward his son and him,
> He will not be so hard as to refuse
> Your liberty to you, and that for nought.
> 'Twill be my care, if I return, to make
> The thing more easy still; for 'tis through you,
> Your kindness and your wisdom and your care,
> That I am able to return; 'twas you
> That told this man about my birth and wealth,
> And so struck off your master's galling chains.

PHILOCRATES: I did as you describe, and I rejoice
> That you remember it. The same is due
> To you, for if, Philocrates, I should
> Relate the good deeds you have done to me,
> The day is all too short, the night would come;
> For had you been my slave, you had not been
> More deferential to me.

HEGIO: Oh, ye gods!
> What faith, what liberality of mind!
> I'm moved to tears; how much they love each other!
> What praise the servant to his master gives!

PHILOCRATES: The praise he gives is not the hundredth part
> That he himself deserves.

HEGIO: Since you have done
> So well, the occasion serves to add still more;
> And see you faithfully discharge his wish.

PHILOCRATES: I cannot wish success in this attempt
> More than I'll try to make it so; and that
> You may believe me, I call you to witness
> That to Philocrates I'll not be false.[4]

HEGIO: An honest man!

PHILOCRATES: Nor will I ever do
> A thing to him I would not to myself.

TYNDARUS (*anxiously*): I wish your actions may make true your words.
> If I said less than I desired of you,
> Please note the reason; be not vexed with me.
> Remember you are sent on my good faith,

That for you here my life remains in pawn.
Do not forget me, when I'm out of sight,
When you have left me here a slave, for you.
Don't think that you are free, and can desert
Your pledge, and not endeavour all you can
To bring again his son in place of me.
Know that your value is at twenty minae.
Be faithful still to those who're so to you.
Beware of broken promises. I know
My father will do all he ought to do.
Make me your constant friend, and find this youth.
By your right hand which now I hold in mine,
Be faithful to me as I am to you.
Do this; you are my master, patron, father;
And to your hands I trust my hopes and fortune.

PHILOCRATES: Enough commands! And will you be content
If I succeed?

TYNDARUS: I will.

PHILOCRATES: I will return
Equipped and furnished as you both can wish.
Is there aught else?

TYNDARUS: That you may soon return,
As soon as may be.

PHILOCRATES: That is evident.

HEGIO (*to* PHILOCRATES): Now follow me that I may get your fare
Out of the bank; and at the same time I
Will get a passport.

TYNDARUS: What passport is that?

HEGIO: To show the army, that he may return.
Now go within.

TYNDARUS: A pleasant journey to you.

PHILOCRATES: Adieu. (TYNDARUS *goes into the house.*)

HEGIO (*to himself*): 'Tis a good bargain I have made,
In buying those men at the quaestor's sale.
My son, if it should please the gods, is saved
From slavery; yet I doubted long if I

Should buy those men or not. (*To* OVERSEER *and
   slaves*) Now, slaves,
Keep that man safe within; let him not stir
Without a guard. And soon I will return.
I go to see my other captives who
Are at my brother's; there I'll ascertain
If any of them knows this same young man.
(*To* PHILOCRATES) Now come, that I may send you
   off; for that
Is the first thing to be attended to. (HEGIO *and* PHI-
   LOCRATES *depart;* OVERSEER *and slaves go inside.*)

Act Three. Scene I

(*Enter* ERGASILUS *from the forum.*)

ERGASILUS (*to himself*): A miserable lot is his, who has
To seek a dinner, and can scarcely find it.
More miserable still is his by far
Who seeks and nothing finds; and yet again
Most miserable is he of all who wants
To eat and nothing has. For, by the gods,
I'd drag the eyes out of this wretched day;
All mortals has it turned against me with
Undying hate! A day more hungerful,
More with starvation crammed, I never saw,
Nor one in which what one begins to do
Has less success; a day on which my throat
And stomach celebrate a famine fast.
The parasite's profession's dead and gone!
So far our modern youths spurn from their side
Poor wags like me! They take no heed of those
Poor buffet-bearers, Spartans forced to sit
At the bottom of the table when they dine;
Whose words today bring them nor meat nor coin,
They ask for those who, when they eat, can make
Return at home; they market for themselves,
Which used to be the parasite's preserve.
They leave the forum, and go to the pimps
Quite unabashed, with just as serious mien
As they would sentence criminals in court.

They do not care a farthing for us wags;
Themselves alone they love. As I just now
Went hence, I met some young men in the market:
"Good day," says I, "where do we dine today?"
But not a word! Who says: "With me," or who
Makes any offer? Still there's no response,
Nor do they even smile. "Where shall we sup?"
I say, and then they simply shake their head.
I tell them one of my best humorous tales,
Which would have got me dinners for a month,
Once on a time; but no one even smiles.
A single glance answers me, it is all
Arranged before. Ev'n if they did not smile,
They might have done just like an angry dog
And shown their teeth a little. So I leave them
On seeing that they only wish to mock me.
Then others I approach, and others still;
But still the same reception! They all act
As pre-arranged, as oil-sellers might do.
And others, too, were walking all about,
But all in vain! Now, by barbaric law
(That is your law), it is my certain right
To prosecute the men who have conspired
To rob us of our life and victuals thus.
I'll set a day, I will demand a fine,
That they give me ten dinners at my choice,
When food is dear. And thus methinks I'll act.
And now to the harbour; that's my only hope
From a dining point of view; if that should fail,
I must again return to this old man,
And face his scurvy supper as I can.

(ERGASILUS *departs to the harbour.*)

Act Three. Scene II

(*Enter* HEGIO *and* ARISTOPHONTES.)

HEGIO (*to himself*): What can more pleasant be than to promote
          The public weal, as I did yesterday
          In purchasing these slaves; where'er I'm seen,
          Men run to greet me. I am quite worn out,

They stop and stay me so; I've just emerged
With life from all their kind civilities.
Then I went to the praetor and demanded
A passport; it was given; and at once
I handed it to Tyndarus, who has left;
And home returned, all things being well arranged.
I go then to my brother where I have
My other slaves; I ask if there is one
Who knows Philocrates; then this one says
He was his friend; I say that he's with me.
And then he straightway asks and prays that he
May see him. So I bid that he may be
Unloosed, and came away. (*To* ARISTOPHONTES) You
      follow me,
That you may have that which you have desired,
To see and have some converse with this man.
      (*They go into the house.*)

Act Three.   Scene III

(TYNDARUS *rushes from the house, as the others go in.*)

TYNDARUS (*to himself*): As things turn out, I'd rather I were dead
            Than yet alive. Now hope and help have gone,
            And left me all alone upon my way.
            This is that day I never wished to see.
            There is not even means to end my life.
            No help, no hope to drive away my fear!
            There is no veil to cover up my lies,
            No covering for my tricks and falsities,
            No prayer for pardon for my perfidy,
            No escape for all my misdeeds, no place where
            My impudence can fly and be not seen,
            No resting-place for all my treachery.
            All, all is now discovered! It remains
            Only to slay myself, and seek the death
            That should have been my master's. I am ruined
            By this Aristophontes who's arrived;
            He knows me, was the friend and relative
            Of our Philocrates; not Providence,
            Ev'n if he wish, can ever save me now.

There is no chance unless I can contrive
Some further cleverness; plague take the thing!
What can I now devise, what think of still?
Folly and silliness I undertake.
I'm in a tight place now, and no mistake.

Act Three. Scene IV

(*Enter* HEGIO *and* ARISTOPHONTES *from the house.*)

HEGIO: Where is that man who dashed out of the house?

TYNDARUS (*aside*): Now I am done for! Tyndarus, the foe
Presses you hard! What shall I speak or say?
What now confess, or what deny? 'Tis all
Uncertain; I can trust to nothing now.
Oh, would that death had taken you away,
Aristophontes, e'er you left your land,
Who thus has made such fatal massacre
Of all our plans. For the whole scheme is wrecked
Unless I can invent some cunning lie.

HEGIO (*to* ARISTOPHONTES): Come here! See, there's the man! Go speak
       to him!

TYNDARUS (*aside*): Is there a man more wretched than I am?

ARISTOPHONTES: How is it, Tyndarus, that you avoid
My looks, and gaze upon me as I were
Unknown? I am a slave as much as you,
Although at home I once was free; while you
From boyhood were a slave in Elis land.

HEGIO: I wonder not if he avoids the sight of you,
Or even hates you, when you say his name
Is Tyndarus and not Philocrates.

TYNDARUS (*drawing* HEGIO *aside*): Hegio, this man was ever counted
       mad,
So do not listen to the tales he tells.
He once attacked his parents with a spear;
Ofttimes too he is ill with that disease
They call the falling sickness, which makes him
Foam at the mouth. Keep farther from him, pray!

HEGIO (*to* ARISTOPHONTES): Keep far from me!

ARISTOPHONTES: They say that I am mad,
        And once attacked my parents? Often have
        Fits of the falling sickness come upon me
        Which makes me foam at mouth?

HEGIO: Be not afraid!
        The disease is common; spitting often cures it.

ARISTOPHONTES: And you, do you believe it?

HEGIO: Believe what?

ARISTOPHONTES: That I am mad.

TYNDARUS (*to* HEGIO):   How savagely he scowls!
        'Twere better, Hegio, to retire at once.
        'Tis as I said; the fit is on him now.
        Look for yourself.

HEGIO: Oh, yes, I thought him mad
        When he began to call you Tyndarus.

TYNDARUS: Even his own name he sometimes forgets,
        And knows not who he is.

HEGIO: He said that you
        Were his companion.

TYNDARUS: He never was;
        If that were so, Alcmaeon and Orestes,
        Aye, and Lycurgus too, were just as much
        Companions as he.[5]

ARISTOPHONTES: And do you dare
        To speak thus ill of me? I did not know you?

HEGIO: 'Tis plain you did not know him, for you call
        Him Tyndarus, and not Philocrates.
        The man you see you know not, but you name
        The man who is not here.

ARISTOPHONTES: 'Tis he pretends
        To be the man that he is not at all,
        Nor owns himself to be the man he is.

TYNDARUS: So you were found to surpass Philocrates
        In speaking truth!

ARISTOPHONTES: Nay, rather you, I think,
Who prove by pure inventions that I'm wrong.
Now look at me!

TYNDARUS: Well!

ARISTOPHONTES: Now do you deny
That you are Tyndarus?

TYNDARUS: Of course I do.

ARISTOPHONTES: And say you are indeed Philocrates?

TYNDARUS: I do indeed.

ARISTOPHONTES (*to* HEGIO):   And you believe it true?

HEGIO: I do believe him more than you or me.
For that man whom you think that this man is
Has left today for Elis, to the father
Of this man.

ARISTOPHONTES: Pray what father? He's a slave.

TYNDARUS: And so are you, although you once were free;
I hope to be so some day, when I've brought
The son of this man back to liberty.

ARISTOPHONTES: You scoundrel, do you say you're freeman born?

TYNDARUS: My name's not Freeman, but Philocrates.[6]

ARISTOPHONTES: This fellow, Hegio, makes game of you.
He is a slave, and is the only slave
His master had.

TYNDARUS: Because at home you are
A pauper and have not the means to live,
You wish that all were like you. 'Tis not strange;
For wretched men are ever evil-minded
And hate and envy men of property.

ARISTOPHONTES: Hegio, take care and do not rashly listen
To all the tales he tells. He seems already
To have tricked you somewhat; for he says that he
Will bring your son back. That I do not like.

TYNDARUS: I know you don't; but if the gods will help,
I'll do it. And this man will send me back

To Elis and my father. So I've sent
A messenger to see him, Tyndarus.

ARISTOPHONTES: But you are he; in Elis there is not
Another slave that bears the name you bear.

TYNDARUS: You still reproach me with my slavery,
A slavery which was the fate of war.

ARISTOPHONTES: I can't contain myself!

TYNDARUS (*to* HEGIO):   Hear you, what he says?
He will attack us here with stones, unless
You have him taken up.

ARISTOPHONTES: I am tormented!

TYNDARUS: His eyes flash fire! Now, Hegio, fetch a rope.
See how he's covered over with black spots;
Black bile is troubling him.

ARISTOPHONTES: If this man's wise,
Black pitch will trouble you, and light you up.

TYNDARUS: He's talking folly and is quite bewitched.

HEGIO: What if I order him to be arrested?

TYNDARUS: You would be wise.

ARISTOPHONTES: I wish I had a stone
To break the rascal's head, who with his tales
Would make me mad.

TYNDARUS: You hear, he wants a stone.

ARISTOPHONTES: Hegio, I wish to see you by yourself.

HEGIO: Speak what you wish; I'll hear you from a distance.

TYNDARUS: If you go nearer to him, he will bite
Your nose off with his teeth.

ARISTOPHONTES: Nay, Hegio,
Think not I'm mad, nor ever have been so,
Or have some foul disease, as this man says.
But, if you fear me, pray let me be bound;
If this man's bound as well, I wish to be.

TYNDARUS: Yes, Hegio, let him be bound.

ARISTOPHONTES: Be quiet!
    You false Philocrates, I'll see that you
    Today are found the real Tyndarus.
    (TYNDARUS *signals to* ARISTOPHONTES *behind* HEGIO's *back*)
    Why do you shake your head?

TYNDARUS: I shake my head?

ARISTOPHONTES (*to* HEGIO): What would he do, if you were not so close?

HEGIO (*to* TYNDARUS): What say you? What if I approach this mad-
      man?

TYNDARUS: He'll talk mere nonsense; chatter so that you
    Can make nor head nor tail of what he says.
    Save for the dress, you see a very Ajax.

HEGIO: Well, never mind. I will approach him now.

TYNDARUS (*aside*): 'Tis quite all over with me! Now I stand
    Between the altar and the priest's sharp knife;
    Nor know I what to do.

HEGIO: I'll listen now,
    Aristophontes, if you've aught to say.

ARISTOPHONTES: From me you'll hear, what now you think is false,
    Is really true; but first I'd make it clear
    I am not mad, and have no fell disease,
    Save that I am a slave. And may the king
    Of gods and men give me my native land,
    As much as that man is Philocrates
    No more than you or I.

HEGIO: Who is he, then?

ARISTOPHONTES: He whom I told you from the very first.
    If it be otherwise, I'll be content
    To lose my parents and my liberty.

HEGIO (*to* TYNDARUS): And what say you?

TYNDARUS: I am your slave, and you
    My master.

HEGIO: 'Tis not that I ask of you,
    But were you free?

TYNDARUS: I was.

ARISTOPHONTES: He never was.
                He's talking nonsense!

TYNDARUS: Pray, how do you know?
                Were you my mother's midwife, that you speak
                So confidently?

ARISTOPHONTES: As a boy I saw you,
                A boy myself.

TYNDARUS: I saw you when grown up.
                Keep to yourself! Don't trouble my affairs!
                I do not trouble yours.

HEGIO: Was this man's father
                Thesauro-Chrysonico-Chrysides?

ARISTOPHONTES: He was not, for I never heard that name
                Before today. Theodoromedes,
                He was the father of Philocrates.

TYNDARUS (*aside*): It is all over! Oh, my heart, be still!
                Be steady; there, you're throbbing now again!
                I scarce can stand upon my legs for fear.

HEGIO: Then are you sure that this man was a slave
                In Elis? And is it not Philocrates?

ARISTOPHONTES: Yes, certain, so that you will never find
                It otherwise. But, pray, where is he now?

HEGIO (*convinced*): Where I the least, and he the most, desired.
                I'm polished off, aye, and torn limb from limb
                By the devices of this wretch, who has,
                Just as he willed, deluded me by wiles.
                But are you sure?

ARISTOPHONTES: Why, yes, the tale I tell
                Is clear and can be proved.

HEGIO: You are quite certain?

ARISTOPHONTES: Nothing you'll find more certain is than this.
                Philocrates and I were friends from youth.

HEGIO: What is he like?

ARISTOPHONTES: Thin-featured, with sharp nose,
Complexion white, eyes black, and reddish hair
In locks, and somewhat curled.

HEGIO: Yes, that agrees.

TYNDARUS (*aside*): Agreed that I have had bad luck today.
Those wretched twigs that on my back will find
An early grave!

HEGIO: I see I've been cajoled.

TYNDARUS (*aside*): Why, chains, do you delay to come to me
And clasp my limbs, that I may hold you fast?

HEGIO: Enough, these captives have beguiled me now,
These wretched slaves! The other said he was
A slave, but this man said that he was free.
I've lost the kernel; he has left the shell.
To be so foolish, to be cheated thus
From first to last! At any rate, this man
Shall not mock me. (*To slaves within*) Here Slap and
Cuff and Knocker!
Go, get the thongs! (*The slaves enter.*)

SLAP: And are we sent for faggots?

Act Three.   Scene V

HEGIO: Put chains at once upon this scoundrel here!

TYNDARUS: What's this? What's my offence?

HEGIO: And do you ask,
You sower, weeder, reaper of my wrongs?

TYNDARUS: Could you not say a harrower as well?
For farmers harrow still before they weed.

HEGIO: Just see what bold effrontery he displays!

TYNDARUS: A slave that's innocent and does no wrong
Should still with confidence present himself
Before his masters.

HEGIO:　　　　　　　　　　　　　　　　Bind his hands, and strongly!

TYNDARUS:　I'm yours, and if you like you can command
To cut them off. But why, I pray, are you
Incensed with me?

HEGIO:　　　　　　　　　　　　Because when I had placed
Myself and my affairs in your hands,
Your wicked lying tricks have mined them all,
And quite destroyed my plans. You've made an end
Of all the things I purposed; by your wiles
You have deprived me of Philocrates.
I thought he was the slave and you were free.
You said so; aye, and even changed your names.

TYNDARUS:　I admit this was the case, and that he did
Escape by treachery with aid for me
And by my cleverness; but is't for this
That you are vexed with me?

HEGIO:　　　　　　　　　　　　　　It shall cost you dear

TYNDARUS:　I count it little, even if I die.
But if I do, and he does not return,
Yet this will be remembered when I'm dead:
That I set free from slavery my master,
Restored him to his native land again,
And to his own father, and preferred to risk
My own head, rather than that he should die.

HEGIO:　　　Go then with glory down to Acheron!

TYNDARUS:　Who dies with glory never dies at all.

HEGIO:　　　When I have made a sad example of you
And put you to a miserable death
For all your wiles, then let them say you died
Or what they like, so long as you are gone.
I shall not care if ev'n they say you live.

TYNDARUS:　Well, if you do it, you will suffer too,
If he returns here, as I think he will.

ARISTOPHONTES (*aside*): Ye gods immortal, now I see it all!
My friend Philocrates is safe at home;
Nor is there any I would rather see
Fare well, not ev'n myself. But I am vexed

That I have done a bad turn to this man
Who has been bound through me, and what I said.

HEGIO: Did I forbid you thus to tell me lies?

TYNDARUS: You did!

HEGIO: Why have you dared to do it, then?

TYNDARUS: Truth would have injured him I wished to save;
But lies have helped him.

HEGIO: And will damage you.

TYNDARUS: 'Tis well! I've saved him whom I wished to save,
Him whom my former master gave to me
To guard; and in this think you I was wrong?

HEGIO: I do. Most wrong!

TYNDARUS: But I, that I was right,
Quite different from you. Just think of it:
If but your slave should do the same as I
For your own son, how grateful you would be!
Would you not set him free? And would he not
Be held the best of all the slaves you had?
Now answer yes or no.

HEGIO: I think it's true.

TYNDARUS: Then why so vexed with me?

HEGIO: Because you were
To him more faithful than you were to me.

TYNDARUS: What, do you think it right, that you should teach
A slave who's been with you a night and day,
Just newly captured, that I should prefer
Your interests to his, with whom I have
Lived since I was a boy?

HEGIO: Then pray thee ask
The favours that you want, from him. (*To slaves*)
Now take him
To where he'll have great heavy chains to wear!
(*To* TYNDARUS) Thence to the quarries you shall go,
and when
The others in the gang quarry eight stones,

Unless you do just half as much again,
Each day you shall be named "Six hundred stripes."

ARISTOPHONTES: I do beseech you, Hegio, by the gods
And men, not to destroy this wretched man.

HEGIO: That shall be looked to! He will be confined
By night in prison; in the day he'll hew
Stones in the quarry. He shall suffer long;
A single day will not excuse his crime.

ARISTOPHONTES: And is this settled?

HEGIO: Yes, as sure as death.
(*To slaves*) Now take him to Hippolytus the smith;
Tell him to load him with thick heavy chains.
Then take him to my freedman Cordalus
Beyond the gate, to place him in the quarry;
And tell him that my wish is that he has
No less than him that gets the very worst.

TYNDARUS: Why do I ask to live in spite of you?
My life I know, if taken, will cost you dear.
And there is nought of ill in death to fright.
Even if I live to the utmost span of life,
Short is the time, to bear the things you threaten.
Farewell! Though you deserve a different wish!
And you, Aristophontes, may you prosper,
As you have done to me; for 'tis your fault,
All this has chanced to me.

HEGIO (*to slaves*):   Now lead him off.

TYNDARUS: One thing I ask, if e'er Philocrates
Return, that I should have the chance to see him.

HEGIO (*to slaves*): Unless you take this fellow from my sight,
May you be hanged! (*They seize* TYNDARUS.)

TYNDARUS: Why, this is force indeed.
To be both dragged and pushed at the same time.
(*The slaves depart with* TYNDARUS.)

HEGIO (*to himself*): He has been taken to the guardroom straight
As he deserves. 'Twill be a lesson to
The other captives lest they do the like.
Had it not been for this man, who made clear

The matter how it was, I should have been
Drawn helpless on by their insidious schemes.
I am resolved to trust no one again;
Once bit, twice shy! I hoped to have redeemed
My son from slavery; the hope is gone.
I lost one son of four years old; a slave
Stole him; I've never found the slave or him.
And now my other son is in the hands
Of the enemy; a piece of ill luck this,
That I should children have, to childless be!
(*To* ARISTOPHONTES) Now follow here. I'll take you
    where you were.
I'll pity no one; no one pities me.

ARISTOPHONTES: My horrid chains were gone, methought, the auspices
    were fair.
But the auspices have failed me, and the chains again
    I wear.
        (HEGIO *and* ARISTOPHONTES *depart*.)

Act Four.   Scene I

(*Enter* ERGASILUS *from the harbour*.)

ERGASILUS (*to himself*): Great Jupiter, thou art my patron god;
    Thou makest me rich, and givest to me wealth
    In sumptuous abundance; honour and gains,
    And games and plays and festivals,
    And trains of servants bringing meat and drink,
    Fulness and joy! 'Tis certain now I need
    To beg of no man. Nay, I now can do
    A good turn to a friend, or ruin a foe.
    This happy day has brought so much of luck!
    An ample heritage is mine, a rose
    Without a thorn! And now I'll take my way
    To Hegio, this old gentleman, to whom
    I bear the glorious news of such a blessing,
    As great as he can ask for from the gods,
    Or more. The thing is safe; I'll throw my cloak
    Close round my neck, and run like any slave
    Upon the comic stage; that he may hear

Of this thing first from me. And then I hope 'twill be
The messenger of everlasting food for me.

Act Four.   Scene II

(*Enter* HEGIO.)

HEGIO (*to himself*): The more I think this matter over now,
          The greater the uneasiness I feel,
          That I was duped today unwittingly.
          When it is known, I am the laughing-stock
          Of all the city. If I should approach
          The forum, they will say at once: "See, there's
          The old man who has been so blindly led,
          So easily cheated." Surely I see there
          Ergasilus, his cloak drawn up to run.
          What is he going to do?

ERGASILUS (*to himself*):   Now no delay,
          Ergasilus, but to your work at once!
          I do forbid, and threaten any one
          Who interrupts, unless indeed he think
          That he's lived long enough; for he who does
          Shall on his face be laid.

HEGIO (*aside*):   He wants to fight.

ERGASILUS: I'm sure to do it. So let each pursue
          His way in peace; nor in this place attempt
          To discuss his own affairs. For know my fist
          Throws stones, my elbow is a catapult,
          And this my shoulder is a battering ram.
          If my knee touches one, why, down he goes;
          And if I strike, you'll see them searching for
          Their teeth upon the ground.

HEGIO (*aside*):   I am amazed.
          I wonder, what does all this menace mean?

ERGASILUS: I'll make him to remember place and hour
          And me as well. Whoe'er impedes my course,
          Something will impede him.

HEGIO (*aside*):   What is't this man
Is going to do with such prodigious threats?

ERGASILUS: I give due notice; if they now are caught,
'Twill be their fault; keep close within the house,
And come not near my way.

HEGIO (*aside*):   Now I'll be sworn,
A well-filled stomach is the cause of all
This confidence. The worse perhaps for him,
At whose free table he has grown so mighty!

ERGASILUS: Then there's the millers who keep pigs to feed
On bran; no one can pass the mill for the stench.
If I see any sow upon the road,
With my own royal fists I will belabour
Its scurfy side.

HEGIO (*aside*):   Right royal edicts these!
An Emperor speaks; the man is full of meat.
He speaks with boldness on a well-filled stomach.

ERGASILUS: Then there are those who sell us stinking fish,
Brought to us by a dull provoking horse,
Whose smell drives all the loiterers inside.
I'll beat their faces with a fishing basket;
One of their own that's made of reeds, that they
May know the trouble that their smells can cause
To other people's noses. Butchers, too,
Who take the lambs from out their mothers' care,
Slaughter and sell them, charging double price,
And pass off tough old ram for primest wethers!
If I should see that ram on the public road,
He and his master shall remember it.

HEGIO (*aside*): These are the edicts of a magistrate;
Surely they have not made him market-clerk.

ERGASILUS: I am no more a parasite! I am
More kingly than the kings! Such ample wealth
Of stores my stomach has! But I delay
To disclose to Hegio all this weight of joy,
Than whom there is no man more fortunate.

HEGIO (*aside*): What is this joy he gives to me so freely?

ERGASILUS (*knocking*): Where are you? Is there any one about
　　　　The door to open?

HEGIO (*aside*):　　　　　He comes back to dine.

ERGASILUS: Here, open both the doors, before I make
　　　　An end to them, and knock them into splinters.

HEGIO (*aside*): I'll speak to him. (*Aloud*) Ergasilus!

ERGASILUS:　　　　　　　　Who calls?

HEGIO: Here, look at me.

ERGASILUS:　　　　　You bid me do that which
　　　　Fortune does not, and will not do for you.
　　　　But who is it?

HEGIO:　　　　Why, I am Hegio.

ERGASILUS: Thou best of all men who are in the world,
　　　　You come just in the very nick of time!

HEGIO: I know not at what port you've touched to dine;
　　　　But this you scorn.

ERGASILUS:　　　　Give me your hand!

HEGIO:　　　　　　My hand?

ERGASILUS: Yes, give it me at once.

HEGIO:　　　　　Well, there it is!

ERGASILUS: Rejoice!

HEGIO:　　　And why?

ERGASILUS:　　　　　Because I tell you to.

HEGIO: My sorrows take precedence of my joys.

ERGASILUS: Now don't be angry. I will take away
　　　　All traces of your sorrows. So rejoice!

HEGIO: I do, although I do not know the reason.

ERGASILUS: I thank you. Order now—

HEGIO:　　　　　And what, I pray?

ERGASILUS: A large fire to be made.

HEGIO: A large fire, is't?

ERGASILUS: Yes, so I say.

HEGIO: D'ye think I'll burn my house,
You greedy fellow, for the sake of you?

ERGASILUS: Now don't be vexed! Will you or will you not
Command the pans to be set near the fire,
The dishes washed, the lard and other viands
Set on the glowing hearth; some one to go
And bargain for the fish?

HEGIO: He dreams awake!

ERGASILUS: Another pork, and lamb, and farmyard cocks?

HEGIO: You know what's good, if but you have the means.

ERGASILUS: Salmon and turbot, mackerel, tunny, trout,
And nice moist cheese?

HEGIO: 'Tis easier to name these things
Than eat them in this house, Ergasilus.

ERGASILUS: Think you I say it for my own sweet sake?

HEGIO: Neither today, nor in much longer time,
Unless there's some mistake, will you eat these things.
Please bring to me your usual appetite.

ERGASILUS: But I'll arrange that you will wish to go
To this expense, ev'n though I should forbid.

HEGIO: I will?

ERGASILUS: Yes, you.

HEGIO: Then you are now my master.

ERGASILUS: And full of good intentions. Do you wish
That I should give you happiness and luck?

HEGIO: Rather than sorrow, yes.

ERGASILUS: Give me your hand.

HEGIO: Then there it is.

ERGASILUS: The gods will bless you much!

HEGIO: I do not mark it.

ERGASILUS: No, you're not yet in
The market; that's why.[7] Bid the vessels be
Prepared for sacrifice; and bid a lamb
Be brought, a fat one.

HEGIO: Why?

ERGASILUS: To sacrifice.

HEGIO: And to what deity?

ERGASILUS: To me, of course.
I now am mighty Jove; thy Providence,
Thy Life, thy Fortune, thy Delight, thy Joy!
So now proceed to appease this Deity
With food.

HEGIO: It seems to me that you are hungry.

ERGASILUS: I hunger for myself, not you.

HEGIO: With that
I easily can bear.

ERGASILUS: And that I know
From boyhood.

HEGIO: Jove and all the gods destroy you!

ERGASILUS: But you should thank me, surely, for my message;
I bring you good news from the port.

HEGIO: You're joking.
Go, fool, you come too late.

ERGASILUS: Had I come sooner,
You might have spoken thus. Now hear from me
The good news that I bring. Just now I saw
Your son within the port all safe and sound,
In a packet boat, and with him that young man.
Aye, and your slave Stalagmus, he who stole
Your son when four years old and ran away.

HEGIO: The deuce! You're joking!

ERGASILUS: So may Sacred Plenty,
The Deity I serve, be kind to me
And bless me always, as 'tis true I've seen—

HEGIO: My son?

ERGASILUS: Your son and my old patron too.

HEGIO: And the Elean captive?

ERGASILUS: By Apollo,
I have seen them.

HEGIO: And that old slave of mine
Who stole my son?

ERGASILUS: Yes, by the town of Cora!

HEGIO: Already?

ERGASILUS: Yes, I swear by famed Praeneste!

HEGIO: He's come?

ERGASILUS: Yes, by Sigaeum, if you like!

HEGIO: You're sure?

ERGASILUS: Why, yes, by Frasinone's town!

HEGIO: Quite sure?

ERGASILUS: Yes, by Alatrium itself!

HEGIO: Why do you swear by all these barbarous towns?

ERGASILUS: Because they are not easy to digest,
Just as you said your dinner too would be.

HEGIO: A plague upon you!

ERGASILUS: For you won't believe
The trouble I take; this slave of yours, Stalagmus,
What country was he of when he left you?

HEGIO: Of Sicily.

ERGASILUS: He is not now; he is
A Boan, with a constrictor round his neck;[8]
They've given him a wife, that he no more
May steal the child of others.

HEGIO: Tell me now,
Is this all true and *bona fide*?

ERGASILUS: Yes.

HEGIO: Ye gods immortal, I shall see again
                    My son, if this your tale is really true.

ERGASILUS: And do you doubt what I so solemnly
                    Have sworn? Now, Hegio, if you think so little
                    Of oaths, come to the port and see.

HEGIO (*eagerly*): Most certainly I will! Do you take care
                    Of all within. Take, ask, produce whate'er
                    You like; I make you butler for the time.

ERGASILUS: Yes, and unless what I have said is true,
                    A pretty dressing I shall get.

HEGIO: But if
                    It is true, I'll dine you till the crack of doom.

ERGASILUS: Who will?

HEGIO: My son and I.

ERGASILUS: You promise that?

HEGIO: I do.

ERGASILUS: And I declare your long-lost son has come.

HEGIO: Take all the care you can.

ERGASILUS: A pleasant walk to you.
                    (*Hegio departs to the harbour.*)

Act Four.   Scene III

ERGASILUS (*to himself*): He's gone and left the pantry in my charge
                    With all the food. What necks I will cut off!
                    What hams destroyed! And what a waste of lard!
                    What pigs' cheek used! What toothsome crackling
                       eaten!
                    What easy times the porksellers will have,
                    And butchers too! The other things that go
                    To feed the stomach take too long to tell.
                    Now to my office! I will fix the price
                    Of lard, and then will go to help those hams
                    Which hang unsentenced and yet uncondemned.

(ERGASILUS *goes into the house; a short time is supposed to elapse
before the next Scene.*)

Act Four.   Scene IV

(*Enter* SLAVE *from the house of* HEGIO.)

SLAVE (*angrily*): The gods destroy you and your stomach too,
          Ergasilus, and all the parasites,
          And all who shall encourage them henceforth!
          Calamity, and misery, and ill luck
          Have visited our house. I feared that he
          Like to a hungry wolf would fall on me.
          I was in dread of him; he gnashed his teeth.
          He came and upset everything at once,
          The meat and rack and all; he drew his sword
          And straight cut off three chunks. He broke
          The pots and cups, excepting only those
          That held a peck; and then he asked the cook
          If larger jars could not be used to boil.
          He broke down all the cupboards in the house,
          And threw the closets open. (*To those within*) Watch
             him now!
          I'll go and see the old man; if he wants,
          He must provide some fresh supplies, for if
          All this goes on, there is or will be nothing left.
             (*The* SLAVE *departs.*)

Act Five.   Scene I

(*Enter* HEGIO, PHILOPOLEMUS, PHILOCRATES, *and* STALAGMUS.)

HEGIO (*to* PHILOPOLEMUS): To Jove and to the gods I give great thanks.
          For that they have restored you to your father,
          And have delivered me from many ills,
          Which pressed me in your absence sore;
          And that they've placed this man in our control,
          And that the other's faithfulness is proved.

I've grieved enough; enough have worn myself
With tears and fasting.

PHILOPOLEMUS: I have heard enough
Of all the troubles that you told me of.
Now to the main point.

PHILOCRATES (*to* HEGIO):   What, since I have kept
Good faith with you and brought your son again,
What will you do?

HEGIO: You've acted so that I
Can never thank you half enough for all
You've done for me and for my son.

PHILOPOLEMUS: Father,
You can and I can too. The gods will give
Us power to recompense a man who well
Deserves reward from us; as you can do
To this man here.

HEGIO: What need of further words?
There is no tongue in which I can refuse
What you demand.

PHILOCRATES: I ask that you restore
To me the slave that I have left behind
In pledge for me, a slave who always was
Far better to me than he was to himself;
That I may pay him for the good he's done.

HEGIO: Let there be thanks for kindness thus received!
That which you ask, and any other prayer
You make, I grant; I do not wish that you
Should still be vexed because I punished him
And lost my temper.

PHILOCRATES: Pray what did you do?

HEGIO: Well, when I found he had deceived me so,
I sent him to the quarries fettered fast.

PHILOCRATES: Alas, alas, through me these troubles have
Oppressed the best of men.

HEGIO: And therefore now
You shall not pay a farthing for his ransom.
Take him; he is free.

PHILOCRATES: Thanks, Hegio, many thanks.
Please have him summoned here.

HEGIO: I will at once.
(*To slaves within*) Where are you? (*Enter slaves*) Go
and fetch him; bring him here.
(*To* PHILOPOLEMUS *and* PHILOCRATES, *as the slaves depart*)
You go within. Meantime I wish to ask
This fellow standing like a whipping post
What happened to the younger of my sons.
Now go and bathe.

PHILOPOLEMUS: And you, Philocrates,
Pray follow me within the house.

PHILOCRATES: I will.
(PHILOPOLEMUS *and* PHILOCRATES *go inside.*)

Act Five.   Scene II

HEGIO (*to* STALAGMUS): And now come hither, my fine slave that was.

STALAGMUS: What can I do, when you, being such a man,
Speak false? Handsome I never was, nor fine,
Nor good, nor of much use, nor ever will be.

HEGIO: But now you know with ease the point at which
Your fortunes stand. If you speak true, your case
Is better than it was. So speak the truth.
You've never done so hitherto at all.

STALAGMUS: D'ye think I am ashamed to tell the tale?

HEGIO: I'll make you blush; I'll make you red all over.

STALAGMUS: I see you threaten stripes, as if I ne'er
Had felt your blows before. Away with them,
And tell me what you want that you may get it.

HEGIO: You're very witty; please speak to the point.

STALAGMUS: Be it so.

HEGIO (*aside*):   He was obedient as a boy.
But not so now. (*Aloud*) Now give your mind to me

To answer what I ask. If you speak truth,
'Twill better be for you.

STALAGMUS: Now pray talk sense!
D'ye think I do not know what I deserve?

HEGIO: At least a portion you might still escape,
If not the whole.

STALAGMUS: 'Twill be but small, I know;
There's much that I deserve, because I fled
From you, and stole your son, and sold him too.

HEGIO: To whom?

STALAGMUS: Theodoromedes, one of
The Goldings, who then lived in Elis land,
For six minae.

HEGIO: Ye gods immortal! He
Was father to Philocrates.

STALAGMUS: I knew
Him better, saw him oftener than you.

HEGIO: Great Jupiter, look down on me and on
My son! (*Calling at the door*) Philocrates, I do be-
seech you
By your good genius to come out! I want you!

Act Five.   Scene III

(*Enter* PHILOCRATES *from the house.*)

PHILOCRATES: Hegio, I'm here. Command me what you will.

HEGIO: He says my son was to your father sold
For six minae.

PHILOCRATES: How long ago was that?

STALAGMUS: 'Tis twenty years since.

PHILOCRATES: He remembers wrong.

STALAGMUS: Or I, or you do; for your father gave
To you a little boy of four years old
To be your playmate.

PHILOCRATES: Pray what was his name?
If you speak truth, you should remember that.

STALAGMUS: Paegnium it was; you called him Tyndarus.

PHILOCRATES: Why did I know you not?

STALAGMUS: Because ofttimes
Men do not recognise, or even know
Those whose goodwill's a thing of nought to them.

PHILOCRATES: Tell me, is he whom you sold to my father,
Who was my playmate, is he Hegio's son?

STALAGMUS: Yes.

HEGIO: Does he live?

STALAGMUS: I took the price for him;
And I know nothing more.

HEGIO (*to* PHILOCRATES): What is't you say?

PHILOCRATES: This Tyndarus, he is indeed your son,
As this man proves. For he from earliest years
With me was brought up till he was a youth
Well and respectably.

HEGIO: If this be true,
I am happy and unfortunate at once.
Unfortunate because I treated ill
My very son. Ah! Why did I inflict
On him more evil and much less of good
Than justice called for? What I did of wrong
Is now my punishment; nor can it be
Recalled. But see, he is coming here again,
Not altogether dressed as he deserves.

Act Five.   Scene IV

(Enter TYNDARUS, *with a crowbar.)*

TYNDARUS *(to himself)*: I've often seen in pictures men pretend
To paint the woes of Acheron; but in truth
Nought is so like to Acheron as to be
Toiling in quarries. That's the place in which
Labour exacts all that the body has
Of strength and health. When I went there,
Just as to high-born boys are given to play with
Jackdaws, or ducks, or quails, so was I given
For my delight this crow. But here's my master
Before the door; and see, my other master
From Elis has returned.

HEGIO: My long-lost son!

TYNDARUS: What's that? My son? I know why you pretend
That you're my father, that I am your son;
Because, as parents do, you give me means
To see the light.

PHILOCRATES: Ah, Tyndarus, good day!

TYNDARUS: And you, for whom I undertook this toil.

PHILOCRATES: But I will straightway make you rich and free.
This is your father; this man here the slave
Who stole you when you were but four years old
And sold you to my father; he did give
You to me as a little boy for playmate.
The slave's confessed; we've brought him back from
     Elis.

TYNDARUS: What? This man's son?

PHILOCRATES: Yes. And of course your brother
Is in the house!

TYNDARUS: [What say you? Have you brought
The captive son of this man?

PHILOCRATES: He's within.

TYNDARUS: In this you've done a right and noble deed.

PHILOCRATES: . He is your father too; this is the thief
Who stole you from him.

TYNDARUS: I am now grown up,
And for his theft will give him to the gallows.

PHILOCRATES: He has deserved it.

TYNDARUS: I will give him now
His fit reward. (*To* HEGIO) But tell me, are you really
My father?

HEGIO: Yes, I am, my son; I am.

TYNDARUS: And now methinks my memory returns.][9]
I think as in a cloud, my father's name
Was Hegio.

HEGIO: I am he.

PHILOCRATES: I ask of you
That lighter may your son's chains now be made,
This slave's made heavier.

HEGIO: I have arranged
This should be done. Now let us go within;
And let the smith be summoned here to knock
The chains from this man, and to place them on
The other.

STALAGMUS: 'Tis well resolved indeed to give
To those who nothing have on which to live.

Epilogue

Spectators all, this story has been made
For chastest ears; and in it will you find
Nothing improper, no illicit loves,
No cheating, nought to shock the modest ear.
Few comedies of this sort you will find,
Where those already good ev'n still may learn
To better be. So you, if we have pleased
And not disgusted you, please make it clear;
Who vote for modesty, applaud our play.

ALLISON'S TRANSLATION has been altered slightly in the following verses: 274, 277, 353, 364, 438, 578, 580, 860, 888, 972; cf. also notes 6, 7, 8.

1. The verse translation of the argument is by E. H. Sugden.

2. A reference to the Porta Trigemina in Rome. Allison's note runs in part as follows: "Although the scene of the play is laid in Aetolia, Plautus, with his habitual disregard of geographical considerations, makes Ergasilus speak as if he was at Rome."

3. The literal meaning of the name is "the son of gold that surpasses treasures of gold." Paul Nixon renders it "Ducatsdoubloonsandpiecesofeightson."

4. Allison's note is as follows: "This, no doubt, would intensely amuse the audience, as there was no difficulty in Philocrates taking the most solemn oaths to be true to himself and his own interests."

5. Three famous madmen of Greek mythology.

6. Sugden's translation of this verse has been adapted; the pun in the original lies between *liber* ("free") and *Liber* (a name of Bacchus).

7. Sugden's translation has been adapted to preserve something of the word-play of the original.

8. Allison translates: "He is Bohemian, with a lady of that land." This fails to reproduce the effect of the original: "He's a Boian, he wears a *boia;*" *boia* signifies both a collar worn by slaves, and a woman of the tribe of the Boii.

9. This passage is bracketed by Lindsay as spurious.

VI
CASINA

Characters in the Play

OLYMPIO, *a slave, the overseer of* LYSIDAMUS
CHALINUS, *slave of* LYSIDAMUS *and armour-bearer of his son*
CLEUSTRATA, *wife of* LYSIDAMUS
PARDALISCA, *her maid-servant*
MYRRHINA, *wife of* ALCESIMUS
LYSIDAMUS, *an aged Athenian*
ALCESIMUS, *his neighbour*
CHYTRIO, *a cook*
Maids and attendants

Acrostic Argument

Two fellow-servants seek to marry a maid-servant; the old man encourages one, his son the other. A decision by lot favours the old man, but he is deceived by a stratagem. A rascally slave is substituted for the maiden, and the slave thrashes both his master and the overseer. The young man marries Casina when she is recognised as a citizen.

INTRODUCTION

THE *Casina*, although not considered one of the better plays of Plautus, is undoubtedly one of his most hilarious farces. The plot centers about the aged Lysidamus who has fallen in love with one of his wife's maids and has arranged to spend a night with her, with the assistance of a slave who is willing to marry the girl. The fact that his son is also in love with the girl merely makes the old gentleman all the more anxious to possess her. Lysidamus is assuredly the most worthless old reprobate in all Roman comedy. In *The Merchant* a father and a son are likewise rivals for the same girl, but the father in that instance does not know of his son's interest. In the *Casina* neither the girl nor the son appears upon the stage, but they are not needed, for the action deals entirely with the successive steps in the frustration of the old man's scheme; he is even double-crossed by his own helper. The impersonation of the bride in the closing scenes brings the comedy to a burlesque and indecent conclusion. The final address to the spectators evinces a low moral tone which is characteristic of the play as a whole.

There is strong evidence that the Greek original by Diphilus had a very different conclusion. Both in the prologue and in the final words the implication is given that Plautus has omitted the return of Euthynicus, the son, and also the recognition of Casina as the daughter of Alcesimus, which made possible her marriage to Euthynicus. In the Greek play, therefore, the farcical elements, if present, were subordinated to the fate of Casina. Plautus has dropped from the action the problem of Casina's identity and has made the play entirely one of comic deception. Many critics believe that much of the rough humour and especially the theme of the false bride have been derived from earlier popular Italian farces, e.g. the *fabula Atellana*, or at least are strongly indebted to them. There is no lack of unity in the action, however, for the lottery in which Lysidamus and his slave are victorious leads naturally to a well-deserved reversal of the situation. One unusual feature of the plot is the important part taken by Cleustrata, the wife; in most Roman comedies of deception it is the wily slave who engineers and supervises the intrigue; here the slaves play a secondary role, and

277

the ridiculous situation in which Lysidamus finds himself is the direct outcome of his wife's ingenuity.

The play is usually dated about 185 B.C. It shows much of the Roman playwright's originality, not only in its rapid action and farcical situations, but also in its unusually large number of lyric songs. No other Roman comedy contains so large a proportion of song, and the concluding scenes of the play (as is also true of *The Girl from Persia* and the *Pseudolus*) are particularly rich in rapidly changing lyric rhythms. Since it is believed that Plautus during his career gradually increased the quantity of lyrical *cantica* in his comedies, we seem justified in dating the play at the very end of his life.

It is to be expected that so amusing a farce would appeal to the average Roman spectator. That this was actually the case is shown by the prologue, part of which, at least, was composed for a later revival of the play about a generation after Plautus' death. Since the prologue states that only the older members of the audience would remember the original production, and comments also upon the worthlessness of contemporary comedy, it is safe to assume that Plautus, Caecilius, and probably Terence, were dead; the revival of the play would then fall somewhere about 150 B.C. Doubtless many other plays of Plautus were presented in this later period, e.g. *The Carthaginian*, which shows by its double conclusion that it has been reworked for a later performance. The *Casina* shows no trace of such reworking, however. After the comedies of Terence with their refinement in language and subtlety of plot, many a Roman spectator undoubtedly wished to see an "old-time" farce that would produce more uproarious and vulgar laughter. For such a purpose the *Casina* was an excellent choice.

CASINA

(SCENE:—*A street in Athens in front of the houses of* LYSIDAMUS *and* ALCESIMUS.)

Prologue

Welcome, excellent spectators, who most highly esteem the goddess Faith, and whom Faith esteems. If I have spoken the truth, give me loud applause that now, from the very beginning, I may know that you are favourably disposed towards me. Those who make use of old wine I consider wise, and those as well who, through choice, are spectators of old plays. Since ancient works and words are pleasing to you, it is right that old plays should please you above all; for the new comedies which are produced at the present time are much more worthless than new coins. Since we have heard the report in public that you eagerly desire the plays of Plautus, we have produced this ancient comedy of his, which you older men approved; I realise that those who are younger are not acquainted with it; still, we shall carefully endeavour to make them acquainted with it. When this play was first produced it surpassed all other plays. In those days there was the very flower of the poets,[1] who have now departed to their common home. But though departed, yet are they of advantage to those now living. I earnestly beg all of you to pay kind attention to our company. Cast from your minds cares and thoughts of debt; let no man stand in dread of his duns. This is a holiday; to the bankers a holiday has been given; there is a calm and these are Halcyon days about the forum. They act reasonably; during the games they ask no one for money; after the games, however, they pay no one. If your ears are disengaged, pay attention; I wish to give you the name of the comedy. In Greek this comedy is called *Clerumenoe;* in Latin, *Sortientes.*[2] Diphilus wrote it in Greek, and after that Plautus with the barking name[3] wrote it over again in Latin.

(*Pointing to the house of* LYSIDAMUS) An old married man is living here; he has a son; the son lives with his father in this house. He has a certain slave who is lying in sickness—or rather, in his bed, to speak the truth. Sixteen years ago, it happened that this slave, at early dawn, saw a baby girl being exposed. He straightway approached the woman who was exposing it and begged her to give it to him; he gained his request and took it away; he carried it straight home, gave it to his mistress, and entreated her to take care of the baby and bring it up. His mistress did this; she reared the girl with great care, as though it had been her own daughter, not much different.

Now that she has grown old enough to attract men, this old gentleman loves her to distraction, and on the other hand, so does his son. Each of them now is gathering his legions, both father and son, each unknown to the other. The father has commissioned his overseer to ask for her as his wife; and he hopes that, if she is given to the overseer, he'll have something to keep him awake away from home without his wife's knowledge; but the son has commissioned his armour-bearer to ask to marry her; he knows that if he gains this request, there will be an object for him to love, within his abode. The wife of the old gentleman has found out that he is giving thought to a love affair, and for that reason she is plotting with her son. But the father, when he found out that his son was in love with this same woman and was in his way, sent the young man abroad on business. His mother, understanding this, still lends him her assistance in his absence. He will not return to the city today in this comedy; don't expect it; Plautus did not wish it, and broke down the bridge that was on his route.

There are some here, I believe, who are now saying among themselves: "What in heaven's name does this mean? The marriage of a slave? Are slaves to be marrying wives, or asking them for themselves? They've introduced something new—a thing that's done nowhere in the world." But I declare that this is done in Greece and in Carthage, and here in our land in Apulia; and the marriages of slaves are usually treated there with more fuss than even those of free persons. If this isn't a fact, whoever wishes shall make a bet for a jug of wine, provided that a Carthaginian is the umpire in my cause, or a Greek in fact, or an Apulian. (*A pause.*) What now? You don't take it? No one's thirsty, I believe.

I'll return to that foundling girl, whom the two slaves wish with all their heart to marry. She'll be found to be both chaste and free, an Athenian girl of freeborn parents, nor will she be guilty of any immodesty—in this comedy, at least. But after the play is over, I suspect that, if any one offers the money, she'll quickly enter into wedlock with him and won't wait for favourable omens. This is all. Farewell, be prosperous in your affairs, and conquer by true valour, as you've done hitherto.

Act One

(*Enter* OLYMPIO, *followed by* CHALINUS.)

OLYMPIO: Can't I speak and think about my own affairs by myself, as I wish, without you prying around? Why the devil are you following me?

CHALINUS: Because I'm determined always to follow you wherever you go, just like your shadow. By heaven, I'm determined to follow you even if you wish to go to the cross. So you figure out whether or not you can secretly keep me from marrying Casina by your tricks, as you expect to do.

OLYMPIO: What business have you with me?

CHALINUS: Look here, you bag of impudence. Why are you crawling about in the city, you good-for-nothing overseer?

OLYMPIO: Because I wish to.

CHALINUS: But why aren't you in the country, in your own bailiwick? Why don't you pay attention to the business that has been entrusted to you, and keep from meddling in city matters? Have you come here to snatch away my betrothed? Be off to the country, be off to your province and be hanged!

OLYMPIO: Chalinus, I haven't forgotten my duty. I've put a person in charge who will look after matters properly in the country. If I gain what I came here to the city for, to marry the girl that you're crazy about—the fair and charming Casina, your fellow-servant—when I've carried her off with me to the country as my wife, then I'll stick fast in the country at my post of command.

CHALINUS: What, you marry her? By heaven, I'd sooner hang myself than have you get possession of her.

OLYMPIO: She's my prize; so you can put yourself into the noose.

CHALINUS: You offscouring of a dungheap, is she to be your prize?

OLYMPIO: You'll find it to be the case.

CHALINUS: Damn you!

OLYMPIO: In how many ways, if I live, I'll make you miserable at my wedding!

CHALINUS: What will you do to me?

OLYMPIO: What will I do to you? First of all, you'll light the wedding torch for this new bride of mine. Then, after that, so that you'll always be worthless and of no account, when you get to the country-house, a single pitcher will be given to you, and a single path, a single spring, a single brass caldron and eight casks; and unless these shall always be filled, I'll fill you with lashes. I'll make you so thoroughly bent from carrying water that a horse's crupper can be made out of you. And after this in the country, unless you eat from a pile of fodder or feed on dirt like a worm, should you wish to taste any food, never, by heaven, is hunger as full of hungriness as I'll make you in the country. After that, when you're weary and famished, I'll see that you go to bed at night as you deserve.

CHALINUS: What will you do?

OLYMPIO: You shall be shut up tight in a little window, where you can listen while I am kissing her, while she is saying to me: "My little soul, my own Olympio, my life, my honey-sweet, my delight, let me kiss your dear eyes, my darling! Do let yourself be loved, there's a dear! Oh, my day of happiness, my sparrow-chick, my dove, my rabbit!" When she utters these sweet little words, then, you rogue, you'll wriggle about in the middle of the wall like a mouse. Now I'm going in, so you needn't try to answer back. I'm tired of your talk.

(*He goes into the house of* LYSIDAMUS.)

CHALINUS: I'll follow you. You'll certainly do nothing here without my knowing it.

(*Follows him into the house.*)

Act Two. Scene I

(*Enter* CLEUSTRATA *and* PARDALISCA *from the house of* LYSIDAMUS.)

CLEUSTRATA (*to servants within*): Seal fast the storerooms, bring back the signet to me. I'm going here to my neighbour next door; if my husband wants me for anything, send for me here.

PARDALISCA: The old gentleman wants his breakfast prepared for him.

CLEUSTRATA: Tut! Hold your tongue and be off. (*To herself, as* PARDALISCA *goes into the house*) I won't prepare it and it shan't be cooked today, since he opposes me and his own son for the sake of his desire and his passion, the foul old duffer! I'll punish that lover with hunger, I'll punish him with thirst, with hard words, with hardships. I'll distress him properly with irritating talk; I'll make him live a life in the future as he deserves—fit food for Acheron, a hunter after iniquity, a stable of infamy! Now I'll go to my neighbour's house to lament my lot. But the door is opening and there she is, coming out. On my word, I've not started for my call at a convenient time.

Act Two.   Scene II

(*Enter* MYRRHINA *from the house of* ALCESIMUS.)

MYRRHINA (*to her servants, at the door*): Follow me here next door, attendants. You there! Does anyone hear what I say? I shall be here, if my husband or anyone seeks me. For when I am home alone, I'm too drowsy to work. Didn't I order my distaff to be brought to me?

CLEUSTRATA: Good morning, Myrrhina.

MYRRHINA: My word, good morning! But why are you sad, pray tell?

CLEUSTRATA: That's the way all usually are who are unhappily married; at home and away from home there's always enough to make them sad. But I was going to your house.

MYRRHINA: And indeed, I was coming here to you. But what is it that now makes you unhappy? For what makes you unhappy likewise distresses me.

CLEUSTRATA: On my word, I do believe you. For with good reason I love no woman neighbour of mine better than yourself, nor in anyone are there more good traits that I should wish for myself.

MYRRHINA: I love you, and I wish to know what this trouble is.

CLEUSTRATA: My husband insults me at home in a most shameful manner.

MYRRHINA: Hah! What is it? Tell me again, I beg (for on my word, I haven't clearly understood your complaints).

CLEUSTRATA: My husband insults me in a most shameful manner, and I have no opportunity to enjoy my own rights.

MYRRHINA: This is surprising, if you tell the truth, for husbands can hardly obtain from their wives what's their own right.

CLEUSTRATA: Why, he demands from me, against my will, a female servant who is mine and has been brought up at my expense, to give her to his overseer—but he's the one in love with her.

MYRRHINA: Please tell me about it, for you can speak frankly now; we're all alone.

CLEUSTRATA: That's true.

MYRRHINA: Where did you get her? For a good wife ought not to have any property without her husband's knowledge, and if she does have any, she hasn't acquired it properly; she's either stolen it from her husband or got it by being unfaithful. I'm of the opinion that whatever you have belongs to your husband.

CLEUSTRATA (*annoyed*): You're certainly saying everything against your friend's interests.

MYRRHINA: Hush now, you simpleton, and listen to me. Please don't keep opposing him; let him love, let him do what he wishes, as long as you lack nothing at home.

CLEUSTRATA: Are you really in your right senses? For you're saying this against your own interests.

MYRRHINA: Silly, always avoid this statement from your husband.

CLEUSTRATA: What statement?

MYRRHINA: "Woman, get out of the house!" [4]

CLEUSTRATA (*looking down the street*): Sh-h! Be quiet!

MYRRHINA: What's the matter?

CLEUSTRATA: There!

MYRRHINA: Whom do you see?

CLEUSTRATA: Look, my husband's coming! Go inside, hurry up, please go!

MYRRHINA: All right, I'll go.

CLEUSTRATA: Later, when we have more leisure, I'll talk with you. Good-bye for the present.

MYRRHINA: Good-bye. (*Goes into her house.* CLEUSTRATA *returns to her doorway.*)

Act Two.   Scene III

(Enter LYSIDAMUS, *very debonair.)*

LYSIDAMUS *(to himself)*: I'm convinced that love surpasses everything, all delights that are delicious; nor can anything be mentioned
that has more relish or flavour. I'm certainly surprised that the cooks
who use spices don't use this one spice that excels all others. For when
love is used as a spice, I believe that the food will please everyone.
Nothing can be salty or sweet unless love is mixed with it. It will turn
bitter gall to honey and make a nice neat fellow out of a grouch. I
venture this prophecy more from my own case at home than from
hearsay. Now that I'm in love with Casina, I've perked up, I'm more
elegant than Elegance itself. I keep the perfumers busy; I use all the
nicest ointments to please her; and I do please her, I believe. But my
wife tortures me—by being alive. *(Catches sight of* CLEUSTRATA) I see
her standing there angry. I'll have to speak smoothly to this wretched
piece of goods. *(Going towards her)* How are you, my wife and my
delight? *(Tries to embrace her.)*

CLEUSTRATA: Get away; don't touch me.

LYSIDAMUS: Look here, my dear Juno, you shouldn't be so cross to
your Jupiter. Where are you going now?

CLEUSTRATA: Let me alone.

LYSIDAMUS: Wait.

CLEUSTRATA: I won't wait.

LYSIDAMUS: Then, by heaven, I'll follow you.

CLEUSTRATA: Look here! Are you sane?

LYSIDAMUS: Of course I'm sane. How I love you!

CLEUSTRATA: I don't want you to love me.

LYSIDAMUS: You can't have your own way there.

CLEUSTRATA: You're tormenting me to death.

LYSIDAMUS *(aside)*: I wish you were speaking the truth.

CLEUSTRATA *(overhearing)*: I believe you in that.

LYSIDAMUS: Please look back, my sweet.

CLEUSTRATA: About as sweet as you are to me. Look here! Where does this smell of ointment come from?

LYSIDAMUS (*aside*): Damnation! I'm caught in the act. I'm slow in wiping off my head with my cloak. May good Mercury curse you, perfumer, for providing me with the stuff.

CLEUSTRATA: Oh, you worthless, hoary-headed gnat! I can't keep from telling you what you ought to hear. Do you walk through the streets reeking with perfume at your time of life, you silly old fool?

LYSIDAMUS: I was just helping a certain friend of mine while he was buying perfume.

CLEUSTRATA (*aside*): How quickly he made that one up! (*Aloud*) Don't you have any shame?

LYSIDAMUS: Any that you wish.

CLEUSTRATA: What low dives have you been lying around in?

LYSIDAMUS (*with an air of innocence*): I, in low dives?

CLEUSTRATA: I know more than you think I do.

LYSIDAMUS: What's this? What do you know?

CLEUSTRATA: That you're the most worthless of all old men. Where are you coming from, you good-for-nothing? Where've you been? Where've you been wandering about? Where've you been drinking? Good heavens! You're drunk; look how wrinkled your cloak is!

LYSIDAMUS: May the gods damn us both, if I have put a drop of wine in my mouth today.

CLEUSTRATA: Well then, keep on as you wish; drink, eat, and squander your property.

LYSIDAMUS: O-ho! Now she's quite the wife; restrain yourself; you're chattering too much. Leave some of your talk for quarreling with me tomorrow. But look here! Have you subdued your temper so that you can do what your husband wants done instead of opposing him?

CLEUSTRATA: About what?

LYSIDAMUS: Do you ask? About your maid Casina, that she be married to our overseer, a worthy slave, where she'll be well off with wood, hot water, food, clothing, and where she can bring up the children she may have, rather than give her to that rascally slave, that worthless and dishonest armour-bearer, who doesn't even have a lead penny in his savings.

CLEUSTRATA: I'm certainly surprised that you don't remember your duty at your time of life.

LYSIDAMUS: How so?

CLEUSTRATA: Because, if you were to act rightly or sensibly, you'd let me take care of the maids—that's my business.

LYSIDAMUS: Why the devil do you want to give her to that shield-carrier?

CLEUSTRATA: Because we ought to help our only son.

LYSIDAMUS: But although he is an only son, he's not a bit more my only son than I am his only father; he ought to yield to my wishes rather than I to his.

CLEUSTRATA: You're certainly seeking trouble for yourself, man.

LYSIDAMUS (*aside*): She suspects, I guess. (*To his wife*) I?

CLEUSTRATA: Yes, you. What are you stammering for? Why are you so eager for this arrangement?

LYSIDAMUS: So she can be married to a good slave instead of a worthless one.

CLEUSTRATA: What if I prevail upon and persuade the overseer for my sake to give her up to the other one?

LYSIDAMUS: But what if I prevail upon the armour-bearer to give her up to the other one? And I think that I can do it.

CLEUSTRATA: Agreed. Do you want me to call Chalinus out here for you? You ask him and I'll ask the overseer.

LYSIDAMUS: I'm willing.

CLEUSTRATA: He'll soon be here. Now we'll find out which of us is the more persuasive. (*She goes into the house.*)

LYSIDAMUS: May Hercules and the gods destroy her—a thing that now I can say. I'm tortured with love, but she opposes me as though on purpose. My wife has some suspicion of this plot of mine; that's why she's purposely helping the armour-bearer.

Act Two.   Scene IV

(Enter CHALINUS *from the house.)*

LYSIDAMUS *(aside, on seeing him)*: May all the powers above destroy him.

CHALINUS: Your wife said that you were calling me.

LYSIDAMUS: Yes, I had you called.

CHALINUS: Tell me what you want.

LYSIDAMUS: First of all, I want you to speak to me with a more cheerful countenance. It's foolish for you to be disagreeable to a person who has more power. *(Speaking more pleasantly)* For a long time now I've considered you a worthy and upright fellow.

CHALINUS: I understand. But if you think so, why don't you give me my freedom?

LYSIDAMUS: That's what I want to do. But my desire in the matter doesn't mean anything, unless you aid me by your actions.

CHALINUS: My only desire is to know your wishes.

LYSIDAMUS: Listen; I'll tell you. I've promised to marry Casina to our overseer.

CHALINUS: But your wife and your son promised her to me.

LYSIDAMUS: I know that. But do you prefer to be single and a free man, or to be married and live, you and your sons, in slavery? The choice is yours; accept whichever condition you wish.

CHALINUS: If I were free, I'd live at my own cost; as it is, I live at yours. As to Casina, I'm determined to yield to no one.

LYSIDAMUS: Go in and call my wife out here at once; and bring out here an urn, with some water, and the lots.[5]

CHALINUS: That's quite satisfactory.

LYSIDAMUS: By heaven, I'll put an end to that attack of yours some way or other; for if I can't get anywhere by persuasion, at least I'll try it by lot. There I'll take vengeance on you and your supporters.

CHALINUS: But the lot will fall to me.

LYSIDAMUS: Yes, so that you can perish in horrible torment.

CHALINUS: She'll marry me, no matter what sort of plot you make.

LYSIDAMUS: Won't you get out of my sight!

CHALINUS (*flippantly*): You don't like the sight of me, but I'll live on. (*He goes into the house.*)

LYSIDAMUS (*to himself*): Well, if I'm not a wretched person! Is everything really against me? Now I'm afraid that my wife has persuaded Olympio not to marry Casina; if that happens, here am I, an old man done for! If she hasn't persuaded him, there's still a ray of hope for me in the lottery. But if the lot fails me, I'll turn my sword into a pillow and lay me down upon it. But look, here's Olympio coming out at just the right time.

Act Two. Scene V

(*Enter* OLYMPIO *from the house.*)

OLYMPIO (*speaking to* CLEUSTRATA *within*): By heaven, you might just as well stick me into a hot oven and bake me there like a brown biscuit, ma'am, as to get me to do what you want.

LYSIDAMUS (*aside*): I'm safe; my hope is saved, judging from his words.

OLYMPIO (*still talking to* CLEUSTRATA *inside*): Why do you keep frightening me about my freedom, ma'am? Even if you and your son are unwilling, for one penny I can become free, against your wishes and in spite of you both.

LYSIDAMUS (*stepping forward*): What's this? Who are you wrangling with, Olympio?

OLYMPIO: With the same person that you always are.

LYSIDAMUS: With my wife?

OLYMPIO: What wife do you mean? You're really a sort of hunter—you spend your life day and night with a bitch.

LYSIDAMUS: What is she doing, what is she talking to you about?

OLYMPIO: She's begging, beseeching me not to marry Casina.

LYSIDAMUS: What did you say after that?

OLYMPIO: I said that I wouldn't give her up to Jupiter himself, if he should beg me to.

LYSIDAMUS: The gods preserve you for me!

OLYMPIO: Now she's in a terrible stew, she's so swollen with anger at me.

LYSIDAMUS: By heaven, I wish she would burst in the middle.

OLYMPIO: By heaven, I think she will, if you're good for anything. But this confounded love affair of yours is a nuisance: your wife is angry at me, your son is angry; the servants are angry.

LYSIDAMUS: What difference does it make to you? As long as this Jupiter (*pointing to himself*) is only favourable to you, don't you pay any attention to those lesser gods.

OLYMPIO: That's great nonsense; as if you didn't know how suddenly these human Jupiters die. And if at length you become a dead Jupiter, when your kingdom falls to the lesser gods, who then will come to the rescue of my back or head or legs?

LYSIDAMUS: Affairs will go better with you than you expect, if we gain this—that I sleep with Casina.

OLYMPIO: But damn it! I don't think it can be; your wife is so bitterly opposed to giving the girl to me.

LYSIDAMUS: This is what I'll do: I'll put the lots in an urn and draw for you and Chalinus. I think the affair has come to this pass: it's necessary to take swords and fight it out.

OLYMPIO: What if the lottery turns out contrary to your wish?

LYSIDAMUS: Speak with good omen. I trust the gods; we'll put our hope in the gods.

OLYMPIO: I wouldn't pay an itty-bitty titbit[6] for that statement; for everyone trusts the gods, but I've seen many of these god-trusting people deceived, just the same.

LYSIDAMUS: Sh-h! Be quiet a bit.

OLYMPIO: What's the matter?

LYSIDAMUS (*pointing*): Look! There's Chalinus coming out with the urn and the lots. Now we'll advance our standards and fight it out.

Act Two. Scene VI

(*Enter* CLEUSTRATA *and* CHALINUS *with the urn and lots.*)

CLEUSTRATA: Chalinus, tell me what my husband wants with me.

CHALINUS: He wants to see you dead and burning outside the gate.

CLEUSTRATA: Dear me, I suppose he does.

CHALINUS: Gad, I don't suppose it; I know it for certain.

LYSIDAMUS: I have more professional men here than I realised; I've got a **fortuneteller** here in my house. What if we move our standards nearer and go to meet them? Follow me. (*Advances to the other pair*) What are you two doing?

CHALINUS: Everything that you ordered is here: wife, lots, urn, and myself.

OLYMPIO: You're one person more than I want here.

CHALINUS: It just seems so to you; I'm stinging you now, I'm pricking your dear little heart; even now you're sweating with fear, you rascal.

LYSIDAMUS: Hush, Chalinus!

CHALINUS: Then you hold him back.

OLYMPIO (*pointing to* CHALINUS): No, that fellow; he likes to be held.

LYSIDAMUS: Place the urn here, give me the lots. Pay attention. And yet I did think, wife, that I could persuade you to have Casina married to me; and even now I think so.

CLEUSTRATA: Have her married to you?

LYSIDAMUS: Yes, to me—oh, I didn't mean to say that; when I said "to him," I meant "to me," and (*somewhat wildly*) while I'm wanting for myself—oh God! now I've got all mixed up.

CLEUSTRATA: You certainly have, and you still are.

LYSIDAMUS: To him—no, to me—Damn! (*Collecting himself*) Now at last I've got back on the right track, with difficulty.

CLEUSTRATA: Upon my word, you're having a lot of difficulty.

LYSIDAMUS: That's what happens, when you desire something terribly. But each of us, he (*pointing to* OLYMPIO) and I, appeal to you, recognising your rights.

CLEUSTRATA: What's this?

LYSIDAMUS: Well, I'll tell you, my sweet. As to this Casina, you should present her to this overseer of ours.

CLEUSTRATA: Well, I don't, and I don't intend to.

LYSIDAMUS: Then I'll divide the lots between them.

CLEUSTRATA: Who hinders you?

LYSIDAMUS: I judge that this is the best and fairest way. We'll be happy afterward, if it turns out as we wish; if not, we'll be calm and make the best of it. (*Giving a lot to* OLYMPIO) Take this lot. See what's written on it.

OLYMPIO: Number one.

CHALINUS: That's not fair, because he has one before I do.

LYSIDAMUS: Take this, will you. (*Giving a lot to* CHALINUS.)

CHALINUS: Give it to me. Wait; one thing just occurred to me. (*To* CLEUSTRATA) Just see that there isn't any other lot at the bottom of the water.

LYSIDAMUS: Rogue! Do you take me for yourself?

CLEUSTRATA: There isn't any; just be calm.

CHALINUS: May this prove lucky and fortunate for me—

OLYMPIO: By gad, it will prove to be a great misfortune for you, I fancy; I know your pious ways. But wait; is that lot of yours of poplar or fir?

CHALINUS: Why do you care about that?

OLYMPIO: Because I'm afraid that it will float on the top of the water.

LYSIDAMUS: Fine! Be on your guard. Now both of you throw in your lots. There they are! Wife, keep everything fair.

OLYMPIO: Don't trust your wife.

LYSIDAMUS: Don't worry.

OLYMPIO: She'll lay a curse on the lots this very day, if she touches them, I'm sure.

LYSIDAMUS: Be quiet.

OLYMPIO: I am quiet. I pray the gods—

CHALINUS: That you may wear the chain and yoke today.

OLYMPIO: —that the lot may fall to me—

CHALINUS: To hang up by your feet, by heaven.

OLYMPIO: That you blow your eyes out of your head through your nose.

CHALINUS: What are you afraid of? You ought to have it ready for you now—a noose, I mean.

OLYMPIO: You're done for.

LYSIDAMUS: Pay attention now, both of you.

OLYMPIO: I'm quiet.

LYSIDAMUS: Now Cleustrata, I entrust it to you, so that you can't say or suspect that I have cheated in this matter; you draw the lot.

OLYMPIO: You're ruining me.

CHALINUS: He profits by that.

CLEUSTRATA (*to* LYSIDAMUS): That's kind of you.

CHALINUS (*to* OLYMPIO): I pray the gods—that your lot may run away from the urn.

OLYMPIO: What's that you say? Just because you're a runaway slave, do you expect everyone to imitate you? I wish that that lot of yours would melt away in the drawing, as that of the descendants of Hercules[7] once did.

CHALINUS: And I wish that you would soon be made so hot with whips that you would melt.

LYSIDAMUS: Pay attention, please, Olympio.

OLYMPIO: If this well-lettered person (*pointing to the brand on the forehead of* CHALINUS) will let me.

LYSIDAMUS: May this prove lucky and fortunate for me.

OLYMPIO: Yes indeed, and for me too.

CHALINUS: No!

OLYMPIO: Yes, by heaven!

CHALINUS: Yes, by heaven—for me!

CLEUSTRATA (*to* OLYMPIO): He'll win, and you'll live in misery.

LYSIDAMUS (*to* OLYMPIO): Punch that fellow in the jaw. Come, what's the matter? (*To* CHALINUS) Don't you raise your hand.

OLYMPIO: Shall I punch him with my fist or my open hand?

LYSIDAMUS: Just as you wish.

OLYMPIO: There, take that!

CLEUSTRATA: What did you hit him for?

OLYMPIO: Because my Jupiter ordered me to.

CLEUSTRATA (*to* CHALINUS): You hit him back, the same way. (CHALINUS *does so eagerly.*)

OLYMPIO: Murder! I'm being punched with his fists, Jupiter.

LYSIDAMUS (*to* CHALINUS): What did you hit him for?

CHALINUS: Because my Juno (*pointing to* CLEUSTRATA) ordered it.

LYSIDAMUS: I have to put up with it, since my wife is boss as long as I live.

CLEUSTRATA: He (*pointing to* CHALINUS) ought to be allowed to speak as much as that fellow.

OLYMPIO: Why does he spoil my omen?

LYSIDAMUS: Chalinus, you'd better be on your guard against a mishap.

CHALINUS: Fine time to tell me, after my face has been smashed.

LYSIDAMUS: Come now, wife, draw the lot. You two pay attention. (*Aside*) I'm so scared I don't know where I am. I'm done for! I've got a heart full of spleen, I guess, it's been jumping around so long; it's working hard, thumping against my chest.

CLEUSTRATA (*putting her hand in the urn*): I have the lot.

LYSIDAMUS: Draw it out.

CHALINUS (*to* OLYMPIO): Aren't you dead now?

OLYMPIO: Show it to me. It's mine.

CHALINUS (*disgusted*): This is certainly a pretty mess.

CLEUSTRATA: You're defeated, Chalinus.

LYSIDAMUS: I'm delighted that the gods have been on our side, Olympio.

OLYMPIO: Thanks to my piety and that of my forefathers.

LYSIDAMUS: Go in, wife, and make arrangements for the wedding.

CLEUSTRATA: I'll do as you order.

LYSIDAMUS: Don't you know that it's a long way from here to the house in the country, where he is to take her?

CLEUSTRATA: I know that.

LYSIDAMUS: Go in and make the arrangements, even though it is distasteful to you.

CLEUSTRATA: Very well (*She goes into the house.*)

LYSIDAMUS: Let's us go in, too; let's urge them to hurry.

OLYMPIO: I'm not delaying you, am I?

LYSIDAMUS: For I don't want to talk any more with this fellow present. (LYSIDAMUS *and* OLYMPIO *go inside.*)

Act Two.   Scene VII

CHALINUS (*to himself*): If I should hang myself now, I'd be wasting my time and in addition to the trouble, I'd have to waste money on a rope, and I'd be giving pleasure to my enemies. What's the need of it, because I'm dead as it is? Now I've been beaten at the lottery, Casina will marry the overseer. And yet this isn't so annoying to have the overseer win out, as it is that the old man was so terribly eager for her to marry him and not me. What a tremble he was in! How he bustled about in anguish! And how he capered about after the overseer won! A-ha! I'll step aside here; I hear the door opening; my friends and well-wishers are coming out. I'll lay a snare here for them from this ambush.

Act Two. Scene VIII

(*Enter* OLYMPIO *and* LYSIDAMUS *from the house.*)

OLYMPIO: Just let him come to the country; I'll send the fellow back to the city to you under the yoke like a charcoal peddler.

LYSIDAMUS: That's what you ought to do.

OLYMPIO: I'll see that it's done properly, too.

LYSIDAMUS: I intended to send Chalinus with you to buy provisions, if he were at home; I wanted to add this unhappiness to our enemy, on top of his present sadness.

CHALINUS (*aside*): I'll snuggle up to the wall, I'll imitate a crab; I must overhear their conversation without their knowing it. For one of them tortures me, the other torments me. This rascal is marching about dressed in white, just ready for a whipping. I'll postpone my own death; I'm determined to send this fellow to Hades first.

OLYMPIO: How helpful I've been to you! I've given you the chance to have what you particularly desired. You'll have your sweetheart with you today without your wife knowing about it.

LYSIDAMUS: May all the gods bless me, I can hardly keep my lips from kissing you for this reason, my darling. (*Prepares to embrace* OLYMPIO.)

CHALINUS (*aside*): What does this "kissing" mean? What goes on here? "Your darling," eh? By gad, I believe he wants to dig out the overseer's bladder.

OLYMPIO: Oh, so you love me a little now, eh?

LYSIDAMUS: Much more than myself, by heaven. Can I embrace you?

CHALINUS (*aside*): What the devil? "Embrace him?"

OLYMPIO: Of course.

LYSIDAMUS (*embracing him*): It's just like tasting honey when I touch you.

OLYMPIO (*pushing him away*): Get the devil off my back, you lover!

CHALINUS (*aside*): That's it, that's the reason why he made him overseer. And once that same person, when I went to bring him home, wanted to make me his chamberlain at the doorway.

OLYMPIO: What a help I've been to you today! What a source of pleasure!

LYSIDAMUS: So that I'll be more devoted to you than to myself, as long as I live.

CHALINUS (*aside*): Lord! These two will have their feet close together today, I'll bet. This old man certainly likes to chase after beards!

LYSIDAMUS: How I'll kiss Casina today! What a grand time I'll have away from my wife!

CHALINUS (*aside*): Oho! Now at last I'm on the right track. He's the one that's crazy about Casina. I've got the men now.

LYSIDAMUS: I'm so damned eager to hug her, to kiss her right now.

OLYMPIO: Let me take her home first. What the devil is your hurry?

LYSIDAMUS: I'm in love.

OLYMPIO: But I don't think that it can be managed today.

LYSIDAMUS: Yes it can, if you think that you can get your freedom to-morrow.

CHALINUS (*aside*): I certainly must make better use of my ears here; I'll make a clever job of catching two boars in one thicket.

LYSIDAMUS: I've a place ready for me here at the house of my friend and neighbour. (*Pointing to the house of* ALCESIMUS) I've entrusted my whole love affair to him; he said that he would find me a room.

OLYMPIO: What about his wife? Where will she be?

LYSIDAMUS: I've fixed that neatly. My wife will invite her over here for the wedding, to be with her, to help her, to sleep with her. I've requested it and my wife said she'd do it. Myrrhina will spend the night at our house, and her husband will be out of the house, I'll see to that. You'll take your wife to the country; but that country shall be in this house, at least long enough for me to have my marriage with Casina. Then tomorrow morning before dawn you'll take her off to the country. Isn't that pretty clever?

OLYMPIO: Neat.

CHALINUS (*aside*): Just keep on with your tricks; you'll suffer for being so damned smart.

LYSIDAMUS: Do you know what you're to do now?

OLYMPIO: Tell me.

LYSIDAMUS: Take this purse; go and buy some provisions; hurry, but I want it done nicely; some delicacies, since she herself is a delicate piece.

OLYMPIO: Very well.

LYSIDAMUS: Buy some little sepias, mussels, cuttle-lets, barley-fish.

CHALINUS (*aside*): No, wheat-fish, if you're wise.

LYSIDAMUS: And some soles.

CHALINUS (*aside*): Why not wooden soles for banging your head with, you wicked old walrus?

OLYMPIO: Do you wish some tongue-fish?

LYSIDAMUS: What need of it, since my wife's at home? She's my tongue-fish, for her tongue is never still.

OLYMPIO: I'll be able to look over the supply of fish in the market and decide what to buy.

LYSIDAMUS: Fair enough; now be off. Don't mind the cost; buy generously. Now I must meet this neighbour of mine again, so that he'll do what I requested.

OLYMPIO: Am I to go now?

LYSIDAMUS: I want you to. (*Exit* OLYMPIO; LYSIDAMUS *enters the house of* ALCESIMUS.)

CHALINUS (*to himself*): I couldn't be hired by three freedoms not to make plenty of trouble for these two today and not to reveal the whole story to my mistress. I have my enemies, they're caught in the act. If my mistress is willing to do her duty, the whole contest is ours. I'll utterly outwit the men. The day advances with favorable omens; though outsmarted we win out. I'll go in to season now in a different way what some other cook has seasoned, so that the stew ready for him won't be ready and one will be ready for him which wasn't ready. (*He goes into the house of* LYSIDAMUS.)

Act Three.   Scene I

(Enter LYSIDAMUS *and* ALCESIMUS *from the latter's house.)*

LYSIDAMUS: Now I'll know whether you're the image of a friend or a foe, Alcesimus; now the proof is placed, now the test is taken. Just stop blaming me for being in love; stop talking about "grey hair," "unfit age;" stop talking about "one who has a wife," too.

ALCESIMUS: I never saw anyone crazier with love than you.

LYSIDAMUS: Make sure that the house is empty.

ALCESIMUS: Heavens, yes! I've decided to send all the menservants and maids to your house.

LYSIDAMUS: Oho! You're a pretty shrewd fellow. But be sure you remember the blackbird's song and have them come "with food, with everything," as though going to Sutrium.[8]

ALCESIMUS: I'll remember it.

LYSIDAMUS: There, that's settled. You're pretty shrewd by yourself. You make the arrangements; I'll go to the forum; I'll soon be back.

ALCESIMUS: Have a pleasant walk.

LYSIDAMUS: Make sure that your house gets a tongue.

ALCESIMUS: Why so?

LYSIDAMUS: That it may invite me in when I return.

ALCESIMUS: Bunk! You need a good basting; you're too full of jokes.

LYSIDAMUS: What's the use of being in love, if I'm not acute and clever? But don't you keep me waiting.

ALCESIMUS: I'll be right here at home. (LYSIDAMUS *departs;* ALCESIMUS *goes into his house.)*

Act Three.   Scene II

(Enter CLEUSTRATA *from her house.)*

CLEUSTRATA *(to herself)*: This was the reason, then, that my husband begged me so earnestly to hurry and invite my neighbour to my house

—that the house would be empty for them to take Casina there. Now I certainly won't invite her and give those two good-for-nothings a place to play in, the decrepit old goats. But there he is coming out, the pillar of the senate, the safeguard of the state, my neighbour who gives my husband a room for his roguery. On my word, he isn't worth the measure of salt that was sold to him.

(*Enter* ALCESIMUS *from his house.*)

ALCESIMUS (*to himself*): I wonder why my wife hasn't been invited over to the house next door; she's been ready and awaiting the invitation for some time. (*Seeing* CLEUSTRATA) But here she is, coming to invite her, I guess. Good-day, Cleustrata.

CLEUSTRATA: The same to you, Alcesimus. Where is your wife?

ALCESIMUS: She's inside, waiting for your invitation; for your husband urged me to send her to help you. Do you wish me to call her?

CLEUSTRATA: Let her be; I don't wish you to, if she's busy.

ALCESIMUS: She's at leisure.

CLEUSTRATA: I don't care about it; I don't want to annoy her; I'll see her later.

ALCESIMUS: Aren't you getting ready for a wedding at your house?

CLEUSTRATA: I'm getting ready for one, making arrangements.

ALCESIMUS: Don't you need an assistant?

CLEUSTRATA: We have enough at home. When the wedding is over, then I'll come to see her. Good-bye and give her my regards. (*Goes to her doorway.*)

ALCESIMUS (*to himself*): What am I to do now? I'm in pretty mess on account of that vile, toothless old goat who got me into this. I promise the aid of my wife away from home as a sort of dish-licker. The foul old buzzard, he told me that his wife would send for her; she says she doesn't want her. Heavens! It's a wonder if my neighbour's wife doesn't suspect this. But on the other hand, when I think about it, if she had any suspicions, she would have asked me about it. I'll go in now and draw the ship back to her dock. (*He goes into his house.*)

CLEUSTRATA (*to herself, entering from the doorway*): Now he's been finely fooled! How the unhappy old men bustle about! Now I'd like to have that useless, decrepit husband of mine appear so that I could

fool him in his turn, after fooling this other. I'd like to stir up a bit
of a quarrel between the two of them. But there he comes. You'd think
him a decent person when you see him so serious.

Act Three.   Scene III

(Enter LYSIDAMUS *from the forum.)*

LYSIDAMUS *(to himself, not seeing* CLEUSTRATA): It's great folly, in
my opinion, for any man in love to go to the forum on the day when
his sweetheart is ready for him; that's what I stupidly did; I've wasted
the day pleading for a certain relative of mine; I'm delighted that he
lost his case; so that he hasn't asked me to plead for him today in
vain. In my opinion, the man who calls for counsel ought to ask and
inquire first whether the man he calls has a mind or not; if he says he
hasn't, he ought to send him home mindless. *(Catching sight of his
wife)* But there's my wife in front of the house. I'm a stupid fool! I'm
afraid that she isn't deaf and has heard this.

CLEUSTRATA *(aside)*: I certainly did hear it, to your great sorrow.

LYSIDAMUS *(aside)*: I'll step a bit nearer. *(To* CLEUSTRATA) How goes
it, my darling?

CLEUSTRATA: I was just waiting for you.

LYSIDAMUS: Are things ready now? Have you brought your neighbour
over here to our house to assist you?

CLEUSTRATA: I sent for her as you requested; but your comrade, that
fine friend of yours, has had some sort of quarrel with his wife; when
I went to get her, he said that he couldn't send her over.

LYSIDAMUS: That's your greatest fault; you aren't enticing enough.

CLEUSTRATA: My good sir, it's not the business of wives but of harlots
to be enticing to the husbands of other women. You go in and get her,
husband; I wish to tend to what's necessary inside.

LYSIDAMUS: Hurry, then.

CLEUSTRATA: Very well. *(Aside)* Indeed, I'll put some fear into his
heart now; I'll make him a most unhappy lover today. *(She goes into
the house.)*

Act Three. Scene IV

(Enter ALCESIMUS *from his house.)*

ALCESIMUS *(to himself)*: I'm going to see if the lover has returned from the forum, the old death's-head who has been making a fool of me and my wife. But there he is in front of his house. (*Addressing* LYSIDAMUS) Look here, I was just coming to see you.

LYSIDAMUS: And I to you, confound you! See here, you insignificant worm! What did I entrust to you? What did I ask you to do?

ALCESIMUS: What's the matter?

LYSIDAMUS: How well you've emptied your house for me! How nicely you've sent your wife over to my house! I'm lost and the opportunity too, all on account of you, eh?

ALCESIMUS: Oh, go hang yourself! You said that your wife would come to get mine.

LYSIDAMUS: Well, she says that she did, and that you said you wouldn't let her go.

ALCESIMUS: Well, she herself told me that she didn't care for her assistance.

LYSIDAMUS: Well, she herself told me to come and get your wife.

ALCESIMUS: Well, I don't care about that.

LYSIDAMUS: Well, you're ruining me.

ALCESIMUS: Well, it's best—well, I'll make you wait a long time—well, I'm eager—

LYSIDAMUS: Well—

ALCESIMUS: —to do you some mischief.

LYSIDAMUS: Well, I'll do that gladly too. Never today will you have a single "well" more than I.

ALCESIMUS: Well, confound it, may the gods finally damn you!

LYSIDAMUS: Look here now! Will you send your wife to my house?

ALCESIMUS: Take her and go to the devil with her, with your own wife, and with that sweetie of yours too. Oh, you go and tend to something else. I'll tell my wife to go to your wife through the garden.

LYSIDAMUS: Now you're truly my friend. (*To himself, as* ALCESIMUS *goes into his house*) Under what auspices did this love come upon me, or how often have I ever sinned against Venus, that so many things should hinder my love affair? (*A noise is heard*) Hey! What in the world is that uproar in our house?

Act Three.   Scene V

(PARDALISCA *rushes from the house in feigned terror.*)

PARDALISCA: I'm gone, I'm gone, I'm totally, totally dead! My heart is heavy with horror; my legs are trembling with terror; I don't know where to get or look for any assistance, safety, refuge, or relief. I've just seen so many strange and amazing things inside, such a new and unusual piece of daring. (*To her mistress inside*) Look out, Cleustrata, get away from her, I beg of you, so she won't harm you in her anger. Get that sword away from her; she's out of her mind.

LYSIDAMUS: Now what's the reason for her jumping out here, so jittery and scared? Pardalisca!

PARDALISCA: I'm dead! Where did that sound come from?

LYSIDAMUS: Just look back at me.

PARDALISCA: I, master—

LYSIDAMUS: What's the matter with you? What are you scared about?

PARDALISCA: I'm dead!

LYSIDAMUS: What do you mean, dead?

PARDALISCA: I'm dead, and so are you.

LYSIDAMUS: What, I'm dead? How so?

PARDALISCA: Woe's to you!

LYSIDAMUS: I'd rather have it to you.

PARDALISCA: Hold me, please, so I won't fall. (*She staggers;* LYSIDAMUS *supports her.*)

LYSIDAMUS: Whatever it is, tell me quick.

PARDALISCA: Hold my breast; fan me, please, with your cloak.

LYSIDAMUS (*aside, fanning her*): I'm worried about this business, unless she's had too strong a sip of the flower of Bacchus.

PARDALISCA: Please hold my ears. (*Her head falls on his shoulder.*)

LYSIDAMUS: Oh, go to the devil! The gods damn you, breast, ears, head, and all! If you don't tell me quickly what the trouble is, I'll smash your head for you, you snake. You've made a laughingstock of me up to now.

PARDALISCA: My master,—

LYSIDAMUS: What do you want, my maid?

PARDALISCA: You're too angry.

LYSIDAMUS: You say that too soon. But whatever it is, tell me; make it brief; what was that uproar inside?

PARDALISCA: Just listen, you'll learn. It was a most foul crime just now inside—that your maid began in this fashion, not at all suited to Attic customs.

LYSIDAMUS (*impatient*): Well, what is it?

PARDALISCA: I'm afraid to tell.

LYSIDAMUS (*angrily*): Can I know from you what the trouble is?

PARDALISCA: I'll tell. Your maid, the one you want to marry to your overseer, well, inside she—

LYSIDAMUS: What did she do inside? What is it?

PARDALISCA: She's imitating the wicked habits of wicked women; she's threatening her husband. His life—

LYSIDAMUS: Well, what about it?

PARDALISCA: Ah!

LYSIDAMUS (*still more impatient*): What is it?

PARDALISCA: His life she wants to take, she says; a sword—

LYSIDAMUS (*alarmed*): What!

PARDALISCA: —a sword—

LYSIDAMUS: What about a sword?

PARDALISCA: She's got one.

LYSIDAMUS: Heaven help me! What's the sword for?

PARDALISCA: She's chasing everybody all over the house and won't let anyone come near her; they're all hiding under chests, under beds, too scared to speak.

LYSIDAMUS: I'm dead and done for! What sort of sickness came on her so suddenly?

PARDALISCA: She's mad.

LYSIDAMUS (*aside*): I'm certainly the most wretched person alive!

PARDALISCA: If you only knew what she said today—

LYSIDAMUS: I want to hear that. What did she say?

PARDALISCA: Listen. She swore by all the gods and goddesses that she would murder the person she slept with this night.

LYSIDAMUS (*frightened and off his guard*): Murder me?

PARDALISCA (*innocently*): Does it concern you in any way?

LYSIDAMUS (*aside*): Confound it!

PARDALISCA: What business do you have with her?

LYSIDAMUS: I made a slip. The overseer, I meant to say.

PARDALISCA: You're purposely leaving the highway for the by-way.

LYSIDAMUS: She isn't threatening me at all, is she?

PARDALISCA: She's more furious at you than at anyone.

LYSIDAMUS (*in alarm*): Why?

PARDALISCA: Because you are marrying her to Olympio; she won't let you or herself or her husband live until morning; I was sent here to tell you this, so that you can look out for her.

LYSIDAMUS: Heavens! I'm dead already.

PARDALISCA (*aside*): You deserve to be.

LYSIDAMUS (*aside*): No lover past or present has ever been as wretched!

PARDALISCA (*aside, to the audience*): I'm deceiving him in fine fashion. For everything that I've told him is a pack of lies. My mistress and the woman next door concocted the scheme; I was sent out to fool him.

LYSIDAMUS: Look here, Pardalisca!

PARDALISCA: What's the matter?

ʟYSIDAMUS: There's a—

PARDALISCA: What?

LYSIDAMUS: There's a question I want to ask you.

PARDALISCA: You're delaying me.

LYSIDAMUS: And you're slaying me. But does Casina still have a sword?

PARDALISCA: Yes, two, in fact.

LYSIDAMUS: What, two?

PARDALISCA: She says she'll murder you with one of them today, the overseer with the other.

LYSIDAMUS: I'm the most murdered person alive. I guess that the best thing for me to do is to put on a breastplate. What about my wife? Doesn't she go and take them away from her?

PARDALISCA: No one dares to come near her.

LYSIDAMUS: She should prevail upon her.

PARDALISCA: She's trying to; but the girl says she won't give them up on any other terms, unless she knows that she won't marry the overseer.

LYSIDAMUS: But she shall marry him today against her will, just because she's unwilling. For why shouldn't I carry out what I've begun, for her to marry me? (*Hastily*) That is, my overseer, I meant to say.

PARDALISCA: You make a lot of mistakes.

LYSIDAMUS: I'm so scared that I can't say what I mean. But please tell my wife that I beg her to beseech the girl to put down the sword, so that I can come back into the house.

PARDALISCA: I'll give her your message.

LYSIDAMUS: You entreat her.

PARDALISCA: I'll entreat her, all right.

LYSIDAMUS: But make a winning appeal, in your usual fashion. And listen; if you manage this, I'll give you a pair of shoes and a gold ring for your finger and lots of nice things.

PARDALISCA: I'll tend to it.

LYSIDAMUS: Be sure to convince her.

PARDALISCA: I'll go now, unless you want me for anything.

LYSIDAMUS: Go on and tend to it. (PARDALISCA *goes into the house*)
Ah! There's my assistant, coming back with the provisions; he's leading
a parade.

Act Three.   Scene VI

(*Enter* OLYMPIO, CHYTRIO, *and assistants with provisions.*)

OLYMPIO (*to* CHYTRIO): Look here, thief, lead on your briars beneath
your banners.

CHYTRIO: How do you mean, these are briars?

OLYMPIO: Because they straightway snatch whatever they touch; if you
try to snatch it from them, instantly they tear it; wherever they come,
wherever they are, they're a two-fold loss to their masters.

CHYTRIO: Bosh!

OLYMPIO (*catching sight of* LYSIDAMUS): Aha! I must give myself a
magnificent and patrician air and go to meet my master.

LYSIDAMUS: Good day, good sir.

OLYMPIO: I admit that I am.

LYSIDAMUS: How goes it?

OLYMPIO: You're in love; I'm hungry and thirsty.

LYSIDAMUS: You've come well provided.

OLYMPIO: Aha! Today . . .[9]

LYSIDAMUS: Wait a minute, even though you are so contemptuous.

OLYMPIO: Phew! Phew! This conversation of yours stinks.

LYSIDAMUS: What's the matter?

OLYMPIO (*pointing to the provisions*): This is the matter. You're still
standing there? You're causing me *trop d'ennui.*

LYSIDAMUS: I'll give you a *grand coup*, I fancy, if you don't stand still.
(*Catches hold of him.*)

OLYMPIO: *O mon Dieu!* Can't you get away from me,—unless you want me to vomit right now. (*Moves away.*)

LYSIDAMUS: Wait.

OLYMPIO: What's the matter? Who is this fellow?

LYSIDAMUS: I'm the master.

OLYMPIO: What master?

LYSIDAMUS: He whose slave you are.

OLYMPIO: I, a slave?

LYSIDAMUS: Yes, and mine, too.

OLYMPIO: I'm a free man, ain't I? Remember, remember.

LYSIDAMUS: Wait and stand still.

OLYMPIO: Oh, stop it!

LYSIDAMUS (*humbly*): I'm your slave.

OLYMPIO: That's very good.

LYSIDAMUS: My dear little Olympio, my father, my patron, I do beg of you—

OLYMPIO: Well, you're quite wise.

LYSIDAMUS: Of course I'm your slave.

OLYMPIO: What do I need of such a worthless slave?

LYSIDAMUS: Well, now! How soon will you give me some pleasure?

OLYMPIO: If only the dinner were cooked!

LYSIDAMUS: Have these fellows go in, then.

OLYMPIO (*to* CHYTRIO *and the assistants*): Go in now in a hurry and show some haste. I'll soon be in; have the meal well soaked. I want it done in a nice, neat fashion, none of your barbarian blither. Still standing there, are you? Go on in, I'm staying here. (CHYTRIO *and the assistants go inside*) There isn't anything else to delay us, is there?

LYSIDAMUS: She says Casina has a sword inside and wants to kill the two of us.

OLYMPIO: I understand; just let her have it. They're joking; I know those worthless baggages. Why don't you go into the house with me?

LYSIDAMUS: Damn it, I'm afraid of trouble. You go in and find out first what's going on inside.

OLYMPIO: My life is just as dear to me as yours is to you. But you go now.

LYSIDAMUS: If you say so, well, I'll go—with you. (*They go into the house; a short time is supposed to elapse before the next Act.*)

Act Four.   Scene I

(*Enter* PARDALISCA *from the house, laughing.*)

PARDALISCA (*to herself*): I don't think I've seen such delightful games at Nemea, or at Olympia,[10] or anywhere else, as the game that's being made inside of our old man and the overseer Olympio. Everybody's hurrying about all over the house; the old man is shouting in the kitchen and urging on the cooks: "Why don't you get to work today? If you're going to serve it, why don't you serve it? Hurry; the dinner should have been cooked before this." The overseer is strutting about with a wreath, dressed in white, scrubbed and all decked out. And the two women are dressing up the armour-bearer to marry him to our overseer in place of Casina. But they're making a clever pretense of not knowing what the outcome will be. And the cooks too, in worthy fashion, are cleverly playing their part, so that the old man won't get any dinner; they upset the pots, pour water on the fire; they're doing it at the request of the women; and the women want to drive the old man out of the house without any dinner, so that they alone can stuff their bellies. I know these female gluttons; they can devour a whole merchant vessel full of victuals. But the door is opening.

Act Four.   Scene II

(*Enter* LYSIDAMUS *from the house.*)

LYSIDAMUS (*speaking to* CLEUSTRATA *within*): If you're wise, wife, you'll have dinner when it's cooked. I'll eat my dinner in the country. I want to escort the new bride and groom to the farm, so that no one will snatch her away; I know how mischievous some people are. You have a pleasant time. But hurry, send the two of them out at once, so that we can get there before dark, at least; I'll be back tomorrow; and tomorrow, wife, I'm going to have myself a banquet.

PARDALISCA (*aside*): It's just as I said it would be. The women are driving the old man out of the house without his dinner.

LYSIDAMUS (*to* PARDALISCA): What are you doing here?

PARDALISCA: Going on an errand for the mistress.

LYSIDAMUS: Really?

PARDALISCA: Seriously.

LYSIDAMUS: What are you looking for here?

PARDALISCA: I'm not looking for anything.

LYSIDAMUS: Be off; you're loitering here; the others are busy inside.

PARDALISCA: I'm off. (*She goes towards the house.*)

LYSIDAMUS: Get away from here then, won't you, you worthless jade? (PARDALISCA *goes into the house*) Has she really gone? Now I can say what I wish. A fellow in love, by heaven, isn't really hungry at all, even if he is hungry. But there he comes with wreath and torch, my buddy, my companion, my co-husband of an overseer!

Act Four. Scene III

(*Enter* OLYMPIO, *dressed as a bridegroom.*)

OLYMPIO (*to the musician on the stage*): Come, piper, make the entire street resound with a sweet wedding-song, as they bring out the new bride.

LYSIDAMUS *and* OLYMPIO (*singing*): *Hymen hymenaee o hymen!*

LYSIDAMUS: How are you, my source of comfort?

OLYMPIO: Damned hungry, and there's no comfort in it either.

LYSIDAMUS: But I'm in love.

OLYMPIO: But I don't give a damn about that. Love is your food. For a long time now my insides have been rumbling with emptiness.

LYSIDAMUS: What are those slow-pokes lingering inside so long for? The more I hurry, the more slowly everything goes—just as if on purpose.

OLYMPIO: What if I sing the wedding-song? Maybe that will bring them out more quickly.

LYSIDAMUS: A good idea, and I'll aid you at this joint marriage of ours.

LYSIDAMUS *and* OLYMPIO (*singing*): *Hymen hymenaee o hymen!*

LYSIDAMUS: I'm done up, poor fool that I am! I can burst myself singing the wedding song; but I don't have a chance to burst myself the way I want to.

OLYMPIO: By gad, if you were a horse, you'd certainly be a wild one.

LYSIDAMUS: Why?

OLYMPIO: You're so persistent.

LYSIDAMUS: You haven't had any experience with me, have you?

OLYMPIO: Heaven forbid! But the door creaked; they're coming out.

LYSIDAMUS: The gods are saving me at last.

Act Four.   Scene IV

(*Enter* CHALINUS, *veiled and dressed as a bride.* PARDALISCA *and maids accompany him.* CLEUSTRATA *stands in the doorway.*)

CHALINUS: He's already got a whiff of this male Casina from a distance.

PARDALISCA: Easy now, lift your feet over the threshold, you newly married bride. Begin this journey safely, that you may always stand over your husband, that you may take him to task and master your mate, that your word and command be supreme; let your husband clothe you, you plunder your husband; and remember, I beg, to trick him by night and by day.

OLYMPIO (*to* LYSIDAMUS): At her own great peril, by heaven, the moment she makes the slightest slip.

LYSIDAMUS: Hush!

OLYMPIO: I won't hush.

LYSIDAMUS: What's the matter?

OLYMPIO: The wicked slut is giving wicked advice to the wretched girl.

LYSIDAMUS: Will you throw this affair into confusion, after it's been all settled? That's what they wish, that's what they're striving for—to undo what's been done.

PARDALISCA: Come, Olympio, when you wish, receive this wife of yours from us. (*They present* CHALINUS *to him.*)

OLYMPIO: Give her to me then, if you're ever going to give her to me today. (*Takes* CHALINUS *from the maids.*)

LYSIDAMUS (*to the maids*): You go on inside.

PARDALISCA: Please be gentle to this innocent and inexperienced maiden.

OLYMPIO: I'll be gentle.

PARDALISCA: Good-bye.

OLYMPIO (*to maids*): Go in, now.

LYSIDAMUS: Yes, go.

CLEUSTRATA: Good-bye. (*The women enter the house.*)

LYSIDAMUS: Has my wife gone now?

OLYMPIO: She's in the house, don't fear.

LYSIDAMUS: Hurrah! Now at last I'm free, by Jove. (*Addressing* CHALINUS *as* CASINA) Now, my little sweetheart, my little honey, my spring-flower!

OLYMPIO: Hey there! You'll avoid trouble, if you're wise. She's mine.

LYSIDAMUS: I know that, but the first enjoyment is mine.

OLYMPIO: Hold this torch.

LYSIDAMUS: No, I'll hold her instead. O mighty Venus, you've given me many blessings, when you gave me possession of her!

OLYMPIO: O you soft little body! My darling wife—what the devil?

LYSIDAMUS: What's the matter?

OLYMPIO (*hopping about*): She stepped on my toes like an elephant.

LYSIDAMUS: Hush, won't you? No cloud is as soft as her breast.

OLYMPIO: Gad! What a beautiful little breast—Ouch! Damn!

LYSIDAMUS: What's the matter now?

OLYMPIO: She hit me in the chest; it was a battering ram, not her elbow.

LYSIDAMUS: Why then do you handle her so roughly, I ask? She doesn't oppose me; I treat her the opposite way. Ow!

OLYMPIO: What's the matter with you?

LYSIDAMUS: Jove! What a strong little thing she is! With her elbow she almost smashed my forehead.

OLYMPIO: That means, she's ready for bed.[11]

LYSIDAMUS: Why don't we go, then?

OLYMPIO (*taking hold of* CHALINUS): Come along, my dear little darling. (*They go into the house of* ALCESIMUS.)

Act Five.   Scene I

(*Enter* MYRRHINA, PARDALISCA, *and* CLEUSTRATA *from the house of* LYSIDAMUS.)

MYRRHINA: After having a nice, pleasant time inside, we've come out to the street to view the wedding games. Dear me, I've never laughed more on any day, nor do I think I'll ever laugh more in time to come.

PARDALISCA: I'd like to know how Chalinus is getting on—the new bridegroom and his new husband.

MYRRHINA: No comic poet ever contrived a more tricky plot than this one which we've invented.

CLEUSTRATA: I'd like to see the old man come along now with his face battered in. There isn't a more worthless old duffer alive . . .[12] unless you think the man who furnished him with a place to go is worse. . . . I want you to be on guard here, Pardalisca, to . . . make fun of the man who comes out.

PARDALISCA: I'll do it gladly . . . in my usual way.

CLEUSTRATA: . . . watch everything from here; tell me what's going on inside.

MYRRHINA: Get behind me, please.

CLEUSTRATA: And you can speak boldly and freely just what you wish.

MYRRHINA: Hush! The door of our house has creaked. (*They hide themselves in* CLEUSTRATA's *doorway.*)

Act Five. Scene II

(OLYMPIO *rushes from the house of* ALCESIMUS, *much dishevelled.*)

OLYMPIO (*to himself*): I don't know where to flee or where to hide or how to conceal my shame. My master and I have been so terribly disgraced at this wedding of ours. I'm so ashamed and I'm so afraid and we're now both so ridiculous! Now in my folly I'm doing something new—I'm ashamed, something I've never been before. (*To the audience*) Pay attention now, while I repeat my exploits; it's well worth your listening; so ridiculous to hear and to repeat are the mishaps I encountered inside. When I took my new bride into the house, I led her straightway to the bedroom. But it was just as dark there as in a well; while the old man was away, I said "Lie down now." I place her in bed, put some pillows under her, utter soft and enticing words, in order to consummate the marriage ahead of the old man. Then I begin to slow up, because. . . .[12] I look around now and then, so that the old man. . . . First of all, to put her in the right mood, I ask her for a nice kiss. . . . She pushed my hand away and didn't let me give her a kiss. Now I'm in more of a hurry; now I'm more anxious to possess Casina. . . . I want to get ahead of the old man; I fasten the door so that he can't catch me at it.

CLEUSTRATA: Come now, you approach him.

PARDALISCA (*stepping up to* OLYMPIO): Tell me, where's your new bride?

OLYMPIO (*aside*): O Lord! I'm done for! They know the whole affair.

PARDALISCA (*overhearing*): Then you ought to admit everything. What's going on inside? What's Casina doing? Is she quite agreeable?

OLYMPIO: I'm ashamed to tell.

PARDALISCA: Tell in detail, as you began.

OLYMPIO: Damn it! I'm ashamed.

PARDALISCA: Speak boldly. After you went to bed, that's what I want to hear about. Tell us what happened.

OLYMPIO: It's disgraceful.

PARDALISCA: It will be a good warning to those who hear you.

OLYMPIO: . . . a great thing.[12]

PARDALISCA: You're wasting time. Why don't you go on?

OLYMPIO: When. . . .

PARDALISCA: What?

OLYMPIO: Terrible!

PARDALISCA: What?

OLYMPIO: Horrible!

PARDALISCA: . . . is it?

OLYMPIO: Oh, it was huge! I was afraid that she had a sword; I began to look for it. While I am hunting for the sword, I seize the hilt. But when I think it over, she didn't have a sword, for it would have been cold.

PARDALISCA: Keep on.

OLYMPIO: Oh, I'm ashamed.

PARDALISCA: It wasn't a radish, was it?

OLYMPIO: No.

PARDALISCA: It wasn't a cucumber, was it?

OLYMPIO: Damn it! It wasn't any vegetable at all. But, whatever it was, no blight had ever touched it. It was enormous, whatever it was.

PARDALISCA: What happened then? Tell me.

OLYMPIO: Then I speak to her; "Casina," say I, "my darling little wife, tell me, why do you scorn me in this fashion, your own husband? I don't deserve to be treated this way, just because I want you for myself." She doesn't say a word and with her clothes she covers that part—which makes a woman of you. When I see this road shut off, I ask to go another way. . . .[13]

MYRRHINA: . . . .

OLYMPIO: A kiss . . . she pricks my lips with a beard just like bristles . . . while I am on my knees, at once she strikes my chest with both feet. I tumble from the bed headlong; she jumps on me and smashes my jaw. Then without saying a word I fled from the house dressed just as you see me, so that the old man can have a dose of the same medicine I had.

PARDALISCA: That's fine. But where's your cloak?

OLYMPIO: I left it inside there.

PARDALISCA: Well now, wasn't that a neat trick that we played on the two of you?

OLYMPIO: We deserved it. But the door creaked. She's not following me out, is she? (*They go to* CLEUSTRATA'S *doorway.*)

Act Five.   Scene III

(LYSIDAMUS *rushes from the house without his cloak;* CHALINUS *follows.*)

LYSIDAMUS (*to himself*): I'm burning with the horrible disgrace and I don't know what to do; nor how to look my wife in the face, I'm so utterly ruined! All my crimes are discovered. In every way I'm done for. . . . I'm caught by the jaws . . .[13] nor how I can clear myself to my wife. . . . I've lost my cloak . . . this is best; I'll go inside to my wife and let her get satisfaction out of—my hide. (*To the audience*) But is there anyone here to perform this task in my place? (*Pauses*) Well, I don't know what to do, except to imitate worthless slaves and run away from home. There's no safety for my shoulders if I return home. (*Again to the audience*) Do you think I'm joking? I do get beaten against my will, even though I have deserved it. I'll dash away in this direction and escape.

CHALINUS: Hey! Stop right there, my fine lover!

LYSIDAMUS: Ruined! Called back! I'll keep on going, just as if I didn't hear.

Act Five.   Scene IV

(CLEUSTRATA, MYRRHINA, *and* OLYMPIO *approach.*)

CHALINUS: Where are you, you imitator of the morals of the Massilians? If you want to fondle me, this is a fine time for it. Just come back to the bedroom. You're ruined, by heaven! Come on, just step this way. Now I'll take an impartial judge to you (*swinging a cane*), apart from the regular session.

LYSIDAMUS: Good Lord! That fellow will soon be shaving my legs with his club. I'll have to go this way, for that way I'll have a hipwreck. (*Turns toward his own house.*)

CLEUSTRATA (*stepping forward*): Greetings, my fine lover.

LYSIDAMUS: And now here's my wife in my way; now I'm between the stone and the sacrifice and I don't know where to go; on one side wolves, on the other, dogs. And the wolf-omen is brandishing a club. Now I'll change the old proverb,[14] I guess; I'll go this way, I hope the dog-omen will prove the better.

MYRRHINA: How are you, double-husband?

CLEUSTRATA: My good husband, where are you coming from in this shape? What did you do with your cane and the cloak that you had?

MYRRHINA: He lost them while making love to Casina, I guess.

LYSIDAMUS (*aside*): Completely ruined!

CHALINUS: Shall we go to bed again? I'm Casina.

LYSIDAMUS: Oh, go to the devil!

CHALINUS: Don't you love me?

CLEUSTRATA: Tell me, won't you, what became of your cloak?

LYSIDAMUS: By heaven, wife, the Bacchantes—

CLEUSTRATA: The Bacchantes?

LYSIDAMUS: Yes, wife, by heaven, the Bacchantes—

MYRRHINA: He's lying, and he knows it. On my word, there are no Bacchantes now.[15]

LYSIDAMUS: I forgot. But still, the Bacchantes—

CLEUSTRATA: What? Bacchantes?

LYSIDAMUS: Well, if that can't be—

CLEUSTRATA: You're certainly frightened.

LYSIDAMUS: I? That's a lie.

CLEUSTRATA: Well, you're awfully pale. . . .[13]

OLYMPIO: . . . who made a poor disgraced wretch of me by his disgusting actions.

LYSIDAMUS: Shut up, won't you?

OLYMPIO: No, by gad! I won't shut up. For you earnestly begged me to ask to marry Casina for the sake of your love affair.

LYSIDAMUS: I did that?

OLYMPIO (*jeering*): No, I suppose Hector of Troy—

LYSIDAMUS (*interrupting him*): Would have shut you up. Did I do those things you say?

CLEUSTRATA: Do you still ask?

LYSIDAMUS (*humbled*): If I did it, I certainly did a wicked thing.

CLEUSTRATA: You just come into the house now; I'll remind you if you don't remember.

LYSIDAMUS: By Jove! I'd rather agree with what you say, I think. But, wife, grant forgiveness to your husband; Myrrhina, you ask Cleustrata; if I ever love Casina after this or even merely think about it—let alone loving her—if I ever do such a thing after this, you have my permission, wife, to hang me up and rake me with rods.

MYRRHINA: I really think that you ought to pardon him, Cleustrata.

CLEUSTRATA: I'll do as you wish. (*To* LYSIDAMUS) I pardon you now with less reluctance for this reason, so that we won't make a long play still longer.

LYSIDAMUS: You're not angry at me?

CLEUSTRATA: No, I'm not angry.

LYSIDAMUS: Can I trust your word?

CLEUSTRATA: You can.

LYSIDAMUS: Not a single person has a more charming wife than I.

CLEUSTRATA (*to* CHALINUS): Come you, give him back his cane and his cloak.

CHALINUS: Take them if you wish. By Jove! A terrible wrong has been done to me today. I've married two husbands; neither treated me as a new bride should be treated.

Epilogue

Spectators, we'll tell you what will happen inside. Casina shall be revealed as the daughter of the man next door, and she'll be married to Euthynicus, our master's son. Now it's only fair that you should give us plenty of well-deserved applause with your hands. Whoever does this will always have the harlot he wishes without his wife's knowledge; but the man that doesn't clap his hands as loud as possible will get in place of a harlot—a goat soused in bilge water.

1. The "flower of the poets" included Plautus, Ennius, Caecilius, and probably Terence.

2. The name of the comedy at its first performance. It means "The men who draw lots," as does the title of the Greek original.

3. An allusion to one explanation of the name "Plautus," "a dog with flat, drooping ears."

4. An expression used on occasions of divorce.

5. The lots were placed in a narrow-necked urn filled with water. Only one lot could come to the top at a time, and the person whose number came up was the winner.

6. An attempt to reproduce the sound of the Latin word, *tittibilicium,* "a worthless trifle."

7. An allusion to the story of Cresphontes who won Messenia by drawing lots; his lot was of terracotta, while his brother's was of sundried clay and dissolved in the water.

8. In the war with the Gauls, the Romans made a hurried march to Sutrium, taking their provisions with them.

9. A short lacuna occurs here.

10. A reference to the Nemean and Olympian Games, held in honour of Jupiter.

11. An attempt to reproduce the word-play between *cubito,* "elbow," and *cubitum* "to go to bed."

12. There are several short lacunae here.

13. There is a gap here of several lines; only a few words are preserved in the manuscripts.

14. "There is no safety between wolves and dogs."

15. Probably a reference to the *senatus consultum de Bacchanalibus* of 186 B.C., which abolished the Bacchic mysteries.

VII
THE CASKET

Characters in the Play

SELENIUM, *a courtesan*

GYMNASIUM, *a courtesan*

A PROCURESS, *mother of* GYMNASIUM

SUCCOUR, *a god, who speaks the Prologue*

ALCESIMARCHUS, *a young man of Sicyon*

A SLAVE, *belonging to* ALCESIMARCHUS

AN OLD GENTLEMAN, *father of* ALCESIMARCHUS

LAMPADIO, *slave of* DEMIPHO

MELAENIS, *a procuress*

PHANOSTRATA, *wife of* DEMIPHO

HALISCA, *maid-servant of* MELAENIS

DEMIPHO, *an old gentleman of Sicyon*

Acrostic Argument

A young man of Lemnos ravishes a woman of Sicyon. After his return to his own land, he marries and begets a daughter. The woman of Sicyon also gives birth to a daughter. A slave carries away this child and abandons it, but watches from a hiding place; a courtesan picks up the baby and gives it to another courtesan. Returning sometime later from Lemnos, the man marries the woman he had ravished, and betroths his Lemnian daughter to a young man already madly in love with the girl that had been abandoned. After a search the slave finds the girl whom he had exposed long before. And so, after she was discovered to be a citizen, Alcesimarchus legally and properly gains possession of the girl whom he had already loved.

INTRODUCTION

The Casket (the *Cistellaria*) takes its name from the *cistella*, or casket, which contains the trinkets whose discovery brings about the recognition of the heroine's identity. The text of the play has come down in a very corrupt state; several hundred lines are either lost or too fragmentary to be intelligible. The play is based on a lost comedy by Menander, *The Women who Dine Together* (*Synaristosae*) and, as far as we can judge, resembles the work of Menander far more closely than any other Plautine comedy. The general tone of the play is not unlike that of Terence's comedies, and the inference seems clear that Plautus here was translating the Greek original far more closely than was his usual procedure.

Although a large section of the play is lost, the general outline of the plot is clear. A young man, Alcesimarchus, has as his mistress a young maiden, Selenium, who is deeply in love with him. She believes herself to be the daughter of Melaenis, a procuress. Alcesimarchus wishes to marry Selenium, but his father insists that he marry another girl, the daughter of Demipho. This situation is not unlike that of Terence's *The Woman of Andros*. Selenium leaves her lover's house, and the unhappiness of the two young people is brought to an end only when the true identity of Selenium is discovered; she too is the daughter of Demipho. Demipho, after the death of his first wife, had married the woman he had wronged many years before; she had given birth to a daughter which had been cast out and picked up by a courtesan, who had given the child to Melaenis. With the discovery that Selenium is Demipho's daughter, all ends well, for Alcesimarchus is now able to carry out his father's wishes. In this respect also *The Woman of Andros* is similar, for the conflict between Simo's wish to have his son marry the daughter of Chremes, and the son's desire to marry Glycerium, is solved by the discovery that Glycerium is the lost daughter of Chremes.

The plot, in its emphasis on mistaken identity and recognition, is thus typically Menandrian, and the play as we have it contains no really farcical scenes. Many of the stock characters so often found in Roman comedy are missing, e.g. the parasite, the braggart warrior, the intriguing slave. The play is one of the most sentimental of Plautus' comedies, and Alcesimarchus and Selenium have been considered the most romantic pair of lovers in Plautus.

The Casket is unusual in the emphasis given to feminine roles. There are six women in the play, and the characters of most of them are carefully delineated, e.g. Gymnasium and her tipsy mother, and the maid Halisca. The best of the women characters is of course Selenium; she is generous and dignified, devoted to Alcesimarchus, and deeply grieved at the separation. Alcesimarchus also is overwhelmed with sorrow and threatens suicide, but his tragic pose becomes comic and is suddenly dropped when he meets Selenium and carries her inside. Other scenes where the humour grows out of the situation are Lampadio's attempt to explain to Melaenis the difference between Demipho's former and later wife, and Halisca's search for the lost casket. It is possible that there may have been considerable humour in the (now fragmentary) scene between the father of Alcesimarchus and Gymnasium whom he took for Selenium. In its present state, however, the play is the most serious of Plautus' comedies.

The Casket was apparently produced at about the end of the second Carthaginian war (cf. the end of the prologue, which appears in Act One, Scene III), and is thus one of the earlier of the extant plays. P. J. Enk suggests that Plautus was here experimenting with a different type of comedy, one which he found did not appeal to his audience. In *The Captives,* another unusually serious play, produced many years later, considerable comic relief was afforded by the character of Ergasilus, the parasite.

THE CASKET

(SCENE:—*A street in Sicyon in front of the houses of* ALCESIMARCHUS *and* DEMIPHO.)

Act One.   Scene I

(*Enter* SELENIUM, GYMNASIUM, *and the* PROCURESS *from the house of* ALCESIMARCHUS; *the* PROCURESS *is somewhat inebriated.*)

SELENIUM: I have long loved you, my dear Gymnasium, and considered that you and your mother were devoted to me; but today the two of you have really shown your affection. If you were my sister, I don't know how you could have treated me better; no, as I think about it, you couldn't possibly have done so. You've laid everything else aside and given me your ready assistance. I love you both for it, and you've made me vastly indebted to you.

GYMNASIUM: Gracious, it's a trifle, considering the way you pay us; it's easy for us to assist you and be useful, when you've given us such a delightful and charming lunch at your house, one that we'll always remember.

SELENIUM: I've been happy to do the things that I think you like, and I'll be glad to do them again.

PROCURESS: Well, as the man said when he was carried over the tranquil sea by a favourable breeze, "I'm glad I breezed along"—to your house, my dear, for you've received us today so very sweetly, and there wasn't a thing at your house that didn't please me, except for the way your servant was trained.

SELENIUM: Please tell me what was wrong.

PROCURESS: He didn't give me nearly enough to drink, and he kept diluting the wine.

GYMNASIUM: Oh, my dear, is that a nice thing to say?

325

PROCURESS: It's quite right and proper. There isn't any stranger here.

SELENIUM: I love you both quite deservedly, since you care for me and make so much of me.

PROCURESS: Heavens, my dear Selenium, it's right for people of our class to be devoted to each other and to keep up friendships; just see how those nobly born women, those society matrons, cherish their friendships and keep them all to themselves. Even if we imitate them and do the same thing, even so we can hardly get along, for they dislike us so much. They want us to be in need of their support. They don't want us to have any resources of our own, but to depend upon them for everything, so that we'll be simply subservient to them. If you go near 'em, you'd rather flee from them than see 'em, for to women like us they're friendly and warm in public, but in private, if they ever have a chance, they deceitfully drop cold water on us. They declare we're in the habit of having affairs with their husbands, and say we're their concubines; they try to crush us. Your mother and I, we both became courtesans, since we were merely freed slaves; she brought you up and I brought up this girl (*indicating* GYMNASIUM); your fathers were men we chanced to come upon. It wasn't through arrogance that I forced her to follow the profession, but to keep me from starving.

SELENIUM: But it would have been better to have her marry some one.

PROCURESS: Come, come! Goodness me, she marries a man every day; she did today, and she'll be marrying again tonight. I've never let her sleep alone; for if she didn't keep marrying, the household would die of dreadful hunger.

GYMNASIUM: I have to be just as you wish me to be, mother.

PROCURESS: Heavens, I don't regret it a bit, if you'll be as you say. For if you'll be the way I want you to be, you'll never get old as I am, and you'll always keep the charm that you now have, and to many you'll bring loss and to me you'll bring profit, without any expense on my part.

GYMNASIUM: The gods grant it!

PROCURESS: The gods can't do any of these things without your help.

GYMNASIUM: I'll certainly promise to do my best. (*Turning to* SELENIUM) But what about you during all this conversation, my dear Selenium, apple of my eye? I've never seen you look more unhappy. Tell me, I beg of you, why does gaiety avoid you? You're not as neat as usual—just look, what a deep sigh!—and you're pale. Please tell us both what your trouble is and what you wish us to do to help, so that we'll understand. Don't cry, my dear, and overwhelm me with such anxiety.

SELENIUM: My dear Gymnasium, I'm tortured and unhappy; I'm terrified and terribly torn with torment! My head pains me, my eyes pain me, my grief causes such pain! What can I say, except that by my own folly I'm being plunged into waves of woe!

GYMNASIUM: Where the folly was conceived, there have it concealed.

SELENIUM (*puzzled*): What am I to do?

GYMNASIUM: Hide it in the dark, in the deepest part of your breast. See that you alone know of your folly, and don't let anyone suspect it.

SELENIUM: But I have such a heartache!

GYMNASIUM: What's this? Where did you get a heart? Please tell me about it, a thing that neither I nor any other woman has, according to what the men say.

SELENIUM: If there is one to ache, it aches; if there isn't any, well, it aches here just the same.

GYMNASIUM (*to her mother*): This girl's in love.

SELENIUM: Ah, please tell me, is it better to be in love if the love is bitter?

GYMNASIUM: Dear me, love just abounds in honey and gall; it gives a taste of sweetness, but piles up bitterness until you can't stand it.

SELENIUM: That's the kind of ailment that tortures me, Gymnasium.

GYMNASIUM: Love is full of trickery.

SELENIUM: And so it's cheating me.

GYMNASIUM: Cheer up, you'll get the better of your malady.

SELENIUM: I hope so, if the doctor comes who can administer medicine to the malady.

GYMNASIUM: He'll come.

SELENIUM: That phrase, "He'll come," is awfully slow to a girl in love, unless he does come. But it's my own fault and foolishness that I'm in such terrible torment, because I've yearned for that one person to spend my life with!

PROCURESS: It's more profitable, Selenium, my dear, for a married woman to love one person and to spend her life with the man she marries. But a courtesan is like a flourishing city; she can't get along alone without plenty of men.

SELENIUM: Please pay attention, both of you. I'll tell you why I sent for you. My mother yielded to my desire, since I didn't wish to be called a courtesan, and obeyed me who am obedient to her; she permitted me to live with the man whom I love passionately.

PROCURESS: Lord, she did a stupid thing! But haven't you ever been intimate with any man?

SELENIUM: Not a one, except for Alcesimarchus. No other person ever violated my chastity.

PROCURESS: Tell me, how did the man work his way into your favour?

SELENIUM: My mother took me to see the procession at the festival of Bacchus. On the way home he spied on me and secretly followed me to the very door; then he won my mother's friendship, and mine as well, by his endearments, his presents, his gifts.

GYMNASIUM: I'd like to have that fellow. How I'd work him!

SELENIUM: No need to say more. From familiarity I began to love him, and he loved me.

PROCURESS: Oh, my dear Selenium, you ought to pretend to be in love; for if you really love, you think much more of the person you love than you do of your own interests.

SELENIUM: But he swore a solemn oath to my mother that he would marry me. (*Weeping*) And now he has to marry another girl, a relative of his from Lemnos, who lives here next door. His father has compelled him. Now my mother is angry at me because I didn't return home to her, when I found out that he was going to marry another girl.

PROCURESS: All's fair in love!

SELENIUM: Now, please let Gymnasium stay here just for the next three days and look after things here for me. Mother has sent for me.

PROCURESS: This will mean a troublesome three days for me, and loss of money; but I'll do it.

SELENIUM: That's kind and friendly of you. Gymnasium dear, if Alcesimarchus comes during my absence, don't upbraid him harshly; no

matter how he has treated me, I still love him. Please be gentle with
him; don't say anything that will cause him pain. Here are the keys.
Take whatever you need to use. (*Weeping*) I want to go.

GYMNASIUM (*weeping*): Look how you've made me cry, too!

SELENIUM: Good-bye, dear Gymnasium.

GYMNASIUM: Take care of yourself, dear. But you're not going in that
dirty dress, are you?

SELENIUM: A dirty dress ought to accompany a filthy fate.

GYMNASIUM: At least, lift up your dress.

SELENIUM: Let it drag, as I'm being dragged.

GYMNASIUM: Well, if you wish it so, good-bye and good luck.

SELENIUM: I'd like it, if it were possible. (SELENIUM *departs*.)

GYMNASIUM: Mother, do you wish anything of me before I go inside?
Dear me, Selenium seemed to be in love!

PROCURESS: And that's the reason I'm repeatedly dinning it into your
ears not to be in love with anyone. Go inside.

GYMNASIUM: Do you wish anything else of me?

PROCURESS: That you may fare well.

GYMNASIUM: Farewell. (*She goes into the house of* ALCESIMARCHUS.)

Act One.   Scene II

PROCURESS (*to the audience*): I've got the same fault that most of us
women have, who follow this profession; as soon as we get well loaded,
we're straightway full of talk; we say more than we should. The girl,
who just went away from here in tears, a long time ago I picked her
up from the street when she was a poor little abandoned baby. There's
a certain youth of very high rank—[why, now that I'm loaded to my
liking and have filled myself with the flower of Bacchus, I want to wag
my tongue more freely; I just can't keep quiet about what I ought to
keep quiet]¹—a man of the best family in Sicyon; his father's alive. The
young man's miserably and madly in love with this poor girl that just
now left here in tears. And she's hopelessly in love with him. I gave her

to a friend of mine, a courtesan, who had often suggested to me that I might find for her somewhere a boy or a girl, just born, that she could pass off as her own. As soon as I had the chance, I gave her what she wanted. After she received the baby girl from me, she immediately gave birth to the same baby that she had received from me, without benefit of a midwife and without the pains of childbirth, which other women have when they bring trouble upon themselves. She said that she had a lover from abroad and that the pretense was on his account. We two are the only ones who know about it, I who gave her the baby, and she who received it from me, except for you spectators, of course. That's the way the affair was managed. I want you to remember it, if the need should arise. I'm going home. (*The* PROCURESS *departs*.)

Act One.   Scene III

(*Enter* SUCCOUR, *who speaks the Prologue*.)

SUCCOUR: This old woman is too confounded loquacious and bibacious! She hardly left anything for the god to say, she was in such a hurry to tell about the substitution of the girl. If she had held her tongue, I would have told you about it just the same, and I could have made it clearer, since I'm a god; my name is Succour. Now, pay attention, so that I'll be successful in setting forth for you the plot of this play.

Many years ago a festival of Bacchus was held at Sicyon. A merchant of Lemnos came here to the games, and while he was here he ravished a maiden late one night along the road, being young and filled with wine. When he found out that he deserved punishment, he at once rescued himself by running away, and fled to Lemnos where he was then living. The girl whom he had made pregnant gave birth to a daughter nine months later. Since she didn't know who was responsible for the deed, she took a slave of her father's into her confidence, and gave the baby girl to the slave to abandon; he left it to its fate. This woman picked up the baby. The slave who had abandoned it watched secretly to see the place to which she took it. As you have just heard the woman herself admit, she gave the baby to the courtesan Melaenis, who raised the child properly and virtuously as her own daughter. The Lemnian later married a neighbour and relative of his. She died, and thereby delighted her husband. After the funeral ceremonies he immediately came here to Sicyon and married the same woman whom he had ravished as a maiden long before, and he recognises her as the one that he had ravished. She tells him that she had given birth to a daugh-

ter as a result of the outrage, and that she at once had handed it over
to a slave to abandon. He immediately orders the same slave to investigate and find if possible the woman who had picked it up. And so
the slave is now constantly devoting himself to this task of locating the
courtesan who picked up the baby when he abandoned it and watched
from his hiding-place. And as for what now remains, I wish to pay you
in full, so that my name can be struck off the debtors' list. There is
a young man here in Sicyon; his father is living. The youth is madly
in love with the girl who was abandoned, the same girl who just left
here in tears to go to her mother's, and she returns his love, which
makes it the sweetest love of all. But nothing is permanent, considering the way life is. The young man's father is anxious to give him a
wife. When the girl's mother learned of this, she sent for her daughter
to come home. That's the way matters stand.

Good-bye, and conquer by your constant courage, as you have done
in the past; aid your allies, both old and new; render greater your resources by just laws; fall on your foes, gain praises and prizes, that
the conquered Carthaginians may pay the penalties they deserve.[2]
(SUCCOUR *departs.*)

Act Two.   Scene I

(*Enter* ALCESIMARCHUS *from the country.*)

ALCESIMARCHUS (*to himself*): I do believe that Love was the first to
invent torture among mankind. I make this surmise from my own experience at home, without looking elsewhere; for I surpass, I excel all
mankind in torturability of soul! I'm tossed, tormented, driven, goaded,
whirled on the wheel of love, made lifeless in my misery! I'm torn, dis-
torted, distracted, distressed, my mind is so beclouded! Where I am,
there I'm not; where I'm not, there my thoughts are, so many different feelings I have! What I like I straightway don't like, Love so tricks
my tired soul; it drives, pursues, seeks, seizes, restrains, deceives, and
dispenses! What it delivers it doesn't deliver; it merely deludes; it
persuades me and then dissuades me; it dissuades me and then urges
me on! It deals with me after the manner of the sea; it wrecks my lovesick soul and, except for the fact that I don't go completely to the
bottom, I'm shattered by every kind of disaster. My father kept me at
his villa in the country for six whole uninterrupted days, and I didn't
have a chance to come to see my sweetheart once. Isn't this a wretched
thing to relate?

(From this point on, the text of the play is very corrupt for several hundred lines. Much has been completely lost, and much is in too fragmentary a condition to be intelligible. The longer fragments have been translated. In the passage which follows, the SLAVE *of* ALCESIMARCHUS *speaks with his master, who reproaches himself for his treatment of* SELENIUM.*)*

SLAVE: But what does this mean?

ALCESIMARCHUS: I want to be abused abundantly.

SLAVE: What for?

ALCESIMARCHUS: For being alive.

SLAVE: I can do that with great ease, if you want me to.

ALCESIMARCHUS: I do.

SLAVE: But don't you plant your fists in my kingdom.

ALCESIMARCHUS: Heavens, I'll never do that!

SLAVE: Promise!

ALCESIMARCHUS: I promise that I won't do it. But first of all, I'm a worthless wretch for being able to stay away from my sweetheart so many days.

SLAVE: God! You are a worthless wretch.

ALCESIMARCHUS: And she loves me so in return!

SLAVE: Damned if you don't deserve a beating!

ALCESIMARCHUS: Ah, that I make her so unhappy at heart!

SLAVE: You'll never be worth anything.

ALCESIMARCHUS: Especially since she promised solemnly and pledged her faith—

SLAVE: Neither god nor man ought to treat you well after this.

ALCESIMARCHUS: —that she would spend her life with me in marriage—

SLAVE: You ought to put on fetters and never take them off.

ALCESIMARCHUS: —and trusted herself to me and believed my word of honour—

SLAVE: Damned if I don't think you deserve a good horsewhipping!

ALCESIMARCHUS: —and she used to call me her little honey, her sweetie-kiss!

SLAVE: For that one phrase you deserve to carry a cross ten times.

ALCESIMARCHUS: Happy thought! But what do you advise now?

SLAVE: I'll tell you. Give her satisfaction; go hang yourself, so that she won't be angry at you. . . .

(*A third person enters, perhaps* GYMNASIUM, *and advises* ALCESIMAR-CHUS *to see* MELAENIS.)

ALCESIMARCHUS: . . . where are you?

SLAVE: Here I am.

ALCESIMARCHUS: Go, bring me weapons!

SLAVE: Weapons?

ALCESIMARCHUS: And bring a corselet!

SLAVE: Bring a corselet?

ALCESIMARCHUS: Run, hurry, bring a horse!

SLAVE: Heaven's name! The poor fellow's gone crazy!

ALCESIMARCHUS: Go! And many spearmen, many light-armed troops, and many, many more—I don't want any excuses! Where are the things I've ordered?

SLAVE (*aside*): This fellow really isn't sane!

GYMNASIUM (*to* SLAVE): Punch-drunk, I guess, judging from his actions!

SLAVE: Tell me, please, are you crazy or dreaming on your feet, when you order me to get a horse, bring a corselet, many spearmen, and then many light-armed troops, and many, many more? That's the kind of crazy talk you've been giving me.

ALCESIMARCHUS: Tell me, did I say that?

SLAVE: You damned well did say it just now.

ALCESIMARCHUS: I'm not really here.

SLAVE: You're a magician, if you can be here and not here at the same time.

GYMNASIUM: Young man, I see that you've been deeply pierced by Love's poisoned arrow; and so I want to give you some advice.

ALCESIMARCHUS: Go ahead.

GYMNASIUM: Be careful never to engage in warfare with Love.

ALCESIMARCHUS: What should I do?

GYMNASIUM: Go to her mother's home; make excuses, give her your oath, make enticing entreaties, beseech her not to be angry at you.

ALCESIMARCHUS: By gad, I'll make excuses until I'm nothing but hoarseness. . . . (ALCESIMARCHUS *and his* SLAVE *perhaps depart at this point.*)

(*The* FATHER *of* ALCESIMARCHUS *enters; he wishes to persuade* SELENIUM *to give up* ALCESIMARCHUS; *he meets* GYMNASIUM, *whom he mistakes for* SELENIUM, *and is attracted by her.*)

FATHER (*to himself*): . . . an attractive little wench. God! She's a little beauty! I may be an old hack, but I suspect that I can still whinny to a little mare like her, if we have a chance to be alone together.

GYMNASIUM (*to herself, pretending to be* SELENIUM): It's just fine for me that Alcesimarchus has returned! No one hates to be alone more than I do.

FATHER (*aside*): Just invite me in, if you don't want to be alone. I'll keep you company; I'll gladly do something to keep you busy.

GYMNASIUM: How beautifully Alcesimarchus decorated this house for me!

FATHER (*aside*): How charming it is when Venus enters! Love is beautiful.

GYMNASIUM: The house is redolent of the fragrance of Venus, since my lover has embellished it.

FATHER (*aside*): Not only is she charming, but her words are damned delightful, too! But as I interpret her remarks, I suspect that she's the very one, by Jove, that's ruining my son! It's only a suspicion, since I've never seen her; but I believe I'm right. For my son rented this house, where she is standing; that's why I think she's the one; and she mentioned his name, too. What if I approach and speak to her. (*To* GYMNASIUM) Good day, you enticer to ruin and destruction! . . .[3]

GYMNASIUM: . . . what you wish.

FATHER: I want to find out from you what it is that my son has done, what injury I or any of mine ever did—tell me that—that you should proceed to plague and plunder me and my son and his mother and our property.

GYMNASIUM (*aside*): The poor fool's mistaken, as I just said! Here's a wonderful chance! I'll have some sport with him, as the occasion demands. (*Aloud*) Can't you stop abusing a poor innocent girl?

FATHER: In heaven's name, haven't you any other lover?

GYMNASIUM: Except for your one and only son, there isn't a single person for me to love. . . .[4]

(*In the next fragment* ALCESIMARCHUS *has returned with* SELENIUM *and* MELAENIS; SELENIUM *refuses to forgive him.*)

SELENIUM: I hate you!

ALCESIMARCHUS: My house needs its little mistress. Let me lead you home.

SELENIUM: Take your hand away!

ALCESIMARCHUS: My own darling little sister!

SELENIUM: I don't want you for my little brother.

ALCESIMARCHUS (*to* MELAENIS): Well then, you, my darling little mother!

MELAENIS: I don't want you for my little boy.

ALCESIMARCHUS: I beg of you—

SELENIUM: Good-bye!

ALCESIMARCHUS: —that you permit—

SELENIUM: I'm not interested!

ALCESIMARCHUS: —me to explain.

SELENIUM: You're wearing me out!

ALCESIMARCHUS: Let me speak.

MELAENIS: I've heard enough of your lies.

ALCESIMARCHUS: They're true!

MELAENIS: Even if they are, it isn't possible now.

ALCESIMARCHUS: I'm willing to make amends.

SELENIUM: And I don't care to receive them from you.

ALCESIMARCHUS: Ah, I'm suffering every possible torture, and I deserve it, unhappy wretch that I am!

SELENIUM: I'm delighted that you are, and you don't deserve to have anyone pity you.

(SELENIUM *departs. After another lacuna in the text, the conversation between* MELAENIS *and* ALCESIMARCHUS *resumes.*)

MELAENIS: Are you joking because you have another bride promised you, the rich Lemnian? You can have her. We haven't as good a family as you, and we haven't as much wealth as you; but just the same I'm not afraid of anyone finding fault with our solemn pledge. And if you suffer any pain, you'll know the reason why you suffer.

ALCESIMARCHUS: May the gods damn me—

MELAENIS (*with sarcasm*): I hope you'll get whatever you pray for!

ALCESIMARCHUS: —if I ever marry that girl my father's engaged me to.

MELAENIS: And me, if I ever let you marry my daughter.

ALCESIMARCHUS: Will you permit me to perjure myself?

MELAENIS: Much more gladly, indeed, than to have myself and my affairs perish and my daughter trifled with. Go away! Find yourself a place where there is an abundance of confidence in your pledges. As far as we're concerned, Alcesimarchus, you've lost your ticket.

ALCESIMARCHUS: Give me just one chance.

MELAENIS: I've done it often, and regretted it.

ALCESIMARCHUS: Give her back to me.

MELAENIS: I'll use an old saying for a new circumstance: "What's given I wish I hadn't given; what's left I shan't give."

ALCESIMARCHUS: Won't you give her back to me?

MELAENIS: You're answering yourself for me.

ALCESIMARCHUS: You won't give her back?

MELAENIS: You've known my entire decision for a long time.

ALCESIMARCHUS: You're really resolved on this at heart?

MELAENIS: Why, I'm not even considering it. Heavens! I'm not even listening to what you're saying.

ALCESIMARCHUS: No? What are you doing, then?

MELAENIS: You pay attention, so that you'll know what I'm doing.

ALCESIMARCHUS (*frantically*): May all the gods and goddesses, the powers of Heaven and the powers of Hell and the middle-in-between powers, and may Juno, the queen and daughter of almighty Jupiter, and may Saturn, his uncle—

MELAENIS (*enjoying his confusion*): His father, you mean.

ALCESIMARCHUS: —and may opulent Ops, his grandmother—

MELAENIS: On the contrary, his mother.

ALCESIMARCHUS: May Juno, his daughter, and Saturn, his uncle, and almighty Jupiter—you're casting a spell on me; it's your fault that I'm making these mistakes!

MELAENIS: Keep right on talking.

ALCESIMARCHUS: Can I know again what your decision will be?

MELAENIS: Keep right on talking. I won't send her back. That's settled.

ALCESIMARCHUS (*wildly*): Now may Jupiter and may Juno and may Janus—I don't know what to say. (*After a pause*) Now I know. You just listen now, woman, so that you'll know my decision. May all the gods, the great gods, the small gods, and even the platter gods[5] keep me from kissing Selenium while we're alive, if I don't kill you and your daughter both today, and if at dawn tomorrow I don't murder the two of you all over again, and if with my third attack I don't completely demolish all of you, by God, unless you give her back to me! I have stated my intention. Farewell! (*He rushes into his house.*)

MELAENIS (*to herself*): He's gone inside in a rage. What am I to do now? If the girl comes back to him, matters will be just as they were before. When he grows weary of her, he'll turn her out and then marry the Lemnian woman. But I'd better go and follow him. I must take care that he doesn't do anything in his passion. In short, since the poor and the rich don't have the same law, I'll waste my time rather than lose my daughter. But who's this that's rushing right up the street in this direction? (*She withdraws to* ALCESIMARCHUS' *doorway*) I'm afraid of the other matter, and I'm frightened at this, and I'm completely torn with terror!

Act Two. Scene II[6]

(*Enter* LAMPADIO *in haste.*)

LAMPADIO (*to himself*): I followed the old woman[7] through the streets with my shouting; I made her miserable! In how many ways today she held her tongue and refused to speak! What allurements, what rewards I promised her! What tricks, what intrigues I invented in questioning her. Finally I did chisel her tongue loose, when I promised to give her a cask of wine.

Act Two. Scene III

(*Enter* PHANOSTRATA *from the house of* DEMIPHO.)

PHANOSTRATA (*to herself*): I thought I heard the voice of my slave Lampadio just now in front of the house.

LAMPADIO (*stepping forward*): You're not deaf, mistress; you heard rightly.

PHANOSTRATA: What are you doing here?

LAMPADIO: Bringing you good news.

PHANOSTRATA: What is it?

LAMPADIO: A little while ago I saw a woman leave the house next door—

PHANOSTRATA (*excited*): The one that picked up my child?

LAMPADIO: That's right.

PHANOSTRATA: What then?

LAMPADIO: I told her how I had seen her pick up the daughter of my mistress at the hippodrome. Then she *was* scared!

MELAENIS (*aside*): Oh, my body's in a tremble! My heart's pounding! For I remember that it was from the hippodrome that the tiny baby was brought to me, and I passed it off as my own.

PHANOSTRATA: Come, continue, please. I'm in a hurry to hear what happened.

MELAENIS (*aside*): I wish that you weren't able to hear.[8]

LAMPADIO: I kept on filling her with advice: "That old woman is calling you from fortune to misery. She's your nurse; don't consider her your mother. I'm to take you back and invite you to great wealth, where you can find a place in a distinguished family, and have a father who will give you a dowry of twenty talents. It isn't that way here, where in Etruscan fashion you have to earn your own dowry by shamefully selling your body."

PHANOSTRATA: Please tell me; is the woman that picked her up a courtesan?

LAMPADIO: No, but she was. Now I'll tell you what happened. I was just winning the girl over by my persuasive arguments; the old woman embraced her knees, begging and beseeching her not to leave her; she swore a solemn oath to me that the girl was her daughter and that she had given birth to her. "The girl that you want," she says, "I gave to a friend of mine to bring up as her own daughter. And she's alive," says she. "Where is she?" says I immediately.

PHANOSTRATA: Save me, gods, I pray of you!

MELAENIS (*aside*): But you're destroying me.

PHANOSTRATA: You should have asked to whom she gave it.

LAMPADIO: I did ask, and she said, to the courtesan Melaenis.

MELAENIS (*aside*): He's mentioned my name! I'm completely ruined!

LAMPADIO: When she mentioned the name, I ask at once: "Where does she live?" says I. "Take me and point her out to me." "She's sailed away to live abroad," says she.

MELAENIS (*aside*): There's cold water to revive me!

LAMPADIO: "We'll sail away after her," says I. "But what nonsense is this? You'll be damned sorry for it, if you don't tell me where she lives." [9] I kept right on insisting, until finally the old woman swore that she would point out Melaenis to me.

PHANOSTRATA: But you shouldn't have let her go.

LAMPADIO: She's safe. She said that she wanted first to meet a certain woman, a friend of hers, who had an interest in this same matter. But I know she'll come.

MELAENIS (*aside*): She'll point me out, and add her own troubles to mine, and reveal the deception to Selenium.[9]

PHANOSTRATA: What do you wish me to do now?

LAMPADIO: Go inside, and be calm. If your husband returns, tell him to remain at home, so that he won't keep me waiting, if I want him for anything. I'm going to hurry back to the old woman.

PHANOSTRATA (*earnestly*): Please, Lampadio, tend to the matter.

LAMPADIO: I'll polish it up for you in fine shape.

PHANOSTRATA: I trust in the gods and you. (*She goes into the house.*)

LAMPADIO: And I in the same gods—that you go home. (*He turns to go.*)

MELAENIS (*coming forward*): Young man, stop and listen!

LAMPADIO: Are you speaking to me, woman?

MELAENIS: Yes, to you.

LAMPADIO: What's your business? I'm fully occupied right now.

MELAENIS: Who lives in that house?

LAMPADIO: My master, Demipho.

MELAENIS: You mean the one that's made such a wealthy match between his daughter and Alcesimarchus?

LAMPADIO: The very one.

MELAENIS: Well, look here! What other daughter are you people now searching for?

LAMPADIO: I'll tell you: not the daughter of his wife, but his wife's daughter.

MELAENIS (*puzzled*): What kind of sentence is that?

LAMPADIO: She's my master's daughter, I say, born of a former woman.

MELAENIS: You certainly said just now that you were searching for the daughter of the woman who was speaking here.

LAMPADIO: It is her daughter that I'm looking for.

MELAENIS: Pray tell me, then, how is she a former woman, when she's now his wife?

LAMPADIO: Woman, whoever you are, you're wearing me out with your questions. It's the in-between wife he had—she's the mother of the girl that is being given to Alcesimarchus. This wife has died. Now do you understand?

MELAENIS: I understand that much. But the thing that bothers me is this: how can the former one be the later one, and the later one the former?

LAMPADIO: I'll explain: he raped her formerly before he married her; Formerly she became pregnant and gave birth to a daughter; after the birth she ordered the baby be exposed; I'm the one that abandoned it. Another woman picked it up. I saw her do it. Later on my master married this same woman. Now we're searching for the girl, his daughter. But why are you now scanning the sky with face upturned?

MELAENIS: Go on now about your business; I won't detain you. I do understand now.

LAMPADIO: Thank heaven for that! For I suppose, if you didn't understand, you'd never let me go. (LAMPADIO *departs.*)

MELAENIS (*to herself*): Now I have to be a noble woman, whether I want to or not, although I'd rather not. The truth is out, I see. Now I'll put them under obligation to me instead of having her point me out to them. I'll go home and bring Selenium back to her parents. (MELAENIS *departs; a short time is supposed to elapse before the next Act.*)

Act Three

(*Enter* MELAENIS, SELENIUM, *and* HALISCA.)

MELAENIS: I've told you the entire story. Follow me, won't you, my dear Selenium, that you may belong to those who ought to have you rather than to me? Although I shall give you up unwillingly, I'll persuade myself that I'm acting in your interest instead of in my own. (*She reveals a little casket*) Here are the trinkets which the woman who gave you to me brought along with you years ago. These will help your parents to recognise you. Halisca, take this casket. (*She hands the casket to the maid*) Hurry up, knock on that door (*indicating the house of* DEMIPHO). Say that I'm anxious to have someone come out here quickly.

(*As* HALISCA *knocks at* DEMIPHO'S *house,* ALCESIMARCHUS *enters from his house, sword in hand.*)

ALCESIMARCHUS (*not seeing the women*): Oh Death, thou who art friendly and devoted to me, take me to thy bosom!

SELENIUM (*to* MELAENIS): Oh, mother dear, we're hopelessly ruined!

ALCESIMARCHUS (*to himself*): Shall I pierce my side here, or on the left?

MELAENIS (*to* SELENIUM): What's the matter?

SELENIUM: Don't you see Alcesimarchus? He has a sword.

ALCESIMARCHUS (*to himself*): What are you about? You're delaying. Leave the light of day!

SELENIUM (*to* MELAENIS *and* HALISCA): Run to his aid, please, or he'll kill himself. (*They run to assist him, and* HALISCA *drops the casket;* SELENIUM *clings to* ALCESIMARCHUS.)

ALCESIMARCHUS: Oh my salvation, more salutary than Salvation herself! You alone make me to live, whether I wish to or not.

MELAENIS: You didn't really intend to do any harm to yourself.

ALCESIMARCHUS: I haven't anything to do with you; as far as you're concerned, I'm dead. (*Embracing* SELENIUM) Now that I have her, I'll never let her go. Damned if I'm not determined to rivet her fast to me all over. (*Calling at the door*) Slaves, where are you? Shut up the house and bolt and bar the doors. I'll go and carry her over the threshold. (*He carries* SELENIUM *inside.*)

MELAENIS: He's gone in! He's carried off the girl! I'll follow him inside and tell him the same story. Perhaps I can calm down his anger. (*She goes inside, followed by* HALISCA.)

Act Four. Scene I

(*Enter* LAMPADIO.)

LAMPADIO (*angrily, to himself*): I don't think I've ever seen a more torturable old hag than that woman is! Why the devil does she deny what she admitted to me just now?

(*Enter* PHANOSTRATA *from her house.*)

But there! I see my mistress. (*Noticing the casket on the ground*) And what's this? A casket lying here with trinkets in it? And I don't see anyone else in the street. I'll have to act like a child now; I'll squat for the casket. (*He stoops down and picks it up.*)

PHANOSTRATA: What are you up to, Lampadio?

LAMPADIO: This casket here, it doesn't come from our house, does it? (*He hands it to* PHANOSTRATA) I just picked it up here in front of the door.

PHANOSTRATA: What news do you bring about the old woman?

LAMPADIO: I've never seen a fouler wretch anywhere on earth; now she denies everything that she admitted a little while ago. Damn it! I'd rather die any sort of death than permit that old hag to make a fool of me.

PHANOSTRATA (*examining the casket*): Ye gods, your protection!

LAMPADIO: Why call on the gods?

PHANOSTRATA: The gods save us!

LAMPADIO: What's the matter?

PHANOSTRATA: These trinkets! They were with my little daughter when you abandoned her to her fate.

LAMPADIO: Are you in your right mind?

PHANOSTRATA: They certainly are the ones.

LAMPADIO: Keeping right on, eh?

PHANOSTRATA: They are the same.

LAMPADIO: If any other woman talked that way to me, I'd say that she was drunk.

PHANOSTRATA: I swear by heaven, I'm telling the truth.

LAMPADIO: Well, tell me, where in the world did they come from? Or do you think some god dumped the casket here in front of our door, intentionally, at just the right time?

PHANOSTRATA: Heavenly Hope, give me your help!

Act Four.　Scene II

(Enter HALISCA *in despair from the house of* ALCESIMARCHUS.*)*

HALISCA *(to herself)*: If the gods don't give me their help, I'm ruined!
And I don't know where to look for aid! How miserable my carelessness makes me! I'm grievously afraid of what my back will feel, if my
mistress finds out that I've been as negligent as this! I held that casket
in my own hands and I took it from her here in front of the house; and
now I don't know where it is; it slipped from my hand somewhere
around here, I suspect. *(To the audience)* Please, dear people, dear
spectators, if any of you saw him, tell me who carried it off, who picked
it up, and whether he went this way or that. *(To herself)* I'm none the
wiser for asking them or tiring them out; they're always delighted to
see a woman in misfortune. Now I'll look to see if there are any footprints here. For if no one passed by here after I went inside, the casket
would be lying right here. But why say "right here?" It's lost,[10] I
guess, it's done for, it's perished! I'm ill-fated and accursed! It's gone,
and I'm a goner! It's lost, and so am I! But I'll keep on as I began;
I'll hunt for it. Inside the house I'm afraid, and outside I'm overcome
with fright! Such fear besets me now on every side! Human beings are
such hopeless creatures! The fellow who has the casket, whoever he is,
is happy now, but it isn't an earthly bit of use to him, and it can be
to me. I'm wasting time by acting slowly. Get to work, Halisca, look at
the ground, look all around! Search with your eyes; survey the spot
shrewdly!

LAMPADIO *(aside to* PHANOSTRATA*)*: Mistress!

PHANOSTRATA: Well?

LAMPADIO: It's—

PHANOSTRATA: What is it?

LAMPADIO: It's she!

PHANOSTRATA: Who?

LAMPADIO: The woman that dropped the casket.

PHANOSTRATA: You're quite right; she's marking the place where she
dropped it; it's obvious.

HALISCA *(to herself)*: But he went this way; I see the mark of his
shoe in the dust. I'll follow this way! Here's a spot where he stood with

another. Here's where we had all the confusion a little while ago. No, he didn't go this way. (*Examining the footprints more carefully*) He stood here, and then he went from here over there. Here was a conference with some one. This concerns two persons, evidently. Aha! Now I see the footprints of just the one. He went this way; I'll investigate. He went from here to here; from here he went—nowhere! Oh dear! I'm done! What's lost is lost; the casket and my hide as well! I'll go inside. (*She goes towards the house of* ALCESIMARCHUS.)

PHANOSTRATA: Wait, my good woman, wait! There are some people here who want to meet you.

LAMPADIO: A good woman and a malevolent male want you.

HALISCA: A good woman and a malevolent male want me, eh? Well, the speaker knows more what he wants than does the person spoken to. I'll go back. Please tell me if you've seen anyone around here with a casket and trinkets in it, which I unfortunately lost here? When we ran in to Alcesimarchus just now, to keep him from killing himself, I must have foolishly dropped it.

LAMPADIO (*aside to* PHANOSTRATA): This is the woman who lost it. Let's keep quiet about it for a moment, mistress.

HALISCA: I'm so completely miserable! What shall I tell my mistress? She told me to guard it so carefully so that Selenium could more easily recognise her parents. The poor girl was adopted by my mistress as her own; a certain courtesan brought the child when she was a tiny baby.

LAMPADIO (*to* PHANOSTRATA): She's talking about this business of ours, all right! She must know where your daughter is, judging from what she says.

HALISCA: Now of her own accord she wants to return the girl to her real father and mother. Mercy me! You have business of your own, my dear sir, and here I am entrusting my troubles to you!

LAMPADIO: This is my business, and those words of yours are food and drink to me! I just answered a question that my mistress here asked, while I was paying attention to this affair of yours. Now I'm back to your business; tell me whatever you need; just command me. What were you looking for?

HALISCA: My greetings to you, good sir, and to you, good lady!

PHANOSTRATA: The same to you. But what are you looking for?

HALISCA: I'm following footsteps where something escaped me.

LAMPADIO: What is it? What sort of thing do you mean?

HALISCA: Something to bring sadness to another and sorrow to us!

LAMPADIO (*to* PHANOSTRATA): Mistress, this woman is a shrewd and worthless piece of goods.

PHANOSTRATA: She certainly seems so.

LAMPADIO: She's imitating a pernicious and pestiferous beast.

PHANOSTRATA: Which one, pray tell.

LAMPADIO: The caterpillar, that turns and twists itself in vine leaves; she's beginning the same sort of twisted talk. (*To* HALISCA) What are you looking for?

HALISCA: Young man, a casket flew away from me here.

LAMPADIO: You should have put it in a cage.

HALISCA: There really wasn't much in it.

LAMPADIO (*with sarcasm*): Strange that there wasn't a whole troop of slaves in the one casket!

PHANOSTRATA: Let her talk.

LAMPADIO: If she only would.

PHANOSTRATA: Come, tell me what was in it.

HALISCA: Merely trinkets.

LAMPADIO: There's a certain man who says that he knows where it is.

HALISCA: Heavens! There's a certain woman who would be awfully grateful if he would show it to her.

LAMPADIO: But that certain man wants to get a reward.

HALISCA: But that certain woman who lost the casket says she hasn't anything to give the certain man.

LAMPADIO: But that certain man prefers a kind favour to money.

HALISCA: Mercy, that certain woman doesn't let a favour go unrewarded.

PHANOSTRATA: Now you're benefiting yourself by your words. We confess that we have the casket.

HALISCA: Salvation save you! Where is it now?

PHANOSTRATA (*producing the casket*): Here it is, safe. But I want to have a talk with you about an important matter of mine. I'll select you to assist in my safety.

HALISCA: What sort of business is this? And who are you?

PHANOSTRATA: I am the mother of the child who wore these trinkets.

HALISCA: Do you live here, then?

PHANOSTRATA: A sound prophecy. But come, my good woman, stop digressing and get to business. Tell me quickly where you got these trinkets.

HALISCA: The daughter of my mistress wore them.

LAMPADIO: You lie! The daughter of my mistress, not yours, wore them.

PHANOSTRATA (*to* LAMPADIO): Don't contradict her.

LAMPADIO: I'll be quiet.

PHANOSTRATA (*impatiently*): Keep on, woman. Where is the girl that wore them?

HALISCA: Right here next door.

PHANOSTRATA: In heavens name! That's where my husband's son-in-law lives.

LAMPADIO (*to* PHANOSTRATA): Now, don't you contradict her.

PHANOSTRATA (*to* HALISCA): Keep right on; how old is she said to be?

HALISCA: Seventeen.

PHANOSTRATA: She's mine.

LAMPADIO: She is, as far as the years are concerned.

HALISCA: Well? I'm looking for my half of the reward.

LAMPADIO: By gee, I'm looking for my third, for there are three of us here.

PHANOSTRATA: And I've found what I was looking for—my daughter.

HALISCA: What was entrusted in good faith ought to be returned, so that a kindness won't be disastrous to the benefactor. The girl is our foster child, and assuredly your daughter. My mistress intends to give your daughter back to you, and that's why she left home. But please ask her about the rest of the matter. I'm merely a servant.

PHANOSTRATA: A just request.

HALISCA: I'd rather have her get the credit for it. But please give that casket back to me.

PHANOSTRATA: What do you think, Lampadio?

LAMPADIO: You'd better keep what's yours.

PHANOSTRATA: And yet I feel sorry for her.

LAMPADIO: This is what I think you ought to do: give her the casket and go inside with her.

PHANOSTRATA: I'll follow your advice. (*To* HALISCA) You take the casket, and let's go in. But what is the name of your mistress?

HALISCA: Melaenis.

PHANOSTRATA: You go first; I'll follow you at once. (*The women enter the house of* ALCESIMARCHUS; LAMPADIO *follows; a short time is supposed to elapse before the next Act.*)

Act Five

(*Enter* DEMIPHO *from the forum.*)

DEMIPHO (*to himself*): What's this story that every one is talking about in the city—that my daughter has been found? And they say that Lampadio has been looking for me in the forum.

(*Enter* LAMPADIO *from the house of* ALCESIMARCHUS.)

LAMPADIO: Master, where are you coming from?

DEMIPHO: From the senate.

LAMPADIO: I'm happy to state that there has been an addition to your family, as a result of my efforts.

DEMIPHO: I'm not pleased by it; I don't care to have any additions through other people's efforts. But what do you mean?

LAMPADIO: Hurry into the house here of your new relative; you'll recognise your daughter inside at once. Your wife's inside there as well.

DEMIPHO: I'm determined to put this matter before everything else. (*They go into the house of* ALCESIMARCHUS.)

Epilogue (*spoken by the company*)

Spectators, don't wait until they come out here to you; no one will come out. They'll all finish the business indoors. When that's done, they'll take off their costumes. After that, the actor who has made mistakes will get a beating, the one who hasn't will get a drink. And now for the rest that remains for you, spectators; in the fashion of your forbears, give us your applause at the conclusion of the play.

1. Lindsay brackets this passage as a later expansion.

2. The play is usually dated shortly before the end of the Second Carthaginian War.

3. About forty lines of the conversation are lost at this point.

4. There is a long break in the text here. The fragments indicate that Lampadio spoke a soliloquy of more than fifty lines which doubtless were concerned with his search for the woman who had found the abandoned baby years before.

5. The "platter gods" were the household gods, to whom offerings were made of platters of food.

6. The conventional division into acts and scenes does not take into account the several scene divisions which occurred in the fragmentary portion of the play.

7. This is the Procuress, whom Lampadio recognised as the woman who had picked up the baby.

8. Lindsay believes that part of the scene is lost at this point. Lampadio tells how he met Gymnasium and wrongly thought her to be Selenium.

9. The Mss. are unintelligible here; the emendation of Schoell has been adopted.

10. *Periit*, the reading of the Mss., seems preferable here to *perii*, suggested by Spengel, and printed by most editors.

VIII
CURCULIO

Characters in the Play

PALINURUS, *slave of* PHAEDROMUS
PHAEDROMUS, *a young man of Epidaurus*
LEAENA, *an old woman, slave of* CAPPADOX
PLANESIUM, *a girl belonging to* CAPPADOX
CAPPADOX, *a pimp*
A COOK
CURCULIO, *a parasite*
LYCO, *a banker*
THE PROPERTY MANAGER
THERAPONTIGONUS, *a captain*

Acrostic Argument

Curculio, sent by Phaedromus, goes to Caria to procure some money. There he makes away with a ring belonging to Phaedromus' rival. He writes and seals a letter. Lyco, upon seeing it, recognises the seal of the captain. He pays the pimp his price to let Phaedromus' sweetheart go. The captain threatens to summon Lyco and the pimp to court. He then discovers that the girl is his long-lost sister, and at her request he gives her in marriage to Phaedromus.

INTRODUCTION

THE *Curculio* is not one of the more popular of Plautus' plays, but it is amusing and has many features of unusual interest. The plot, which combines both trickery and mistaken identity, has in itself little originality. A young man (Phaedromus) is in love with a girl (Planesium) who is in the possession of a pimp (Cappadox). She is about to be handed over to a soldier (Therapontigonus) who has deposited the money for her with a banker (Lyco). By means of a ring which a parasite (Curculio) steals from the soldier, the young man secures the girl. The soldier arrives in anger, but recognises Planesium as his sister. The tables are turned and the pimp becomes the victim, since he must reimburse the soldier, now that Planesium has been discovered to be freeborn.

The play is rich in the usual comedy types: young lover, sweetheart, impudent slave, parasite, pimp, boasting soldier, drunken old woman. There is nothing mechanical about their parts, however; each is portrayed with vivacity and humour. Curculio is one of the most active parasites in Roman comedy; he plays the part of a running slave, and manages the deception with cleverness and cunning; his account of the meeting with the soldier is a little masterpiece of vivid narrative. Cappadox is a ridiculous rather than a vicious pimp, Planesium is a decent girl who in spite of her surroundings has preserved her chastity (a necessary feature since she will prove to be of free birth), Therapontigonus has the qualities of a boastful soldier, but is far less ridiculous than such a figure as Pyrgopolynices in *The Braggart Warrior*.

The *Curculio*, like *The Comedy of Asses,* moves rapidly and has few dull scenes. There are many puns and jests, and somewhat more obscenity than usual. The plot is well constructed; the two elements of intrigue and recognition are closely knit, since it is the stolen ring of the soldier that brings about both the tricking of the pimp and the revelation of Planesium's real identity.

The comedy has several striking features which make it stand out among the lesser known plays of Plautus. The setting is unusual, for the action takes place at Epidaurus, where the pimp hopes to cure himself of his many ailments by spending the night in the temple of

353

Aesculapius. The play has no prologue, but an excellent opening scene in which Phaedromus and his slave bring an offering of wine to the old woman who has charge of Planesium. Like the *Amphitryon,* the action of the play begins before dawn. The address of the property manager to the audience is an innovation which appears in no other Plautine comedy. There is no foreshadowing of the later action, and the recognition of Planesium as the soldier's sister comes as a complete surprise. In most recognition plays of Plautus, some hint of the true relationship is given either by the prologue or by the words of the characters. Since no one of the characters has any idea of Planesium's identity, it has been conjectured that the play originally had a prologue which has been lost.

The date of the Greek original is thought to be 303-2 B.C. since there is a reference to the taking of Sicyon in lines 394-5. The author of the original is not known, but both Posidippus and Diphilus have been suggested as possibilities. G. W. Elderkin believes that the author must have been Philippides and that the purpose of the play was to hold up Demetrius Poliorcetes and his mistress Lamia to the ridicule of the Athenians. If this be true, the *Curculio* in its original form contained far more political satire than do most of the plays of the Greek New Comedy. The date of the Roman production is usually assumed to be shortly after 194 B.C.

CURCULIO

(SCENE:—*A street in Epidaurus on which are the houses of* CAPPADOX *and* PHAEDROMUS *and a temple of Aesculapius.*)

Act One. Scene I

(*The action begins before daybreak.* PHAEDROMUS *enters, carrying a lighted candle; he is followed by* PALINURUS *and slaves with wine and provisions.*)

PALINURUS: Where am I to think you're bound for at this hour of the night, Phaedromus, all dressed up as you are, and with this procession behind you?

PHAEDROMUS (*cheerfully*): Whither Venus and Cupid summon me, and whither Love persuades. Whether 'tis midnight or early twilight, when the day is fixed and agreed upon for meeting your enemy, you have to go whither they command, even against your will.

PALINURUS: But still—but still—

PHAEDROMUS: But still you're bothering me.

PALINURUS: This really isn't a pretty sight, nor one to be spoken about: you're acting as your own slave; here you are, all dressed up, lighting your way with a candle.

PHAEDROMUS: Isn't it fitting for me to take to my sweet little honey that which is produced from sweets and gathered by the labours of the little bees?

PALINURUS: Well, where am I to say you're going?

PHAEDROMUS: If you should ask me, I might give you the information.

PALINURUS: If I should ask you, what would you reply?

PHAEDROMUS: This is the temple of Aesculapius.

PALINURUS: I've known that for more than a year.

PHAEDROMUS: And next to it (*pointing to the house of* CAPPADOX) is that doorway, dearest and closest to me of all doors. Good day, door! Have you been well of late?

PALINURUS (*mocking him*): Ah, door, most closed to me of all doors! Did your fever leave you yesterday or the day before? And did you dine yesterday?

PHAEDROMUS: Are you making fun of me?

PALINURUS: Why, then, are you asking whether the door is well or not, you idiot?

PHAEDROMUS: Heavens! It's the most beautiful and the most tactful door I've ever seen. It never whispers a single word. When it's opened, it's silent; when she comes forth secretly to me by night, it's silent.

PALINURUS (*troubled*): Look here, you're not doing, or planning to do, some deed that will disgrace you or your family, are you? You're not laying a snare for some chaste maiden, or for someone who ought to be chaste?

PHAEDROMUS: Of course not! May Jupiter forbid!

PALINURUS: My sentiments, exactly! Always arrange your love affairs, if you're wise, so that you won't be in disgrace, if every one learns about them. And always be sure that you don't lose your power.[1]

PHAEDROMUS: What do you mean by that?

PALINURUS: Go down your road cautiously. Love what you love, but keep your power to love.

PHAEDROMUS: But it's a pimp who lives here.

PALINURUS: No one keeps you from here then, nor prevents your buying what's on the open market, if you have the money. No one forbids any person from going along the public highway. Provided you don't make a path across fenced-in property, provided you keep away from married women, widows, virgins, young people, and respectable children, love anyone you wish.

PHAEDROMUS: This house belongs to a pimp.

PALINURUS: May it be damned!

PHAEDROMUS: Why?

PALINURUS: It's enslaved in the service of a scoundrel.

PHAEDROMUS: Interrupt me, will you?

PALINURUS: By all means!

PHAEDROMUS: Won't you hold your tongue?

PALINURUS: Why, you told me to interrupt you.

PHAEDROMUS: And now I forbid it. But, as I started to say, he has a young slave girl.

PALINURUS: The pimp, you mean, who lives here?

PHAEDROMUS: You've got it exactly.

PALINURUS (*grinning*): Then I won't be afraid of losing it.

PHAEDROMUS: You're a nuisance. The pimp wants to make her a courtesan. She's madly in love with me. But I don't want to return her love.

PALINURUS: Why not?

PHAEDROMUS: Because I want it for keeps! I love her just as much as she loves me.

PALINURUS: A secret love affair is a bad business; it's utter ruin.

PHAEDROMUS: You're certainly right about that.

PALINURUS: Does she bear the yoke yet?

PHAEDROMUS: As far as I'm concerned, she's just as chaste as if she were my sister—unless there's something unchaste in a few kisses.

PALINURUS: Always remember, where there's smoke, there's fire. Nothing can be burned with smoke, but it can with fire. The man who wants to eat the kernel cracks the nut first. The man who wants to sleep with a girl smooths the way with kisses.

PHAEDROMUS: But this girl is chaste; she doesn't sleep with men yet.

PALINURUS: I'd believe it, if a pimp had any regard for chastity.

PHAEDROMUS: Well, what do you think of her? Whenever she has a chance she steals out to me; when she has given me a kiss, away she runs. And it's all because of the pimp here, who is lying sick in the temple of Aesculapius; he's the one that's torturing me.

PALINURUS: How so?

PHAEDROMUS: At one time he wants thirty minae for the girl, at another a whole talent; I can't get any fair and just treatment from him.

PALINURUS: You're foolish to try to get from a pimp what no pimp has.

PHAEDROMUS: Now I've sent my parasite off to Caria to seek a loan from a friend of mine there. If he doesn't bring it, I don't know which way to turn.

PALINURUS: To the right, I'd suggest, if you're going to pay your respect to the gods.

PHAEDROMUS (*pointing to the altar in front of the house of* CAPPADOX): Here is the altar of Venus in front of their door. I made a vow to bring me a breakfast to my Venus.

PALINURUS: What's this? You're going to bring yourself to Venus as a breakfast?

PHAEDROMUS: Yes, myself, and you, and all these slaves.

PALINURUS: Then you must want Venus to vomit.

PHAEDROMUS (*to one of the slaves*): Here, boy, give me the bowl.

PALINURUS: What are you going to do?

PHAEDROMUS: You'll see in a minute. An old hag usually sleeps here, the keeper of the door. Her name's Leaena, and what a swigger and swiller of wine she is!

PALINURUS: You ought to name her Flagona; that's where Chian wine is usually kept.

PHAEDROMUS: Why say more? She is the essence of vinosity; the very moment that I've sprinkled this door with wine, she knows from the odour that I'm here, and she opens it immediately.

PALINURUS (*disappointed*): Is this bowl of wine brought for her?

PHAEDROMUS: If you have no objection.

PALINURUS: I have, damn it! I wish the fellow carrying it would break his neck! I thought it was being brought for us.

PHAEDROMUS: Be still, won't you? Whatever's left over when she's finished will be enough for us.

PALINURUS: Is there any river that the sea doesn't hold?

PHAEDROMUS: Follow me here to the door, Palinurus; be obedient.

PALINURUS: All right. (*They approach the door.*)

PHAEDROMUS (*sprinkling the door with wine*): Come drink, ye doors of delight! Come drink, be gracious and propitious to me!

PALINURUS (*mocking his master*): What will you have, doors—olives, croquettes, capers?

PHAEDROMUS (*to the door*): Arouse your keeper for me.

PALINURUS (*in alarm*): You're wasting the wine! What the devil possesses you?

PHAEDROMUS: Let me alone. Don't you see how the darling doors are opening? The hinge is creaking, isn't it? Oh, charming hinge!

PALINURUS: Why don't you give it a kiss?

PHAEDROMUS: Hush! Let's hide the light and keep still.

PALINURUS: All right. (*They withdraw from the door.*)

Act One. Scene II

(*Enter* LEAENA *from the house of* CAPPADOX, *sniffing.*)

LEAENA (*to herself*): The savour of aged wine has reached my nostrils. My love for it has enticed me hither in the dark; I'm so eager for it! Wherever it is, it's near me. Hurrah! I've found it! (*She sniffs at the door*) There you are, my soul, my delightful drink! I'm old and I love you when you're old! Compared to your fragrance, the odour of all perfumes is mere bilge water. You are my myrrh, my cinnamon, my rose, my saffron, my casia, my fenugreek! Where you are sprinkled, there may I be buried! Fragrance, so far you've favoured only my nostrils; tickle my throat with your delight also! (*To the door*) I'm getting nowhere with you. Where is the bowl itself? It's you I want to touch, bowl; I want to pour your liquid into me, gurgle, gurgle! But it went this way; I'll follow it. (*Moves towards the others.*)

PHAEDROMUS (*aside to* PALINURUS): This old woman's thirsty.

PALINURUS (*anxiously*): Not very, I hope.

PHAEDROMUS: Oh, moderately so; she'll take about six gallons.

PALINURUS: Jove! According to your reckoning, an entire vintage isn't enough for this one old woman alone. She really should have been a dog;[2] she has a keen scent.

LEAENA: Heavens! Whose voice do I hear at a distance?

PHAEDROMUS (*aside to* PALINURUS): I suppose I ought to hail the hag. I'll hurry to her. (*To* LEAENA) Go back, Leaena, and gaze this way.

LEAENA (*looking around*): Who's in command here?

PHAEDROMUS: Beautiful Bacchus, lord of the vine, who brings a drink to your parched, snivelling, sleepy self, and who comes to quench your thirst.

LEAENA: How far away from me is he?

PHAEDROMUS (*holding up the candle*): Behold this light!

LEAENA: Make stronger your steps towards me, I beg.

PHAEDROMUS: Good health to you!

LEAENA: How can I have health, when I'm torn with thirst?

PHAEDROMUS: Soon you shall drink.

LEAENA: 'Tis a long time coming.

PHAEDROMUS (*extending the bowl*): Here you are, sweet lady!

LEAENA: Your health, you dearest of men!

PALINURUS: Come on, pour it quickly down your chasm; flush out the sewer speedily.

PHAEDROMUS (*to* PALINURUS): Hush! I don't want her abused.

PALINURUS (*to* PHAEDROMUS): All right; I'll misuse her, then.

LEAENA (*pouring a small libation on the altar*): Venus, of the little I have, I'll give you a very little—much against my will. For all lovers, as they drink, give you wine to win your favour; but windfalls such as this don't often fall to me. (*She drinks.*)

PALINURUS: Just look how the greedy hag gulps it down clear, with mouth wide open!

PHAEDROMUS: I'm damned! I don't know what to say to her first.

PALINURUS: Well, tell her what you just told me.

PHAEDROMUS: What's that?

PALINURUS: Tell her you're damned.

PHAEDROMUS: The gods curse you!

PALINURUS: Go on, tell her.

LEAENA (*after a long drink*): Ah!

PALINURUS: How is it? Do you like it?

LEAENA: I like it. (*She drinks again.*)

PALINURUS: And I'd like to poke you with a prick.

PHAEDROMUS (*to* PALINURUS): Stop that! (*Threatens him.*)

PALINURUS (*frightened*): Don't! I'll stop. (*He points to* LEAENA *who bends backward as she drinks*) Just look at the old rainbow drink! We're going to have plenty of rain today, I'll bet.

PHAEDROMUS: Am I to speak to her now?

PALINURUS: What will you say?

PHAEDROMUS: That I'm damned.

PALINURUS: Go on, say it.

PHAEDROMUS: Listen here, old lady; I want you to know this: I'm a poor damned wretch!

LEAENA: But I've attained complete salvation! Tell me, what's the matter? Why do you want to say you're damned?

PHAEDROMUS (*pretending to weep*): Because I'm deprived of the one I love.

LEAENA: Phaedromus, my dear, don't cry, please. You keep me from being thirsty, so I'll bring out here the girl you love. (*She goes into the house.*)

PHAEDROMUS (*calling after her*): If you keep your promise, I'll set up for you, instead of a golden statue, a statue of wine, as a memorial to your gullet. Oh, Palinurus, who in the world will be a luckier man than I, if she really does come out to me?

PALINURUS: A lover is in a damned bad way, if he's out of money.

PHAEDROMUS: That's not the case with me, for I'm sure that the parasite will return to me today with the money.

PALINURUS (*with sarcasm*): That's a mighty undertaking, to wait for what doesn't exist.

PHAEDROMUS: What if I should approach the door and sing a serenade?

PALINURUS: As you please. I neither bid it nor forbid it, master, since I see how your character and disposition have changed.

PHAEDROMUS (*singing*):
> Bolts and bars, bolts and bars, gladly I greetings bring.
> Hear my love, hear my prayer; you I beg and entreat;
> Yield to me and be kind; favour me, charming bolts.
> Dancers be, for my sake;
> Spring apart, I beseech; open wide, send her out,
> She who drains all my blood. I am in such distress!
> But the bars stay asleep, villains all! And for me
> Not a move do they make.[3]

I can plainly see that you doors have no regard for my good will. But hush, hush!

PALINURUS: Damn it! I am hushing.

PHAEDROMUS: I hear a sound. Heavens above! The bolts are obedient to me at last.

Act One.   Scene III

(The door opens and LEAENA *and* PLANESIUM *appear.)*

LEAENA: Come out quietly, Planesium darling, and keep the door from rattling and the hinges from creaking; we don't want master to find out what we're doing here. Wait, I'll pour a little water on them. (*She does so.*)

PALINURUS (*aside to* PHAEDROMUS): D'ye see what a doctor the feeble old hag is becoming? She's learned to drink wine clear, herself, but she gives the door water to drink.

PLANESIUM (*looking around, as* LEAENA *goes inside*): Where are you, who have cited me to the court of Venus? I present myself to you, and urge you likewise to present yourself.

PHAEDROMUS (*stepping forward*): Here I am; if I weren't here, I wouldn't complain at any sort of misfortune, my honey.

PLANESIUM: Oh, my darling, it isn't right for my lover to be so far from me.

PHAEDROMUS (*overjoyed*): Oh, Palinurus, Palinurus!

PALINURUS: Tell me, what are you calling Palinurus for?

PHAEDROMUS: She's a dear.

PALINURUS (*dryly*): Yes, very dear.

PHAEDROMUS: Oh, I'm an immortal!

PALINURUS: Rather, a mortal, and a pretty worthless one, at that.

PHAEDROMUS: What have you ever seen, what will you ever see, more comparable to the gods?

PALINURUS: I see that you're in a bad way, and I'm pretty unhappy about it.

PHAEDROMUS: Oh, shut up! You won't agree with me at all.

PALINURUS (*helpfully*): The man who sees his loved one and doesn't get her while he can is torturing himself.

PHAEDROMUS (*to* PLANESIUM): Rightly reproached! There isn't a thing that I've wanted more for a long time.

PLANESIUM: Take me, then; embrace me.

PHAEDROMUS (*embracing her*): This is the real reason I have for living. I get you secretly, since your master keeps you from me.

PLANESIUM: Keeps me? He can't keep me, he won't keep me from you, unless death should separate my soul from yours.

PALINURUS (*aside*): I just can't keep from finding fault with my master. Sane love in moderation is all right; insane passion isn't good; and to go completely off one's nut, well, that's just what my master is doing!

PHAEDROMUS (*in an ecstasy of delight*): The kings may have their kingdoms; the rich may have their riches; they may have their honours, their brave deeds, their combats, their battles. As long as they don't envy me, they can all have whatever they have.

PALINURUS: Look here, sir! Did you vow to keep a vigil all night in honour of Venus? By gad, before very long dawn will be breaking.

PHAEDROMUS: Hush!

PALINURUS: What, hush? Why don't you go to sleep?

PHAEDROMUS (*still embracing* PLANESIUM): I am asleep; don't make so much noise.

PALINURUS: Why, you're wide awake.

PHAEDROMUS: I'm sleeping in a manner of my own; this is my slumber.

PALINURUS (*to* PLANESIUM): Look here, miss; it's stupid to mistreat a person who hasn't done anything amiss.

PLANESIUM: You'd be angry if your master drove you away from the food you were eating.

PALINURUS (*aside*): It's all up! I can see that both of them are perishing with passion; they're both crazy! Such passionate embraces! They can't hug each other enough! (*To the couple*) Break it up, won't you?

PLANESIUM: No blessing lasts forever for any human being; to this pleasure of ours has come this plague.

PALINURUS: What's that, you hussy? You with your owl eyes, do you call me a plague? You tipsy little fright! You worthless baggage!

PHAEDROMUS (*angrily*): What, you abuse my own Venus? A servant that's been raked with rods to insert such speeches! Damned if you didn't say that at your own peril! (*Striking him*) Take that for your abuse, since you can't control your language.

PALINURUS: Help me, you owl—I mean—all-night-vigilant Venus!

PHAEDROMUS: Keeping right on, eh, you scoundrel?

PLANESIUM: Please don't strike a stone; you'll hurt your hand.

PALINURUS: Phaedromus, you're committing a shameful and sinful crime; you punch with your fists a person who gives you good advice, you make love to a girl here that's worthless trash. Is this the right thing to do, to behave in such an immoderate manner?

PHAEDROMUS: Find me a lover that shows moderation, and I'll pay you his weight in gold.

PALINURUS: Find me a master that shows some sanity, and I'll pay you his weight in platinum.[4]

PLANESIUM: Good-bye, my love! I hear the sound and the rattle of the bolts. The priest is opening the temple next door. Oh dear, how long must we go on this way, always snatching love by stealth?

PHAEDROMUS: Not very long. Three days ago I sent my parasite to Caria to get some money. He'll be here today.

PLANESIUM: Your plans take too long.

PHAEDROMUS: So love me Venus, I'll never let you stay three days in that house, without procuring for you a fitting freedom.

PLANESIUM: Be sure to remember that. Now kiss me once again before I leave. (*They do so.*)

PHAEDROMUS: Heavens! If a kingdom were offered to me now, I wouldn't procure it with greater pleasure. When shall I see you again?

PLANESIUM: Well, the answer to that is to make me free. If you love me, buy me. Don't keep asking; see that you have the courage of your convictions. Good-bye! (*She goes into the house of* CAPPADOX.)

PHAEDROMUS: Am I left alone now? Oh, Palinurus, it's a beautiful death!

PALINURUS: Yes, for me too; I'm dead from blows and lack of sleep.

PHAEDROMUS: Follow me. (*They go into the house of* PHAEDROMUS.)

Act Two.   Scene I

(*Enter* CAPPADOX *from the temple of Aesculapius.*)

CAPPADOX (*to himself*): I've decided to leave the temple right now, for I know what Aesculapius thinks of me; he has no regard for me and doesn't want me to get well. My strength is decreasing, my pain is increasing! I walk along here with my spleen as tight as a girdle, and I feel in my belly as if I were carrying twins. The one thing that I'm afraid of is that in my misery I'll burst in the middle.

(*Enter* PALINURUS *from the house of* PHAEDROMUS.)

PALINURUS (*to* PHAEDROMUS *within*): If you were sensible, Phaedromus, you'd drive away that distress from your mind. You're panicky because the parasite hasn't returned from Caria. I guess he's bringing the money; for if he weren't he couldn't be kept by an iron chain from hurrying back here to his manger to eat.

CAPPADOX (*turning*): Who is the person talking here?

PALINURUS (*aside*): Whose voice do I hear?

CAPPADOX: This is Palinurus, Phaedromus' slave, isn't it?

PALINURUS (*aside*): Who's this fellow with a swollen belly and eyes like grass? I recognise him from the shape, but I'm not sure about the complexion. Ah, yes! Now I know him. It's the pimp Cappadox. I'll approach him.

CAPPADOX: Good day, Palinurus!

PALINURUS: Good day to you, assortment of villainies! How are you?

CAPPADOX (*dolefully*): Alive.

PALINURUS: As you deserve, to be sure. But what's the matter with you?

CAPPADOX: My spleen is killing me, my kidneys ache, my lungs are torn to pieces, my liver is in torment, my heartstrings are giving way, all my intestines are filled with pain.

PALINURUS: Some sort of liver complaint, no doubt.

CAPPADOX: It's easy to laugh at a person that's miserable.

PALINURUS: Why not hold out for a few days more, until your intestines get rotten, now that the pickling season is on? If you do that, your intestines will be worth more than you are.

CAPPADOX: My spleen is split in two!

PALINURUS: Take a walk; that's the best thing for your spleen.

CAPPADOX: Oh, come, drop this chatter, and answer this question for me. Can you give me an explanation, if I tell you the dream I had in my sleep last night?

PALINURUS: Ah! You have right here the one person who's really skilled in divination. Why, all the dream interpreters come to me for advice, and they all stand on the opinion that I hand out to them.

Act Two.   Scene II

(*Enter a* COOK *from the house of* PHAEDROMUS.)

COOK: Palinurus, what are you standing here for? Why don't you get me the things I need, so that lunch will be ready for the parasite when he arrives?

PALINURUS: Wait a minute, until I interpret this fellow's dream.

COOK: And you're always bringing any dreams you have to me!

PALINURUS: I admit it.

COOK: Be off, then, get the provisions.

PALINURUS (*to* CAPPADOX): Now, you! In the meantime you tell him your dream. I'm giving you a substitute better than I am. For everything that I know I learned from him.

CAPPADOX: I hope he can help me.

PALINURUS: He will. (PALINURUS *departs*.)

CAPPADOX (*looking after him*): He's doing what few do, obeying his teacher. (*To the* COOK) Well, then, give me your help.

COOK: I'll do it, even though I don't know you.

CAPPADOX: Well, last night in my sleep I seemed to see Aesculapius sitting far away from me, and he didn't seem to come near me or have any regard for me.

COOK: The other gods will do the same, you may be sure; in fact, there is an amazing agreement among them. There's nothing remarkable in the fact that you get no better. You should have spent the night in the temple of Jupiter, since he has been so helpful to you in your solemn oaths.

CAPPADOX: If all the people who have committed perjury wanted to spend the night there, it wouldn't be possible to find a place for them on the Capitol.

COOK: Take my advice; seek the favour of Aesculapius, so that the terrible disaster which your dream portended won't descend on you.

CAPPADOX: Good advice! I'll go in and pray. (*He enters the temple*.)

COOK: And I hope you have bad luck! (*He returns to the house of* PHAEDROMUS.)

(*Enter* PALINURUS, *much excited*.)

PALINURUS: Ye immortal gods, whom do I see? Who is that fellow? Isn't he the parasite who was sent to Caria? (*Calling at the door*) Hey, Phaedromus! Come out, come out, come out, I say, this very instant.

(*Enter* PHAEDROMUS *from his house*.)

PHAEDROMUS: Why are you making all this uproar?

PALINURUS: Your parasite! I see him running down at the end of the street. Let's listen from here what he's up to.

PHAEDROMUS: I quite agree.

Act Two. Scene III

(Enter CURCULIO *in great haste.)*

CURCULIO *(to imaginary passers-by)*: Friends, strangers, make way for me, while here I do my duty! Hurry away, all of you, scatter, get off the street, or in my haste I'll strike someone with my head or my elbow or my chest or my knee! It's a sudden, quick, speedy business that I have on hand now, and there isn't a man anywhere rich enough to stop me, neither any general, nor despot, nor market inspector, nor tribune, nor burgomaster, nor anyone so important, but that down he'll go and tumble headfirst from the sidewalk to the street. And then those Greeks who stroll about in cloaks with heads covered, who stride along stuffed out with books and baskets, who loiter together and gossip together, the gadabouts, who stand in your way, who get in your way, who walk along with their wearisome opinions, whom you can always see drinking in a tavern when they have scraped together something; with their pates covered they take hot drinks, and then depart sad and soggy! If I bump into them, I'll knock the barley-fed wind out of every one of them. And then those servants of the city idlers that play ball in the street; pitchers and catchers both, I'll grind them under my feet! So let them stay at home and avoid trouble.

PHAEDROMUS *(aside to* PALINURUS*)*: He has the right idea, if he can only back it up. That's the way things are these days; that's the way it is with the servants; there's just no controlling them at all.

CURCULIO *(running about)*: Won't someone please point out to me Phaedromus, my good genius? I need to meet him at once.

PALINURUS *(to* PHAEDROMUS*)*: He's looking for you.

PHAEDROMUS *(to* PALINURUS*)*: What if we approach him? *(To* CURCULIO*)* Hallo, Curculio! I want you.

CURCULIO: Who's calling me? Who speaks my name?

PHAEDROMUS: One who wants to meet you.

CURCULIO *(recognising him)*: Not a bit more than I want to meet you.

PHAEDROMUS: Oh, my Opportunity! My much-desired Curculio! How do you do?

CURCULIO: How d'ya do?

PHAEDROMUS: I'm delighted that you've arrived safely. Give me your right hand. Where are my hopes? Tell me, I beg of you, in heaven's name.

CURCULIO: You tell me, I beg of you, where are mine? (*He staggers, as if about to fall.*)

PHAEDROMUS: What's the matter with you?

CURCULIO: Darkness comes upon me; my knees give way from lack of food.

PHAEDROMUS: Jove! It's fatigue, I suppose.

CURCULIO: Hold me, hold me up, please!

PHAEDROMUS: Do you see how pale he's grown? (*To slaves within*) Bring him a chair, quick, so he can sit down, and a bowl of water. Hurry up, won't you?

CURCULIO: Oh! I feel faint. (*The slaves enter with chair and water.*)

PALINURUS (*seating him*): Do you want some water?

CURCULIO: If it has some food in it, give it to me, for heaven's sake! Let me gulp it down.

PALINURUS (*disgusted*): The devil with you!

CURCULIO: Heavens! A good wind has blown me here, I hope.[5]

PALINURUS: Certainly! (*They fan* CURCULIO *vigorously.*)

CURCULIO: What are you two doing, I'd like to know?

PALINURUS: Giving you a good wind.

CURCULIO: But I don't want a bit of wind.

PHAEDROMUS: What do you want, then?

CURCULIO: To eat; then I'll know it's a good wind.

PALINURUS: Jupiter and the other gods damn you!

CURCULIO: I'm dead and gone! I can hardly see! My teeth are rheumatic, my jaws are bleary from being starved! My bowels are so lean and weary from lack of nourishment!

PHAEDROMUS: You'll soon have something to eat.

CURCULIO: I don't want "something," damn it! I prefer a certain thing to "something."

PALINURUS: But if you only knew what leavings there are!

CURCULIO: I certainly want to know where they are; my teeth have great need of making their acquaintance.

PHAEDROMUS: Ham, tripe, sow's udder, sweetbreads—

CURCULIO: All this, really? But I suppose you mean they're in the pantry.

PHAEDROMUS: No, right on the platter; they were all prepared for you after we learned that you were coming.

CURCULIO: You wouldn't fool me, would you?

PHAEDROMUS: I swear by the love of the girl I love, I'm telling the truth. But I still know nothing about your mission.

CURCULIO: I've brought nothing.

PHAEDROMUS: I'm completely lost!

CURCULIO (*with assurance*): I can find you again, if you follow me with attention. After setting out at your request, I arrived in Caria, I saw your friend, and asked him to loan the money. He wanted your good will, you may be sure; he didn't wish to disappoint you, and he desired to act as a friend should and assist you. He answered me briefly and quite sincerely, that he had the same trouble you have—a complete lack of cash.

PHAEDROMUS: You're killing me with your words!

CURCULIO (*with confidence*): Why no; I'm saving you, and that's what I want to do. After I got his answer, I go off to the forum, very depressed at having had my trip for nothing. There I happen to see a military officer; I go up to him, and as I come near him, I bid him good day. "Good day," he says to me; he takes my right hand, draws me aside, and asks why I have come to Caria. I reply that I've come there to have a good time. Then he asks me if I know a banker in Epidaurus named Lyco. "I know him," says I. "Well then! The pimp Cappadox?" he adds. I admit that I've seen him. "What do you want of him?" I ask. "Well," says he, "I bought a girl of him for thirty minae; then there were some clothes and jewelry, which cost ten minae more."

"Have you paid the money?" I ask. "No," says he, "the money's deposited with the banker Lyco whom I mentioned, and I've arranged with him that the person who brings a letter sealed with my ring is to receive the girl with her clothes and jewelry from the pimp." After he told me this, off I go. But he calls me back at once and asks me to dinner. I had scruples about it, and didn't want to refuse. "What if we go and take our places at the table?" says he. I consider it a fine idea; "We dare not delay the day, nor injure the evening hour." "Everything's ready," says he. "And we're on hand, for whom it's ready," says I. After we have dined and drunk, he calls for dice and challenges me to a game of chance. I stake my cloak; he stakes his ring against it, and invokes Planesium.

PHAEDROMUS (*in amazement*): What! My sweetheart?

CURCULIO: Keep quiet a minute. He throws four vultures. I seize the dice, invoke my fostering nurse Hercules,[6] and then make the royal throw.[7] I drink a huge bumper to his health; he drinks, drops his head, falls fast asleep. I slip the ring off his finger, quietly slide my feet down from the couch, so the captain won't hear me. The slaves ask me where I'm going. I say I'm going where people usually go when they're full. When I saw the door, I dashed through it at once.

PHAEDROMUS: Admirable!

CURCULIO: Save your admiration until I've done what you want. Let's go in now and use the seal on a letter.

PHAEDROMUS: No delay from me, is there?

CURCULIO: And let's gulp down some food first—ham, sow's udder, sweetbreads. This is the way to sustain the stomach—bread, roast beef, a large cup, a huge pot—so that we'll have plenty of ideas. You seal the letter, Palinurus will serve me, I'll do the eating. I'll tell you how to write the letter. Come along inside.

PHAEDROMUS: Coming. (*They go into the house of* PHAEDROMUS; *a short time is supposed to elapse before the next Act.*)

Act Three

(*Enter* LYCO *from the forum.*)

LYCO (*to himself*): I seem to be doing well; I've done a bit of figuring, to see how much money I have and how much I owe. I'm really rich—

if I don't pay my creditors; if I do pay them, I owe a lot of money.
But hell! When I consider the matter carefully, if they press me too
hard, I'll go into bankruptcy. Most bankers have this habit of dunning
everyone and repaying no one, of settling the accounts with their fists,
if anyone gets too noisy in his demands. If a man makes money
quickly and doesn't save it quickly, he'll quickly go hungry. I want
to buy myself a slave, but now I'd better rent the use of one; I have
use for my money.

(*Enter* CURCULIO *and a slave from the house of* PHAEDROMUS.)

CURCULIO (*to* PHAEDROMUS *within*): Don't give me any advice while
my stomach is full. I remember and understand. I'll carry out this
business for you in clever fashion. You just keep quiet! (*To himself*)
Gad! I certainly stuffed myself indoors to my satisfaction; but I left
one little corner of my belly empty, in which I can stow away what's
left of the leavings. (*Seeing* LYCO) Who's this fellow greeting Aesculapius with covered head? Aha! The very man I was looking for! (*To
the slave*) Follow me; I'll pretend that I don't know him. (*To* LYCO)
Hey, you! I want you.

LYCO: Good day, One-eye! [8]

CURCULIO: Look here, are you making fun of me?

LYCO: I suppose you belong to the Cyclops family; they have only one
eye.

CURCULIO: This was struck by a shot from a catapult in Sicyon.

LYCO: It can have been knocked out by a broken pot of cinders, for all
I care.

CURCULIO (*aside*): This fellow's a wizard! He's telling the truth; for
that's the kind of catapult that commonly comes at me. (*Aloud*) Young
man, it's in the service of the state that I have gained this honourable
wound; please don't insult me in public.

LYCO (*leering*): Can I do a little private consulting with you, if you
don't want it in public?

CURCULIO: Keep your private things to yourself; I don't care about
your public interests, or your private ones either. But if you can point
out to me the man I'm looking for, you'll get from me my good and
substantial—gratitude. I'm looking for the banker Lyco.

LYCO (*suspiciously*): Tell me, why are you looking for him? Where
are you from?

CURCULIO: I'll tell you. I'm from Captain Therapontigonus Platagidorus.

LYCO (*aside*): Heavens! I remember that name, for I filled four entire pages with it, writing it down. (*To* CURCULIO) But what do you want Lyco for?

CURCULIO: I've been ordered to bring him this letter.

LYCO: And who are you?

CURCULIO: His freedman; everybody calls me "Piddler."[9]

LYCO: Piddler, good day! But why "Piddler?" Inform me.

CURCULIO: Because, when I go to sleep drunk, I piddle in my pants; that's why everyone calls me "Piddler."

LYCO: You'd better hunt a lodging for yourself elsewhere; I certainly haven't any room for a "Piddler" in my house. But I am the person you're looking for.

CURCULIO: Tell me, are you really Lyco, the banker?

LYCO: I am.

CURCULIO: Therapontigonus asked me to give you his best greetings and to deliver this letter to you.

LYCO: To me?

CURCULIO: That's right. (*Handing him the letter*) Take it; notice the seal. Do you recognise it?

LYCO (*examining it*): Naturally. A man with a shield splitting an elephant in two with his sword.

CURCULIO: As to what's written there, he asked me to beg you to do it at once, if you wish his good will.

LYCO: Get back; let me read what's written here.

CURCULIO (*stepping back*): Certainly, as you wish, provided I get from you what I want.

LYCO (*reading*): "Captain Therapontigonus Platagidorus sends his very best greetings to Lyco, his host in Epidaurus."

CURCULIO (*aside*): I've got him; he's swallowing the hook.

LYCO: "I beg and beseech you to see that the bearer of this letter receives the girl I bought there, and the jewelry and the clothes; the transaction was done in your presence and through your agency. You already know the details of the agreement; you are to give the money to the pimp and the girl to this man of mine." (LYCO *frowns*) Where's the Captain himself? Why doesn't he come?

CURCULIO: I'll tell you; we just got back to Caria from India three days ago. Now he wants to have a solid gold statue made there, all of good gold of Philip; it's to be seven feet high; a memorial to his wonderful deeds.

LYCO: What's the reason for it?

CURCULIO: I'll explain. It's because the Persians, Paphlagonians, Sinopians, Arabs, Carians, Cretans, Syrians, Rhodes and Lycia, Eatonia and Tipplearia, Centaurfightiglia and Onenipplehostania, all the coast of Libya, all Winepressbacchanalia, half of the nations on earth, were all conquered by him singlehanded in less than twenty days.

LYCO (*in apparent admiration*): Whew!

CURCULIO: Why are you surprised?

LYCO: Because if all those people were penned up in a coop like chickens, a man still couldn't walk around them in one year. Damned if you don't come from him, for you jabber such nonsense!

CURCULIO: Oh, I can keep right on, if you like.

LYCO: I don't care for it. But come this way; I'll settle the business that you came on.
(*Enter* CAPPADOX *from the temple of Aesculapius.*)
But there, I see our man! Good day, pimp.

CAPPADOX: The gods bless you!

LYCO: What about my business with you?

CAPPADOX: Tell me what you wish.

LYCO: You are to receive the money, and send the girl away with this man here.

CAPPADOX: What about my oath?

LYCO: What do you care, so long as you get the money?

CAPPADOX: One who advises is as good as a helper. Come along.

CURCULIO: Take care, pimp, that you don't delay me. (*They go into the house of* CAPPADOX.)

Act Four. Scene I

(Enter the PROPERTY MANAGER.*)*[10]

PROPERTY MANAGER: 'Twas damned clever of Phaedromus to find this clever rascal. I really don't know whether to call him a sharp slicker or a slick sharper. I'm afraid that I won't get back the costumes I hired out. I had no business dealings with him myself; I trusted them to Phaedromus; just the same, I'll keep on watch. Now, before he comes back here, I'll show you where you can easily find every sort of person, so that no one will waste too much time if he wants to meet someone vicious or virtuous, or decent or indecent. If you want to meet a perjurer, go to the law-courts; if you want a liar and a braggart, go to the temple of Venus the Purifier; for wealthy, wasteful husbands, seek around the Basilica. There too will be the haggard harlots, and the men who habitually haggle for them; the contributors to the eating clubs you'll find in the fish market. In the lower forum good substantial citizens stroll about; in the middle forum, near the Canal, they are mere exhibitionists; above the Lake are the impudent, talkative, spiteful fellows, who boldly abuse others for no good reason, and who have plenty of things that could truthfully be said against themselves. Below the old shops are those who lend and borrow at interest. Behind the temple of Castor are those whom you would trust quickly to your sorrow. In the Tuscan quarter are the men who sell themselves. In the Velabrum you can find a baker or butcher or soothsayer, or those who themselves turn or who give others a chance to turn.[11] [Rich, wasteful husbands you'll find at the home of Oppian Leucadia.][12] But now the door creaks; I must hold my tongue. (*The* PROPERTY MANAGER *departs.*)

Act Four. Scene II

(Enter CURCULIO, *his slave,* CAPPADOX, LYCO, *and* PLANESIUM *from the house of* CAPPADOX.*)*

CURCULIO (*to* PLANESIUM): Girl, you go first; I can't watch what's behind me. (*To* CAPPADOX) All her jewelry and clothing he said was his, too.

CAPPADOX: No one denies it.

CURCULIO: Well, I thought it wise to warn you, anyway.

LYCO: Remember that you promised, in case anyone should prove in court that she's freeborn, that you would return all the money to me, thirty minae.

CAPPADOX: I'll remember; you just be easy about it. I say the same thing now.

CURCULIO: And I shall want you to remember this also.

CAPPADOX: I remember; I'll transfer her to you in due, legal form.

CURCULIO: What? Receive anything in due, legal form from a pimp? People who don't own a damned thing except a tongue with which they deny on oath anything that's been entrusted to them! It's other people's property that you're transferring in due, legal form, that you're setting free, that you're giving commands to. No one guarantees your ownership and you can't give title to anyone. In my opinion, pimps as a class rate among men just about like flies, gnats, bugs, lice, and fleas; you're all a plague, a mischief, and a nuisance, and you're no earthly use to anyone. No respectable person dares to stand near you in the forum; anyone who does is censured, criticised, abused; all say that he is ruining his property and his credit, even though he hasn't done a thing.

LYCO (*amused*): Damned if I don't think you know your pimps to perfection, my one-eyed friend!

CURCULIO (*turning on him*): And, by gad, I put you bankers in the very same class! You're a perfect match for them. At least, they do their dirty business in dark corners; you do yours in the forum itself. You mangle men with your high interest rates, they with their evil persuasions and their dens of iniquity. The people has passed against you many a bill of prevention, but when the bills are passed you break them; you always look for some loophole. You think that laws are like boiling water that soon becomes cold.

LYCO (*aside*): I wish I'd kept still.

CAPPADOX: There's some sound sense in your abusive speech.

CURCULIO: If those who don't deserve it are abused, then I admit I've spoken abusively; but if they do deserve it, then I've spoken ably, at least, in my own opinion. I certainly don't want you as a guarantor of title, or any other pimp. Anything else, Lyco?

LYCO: A hearty farewell.

CURCULIO: Good-bye, then. (*He turns to go.*)

CAPPADOX (*to* CURCULIO): Hey, you! I'm speaking to you.

CURCULIO (*wearily*): Speak out; what do you want?

CAPPADOX: Be sure to see that the girl's well treated. I've brought her up carefully and chastely at my house.

CURCULIO: If you feel sorry for her, will you give me anything to see that she's well treated?

CAPPADOX: Damnation!

CURCULIO: You ought to provide that for yourself.

CAPPADOX (*to* PLANESIUM, *who is weeping*): What are you crying for, you silly girl? Don't be afraid, for heaven's sake! I've made a splendid sale for you. Just you be a good girl now, my pretty one, and go along with him in a pretty manner.

LYCO: Piddler, you don't want me for anything else now, do you?

CURCULIO: Good-bye and the best of health to you. You've been most kind to furnish me with your time and your money.

LYCO: Give my best regards to your patron.

CURCULIO: I'll do that. (*He departs with* PLANESIUM *and the slave; they dart quickly into the house of* PHAEDROMUS *while* LYCO *and* CAPPADOX *are engaged in conversation.*)

LYCO: Anything else you wish, pimp?

CAPPADOX: I'd like those ten minae to get along with until things go better with me.

LYCO: They'll be paid; have them sent for tomorrow. (LYCO *departs.*)

CAPPADOX (*to himself*): I want to make a prayer here in the temple, since I've carried out the business successfully. For I bought the girl long ago when she was a tiny little thing for only ten minae, and the fellow who sold her to me I've never seen since that time. I suppose he's dead. Well, what's that to me? I have the money. When the gods are favourable to anyone, they certainly throw profit in his direction. Now I'll turn my attention to the sacrifice; I've decided to take good care of myself. (*He goes into the temple.*)

Act Four.   Scene III

(*Enter* THERAPONTIGONUS *and* LYCO.)

THERAPONTIGONUS (*in great anger*): It's no ordinary rage with which I'm raving as I rush here, but that same rage which has enabled me to deal destruction to cities. Now, if you don't make haste and hand over to me the thirty minae which I deposited with you, you can make haste to meet your Maker.

LYCO (*imitating him*): By gad, it's no ordinary penalty with which I'll punish you now, but the very same one with which I punish the man to whom—I owe nothing.

THERAPONTIGONUS: Don't you get tough with me, or think you can win me over.

LYCO: And don't you ever force me to pay you what's already been paid; I won't do it.

THERAPONTIGONUS: Just what I thought when I entrusted it to you, that you wouldn't pay anything back.

LYCO: Then why do you ask me for it now?

THERAPONTIGONUS: I want to know to whom you paid it.

LYCO: To your one-eyed freedman; he said his name was Piddler; he's the one I paid it to. He brought me this letter with your seal, which you—

THERAPONTIGONUS: What one-eyed freedman, what Piddlers are you babbling about? I don't own a single freedman.

LYCO: You act more wisely than do part of the pimps, who have freedmen and then forsake them.

THERAPONTIGONUS: What have you done?

LYCO: I've done for your sake just what you requested; I didn't reject the messenger who brought me your seal.

THERAPONTIGONUS: You were crazier than a fool to put any trust in a letter.

LYCO (*indignant*): What! Not trust letters, when all public and private business is carried on by them? I'm leaving. Your business has been settled beautifully. Warrior, farewell.

THERAPONTIGONUS: What d'ya mean, "farewell"?

LYCO: Fare ill then, if you prefer; all your life, for all I care. (LYCO *departs*.)

THERAPONTIGONUS (*to himself*): What am I to do now? What's the advantage of having kings give me their allegiance, if this lazy loafer is to laugh at me today?

Act Four.   Scene IV

(*Enter* CAPPADOX *from the temple of Aesculapius*.)

CAPPADOX (*to himself*): When the gods are favourable to a man, then, I guess, they're not angry at him. After I finished my sacrifice, it occurred to me that the banker might abscond and that I'd better get my money. Better for me to have plenty to eat than for him.

THERAPONTIGONUS: Good day to you!

CAPPADOX: Therapontigonus Platagidorus, good day! Since you have arrived safely in Epidaurus, today here at my house—you'll never lick a grain of salt.

THERAPONTIGONUS: Thanks for the kind invitation, but I've made arrangements—for you to suffer plenty. Well, how fares this merchandise of mine at your house?

CAPPADOX: There's nothing of yours at my house. Now, don't send for witnesses; I don't owe you a single thing.

THERAPONTIGONUS: What's this?

CAPPADOX: I've done what I swore to do.

THERAPONTIGONUS: Will you give me back the girl or not, you rascal, before I stick you with this sword of mine?

CAPPADOX (*unmoved by the threat*): I'm in favour of giving you a good sound flogging. Don't you try to frighten me. The girl's been led away, and if you keep on abusing me, you'll certainly be carried away from here; I don't owe you a single thing but a thrashing.

THERAPONTIGONUS: What's this? You threaten me with a thrashing?

CAPPADOX: Hell! I won't threaten you, I'll give it to you, if you continue to make a nuisance of yourself.

THERAPONTIGONUS: A pimp to threaten me? And my many brilliant battles to lie battered in the dust? May my sword and my shield aid me well as I fight on the field; if the girl isn't restored to me, I'll make such mincemeat of you that the ants can carry you away from here bit by bit.

CAPPADOX (*imitating him*): And may my tweezers, comb, mirror, curling iron, scissors, bath towel love me well; I don't give any more of a damn for your defiant words and dreadful threats than I do for the dirty wench of mine that cleans out the privy. I gave the girl to the man who brought the money from you.

THERAPONTIGONUS: What man do you mean?

CAPPADOX: He said that he was Piddler, your freedman.

THERAPONTIGONUS: Mine? (*He reflects a minute*) Ouch! Now that I think about it, it's Curculio that's tricked me, by gad! He stole my ring.

CAPPADOX: Lost your ring, eh? (*Aside*) Fine captain he is, assigned to a disbanded company!

THERAPONTIGONUS: Where can I find Curculio now?

CAPPADOX: Some wheat would be the easiest place; you can find five hundred Curculios there instead of one, I'm sure.[13] I'm going now. Farewell; good luck to you! (CAPPADOX *departs in the direction of the forum.*)

THERAPONTIGONUS (*calling after him*): Fare ill, bad luck to you! (*To himself*) What am I to do? Stay here or depart? To have been bamboozled in this way! I want to give a reward to the person who can tell me where that fellow is. (*He departs in anger.*)

Act Five. Scene I

(*Enter* CURCULIO *from the house of* PHAEDROMUS.)

CURCULIO (*to himself*): I've heard that an ancient dramatist once wrote in a tragedy that two women are worse than one. It's the truth. But I've never seen or heard of a worse wench than this woman that Phaedromus has; I don't think a worse one can be described or imagined. When she saw that I had this ring (*displaying the Captain's ring*), she asks me where I got it. "What are you asking for?" says I. "Because I have to know," says she. I refuse to tell her. To get it away from me she tore my hand with her teeth. I just barely got out of the house and made my escape. Damn the little bitch!

Act Five.   Scene II

(*Enter* PLANESIUM *from the house, followed by* PHAEDROMUS.)

PLANESIUM (*looking back*): Hurry, Phaedromus.

PHAEDROMUS: Why hurry?

PLANESIUM: So that you won't lose your parasite. It's awfully important.

CURCULIO (*aside*): Not to me; anything that I have of importance is quickly consumed.

PHAEDROMUS (*seizing* CURCULIO): I've got him. What's the trouble?

PLANESIUM (*excited*): Ask him where he got that ring. My father used to wear it.

CURCULIO: And so did my mother's sister.

PLANESIUM: My mother let him wear it.

CURCULIO: And your father gave it to you, I suppose.

PLANESIUM: You're talking nonsense.

CURCULIO: I usually do. That's the way I make an easy living.

PLANESIUM: Well, now? Please don't keep my parents from me?

CURCULIO: What am *I* doing? (*Examining the ring*) I don't have your father and mother hidden away under the stone, do I?

PLANESIUM: I was born a free woman.

CURCULIO: So were many others who are now in slavery.

PHAEDROMUS (*advancing on* CURCULIO): Now I'm really getting angry at you.

CURCULIO: Well, I told you how the ring came into my possession. How often do I have to explain it? I tricked the Captain at dice, I say.

(*Enter* THERAPONTIGONUS.)

THERAPONTIGONUS (*seeing* CURCULIO): I'm saved! There's the fellow I was looking for. What are you up to, my good sir?

CURCULIO (*grinning*): Listening to you. How about fooling with the dice again, three throws for your cloak?

THERAPONTIGONUS: Oh, go to the devil, won't you, with your foolery and your jewelry? Give me back the money or the girl right now!

CURCULIO: What money? What nonsense are you talking about? What girl are you demanding?

THERAPONTIGONUS: The one that you took from the pimp today, you confounded rascal.

CURCULIO: I took no girl.

THERAPONTIGONUS: You certainly did. (*He points to* PLANESIUM) There she is right now.

PHAEDROMUS: This girl is free.

THERAPONTIGONUS: How can my maidservant be free, when I never freed her?

PHAEDROMUS: Who gave you title to her? Where did you buy her? Just tell me that.

THERAPONTIGONUS: Why, I paid for her through my banker. And I'll get the money back from you and the pimp four times over.

PHAEDROMUS: Since you know how to traffic in kidnapped and freeborn girls, just go to court!

THERAPONTIGONUS: I won't.

PHAEDROMUS (*to* CURCULIO): Can I call on you to be witness?

THERAPONTIGONUS (*interrupting*): No, you can't.

PHAEDROMUS: Jupiter damn you! Live minus witnesses to your manhood. (*To* CURCULIO) And I call on you as a suitable witness. Come here.

THERAPONTIGONUS: What? A slave serve as witness?

CURCULIO (*as* PHAEDROMUS *touches his ear*): See! There, now you know I'm a free man! So just march off to court.

THERAPONTIGONUS (*striking him*): There, take that!

CURCULIO: Citizens, citizens, help!

THERAPONTIGONUS: What are you shouting for?

PHAEDROMUS: What did you strike him for?

THERAPONTIGONUS: Because I felt like it.

PHAEDROMUS (*to* CURCULIO): Come here; I'll give him over to you. Just be quiet.

PLANESIUM: Phaedromus, I beg of you, save me!

PHAEDROMUS: As I would myself and my own good Genius. (*To* THERAPONTIGONUS) Captain, I ask you to tell me where you got that ring, the one that the parasite tricked you of.

PLANESIUM (*kneeling before* THERAPONTIGONUS): As I clasp these knees, I beg you to give us the information.

THERAPONTIGONUS: How does it concern you two? Suppose you ask where I got my cloak and my sword.

CURCULIO (*aside*): What airs the braggart gives himself!

THERAPONTIGONUS (*overhearing*): Ignore that fellow. I'll tell you everything.

CURCULIO: The everything that he says is still nothing.

PLANESIUM: Do let me know, I beseech you.

THERAPONTIGONUS: Rise up. I'll explain. Listen now and pay close attention. My father Periplanes had the ring; before he died he gave it to me, naturally, as his own son.

PLANESIUM: Oh, Jupiter!

THERAPONTIGONUS: And he made me his heir.

PLANESIUM: Oh goddess of filial devotion, save me, as I have carefully cherished you! Welcome, my dear brother!

THERAPONTIGONUS (*taken by surprise*): How am I to believe that? Tell me, if you speak the truth, who was your mother?

PLANESIUM: Cleobula.

THERAPONTIGONUS: And your nurse?

PLANESIUM: Archestrata. She took me to see the show at the festival of Dionysus.[14] After we arrived there and she found me a seat, a terrific whirlwind arose; the seats collapsed. I was awfully frightened. Then some person or other grabbed me up, scared and trembling, neither alive nor dead; and I can't say how he got me away from there.

THERAPONTIGONUS: I remember the excitement. But tell me this: where is the man that snatched you away?

PLANESIUM: I don't know. (*Showing a ring*) But here's a ring that I've always kept with me. I had it on when I was lost.

THERAPONTIGONUS: Let me look at it.

CURCULIO (*to* PLANESIUM): Are you crazy, to trust it to him?

PLANESIUM: Just let me be. (*She hands over the ring.*)

THERAPONTIGONUS: Almighty Jupiter! This is the one I sent you on your birthday. I know it as well as my own self. How are you, my sister?

PLANESIUM: My brother, welcome! (*They embrace.*)

PHAEDROMUS: I trust the gods will bring happiness to you both.

CURCULIO: To all of us, I hope. (*To* THERAPONTIGONUS) Since you've arrived today, you should give a dinner for your sister, a sorority banquet; Phaedromus will furnish a nuptial banquet tomorrow. (*Grinning*) We promise to attend.

PHAEDROMUS: Hush, you!

CURCULIO: I won't hush, since everything is turning out so nicely. Captain, promise your sister in marriage to this man. I'll give a dowry.

THERAPONTIGONUS: What kind of dowry will you give?

CURCULIO: I? The privilege to endow me with food, forever, as long as he lives. And I really mean it.

THERAPONTIGONUS: You have my permission to do it. (*To the others*) The pimp here owes us thirty minae.

PHAEDROMUS: For what reason?

THERAPONTIGONUS: Well, he made this agreement with me: if anyone should claim the girl to be freeborn, he would return all the money without argument. Now, let's go after the pimp!

CURCULIO: Approved!

PHAEDROMUS: I want this first, to finish my own affair.

THERAPONTIGONUS: What is it?

PHAEDROMUS: Promise me your sister.

CURCULIO: Why hesitate, Captain, to let him marry her?

THERAPONTIGONUS: If she wishes.

PLANESIUM: Oh, my dear brother, I'm eager to.

THERAPONTIGONUS: All right, then.

CURCULIO: Very kind of you.

PHAEDROMUS: Captain, do you promise her to me as my wife?

THERAPONTIGONUS: I promise.

CURCULIO: And I say the same thing: "I promise."

THERAPONTIGONUS (*with sarcasm*): Charming of you. (*Looking down the street*) But there comes the pimp, my treasure chest!

Act Five.   Scene III

(Enter CAPPADOX *from the forum.)*

CAPPADOX (*to himself*): Those who say you make bad investments with bankers talk nonsense. I say you can make both good and bad investments; that at least has been my experience today. It's not a bad investment when they never repay you—it's downright loss. For instance, while Lyco was trying to find ten minae for me, he went to all the banks. When he got nowhere, I start dunning him in a loud voice. Then he summons me to court; I was terribly afraid that he'd begin bankruptcy proceedings today before the praetor. Then his friends applied some force, and he paid me the money at his house. But now I'd better hurry home. (*He goes towards his house.*)

THERAPONTIGONUS: Hey, there, you pimp! I want you.

PHAEDROMUS: And I want you too.

CAPPADOX: But I want neither of you.

THERAPONTIGONUS: Stop right there, if you please.

PHAEDROMUS: And make haste to disgorge the money.

CAPPADOX (*to* THERAPONTIGONUS): What business with me do you have? (*To* PHAEDROMUS) Or you?

THERAPONTIGONUS: Well, I'm going to turn you into an arrow today and twist you with the string, the way catapults do.

PHAEDROMUS (*to* CAPPADOX): And I'm going to turn you into a little darling today and make you sleep with a dog—an iron one, I mean.

CAPPADOX (*coolly*): And I'm going to put you both into a strong prison cell and let you rot.

PHAEDROMUS: Seize his throat; drag him off to the devil!

THERAPONTIGONUS: Whatever happens, he'll go there of his own accord. (*He seizes* CAPPADOX.)

CAPPADOX: Protect me, ye gods and men! Am I to be dragged off in this way without trial or testimony? I beseech you, Planesium, and you Phaedromus, aid me!

PLANESIUM: Brother, please! Don't have him condemned and ruined. He treated me kindly and modestly at his house.

THERAPONTIGONUS: No thanks to him for that. You can thank Aesculapius here for your chastity; for if the pimp's health had been better, he'd have sent you off wherever he could long ago.

PHAEDROMUS: Attention, now! Perhaps I can settle this dispute of yours. (*To* THERAPONTIGONUS) Let him go. (*To* CAPPADOX) Come here, pimp. I'll give you my opinion, if you're willing to abide by my decision.

THERAPONTIGONUS (*releasing the pimp*): We leave it to you.

CAPPADOX: Yes, provided—by Jove!—that you decide no one is to get any money away from me.

THERAPONTIGONUS: Money that you promised?

CAPPADOX: How did I promise?

PHAEDROMUS: With your tongue.

CAPPADOX: Well, I deny it now the same way. Nature gave me a tongue to talk with, not to lose money with.

PHAEDROMUS (*to* THERAPONTIGONUS): He's not doing anything. Grab him by the throat.

CAPPADOX (*in terror*): Wait, wait! I'll do as you order.

THERAPONTIGONUS: Since you're such a fine fellow, answer my questions.

CAPPADOX: Ask whatever you wish.

THERAPONTIGONUS: Didn't you promise to pay back all the money, if anyone should claim this girl as freeborn?

CAPPADOX: I don't remember saying it.

THERAPONTIGONUS: What? You deny it?

CAPPADOX (*more boldly*): Yes, damn it! I certainly do deny it. Who was present? Where was it done?

THERAPONTIGONUS: Lyco the banker and I were both present.

CAPPADOX: Won't you shut up?

THERAPONTIGONUS: No, I won't.

CAPPADOX: I don't care a straw for you. Don't you try to terrify me.

THERAPONTIGONUS (*to* PHAEDROMUS): Lyco and I were present when he made the promise.

PHAEDROMUS: I quite believe you. (*To* CAPPADOX) And now, pimp, that you may know my opinion: this girl is free; this man is her brother and she's his sister; she's going to marry me; and you refund the money to him. This is my decision.

THERAPONTIGONUS: Moreover, you'll soon find yourself in prison, if the money isn't returned to me.

CAPPADOX (*angrily*): That's a damned dirty decision, Phaedromus, and you'll be sorry for it. And as for you, Captain, I hope the gods and goddesses curse you. Come along.

THERAPONTIGONUS: Come along where?

CAPPADOX: To my banker, the praetor. That's where I pay all my creditors.

THERAPONTIGONUS: I'll drag you off to the prison, not the praetor's, if you don't pay back the money.

CAPPADOX: I certainly want you to come to a bad end; now you know how I feel.

THERAPONTIGONUS: Is that so?

CAPPADOX: Yes, damn it! That's so.

THERAPONTIGONUS (*raising his arms*): I'm well acquainted with these fists of mine.

CAPPADOX: What of it?

THERAPONTIGONUS: "What of it?" you ask. If you provoke me, I'll calm you down with them today.

CAPPADOX (*subsiding*): Well, then, take it. (*He produces the money.*)

THERAPONTIGONUS: And at once.

CAPPADOX: All right. (*He hands him the money.*)

PHAEDROMUS: Captain, you'll dine with me; the wedding will take place today. And may it turn out well for me and for you! (*To the audience*) Spectators, your applause.

1. The Latin *intestabilis* means both one who has lost the power to bear witness in court, and one who has lost his manhood, with reference here to the punishment of castration inflicted by an injured husband. Cf. *The Braggart Warrior*, Act Five.

2. Palinurus has in mind the literal meaning of the name Leaena, "lioness."

3. This song is the earliest example in Latin literature of the *paraclausithyron*, or serenade to a sweetheart's door. Such songs are often found in Greek and Latin love poetry. Phaedromus' song has been rendered in the cretic meter of the original.

4. *Orichalcum*, "mountain-copper," was also written *aurichalcum*, as if from *aurum*, "gold." Plautus here apparently thinks of it as more valuable than gold.

5. Curculio means by the words *facite ventum ut gaudeam* "give me cause to rejoice at my arrival"; but the phrase can also mean "make a wind that I may rejoice," and Phaedromus and Palinurus so understand it.

6. Hercules was a great eater.

7. The royal, or Venus, throw occurred when the four dice all came up different (cf. *The Comedy of Asses*, note 12); the poorest throw was when the four dice came up the same. The "four vultures" are believed to have been four aces.

8. Curculio wears a patch over one eye.

9. The name in Latin is *Summanus*, which contains a play upon *Summanus*, a Roman deity, and *summanare*, "to piddle, to wet."

10. This address to the audience by the property manager is unique in the plays of Roman comedy, and has often been likened to the *parabasis* in the plays of Aristophanes. There are numerous references to the topography of Rome in this speech; cf. *The Captives*, note 2.

11. The significance of this is not clear.

12. Lindsay brackets this verse as spurious.

13. The literal meaning of the name Curculio is "weevil."

14. It was at the festivals of Dionysus (Bacchus) that the great Athenian tragedies and comedies were produced.

IX
EPIDICUS

CHARACTERS IN THE PLAY

EPIDICUS, *slave of* PERIPHANES
THESPRIO, *orderly of* STRATIPPOCLES
STRATIPPOCLES, *son of* PERIPHANES
CHAERIBULUS, *a young Athenian, friend of* STRATIPPOCLES
PERIPHANES, *an aged Athenian*
APOECIDES, *an aged Athenian, friend of* PERIPHANES
A SLAVE *of* PERIPHANES
A MUSIC GIRL
A SOLDIER
PHILIPPA, *a woman of Epidaurus, mother of* TELESTIS
ACROPOLISTIS, *a music girl*
A MONEYLENDER
TELESTIS, *daughter of* PHILIPPA *and* PERIPHANES

ACROSTIC ARGUMENT

A slave persuades his aged master to buy a music girl under the impression that she is his own daughter, and again this slave deceives him by palming off as his son's sweetheart a girl hired for the purpose. He gives the money to his master's son. With it the young man, without knowing it, purchases his own sister. With the aid of a woman he had wronged and of a soldier, the old man discovers that he has been tricked; the soldier was hunting for his mistress, the woman for her daughter. When the daughter is found, he gives the slave his freedom.

INTRODUCTION

THE *Epidicus* resembles the *Curculio* in many respects: both plays are short, both contain recognitions as well as trickery, in both the recognition scene is sudden and unexpected; since neither play has a prologue, it has been assumed that the original prologue of each has been lost. The differences between the two plays are equally striking. The intrigue of the *Epidicus* has far more originality and complexity, and the wily slave who gives his name to the comedy is one of the most resourceful of Plautus' creations. He resembles Tranio (in *The Haunted House*) rather than Palaestrio (in *The Braggart Warrior*) or Pseudolus, however. While the schemes of the latter two slaves are not only amusing and ingenious but successful as well, Epidicus' inventions, like Tranio's lies and Chrysalus' first trick (in *The Two Bacchides*), are only temporary expedients at best, and the discovery of the truth is sooner or later inevitable.

The action of the *Epidicus* is double, but not in the Terentian sense of the weaving together of two problems and two sets of characters; it results from the use of two different methods of deception, as in *The Braggart Warrior* and *The Two Bacchides*. In the latter play, the first deception is brought to an end by Mnesilochus' revelation of the truth to his father. In the *Epidicus* the first intrigue is rendered useless by the fact that the youthful lover shifts his affection to a different girl. Epidicus' trickery is not discovered, however, and as a result he is able to erect a second and more ingenious plan on the structure of the first. The intrigue of the play is complicated, involving considerable mistaken identity, but it does not have the difficulty and obscurity that critics have sometimes claimed.

Stratippocles, in love with a music girl named Acropolistis, has gone to war after commissioning his slave, Epidicus, to buy the girl. Since Periphanes, the father of Stratippocles, is seeking a daughter who was born out of wedlock as the result of a youthful indiscretion, Epidicus procures the money to buy the music girl by persuading the old man that Acropolistis is in reality Telestis, his lost daughter and the half-sister of Stratippocles. The girl is installed in the house as Telestis. This first intrigue was completed before the opening of the play. The action begins with the return of Stratippocles from war. He has fallen in love with another girl, a captive, and has borrowed money from a moneylender for her purchase. Stratippocles appeals to Epidicus for aid a second time, and the second deception is twofold; not only must Epidicus raise the necessary sum for the moneylender, but he must get rid of Acropolistis, who is posing as Periphanes' daughter. With an excellent yarn about Stratippocles and his sweetheart Acropolistis, he persuades Periphanes to outsmart his son by buying the music girl, i.e. Acropolistis, before Stratippocles can free her, and by selling her to a soldier who is in love with her. Epidicus hires for this purpose a second music girl, and the money which he receives from Periphanes for the supposed purchase is given to Stratippocles to pay for the new girl, the captive. It is all the more amusing when, as here, the butt of the deception thinks that he is deceiving someone else. The revelation of the truth comes soon after the completion of the trickery; the soldier comes from Acropolistis and indignantly rejects the hired music girl; Philippa, the mother of Telestis, likewise is heartbroken when she finds that the supposed daughter is not Telestis. These two scenes are among the best in the play. The moneylender arrives with the captive maiden who proves to be the real Telestis, and Periphanes' desire to punish Epidicus for his knavery vanishes when he learns the truth.

The conclusion of the play is highly unsatisfactory for Stratippocles. Instead of getting the girl he loves, he finds that he has gained a half-sister, and the only reference to his later fate is Epidicus' suggestion that he return to his first love, Acropolistis, who is still in the house. The spectators are left in uncertainty also about Periphanes, since it is not clear whether he marries Philippa or not. Epidicus as the chief character holds the center of attention at the close, and his impudence and apparent desire for punishment provide an amusing finale. The author of the Greek original is unknown, but it is possible that the Greek comedy had a very different ending. Karl Dziatzko put forth the theory, which has been accepted by many scholars, that the curious and unsatisfactory conclusion of the *Epidicus* was the result of alterations and omissions on the part of Plautus. He suggested that the original may have ended with the marriage of Stratippocles and Telestis, his half-sister; marriages between brothers and sisters of the same father were permitted in Greece, but were viewed by the Romans as incestuous; Plautus therefore would feel it necessary to eliminate the happy ending, the marriage of Stratippocles and Telestis. In the Greek play Acropolistis may have joined the soldier who was in love with her. W. E. J. Kuiper believes that the real purpose of the first deception was to have Stratippocles marry his supposed half-sister (Acropolistis) and that this was the marriage to which Apoecides and Periphanes refer in line 190. The

theories of Dziatzko and Kuiper are attractive, but not necessarily con-
clusive. Telestis' non-Athenian citizenship may well have been an im-
pediment to her marriage with her half-brother in the Greek original, as
C. W. Keyes has recently shown; in this case, there is less reason for
believing that Plautus made extensive alterations in his reworking of
the Greek comedy.

The numerous cases of mistaken identity in the play produce much
humour and irony. Although the *Epidicus* is not considered today as
one of Plautus' best plays, it was apparently Plautus' own favourite
(cf. *The Two Bacchides*, lines 214 f.). Whether his fondness for the play
was due to the cleverness and complexity of the intrigue, to the character
of Epidicus himself, or to the lyrical element in the play is not known.
The date of the production is uncertain; it is earlier than *The Two
Bacchides*, and is probably to be placed in the first decade of the second
century B.C.

Many traits of the intriguing slave or valet of Italian and French
comedy recall the character of Epidicus, e.g. Mascarille in Molière's
L'Etourdi and Scapin in *Les Fourberies de Scapin*. Cieco's *Emilia* (1579)
was primarily an adaptation of the *Epidicus*, as was Lemercier's *Plaute*
(1808). Cailhava's *Le Mariage Interrompu* (1769) was drawn in part
from the *Epidicus*, in part from *The Two Bacchides*.

EPIDICUS

(SCENE:—*A street in Athens in front of the houses of* PERIPHANES *and* CHAERIBULUS.)

Act One.   Scene I

(*Enter* THESPRIO *from the harbour, running; he is followed by* EPIDICUS, *who catches up with him and seizes his cloak.*)

EPIDICUS: Hey there, young fellow!

THESPRIO (*without stopping or turning*): Who's clutching me by the cloak when I'm in a hurry?

EPIDICUS: One of the family.

THESPRIO: I'm sure of that. You're too damned familiar, the way you annoy me.

EPIDICUS: Just look back, Thesprio.

THESPRIO (*stopping and turning*): Oh, is it you I see, Epidicus?

EPIDICUS (*grinning*): Your eyesight's pretty good.

THESPRIO: Good day to you.

EPIDICUS: The gods grant your wishes. I'm glad you're back safe.

THESPRIO: What about the rest of it?

EPIDICUS: Oh, the usual thing: you'll receive a dinner.

THESPRIO: I promise—

EPIDICUS (*interrupting*): What?

THESPRIO: To accept, if you'll provide the dinner.

EPIDICUS: Well, how are you? Your health good?

THESPRIO: You can see the proof—

396

EPIDICUS (*cutting him short*): I know, I know! Fine! You seem quite plump and hearty.

THESPRIO (*with a grin, indicating his left hand*): Yes, thanks to this.

EPIDICUS: That's something you should have lost long ago.

THESPRIO: Oh, I'm not as much of a thief as I used to be.

EPIDICUS: How's that?

THESPRIO (*grinning*): I plunder in the open now.

EPIDICUS (*with apparent annoyance*): The immortal gods blast you! You hurry along with such huge steps. When I saw you at the harbour, I began to chase after you, and I was hardly able to overtake you just now.

THESPRIO: You're just a city softy.

EPIDICUS (*with sarcasm*): And you're a military man, to be sure.

THESPRIO (*missing the point*): You can speak as boldly as you wish.

EPIDICUS: How are you, anyway? Your health been good all along?

THESPRIO: Oh, sort of spotty.

EPIDICUS: I don't care much for folks with spotty health—the goatish or pantherish kind.[1]

THESPRIO: Well, what d'ye want me to say except the truth?

EPIDICUS: How about the campaign?[2]

THESPRIO: Just fine.

EPIDICUS: And how's our young master?

THESPRIO: Stout as a boxer and an athlete.

EPIDICUS: That's delightful news you announce on your arrival, Thesprio. But where is he?

THESPRIO: He came when I did.

EPIDICUS: Where is he then? (*Looking around*) Unless maybe you brought him in your wallet or your knapsack.

THESPRIO (*good-naturedly*): You be damned!

EPIDICUS: You, I'd prefer (*changing his tone*) to answer some questions. Pay attention; I'll return the favour.

THESPRIO: You talk like a judge.

EPIDICUS: That's the way I should.

THESPRIO: You hold the praetorship now, eh?

EPIDICUS: Can you think of anyone else in Athens today that's more deserving?

THESPRIO (*chuckling*): Well, Epidicus, there's one thing your praetorship lacks.

EPIDICUS: What's that?

THESPRIO: I'll tell you. Two lictors and two bundles of switches.

EPIDICUS: Oh, go hang! But look here!

THESPRIO: What is it?

EPIDICUS: Where are Stratippocles' arms?

THESPRIO: Heavens! They fled to the enemy.

EPIDICUS: What? His arms?

THESPRIO: Yes, and in a hurry, too.

EPIDICUS: You mean it seriously?

THESPRIO: Yes, seriously. The enemy have them.

EPIDICUS: Damned disgraceful, that is!

THESPRIO: Oh well, others have done the same thing before this. The deed will bring him honour.

EPIDICUS: How?

THESPRIO: Because it brought honour to those others.[3] Vulcan made the arms that Stratippocles had, I guess; that's why they flew to the enemy.[4]

EPIDICUS: Then let this son of Thetis lose them; the daughters of Nereus will bring him others. But he must see to it that there's plenty of raw material for the shield makers, if he's going to present the enemy with spoils on every campaign.

THESPRIO: Come now, stop this idle talk.

EPIDICUS: Stop it yourself, when you wish.

THESPRIO: Don't ask so many questions.

EPIDICUS: You do the talking, then. Where is Stratippocles?

THESPRIO: Well, there's a certain reason why he was afraid to come along with me.

EPIDICUS: What in the world is it?

THESPRIO: He doesn't want to see his father just yet.

EPIDICUS: Why not?

THESPRIO: I'll tell you. Because he bought from the booty a young captive, a very lovely and ladylike girl.

EPIDICUS (*in alarm*): What's this I hear?

THESPRIO: Just what I'm telling you.

EPIDICUS: Why did he buy her?

THESPRIO: To please his fancy.

EPIDICUS: How many fancies does that fellow have? Why, before he left home to join the army, he certainly commissioned me to buy from a pimp a music girl he was in love with; I did the trick for him.

THESPRIO (*sententiously*): Just as the wind blows on the sea, Epidicus, that's the way the sails are set.

EPIDICUS: Damn me for a poor fool! He's fixed me in fine style!

THESPRIO: Why, what's the trouble? What on earth is it?

EPIDICUS (*ignoring the question*): That girl that he bought, how much did he pay for her?

THESPRIO: Not much.

EPIDICUS: I'm not asking you that.

THESPRIO: What, then?

EPIDICUS: How many minae?

THESPRIO (*holding up his fingers four times*): This many. Forty minae. He borrowed the money from a moneylender in Thebes at interest— two per cent a day.

EPIDICUS: Whew!

THESPRIO: And the moneylender came along with him to get the money.

EPIDICUS: Immortal gods! How royally I'm ruined!

THESPRIO: What now? What's the trouble, Epidicus?

EPIDICUS: He's done for me.

THESPRIO: Who has?

EPIDICUS: The man who did for his arms.

THESPRIO: How so?

EPIDICUS: Because he kept sending me letters every day from the army —but I'd better hold my tongue. It's proper for a slave to know more than he tells; that's true wisdom.

THESPRIO: Dear me, Epidicus, you seem to be troubled about something; you're in a tremble. Judging from your expression, I suspect that you've got into some sort of scrape here in my absence.

EPIDICUS: Can't you stop pestering me?

THESPRIO: I'm going now. (*He moves away.*)

EPIDICUS: Stop! (*Seizing his arm*) I won't let you go.

THESPRIO: What are you holding me back for?

EPIDICUS: Is he in love with the girl he bought from the booty?

THESPRIO: You ask? . . .[5] He's crazy about her.

EPIDICUS: Then he's skinning the hide right off my back.

THESPRIO (*flippantly*): He loves her more than he ever loved you.

EPIDICUS: Jupiter damn you!

THESPRIO: Let me go now; he told me not to go home; he wanted me to go here next door, to the house of Chaeribulus. He told me to wait there; he's going to come there himself.

EPIDICUS: Why so?

THESPRIO: I'll tell you. He doesn't want his father to meet him or to see him until he's paid off the money he owes for the girl.

EPIDICUS: God! What a horrible mess this is!

THESPRIO: Let me go in now.

EPIDICUS: When the old man finds all this out, there's one raft that'll be an utter wreck.

THESPRIO: What difference does it make to me how you meet your end?

EPIDICUS: Why, I don't want to die alone, I want you to die with me, two well-wishers together.

THESPRIO: Oh, go to the devil with that proposal of yours! Leave me alone.

EPIDICUS: Go on in, then, if you're in such a hurry.

THESPRIO (*with a sigh of relief*): I never met a fellow that I was gladder to get away from. (*He hurries into the house of* CHAERIBULUS.)

EPIDICUS (*to himself*): He's gone. Now you're alone. Epidicus, you can see the state that affairs are in. If you don't have some aid for yourself, you're ruined. So much destruction overhangs your head; if you don't give it firm support, you can't survive; such mountains of misery are toppling upon you. And I don't see any plan now to enable me to disentangle myself from my entanglements. Fool that I was, I deceived the old man into believing he was buying his own daughter. Actually, he bought a music girl for his son, the one the young man was in love with, the one he entrusted to my care when he went away. If now he's brought back another girl from the army to suit his fancy, I've lost my hide. For when the old man learns that he was tricked, he'll polish off my posteriors with good stout rods.— (*Carrying on an imaginary conversation with himself*) You look out for yourself.—Oh, well! Oh, hell! That's no good. My head's completely confused.—You're a worthless wretch, Epidicus.—But what pleasure is there in being abusive?— Because you leave yourself in the lurch.—What am I to do?—You ask *me*? *You're* the one who used to give advice to others.—(*Resuming his normal tone*) Well, I'll have to devise something somehow. But why don't I go to meet my young master and find out how things stand? (*Looking down the street*) Look, there he is! Dejected, too. He's coming along with his friend Chaeribulus. I'll step back here, where I can easily overhear their conversation. (*He withdraws.*)

Act One. Scene II

(*Enter* STRATIPPOCLES *and* CHAERIBULUS.)

STRATIPPOCLES: I've told you the whole story, Chaeribulus, and I've given you a full account of my passions and my pains.

CHAERIBULUS: You're a fool, Stratippocles, in spite of your age and valour. Is this why you're ashamed? Because you've bought a wellborn captive in the booty? Who will find fault with you for that?

STRATIPPOCLES: All who are envious have become my enemies because of it. But never have I marred or scarred her innocence in any way.

CHAERIBULUS: All the more credit to you, as I see it, for being so restrained in your love.

STRATIPPOCLES (*sadly*): It does no good to comfort a despairing man with words; a real friend in an emergency is a friend in deed, when there is need of the deed.

CHAERIBULUS: What do you want me to do?

STRATIPPOCLES: To give me forty minae to give to the moneylender from whom I borrowed the money at interest.

CHAERIBULUS: Heavens! I'd give it to you if I had it.

STRATIPPOCLES: Well, what's the use of being generous in speech, if all real aid of yours is dead?

CHAERIBULUS: But, confound it, I'm being distressed, dis-troubled, by creditors myself.

STRATIPPOCLES: I'd rather have friends like you baked up than bankrupt. (*Reflecting*) I'd be willing to pay a pretty price now for help from Epidicus. Gad, I'll irrigate his back with blows and send him off to the mill, if he doesn't produce forty minae for me this very day before I can say the last syllable of the sum.

EPIDICUS (*aside, ironically*): I'm safe! He's making a fine promise. He'll keep his word, too, I suppose. A picnic's being prepared for my back without any payment on my part. I'll approach him. (*To* STRATIPPOCLES) Slave Epidicus bestows his best greetings upon his master Stratippocles on his return from abroad.

STRATIPPOCLES (*looking about*): Where is he?

EPIDICUS (*coming forward*): Here I am. Your safe arrival here—

STRATIPPOCLES (*interrupting*): I believe you in that just as I would myself.

EPIDICUS: Your health been good up to now?

STRATIPPOCLES: Yes, in body, but I've been sick at heart.

EPIDICUS: The work that concerned me has been tended to, sir. Your commission has been carried out; the slave girl that you kept sending me letters about was purchased.

STRATIPPOCLES: You've wasted all your labour.

EPIDICUS (*pretending ignorance*): Wasted it? How?

STRATIPPOCLES: Because I neither love her now nor care for her.

EPIDICUS: What was the point then of giving me so many orders and sending me so many letters?

STRATIPPOCLES: At that time I was in love with her; but now another love o'erhangs my heart.

EPIDICUS: Damn it! It's a wretched business for a man to be ungrateful when you do him a kindness. My good deed proves to be a bad deed, all because your love has shifted.

STRATIPPOCLES: I was crazy in my head when I sent you those letters.

EPIDICUS (*indignant*): Must I be the victim because you were a fool? Are you going to substitute my back as a sacrifice to your folly?

CHAERIBULUS (*impatiently*): Why waste words here? This fellow needs forty minae, hot ones, procured in haste, to pay the moneylender.

EPIDICUS (*with sarcasm*): All right, tell me: where do you want me to get them? What banker am I to ask?

STRATIPPOCLES: Get it wherever you wish. But if you don't have it before sunset, don't expect to enter my house. Off to the mill you go!

EPIDICUS: It's easy enough for you to say that, without any risk or worry or anxiety on your part. But I know what our folks are like; I'm the one that gets hurt when I get a beating.

STRATIPPOCLES (*plaintively*): What do you want now? To let me destroy myself?

EPIDICUS: Oh, don't do that. (*Resolutely*) It's up to me rather to take the risk and do the daring deed.

STRATIPPOCLES: Now you're a fine fellow, now I approve of you.

EPIDICUS: I'll put up with anything you wish.

STRATIPPOCLES: What's to become of the music girl now?

EPIDICUS: I'll think up something, there'll be some way for you to escape, I'll extricate you by some means.

STRATIPPOCLES: You're full of tricks; I know you.

EPIDICUS (*pondering*): There's a rich soldier from Euboea, with loads of money; when he learns that you've bought this girl inside (*pointing to* PERIPHANES' *house*), and that you've brought another one with you, he'll come at once and ask you to turn the first one over to him. But where is the girl that you brought with you?

STRATIPPOCLES: She'll soon be here, I promise you.

CHAERIBULUS: What are we to do here now?

STRATIPPOCLES: Let's go into your house here and make this present day a jolly one.

EPIDICUS: Yes, go on in. (*To himself, as* STRATIPPOCLES *and* CHAERIBULUS *go into the latter's house*) Now I'll summon the senate inside my chest to hold a special session on financial policy and decide whom to declare war on and get money from. Look where you're going, Epidicus; it's a tough business that's been dropped into your lap. No chance now for sleeping or loitering! Up and at 'em! I must lay siege against the old man, that's sure. I'll go inside and tell my young master not to ramble out of the house or get in the old man's way. (EPIDICUS *goes into the house of* CHAERIBULUS.)

Act Two. Scene I

(*Enter* APOECIDES *and* PERIPHANES.)

APOECIDES: Most men feel ashamed when there's no need of it, and when there is, then they lose their sense of shame and don't feel the shame they should. That's just the sort of person you are. Why should you be ashamed at the thought of marrying a poor woman of noble birth? Especially when you say that she's the mother of the girl here in your house.

PERIPHANES: I have respect for my son's feelings.

APOECIDES (*ironically*): Dear me, I thought it was your respect for your dead wife. (*Laughing*) Why, whenever you catch sight of her tomb, you immediately present Pluto with gifts, and it's a good idea, too, because you were allowed to outlive her.

PERIPHANES: Oh, what a Hercules I was while she was living with me! His sixth labour[6] wasn't any more difficult than the labour allotted to me.

APOECIDES: Still, a fat dowry is damned good money to have.

PERIPHANES: Heavens, yes, if it comes without a wife.

Act Two.   Scene II

(*Enter* EPIDICUS *from the house of* CHAERIBULUS.)

EPIDICUS (*to* STRATIPPOCLES *and* CHAERIBULUS *inside*): Hush! Quiet now, and cheer up, both of you! (*To himself*) I'm coming out under favourable auspices, with a bird on my left! I have a sharp knife and I'll eviscerate the old man's purse with it. (*Noticing* PERIPHANES *and* APOECIDES) Ah! Here he is in front of the house, and Apoecides with him; just the pair of greybeards I want. I'll turn myself into a leech and suck the blood out of these so-called senate-props.

PERIPHANES: . . . .[5]

APOECIDES: . . . that he be married at once.

PERIPHANES: An excellent plan! I've heard that he was tangled up in a love affair with some music girl or other; it distresses me.

EPIDICUS (*aside*): By Jupiter, how all the gods aid me, assist me, adore me! These two men themselves are showing me the way to get their money. Come now, Epidicus, get yourself set; throw your cloak over your shoulder (*doing so*) and pretend that you've been hunting the man all over the city. Act now, if ever! (*To himself, as if running from the forum*) Immortal gods! I hope I can find Periphanes at home. I'm just exhausted with looking for him all over the city—in doctors' offices, barbers' shops, the gymnasium and the forum, in perfumers' shops and meatmarkets and around the banks. I'm hoarse from shouting, I fairly fainted from running.

PERIPHANES (*seeing him*): Epidicus!

EPIDICUS (*without looking*): Who is it calling Epidicus back?

PERIPHANES: I'm Periphanes.

APOECIDES: And I'm Apoecides.

EPIDICUS (*stopping*): And I'm Epidicus, to be sure. Master, the two of you have turned up at the most opportune occasion.

PERIPHANES: What's the matter?

EPIDICUS (*panting*): Wait; let me get my breath, please.

PERIPHANES: Why of course, take a rest.

EPIDICUS: I feel faint. Let me have a breathing spell.

PERIPHANES: Take it easy. Rest yourself.

EPIDICUS (*as if recovering*): Listen, both of you. The soldiers have all been sent back home from Thebes.

APOECIDES: Who says so?

EPIDICUS: I say so.

PERIPHANES: You know it to be the case?

EPIDICUS: I do.

PERIPHANES: How do you know?

EPIDICUS: Why, I saw the streets just crowded with soldiers; they're bringing back their arms and leading their baggage animals.

PERIPHANES: Excellent!

EPIDICUS: And then, the captives they have with them! Boys, girls, two apiece, three apiece, another with five. The streets are crowded, everybody's going to see their sons.

PERIPHANES: Gad, what a successful campaign!

EPIDICUS: Then, too, all the harlots in the whole city were hurrying to meet their own special lovers, all decked out in their best, all trying to lure them back. And how did I happen to notice this particularly? Most of them had charms with them—under their clothes. When I get to the gate, there I see her waiting for him, and there were four flute girls with her.

PERIPHANES: With whom, Epidicus?

EPIDICUS: Why, that woman that your son's been perishing with passion for this many a year; for whom he's rushing to ruin his credit and his cash and himself, and you too. She was waiting for him at the gate.

PERIPHANES: Imagine that, the witch!

EPIDICUS: And the way she was begarbed, bejewelled, bedecked! So splendidly, so tastefully, so fashionably!

PERIPHANES: How was she dressed? In royal cloth, or beggar style?

EPIDICUS: Sky-light style, according to the way the women name their clothes.

PERIPHANES: What? She wore a sky-light?

EPIDICUS: What's so strange about that? Just as if lots of women didn't parade through the streets wearing whole estates. When there's an assessment of taxes, the men say they can't pay it; but they're able to hand over far heavier taxes to these wenches, all right. (*Scornfully*) Why, what new names those women invent yearly for their garments! The Looseknit tunic, the Tightknit tunic, the Kerchiefblue, the Innerweave, the Goldedge weave, the Marigold or Crocus tunic, the Slip or the Slippery, the Mantilla, the Royal or the Exotic, the Wavy or the Watery, the Nutty or the Waxy—and it's all pure tommyrot. Why, they've even taken the name of a dog.

PERIPHANES: How's that?

EPIDICUS: They call a tunic Greyhound. It's terms like these that drive husbands to bankruptcy.

APOECIDES: Why don't you continue your story?

EPIDICUS: Well, two other women began to chatter behind me. I purposely drew away a bit and pretended not to pay any attention to their words; I couldn't hear all they said, but I didn't miss much they said, either.

PERIPHANES: I want to hear about this.

EPIDICUS: Then one of them said to the woman who was with her—

PERIPHANES (*impatiently*): What?

EPIDICUS: Just keep quiet and you'll hear. After they caught sight of the girl your son's crazy about, "Gracious," says she, "What favour and what fortune a girl like that has, when her lover wants to set her free." "Who in the world is he?" says the other. Thereupon the first one mentions the name of Stratippocles, the son of Periphanes.

PERIPHANES: O God, I'm done for! What's this I hear?

EPIDICUS: The very truth, sir. After I heard them say this, I began to back up towards them little by little, as if a crowd of people was pushing me back against my will.

PERIPHANES: I understand.

EPIDICUS: Then the second asked the other, "How do you know? Who told you this?" "Why," says she, "a letter was brought to her from Stratippocles this very day, saying he'd borrowed money on interest from a moneylender in Thebes, that the money was all ready, and that he himself was bringing it for this very purpose."

PERIPHANES: Death and destruction!

EPIDICUS: Yes, she said she'd learned it from the girl herself and from the letter.

PERIPHANES: What am I to do now? (*To* APOECIDES) I need your advice, Apoecides.

APOECIDES: We must think up some plan that's hot and helpful. Damn it! The young rascal will soon be here, I suppose, or else he's here already.

EPIDICUS (*modestly*): If it were right for me to show more wisdom than you, I could concoct a clever trick, I suspect, that you'd both approve of.

PERIPHANES (*eagerly*): Well, well! What is it, Epidicus?

EPIDICUS: And one that would be helpful in this situation.

APOECIDES: Why hesitate to tell it, then?

EPIDICUS: You two ought to speak first and I second; you have much more wisdom.

PERIPHANES: Oh, bosh! Come, speak up.

EPIDICUS (*bashfully*): You gentlemen will make fun of me.

APOECIDES: We won't do it, I swear.

EPIDICUS: Well, if you like my plan, use it; if not, scrape up a more satisfactory one. (*Indifferently*) I'm not doing any sowing or reaping for myself here; I'm merely trying to help you out.

PERIPHANES (*slightly ironical*): I'm duly grateful. Bestow upon us the benefits of your wisdom.

EPIDICUS: Have a wife selected for your son at once; and as for the music girl he wants to set free, the one that's ruining him for you, you should take vengeance on her and make sure she's a slave to her dying day.

APOECIDES: That's just the thing.

PERIPHANES: I'm willing to do anything you say, if only it will work out.

EPIDICUS: Well, now's the chance to do it, before he gets back to the city; he'll be here tomorrow, in fact; he's not coming today.

PERIPHANES: How do you know?

EPIDICUS: I'm sure of it, because another man from there told me that he'll be here in the morning.

PERIPHANES: Tell us, then, won't you? What are we to do?

EPIDICUS: Well, I think you ought to act as if you were eager to free the girl for your own enjoyment and as if you were head over heels in love with her.

PERIPHANES: What's the advantage of that?

EPIDICUS: Can you ask? So that you can buy her first, before your son returns, and you can say you purchased her to set her free.

PERIPHANES: I understand.

EPIDICUS: And then, when she's bought, you can get her away from the city somewhere, that is, unless you have a different idea.

PERIPHANES: Oh, no! That's quite clever.

EPIDICUS (*to* APOECIDES): And what do you think, Apoecides?

APOECIDES: What indeed, except that it's a damned shrewd invention, I'm sure.

EPIDICUS: And then all his hesitation concerning marriage will be at an end, and he won't oppose your wishes.

PERIPHANES: You're certainly a smart one! I like it.

EPIDICUS: Then you must do in hot haste whatever you're going to do.

PERIPHANES: Gad, you hit the nail there.

EPIDICUS: And I've found a way to keep you from being suspected.

PERIPHANES: Let me know it.

EPIDICUS: You shall, just listen.

APOECIDES (*to* PERIPHANES): This fellow's just saturated with good sense.

EPIDICUS: We need a man to take the money for the music girl to her owner. I don't want you to do it, and there's no need for it, either.

PERIPHANES: How's that?

EPIDICUS: I don't want him to think you're acting for your son's welfare—

PERIPHANES: Very sound!

EPIDICUS: —and trying to separate him from her; we don't want any difficulty to arise from such a suspicion.

PERIPHANES: What man can we find suitable for the purpose?

EPIDICUS (*indicating* APOECIDES): He'll be an excellent person; he has a good understanding of laws and legal matters and will be able to take the proper precautions.

PERIPHANES (*to* APOECIDES): You should be grateful to Epidicus.

EPIDICUS: But I'll use great care here, too. I'll meet the owner of the music girl, and I'll bring the girl herself here to you, (*as an afterthought*) and I'll go with Apoecides and take the money.

PERIPHANES: What's the lowest price I can buy her for?

EPIDICUS: The girl? Oh, I think possibly she can be bought for about forty minae, at the lowest. But if you give me too much, I'll bring it back; there's no catch here at all. And that money of yours won't be tied up ten days.

PERIPHANES: How's that?

EPIDICUS: Why, there's another young man madly in love with her, a fellow just rolling in money, a famous fighter from Rhodes, a plunderer of the enemy, a braggart. He'll buy the girl from you and be glad to give you his gold. Just do your part; there'll be a big profit here for you.

PERIPHANES: I hope to God there is.

EPIDICUS: Your prayer is answered.

APOECIDES (*to* PERIPHANES): Why not go in and get the money for him? I'll take a look in the forum. (*To* EPIDICUS) Meet me there, Epidicus.

EPIDICUS: Don't go away before I join you.

APOECIDES: I'll wait until then. (*He departs in the direction of the forum.*)

PERIPHANES: Come on in with me.

EPIDICUS: You go in and count out the money; I won't delay you. (PERIPHANES *goes into his house.*)

Act Two.   Scene III

EPIDICUS (*to himself*): I don't think there's a single field in Attica as fertile as this Periphanes of ours. Why, his chest is shut up and sealed, but I shake out of it just as much money as I wish. (*Reflecting*) By Jove, though, if the old man finds out the truth, I'm afraid he'll turn the elm switches into parasites and let them gnaw me to the bone. But the one difficulty that really disturbs me is what hired music girl I'm to provide for Apoecides. (*After a pause*) Ah, I have that, too The old man ordered me this morning to hire a music girl and bring her home to play for him while he was offering sacrifice. I'll hire her and instruct her beforehand how to deceive the old fellow. I'll go in now and get the money from the wasteful old wretch. (*He goes into the house of* PERIPHANES.)

Act Three.   Scene I

(*Enter* STRATIPPOCLES *and* CHAERIBULUS *from the latter's house.*)

STRATIPPOCLES: I'm wretched and worn out with waiting to see how the smooth words of Epidicus will turn out. I've been tortured too long; I want to know if there's any hope or not.

CHAERIBULUS: As far as his help is concerned, you'd be wise to get some help elsewhere. Why, I knew right at the very beginning that he wouldn't be able to do anything for you.

STRATIPPOCLES: Oh, hell! I'm done for!

CHAERIBULUS: It's disgusting for you to be so distressed. Gad, if I ever get my hands on him, I'll never let that rascal of a slave have the laugh on us without paying for it.

STRATIPPOCLES (*bitterly*): What do you expect him to do? You're the one with lots of wealth at home, and yet you don't have a cent and can't give any assistance to your friend.

CHAERIBULUS: I swear, if I had it, I'd promise it gladly. But somehow, some way, in some manner, from somewhere, from some one, there's some hope of your having good luck along with me.

EPIDICUS: Oh, go to the devil, you good-for-nothing!

CHAERIBULUS: Why do you wish to abuse me?

STRATIPPOCLES: Because you keep jabbering to me about something, some way, from somewhere, from some one, and there isn't a thing anywhere. I won't let you fill my ears with it. You don't give me any more assistance than a man who's never even been born.

Act Three.   Scene II

(*Enter* EPIDICUS, *with a bag of money, from the house of* PERIPHANES.)

EPIDICUS (*to* PERIPHANES *within*): Yes, you've done your part; now I must do mine. As far as the money is concerned, you can rest easy, (*as the door closes*) for it's already dead. Don't expect to get any of this back; it's laid out for burial, every bit of it. Just trust me; it's the way I act; it's the way my forefathers acted. (*To himself*) Ye immortal gods! What a glorious day you have granted me! What a charming and an agreeable day! But why not tramp away from here and transport these supplies to the colony under my own auspices? I delay myself by standing here. (*Noticing the young men*) But what's this? I see the two buddies, master and Chaeribulus, in front of the house. (*Approaching*) What are you two doing here? (*Handing the bag of money to* STRATIPPOCLES) Take this, please.

STRATIPPOCLES (*taking it eagerly*): How much is in it?

EPIDICUS: Sufficient and more than sufficient—a superabundance. I've brought you ten minae more than you owe the moneylender. Provided I can satisfy and oblige you, I don't care a damn for my own hide.

STRATIPPOCLES: How do you mean?

EPIDICUS: Why, I'm going to make your father a parenticide.

STRATIPPOCLES: What kind of word is that?

EPIDICUS: I'm tired of the old, ordinary words, like "to cheat him out of his purse." I'm going to take him in in a sack.[7] The pimp's collected his cash for the music girl there (*indicating* PERIPHANES' *house*); I paid it myself. [I counted out the money with my own hands for the girl your father believes to be his daughter.][8] Now I've found the way to deceive your father a second time and to afford you assistance. I persuaded the old man and delivered a lengthy discourse to this effect, that you should have no access to her[9] on your return.

STRATIPPOCLES: Splendid!

EPIDICUS: The music girl is in the house now, posing as his daughter.

STRATIPPOCLES: I understand.

EPIDICUS: He's given me Apoecides to be his agent in the transaction, as if he were on his guard against me; Apoecides is in the forum waiting for me.

STRATIPPOCLES: Not a bad idea!

EPIDICUS: I've made game of the guarder now. Why, your father himself placed the purse on my neck. He's making preparations for you to be married as soon as you arrive home.

STRATIPPOCLES: There's only one way of persuading me to be married; Hades must first snatch away the girl I brought here with me.

EPIDICUS: Now here's the cunning plot I've planned: I'll go all alone to the house of the pimp and instruct him to say, in case any one should come to him, that he has received the money for the music girl and that he was paid the sum of fifty minae of silver.[10] As a matter of fact, I paid out the money with my own hands just the day before yesterday for that sweetheart of yours that your father thinks is his own daughter. In that way the pimp unwittingly will swear by his filthy head and give the impression he has received the money, which is actually going for the girl you've now brought with you.

STRATIPPOCLES: You've got more turns than a potter's wheel.

EPIDICUS: And now I'll hire some wily music girl for a few cents and get her to pretend that she's been bought; she'll trick the two old men in fine fashion. Apoecides will bring her along with him to your father.

STRATIPPOCLES: How well thought out!

EPIDICUS: I'll send her to him well coached, too, just loaded down with my tricks and deceits. But I'm talking too much; you've both delayed me a long time. You know now what'll happen. I'm off. (*He hurries away towards the forum.*)

STRATIPPOCLES (*calling after him*): Have a good trip.

CHAERIBULUS (*admiringly*): He's certainly a clever one at cooking up schemes.

STRATIPPOCLES: Well, he's saved me with his plans, I know that for sure.

CHAERIBULUS: Let's go into my house.

STRATIPPOCLES: Yes, and rather more cheerfully than I came out of it. Thanks to the bravery and auspices of Epidicus, I'm going back to camp laden with plunder. (*They enter the house of* CHAERIBULUS. *A short time is supposed to elapse before the next Act.*)

Act Four. Scene I

(*Enter* PERIPHANES *from his house.*)

PERIPHANES (*to himself*): Men ought to have a mirror for themselves, not merely for the sake of scrutinising their countenance, but to be able to perceive [the source of their wisdom, and then be able to perceive][11] the resources of their mind. And when they had inspected that, they should then consider the sort of life they lived long ago in their youth. This has been advantageous, according to my way of thinking. For instance, here I've begun to be distressed at heart about my son, just as if he had committed some offence against me, or just as if my own misdeeds hadn't been plentiful and serious when I was a youth. At times we old fellows are positively deranged. (*Looking down the street*) But here's my good friend Apoecides with the booty.
(*Enter* APOECIDES *with a* MUSIC GIRL.)
I'm glad to see our merchant back safe and sound. How's everything?

APOECIDES: The gods and goddesses are on your side.

PERIPHANES: That's a good omen.

APOECIDES: Yes, and the omen is supported by success, too. Have this girl led off inside, if you please.

PERIPHANES (*calling at his door*): Hey! Come outside here, some one!
(*Enter a* SLAVE *from the house of* PERIPHANES.)
(To the SLAVE) Just take that woman inside. And listen, will you?

SLAVE: What do you wish?

PERIPHANES: Be sure you don't let her come in contact with my daughter, or even catch sight of her. Do you understand? I want her shut off by herself in a small room. (*The* SLAVE *and the* MUSIC GIRL *go into the house*) There's a great difference between the character of a maiden and of a slut[12] like that.

APOECIDES: Wisely and cleverly spoken! A man can never be careful enough about his daughter's chastity. Gad! Our transaction got her away from your son just in time.

PERIPHANES: How so?

APOECIDES: Because a man told me he had just seen your son here in the city, and, by Jove, this (*glancing at the door*) was the very business he was after.

PERIPHANES (*grimly*): There isn't much doubt about that, damn it!

APOECIDES: Well, you certainly have an old master of a slave, cheap at any price; why, he's worth his weight in gold. The way he kept that music girl from knowing she had been bought for you![13] She was as full of laughter and gaiety as she could be when he brought her along with him.

PERIPHANES: It's surprising that he could do it.

APOECIDES: He told her that you were going to offer sacrifice at your house to celebrate your son's safe return from Thebes.

PERIPHANES: He was on the right road there.

APOECIDES: And he really convinced her that she had been hired to assist you here at your sacrifice. [He said that you were going to offer sacrifice at your house.][11] At that point I began to look like this (*assuming a stolid expression*), and I made myself sort of stupid and dull-witted.

PERIPHANES: Quite right, too.

APOECIDES (*suddenly remembering*): A friend of mine's got an important case on in the forum now; I must go and give him my support.

PERIPHANES: Come back to me, please, as soon as you're free.

APOECIDES: I'll be back here directly. (*He hurries off towards the forum.*)

PERIPHANES (*to himself*): A friend in need is the finest thing a man can have. With no labour on your part, your wishes are carried out just the same. If I had employed for this business some fellow less skilled and less clever in tricks of this sort, I'd have been nicely hoodwinked, and then my son could show his white teeth and laugh at me, and I'd deserve it, too. (*Reflecting*) But it's foolish of me to find fault with him for doing just what I was always doing myself in my youth, when I was a soldier; I used to wear out men's ears with the tales of my exploits, once I'd begun. (*Looking down the street*) But who's this I see headed this way, swaggering so that his cloak fairly undulates?

Act Four. Scene II

(*Enter a* SOLDIER, *followed by his servant.*)

SOLDIER (*to his servant*): Don't you pass by a single house without asking where old man Periphanes Platenius lives. Don't you return to me until you've found it out.

PERIPHANES (*stepping up*): Young man, if I point out to you the person you're looking for, will I get any thanks from you for the favour?

SOLDIER (*loftily*): By my military valour, I have in arms won the right to have all people give *me* their thanks.

PERIPHANES: Young man, you haven't found a very tranquil spot in which to unfold your valorous deeds, as you'd like to do. When an inferior boasts of his battles to his superior, they seem cheap by comparison. But as to that Periphanes Platenius you're looking for, I am he, if you wish him for anything.

SOLDIER (*in a tone of awe*): You mean the one that they say served as a youth with kings and won great wealth by his deeds and his knowledge of warfare?

PERIPHANES: Why, if you should hear of my battles, you'd dash home with your arms out like a sprinter.

SOLDIER: Damn it, I'm looking for some one to whom I can narrate my own battles, not for one to tell me about his.

PERIPHANES: This isn't the right place for you, then. Go hunt some other person to patch together your lies for.

SOLDIER (*promptly changing the subject*): Pay attention, now, and I'll inform you why I've come here. I hear that you have purchased my sweetheart.

PERIPHANES (*aside*): Aha! Now at last I know who this fellow is—the soldier that Epidicus told me about a while ago. (*Aloud*) That's right, young man. I bought her.

SOLDIER: I'd like a few words with you, if you don't mind.

PERIPHANES: Gad, I don't know whether I mind or not, unless you tell me what you want.

SOLDIER: I want you to turn the girl over to me and let me pay you for her.

PERIPHANES: You've the money with you, eh?

SOLDIER: Why shouldn't I speak frankly with you? I want to make her my freedwoman this very day and keep her as my mistress.

PERIPHANES: A few words will be sufficient. She cost me fifty minae; you pay sixty over to me, and the woman will keep you busy in your spare time, I'll guarantee. But the deal is on this condition, that you unload this region of her.

SOLDIER: Is she mine, then, on those terms?

PERIPHANES: Yes, you may have her. You've made a good bargain. (*Calling at the door*) Hey! Bring out that music girl you took inside. (*To the* SOLDIER) And I'll even throw in the lute that came with her as a gift to you, free of charge.

Act Four. Scene III

(*Enter slaves of* PERIPHANES *with the* MUSIC GIRL; *the slaves return to the house.*)

PERIPHANES: Here she is. Take her, please.

SOLDIER (*to* PERIPHANES, *after a look at the* MUSIC GIRL): Are you crazy? What type of trick are you palming off on me? Why don't you have the music girl brought out from the house?

PERIPHANES: This is the music girl. There's no other one here.

SOLDIER (*hotly*): You can't trifle with me. Bring out the music girl Acropolistis, won't you?

PERIPHANES: This is she, I say.

SOLDIER: This is not she, I say. Do you think I don't know my own sweetheart?

PERIPHANES: This is the music girl my son was in love with, I tell you.

SOLDIER: She is not the one.

PERIPHANES (*astonished*): What? She isn't?

SOLDIER: No, she isn't.

PERIPHANES: Where in the world does this one come from, then? I paid good money for her, confound it!

SOLDIER: I think you were a fool to pay it; there's been a fine blunder here.

PERIPHANES (*unconvinced*): No, this is the one. Why, I sent the slave who always attends my son; and the slave himself bought the music girl.

SOLDIER: Hm-m! Old man, the fellow has cut you up joint by joint, that slave of yours has.

PERIPHANES: What do you mean, "cut me up"?

SOLDIER: That's my suspicion; this young deer[14] has been palmed off on you in place of the music girl. Old man, the wool has been pulled over your eyes in cunning and clever style. I'm going now to look for her, wherever she is. (*The* SOLDIER *departs, followed by his servant.*)

PERIPHANES (*calling after him*): Good-bye, warrior. (*To himself, bitterly*) Bravo, bravo, Epidicus! You're a fine fellow, a good fighter, a real man! You've wiped me out, snivelling good-for-nothing that I am! (*To the* MUSIC GIRL) Did Apoecides buy you from the pimp today?

MUSIC GIRL: I've never heard the man mentioned before today, and besides, no one could buy me at any price. I've been a free woman for more than five years.

PERIPHANES: What business do you have in my house, then?

MUSIC GIRL: I'll tell you. I was hired to come and sing to the lute for an old man while he offered sacrifice.

PERIPHANES (*aside*): I'm the most worthless old idiot in all Attic Athens, I realise it. (*To the* MUSIC GIRL) Look here, you, do you know the music girl Acropolistis?

MUSIC GIRL: As well as I know myself.

PERIPHANES: Where does she live?

MUSIC GIRL: I can't really say where she does live, now that she's free.

PERIPHANES: What's that? She's free? Who freed her, I want to know. in case you know.

MUSIC GIRL: I'll tell you what I've heard. They say that Stratippocles, the son of Periphanes, arranged to have her freed during his absence.

PERIPHANES (*aside*): Jupiter! I'm royally ruined, if this is true. Epidicus has eviscerated that purse of mine, no doubt about it.

MUSIC GIRL: That's what I've heard. (*Sweetly*) There isn't anything else you wish, is there?

PERIPHANES (*shouting*): Yes, that you die a horrible death and get out of here at once.

MUSIC GIRL: Won't you give me back my lute?

PERIPHANES: Neither lutes nor flutes! Hurry up and get out of here, if the gods love you!

MUSIC GIRL: I'll be off. But you'll give it back later, just the same, and there'll be a bigger scandal when you do. (*The* MUSIC GIRL *departs.*)

PERIPHANES (*to himself, bitterly*): What now? Am I to let her go unpunished, I, a man whose name figures in so many important decisions? On the contrary, if I had to lose the same amount all over again, I'd rather lose it than let myself be laughed at with impunity and be looked upon as an object of plunder. Ah! That I should be tricked openly, to my very face! And yet I think less of my own case than of his, for he is called a doctor and concocter of laws and legal principles. He even talks about his wisdom; why, I've seen a hammer with its handle off show more wisdom than he does!

Act Four.   Scene IV

(*Enter* PHILIPPA *in distress.*)

PHILIPPA (*to herself, not seeing* PERIPHANES): If a human being is in misery that deserves commiseration, he is truly miserable! This now is my experience, on whom so many woes converge and batter my breast at one time; sufferings of many a kind keep me in anguish; poverty and apprehension terrify the thoughts of my mind, nor have I anywhere a place of refuge wherein I can place my hopes. My daughter has fallen into the power of the enemy, and I know not where she is.

PERIPHANES (*aside*): Who is this woman coming from abroad, bewailing her fate in such terror?

PHILIPPA: They told me that Periphanes lived in this neighbourhood.

PERIPHANES (*aside*): She mentions my name; she has need of hospitality, I suppose.

PHILIPPA: I'd gladly reward anyone who could point the man out to me or show me where he lives.

PERIPHANES (*aside*): I'm trying to recognise her; it seems to me that I've seen her before somewhere or other. (*As suspicion of her identity grows*) Is she the one my mind believes, or is she not?

PHILIPPA (*catching sight of* PERIPHANES): Merciful gods! Haven't I seen him before? . . . .[15]

PERIPHANES (*aside*): She is certainly the one, the poor girl in Epidaurus that I remember wronging.

PHILIPPA (*aside*): He is surely the one, the man who violated my virginity in Epidaurus.

PERIPHANES (*aside*): The one who, from my embrace, gave birth to the daughter I now have in my house. What if I should go up—

PHILIPPA (*aside*): I don't know whether to approach—

PERIPHANES (*aside*): —if she is the one?

PHILIPPA (*aside*): —if he is the man, but the lapse of so many years makes me uncertain.

PERIPHANES (*aside*): So long a time has passed, my mind's in doubt. But if she's the one I half-suspect her to be, I shall approach craftily.

PHILIPPA (*aside*): Now I must bring the wiles of women to my aid.

PERIPHANES (*aside*): I'll speak to her.

PHILIPPA (*aside*): I'll direct the strength of my discourse at him.

PERIPHANES (*stepping up*): Good health to you.

PHILIPPA: I accept good health for me and mine.

PERIPHANES: Anything else?

PHILIPPA: Good health to you; I return your loan.

PERIPHANES (*smiling*): I approve of your honesty. But don't I know you?

PHILIPPA: If I know you, I shall persuade myself that you know me.

PERIPHANES: Where have I seen you?

PHILIPPA: You're unfair and unjust.

PERIPHANES: How so?

PHILIPPA: In expecting me to be the prompter of your memory.

PERIPHANES: A neat point!

PHILIPPA: Strange things you speak of. . . .[15]

PERIPHANES: There! That's better. Do you remember?

PHILIPPA: I remember what I remember.

PERIPHANES: But in Epidaurus—

PHILIPPA: Ah! You've dashed a drop of water on my burning breast!

PERIPHANES (*continuing*): —for you, a poor young innocent, and your mother, I relieved your poverty, you recall?

PHILIPPA: Are you the man who, for your own pleasure, sowed grievous suffering in me?

PERIPHANES: I am he. I hope you're well.

PHILIPPA: I am well, since I perceive that you're well.

PERIPHANES: Give me your hand.

PHILIPPA (*doing so*): Take it. You hold the hand of a grieving and miserable woman.

PERIPHANES (*concerned*): Why is it that you look so distressed?

PHILIPPA: The daughter that I had by you—

PERIPHANES: What about her?

PHILIPPA: After I brought her up, I—I lost her. (*Weeping*) She was captured by the enemy.

PERIPHANES: Keep your mind calm and peaceful! Hush, now! She's here safe and sound in my house. As soon as I heard from my slave that she had been captured, I gave him money immediately for her purchase. He attended to the matter as discreetly and as thriftily as —(*suddenly recalling the scene with the* SOLDIER)—as he is disgustingly dishonest in other matters.

PHILIPPA: Let me see if she is mine, if you wish me well.

PERIPHANES (*calling at the door*): Ho, there, Canthara! Tell my daughter Telestis to come out here in front of the house to see her mother.

PHILIPPA: Now at last I breathe again.

Act Four.　Scene V

(*Enter* ACROPOLISTIS *from the house of* PERIPHANES.)

ACROPOLISTIS: Why is it, father, that you called me out of the house?

PERIPHANES: For you to see your mother, go up to her and greet her on her arrival, and give her a kiss.

ACROPOLISTIS (*insolently*): Eh? What mother?

PERIPHANES: The mother who is half dead from seeking the sight of you.

PHILIPPA (*to* PERIPHANES, *in amazement*): Who is that person you're telling to give me a kiss?

PERIPHANES: Your daughter.

PHILIPPA: This girl?

PERIPHANES: Yes.

PHILIPPA (*indignantly*): And I'm to kiss her?

PERIPHANES: Why not? She's your own child.

PHILIPPA: Man, you're crazy!

PERIPHANES (*astonished*): I?

PHILIPPA: Yes, you.

PERIPHANES: Why?

PHILIPPA: Because I don't know who this girl is, and I don't recognise her, and I never laid eyes on her before this day.

PERIPHANES: I know why you're mistaken; she has different clothing and jewelry. . . .[15]

PHILIPPA (*contemptuously*): Puppies and pigs have a very different smell. I tell you, I don't know who this girl is.

PERIPHANES (*enraged*): By the honour of gods and mortals! What is this? Am I going into the pimp business here, keeping strange girls in my home and fairly egurgitating money from the house? (*To* ACROPOLISTIS) Here you, who kiss me and call me your father, why do you stand there so stupid? What are you silent for?

ACROPOLISTIS: What do you want me to say?

PERIPHANES: This lady denies being your mother.

ACROPOLISTIS (*calmly*): She needn't be, if she doesn't want to. But in spite of her, I'll be my mother's daughter just the same.

PERIPHANES: Why did you keep calling me father, then?

ACROPOLISTIS: That's your fault, not mine. Why shouldn't I say you're my father, when you call me your daughter? This woman too—why, if she'd consider me her daughter, I'd call her mother. She says I'm not her daughter; well, then, she's not my mother. And anyway, this isn't my fault; I've merely recited the lessons I learned. Epidicus was my teacher.

PERIPHANES (*realising the truth*): Damnation! I've upset the apple-cart.

ACROPOLISTIS (*sweetly*): I haven't done anything wrong, have I, father?

PERIPHANES (*hotly*): By God, I'll kill you, if I ever hear you call me father again!

ACROPOLISTIS: I won't, then. You shall be my father when you wish; when you don't wish to, don't be my father.

PHILIPPA: Well, if you bought her under the impression she was your daughter, what means of identification did you use?

PERIPHANES: None.

PHILIPPA: Then how were you convinced she was our daughter?

PERIPHANES: My slave Epidicus told me she was.

PHILIPPA: But, heavens above, couldn't *you* recognise her, even if your servant had been mistaken?

PERIPHANES: How could I? I never saw her except once.

PHILIPPA (*beginning to weep*): Oh, dear me! I'm so unhappy!

PERIPHANES: Don't cry, my dear woman. Go inside and keep your spirits up. I'll find her for you.

PHILIPPA: An Athenian citizen from here bought her, a young man, so they said.

PERIPHANES: I'll find her; just hush! You go in and keep guard over this Circe,[16] this daughter of the Sun. (*To himself, as* PHILIPPA *and* ACROPOLISTIS *go into his house*) And I'm going to drop everything else and turn my attention to hunting down Epidicus. If I find him, I'll make this his day of destruction. (PERIPHANES *departs towards the forum. A short time is supposed to elapse before the next Act.*)

Act Five.　Scene I

(*Enter* STRATIPPOCLES *from the house of* CHAERIBULUS.)

STRATIPPOCLES (*to himself*): That moneylender is frightfully unaccommodating; he doesn't come to get his money from me, and he doesn't bring the girl that was bought from the booty. (*Looking down the street*) But here comes Epidicus. I wonder why it is his brow's so wrinkled with gloom.

(*Enter* EPIDICUS *from the forum.*)

EPIDICUS (*to himself, not seeing* STRATIPPOCLES): If Jupiter were to bring the other eleven gods along with him, all of them together wouldn't be able to rescue Epidicus from torture. I saw Periphanes buying straps, and Apoecides was along with him. The two men are looking for me right now, I suppose. They've found it out; they realise they've been deceived.

STRATIPPOCLES (*cheerfully*): How goes it, friend Timeliness?

EPIDICUS (*glumly*): The way it does with every poor wretch.

STRATIPPOCLES: What's your trouble?

EPIDICUS: Just give me some funds for flight, won't you, before I meet destruction? Two de-fleeced old rams are hunting for me all over the city; they're carrying straps with them, too.

STRATIPPOCLES: Keep your courage up.

EPIDICUS (*with sarcasm*): Oh, sure! I'm a man who has liberty in store for him!

STRATIPPOCLES: I'll keep you safe.

EPIDICUS: Gad, they'll do a better job of that, if they find me. (*Looking down the street*) But who is this slip of a girl and that grey-headed little fellow coming this way?

STRATIPPOCLES (*excited*): He's the moneylender, and she's the girl I bought from the booty.

EPIDICUS (*looking at* TELESTIS *with interest*): So she's the one, eh?

STRATIPPOCLES: The very one. Isn't she just as I described to you? (*Entranced*) Gaze upon her, observe her closely, Epidicus; from the tip of her toe to the crown of her head she's perfectly charming! Isn't it just like looking at a beautifully painted picture?

EPIDICUS: It's my skin that will be beautifully painted, judging from what you say; Apelles and Zeuxis, the two of them,[17] will paint me with pigments of elm.

(*Enter the* MONEYLENDER *and* TELESTIS.)

STRATIPPOCLES (*to the* MONEYLENDER): Immortal gods! Is this the way I told you to come to me? A man with feet of lead would have arrived here before you have.

MONEYLENDER: The girl here delayed me, confound it!

STRATIPPOCLES: Well, if it's on account of her that you're delayed and it was her wish, then you've arrived too soon.

MONEYLENDER: Come, come! Pay me, count out the money; I mustn't delay my companions.

STRATIPPOCLES: It's all counted out.

MONEYLENDER (*handing him a purse*): Take this purse and put the money in it.

STRATIPPOCLES: You come wisely prepared. Wait till I bring it out to you.

MONEYLENDER: Hurry up.

STRATIPPOCLES: It's in the house. (*He goes into the house of* CHAERI-BULUS.)

EPIDICUS (*gazing intently at* TELESTIS): Do I have really good eyesight or don't I? Is it you I see, Telestis, the daughter of Periphanes and Philippa, born in Thebes and conceived in Epidaurus?

TELESTIS (*in surprise*): Who are you, who mention the name of my parents and my own name?

EPIDICUS: You don't know me?

TELESTIS: Not so far as I can recall right now, I'm sure.

EPIDICUS: Don't you remember my bringing you on your birthday a little gold crescent and a little gold finger-ring?

TELESTIS: I do remember, my dear man! Were you the one?

EPIDICUS: I was, and the man who purchased you is your brother. . . .[15] by a different mother and the same father.

TELESTIS (*eagerly*): What about my father? Is he alive?

EPIDICUS: Hush, now! Keep your mind calm and tranquil.

TELESTIS (*reassured*): The gods have saved me from destruction, if you speak the truth.

EPIDICUS: There's no reason why I shouldn't tell you the truth.

(*Re-enter* STRATIPPOCLES *with the purse.*)

STRATIPPOCLES: Here, moneylender, take the money. There are forty minae there. If any coin is questionable, I'll change it.

MONEYLENDER (*taking the purse and examining the money*): Very kind of you. Good-bye, sir. (*The* MONEYLENDER *departs.*)

STRATIPPOCLES (*to* TELESTIS): And now you are really mine.

TELESTIS: Goodness, yes! Your sister, that is—that you may know the truth too. I greet you, my brother.

STRATIPPOCLES (*to* EPIDICUS): Is she in her right mind?

EPIDICUS: Yes, indeed, if she calls you her brother.

STRATIPPOCLES (*aghast*): What? Have I just turned into her brother while stepping in and out of the house?

EPIDICUS: You should accept your good luck quietly, keep quiet about it, and be happy.

STRATIPPOCLES (*sadly*): You have both lost me and found me, sister.

EPIDICUS: You're a fool. Hush, now! Through my endeavours there's some one already at home for you to love—the music girl. And likewise through my endeavours your sister is regaining her liberty.

STRATIPPOCLES: Epidicus, I admit—

EPIDICUS: Go in and have some water heated for her. I'll explain everything else to you later, when there's more time.

STRATIPPOCLES: Come this way with me, sister.

EPIDICUS: I'll have Thesprio come over here. Remember now, if the old men get savage, you and your sister are to give me your support.

STRATIPPOCLES: That will be easy. (STRATIPPOCLES *and* TELESTIS *go into the house of* PERIPHANES.)

EPIDICUS (*calling at* CHAERIBULUS's *door*): Thesprio, cross over through the garden and give me your assistance at home. (*To himself*) Big doings! I'm not as worried about the old men as I was. I'll go back in to arrange things for the guests on their arrival. At the same time I'll tell Stratippocles inside what I know. I won't run away; I've made up my mind to stay at home, and that master of mine shan't accuse me of challenging him to a foot race. I'm talking too much here; I'm going in. (*He goes into the house of* PERIPHANES.)

Act Five.   Scene II

(*Enter* PERIPHANES *and* APOECIDES.)

PERIPHANES (*angrily*): So that fellow is making a laughingstock of us two decrepit old men, eh?

APOECIDES (*extremely weary*): Gad, no! You're the one that's making me miserable with this miserable business.

PERIPHANES: Oh, keep quiet, won't you? Just let me get hold of the rascal.

APOECIDES: I'll tell you this right now, so you'll know it: you'd better get yourself another companion. (*With a groan*) I'm so weary from following you around that the swelling in my ankles has spread to my knees.

PERIPHANES: How many ways that fellow tricked me today, and you too! And how he did eviscerate my finances!

APOECIDES: To hell with him, as far as I'm concerned! Why, he's the son of Vulcan, and an angry Vulcan, at that! Whatever he touches is entirely consumed. Stand near him, and he scorches you with his heat.

(*Enter* EPIDICUS *from the house without being seen.*)

EPIDICUS (*to himself*): All the immortal gods in heaven, and another twelve besides, are aiding me with their assistance and fighting on my side. Whatever my misdeeds have been, I have allies and reserves at home. I give all my enemies a good swift kick.

PERIPHANES: Where on earth am I to look for him?

APOECIDES: So long as you look for him without me, you can go look in the middle of the sea, for all I care.

EPIDICUS (*stepping forward and addressing* PERIPHANES): Why look for me? Why bother yourself? Why worry this man? Here I am. I haven't run away, have I? Or left the house? Or vanished from your sight? . . . .[18] I don't beg you for mercy, either. You want to bind me? Well, here are my hands. (*Holding them out*) You have straps; I saw you buy them. Why the delay now? Bind me.

PERIPHANES (*puzzled*): It's no use; he's offering me bail of his accord.

EPIDICUS: Why don't you bind me?

APOECIDES: Jove, what a wicked bit of property!

EPIDICUS (*ironically*): Apoecides, I certainly don't want you to intercede in my behalf.

APOECIDES: It's easy to comply with your wishes, Epidicus.

EPIDICUS (*to* PERIPHANES): Going to do anything?

PERIPHANES: As you wish it, eh?

EPIDICUS: Yes, by Jove! You must bind these hands of mine today according to my wish, not yours.

PERIPHANES: But I don't care to; I won't bind them.

APOECIDES (*to* PERIPHANES): He's ready to hurl his dart at you; he's up to some sort of trick.

EPIDICUS (*still holding out his hands*): You're delaying yourself by letting me stand here loose. Come, bind me, I say!

PERIPHANES: But I really prefer to question you unbound.

EPIDICUS: You won't find anything out, then.

PERIPHANES (*appealing to* APOECIDES): What am I to do?

APOECIDES: Do? Let him have his way.

EPIDICUS (*approvingly*): You're a worthy fellow, Apoecides.

PERIPHANES: Give me your hands, then.

EPIDICUS: No delay about that. (*As* PERIPHANES *binds his wrists*) And bind them tightly, too. And don't have any compassion.

PERIPHANES (*pulling the straps tighter*): You can decide about that when the job is done.

EPIDICUS (*surveying the result*): That does it nicely. Go ahead, now, question me, ask anything you wish.

PERIPHANES: In the first place, how did you have the nerve to tell me that the girl who was bought the day before yesterday was my daughter?

EPIDICUS (*insolently*): I wanted to; that was how.

PERIPHANES: That's what you say, eh? You wanted to!

EPIDICUS: That's what I say. Just make a bet with me that she isn't a daughter.

PERIPHANES: When her mother says she doesn't know her?

EPIDICUS: Well, make your bet—three thousand to one—that she isn't her mother's daughter.

PERIPHANES: Ah, yes! I see the catch. But who is this woman?

EPIDICUS: Your son's mistress, to tell you the truth.

PERIPHANES (*hotly*): Didn't I give you thirty minae for my daughter?

EPIDICUS: Admitted; and I used the money to buy that music girl, your son's mistress, in place of your daughter. That's why I did you out of your thirty minae.

PERIPHANES: And how you tricked me about that hired music girl!

EPIDICUS: Yes, I did it, and a damned good job, too, I think!

PERIPHANES: What became of the last money I gave you?

EPIDICUS: I'll tell you. I gave it to a fellow that's neither a rogue nor a saint, your own son Stratippocles.

PERIPHANES: How did you dare to give it away?

EPIDICUS: Because I wanted to.

PERIPHANES: Confound it! What sort of insolence is this?

EPIDICUS: What? Am I being scolded like a slave?

PERIPHANES (*with sarcasm*): I'm happy to hear that you are a free man now.

EPIDICUS: Well, I've deserved to be.

PERIPHANES: You? Deserved it?

EPIDICUS: Go look inside the house; then you'll know it's true, I'll guarantee.

PERIPHANES (*more puzzled*): What's the meaning of this?

EPIDICUS: The fact will speak for itself. Just go on inside.

APOECIDES (*to* PERIPHANES): Go in; there's some good reason for this.

PERIPHANES: Keep your eye on him, Apoecides. (*He goes into his house.*)

APOECIDES: What's the meaning of all this, Epidicus?

EPIDICUS: By heavens, it's downright injustice for me to stand here bound, when his daughter has been discovered today as a result of my labours.

APOECIDES (*incredulous*): You say that you discovered his daughter?

EPIDICUS: I did, and she's at home. Ah, it's a bitter thing to reap a crop of cruelty, when you've sown nothing but kindness.

APOECIDES: You mean the girl that we both hunted for all over the city today, and wore ourselves out doing it?

EPIDICUS: I wore myself out finding her; you wore yourselves out hunting for her.

(*Re-enter* PERIPHANES *from his house.*)

PERIPHANES (*to* STRATIPPOCLES *and* TELESTIS *within*): Why so many entreaties? I realise now that I must treat him according to his deserts. (*To* EPIDICUS) Hold out your hands and let me untie them.

EPIDICUS: Don't touch them.

PERIPHANES: Come, stretch them out.

EPIDICUS: I don't wish to.

PERIPHANES: That's not fair of you.

EPIDICUS (*angrily*): By Jove, I'll never let you untie me today, unless you give me satisfaction.

PERIPHANES (*meekly*): A very fair and just request. I'll give you shoes, a tunic, and a cloak.

EPIDICUS: And then what?

PERIPHANES: Your liberty.

EPIDICUS: And what after that? A new freedman needs a bit of grub.

PERIPHANES: You'll get it. I'll furnish you with food.

EPIDICUS: Even so, damn it, you shan't untie me today, unless you beg my pardon.

PERIPHANES (*humbly*): I do beg you to pardon me, Epidicus, if unwittingly I have been guilty of any wrongdoing. And now, in return, you shall be free.

EPIDICUS: As much as I hate to do it, I'll pardon you; circumstances make it necessary. (*Holding out his hands*) Untie me now, by all means, if you so desire.

Epilogue

This is the fellow whose cunning brought him his freedom. Give us your applause and fare you well. Stretch your limbs and rise.

1. Epidicus alludes here to slaves whose backs are mottled or spotted from frequent whippings.

2. The text of this speech is corrupt.

3. Thesprio probably alludes here to the famous cases of Archilochus and Alcaeus who fled from battle, leaving their weapons behind.

4. That is, the arms moved of their own accord as did the automatic tripods made by Hephaestus (Vulcan) and described in Homer's *Iliad,* XVIII, 373 ff.

5. There is apparently a lacuna of two verses at this point.

6. The labour of Hercules to which Periphanes refers is usually thought to be his victory over Hippolyta, the queen of the Amazons.

7. This jest, which is prepared for by the newly coined word "parenticide," alludes to the early Roman custom of punishing parricides by sewing them up in sacks and drowning them.

8. This verse is bracketed as spurious; it appears in much the same form a few verses later.

9. The girl in question is the former sweetheart, Acropolistis, who, as Stratippocles knows, is in the house posing as the daughter of Periphanes. Periphanes, however, thinks that Epidicus will bring Acropolistis to him later, in accordance with the arrangements made in Act Two, Scene II.

10. Actually, the pimp at the earlier transaction had received only thirty minae; cf. line 700. But the pimp's story must now agree with the fictitious sale, for which Epidicus has just received fifty minae from Periphanes.

11. This passage is bracketed as spurious.

12. Literally, a "she-wolf," a slang expression for a harlot; cf. *Truculentus,* line 657 and note.

13. This reveals one important aspect of the cleverness and the complicated nature of the deception. Epidicus hires a music girl, pretends to the two old men that he has bought her, but convinces them that he has deceived the girl into thinking she was hired. Thus the music girl, by maintaining she has been hired, gives the old men the impression that she herself is the victim of deception. When Periphanes later discovers the truth, the music girl proves to be what she has always claimed to be.

14. This is an allusion to the substitution of a stag for Iphigenia

when she was about to be sacrificed by her father Agamemnon at Aulis.

15. There is a short lacuna here.

16. Periphanes probably calls Acropolistis by the name of Circe because Circe was a sorceress; others explain it on the ground that Circe knew neither her father nor her mother.

17. Apelles and Zeuxis were famous Greek painters. Epidicus, of course, has in mind Periphanes and Apoecides.

18. One verse is missing at this point.

X

THE TWIN MENAECHMI

Characters in the Play

BRUSH (PENICULUS), *a parasite*
MENAECHMUS I, *a young man of Epidamnus*
EROTIUM, *a courtesan*
CYLINDRUS, *cook of* EROTIUM
MENAECHMUS II (SOSICLES), *a young man of Syracuse*
MESSENIO, *slave of* MENAECHMUS II
MAID *of* EROTIUM
WIFE *of* MENAECHMUS I
FATHER, *an old man, father-in-law of* MENAECHMUS I
A DOCTOR
SLAVES

Acrostic Argument

A Sicilian merchant had twin sons and died when one was stolen from him. His paternal grandfather gave the boy at home the name of the stolen twin and called him Menaechmus instead of Sosicles. When this boy grew up, he began to search for his brother in every land. At last he comes to Epidamnus; it was here that his stolen brother had been reared. Everyone thinks that the stranger is Menaechmus, their own fellow-citizen, and his brother's mistress, wife, and father-in-law so address him. Finally the two brothers recognise each other.

INTRODUCTION

ONE of the most effective sources of laughter in comedy of all ages has been the confusion resulting from the existence of twins or persons of similar appearance. Plautus in his *Amphitryon* made excellent use of the humorous possibilities afforded by the two sets of doublets, and in *The Braggart Warrior* used the device of a non-existent twin sister to good effect. It is *The Twin Menaechmi,* however, that is his most successful comedy of errors. This play is one of the best known and one of the most amusing of Roman comedy. Menaechmus of Syracuse, searching for his twin brother, comes to Epidamnus where his brother lives and is mistaken for his brother by a cook, a courtesan, a parasite, his brother's wife, and his brother's father-in-law. The farcical situations which develop follow one another in rapid succession. The play is, as J. W. Duff says, "a triumph of fun without challenge."

The basic weakness of such a plot is the improbability that Menaechmus of Syracuse, who knows of the existence of his brother, should not be more suspicious when he is accosted as a friend, a lover, or a husband. The continuance of the action is dependent upon his failure to realise the truth. And yet Plautus has avoided making him appear excessively stupid. The suggestions of his slave Messenio that Epidamnus is a town where sharpers and harlots are on the lookout for strangers pave the way for the misunderstandings, and as Menaechmus grows more and more confused and angry his failure to think of the true explanation is less noticeable. The actions of Menaechmus of Epidamnus are far more natural. He has no idea of the presence of his twin brother and cannot understand why his sweetheart, his wife, and many others accuse him of actions and words of which he is not guilty. The best situations of the play occur when he returns from the forum to find himself shut out of the houses of both his wife and his mistress, and later when he comes back to find himself accused of madness by his father-in-law and the doctor. He has no way of knowing that his twin brother has pretended insanity and has threatened both his wife and father-in-law as a means of putting a stop to their unintelligible accusations.

The characters of the two brothers are somewhat colourless, as is perhaps inevitable if they are to resemble each other closely. Neither is a very noble character; one steals a dress from his wife to give to his mistress, and the other takes full advantage of the courtesan's mistake. The minor characters are much more vividly drawn: the mercenary Erotium, Brush the parasite, the shrewish wife, the easygoing and reasonable father-in-law, the pompous doctor, the faithful Messenio— all stand out among the characters in Plautine comedy. In a farce of this type, however, the action is the main thing, and it is here where Plautus excels. There is no slackening of the pace until the final scene, where the recognition is perhaps unduly prolonged. The entrances and exits of the characters are well handled; Plautus has taken unusual pains to make the identity of each Menaechmus clear whenever he enters. The stolen dress helps to unify the action and serves as a pretext for many of the misunderstandings when it falls into the hands of the wrong Menaechmus. Few plays of Plautus reveal more skill in the handling of the plot.

The author of the Greek original is not known. Several poets of Greek comedy produced plays dealing with twins and any one of these may have provided Plautus with the subject of his play. If the reference to Hiero as king of Syracuse (411 f.) comes from the Greek play, the original must have been composed in the second half of the third century B.C., almost contemporaneous with Plautus. Some scholars consider the reference a Plautine addition, but this would date the composition of the Roman play before 215 B.C., the date of Hiero's death. *The Twin Menaechmi* would in this case be the earliest of Plautus' extant plays. This date is not impossible and has been accepted by several, but a later date seems preferable in view of the technical perfection of the play, its rapid and farcical action, and its complicated metrical structure.

The influence of *The Twin Menaechmi* on later drama has been considerable. Among the more important plays based on the Plautine comedy are Trissino's *I Simillimi* (1547), Sachs' *Monechmo* (1548), Firenzuola's *I Lucidi* (1549), Cecchi's *La Moglie* (1585) which drew material also from Plautus' *The Three Penny Day* and Terence's *The Woman of Andros*, Rotrou's *Les Ménechmes* (1636), Regnard's *Les Ménechmes* (1705) and Goldoni's *I Due Gemelli Veneziani*. The most famous of the imitations is Shakespeare's *The Comedy of Errors* (1589?), usually considered inferior to its Latin original. By introducing a second pair of twins Shakespeare greatly increased the number of possible misunderstandings, but at the same time he heightened the improbability of the situation and made the play far more perplexing for the spectators. The idea of the two pairs of twins was probably suggested by the two sets of doublets in Plautus' *Amphitryon*. Shakespeare added Luciana, the sister, to increase the love interest; he multiplied the recognitions at the end by bringing in the story of Aegeon and Aemilia, the father and mother of the two Antipholuses, and enclosed the farcical comedy of errors in a framework full of sentiment and pathos. His play thus contained much of the romantic spirit of Elizabethan comedy and had an effect very different from that of the Plautine farce.

The recent New York production, *The Boys from Syracuse*, a Rodgers and Hart musical comedy, was adapted by George Abbott from Shakespeare's comedy, but in its emphasis on farcical situations and on song and dance resembled in spirit Plautus' *The Twin Menaechmi* more closely than the comedy on which it was based.

THE TWIN MENAECHMI

(SCENE:—*A street in Epidamnus in front of the houses of* MENAECH-
MUS I *and* EROTIUM.)

Prologue

Now first and above all, spectators, I'm bringing a few
Of the best of good wishes to me—and then also to you;
I'm bringing you Plautus—by mouth, of course, not in person,
And therefore I pray you receive him with kindliest ears.
To the argument gird up your minds, as I babble my verse,
And I shall explain it—in briefest of terms, have no fears.
   And this is the thing that poets do in their plays:
The action has all taken place in Athens, they say,
That the setting will seem to be Greek to you all the more.
But from me you'll hear the truth—where it actually happened.
The plot of the play, to be sure, is Greek, but not
Of the Attic variety; Sicilian, rather.
I've given you now of the argument merely the preface;
And next the plot I'll generously pour out
Not merely by peck or bushel, but by the whole barn,
So kindly a nature I have for telling the plot.
   Now, an old merchant was living in Syracuse city,
And he by some chance had a couple of twin sons—yes, two of 'em—
And they looked so alike that the nurse couldn't tell (more's the pity)
Which one she gave suck to; no more could their mother, for whom
The nurse was called in, no, not even their mother who'd borne 'em.
Much later, the boys being now about seven years old,
Their father filled up a big ship with a lot of his goods
And, putting one twin in safekeeping with them in the hold,
Betook himself off to Tarentum to market, to turn 'em
To cash; and the other twin stayed at home with his mother.
When they got there, Tarentum was holding some games, as it happened,
And people were flocking to town, as they do for the games.
The little boy strayed from his father among all the crowds;
The lost was soon found by a rich Epidamnian merchant

Who seized him and took him off home. But the father
Was sadly dejected at heart at the loss of the boy,
And only a little while later he died of despair.
Syracuse at last heard the bad news that the father was dead
And that someone had stolen the twin who had wandered away.
So the grandfather changed the remaining twin's name then and there,
Since the other had been so beloved—the one stolen away.
The other one's name he bestowed on the twin safe at home,
And called him Menaechmus, the same as the one I have said.
The grandfather's name was Menaechmus too, it so happened,
And with ease I remember the name, as they called it aloud.
And lest you get muddled, both twins now have the same name.

　　But now on the poet's rude feet I must seek Epidamnus,
To speed on my tale. Should anyone wish to have business
Transacted there, let him be bold and speak forth and give me
The money with which I may carry out all his commands.
But unless the money's forthcoming, he's wasting his time,
And he's wasting his time even more, should the money be given.
And while standing still I've returned to my point of departure.

　　The old merchant I told you about, who kidnapped the boy,
Had no children whatever, unless you should count all his money.[1]
He adopted the stolen young twin as his son, and to him
Gave a wife and a dowry, and made him his heir when he died.
For, wandering into the country not far from the town, the
Epidamnian stepped in a freshet, where torrents of rain
Had been falling; the current caught quickly the kidnapper's feet
And carried him off to the place where he'll get his deserts.
So from him the young man inherits a plentiful fortune,
And this is the house where the rich kidnapped twin is now dwelling.

　　The other twin, living in Syracuse, comes with his slave
To find his own twin brother here, for whom he's been searching.
While the play's being acted, the town's Epidamnus, you see;
When another play comes, 'twill turn into some other town.
And then the families in the houses will change;
The inhabitant is now a pander, and now a youth,
Or a pauper, a beggar, a parasite, or a prophet.

Act One. Scene I

(*Enter* BRUSH, *who addresses audience.*)

BRUSH: My nickname's Brush, because when I eat I sweep the table clean.

People who keep prisoners in chains and put shackles on runaway slaves do a very foolish thing, if you ask me. You see, if you add insult to injury, a poor fellow will want all the more to escape and go wrong. He'll get out of his chains somehow, you can be sure—file away a link, or knock out a nail with a stone. That way's no good.

If you really want to keep somebody so he won't get away, you'd better tie him with food and drink: hitch his beak to a full dinnerpail. Give him all he wants to eat and drink every day, and he'll never try to run away, not even if he's committed murder. The bonds of food and drink are very elastic, you know: the more you stretch them, the tighter they hold you.

(*Going towards the house of* MENAECHMUS I) Now take me—I'm on my way over to Menaechmus', where I've been doing a long stretch; I'm giving myself up to let him bind me. He doesn't only feed you, you see: he builds you up and makes a new man of you. There's no better doctor alive. Just to show you what sort of fellow he is—he has wonderful meals, regular Thanksgiving dinners: he builds up such skyscrapers of dishes you have to stand on your couch if you want to get anything off the top.

But it's quite a few days since I've been over there. I've been kept at home with my dear ones—I don't eat or buy anything but what it's very dear. But now my army of dear ones is deserting, and so I'm going to see him. (*He approaches the door*) But the door's opening. There's Menaechmus—he's coming out. (*Withdraws.*)

Act One. Scene II

(*Enter* MENAECHMUS I *from his house, wearing a dress of his wife's under his own cloak. He calls back to his wife inside.*)

MENAECHMUS I: If you were not
                  Stubborn, bad,
               Stupid, and a
               Little mad,

> What your husband hates, you'd see
> And behave accordingly.
> Act the way you have today
> And back you go to dad to stay.
> If I say I'm going out,
> You're on hand to ask about
> Where I'm going,
>   What to do,
> What's my business,
>   What's for you.
> I can't get out anywhere
> But you want me to declare
> All I've done and all I do.
> Customs officer—that's you!
> I've handled you with too much care;
> Listen what I'm going to do:
> Food I give you,
>   Maids, indeed,
> Money, dresses—
>   All you need;
> Now you'll keep your spying eyes
> Off your husband, if you're wise.

And furthermore I'll see that you don't have your watching for nothing: I'm going to get even with you and take a woman out to dinner somewhere.

BRUSH (*aside*): The fellow pretends he's cursing his wife, but he's really cursing me. It's me he hurts if he eats out, not his wife.

MENAECHMUS I: Gosh! At last I've scolded my wife away from the door. (*To the audience*) Where are all you philandering husbands? What are you waiting for? Come on up and congratulate me and reward me for the good fight I've put up—I've just stolen this dress from my wife in there and I'm taking it to my mistress. This is a fine way to cheat this clever guardian of mine. An excellent job, an honest job, an elegant job, a workmanlike job! I risked my life and robbed my wife, and the thing's going to be a total loss. But I got the spoils from the enemy and didn't lose a man.

BRUSH (*accosting him*): Hey, young fellow, is any of that stuff for me?

MENAECHMUS I: It's all over. I've fallen into a trap.

BRUSH: Oh no, sir, just into protective custody. Don't be alarmed.

MENAECHMUS I: Who are you?

BRUSH: Myself.

MENAECHMUS I (*turning*): Why, you sight for sore eyes, you chance that comes once in a lifetime! Good morning.

BRUSH: Good morning.

MENAECHMUS I: What are you doing?

BRUSH: I'm shaking hands with my best friend.

MENAECHMUS I: You couldn't have come at a better time than this.

BRUSH: That's just like me: I'm quite an expert on opportune moments.

MENAECHMUS I: Want to see something gorgeous?

BRUSH: What cook cooked it? I'll know if he slipped up when I see what's left.

MENAECHMUS I: Say, did you ever see the painting on the temple wall where the eagle steals Ganymede, or where Venus gets away with Adonis?

BRUSH: Plenty of times. But what have those pictures got to do with me?

MENAECHMUS I (*revealing the dress*): Take a look at me. Do I look like them at all?

BRUSH: What's that outfit you're wearing?

MENAECHMUS I: Say I'm a clever fellow.

BRUSH: When do we eat?

MENAECHMUS I: You just say what I tell you.

BRUSH: All right. "Clever fellow."

MENAECHMUS I: Can't you add anything of your own?

BRUSH: Well—life of the party.

MENAECHMUS I: Go on, go on.

BRUSH: I certainly will not go on unless I know what I'm going to get out of it. You've had a quarrel with your wife and I'm staying on the safe side.

MENAECHMUS I: What do you say we find a place away from my wife where we can have a funeral—and then we burn up the day?

BRUSH (*enthusiastically*): Wonderful! Let's get going. How soon do I light the pyre? The day's already dead up to the waist.

MENAECHMUS I: You'll wait if you interrupt me.

BRUSH: Knock my eye out, Menaechmus, if I say a word except when you tell me.

MENAECHMUS I: Come over here away from the door.

BRUSH: Sure.

MENAECHMUS I: Farther still.

BRUSH: All right.

MENAECHMUS I: Now come boldly away from the lion's den.

BRUSH: Say there, I've got an idea you'd make a good racing driver.

MENAECHMUS I: How come?

BRUSH: Well, you're always looking back to see that your wife isn't following you.

MENAECHMUS I: But what do you say—

BRUSH: What do I say? Why, anything you want, my friend.

MENAECHMUS I: I wonder if you could make a guess from the odour of a thing if you smelt it.

BRUSH: . . .[2] if you got the whole staff.

MENAECHMUS I: Well, take a sniff of this dress I've got. How does it smell? Don't hang back.

BRUSH: You ought to smell the top of a woman's dress; the smell down there is awful.

MENAECHMUS I: Then smell here, Brush. How dainty you are!

BRUSH: This is better.

MENAECHMUS I: How about it? What does it smell like? Tell me.

BRUSH: A moocher, a mistress, and a meal! . . .[2]

MENAECHMUS I: Now I'll take this to my lady Erotium here, and I'll order dinner for all three of us.

BRUSH: Swell!

MENAECHMUS I: After that we'll drink right through till daylight tomorrow.

BRUSH: Swell! You've said a mouthful. Do I knock now?

MENAECHMUS I: Go ahead. Or wait a minute.

BRUSH: Oh, you're holding up our drinking a mile.

MENAECHMUS I: Knock softly.

BRUSH: I suppose you're afraid the door is made of Samian ware.

MENAECHMUS I: Wait, for heaven's sake, wait! Look. She's coming out herself. Do you see how dim the sun is compared to the splendour of her beauty?

Act One.   Scene III

(*Enter* EROTIUM *from her house.*)

EROTIUM: Good morning, Menaechmus, my sweet.

BRUSH: How about me?

EROTIUM: You don't count with me.

BRUSH: That's what usually happens to the reserves in an army.

MENAECHMUS I: I'd like you to do something for him and me over at your house—get ready a battle.

EROTIUM: It shall be done.

MENAECHMUS I: And we'll both drink in this battle, and which is the better battler will be found by the bottle. You're head of the army, and you'll decide which of us—you'll spend the night with. O my heart's delight, how I detest my wife when I set my eyes on you!

EROTIUM (*noticing the dress*): Still, you can't keep from wearing her clothes. What's this?

MENAECHMUS I: Your dress and my wife's *un*dress, rosebud.

EROTIUM: You're an easy winner over all the others who possess me.

BRUSH (*aside*): The woman flatters him as long as she sees what he's stolen. (*To* EROTIUM) Now, if you really loved him, you'd have bitten his nose off with kisses.

MENAECHMUS I: Hold this, Brush. (*Handing him his cloak*) I want to make the offering I have vowed.

BRUSH: Let's have it. But please, dance with that dress on like that.

MENAECHMUS I: Me dance? You're as crazy as they come.

BRUSH: Maybe you're the crazy one. But if you won't dance, take the thing off.

MENAECHMUS I (*removing dress*): I took a big chance stealing this— bigger than Hercules did, I guess, when he stole Hippolyta's girdle. (*Handing the dress to* EROTIUM) Here, my dear. You're the only one who really understands me.

EROTIUM: That's how true lovers should feel.

BRUSH (*aside*): At least ones who are on their way to the poorhouse.

MENAECHMUS I: That cost me four minae last year when I bought it for my wife.

BRUSH (*aside*): Four minae gone to the devil, when you add up your accounts.

MENAECHMUS I: Do you know what I want you to do?

EROTIUM: Tell me; I'll do anything you wish.

MENAECHMUS I: Then have a dinner for the three of us at your house. And get some fine food at the market—

> The son of a glandule of pork,
> The son of a fattened ham,
> Or the jowl of a hog—
> Some food of that sort
> Which set on the table
> Will tickle my palate
> And give me the gorge of a kite.

And hurry up.

EROTIUM: Very well.

MENAECHMUS I: We'll go on downtown, but we'll be back soon. While the dinner's being cooked, we'll pass the time drinking.

EROTIUM: Come whenever you wish; everything will be ready.

MENAECHMUS I: Hurry now. (*To* BRUSH) You follow me.

BRUSH: I'll watch you and follow you, all right. I wouldn't lose you for all the wealth of heaven. (MENAECHMUS *and* BRUSH *depart*.)

EROTIUM (*to those inside*): You in there, call out my cook Cylindrus at once.

Act One. Scene IV

(*Enter* CYLINDRUS.)

EROTIUM: Take a basket and some money. Here are three nummi.

CYLINDRUS: Yes, ma'am.

EROTIUM: Go and get some provisions. See that there's enough for three, not too little and not too much.

CYLINDRUS: What kind of people will they be?

EROTIUM: Menaechmus and his parasite and I.

CYLINDRUS: That makes ten, then, because a parasite does as well as eight ordinary men.

EROTIUM: I've told you the guests; take care of the rest.

CYLINDRUS: All right. Everything's done. Tell them dinner is served.

EROTIUM: Hurry back. (*She goes into her house*.)

CYLINDRUS: I'm practically back now. (CYLINDRUS *departs*.)

Act Two. Scene I

(*Enter* MENAECHMUS II, *and his slave* MESSENIO *carrying a bag, followed by sailors with luggage*.)

MENAECHMUS II: I think, Messenio, that there is no greater joy for sea travellers than sighting land.

MESSENIO: Yes, but it's still better if it's your own land. Why, I ask you, have we come here—why Epidamnus? We might as well be the ocean: we never miss a single island.

MENAECHMUS II (*sadly*): We are searching for my twin brother.

MESSENIO: Is this search ever going to end? It's six years now that we've spent on it. We've seen 'em all—Istrians, Iberians, the people of Marseilles, Illyrians, the whole Adriatic, all of Magna Graecia, the whole Italian seacoast. If you'd been hunting for a needle you'd have found it long ago, if there had been one. We're looking for a dead man among the living; if he were alive you'd have found him long ago.

MENAECHMUS II: If I can find somebody who can prove that, who can say he knows for certain that my brother is dead, then I shall seek no further. But otherwise I shall go on as long as I live; I know how dear he is to my heart.

MESSENIO: You might as well try to find a knot in a bulrush. Let's clear out of here and go home. Or are we going to write a book—"Our Trip around the World"?

MENAECHMUS II: You do what you're told, take what's given you, and keep out of trouble. Don't annoy me. I'm running this, not you.

MESSENIO (*aside*): Hm-m, that puts me in my place all right. Neat, complete; it can't be beat. But just the same, here I go again. (*Aloud*) Look at our purse, Menaechmus; our money is feeling the heat: it's getting as thin as a summer shirt. If you don't go home, you'll be hunting for that blessed brother of yours without a cent to bless *yourself* with. That's what Epidamnus is like, full of rakes and tremendous drinkers; a lot of swindlers and spongers live here, and everybody knows their women are the most seductive in the whole world. That's why the place is called Epidamnus; scarcely anybody can come here without getting damned.

MENAECHMUS II: I'll take care of that: just hand the purse over to me.

MESSENIO: What for?

MENAECHMUS II: What you say makes me worried—about you.

MESSENIO: Makes you worried?

MENAECHMUS II: That you may get yourself damned in Epidamnus. You are very fond of the ladies, Messenio, and I have a bad temper and lose it very easily. So if I have the money, you get double protection: your foot doesn't slip, and my temper doesn't either.

MESSENIO (*handing it over*): Take it, keep it; it's all right with me.

Act Two. Scene II

(*Enter* CYLINDRUS *the cook, with his market-basket.*)

CYLINDRUS (*to himself*): I've done a good job of marketing—just what I like myself. I'll give the company a fine dinner.—Glory, there's Menaechmus! Now I'm in for it! Here are the guests at the door before I'm back from the market. I'll go up and speak to him. (*To* MENAECHMUS II) Good day, Menaechmus.

MENAECHMUS II: Why, thank you. (*To* MESSENIO) He seems to know my name. Who is he? [3]

MESSENIO: I don't know.

CYLINDRUS: Where are the other guests?

MENAECHMUS II: What guests?

CYLINDRUS (*grinning*): Your parasite.

MENAECHMUS II (*to* MESSENIO): My parasite? The man's crazy.

MESSENIO: Didn't I tell you there were a lot of swindlers here? . . .[4]

MENAECHMUS II (*to* CYLINDRUS): What do you mean "my parasite," young man?

CYLINDRUS: Why, 'Brush.'

MESSENIO (*peering into the bag*): Nonsense, I have your brush safe right here in the bag.

CYLINDRUS: You are a little early for dinner, Menaechmus; I'm just back from the market.

MENAECHMUS II: Tell me, young man: how much do pigs cost here? Grade A pigs, for sacrifice.

CYLINDRUS: A drachma.

MENAECHMUS II: Well, here's a drachma; go get yourself cured at my expense. Because you certainly must be crazy, what's-your-name, to be bothering a perfect stranger like me.

CYLINDRUS: "What's-your-name"! Don't you remember me? I'm Cylindrus.

MENAECHMUS II: The devil take you, whether your name is Cylinder or Colander. I don't know you, and I don't want to.

CYLINDRUS (*persisting*): Your name is Menaechmus.

MENAECHMUS II: You're in your right mind when you call me by name, anyway. But where did you ever see me before?

CYLINDRUS: Where did I ever see you before—when my mistress, Erotium, is your mistress?

MENAECHMUS II: Confound it, she's not my mistress, and I don't know you, either.

CYLINDRUS: All the drinks I've poured for you in the house here, and you don't know me?

MESSENIO: I wish I had something to break his head with.

MENAECHMUS II: You pour my drinks for me, do you? When I've never set foot in Epidamnus before today and never even seen the place?

CYLINDRUS: You deny it?

MENAECHMUS II: Of course I deny it.

CYLINDRUS: Don't you live in that house over there?

MENAECHMUS II: The devil take the people that do!

CYLINDRUS (*aside*): If he curses himself like this, *he's* crazy. (*Aloud*) Menaechmus!

MENAECHMUS II: Well?

CYLINDRUS: If you ask me, you ought to take that drachma you—promised me a minute ago and order *yourself* a pig, because your head isn't on straight either, you know, if you curse your own self.

MENAECHMUS II: Confound your cheek, you chatterbox! (*Turns away.*)

CYLINDRUS (*aside*): He likes to joke with me like this. Always full of laughs—when his wife's not there! (*To* MENAECHMUS II) Well, sir— (*No response*) Well, sir— (MENAECHMUS II *turns*) Is this enough for the three of you—you, the parasite, and the lady—or shall I get some more?

MENAECHMUS II: What "ladies"? What "parasites"?

MESSENIO (*to* CYLINDRUS): Here, what's the matter with you? Why are you pestering the gentleman?

CYLINDRUS: Who are you, and what's it to you? I'm talking to *him*; he's a friend of mine.

MESSENIO: You're cracked, that's certain.

CYLINDRUS (*to* MENAECHMUS II): I'll get these things into the pot right away, so don't wander off too far from the house. Anything else I can do for you?

MENAECHMUS II: Yes. Go to the devil.

CYLINDRUS: Oh, better that you should—go inside and make yourself comfortable on your couch, while Vulcan is getting violent with the food. I'll go in and tell Erotium that you're here. I know she'd rather take you in than make you wait outside. (*He goes into the house of* EROTIUM.)

MENAECHMUS II: Is he gone? Good. Whew! I see there was a lot in what you said.

MESSENIO: Yes, but look out. I think one of those fancy women lives here, just as that crackpot said.

MENAECHMUS II: All the same, I wonder how he knew my name.

MESSENIO: Nothing strange in that; it's just the way these women have. They send their maids and slave-boys to the harbour; and if a foreign ship comes in, they find out the name of the owner and where he's from, and then, bingo! they fasten onto him and stick to him like glue. If he falls for it, they send him home a ruined man. (*Pointing to house of* EROTIUM) Now in that harbour rides a pirate craft, of which we must beware.

MENAECHMUS II: That's good advice.

MESSENIO: Yes, but it's no good unless you take it. (*The door starts to open.*)

MENAECHMUS II: Quiet a minute; I hear the door opening. Let's see who comes out.

MESSENIO (*putting down the bag*): I'll set this down then. You sailors, keep an eye on the luggage.

Act Two.   Scene III

(Enter EROTIUM *from her house.)*

EROTIUM *(to slaves within)*:
  Go in, and do not close the door,
   I want it left just so.
  See what there is to do inside
   And do it all—now go.
  The couches must be spread, and perfumes burned:
  Neatness entices lovers, I have learned.
  Splendour to lovers' loss, to our gain is turned.
(Coming forward)
  But where is the man they said was before my door?
  Ah, there he is; he's been of use before;
  Yet is, as he deserves, my governor.
  I'll go and speak to him myself.—My dear,
  I am amazed to see you standing here;
  My home is always yours when you appear.
   Now all you ordered is prepared,
    The doors are opened wide,
   Your dinner's cooked, and when you like
    Come take your place inside.

MENAECHMUS II *(to* MESSENIO*)*: Who's this woman talking to?

EROTIUM: To you!

MENAECHMUS II: But why? We've never—

EROTIUM: Because it is the will of Venus that I exalt you above all others; and so I should, because you're the one who keeps me blooming with your loving favours.

MENAECHMUS II *(to* MESSENIO*)*: This woman is either insane or drunk, Messenio. Such language, to a perfect stranger!

MESSENIO *(to* MENAECHMUS II*)*: Didn't I tell you that was the way here? Why, these are just falling leaves; stay here a couple of days, and there'll be *trees* falling on you. These women look like pick-ups, but they're not; they're just stick-ups.—Let me talk to her. *(To* EROTIUM*)* Listen, lady—

EROTIUM: What?

MESSENIO: Where did you get so familiar with the gentleman?

EROTIUM: In the same place where he got so familiar with me—here, in Epidamnus.

MESSENIO: In Epidamnus? He never set so much as his foot in the place until today.

EROTIUM: Oh, what a ravishing sense of humour! (*To* MENAECHMUS II) Menaechmus dear, won't you come in? We can straighten this out so much better inside.

MENAECHMUS II (*to* MESSENIO): And now she calls me by name too. What's going on here?

MESSENIO (*to* MENAECHMUS II): She's got a whiff of that purse of yours.

MENAECHMUS II (*to* MESSENIO): You're probably right. Here, take it. (*Hands him the purse*) Now I'll see which she loves, me or the money.

EROTIUM: Let's go in to dinner.

MENAECHMUS II: You are very kind, but (*backing away*) no, thank you.

EROTIUM: But you just told me to fix a dinner for you.

MENAECHMUS II: I told you to?

EROTIUM: Why, yes, for you and your parasite.

MENAECHMUS II: What parasite, confound it? (*To* MESSENIO) She's crazy.

EROTIUM: Brush.

MENAECHMUS II: What is this brush you all keep talking about? You mean my shoe-brush?

EROTIUM: No, of course I mean the Brush who came with you when you brought me the dress you had stolen from your wife.

MENAECHMUS II: What? I gave you a dress that I had stolen from my wife? You're out of your mind! (*To* MESSENIO) Why, this woman dreams standing up, like a horse.

EROTIUM: Why do you make fun of me, and deny what you did?

MENAECHMUS II: Well, what *did* I do?

EROTIUM: You gave me a dress of your wife's, today.

MENAECHMUS II: I still deny it. I haven't got a wife and I never had one, and I never set foot in this house before. I had dinner on the boat, came ashore, walked by here, and ran into you.

EROTIUM (*frightened*): Oh, my goodness, what boat?

MENAECHMUS II: A wooden boat—oft sprung, oft plugged, oft struck with maul,
And peg lies close by peg, as in a furrier's frame.

EROTIUM: Oh, please stop joking and come in.

MENAECHMUS II: But madam, you are looking for somebody else, not me.

EROTIUM: Do you think I don't know Menaechmus, son of Moschus, born at Syracuse in Sicily where Agathocles was king, and then Phintia, and then Liparo, who left it to Hiero, who is king now? [5]

MENAECHMUS II: That's all correct.

MESSENIO (*to* MENAECHMUS II): Good lord, the woman can't be from there herself, can she? She certainly has you down pat.

MENAECHMUS II (*weakening*): You know, I don't see how I can refuse. (*He starts towards the door.*)

MESSENIO: Don't! If you go in there, you're done for!

MENAECHMUS II: Be quiet. Things are going nicely. Whatever she says, I'll agree to it, and see if I can pick up some entertainment! (*To* EROTIUM) I've had a reason for contradicting you all this time: I was afraid this man would tell my wife about the dress and the dinner. But now let's go in, anytime you want.

EROTIUM: Are you going to wait for the parasite any longer?

MENAECHMUS II: No! I don't give a rap for him, and if he comes I don't want him let in.

EROTIUM: That's quite all right with me. But there's something I wish you'd do for me, will you?

MENAECHMUS II: Anything; command me.

EROTIUM: That dress you just gave me—take it to the place where they do that lovely gold embroidery and get them to fix it up and put on some new trimming.

MENAECHMUS II: Splendid idea! And that'll keep my wife from recognising it, if she sees it on the street.

EROTIUM: You can take it with you when you go.

MENAECHMUS II: I certainly will!

EROTIUM: Let's go in.

MENAECHMUS II: I'll be right with you. I just want to speak to this man a minute. (EROTIUM *goes into her house*) Hi there, Messenio, come here.

MESSENIO: What's going on here? Come to your senses! [3]

MENAECHMUS II: What **for?**

MESSENIO: Because—

MENAECHMUS II: Oh, I know, don't say it.

MESSENIO: So much the worse.

MENAECHMUS II: The booty is as good as in my hands right now; the siege has just begun! (*Pointing to the sailors*) Come on now, hustle these men off to an inn somewhere, and then come back for me here before sunset.

MESSENIO: Master, you don't know what these women are!

MENAECHMUS II: None of that! If I do anything foolish, it's my loss, not yours. This woman is a silly fool. The way things look so far, there's booty to be had! (*He goes into the house of* EROTIUM.)

MESSENIO: God help me! (*Calling after* MENAECHMUS II) Sir! (*To himself*) God help him, too! The pirate ship has got the pinnace steered straight on the rocks! But I'm a fool to expect to control my master. He bought me to obey him, not to give him orders. (*To the sailors*) Come along you, so I can come back and pick him up in time. Orders is orders! (*They depart.*)

Act Three.   Scene I

(*Enter* BRUSH *from the forum.*)

BRUSH (*to himself*): Here I am over thirty years old, but I never got into a worse mess than I did today. I pushed into the middle of the

assembly, like a darn fool, and while I was watching things, Menaechmus sneaked away from me. He probably went off to his mistress and
didn't want to take me.—Damn the man who first got the idea of holding assemblies and taking up the time of busy men! Why couldn't they
pick people who aren't tied up for this sort of thing, and then if they
didn't show up when the roll was called, they could pay a fine right off? [4]
. . . There are plenty of men who only eat once a day and never get
asked out to dinner or ask anyone else in. They're the ones who ought
to have the job of sitting in assemblies and law courts. If things were
run that way, I wouldn't have lost my dinner today. As sure as I'm
alive, he would have given it to me.—I'll go on, anyway. Maybe
there'll be something left, and just the idea makes my mouth water.
(*Enter* MENAECHMUS II *from* EROTIUM'S *house, carrying the dress, very
    drunk.*)
But what's this? There's Menaechmus coming out with a wreath on.
The dinner's over, and I've come just in time to take him home. I'll
see what he's up to, and then go and speak to him. (*He withdraws.*)

Act Three.   Scene II

MENAECHMUS II (*to* EROTIUM *within*): Oh, can't you keep quiet? I'll
have it nicely fixed for you, all right, and I'll bring it back on time. I
bet you won't recognise it, it'll be so different.

BRUSH (*aside*): He's taking the dress to the embroiderer's. He's finished
his dinner, drunk his wine, and shut his parasite outside. I'll get even
for this trick, all right, or my name's not Brush! Just watch what's
coming to him!

MENAECHMUS II (*to himself*): Gods above, did you ever give more luck
in a single day to a man who didn't expect it? I wined and dined with
the woman, and got away with this thing (*indicating the dress*), and
she won't ever see it again.

BRUSH: I can't hear what he's saying from over here. Is he full of
food and talking about me and my dinner?

MENAECHMUS II: She said I stole this from my wife and gave it to her.
The moment I saw she was wrong, I began to agree with her, as if
we'd had some sort of deal. Whatever the woman said, I said too. Why
waste words? I never had a better time at less expense.

BRUSH: I'm going up to the fellow. I'm itching to smack him one.

MENAECHMUS II: Who's this coming towards me?

BRUSH: What are you talking about, you feather-weight, you scum, you crook, you disgrace to humanity, you sneak, you bum? What did I ever do to you that you should wipe me out? So you sneaked away from me downtown a while ago, did you? And you had the funeral of the dinner when I wasn't there? How did you have the nerve, when it was mine as much as it was yours?

MENAECHMUS II: See here, young fellow, what's the idea of going around and insulting a perfect stranger like me? Are you an idiot? Or do you want to get beaten up for your words?

BRUSH: Huh! After the beating you've already given me!

MENAECHMUS II: Tell me, young fellow, what's your name?

BRUSH: Are you making fun of me too, as if you didn't know my name?

MENAECHMUS II: Well, as far as I know, I never saw you or knew of you before today. But let me tell you, whoever you are, if you want to do the right thing, don't make a nuisance of yourself.

BRUSH: Menaechmus, wake up!

MENAECHMUS II: Damn it, I am awake as far as I know.

BRUSH: You don't know me?

MENAECHMUS II: I wouldn't deny it if I did.

BRUSH: You don't know your own parasite?

MENAECHMUS II: I think you're not all there, young fellow.

BRUSH: Answer me this: did you steal that dress from your wife today and give it to Erotium?

MENAECHMUS II: Damn it, I haven't got any wife, and I didn't give any dress to Erotium or steal one.

BRUSH: Are *you* all there? (*Aside*) This thing's done for! (*To* MENAECHMUS II) Didn't I see you come out of there with a dress on?

MENAECHMUS II: Go to the devil! Do you think everybody is a rotter just because you are? Do you mean to say that I had a dress on?

BRUSH: I do, all right.

MENAECHMUS II: Why don't you go where you belong, or else get yourself purified, you imbecile?

BRUSH (*furious*): By God, no one will ever stop me from telling your wife the whole business, just the way it happened. All your insults will come back on you. I'll see to it that you don't get away with eating that dinner. (*He goes into house of* MENAECHMUS I.)

MENAECHMUS II: What's the matter? Why is it that everyone I meet makes fun of me? But I hear the door opening.

Act Three.   Scene III

(*Enter* MAID *from house of* EROTIUM *with a bracelet in her hand.*)

MAID: Menaechmus, Erotium says she would like to have you take this bracelet along to the jeweler's. She wants you to have an ounce of gold added to it and have it done over.

MENAECHMUS II: Tell her I'll tend to it and anything else she wants tended to, anything at all. (*He takes the bracelet.*)

MAID: Do you know what bracelet this is?

MENAECHMUS II: Only that it's a gold one.

MAID: It's the one you said once you stole from your wife's jewel-box.

MENAECHMUS II: I never did.

MAID: Come on, don't you remember? Give the bracelet back if you don't remember.

MENAECHMUS II: Wait a minute. Why, of course I remember. It must be the one I gave her. That's it. Where are the armlets I gave her with it?

MAID: You never gave her any.

MENAECHMUS II: Right you are; this was all I gave her.

MAID: I'll say you'll tend to it, then?

MENAECHMUS II: Yes, it'll be tended to. I'll see that the dress and the bracelet are brought back together.

MAID (*coaxingly*): Please, Menaechmus dear, give me some earrings. Have them made to weigh two nummi. Then I'll be glad to see you when you come to see us.

MENAECHMUS II: Surely. Give me the gold and I'll pay for the work.

MAID: Oh, please, *you* give the gold, and I'll pay you back later.

MENAECHMUS II: No, you give it. Later I'll pay you back double.

MAID: I haven't got any.

MENAECHMUS II: Well, when you get some, give it to me then.

MAID: Anything else, sir?

MENAECHMUS II: Tell her I'll tend to the things, (*to himself, as the* MAID *goes inside*) and sell 'em for all they'll bring. Has she gone in? Yes; the door's shut. The gods are certainly supporting and supplying and sustaining me. But what am I waiting for when I've got a good chance to get away from this woman's place? Hurry up, Menaechmus. Forward, march! I'll take off this wreath and throw it away towards the left; then if they follow me, they'll think I've gone that way. I'll go and find my slave, if I can, and tell him myself about the luck the gods are giving me. (*He departs in the direction of the harbour.*)

Act Four.   Scene I

(*Enter* WIFE *and* BRUSH *from house of* MENAECHMUS I.)

WIFE: How can I put up with married life any longer? My husband sneaks off with anything there is in the house and carries it off to his mistress.

BRUSH: Oh, keep quiet. I'll show you how to catch him with the goods. He had on a wreath, he was reeling drunk, and he was taking the dress he stole from you today to the embroiderer's. But look, there's the wreath. Now will you believe me? See, this is the way he went, if you want to track him down. (*Looking down the street*) Well, for heaven's sake, there he is now, coming back. But he hasn't got the dress.

WIFE: What'll I do to him now?

BRUSH: The same as usual—treat him rough. That's my advice. Let's get over here and hide from him. (*They step aside.*)

Act Four.   Scene II

(Enter MENAECHMUS I *from the forum.)*

MENAECHMUS I: It's a very silly fashion and an awful nuisance, too,
That all of us obey, especially the well-to-do.
We want a lot of hangers-on, who may be good or bad:
Reputation doesn't matter when there's money to be
    had.
You may be poor and honest—as a fool you're sent
    away.
But if you're rich and wicked, you're a worthy pro-
    tégé.
The lawless man, who when he's trusted with a thing
    will swear
He never saw it—that's the man for whom we patrons
    care:
The contentious man, the trickster, who by means of
    perjury
Or bribes supports a life of lawsuits, greed, and
    luxury.
But the patron has no holiday when law-days are
    decreed;
He must defend the guilty man and see that he is
    freed.
In just this way was I detained today by one poor
    sinner,
And now I've missed my mistress, to say nothing of
    my dinner.
I spoke before the aediles to allay their just sus-
    picions,
And proposed a set of intricate and tortuous condi-
    tions
Which, if we could have proved 'em, would have
    surely won the case.
But then this brainless boob brought in a bondsman
    to the place!
I'm sure I never saw a man more clearly caught than
    he:
Three witnesses were there who swore to all his
    deviltry.

May heaven destroy the man who's made a ruin so
 complete
Of all my day—and me, who in the law-courts set
 my feet!
As soon as it was possible, I came directly here.
I've ordered dinner, and she's waiting for me; yet I
 fear
 She's mad at me now.
  But the dress ought to move her
  That I stole from my wife
  And took to my lover.

BRUSH (*aside to* WIFE): What have you got to say now?

WIFE: I'm blessed with a bad marriage and a bad husband.

BRUSH: Do you hear what he's saying all right?

WIFE: I should say so.

MENAECHMUS I: Now the best thing for me to do is to go in here where I can have a good time. (*He starts towards* EROTIUM's *door, but* BRUSH *stops him.*)

BRUSH: Just a minute. You'll have a bad time first.

WIFE: You'll pay interest on what you stole, I promise you.

BRUSH: Now he's getting it.

WIFE: So you thought you could get away with all that crooked business, did you?

MENAECHMUS I: What's the matter, dear?

WIFE: That's a fine thing to ask *me!*

MENAECHMUS I: Do you want me to ask *him*, then? (*He attempts to fondle* WIFE.)

WIFE: Cut out the pawing!

BRUSH: Keep after him, ma'am!

MENAECHMUS I: Why are you angry at me?

WIFE: You ought to know.

BRUSH: He does, the scum, but he's making out he doesn't.

MENAECHMUS I: What's the matter?

WIFE: A dress.

MENAECHMUS I: A dress?

WIFE: A dress that someone—

BRUSH: What are you shaking about?

MENAECHMUS I: I'm not shaking about anything.

BRUSH: Only this: the dress does impress!—You would sneak away from me and eat dinner! (*To* WIFE) Keep after the fellow!

MENAECHMUS I: Won't you shut up?

BRUSH: No, by George, I will not shut up. (*To* WIFE) He's shaking his head at me to shut up.

MENAECHMUS I: I am not, or winking either.

WIFE: Oh dear, I am an unhappy woman!

MENAECHMUS I: Why unhappy? Tell me about it.

BRUSH: What a nerve! Why, he won't admit a thing is so when you can see it is.

MENAECHMUS I: By Jupiter and all the gods (is that enough for you, dear?) I swear I didn't shake my head at him.

BRUSH: She'll believe you about that. Now get back to business.

MENAECHMUS I: What business?

BRUSH: Oh, maybe the embroiderer's. And give back the dress.

MENAECHMUS I: What dress are you talking about?

BRUSH: Oh, I give up! He can't even remember his own affairs.

MENAECHMUS I (*to* WIFE): Has one of the slaves been cutting up? Are the maids or the menservants answering back? Tell me. They won't get away with it.

WIFE: Nonsense!

MENAECHMUS I: She's really mad. I don't like this much—

WIFE: Nonsense!

MENAECHMUS I: You must be angry with one of the servants.

WIFE: Nonsense!

MENAECHMUS I: Well, are you angry with me, then?

WIFE: Now that's not nonsense.

MENAECHMUS I: What the devil! I haven't done anything.

WIFE: More nonsense again!

MENAECHMUS I: Tell me, my dear, what's upsetting you?

BRUSH: Apple-sauce!

MENAECHMUS I: Can't you quit bothering me? Do you think I'm talking to you? (*He goes to* WIFE.)

WIFE: Take away your hand.

BRUSH: Now you're getting it. Go and eat dinner without me, will you? Then come out drunk, with a wreath on your head, and make fun of me in front of the house, will you?

MENAECHMUS I: What the devil! I haven't had dinner or set foot in that house today.

BRUSH: Do you mean to say that?

MENAECHMUS I: I certainly do.

BRUSH: This fellow's the worst yet. Didn't I just see you standing here in front of the house with a wreath on? You said I wasn't all there and you didn't know me and you were a foreigner.

MENAECHMUS I: See here, since I left you, I haven't been home until just now.

BRUSH: Oh, I know you. You didn't think I had any way of getting even with you. All right for you—I've told everything to your wife.

MENAECHMUS I: What did you tell her?

BRUSH: I don't know; ask her yourself.

MENAECHMUS I (*to* WIFE): What's the matter, dear? What stories has he been telling you? What is it? Why don't you say something? Why don't you tell me what's the matter?

WIFE: As if you didn't know! A dress has been stolen from me out of the house.

MENAECHMUS I: A dress has been stolen from you?

WIFE: Are you asking me?

MENAECHMUS I: Well, I certainly wouldn't be asking you if I knew.

BRUSH: Look at the man! What a snake in the grass! You can't hide anything; she knows the whole story. I spilled everything, all right.

MENAECHMUS I (*to* WIFE): What's the matter?

WIFE: Well, since you're not ashamed and won't own up yourself, listen and learn. I'll explain what I'm angry about and what he told me. A dress has been stolen from me out of the house.

MENAECHMUS I: A dress has been stolen from me?

BRUSH (*to* WIFE): See how the fellow's trying to catch you. (*To* MENAECHMUS I) It was stolen from her, not from you. Now if it had really been stolen from you—it wouldn't be all right.

MENAECHMUS I: I'm not dealing with you. (*To* WIFE) What have you got to say, madam?

WIFE: A dress, I tell you, is gone from the house.

MENAECHMUS I: Who stole it?

WIFE: I expect the person who stole it knows that.

MENAECHMUS I: Who is this person?

WIFE: Somebody named Menaechmus.

MENAECHMUS I: It's a dirty trick. But who is this Menaechmus?

WIFE: You, I tell you.

MENAECHMUS I: Me?

WIFE: Yes, you.

MENAECHMUS I: Who says so?

WIFE: I do.

BRUSH: So do I. And you took the thing over to your friend Erotium.

MENAECHMUS I: What? I gave it to her?

WIFE: Yes, you, you, I say.

BRUSH: Do you want us to get an owl to keep on saying, "You, you!" to you? We're getting tired, you see.

MENAECHMUS I: By Jupiter and all the gods (is that enough for you, my dear?) I swear I didn't give—

BRUSH: All right, and we swear we're not lying.

MENAECHMUS I: But I didn't give it to her; I only lent it.

WIFE: Maybe you did, but I certainly never lend your dress suit or your overcoat to anybody. It's the wife's business to lend her clothes, and the husband's to lend his. Now go and bring that dress back home.

MENAECHMUS I: I'll get it back.

WIFE: Well, you'd better. You won't get into this house again unless you bring my dress with you. I'm going home.

BRUSH: What do I get for going to so much trouble for you?

WIFE: You'll be repaid when something is stolen from your house. (*She goes inside.*)

BRUSH: That'll never happen; I haven't got anything at home to lose. Damn the husband and the wife, too! I'll go along downtown. I can see I'm done with this family. (*He departs.*)

MENAECHMUS I (*to himself*): My wife thinks she's punished me by shutting me out—as if I didn't have a better place to go where they'd let me in. If you don't like me, that's your hard luck; Erotium here likes me. She won't shut me out from her; she'll shut me in *with* her. Now I'll go and ask her to give back that dress I gave her this morning. I'll buy her a better one. (*Knocking at* EROTIUM's *door*) Hey, there, where's the doorman? Open the door, somebody, and call Erotium outside.

Act Four.   Scene III

(*Enter* EROTIUM *from her house.*)

EROTIUM: Who is asking for me?

MENAECHMUS I: More of an enemy to himself than to your tender years.

EROTIUM: Menaechmus, my love, why are you standing out there? Come on in.

MENAECHMUS I: In just a minute. Do you know what I've come to see you for?

EROTIUM: Why, of course: to enjoy yourself with me.

MENAECHMUS I: No; it's that dress I gave you this morning. Be a good girl and give it back to me. I'll buy you any dress you want, twice as expensive.

EROTIUM: Why, I just gave it to you to take to the embroiderer's. I gave you the bracelet, you know, too, to take to the jeweler's to be done over.

MENAECHMUS I: How could you have given me the dress and the bracelet? I gave you the dress just a little while ago and went downtown, and this is the first time I've come back and seen you since then.

EROTIUM: Oh, I see your game. You're trying to cheat me out of what I let you take.

MENAECHMUS I: No, no, I'm not asking for the dress to cheat you. I tell you, my wife's found out about it.

EROTIUM (*angrily*): And I didn't ask you to give it to me in the first place. You brought it to me yourself, and you gave it to me for a present. And now you want it back. All right. Have the old thing. Take it. Wear it yourself, or let your wife wear it, or lock it up in a trunk if you want to. After today you won't set foot inside this house again— don't fool yourself. You trifler with the affections of an innocent woman! Unless you bring me money, you haven't got a chance to see me again. Now go and find some other poor girl you can deceive. (*She goes into her house.*)

MENAECHMUS I: Say, she's really mad this time. (*Rushing to her door*) Hey there, wait a minute, I tell you. Come back. Won't you stay? Won't you please come back for my sake? (*To himself*) She's gone in and closed the door. Now I am the most shut out of men! They won't believe anything I say at home or at my mistress's. I'll go and see what my friends think I'd better do about this. (*He departs in the direction of the forum.*)

Act Five.   Scene I

(*Enter* MENAECHMUS II *along the street; he still has the dress.*)

MENAECHMUS II (*to himself*): That was a fool thing I did a while ago, giving Messenio the purse with all my money in it. He's landed him‧ self in a clip-joint somewhere, for sure.

(*Enter* WIFE *from her house.*)

WIFE (*to herself*): I'll just have a look outside; that husband of mine should be back soon. Ah ha, there he is. And he's bringing back the dress. That's just fine.

MENAECHMUS II (*to himself*): I wonder where Messenio can be headed now.

WIFE (*to herself*): I'll step up and give him the welcome he deserves. (*Aloud*) You scoundrel, how dare you come into my sight with that dress?

MENAECHMUS II: Huh? What's the matter, lady, seen a ghost?

WIFE: Impudence, how dare you utter one single syllable? How dare you speak to me?

MENAECHMUS II: Here, what have *I* done? Why shouldn't I?

WIFE: You ask me! The cheek, the impudence of the man!

MENAECHMUS II: I suppose you know why the Greeks used to call Hecuba the bitch?

WIFE: *No!*

MENAECHMUS II: Because she acted just like you: she showered abuse on everybody in sight. That's how she got to be called the bitch—and she deserved it, too.

WIFE: This is outrageous! I won't stand for it! No husband is worth it. It's outrageous!

MENAECHMUS II: What's it to me? You can't stand marriage, you're going to leave your husband—what is it, the custom of the country to babble this kind of nonsense to perfect strangers?

WIFE: Babble? I won't stand for this a minute longer. I'll get a divorce.

MENAECHMUS II: *Get* a divorce. As far as I care, you can stay single till hell freezes over.

WIFE (*pointing to the dress*): And a minute ago you denied you stole this from me, and now you dangle it under my very nose. Haven't you any shame?

MENAECHMUS II: My God, woman, you certainly have an awful nerve. I didn't steal this dress from you. Another woman gave it to me; she wanted me to get it made over for her.

WIFE: That settles it! I'm going to send for my father and tell him how outrageously you behave. (*Calls into the house to a slave*) Decio! Go find my father and bring him here to me. Tell him it's important! (*To* MENAECHMUS II) I'll tell him how outrageous you are.

MENAECHMUS II: Are you insane? What do you mean, outrageous?

WIFE: You steal dresses and jewelry from your wife and take them to your mistress! And that's not babbling, either!

MENAECHMUS II: I wish you'd tell me some good medicine for me to take against that tongue of yours! I don't know who you think I am, but I don't know you from Hercules' wife's grandfather.

WIFE (*pointing down the street*): You may make fun of me, but not of *him*—my father! Here he comes. Look at him. Do you know *him*?

MENAECHMUS II: Oh yes, I remember meeting the two of you the same day I met Methuselah.

WIFE: You deny you know me? And my father too?

MENAECHMUS II: And your grandfather too, if you want to drag him in.

WIFE: You're impossible and always were.

Act Five.   Scene II

(*Enter* FATHER.)

FATHER: As fast as my age will permit and this business requires, I'm
                getting along,
          But if some of you think that it's easy for me, very briefly
                I'll prove that you're wrong.
          My body's a burden, my nimbleness gone, and of strength I've
                a notable lack,
          I'm quite overgrown with my years—oh, confounded old age
                is a curse on the back!
          Why, if I were to tell all the terrible evils that age, when it
                comes, brings along,
          I'm certain as certain can be that past suitable limits I'd
                lengthen this song.
          However, my mind is a little disturbed at this thing, for it
                seems a bit queer

That my daughter should suddenly send to my house with
    directions for me to come here.
And how this affair is related to me, she has not let me know
    up to now;
But I'm a good guesser, and I'm pretty sure that her husband
    and she've had a row.
That's what usually happens when men are enslaved by their
    wives and must come when they call;
And then it's the wives who are mostly to blame, while the
    husbands aren't guilty at all.

And yet there are bounds, which we all must observe, to the
    things that a wife can endure,
And a woman won't call in her father unless the offence of her
    husband is sure.
But I think very soon the suspense will be over, and then
    I'll know what is the matter—
But look, there's my daughter in front of the door, and her
    husband; he's not looking at her.
                 It's just as I suspected.
I'll start with her.

WIFE (*to herself*): I'll go to meet him. (*To* FATHER) How do you do,
father.

FATHER: How d'ye do, how d'ye do. Now what's this how d'ye do?
Why did you send for me? What are you so sad about? Why is he
standing off from you angry? The two of you have had a fight. Tell me,
which of you is in the wrong? But be brief about it: no long speeches.

WIFE: I haven't done anything, not a thing, believe me. But I can't live
here, I just can't stand it. Take me away!

FATHER: Eh, what's this?

WIFE: He makes a laughingstock of me.

FATHER: Who does?

WIFE: The man you entrusted me to—my husband!

FATHER: Tch, tch, tch! A squabble! How many times have I told you
not to come to me with your complaints, either of you?

WIFE: How can I help it, father?

FATHER: You ask me that!

WIFE (*timidly*): Yes.

FATHER: I've told you often enough—humour your husband; don't always have your eye on what he's doing, where he's going, what he's up to.

WIFE: But he has a mistress, right next door!

FATHER: Sensible man. And the more you make of it, the more he'll love her. No doubt of it.

WIFE: And he drinks there too.

FATHER: Suppose it's there, suppose it's somewhere else: can you stop him? Confound your impudence! Why not forbid him to go out to dinner, or to have his friends in for a meal? Do you want husbands to be slaves? You might as well give him piecework, and make him sit with the maids and card wool.

WIFE: Father, I brought you here to be *my* lawyer, not his; but now you're arguing on his side instead of mine.

FATHER: If he's been at fault in any way, I'll be much harder on him than I was on you. But he keeps you in clothes and jewelry, and gives you proper food and service, and so you oughtn't to be so fussy about things, my girl.

WIFE: But he steals my jewelry and dresses right out of the house! He takes all my nice things and sneaks them off to his mistress!

FATHER: If he's up to that, he's up to no good; if he's not up to that, *you*'re up to no good; that would be slander.

WIFE: But, father, he has the dress this very minute, and the bracelet he took her, too; he's bringing them back because I found out.

FATHER: I must have his account of it now. I'll speak to him. (*To* MENAECHMUS II) Tell me, Menaechmus, what are you two quarreling for? What are you so sad about? Why is she standing off from you angry?

MENAECHMUS II (*in legal style*): Old man, whoever you may be, by highest Jupiter and the gods I swear—

FATHER: Well sworn. But what?

MENAECHMUS II: —firstly, that I have done no wrong to this your daughter who accuses me of stealing and purloining from her house this dress—

WIFE: Perjury!

MENAECHMUS II: —and secondly, if I have ever set my foot within the house in which she lives, I pray that I may be the most miserable of miserable men.

FATHER: That's a fool's prayer, if you deny you ever set foot in the house you live in, you utter madman.

MENAECHMUS II: Old man, do you say I live in that house?

FATHER: Do you deny it?

MENAECHMUS II: I deny it and that's the truth.

FATHER: No, no, you deny it and it's *not* the truth. Unless, of course, you've moved since yesterday. (*To* WIFE) Come here, daughter. Tell me, you haven't moved, have you?

WIFE: For goodness sake, what for, and where to?

FATHER: I don't know.

WIFE: He's playing games with you. Don't you see?

FATHER: Menaechmus, that's enough joking. Now get down to business.

MENAECHMUS II (*hotly*): What business have we got to get down to? Who are you, anyway? You haven't got anything on me, and neither has that daughter of yours; and besides, she's a first class pest.

WIFE (*frightened, to* FATHER): Look at the green in his eyes! He's getting green in the face! See how his eyes glitter!

MENAECHMUS II (*aside*): Fine! They say I'm crazy: I'll pretend I *am*, and scare them away! (*He starts a mad-scene.*)

WIFE: See how he stretches and gapes! What shall I do, father?

FATHER: Come over here, child; keep as far away from him as you can.

MENAECHMUS II: Hola hola, Bromius! You call me to the forest, to the hunt? I hear; but I cannot leave this place: I am beset upon the left by this rabid bitch-woman, and behind her is that stinking goat who ruins innocent citizens with perjury.

FATHER: Woe to your head!

MENAECHMUS II: Lo! Apollo from his oracle bids me burn her eyes out with flaming torches!

WIFE: Help, father! He's threatening to burn my eyes out!

MENAECHMUS II (*aside*): Ha, they think I'm crazy, but they're the crazy ones.

FATHER: Psst! Daughter!

WIFE: What?

FATHER: What shall we do? Suppose I get some slaves. Yes, they can grab him and chain him up in the house before he raises any more commotion.

MENAECHMUS II (*aside*): Caught! If I don't work fast, they'll have me carried into the house with them. (*Aloud*) Yes, Apollo? I must punch her face in with my fists unless she gets the hell out of my sight? I'll do your orders!

FATHER: Run home as fast as you can, or he'll smack you.

WIFE (*retreating to her house*): Please, father, watch him, don't let him get away! That I should live to hear such language! Poor me! (*She goes into her house.*)

MENAECHMUS II (*aside*): I fixed her all right! Now for the other one. (*Aloud*) Now this dirty wretch, this bearded tremulous Tithonus, this son of Cycnus;[6] you want me to take that staff he has and beat him to pieces, joint from joint and bone from bone and limb from limb?

FATHER (*retreating*): If you touch me or come a step closer, there'll be trouble.

MENAECHMUS II: I'll do your orders: I'll take a double axe and hack this old fellow's guts to mincemeat, down to the very bone.

FATHER: Then I must beware and take care of myself. The way he threatens me, I'm afraid he will do me harm.

MENAECHMUS II: New commands, Apollo! Now I am to yoke my wild ungovernable horses and mount my chariot, to trample down this stinking old toothless lion! Now I stand in the chariot; now I have the reins; now the goad is in my hand. Forward, my steeds! Ring out the clatter of your hoofs! Fleet feet, speed swift with tireless tumult!

FATHER: Threaten me with a chariot!

MENAECHMUS II: Another charge at him, Apollo, to the death? (*Pretending to have a change of fit*) But who is this who drags me from the chariot by the hair? O edict of Apollo, thy command is maimed! (*He falls and is still.*)

FATHER (*to himself*): A violent and severe disease![2] . . . The gods preserve us from the like. See now, how strong he was a moment since, and now is mad with sudden access of disease. I'll go and get a doctor, as fast as I can. (*He departs.*)[7]

MENAECHMUS II (*rising*): Are they out of sight, I wonder, these people that make me pretend I'm crazy? I'd better get back to the ship while the going is good. (*To the audience*) Please, all of you, if the old man comes back, don't tell him which way I went. (*He departs. Considerable time is supposed to elapse before the next scene.*)

Act Five.   Scene III

(*Enter* FATHER.)

FATHER: I've got pains in my back and pains in my eyes, waiting and watching for the doctor to be free. He didn't want to leave his patients; I had a hard time persuading him to come. He says he set a broken leg for Aesculapius and a broken arm for Apollo.[8] Have I got a doctor, I wonder, or a joiner? Here he comes now. Get along, you ant!

Act Five.   Scene IV

(*Enter the* DOCTOR.)

DOCTOR: Tell me, sir, what did you say was his disease? Has he hallucinations, or madness? Pray inform me. Has he the lethargy, or the subcutaneous humours?

FATHER: That's what I brought you here for: to tell me what's wrong with him, and cure him.

DOCTOR: Ah, that is quite simple. He shall be cured, I promise you.

FATHER: I want a careful treatment for him; spare no pains.

DOCTOR: No pains shall be spared; why, I will spend at least six hundred sighs a day on it.

FATHER (*seeing* MENAECHMUS I *approaching*): Here he comes himself. Let's watch him.

Act Five. Scene V

(*Enter* MENAECHMUS I, *not seeing the others.*)

MENAECHMUS I (*to himself*): What a day! Everything going wrong, and getting me in wrong! I thought I was getting away with something; but that parasite of mine has let it all out and made a quaking criminal of me—the smart alec, biting the hand that feeds him. Sure as I live, it'll cost him his life. I'm a fool to call it *his* life though; it's mine: he lives on me and what I feed him. Well then, I'll cut his greedy throat. My mistress was just as bad; these girls are all alike. When I asked for the dress so I could take it back to my wife, she pretended she'd given it to me already. Ugh! I certainly lead a miserable life!

FATHER (*to* DOCTOR): Can you hear what he's saying?

DOCTOR: He says he is miserable.

FATHER: Go on up to him.

DOCTOR (*complying*): Good afternoon, Menaechmus. Tch tch, why do you leave your arm uncovered like that? Don't you know how bad that is for a man in your condition?

MENAECHMUS I: Go hang yourself! (*The* DOCTOR *retreats.*)

FATHER: Notice anything?

DOCTOR: Notice anything! This case will take an *acre* of hellebore, at least![9] (*Returning to* MENAECHMUS I) Now, Menaechmus—

MENAECHMUS I: Well?

DOCTOR: Just a few questions, please. Do you drink red wine or white wine?

MENAECHMUS I: Why not ask about the bread I eat, if it's purple, pink, or scarlet? Or whether I eat scaly birds and feathered fish?

FATHER: My goodness, hear the way he raves! Hurry up and give him some medicine before he goes completely crazy.

DOCTOR: Just a minute; I want to finish my questions.

FATHER: You talk a man to death.

DOCTOR (*to* MENAECHMUS I): Tell me, are you ever troubled with a hardening of the eyes?

MENAECHMUS I: What, you idiot! Do you take me for a lobster?

DOCTOR: Tell me this: are you subject to rumbling of the bowels—as far as you know?

MENAECHMUS I: After a good meal, no; but if I'm hungry, then they do.

DOCTOR (*aside*): Nothing crazy in that answer. (*To* MENAECHMUS I) Do you sleep soundly all night? Do you fall asleep readily on retiring?

MENAECHMUS I: I sleep like a log—if I've paid my bills! (*Losing his temper*) Oh, the devil take you and all your questions!

DOCTOR (*to* FATHER): The madness is beginning. You hear the way he talks; be careful.

FATHER: Why he's talking like a perfect Nestor now, compared to the way he was a little while ago. Just a few minutes ago he called his wife a rabid bitch.

MENAECHMUS I: I said *what*?

FATHER: You were raving, I say.

MENAECHMUS I: *I* was raving?

FATHER: Yes, *you*. And you threatened to run over me with a chariot. I saw you; I accuse you.

MENAECHMUS I (*furious*): And you stole a wreath out of the temple of Jupiter, I know, and you were thrown into jail for it, I know, and after you were let out of there you were strung up and whipped, I know, and you murdered your father and sold your mother into slavery, I know. Right back at you with your dirty insults! I'm sane enough for that, all right.

FATHER: For God's sake, doctor, hurry! Whatever you're going to do, do it. Don't you see the man is raving?

DOCTOR: The best thing for you to do is to have him taken to my house.

FATHER: You think so?

DOCTOR: Definitely. Then I'll have a free hand with his treatment.

FATHER: Just as you like.

DOCTOR (*gloatingly, to* MENAECHMUS I): I'll have you drinking hellebore for something like three weeks!

MENAECHMUS I (*savagely*): And I'll have you strung up and jabbed with ox-goads for a month!

DOCTOR (*to* FATHER): Get some men to bring him there.

FATHER: How many?

DOCTOR: Judging by the extent of his madness, four; no less.

FATHER: They'll be right here. (*Starts to go*) Watch him, doctor.

DOCTOR (*hurriedly*): No no; I must go back and get things ready. Tell the slaves to bring him to me.

FATHER: I'll have him there right away.

DOCTOR: I'm on my way. (*The* DOCTOR *hurries down the street.*)

FATHER: Good bye. (*The* FATHER *departs.*)

MENAECHMUS I (*to himself*): Father-in-law gone, doctor gone; now I'm alone. Good God, why do these people say I'm crazy? All my life I've never had a day's illness; I don't lose my head and pick fights, or lawsuits either. I lead a normal life with normal people; I recognise my friends, and talk to them. Must be that *they're* crazy, the ones that say I am. What do I do now? I want to go home, but my wife won't have it. And I can't get in here. (*He points to the house of* EROTIUM) A nice situation! I'll be stuck here forever! Well, maybe I'll get in at home by nightfall.

Act Five.   Scene VI

(*Enter* MESSENIO.)

MESSENIO (*to himself, not seeing* MENAECHMUS I):
    It's a proof of an excellent slave,
    If, his master's belongings to save,
        He'll use as much care
        When his master's not there
    As when master is watching the slave.

    For his back and his shins he must fear,
    The demands of his stomach not hear,

And the punishment know
Of the slothful and slow—
This servant whose conscience is clear.

There are beatings, and chains, and the mills,
Hunger, weariness, terrible chills—
The reward of the lazy;
But since I'm not crazy
I'm good, and avoid all these ills.

I can stand a tongue-lashing, but I don't like a whip-lashing; and I'd rather eat the meal than turn the mill. So I obey my master; it's worth my while. Others can take the easy way if they want to; I'll take the hard way. I'll keep out of trouble by worrying about being on the spot wherever my master needs me. Slaves who worry while they're *out* of trouble are the ones that serve their masters best: because the ones who don't worry then still have plenty to worry about when they're *in* trouble, but then the harm's done. But I don't have to worry much— my master will reward me before long. Beware of a beating, that's my motto. I've left the baggage and the slaves at an inn as he ordered, and now I'm back to meet him. I'll knock and let him know I'm here, in hopes I'm in time to get him safely out of this pirate lair. But I'm afraid the fight may be over already. (*He goes toward* EROTIUM'S *door.*)

Act Five.   Scene VII

(*Enter* FATHER *with* SLAVES. MESSENIO *withdraws to one side.*)

FATHER (*to* SLAVES): Now by all that's holy, don't bungle your orders. I repeat: pick that man up and carry him to the doctor's, or your shanks and sides will smart for it. Pay no attention to his threats. Why do you stand there? What are you waiting for? You should have had him up and off already. I'm going to the doctor's; I'll be there when you come. (*He departs.*)

MENAECHMUS I (*finding himself surrounded*): Good lord, what's going on here? Why are these men making for me? What do you want? What are you after? Why are you surrounding me? Why are you grabbing me? Where are you taking me? Murder! Help! Good folk of Epidamnus, help! Let me go!

MESSENIO: Great heaven, what is this I see? A gang of strangers carrying off my master! Shame!

MENAECHMUS I: Doesn't anybody dare help me?

MESSENIO: I do, master, I dare most daringly! (*To the audience*)
        Oh! What an outrageous crime I see!
        Epidamnians, this man was free,
        My master, when he came today;
        And now they're carrying him away,
        While you're at peace, by light of day!
(*To the* SLAVES) Let go of him!

MENAECHMUS I: I implore you, stranger, help me! Make them stop this criminal outrage!

MESSENIO: You bet I will! I'll be your helper, your defender, your ally! I won't let them murder you; better me than you. That one who has you by the shoulder, gouge out his eye. I'll garden up these fellows' faces and plant my fists there. (*General scuffle*) Try to kidnap him, would you? This is what you get for it! Hands off him!

MENAECHMUS I: I've got him by the eye.

MESSENIO: Gouge it out! (*To* SLAVES) Villains! Robbers! Bandits!

SLAVES: Murder! Stop, for God's sake!

MESSENIO: Then let go of him! (*The* SLAVES *drop* MENAECHMUS I.)

MENAECHMUS I: Take your hands off me! (*To* MESSENIO) Keep on hoeing with those fists.

MESSENIO: Go, beat it! Get the devil out of here! Here's a prize for *you*, for being the last to go! (*The* SLAVES *run off*) I mapped out those faces pretty well, I think! Well, master, I got here just in time, didn't I?

MENAECHMUS I: May heaven reward you, young man. If it hadn't been for you, I'd never have lived to see the sun go down today.

MESSENIO: Well then, if you did the right thing, you'd set me free.

MENAECHMUS I: I'd set you free?

MESSENIO: Yes master, because I saved your life.

MENAECHMUS I: What is this? Young man, you are mistaken.

MESSENIO: What do you mean?

MENAECHMUS I: By father Jupiter, I swear I am not your master.

MESSENIO: You're joking!

MENAECHMUS I: No, I mean it. And no slave of mine ever served me as well as you have.

MESSENIO: Then if you say I don't belong to you, let me go free.

MENAECHMUS I: So far as I am concerned, I declare you free to go anywhere you want.

MESSENIO: My Patron! "Congratulations on your freedom, Messenio." "Thank you." But please, Patron, I'm still at your service just as much as when I was your slave. I'll live with you and go with you when you go back home.

MENAECHMUS I (*to himself*): I guess not!

MESSENIO: I'll go to the inn now and get your baggage and the money. The purse and the passage-money are sealed up safely in your bag. I'll have it all here right away.

MENAECHMUS I: Do, by all means.

MESSENIO: I'll give it back to you all safe, just as you gave it to me. Wait for me here. (*He departs.*)

MENAECHMUS I (*to himself*): A lot of strange things have certainly been happening to me today in strange ways. People denying that I am I, and locking me out of the house; and then this fellow saying he was my slave, and I set him free; and now he says he'll bring me a bag of money. If he does, I'll tell him he's free to go wherever he wants, so that when he comes to his senses he won't try to get the money back. And my father-in-law and the doctor saying I was insane! Heavens knows what it all means; it all seems like a dream.—Well, I'll try at Erotium's again. I suppose she's still angry at me, but I've got to try to get that dress and take it home. (*He goes into the house of* EROTIUM.)

Act Five.   Scene VIII

(*Enter* MENAECHMUS II *with* MESSENIO.)

MENAECHMUS II: You brazen rascal, you dare tell me you've seen me anywhere today since I told you to come here?

MESSENIO: Why, I rescued you just a few minutes ago, when four men were carrying you off bodily, right in front of this very house. You were yelling for help to all heaven and earth, and I ran up and rescued you with my fists, in spite of them. And you set me free, because I saved your life. I said I'd get the money and the luggage, and then you doubled round the block so you could meet me and deny the whole thing!

MENAECHMUS II: I set you free?

MESSENIO: You did.

MENAECHMUS II: I'd turn slave myself sooner than free you. And that's that!

Act Five.   Scene IX

(*Enter* MENAECHMUS I *from the house of* EROTIUM.)

MENAECHMUS I (*to those within*): Swear by your eyes if you want to, but you did *not* give me the dress or the bracelet either, you trollops!

MESSENIO: Immortal gods, what's this I see!

MENAECHMUS II: What do you see?

MESSENIO: Your mirror!

MENAECHMUS II: What's this?

MESSENIO: He's the very image of you, as like as can be.

MENAECHMUS II: Well! He's certainly not unlike me, now that I take stock of myself.

MENAECHMUS I (*catching sight of* MESSENIO): Oh, the young man who saved my life. How are you?

MESSENIO: Please sir, if you don't mind, tell me what your name is, for goodness sake!

MENAECHMUS I: Indeed I don't mind, after what you did for me. My name is Menaechmus.

MENAECHMUS II: No, that's *my* name.

MENAECHMUS I: I am a Sicilian, from Syracuse.

MENAECHMUS II: That's where *I* come from.

MENAECHMUS I: What's that?

MENAECHMUS II: That's the truth.

MESSENIO (*pointing to the wrong man*, MENAECHMUS I): This is the man I know, of course, this is my master. I'm his slave, but I thought I was that other man's. (*To* MENAECHMUS I) I thought he was you, and bothered him. (*To* MENAECHMUS II) Please excuse me if I said anything foolish without realising it.

MENAECHMUS II: You must be crazy. Don't you remember leaving the ship with me today?

MESSENIO (*to* MENAECHMUS II): You are right. *You* are my master. (*To* MENAECHMUS I) *You* must look for another slave. (*To* MENAECHMUS II) Greetings to you. (*To* MENAECHMUS I) Good bye to you. (*Pointing to* MENAECHMUS II) I say *this* man is Menaechmus.

MENAECHMUS I: But I say *I* am.

MENAECHMUS II: What is this nonsense? *You* Menaechmus?

MENAECHMUS I: Yes; Menaechmus, son of Moschus.

MENAECHMUS II: The son of my father?

MENAECHMUS I: No, sir, mine, not yours. You may have your father; I don't want to deprive you of him.

MESSENIO (*to himself*): Immortal gods, fulfil this unhoped-for hope! Unless my mind has failed me, these are the two twin brothers! Both of them claim the same father and country. I'll tell my master about it first. (*Aloud*) Menaechmus!

MENAECHMUS I *and* II (*together*): What is it?

MESSENIO: I don't want both of you; just the one that came with me on the boat.

MENAECHMUS I: I didn't.

MENAECHMUS II: I did.

MESSENIO: Then it's you I want. (*Drawing him to one side*) Come over here.

MENAECHMUS II: Well, what is it?

MESSENIO: That man is either a swindler or your twin brother! I never saw two men look so much alike. You're as hard to tell apart as two drops of water or two drops of milk. And besides, he claims the same father and the same country. We'd better ask him about this.

MENAECHMUS II: That's good advice, and thanks! Keep on helping, do! If you prove he is my brother, you shall be a free man.

MESSENIO: That's what I hope.

MENAECHMUS II: I hope so too.

MESSENIO (*to* MENAECHMUS I): You, sir: you said your name was Menaechmus, I believe.

MENAECHMUS I: Yes, it is.

MESSENIO: His name is Menaechmus too. You said you were born at Syracuse in Sicily; that's where he was born. Moschus was your father, you said; his too. Now both of you can help me, and help yourselves too.

MENAECHMUS I: I am in your debt; ask me whatever you want, and you shall have it. I'm at your service, just as if you had bought and paid for me.

MESSENIO: I hope to prove that you two are twin brothers, born on the same day to the same father and mother!

MENAECHMUS I: Amazing! I certainly wish you could prove that.

MESSENIO: I can. But come now, both of you, answer my questions.

MENAECHMUS I: Ask away, I'll answer; I won't conceal anything I know.

MESSENIO (*questioning each in turn*): Your name is Menaechmus?

MENAECHMUS I: It is.

MESSENIO: And yours too?

MENAECHMUS II: Yes.

MESSENIO: You say you are the son of Moschus?

MENAECHMUS I: Quite so.

MENAECHMUS II: So am I.

MESSENIO: You are from Syracuse?

MENAECHMUS I: Yes.

MESSENIO: And you?

MENAECHMUS II: Of course.

MESSENIO: It checks very well so far. Now to proceed: what is the earliest thing you can remember of your life in Sicily?

MENAECHMUS I: Going with my father to the market in Tarentum; and then getting separated from him in the crowd, and being brought here.

MENAECHMUS II: God save us!

MESSENIO (*to* MENAECHMUS II): What are you shouting for? Be quiet. (*To* MENAECHMUS I) How old were you when you went on this trip with your father?

MENAECHMUS I: Seven: I was just beginning to lose my teeth. I never saw my father again.

MESSENIO: Now then: how many sons did your father have at this time?

MENAECHMUS I: To the best of my recollection, two.

MESSENIO: Which was the older, you or the other one?

MENAECHMUS I: Both the same age.

MESSENIO: How is that possible?

MENAECHMUS I: We were twins.

MENAECHMUS II: Thank God!

MESSENIO (*to* MENAECHMUS II): If you interrupt, I'll stop.

MENAECHMUS II: No, no, I'll be quiet.

MESSENIO (*to* MENAECHMUS I): Tell me, did you both have the same name?

MENAECHMUS I: Oh, no. I was the one who was called Menaechmus then, as I still am. His name was Sosicles.

MENAECHMUS II: That's proof enough! No more delay! O my own twin brother, come to my arms! I am Sosicles!

MENAECHMUS I (*doubting*): Then how does it come you're named Menaechmus?

MENAECHMUS II: After we got the news that you were lost . . .[10] and that our father was dead, our grandfather changed my name and gave me yours.

MENAECHMUS I: I believe you. But one more question.

MENAECHMUS II: Ask it.

MENAECHMUS I: What was the name of our mother?

MENAECHMUS II: Teuximarcha.

MENAECHMUS I (*convinced*): Exactly so! Oh, welcome, beyond all hope, after all these years!

MENAECHMUS II: Welcome, dear brother! Sought with such misery and toil, and found with joy at last! (*They embrace.*)

MESSENIO (*to* MENAECHMUS II): So that's why the woman here called you by name! She took you for him, and asked you to dinner.

MENAECHMUS I: Yes, I told her to have a dinner for me there today (putting one over on my wife), and I gave her a dress that I'd stolen from my wife too.

MENAECHMUS II (*producing the dress*): Do you mean this dress?

MENAECHMUS I: That's the one! How did you get it?

MENAECHMUS II: The woman dragged me in to dinner and said the dress was mine, I'd given it to her. So after some excellent wine, women, and song, I took it away with me, and a gold bracelet too.

MENAECHMUS I: She thought she was getting *me* in, of course. But I'm certainly glad I got you fixed up so well.

MESSENIO: I suppose you're still willing to set me free as you promised?

MENAECHMUS I: A very good and fair request, brother; grant it for my sake.

MENAECHMUS II (*complying, with the correct legal formula*): I declare you free.

MENAECHMUS I: Congratulations on your freedom, Messenio.

MESSENIO: I hope it lasts better this time.

MENAECHMUS II: Well, brother, now that everything has turned out the way we wanted, let's both go back to Syracuse.

MENAECHMUS I: Agreed! I'll have an auction and sell all my Epidamnus property. In the meantime, brother, won't you come in?

MENAECHMUS II: Good. (*They move towards the house of* MENAECHMUS I.)

MESSENIO: Do me a favour!

MENAECHMUS I: What is it?

MESSENIO: Give me the job of auctioneer.

MENAECHMUS I: You shall have it.

MESSENIO: You want the auction cried at once?

MENAECHMUS I: Yes, for a week from today. (*The brothers go into the house.*)

MESSENIO: EXTRAORDINARY AUC—TION
                WEEK FROM TODAY
          MENAECHMUS SELLS HIS PROPERTY
                CASH AND NO DELAY
          ALL MUST GO—HOUSE AND LOT
             SLAVES AND FURNITURE
           WIFE GOES TOO IF ANY ONE
              TAKES A FANCY TO HER

He'll be lucky if he gets a quarter of a million for the whole lot. (*To the audience*) And now, spectators, fare ye well, and lustily applaud us all.

THE TRANSLATION of *The Twin Menaechmi* by Edward C. Weist and Richard W. Hyde is not a reprinting of their 1930 version, published by the Harvard Press, but a new translation. Acts Two and Five were translated by Weist, Acts One, Three, and Four by Hyde. The prologue, which in the original version was translated by Spencer Brown, contained many insertions and omissions and has been revised by the editor.

1. There was apparently a jest here in the Greek original. The Greek word τόχος means both "children" and "interest on money."

2. There is a short lacuna in the text here.

3. The text is corrupt at this point.

4. Lindsay indicates a lacuna after this speech.

5. This list of Syracusan rulers is incomplete and inaccurate. Agathocles ruled from 317 to 289 B.C., Hiero from 265 to 215. Between them were two princes Hicetas and Pyrrhus. Phintia and Liparo are not known and are doubtless inventions.

6. Lindsay reads *Titanum* here with the Mss. Most editors prefer *Tithonum;* Tithonus was granted immortality but not eternal youth, and his name became proverbial for age and infirmity. He was the son of Laomedon; the mistake was probably intentional on the part of Plautus.

7. Lindsay begins Act Five, Scene III at this point.

8. This is all the more amusing, since both Aesculapius and Apollo were gods of healing.

9. Hellebore was used by the ancients as a remedy for insanity.

10. Lindsay indicates a lacuna of one verse here.

XI
THE MERCHANT

Characters in the Play

CHARINUS, *son of* DEMIPHO, *and lover of* PASICOMPSA
ACANTHIO, *slave of* CHARINUS
DEMIPHO, *father of* CHARINUS
LYSIMACHUS, *neighbour of* DEMIPHO *and father of* EUTYCHUS
A SLAVE *of* LYSIMACHUS
EUTYCHUS, *son of* LYSIMACHUS *and friend of* CHARINUS
PASICOMPSA, *mistress of* CHARINUS
DORIPPA, *wife of* LYSIMACHUS
SYRA, *slave of* DORIPPA
A CATERER

Argument I (Acrostic)

A young man was sent by his father on a business-trip; he purchases and brings home a nice-looking girl. After seeing her, the old man asks who she is; the slave pretends that she was bought as an attendant for the youth's mother. The old man falls in love with her, pretends to sell her, and hands her over to his neighbour; the neighbour's wife thinks that he's brought home a harlot. Then his friend brings Charinus back from exile after finding the girl.

Argument II

A father sends his dissolute son off on a commercial venture. The son goes abroad, buys his host's serving-girl, with whom he is in love, and brings her home. He leaves his ship; his father comes, sees the girl, and falls madly in love. He inquires, "Whose is she?" The slave replies that she's an attendant whom the youth bought for his mother. The old man, looking out for Number One, begs his son to sell her to a friend of his; the son wants to sell her to his own friend. The son sets up their neighbour's son as proxy, the old man sets up the neighbour himself. The old man gets in first and buys the girl. The neighbour's wife catches the girl in the house, accuses her of being her husband's mistress, and kicks the old man out. The youthful merchant, in despair, decides to leave home, but is checked by his friend, who, aided by his father, prevails on the old man to give in to his son.

INTRODUCTION

The Merchant, based upon a Greek comedy of the same name by Phile-mon, is generally considered one of the earliest of Plautus' plays and one which, like *The Casket*, reproduces most closely the language and tone of the Greek original. It contains little of the robust humour and the elaborate lyrical structure so characteristic of Plautus' later work.

The plot of the comedy is relatively simple and has very little intrigue. There are no deceptions engineered by cunning slaves and no kidnapped daughters to be recognised at the end. The play resembles the *Casina* in that the action deals primarily with the attempt of a father (Demipho) to gain possession of the sweetheart of his son (Charinus). Demipho is successful and arranges for the girl to stay at the home of his neighbour Lysimachus, whose wife returns and accuses her husband of keeping a harlot in his house during her absence. Demipho is ridicu-lous as an aged lover, but cannot be considered so worthless an old reprobate as Lysidamus in the *Casina*, since he claims to be ignorant of his son's love for the girl. Demipho repents at the end and is forgiven without suffering any such ignominious treatment as was accorded to Lysidamus.

The play lacks the boisterous fun and burlesque conclusion of the *Casina* and has been considered by various critics as "dull and sordid," "one of the feeblest works of Plautus." Gilbert Norwood, on the con-trary, maintains that it is the best of Plautus' plays, for the dramatist here is merely translating and so allows the splendour of the Greek original to shine forth unpolluted by his own bad workmanship. He says that *The Merchant* "comes near perfection in its own class . . . sparkling, sophisticated, immoral, light comedy. . . . It is buoyant, rapid, clear, sparkling in plot, dialogue and situations." Few critics will agree with Norwood's exaggerated claims for the comedy, but it is equally wrong to consider it "dull and sordid." Many of the faults which Norwood attributes to other plays of Plautus are present here, e.g. the protatic character used merely for purposes of exposition, weakness of characterisation (with the exception of the portrayal of Pasicompsa, the pert and amusing courtesan), and an undramatic solution. It is true, however, that there is little padding and few irrelevant jests. The action moves rapidly and many of the scenes are rich in humour arising from the situations. Among the most effective scenes are the sham auction between father and son in Act Two, the return of the neighbour's wife in Act Four, and the cook's amusing attempts to mollify her under the impression that she is Lysimachus' mistress. The scene of Charinus' farewell in Act Five, which Norwood considers "a marvellous blend of beauty, pathos, and absurdity," seems unnatural and pointless and as a mad scene is far inferior to the pretended madness of Menaechmus in *The Twin Menaechmi*.

Norwood is clearly wrong in exalting *The Merchant* above all the other plays of Plautus, but he has done a good service in bringing to the attention of readers the many excellent features of the play. P. J. Enk in his introduction to the comedy renders a sane judgment when he rates *The Merchant* among the better plays of Plautus, but not among his best.

THE MERCHANT

(SCENE:—*A street in Athens in front of the houses of* DEMIPHO *and* LYSIMACHUS; *there is an altar of Apollo before the home of* DEMIPHO.)

Act One.   Scene I

(*Enter* CHARINUS *from the house of* DEMIPHO.)

CHARINUS (*to the audience*): I'm now going to kill two birds with one stone: I'll tell you both the plot of our play and about my love affair. And I'm not going to do what I've seen other love-stricken characters in comedy do, when they tell their troubles to Night or Day, to Sun or Moon. Good heavens! They, I'm sure, don't give *that* for our mortal complaints, for our likes and dislikes. I'm going to tell my troubles to you, instead.

In Greek this play is called *The Merchant* of Philemon; it's just the same in Latin: *The Merchant* of Maccius Titus.

My father sent me off to Rhodes on business; it's now two years since I left home. There I fell in love with a girl of wondrous beauty. But I'll tell you how I got involved with her, if you'll lend me your ears, and have the kindness to pay strict attention. By George! I haven't quite followed the fashion of lovers here: I've set forth my facts badly from the very beginning.[1] Well, then, Love is usually accompanied by all these faults: care, sorrow, and excessive luxury (although this fault ruins not only the lover, but whomsoever it touches it affects with complete and utter ruin, and no one in the world ever set his heart on luxury beyond his means without causing himself great loss). But Love has in addition these faults which I omitted: insomnia, grief, mistakes, fear, and flight; then there's stupidity, folly, and thoughtlessness, insane inconsiderateness, immoderation, impudence, lust, and ill will; you'll also find there greed, laziness, insult, want, abuse, extravagance, multiloquence and pauciloquence: the one, because a lover often blurts out something useless and irrelevant at the most inopportune moment; the other, pauciloquence, I mention because no lover is

493

ever eloquent enough to speak to his own advantage. Now you mustn't
be angry at me for my multiloquence; Venus bequeathed this to me on
the day she sent me Love. But I must go back to that and finish my
story.

To begin with, when I came of age and gave up childish pursuits, I
fell violently in love with a courtesan here in Athens. Right away my
father's cash began sneaking off into exile; the insistent pimp who
owned the girl grabbed whatever he could lay his hands on. My father
scolded night and day, shouting about the faithlessness and wickedness
of pimps at the top of his voice, and complaining that his property
was being ruined to enrich a pimp! At other times he'd mutter to himself; he'd shake his head and disown me as a son. He bawled through
all the city, telling all to guard against lending me anything. Love, he
said, had enticed more than one man to his ruin; I was a prodigal, reck-
less villain, who grabbed and spirited off from the house whatever I
could; it was terrible, the way I, on account of my love affair, was
squandering and ruining his honest acquisitions, the fruit of years of
patient toil. He'd brought me up, he said, and I was turning out to be
a reproach to him; if I weren't ashamed of such behaviour, I ought to
die without regret. As for himself, he said, as soon as he grew up, he
didn't devote himself, like me, to love affairs and idleness—he had no
chance for that; his father kept him in check too tightly. He was kept
busy at dirty jobs on the farm, and only saw the city once in four
years, and even then, when once he'd seen the festival, was usually
hustled back to the country by his father. There he was by far the
most industrious member of the household, and his father kept on telling
him: "You are ploughing for yourself; for yourself you harrow, for
yourself you sow, for yourself you reap; for yourself your toil will be
fruitful with joy." After his father left this mortal life, he said, he sold
his farm and with the money equipped a three hundred-ton ship and
shipped his cargoes for all ports, until he amassed his present fortune;
I ought to do the same, if I were the man I ought to be.

When I realised that I was incurring the dislike of my own father
and was annoying to the very man who ought to be pleased with me,
daft with desire as I was, I made a violent effort to strengthen my
resolve and said I'd go away on business, if he wished, and say good-
bye to love to humour him. He thanked me and praised my spirit, but
he jumped at my offer; he prepared a packetboat, purchased a cargo,
loaded the vessel, when it was ready, and counted out a talent in cash
from his own pocket. He sent along a slave who had been my attendant
as a little boy, to keep an eye on me. When all was ready we cast off;
we sailed to Rhodes, where I sold all my cargo on my own terms. I
gained a considerable profit over and above the valuation my father

had set on the cargo, so I made a large amount of private profit for myself. While I was walking around the harbour there, an old friend of the family recognised me and asked me to dinner. I went, and enjoyed a jolly and sumptuous repast. When we went to bed, a girl came in to me—the prettiest girl I had ever seen. She spent the night with me, by my host's order. You can see for yourselves how much I liked her: in the morning I went to my host, begged him to sell her to me, and promised to be eternally grateful and always at his service in return for this kindness. To cut the story short, I bought her and yesterday brought her here; but I don't want my father to find out that I've brought her, so I left her and my slave in port on the ship. (*Looking off towards the harbour*) But what's this? I see my slave running up from the harbour. I forbade him to leave the ship. I'm afraid something's the matter!

Act One.   Scene II

(*Enter* ACANTHIO *running from the direction of the harbour.*)

ACANTHIO (*to himself, without seeing* CHARINUS): Use every effort; summon every ounce of energy to save young master; come on, come on, Acanthio; away with weariness; don't give in to indolence. (*Stops and pants loudly*) This is killing me; I'm completely winded—can't get my breath—and the streets are filled with people in my way. (*Staggering blindly*) One side, there; shove 'em away, push 'em in the gutter. That's the vilest of all customs in this town: if a man's in a hurry and running, no one has the decency to get out of his way. So now I've got to do three things at once, instead of the one I began: I've got to run and fight and argue all along the street.

CHARINUS (*aside*): What in the world makes him so anxious to take up sprinting? I'm worried: what can the matter be, and what's the news?

ACANTHIO (*still without seeing* CHARINUS): I'm getting nowhere. The more I stand here, the more critical our danger gets.

CHARINUS (*aside*): He's got some bad news, all right.

ACANTHIO (*trying to start running again*): My knees desert me; I can't run. (*Crying*) Oh, I'm done for; my guts have started a revolution and have seized my midriff. O God, I can't breathe—I'd make a wretched flute-player.

CHARINUS (*aside*): For heaven's sake, take the edge of your shirt and wipe the sweat off.

ACANTHIO (*to himself*): All the baths in the world will never wash away this tired feeling. But I wonder if master Charinus is at home or out?

CHARINUS (*aside*): This is torturing me! I want to know what this is, and be relieved of my fears.

ACANTHIO: Am I still standing here? Do I hesitate to smash the door to splinters? (*Runs up to door of* DEMIPHO's *house and knocks*) Open up, someone! Where's master Charinus? Is he at home or out? (*Exasperated*) Won't anyone have the decency to come to the door?

CHARINUS (*to* ACANTHIO): Here I am, Acanthio, the man you're looking for.

ACANTHIO (*without seeing* CHARINUS): The service here is terrible!

CHARINUS (*approaching* ACANTHIO): What's the trouble with you?

ACANTHIO (*turning and recognising* CHARINUS): Plenty of trouble, master, for you and me too.

CHARINUS: What's the matter?

ACANTHIO: It's all up with us.

CHARINUS: Save that greeting for our enemies.

ACANTHIO: But it's been allotted to you.

CHARINUS: Tell me what the trouble is.

ACANTHIO: Take it easy; I need a rest. I've burst a blood-vessel for you, and I'm spitting blood.

CHARINUS (*impatiently*): Drink some Egyptian resin with honey; that will fix you up.

ACANTHIO: You just drink some hot tar; your troubles will be all over.

CHARINUS: I've never known a more irritable fellow than you.

ACANTHIO: I've never known a more insulting fellow than you.

CHARINUS (*soothingly*): But suppose I'm telling you what I think will cure you?

ACANTHIO: Away with cures like that; they bring pain with them.

CHARINUS: Tell me, is there any good which anyone can have without some evil in it, or which you can enjoy without taking some discomfort therein?

ACANTHIO: I don't know about that stuff: I never took a course in philosophy. All I know is that a good with a joker in it is a gift I don't yearn for.

CHARINUS: Come, Acanthio, give me your hand.

ACANTHIO: There; take it.

CHARINUS: Do you want to be obliging or not?

ACANTHIO: You can find that out from my actions: I've got a rupture from running for your sake, so you could learn promptly what I know.

CHARINUS: I'll make you a free man—in a few months.

ACANTHIO: You're wheedling me.

CHARINUS: Could I bring myself to tell you a falsehood about anything? Why, before I even speak, you know if I want to lie.

ACANTHIO: This talk of yours increases my fatigue; you're killing me!

CHARINUS (*impatiently*): Is this the way you oblige me?

ACANTHIO: What do you want me to do?

CHARINUS: Do? What I want.

ACANTHIO: Well then, what do you want?

CHARINUS: I'll tell you.

ACANTHIO: Tell me.

CHARINUS: But quietly, if you please.

ACANTHIO (*with a wink at the spectators*): Are you afraid of waking up the audience?

CHARINUS (*angrily*): Curse you!

ACANTHIO (*angrily*): And you—(*more calmly*) will curse the news I'm bringing you from the harbour.

CHARINUS: What are you bringing? Tell me.

ACANTHIO (*melodramatically*): Violence, Fear, Torture, Care, Brawls, and Want.

CHARINUS: The devil! Quite a treasure-chest of troubles you've brought. I'm a goner!

ACANTHIO: No, you're— (*He breaks off and leaves his sentence unfinished.*)

CHARINUS: I know; you'll say I'm a miserable wretch.

ACANTHIO: I said it—under my breath.

CHARINUS: What is this trouble?

ACANTHIO: Don't ask; it's a terrible misfortune.

CHARINUS: Please don't keep me in suspense any longer; I've been anxious too long.

ACANTHIO: Take it easy; there are several questions I want to ask before I get my—beating.

CHARINUS: Indeed you will get a beating unless you either speak up or get out.

ACANTHIO: Just look at that, will you? How he coaxes! He's as smooth as they come, when he sets his mind to it.

CHARINUS (*earnestly*): Heavens above! I beg and beseech you to tell me at once what it is; for I see I've got to humble myself to my own slave.

ACANTHIO (*with dignity*): And don't I seem to deserve it?

CHARINUS (*humbly*): Yes indeed.

ACANTHIO: So I supposed.

CHARINUS: Please tell me: the ship hasn't been wrecked, has it?

ACANTHIO: The ship's all right, don't worry.

CHARINUS: What about the gear and tackle?

ACANTHIO: They're quite sound, too.

CHARINUS: Why don't you tell me why you were running all over the town looking for me just now?

ACANTHIO: You keep interrupting me and take the words out of my mouth.

CHARINUS: I'll keep quiet.

ACANTHIO: Quiet, then! (*Conversationally*) I suppose that if I had any good news for you, you'd squeeze it right out of me, seeing how anxious you are for me to tell you the bad news you've got to hear.

CHARINUS (*in desperation*): For heaven's sake, I entreat you to disclose that bad news of yours.

ACANTHIO: I'll tell you, since you beg me to. Your father—

CHARINUS (*frightened*): What about my father?

ACANTHIO: And your mistress—

CHARINUS (*still more alarmed*): What about her?

ACANTHIO: Have met!

CHARINUS: Met? I'm ruined! (*After a pause*) Answer me this one question.

ACANTHIO: Ask anything you like.

CHARINUS: How could he see her?

ACANTHIO: With his eyes.

CHARINUS: In what way?

ACANTHIO: Popping right out of his head.

CHARINUS: Go to the devil! Are you being funny when my life's at stake?

ACANTHIO: How the devil am I being funny if I only answer your questions?

CHARINUS: Are you sure he saw her?

ACANTHIO: As sure as that you and I see each other.

CHARINUS: Where did he see her?

ACANTHIO: On board the ship, standing near her; he talked with her, too.

CHARINUS (*dramatically*): O father, you've killed me! (*Turning savagely on* ACANTHIO) You there—see here, you: why didn't you keep him from seeing her, you rascal?

ACANTHIO: Because we were busy at our own tasks—folding up and storing away the tackle. While we were doing this, your father rowed out in a little skiff and no one saw him until he boarded the ship.

CHARINUS: In vain, O Sea, have I escaped from your storms! I thought that now I was on land, in safety, but I see the wild waves driving me on the reef. (*To* ACANTHIO) Tell me what happened next.

ACANTHIO: When he saw the girl, he first asked whose she was.

CHARINUS: What did she say?

ACANTHIO: At once I ran up and interrupted; I said that you had bought her as a maid for your mother.

CHARINUS (*hopefully*): Do you think he believed you?

ACANTHIO (*scornfully*): What a question! But then the dirty old fellow tried to make her.

CHARINUS: Good heavens! My mistress?

ACANTHIO: Strange he didn't try to make *me*!

CHARINUS: Alas, my heart, my poor heart! Drop by drop, it melts away, like salt in water. It's all up with me!

ACANTHIO: You never spoke a truer word. (*More hopefully*) But that's all nonsense.

CHARINUS: What shall I do? I'm sure my father won't believe me if I say I bought her for my mother. Besides, it seems a crime to tell a falsehood to my father. Anyway, neither he nor anyone else would believe that I bought such a lovely girl for my mother.

ACANTHIO (*encouragingly*): Oh, hush, you silly fool! He'll believe you; why, he believed me.

CHARINUS (*miserably*): Oh, dear, I'm just afraid he'll be suspicious about the affair. Answer this question, please.

ACANTHIO: What is it?

CHARINUS: You don't think he suspected she was my mistress, do you?

ACANTHIO: No, he didn't seem to. Why, he believed everything I told him.

CHARINUS: You mean, you think he did.

ACANTHIO: No, he really did believe me.

CHARINUS: Alas, I'm done for, ruined completely! But why do I waste time in weeping here? Why not go to the ship? Come on.

ACANTHIO (*stopping him as he starts for the harbour*): If you go that way, you'll run up against your father; then he'll see you're frightened and distracted; straightway he'll stop you, ask you where you bought her, what you paid; he'll pump you while you're scared.

CHARINUS: I'll go this way, then. (*Starts off towards the city*) Do you think father has left the harbour?

ACANTHIO: Yes, that's why I ran on ahead: I didn't want him to catch you unawares and worm it out of you.

CHARINUS: Very good. (*They depart to the forum.*)

Act Two.   Scene I

(*Enter* DEMIPHO *from the harbour.*)

DEMIPHO (*to the audience*): It's wonderful how the gods make sport of us men, and wonderful are the dreams they send us in our sleep. For example, in this past night I was pretty active in my sleep and kept quite busy. I dreamed I bought a beautiful nanny-goat; now I didn't want the nanny-goat I already had at home to hurt her, or the two of them to fight if they were brought together, so after I'd bought her I dreamed I'd entrusted her to the keeping of a monkey. Then a little later that monkey came to me, cursed me roundly, and started a quarrel: he said that thanks to the coming of that nanny-goat he'd suffered considerable disgrace and loss; for the goat (he said) which I'd given him to keep, had immediately eaten up his wife's dowry. I thought it very strange that a goat should have eaten the dowry of a monkey's wife. But the monkey assured me that it was so, and finally announced that if I didn't hurry up and take that goat away from his house, he'd take her to my house and my wife. Now I seemed to have a great liking for that nanny-goat, but I didn't have any place to keep her; what was I to do? I was in torment. Meanwhile I dreamed a billy-goat came up to me and told me he'd stolen that nanny-goat from the monkey, and he began to laugh at me. And I was miserable, and could hardly stand the loss of my goat.

Now I can't discover how this dream applies to me; but I suspect I've already found out who that nanny-goat is and what it means. I went off at dawn to the harbour; when I'd transacted my business there, I saw the ship on which my son came from Rhodes yesterday. A fancy struck me, for some reason or other, to visit it; I boarded a skiff, rowed out to the ship; and there I saw a stunning girl whom my son had brought as a maid for my wife. It was love at first sight—not the ordinary kind of sensible love, but the love of an absolute madman. I've been in love before, to be sure, in my youth, but never in the crazy sort of way that I am now. Well, I'm sure of this: I'm done for! You yourselves can see what I'm worth.

Well, this is how it is: the girl is that nanny-goat; but that monkey and billy-goat are bringing me some trouble, and I don't know who they are. But hush—here comes my neighbour out of his house.

Act Two. Scene II

(*Enter* LYSIMACHUS *from his house, attended by a* SLAVE.)

LYSIMACHUS (*to his slave*): I want that buck-goat castrated—the one that's been giving you so much trouble at the farm.

DEMIPHO (*to himself*): That's an ill-omened beginning; I don't like it. I'm afraid my wife may castrate me, like a goat, and play the part of the monkey, herself.

LYSIMACHUS (*to the slave*): Go out to the farmhouse and give those rakes to my overseer; see that you hand them over to Pistus himself, in person. And tell my wife that I have some business in the city, and not to look for me; say I've got to try three cases today. Go, and don't forget the message.

SLAVE: Anything else?

LYSIMACHUS: That's all. (*The slave departs.*)

DEMIPHO (*approaching* LYSIMACHUS): Good day, Lysimachus.

LYSIMACHUS: Well there, Demipho, good day. How are you? How's everything?

DEMIPHO: Pretty wretched.

LYSIMACHUS: God forbid.

DEMIPHO: But God does just this.

LYSIMACHUS: What is it?

DEMIPHO: I'll tell you, if you are interested and have nothing to do.

LYSIMACHUS: I am busy, Demipho, but if you want anything, I'm never too busy to oblige a friend.

DEMIPHO: I know how obliging you are; you needn't tell me. (*Confidentially*) How old do I seem to you?

LYSIMACHUS: Old enough for the undertaker; a senile, decrepit old man.

DEMIPHO: Take another look. I'm a boy, Lysimachus—seven years old.

LYSIMACHUS: Are you crazy? Calling yourself a boy!

DEMIPHO: It's true.

LYSIMACHUS: Oh, now I get what you mean; when a man is old, and loses his senses and his wits, people usually say he's in his second childhood.

DEMIPHO: No, I'm twice as strong as I ever was.

LYSIMACHUS: That's fine; I congratulate you.

DEMIPHO: Why, if you only knew—my eyesight's much keener than it was before.

LYSIMACHUS: Very good.

DEMIPHO: For something wicked, I mean.

LYSIMACHUS: Not so good.

DEMIPHO: Can I speak out to you, in confidence?

LYSIMACHUS: Trust me.

DEMIPHO: Pay attention.

LYSIMACHUS: I'll do so.

DEMIPHO: Today I started grammar-school, Lysimachus; already I know five letters.

LYSIMACHUS: Which five?

DEMIPHO (*coyly*): I L-O-V-E.

LYSIMACHUS: What, you, with that grey head, are in love, you worthless dotard?

DEMIPHO: Whether it's grey or red or black, I love.

LYSIMACHUS: You're kidding me, Demipho.

DEMIPHO: Cut my head off right on the spot, if I'm lying. Or, to prove I'm in love, take a knife: cut my finger, or my ear, or my nose, or lips; if I budge or feel the wound, you have my permission to slay me— (*with a lingering sigh*) with love.

LYSIMACHUS (*to the audience*): If you've never seen a picture of a lover, there's one for you. In my opinion, a senile, decrepit old man is just as good a lover as a mural.

DEMIPHO: You're going to scold me, I suppose.

LYSIMACHUS: Scold you?

DEMIPHO: There's no reason to be angry at me; many other distinguished men have done the same. 'Tis human to be in love, and it's human to be forgiving.[2] . . . Don't scold me; it wasn't my idea to fall in love.

LYSIMACHUS: Why, I'm not scolding you.

DEMIPHO: I don't want to lose your good opinion because of this.

LYSIMACHUS: My good opinion? God forbid!

DEMIPHO: Please think it over.

LYSIMACHUS: I've done so.

DEMIPHO: Are you sure?

LYSIMACHUS: Don't be a nuisance. (*Aside*) The fellow's crazy with love. (*To* DEMIPHO) Anything else?

DEMIPHO: Farewell.

LYSIMACHUS (*starting to leave*): I'm in a hurry to get to the harbour; I've some business there.

DEMIPHO: Have a good walk.

LYSIMACHUS: Good luck and good-bye. (LYSIMACHUS *departs.*)

DEMIPHO: Good luck to you. (*To himself*) Why, I've got some business at the harbour, too. I'll go there now. (*Looking down the street*) But here's my son coming; excellent! I'll wait for him. I've got to see to this, how I can persuade him to sell the girl to me and not give her to his mother; he's brought her as a gift for her, I hear. But I must take care he doesn't notice that I've taken a liking to her.

Act Two.   Scene III

(Enter CHARINUS, *very disconsolate; he does not see* DEMIPHO.)

CHARINUS *(to himself)*: There's no more wretched man alive, I'm sure; everything's always going against me. No matter what I start out to do, I can never attain to my heart's desire; some nuisance always gets in my way, and thwarts my careful schemes. Alas! I got myself a mistress, to delight my heart, and paid a good price for her; I thought I could keep her without my father's knowledge. But he has found her out, has seen her, and ruined me. When he begins to question me, I've no idea what to say; a dozen ideas struggle in confusion in my head. I don't know what plan I can make; my mind is wandering and is so upset. At times my slave's plan pleases me, and then again I don't like it and don't believe that my father can be brought to think that I bought her for my mother. Well now, if I tell him the truth, and say that I bought her for myself, what will he think of me? And further, he'd take her away and send her abroad to be sold. I know how strict he is from my own experience. If this be love, I'd rather dig a trench than ever kiss a wench again.[3] He's already driven me out of the house once, for all my reluctance, and made me go off on a business trip; that's how I got into this mess. When the pain is greater than the pleasure, what charm is left? To no avail I hid her, buried her away, kept her out of sight; my father is a ferret,[4] you can't keep anything from him; nothing is so hallowed or so profane but that he puts his nose in it. I have no confidence in my fortunes, and no hope in my heart.

DEMIPHO *(aside)*: Why is my son talking to himself? He seems upset about something or other.

CHARINUS *(suddenly noticing* DEMIPHO): Ye gods! Here's my father. I'll go up and speak to him. *(Approaching* DEMIPHO) How goes it, father? *(Tries to escape into the house.)*

DEMIPHO: Where have you been, and what's your hurry, son?

CHARINUS *(embarrassed)*: Oh, it's all right, father.

DEMIPHO: I hope so, but what's the matter with you? You're changing colour. Have you a pain somewhere?

CHARINUS: I feel a little queer, somehow; I didn't sleep very well last night.

DEMIPHO: You've been travelling by sea; your eyes aren't used to the land yet.

CHARINUS: I rather think—

DEMIPHO (*eager to finish with the subject*): Yes, indeed, that's it. It will leave you soon. That's why you're pale. You'd be wise to go lie down at home.

CHARINUS: I haven't time; I want to attend to some commissions first.

DEMIPHO: Do it tomorrow, or the day after tomorrow.

CHARINUS: I've often heard you say a wise man should attend to his commissions first of all.

DEMIPHO: Do so, then; I won't oppose your wishes.

CHARINUS (*aside*): I'm saved, if I can always count on that remark.

DEMIPHO (*aside*): Why is he taking counsel with himself, apart from me? But I have nothing to fear; he can't have found out that I'm in love with her. For I've done nothing stupid, like an ordinary lover.

CHARINUS (*aside*): Everything is still all right, by George! I'm quite sure he doesn't know about my mistress; if he knew it, he'd sing another tune.

DEMIPHO (*aside*): Why not approach him about her?

CHARINUS (*aside*): Why don't I get out of here? (*To* DEMIPHO) I'm going to complete my friend's commissions, like a true friend.

DEMIPHO: No, wait a minute. There are a few little matters I want to ask about first.

CHARINUS: Tell me what you want.

DEMIPHO (*embarrassed, with some hesitation*): Have you kept well?

CHARINUS: Very well, all the time I was at Rhodes; but since I sailed back to port here, I've been a little upset, somehow.

DEMIPHO: Sea-sickness, I suppose; it will soon go away. (*Fidgeting with embarrassment*) But I say; did you bring a maid for your mother from Rhodes?

CHARINUS (*startled*): Yes, I did.

DEMIPHO: Well—what kind of a girl is she, in your opinion?

CHARINUS (*trying to appear indifferent*): Not bad.

DEMIPHO: Good character?

CHARINUS: I've never seen a better, to my knowledge.

DEMIPHO: Indeed, that's what I thought, when I saw her.

CHARINUS: What? Have you seen her, father?

DEMIPHO: Yes. But she's no good for us; I don't like her.

CHARINUS: Why not?

DEMIPHO (*hesitating*): Because—well, because her appearance doesn't suit our household. The only girl we need is one who can weave, grind the meal, split the wood, work at wool, sweep the house, take her beatings, and cook the family's meals every day. That girl couldn't do any of this.

CHARINUS: Exactly. That's why I bought her; she's a gift for mother.

DEMIPHO: Don't give her, and don't tell your mother you've brought her.

CHARINUS (*aside, with great delight*): The gods are on my side.

DEMIPHO (*aside*): He's slipping, bit by bit. (*Aloud*) But I forgot to mention this: it wouldn't be quite decent for her to accompany your mother, and I wouldn't permit it.

CHARINUS: Why?

DEMIPHO: Because it would be a disgrace for such a pretty figure to attend a respectable matron. When she'd walk down the street, everybody would look her over, stare at her, nod, wink, and whistle; they'd nudge her, yoo-hoo at her, and make a nuisance of themselves; they'd sing serenades at the door, and chalk the house with gallant verses. And people gossip so now, they'd accuse my wife and me of running an "establishment." We don't want that.

CHARINUS: Good heavens! You're quite right, and I agree with you. But what's to become of the girl?

DEMIPHO: That's all right. I'll buy your mother a stout, ugly wench, as befits a matron,—a Syrian or Egyptian; she'll grind and cook and spin and be cudgelled, and won't bring any scandal to our doors.

CHARINUS: What if I return the other girl to the seller?

DEMIPHO (*vehemently*): Not on your life!

CHARINUS: He said he'd take her back if we didn't like her.

DEMIPHO: There's no need for that; I don't want any lawsuits, or your credit to be hurt. I much prefer to take my loss, if necessary, rather than have any reproach or scandal over a woman originate in our family. I think I can sell her for you for a handsome sum.

CHARINUS: Providing that you don't sell her for less than I paid, father—

DEMIPHO (*interrupting*): Just keep quiet; there's an old man who commissioned me to buy her—I mean, one like her.

CHARINUS (*desperately*): But a young man has commissioned me to buy one of her sort, exactly like her, father.

DEMIPHO: I think I can sell her for twenty minae.

CHARINUS (*hastily*): If I'd take them, he's already offered me twenty-seven minae.

DEMIPHO: But I—

CHARINUS: No, I say, I can—

DEMIPHO (*angrily*): You don't know what I'm going to say; shut up! (*Looking down the street*) I can scrape up another three minae and make it thirty.

CHARINUS: What are you looking at?

DEMIPHO: At my customer.

CHARINUS (*straining to see*): Where in the world is the fellow?

DEMIPHO: There he is: I see him. He bids me add five more minae.

CHARINUS: God damn him, whoever he is!

DEMIPHO (*still gazing down the street*): He now signals to me to add six more minae.

CHARINUS (*looking down the street in the other direction*): Seven more from my customer!

DEMIPHO: By God, you'll never outbid me!

CHARINUS: He offers to pay in gold, father.

DEMIPHO: His offer's useless; I *will* have her!

CHARINUS: But he promised first.

DEMIPHO: I don't care.

CHARINUS (*looking down the street again*): He bids fifty.

DEMIPHO: He won't get her for a hundred! (*In a burst of rage*) Can't you stop trying to sell her against my wishes? You'll get an outrageous profit. That old man I'm buying her for is just crazy with love. You can name your own price.

CHARINUS: But good heavens, the young man I'm buying her for is dying with love.

DEMIPHO: The old man is much worse off, believe me.

CHARINUS: The old man never was, and never will be, more crazy with love than that youth for whom I'm acting, father.

DEMIPHO: Be quiet, I say. I'll attend to this affair properly.

CHARINUS (*as a sudden thought strikes him*): I say!

DEMIPHO: What is it?

CHARINUS: I took her without legal title.

DEMIPHO: He'll take her anyway. Forget it.

CHARINUS: But you can't sell her legally.

DEMIPHO: I'll think up something.

CHARINUS (*trying another tack*): Besides, another fellow has a share in her. How do I know his mind, or whether he is willing to sell or not?

DEMIPHO: I know he's willing.

CHARINUS: Well, I'm sure there's someone who isn't willing.

DEMIPHO: What do I care about that?

CHARINUS: Because it's only fair that he should manage his own property.

DEMIPHO: What do you say to—

CHARINUS (*paying no attention*): That other fellow is joint owner of her; he's not here now.

DEMIPHO (*annoyed*): You answer before I ask my question.

CHARINUS: And you buy before I sell. I tell you, I don't know if he wants to give up possession or not.

DEMIPHO: What? If she is to be bought for that party who gave you the commission, then he'll be willing, but if I buy her for my party, then he won't be willing? Nonsense! Damn it! No one shall have her except the fellow I wish.

CHARINUS (*sullenly*): Is that your decision?

DEMIPHO: Do you suppose it isn't? Why, I'm going right away to the ship, and she'll be sold right there.

CHARINUS: Do you want me to go with you?

DEMIPHO: No, I don't.

CHARINUS: You're very unpleasant about it.

DEMIPHO: You'd better go attend to those commissions of yours.

CHARINUS: You're keeping me.

DEMIPHO: Blame me, then; say you did your best. Don't go to the harbour, I tell you.

CHARINUS: I hear you.

DEMIPHO (*aside*): I'll go to the harbour. I must take care he doesn't find out; I won't buy her myself, I'll commission my friend Lysimachus. He said some time ago he was going to the harbour; I'm holding myself up by standing here. (DEMIPHO *departs to the harbour.*)

CHARINUS: I'm done for! I'm ruined!

Act Two. Scene IV

(*Enter* EUTYCHUS *from his house; he is not perceived at first by* CHARINUS.)

CHARINUS (*wildly*): Pentheus was torn to shreds by the Bacchantes, they say; that was the merest trifle, I think, in comparison to the way I'm torn to pieces. Why do I live? Why not die? What good is left for me in life? My mind's made up: I'll go to a doctor and end my life with poison, since I've been bereft of that for which I desire to live. (*He starts to leave.*)

EUTYCHUS: Wait, wait, Charinus; please!

CHARINUS: Who calls me back?

EUTYCHUS: Eutychus, your friend and companion, your next-door neighbour.

CHARINUS: You don't know how heavy a burden I have to bear.

EUTYCHUS: Yes I do; I heard from the doorway everything you said; I know all about it.

CHARINUS: What is it you know?

EUTYCHUS: Your father wants to sell—

CHARINUS: You've got the whole story.

EUTYCHUS: —your mistress—

CHARINUS: You know too much.

EUTYCHUS: —against your will.

CHARINUS: You know everything. But how do you know she's my mistress?

EUTYCHUS: You yourself told me yesterday.

CHARINUS: Pretty funny that, forgetting that I'd told you.

EUTYCHUS: It's no wonder.

CHARINUS: Now I want your advice. Tell me: by what method do you think it would be best for me to die?

EUTYCHUS: Won't you be still? Don't say that.

CHARINUS: What do you want me to say?

EUTYCHUS: Do you want me to put one over on your father?

CHARINUS: Of course I do.

EUTYCHUS: Do you want me to go to the harbour—

CHARINUS: Do I? Why, fly there!

EUTYCHUS: —and get the girl away from him with money?

CHARINUS: Why, pay her weight in gold!

EUTYCHUS: Where's the money?

CHARINUS: I'll beg Achilles to give me the gold with which Hector was ransomed.

EUTYCHUS: Are you crazy?

CHARINUS: If I were sane, I wouldn't take you for my doctor.

EUTYCHUS: No matter what he bids, do you want me to match it and buy her?

CHARINUS: You can add a thousand to whatever he bids.

EUTYCHUS: Oh, hush! (*Starts to leave*) Say! Where am I to get the money for you to pay when your father asks for it?

CHARINUS: It will be found; it will be discovered; something will turn up; you're killing me.

EUTYCHUS: I'm afraid of that, "something will turn up."

CHARINUS: Why don't you keep still?

EUTYCHUS: I'm mute.

CHARINUS: Are your orders sufficient?

EUTYCHUS: Can't you stop worrying?

CHARINUS: No, I can't.

EUTYCHUS: Good luck.

CHARINUS: No luck for me until you return.

EUTYCHUS: Better try to be sensible.

CHARINUS: Good-bye, good luck, and preserve me.

EUTYCHUS: I'll do so; wait for me at home.

CHARINUS: See that you come back soon with the spoils.

(EUTYCHUS *departs to the harbour;* CHARINUS *goes into his father's house. A short time is supposed to elapse before the next Act.*)

Act Three. Scene I

(*Enter* LYSIMACHUS *with* PASICOMPSA *from the direction of the harbour.*)

LYSIMACHUS: Like a friend in need, I've done my friend this service; as my neighbour asked, I've made this purchase. (*To the girl*) You're mine; come along. Don't weep; it's just too silly, to spoil such lovely eyes. Why, as far as you're concerned, you ought to laugh rather than weep.

PASICOMPSA: Please, my dear old fellow, tell me—

LYSIMACHUS: Ask whatever you will.

PASICOMPSA: Why have you bought me?

LYSIMACHUS: Bought you? That you may do my bidding, (*with an amorous look*) just as I'll do whatever you bid.

PASICOMPSA: I'm resolved to do whatever I think you wish, as far as I can and know how.

LYSIMACHUS: No hard task shall be imposed on you, my dear.

PASICOMPSA: You see, dearie, I don't know how to carry heavy burdens or tend the sheep or nurse children.

LYSIMACHUS: If you're a good girl, you'll be well off.

PASICOMPSA: Oh dear! Then I'm ruined.

LYSIMACHUS: Why?

PASICOMPSA: Because where I come from, the naughty girls are usually well off.

LYSIMACHUS: You mean to say no woman is any good?

PASICOMPSA: Oh, no; it's not my way to say what everybody knows.

LYSIMACHUS (*aside*): By Jove, her conversation's worth more than I paid for her. (*Aloud*) I want to ask you one question.

PASICOMPSA: If you ask, I'll answer.

LYSIMACHUS: I say, what's your name?

PASICOMPSA: Pasicompsa.

LYSIMACHUS: You got your name from your appearance.[5] But see here, Pasicompsa! (*Leering, with an indecent gesture*) If you get a chance, could you thread a fine needle? [6]

PASICOMPSA: Oh, yes.

LYSIMACHUS: If you can deal with a fine thread, I'm sure you could handle a coarse one.

PASICOMPSA (*coyly*): As far as *sewing* goes, I'm not afraid of anyone of my own age.

LYSIMACHUS: I see you're a good girl, and plenty old enough, since you know your business, my girl.

PASICOMPSA: Oh, I've been well taught. I won't let anyone complain about my—work.

LYSIMACHUS: Well, that's just it. I'm going to give you a little lamb, just sixty years old, for your very own.

PASICOMPSA: So old, dearie?

LYSIMACHUS: It's of Greek stock. If you take good care of it, it will be very good; you can shear it very nicely.

PASICOMPSA: For your sake, I'll be very grateful for whatever is given me.

LYSIMACHUS (*adopting a more serious tone*): See here, my girl; don't fool yourself; you're not mine—don't imagine it.

PASICOMPSA: Why then, tell me, please, whose am I?

LYSIMACHUS: Your own master has bought you back; I bought you for him as he requested.

PASICOMPSA (*delighted, thinking* CHARINUS *is meant*): Ah, I'm coming back to life; he's kept his promise to me.

LYSIMACHUS: Cheer up; he'll set you free; he's crazy about you, and he never saw you before today.

PASICOMPSA: For mercy's sake, it's two years since he started this affair with me. Since I see you're his friend, I'll tell you about it.

LYSIMACHUS: What's that? For two years he's had an affair with you?

PASICOMPSA: Certainly; and we made a solemn promise to each other— I to him and he to me: neither of us would ever pet or sleep with any other man or woman.

LYSIMACHUS: Good heavens! Wouldn't he even sleep with his wife?

PASICOMPSA: Please, sir, is he married? He isn't and he shan't be!

LYSIMACHUS: I wish he weren't. By George, what a liar the man is!

PASICOMPSA: There's no young man I love better.

LYSIMACHUS: He's a mere child, you silly girl; for it wasn't long ago that his teeth fell out.

PASICOMPSA: What, his teeth?

LYSIMACHUS: Never mind. Come along please. (*To the audience*) He begged me to find a place for her in my house for one day, since my wife is at the country. (*They go into the house of* LYSIMACHUS.)

Act Three.   Scene II

(*Enter* DEMIPHO *from the harbour.*)

DEMIPHO (*to himself*): At last I've succeeded in finding the road to ruin: I've bought a mistress without my wife or son knowing it. I've made up my mind to return to my old habits and indulge myself. I have but a short time of life left; why then, I'll enliven it with wine, women, and good living. It's much more fair that a man of my years should have a good time. When you're young, when your blood is vigorous, it's proper to devote your energies to making money; but when you finally reach old age, then you ought to take it easy and make love while you can; life itself is then pure profit. And I'm going to follow out my words with actions. Meanwhile I'll go look in at my house here. (*Pausing*) My wife is waiting for me at home; she's probably starving by now. She'll kill me with her nagging, if I go in. (*Making up his mind*) Well then, however it may be, I won't go home after all; I'll first stop in here to see my neighbour. I want him to rent a little apartment for me, where the girl can live. But here he comes out of his house.

Act Three.   Scene III

(*Enter* LYSIMACHUS *from his house.*)

LYSIMACHUS (*to* PASICOMPSA, *within the house*): I'll bring him to you, if I meet him.

DEMIPHO (*with a fatuous grin*): He means me.

LYSIMACHUS (*turning and seeing* DEMIPHO): Oh, I say, Demipho.

DEMIPHO: Is the girl at your house?

LYSIMACHUS: What do you think?

DEMIPHO: How about going in to see her?

LYSIMACHUS: What's your hurry? Wait.

DEMIPHO: What shall I do?

LYSIMACHUS: Just consider carefully what you ought to do.

DEMIPHO: Consider? Why, good heavens! *This* is what I ought to do, go right in to see her.

LYSIMACHUS: You think so, you mutton-head? Go into her?

DEMIPHO: What else?

LYSIMACHUS: First listen to me and pay attention: there's something else I think you ought to do first. If you go in there now, you'll want to hug her, chat with her, and kiss her.

DEMIPHO: You're a mind-reader; you know just what I'm going to do.

LYSIMACHUS: You'll be making a big mistake.

DEMIPHO: But if you love a girl—

LYSIMACHUS: So much the less. With your sallow complexion, your stinking breath, smelling like a goat, will you kiss a girl? Do you want to make her throw up? I'm sure you must be in love, to tell me such a plan as that.

DEMIPHO: Well then, how about doing this? If you agree, let's get a caterer to cook dinner for us at your house tonight.

LYSIMACHUS (*enthusiastically*): That's just what I'd advise. Now you're talking sensibly and not like a silly lover.

DEMIPHO: What are we waiting for? Why not go and look for some provisions, so we can have a party?

LYSIMACHUS: I'm right with you. And you'll find some place for her, if you're wise; not one day more will she spend in my house, after today. I'm afraid my wife will find her here if she returns from the country tomorrow.

DEMIPHO: Everything has been attended to; just come along. (*They depart to the forum.*)

Act Three.   Scene IV

(Enter CHARINUS *from his father's house.)*

CHARINUS *(to himself)*: How wretched and miserable I am! I can't relax a minute. If I'm at home, my mind is out of doors; if I'm out, my mind's at home. Love blazes up in my heart and soul; if my tears didn't prevent it, I'm sure my head would be on fire. I hold fast to hope, but I've lost my life; I don't know whether she'll return or not. If my father puts his threats into force, my life's gone off into exile; but if my friend carries out his promise, my life's not gone. But even if Eutychus had gout in both feet, he could have come back from the harbour by now. He has that one bad fault: he's too slow for my wishes. *(Seeing* EUTYCHUS *approaching down the street)* But isn't that Eutychus I see running up? It's he! I'll go to meet him. [O Lady Luck, mistress of men and gods, since you have brought me this longed-for hope, receive my thanks!][7] Now, what's he stopping for? Oh, damn it! I don't like his expression. He walks sadly (Oh, my heart's afire, I'm numb!), he shakes his head. Oh, Eutychus!

(Enter EUTYCHUS *from the harbour.)*

EUTYCHUS: Well, Charinus!

CHARINUS: Before you catch your breath, tell me in one word: where am I? Here or with the dead?

EUTYCHUS: You're neither here nor with the dead.

CHARINUS *(joyfully)*: I'm saved; I've become an immortal! He has bought her, he's neatly hoodwinked my father. There's no man alive better able to get what he's after. *(Slightly worried, as* EUTYCHUS *still looks glum)* Tell me, please; if I'm neither here nor in Hell, where am I?

EUTYCHUS *(mournfully)*: Nowhere at all.

CHARINUS: I'm ruined! That remark has done for me.

EUTYCHUS: It's tiresome to keep on talking when you're busy.

CHARINUS: Whatever it is, come to the point.

EUTYCHUS: First of all: we're lost.

CHARINUS: Why don't you tell me something I don't know?

EUTYCHUS: Your girl's been disposed of.

CHARINUS: Eutychus, you're guilty of a capital offence.

EUTYCHUS: Why?

CHARINUS: You're killing your best friend, and a free citizen.

EUTYCHUS: God forbid!

CHARINUS: You've plunged the knife in my throat; I'm going to fall.

EUTYCHUS: For heaven's sake, don't lose heart.

CHARINUS: I've none to lose. Go on; tell me some more bad news. To whom was she sold?

EUTYCHUS: I don't know. She'd already been handed over and led away when I reached the harbour.

CHARINUS: Alas for me! These are very mountains of burning misery you've been hurling on me. Go on, torture me, you butcher, since you've started.

EUTYCHUS: It's no more upsetting for you than it was for me.

CHARINUS: Tell me; who bought her?

EUTYCHUS: I don't know, I tell you.

CHARINUS: Well, is that what you call doing a favour for a friend?

EUTYCHUS: What do you want me to do?

CHARINUS: What you see me doing: die on the spot! Why didn't you ask for a description of the man who bought her? In that way the girl could have been traced. (*Weeping*) Oh, dear; oh, dear!

EUTYCHUS: Stop crying like that. What have I done?

CHARINUS: You've ruined me and my faith in you.

EUTYCHUS: God knows, it's not my fault.

CHARINUS: Fine! You call God to witness. Why should I believe you?

EUTYCHUS: Because you can control what you should believe, but I can't control what I have to tell you.

CHARINUS: You're clever enough at giving tit for tat, but when it comes to my commission, you're lame, blind, mute, crippled, and weak. You promised to put one over on my father; I supposed I was trusting my affair to a clever fellow, but he turns out to be a lump of earth.

EUTYCHUS: What was I to do?

CHARINUS: What were you to do? What a question! You should have made inquiries, asked who he was, where he came from, what his family was, whether he was a citizen or a foreigner.

EUTYCHUS: They said he was an Attic citizen.

CHARINUS: You should have found out where he lived, at least, if you couldn't find out his name.

EUTYCHUS: Everyone said they didn't know.

CHARINUS: Well, at any rate, you could have got a description.

EUTYCHUS: I did.

CHARINUS: What did they say he looked like?

EUTYCHUS: I'll tell you: he was grey-haired, knock-kneed, pot-bellied, big-mouthed, short, black-eyed, slanting-jawed, and a little flat-footed.

CHARINUS: That's not a man, but some chamber of horrors you're describing. Is there anything else you can say about him?

EUTYCHUS: That's all, as far as I know.

CHARINUS: Good God, that fellow with his slanting jaws has certainly hung one on my jaw! [8] I can't endure it! I've decided to go into exile. What state should I choose? Megara, Eretria, Corinth, Chalcis, Crete, Cyprus, Sicyon, Cnidus, Zacynthus, Lesbia, Boeotia?

EUTYCHUS: Why have you made that plan?

CHARINUS: Because love afflicts me.

EUTYCHUS: But tell me this: when you reach this destination which you're now choosing, if by chance you fall in love there and can't get your own way, will you go into exile again from there, and then again from the next place, if the same thing happens? What end will ever come to your exile, what limit to your flight? What country or what home can ever be lasting? Tell me that. Come then, if you leave this city, do you think you'll leave love here? If you're convinced that this will be so, if you're sure, if you're absolutely certain of it, how much better it would be for you to go off to the country somewhere and live there for awhile until your passion and love for her lose their hold on you.

CHARINUS: Are you through talking?

EUTYCHUS: I am.

CHARINUS: Your talking is useless. My mind's made up: I'm going home to greet my father and mother; then, without telling my father, I'll leave the country, or (*gloomily*) find some other plan. (*He goes into the house.*)

EUTYCHUS (*to himself*): How hastily he tore himself away and left! Oh, dear me! If he goes away, everyone will say it happened through my negligence. I'd better go hire a large force of private detectives to search for her. Then I'll go to the magistrates and beg them to give me search-warrants for all the precincts; there's no other course left to me now, I guess. (*He departs towards the forum.*)

Act Four. Scene I

(*Enter* DORIPPA *from the country.*)

DORIPPA: Since my husband sent me a message that he wasn't coming to the farm, I've followed my hunch and have come back to track down this fellow who runs away from me. (*Looking back*) But I don't see old Syra with me. Oh, there she comes at last. Hurry up!

(*Enter* SYRA, *very deliberately.*)

SYRA: I can't, for heaven's sake, with this heavy load I'm carrying.

DORIPPA: What load?

SYRA: My eighty-four years; add to that slavery, sweat, and thirst; and these bundles are a heavy burden too.

DORIPPA: Give me something to offer to this altar of our neighbour's. There, give me that laurel branch. Go on inside.

SYRA: I'm going. (SYRA *goes into the house of* LYSIMACHUS.)

DORIPPA (*approaching the altar in front of* DEMIPHO'S *house*): Apollo, grant, I pray, thy favour and thy mercy; grant safety and health to our household, and with thy mercy and kindness spare my son.

(*Enter* SYRA *hastily from the house.*)

SYRA: Oh, mercy me! Oh, dear, alas!

DORIPPA: Are you crazy? What are you crying about?

SYRA: O Dorippa, my poor Dorippa!

DORIPPA: What are you shouting for, if you please?

SYRA: There is some woman here, in the house.

DORIPPA: What's that? a woman?

SYRA: Yes, a harlot!

DORIPPA: Really?

SYRA: It was very smart of you not to stay in the country. The most stupid woman in the world could guess that she's the mistress of that fine husband of yours.

DORIPPA: Good heavens, I believe you're right.

SYRA: Come in with me, my lady Juno, to see your rival, your Alcmena.[9]

DORIPPA: My goodness, I'm coming just as fast as I can. (*They hurry into the house.*)

Act Four.   Scene II

(*Enter* LYSIMACHUS *from the forum.*)

LYSIMACHUS (*to himself*): Isn't it troublesome enough that Demipho's in love, without his becoming a spendthrift too? Why, if he'd invited ten guests to dinner, he's still bought too much. But the caterer, just like a coxswain urging on his crew, kept urging him on. Well, I've hired the caterer myself. I wonder that he hasn't come, as I ordered. But who's this coming out from my house? The door's open. (*He retires.*)

Act Four.   Scene III

(*Enter* DORIPPA *in great distress.*)

DORIPPA (*to herself*): There never was a more wretched woman than I, to be married to such a man! (*Crying*) Oh, dear me! Just look at the man! There's a fellow you can trust yourself and your possessions to, there's the fellow to whom I brought ten talents dowry! To think that I should see such a sight, to think that I should endure such an insult!

LYSIMACHUS (*aside*): Good Lord, I'm done for! My wife's come back from the country. I suppose she's seen the girl in the house. But I can't hear what she's saying from here; I'll move up closer.

DORIPPA (*to herself*): Oh, heaven help me!

LYSIMACHUS (*aside*): No, help me!

DORIPPA: I'm ruined.

LYSIMACHUS (*aside*): By Jove, I'm completely done for. She has seen her. The gods damn you, Demipho!

DORIPPA: So that's why my husband didn't want to come to the country.

LYSIMACHUS (*aside*): What can I do now, except go up and speak to her? (*Approaching* DORIPPA *with a pompous air*) Your husband bids his wife good day. Have our country-folk become citified?

DORIPPA (*savagely*): They act more decently than those who don't become countrified!

LYSIMACHUS (*pretending not to understand*): The country-folk haven't done anything wrong, have they?

DORIPPA: Not nearly so much as the city-folk, and (*threateningly*) they're not piling up nearly so much trouble for themselves, either!

LYSIMACHUS: Why, what wrong have the city-folk done? Tell me, I really want to know.

DORIPPA: You're pumping me, though you know all the time. (*Bluntly*) Who's that woman in there?

LYSIMACHUS (*innocently*): Oh, have you seen her?

DORIPPA: Yes, I have.

LYSIMACHUS: You want to know who she is?

DORIPPA: Yes, and I'll find out, too.

LYSIMACHUS (*in confusion*): You want me to tell who she is? She's— she is— (*Aside*) Oh, dear! I don't know what to say.

DORIPPA: You're stuck!

LYSIMACHUS (*aside*): Never saw a man more so.

DORIPPA: Why don't you tell me?

LYSIMACHUS: Why, if you'd let me—

DORIPPA: You should have told me long ago.

LYSIMACHUS: I can't, you interrupt me so; you jump on me as if I were guilty.

DORIPPA (*sarcastically*): I know; you're not guilty.

LYSIMACHUS: You can say that with every assurance.

DORIPPA: Then tell me.

LYSIMACHUS: I'll tell you. (*Hesitates for a long time.*)

DORIPPA: And yet, you've got to tell me.

LYSIMACHUS: She is— Do you want to know her name?

DORIPPA: You're talking nonsense; I've caught you in the act.

LYSIMACHUS: What act? She's the girl who— (*Pauses again.*)

DORIPPA: The girl who—*what*?

LYSIMACHUS: She— (*Another long pause.*)

DORIPPA: Bah! [1]

LYSIMACHUS: Well—if it weren't necessary, I shouldn't tell you.

DORIPPA: Don't you know who she is?

LYSIMACHUS: Oh, yes, I remember now; I've been made a referee in her case.

DORIPPA: A referee? Now I see; so now you've called her into a huddle with yourself!

LYSIMACHUS: No, it's this way: she's been deposited with me for safe-keeping.

DORIPPA (*sarcastically*): I understand.

LYSIMACHUS (*desperately*): It's not at all what you think.

DORIPPA: Quite prompt with denials, aren't you?

LYSIMACHUS (*aside*): This is too much for me. I'm stuck!

Act Four. Scene IV

(*Enter a* CATERER *with several attendants carrying baskets of provisions.*)

CATERER (*to his attendants*): Come on there; hurry up, you! We've got to cook a dinner for a lovesick old man. And yet, on second thought, it's for ourselves we've got to cook it, not for the man who hired us. For if a man in love has his beloved, he takes this for food: seeing, hugging, kissing, talking; I'm sure we'll go back home well-laden. Come on here. (*Noticing* LYSIMACHUS) But there's the old fellow who hired us.

LYSIMACHUS (*aside*): Good God, here's the caterer!

CATERER (*approaching* LYSIMACHUS): Here we are.

LYSIMACHUS: Go away!

CATERER: What? Go away?

LYSIMACHUS: Hush! Go away!

CATERER: Go away?

LYSIMACHUS: Get out!

CATERER: Aren't you going to dine?

LYSIMACHUS: I'm fed up already.

CATERER: But—

LYSIMACHUS: Oh, damn it!

DORIPPA: I say, there; did these men for whom you're acting as referee send you these things too?

CATERER: Is this your mistress, the one you told me you were in love with, when you were buying the food?

LYSIMACHUS: Shut up!

CATERER (*looking over* DORIPPA *with an appreciative air*): A fine figure of a woman. She's a little old, though.

LYSIMACHUS: Go to the devil!

CATERER (*apologetically*): Oh, she's all right.

LYSIMACHUS: Well, you're all wrong!

CATERER (*still trying to make up for his disparaging remark*): I'm sure she's dandy in bed.

LYSIMACHUS: Won't you get out! I'm not the fellow who hired you.

CATERER (*looking him over carefully*): What's that? Oh, yes, indeed you are—the very one.

LYSIMACHUS (*aside*): God help me!

CATERER: Your wife's in the country; and you said you hated her like a snake.

LYSIMACHUS: I told you that?

CATERER: Yes indeed, you told me.

LYSIMACHUS (*to* DORIPPA): So help me God, I never said that, (*with a meaningful wink at the* CATERER) my dear *wife*.

DORIPPA: Do you still deny it? Why, it's plain as day that you hate me.

LYSIMACHUS: Of course I deny it.

CATERER (*helpfully, to* DORIPPA): Now, no; he didn't say he hated you, but his wife; and he said his wife was in the country.

LYSIMACHUS (*to* CATERER, *in a low voice*): This is she. Why are you such a nuisance?

CATERER: Because you said you didn't know me; but perhaps you're afraid of her.

LYSIMACHUS (*aloud*): And wisely, too; for she's my only sweetheart.

CATERER: Do you want to try my talents?

LYSIMACHUS: No.

CATERER: Give me my wages then.

LYSIMACHUS: Come back tomorrow; you'll get them. And now get out.

DORIPPA: Oh, Lord help me!

LYSIMACHUS (*aside*): Now I am learning the truth of that old proverb: it's a bad business to have a bad neighbour.

CATERER (*to attendants*): Why are we standing around here? Let's go. (*To* LYSIMACHUS) If you've got into trouble, it's not my fault.

LYSIMACHUS: Why, you're just killing me.

CATERER (*slyly*): I know what you want; you want me to get out of here, don't you?

LYSIMACHUS: Yes, indeed.

CATERER: We'll go. But—give me a drachma.

LYSIMACHUS: You shall have it.

CATERER: Well then, bid someone pay it to me now. It can be paid me while my attendants are setting down the provisions.

LYSIMACHUS: Won't you get out? Can't you stop making a nuisance of yourself?

CATERER (*to his attendants*): Come on; set the food down there at the feet of the old fellow. I'll have someone fetch these utensils by and by —tomorrow. Come along. (*The* CATERER *and his attendants depart.*)

LYSIMACHUS (*hesitantly*): Perhaps you're wondering about that caterer —why he came and brought all this. I'll tell you what it is.

DORIPPA: I don't wonder at any of your ruinous and disgraceful actions. I won't put up with it—to be married like this and have whores taken into my house! (*Calling into the house*) Syra, go and ask my father in my name, to come back here with you.

(*Enter* SYRA *from the house.*)

SYRA: Yes, ma'am. (*She departs.*)

LYSIMACHUS (*desperately*): Please, my dear, you don't understand the affair. I'll swear a solemn oath that I never had anything to do with —has Syra left already? (DORIPPA *stalks into the house*) God damn it! Now *she's* gone too. Oh dear, oh dear! May all the devils in Hell ruin you, neighbour, with your mistress and love-life too! He's overwhelmed me with the most unfair suspicions, and stirred up my house against me. And my wife has a fierce temper. I'll go to the market and tell Demipho I'll drag the girl out into the street by the hair, unless he takes her off somewhere from my house. (*Calling into the house*) Hello there, wife! Even though you're mad at me, you'll have these provisions taken inside, if you're smart; we'll have a better dinner on them by and by. (*He departs to the forum.*)

Act Four. Scene V

(*Enter* SYRA.)

SYRA (*to herself*): My mistress sent me to her father's, but he's not at home; they said he'd gone to the country. I'll go now and tell her.

(*Enter* EUTYCHUS, *very discouraged.*)

EUTYCHUS (*to himself*): I'm worn out from searching through the city; I can't find a trace of that girl anywhere. (*Noticing* SYRA) But mother's returned from the country; I see Syra standing in front of the house. O Syra!

SYRA: Who calls me?

EUTYCHUS: Your master and foster-child.

SYRA: Greetings, my dear child.

EUTYCHUS: Has mother returned from the country already? Answer me.

SYRA: Yes, and lucky for the whole house, too.

EUTYCHUS: Why, what's the matter?

SYRA: That fine father of yours has brought a mistress into the house.

EUTYCHUS: How's that?

SYRA: When your mother returned from the country she found her at home.

EUTYCHUS: Wow! I didn't think father was like that. Is the woman still in the house?

SYRA: Yes.

EUTYCHUS: Come with me. (*He goes into the house.*)

Act Four. Scene VI

SYRA (*to herself*): My goodness! It's a harsh law that women live by, and much more unfair, poor things, than the men's. If a man secretly takes a harlot, and his wife finds it out, the man goes unpunished. But if a wife even goes out of the house without her husband's knowledge, the man has grounds for divorce, and she's driven out. There ought to be the same law for husbands as for wives! For a good wife is satisfied with one husband; why shouldn't a man be satisfied with one woman? Goodness me, if men who secretly took harlots were punished in the same way as women who are divorced for committing some fault, I'll wager that more men would now be living alone than women. (*She goes into the house.*)

Act Five. Scene I

(*Enter* CHARINUS *from his father's house, with a sword, travelling clothes, and luggage.*)

CHARINUS (*tragically, addressing the door of his house*): O doorsills, above and below, hail and fare ye well. Today for the last time I lift my foot from mine ancestral home. All use, enjoyment, living, and nurture from this house have perished for me, have died, have passed away. Alas, I die! O ye gods of my hearth, gods of my parents, O Father Lar of this house, to you I entrust the care of my parents; see you guard them well. I shall seek another hearth and home, other household gods, another city, another state; for Attica makes me shudder. Where characters deteriorate day by day, where you cannot tell true friend from faithless foe, where your heart's desire is snatched away from you, such a state is undesirable even though you are offered a tyranny there.

Act Five. Scene II

(*Enter* EUTYCHUS *from the house of* LYSIMACHUS.)

EUTYCHUS (*to himself, without seeing* CHARINUS): O Lady Luck, mistress of men and gods, since you have brought me this longed-for hope, receive my thanks! What god is there who feels joy like mine? What I sought was at home; I have found there six good friends: Life, Friendship, Country, Joy, Sport, and Mirth. And in finding them I have sent to the devil these devilish fellows: Wrath, Enmity, Grief, Tears, Exile, Want, Loneliness, Folly, Destruction, and Obstinacy. O ye gods, just let me meet him soon!

CHARINUS (*to the audience, without seeing* EUTYCHUS): I am equipped, as you see; I cast away all pride. I am my own messmate and orderly, my own horse and groom, my own armour-bearer; I am my own commander-in-chief, and I'm the private too. I carry all I need. (*Tragically*) O Cupid, how mighty art thou! For by thy deeds, a man can reach the heights of confidence, and then again fall from security into despair!

EUTYCHUS (*to himself*): I wonder where I should go to find him.

CHARINUS: I'm determined to keep on seeking her, no matter where she's been taken. No river shall stay me, nor mountain nor sea; I fear no heat or cold, no wind or hail; I'll endure the rain, I'll suffer toil and sun and thirst. I'll not give in nor shall I rest by night or day until I find my mistress or my grave!

EUTYCHUS: I hear somebody's voice.

CHARINUS (*picking up his luggage and starting to leave*): Ye Saints who guard the traveller, watch over me, I pray.

EUTYCHUS (*noticing* CHARINUS): Ye gods, is that Charinus?

CHARINUS (*to the audience*): My fellow-citizens, farewell!

EUTYCHUS: Charinus, stop there.

CHARINUS: Who calls me back?

EUTYCHUS: Hope, Health, and Victory.

CHARINUS (*without turning*): What do you want of me?

EUTYCHUS: To go with you.

CHARINUS: Look for some other companion; these companions of mine have got me in their grip and won't let me go.

EUTYCHUS: Who are they?

CHARINUS: Care, Misery, Grief, Tears, and Sorrowing.

EUTYCHUS: Dismiss those companions; look here and come back.

CHARINUS (*resuming his journey*): If you want to talk to me, come along.

EUTYCHUS: Stop right there!

CHARINUS: You're a damn nuisance, to hold me up when I'm in a hurry. It's nearly sundown.

EUTYCHUS: If you'd hurry back here as fast as you're hurrying off there, you'd be better off: there's a fine stern wind over here; hard a-lee there! Here there's a nice, fair west wind; over there you have a foul easterly. Here there's a calm; over there you're in the midst of white-caps. Put in to shore, Charinus; don't you see that black cloud and rain looming up on the port bow? Don't you see how the heavens are filled with sunlight on the other side?

CHARINUS (*stopping*): I'm superstitious; his words worry me. I'll go back to him.

EUTYCHUS: You're a smart fellow. O Charinus, just step here to meet me; approach and give me your hand.

CHARINUS: Take it. Have you got it?

EUTYCHUS: I have.

CHARINUS: Hold on.

EUTYCHUS: Where were you going just now?

CHARINUS: Into exile.

EUTYCHUS: And how did you expect to fare there?

CHARINUS: Miserably.

EUTYCHUS: Hush! Don't fear, I'll restore you to your former happiness. You shall hear just what you most want to hear, and what will make you happy. Stay right there; I'm coming to you as a true friend, with the best wishes in the world. Your mistress—

CHARINUS: What about her?

EUTYCHUS: I know where she is.

CHARINUS: You do, for heaven's sake?

EUTYCHUS: She's safe and sound.

CHARINUS: *Where's* she safe and sound?

EUTYCHUS (*teasing*): I know.

CHARINUS: I'd rather *I* knew.

EUTYCHUS: Can't you keep your mind calm?

CHARINUS: But what if it's all at sea?

EUTYCHUS: I'll bring it into a calm and safe haven. Don't worry.

CHARINUS (*more and more excited*): For heaven's sake, please tell me at once where she is, where you saw her. Why are you silent? Tell me. You're killing me with your silence!

EUTYCHUS: She's not far away from us.

CHARINUS: Well, just show her to me, if you see her.

EUTYCHUS: I don't see her now, but I saw her a moment ago.

CHARINUS: Why don't you let me see her?

EUTYCHUS: I shall.

CHARINUS: That "shall" is a long time for a lover.

EUTYCHUS: Are you still afraid? I'll show you everything. I've no better friend alive than the man who has her; there's no one I ought to like better.

CHARINUS: I don't give a damn about *him;* I'm asking about her.

EUTYCHUS: Well, I'm telling you about her. To be sure, I did forget just now to tell you where she is.

CHARINUS: Tell me, where is she?

EUTYCHUS: In our house.

CHARINUS: O lovely house—if you're telling me the truth—a well-built house, in my opinion! (*Suspiciously*) But why should I believe you? Did you see her, or is this hearsay?

EUTYCHUS: I saw her.

CHARINUS: Who took her to your house? Tell me.

EUTYCHUS (*embarrassed*): You're asking that?

CHARINUS: Yes, I am.

EUTYCHUS: It's nothing for you to feel ashamed of, Charinus. What does it matter to you who came with her?

CHARINUS: Oh, well, provided she is there.

EUTYCHUS: She is indeed.

CHARINUS: Make whatever wish you like in return for this information.

EUTYCHUS: What if I do make a wish?

CHARINUS: Then pray the gods to grant it.

EUTYCHUS: You're making fun of me.

CHARINUS: I'm saved at last, if I see her. (*Looking at his travelling clothes*) But why don't I throw away this get-up? (*Calling into his house*) Hey there! Someone come out here and bring me a coat.

EUTYCHUS: Ah, that's the way I like to see you.

(*Enter a slave from the house of* DEMIPHO.)

CHARINUS: You've come in the nick of time, my boy. (*He takes off his heavy travelling-coat*) Take this overcoat and stand here. If this story isn't true, I'll continue my journey.

EUTYCHUS: Don't you believe me?

CHARINUS: I believe everything you tell me. But why don't you take me in to see her.

EUTYCHUS: Wait a minute.

CHARINUS: Why should I wait?

EUTYCHUS: It's not time to go in.

CHARINUS: You're killing me!

EUTYCHUS: There's no need to go in now, I say.

CHARINUS: Answer me this: why not?

EUTYCHUS (*somewhat embarrassed*): She's not free.

CHARINUS: Why not?

EUTYCHUS: Because it isn't convenient for her.

CHARINUS (*sarcastically*): Really? It's not convenient for her, when she loves me and I love her? (*To himself*) The fellow's making a complete fool of me. I'm an idiot to believe him. He's holding me up. I'll put on my heavy-coat again. (*Removes his civilian coat.*)

EUTYCHUS: Wait a minute and listen to me.

CHARINUS: Take this coat, please, my boy. (*Hands coat to the slave.*)

EUTYCHUS (*desperately*): Mother's terribly angry at father because he brought a harlot into her house under her very nose, while she was in the country; she suspects that she's his mistress.

CHARINUS (*paying no attention*): I'm buckling my belt.

EUTYCHUS: Now she's looking into the matter.

CHARINUS: Now I've got my sword in hand.

EUTYCHUS: You see, if I take you in—

CHARINUS: Now for my water-bottle, and then away!

EUTYCHUS: Wait, wait, Charinus!

CHARINUS: You're wrong; you can't fool me that way.

EUTYCHUS: I don't even want to.

CHARINUS: Well then, why don't you let me proceed on my journey?

EUTYCHUS: I won't let you.

CHARINUS: I'm delaying myself. (*To the slave*) Go into the house, you! (*The slave goes in;* CHARINUS *dashes wildly to the front of the stage and strikes an attitude*) Now I've mounted my chariot; I've got the reins in my hands.

EUTYCHUS (*backing away timidly*): You're crazy!

CHARINUS (*wildly*): Now then, feet; spur yourselves and sprint for Cyprus, since my father orders my exile.

EUTYCHUS: You're silly; don't say that.

CHARINUS: I've determined to follow out my plan and undertake the task of tracking down my love.

EUTYCHUS: Why, she's at home.

CHARINUS: For yonder fellow tells nought but lies.

EUTYCHUS: I'm telling you the truth, I say.

CHARINUS (*dashing around the stage*): Now I've come to Cyprus.

EUTYCHUS (*timorously plucking at his mantle*): Just come with me to see the girl you're seeking.

CHARINUS (*paying no attention*): I've inquired, but did not find her.

EUTYCHUS: I don't care about mother's temper.

CHARINUS: I continue on my quest. Now I've come to Chalcis; I see there a friend from Zacynthus; I tell him why I've come; I ask him who has taken her and if he's heard who has her.

EUTYCHUS: Why don't you stop that nonsense and walk right into the house here with me?

CHARINUS: My friend tells me that Zacynthian figs aren't bad.

EUTYCHUS: That's no lie.

CHARINUS: But as for my mistress, he says he heard she was here in Athens.

EUTYCHUS: That Zacynthian is a regular Calchas.

CHARINUS: I board ship, set out for there. Now I'm home, I've returned from exile. (*Looking around and apparently noticing* EUTYCHUS *for the first time*) Greetings, my dear friend; how are you, Eutychus? How are my parents? Mother and father well? Very kind of you to ask me; thank you very much. Tomorrow I'll dine with you; today I must dine at home. That's the way it ought to be.

EUTYCHUS (*a little overpowered*): Gracious! Are you dreaming? The fellow's crazy!

CHARINUS (*cheerfully*): Why then, hurry up and give me a treatment, like a good fellow.

EUTYCHUS: Follow me, please.

CHARINUS: I'm coming. (*They start for* LYSIMACHUS' *house.*)

EUTYCHUS: Take it easy, please; you're stepping on my heels. (*As* CHARINUS *pays no attention*) Do you hear?

CHARINUS: I heard you long ago.

EUTYCHUS (*pausing at the door*): I want father to make up with mother; for now she's so angry—

CHARINUS (*impatiently*): Go on!

EUTYCHUS: —because of your—

CHARINUS: *Go on!*

EUTYCHUS: Well then, take care.

CHARINUS: Why don't you go on? I'll make her as gentle as Juno is to Jupiter—when she is gentle. (*They go into the house of* LYSIMACHUS.)

Act Five.   Scene III

(*Enter* DEMIPHO *and* LYSIMACHUS *from the forum.*)

DEMIPHO: As if you never did anything like this!

LYSIMACHUS: Never, by God! I took good care not to do anything. (*Plaintively*) Oh, dear, I'm nearly dead! My wife's just boiling over on account of that girl.

DEMIPHO: I'll get you out of it; she won't be angry.

LYSIMACHUS: Come along with me. But here's my son coming out.

Act Five.   Scene IV

(*Enter* EUTYCHUS *from his father's house.*)

EUTYCHUS (*speaking to* CHARINUS *within the house*): I'll go to father and tell him that mother has quieted down. I'll be right back.

LYSIMACHUS: I like that beginning. (*To* EUTYCHUS) How are you? What's new, Eutychus?

EUTYCHUS: Good! You've both come in the nick of time.

LYSIMACHUS: What's the matter?

EUTYCHUS: Your wife has been appeased and calmed down. Give me your hands.

LYSIMACHUS (*shaking his son's hand*): God bless me!

EUTYCHUS (*to* DEMIPHO): As for you, I announce that you have no mistress.

DEMIPHO: God damn *you*! What business of yours is that, if you please?

EUTYCHUS: I'll tell you. Pay attention, both of you.

LYSIMACHUS: Why, we're both at your service.

EUTYCHUS (*impressively*): When men of noble birth have bad characters, it's their own fault if they suffer loss and disgrace their birth.[1]

DEMIPHO: That's very true.

LYSIMACHUS: It's for you that he says it.

EUTYCHUS: In this case it's even more true. (*To* DEMIPHO) It wasn't fair for you, at your age, to take away your son's mistress, when he'd bought her with his own money.

DEMIPHO (*in surprise*): What's that you say? Is she Charinus' mistress?

EUTYCHUS: As if he didn't know, the rogue!

DEMIPHO: But he said he'd bought her as a maid for his mother.

EUTYCHUS: So that's the reason *you* bought her, you young lover, you ancient Don Juan?

LYSIMACHUS: Bravo! Go on! I'll stand here on his other side, and we'll both load him with the remarks he deserves.

DEMIPHO (*weakly*): I'm a goner!

LYSIMACHUS: To harm his innocent son so!

EUTYCHUS: Yes indeed; and he was going into exile too, but I brought him home; for he really was going.

DEMIPHO: He was going?

LYSIMACHUS: Are you still talking, you goblin? At your age you ought to refrain from such practices.

DEMIPHO: I've done wrong; I admit it.

EUTYCHUS: Still talking, you goblin? At your age you ought to be free from such vices. Like the seasons of the year, each age has its fitting task; now, if it were the rule for old men to go with harlots, where in the world would our country be?

DEMIPHO: Oh, dear! I'm done for.

LYSIMACHUS: This sort of activity is more the practice of young men.

DEMIPHO: For mercy's sake, keep her for yourselves, bag and baggage.

EUTYCHUS: Give her back to your son.

DEMIPHO: Let him have her; as far as I'm concerned, he can have her as he likes.

EUTYCHUS (*ironically*): It's about time, since there's no chance for you to do anything else.

DEMIPHO: I'll suffer any punishment he wants for this injury; only do appease him for me, so he won't be angry at me. By Jove, if I'd only known, or if he'd told me even in jest that he loved her, I'd never have taken her away from him, since he loves her. Eutychus, I beg you: you're his best friend; save me and come to my aid. I put my case into your hands; you'll find me eternally grateful for the kindness.

LYSIMACHUS (*ironically*): Beg him to pardon your mistake and your extreme youth.

DEMIPHO: Are you still at it? Bah! What a haughty prosecutor! I just hope some day the time will come when I can repay you in kind.

LYSIMACHUS: I've said good-bye to all that.

DEMIPHO: And so have I, from this moment on.

EUTYCHUS: Nonsense! You've got the habit now; you'll go right back to it.

DEMIPHO: For heaven's sake, haven't you had enough? Why, you can whip me into little pieces, if you like.

LYSIMACHUS: Right you are. But your wife will do that, when she finds out about this.

DEMIPHO (*frightened*): There's no need for her to know.

EUTYCHUS: All right. She won't find out; don't worry. Let's go in; this spot isn't well-chosen: while we are talking the passersby can learn all about your business.

DEMIPHO: By Jove, you're right. At the same time, our play will be shorter. Let's go.

EUTYCHUS: Your son is here at our house.

DEMIPHO: Excellent. We'll cross over to my house through the garden there.

LYSIMACHUS (*nervously*): Eutychus, there's a little matter I want discussed before I step into the house.

EUTYCHUS: What is it?

LYSIMACHUS: Every man looks out for himself. Now answer this question: are you certain your mother isn't angry at me?

EUTYCHUS: I'm certain.

LYSIMACHUS: Just think a minute.

EUTYCHUS: I give you my word.

LYSIMACHUS: I'm content. (*After a pause*) Please, consider it again.

EUTYCHUS: Don't you believe me?

LYSIMACHUS: Oh, yes, I believe you, but I'm just so scared.

DEMIPHO: Let's go in.

EUTYCHUS: Wait. I move we pass a new law for old men before we go; let them keep and abide by the following law: (*in a formal, singsong tone*)

"WHEREAS men over sixty years of age, whether married or single, do, with evil intent and malice aforethought, consort with harlots,

BE IT RESOLVED THAT in the future they shall be dealt with according to the law, as follows:

Item one: they shall be considered stupid.

Item two: they shall come to want, in so far as in us lies, when they have wasted their property and possessions.

FURTHER, BE IT RESOLVED THAT no one shall prevent a young son from falling in love or having a mistress, within decent limits. If anyone tries to prohibit this, he shall lose more than if he had openly provided the necessary cash.

This law is to be in force from this night on."

(*To the audience*) Fare you well; and if this law pleases you, young men, in honour of the old men you ought to give us a hearty applause.

1. The text is corrupt here.
2. There is a slight lacuna in the text at this point.
3. There is a play in the original between *arare*, "to plough," and *amare*, "to love."
4. The literal meaning is "a fly."
5. Pasicompsa, a Greek name, means literally "altogether charming."
6. The passage in the original plays on words taken from the task of weaving; the more familiar idea of threading a needle has been substituted.
7. These two verses seem out of place here; they occur again in lines 842-3.
8. There is a pun in the Latin on *mala*, "jaws," and *malum*, "evil."
9. Jupiter's love affair with Alcmena is treated by Plautus in his *Amphitryon*.

XII
THE BRAGGART WARRIOR

Characters in the Play

PYRGOPOLYNICES, *the braggart warrior*
ARTOTROGUS, *his parasite*
PALAESTRIO, *slave of* PLEUSICLES, *now in the power of* PYRGOPOLYNICES
PERIPLECTOMENUS, *an old gentleman of Ephesus*
SCELEDRUS, *slave of* PYRGOPOLYNICES
PHILOCOMASIUM, *a girl abducted by* PYRGOPOLYNICES
PLEUSICLES, *a young Athenian, in love with* PHILOCOMASIUM
LURCIO, *a slave boy, belonging to* PYRGOPOLYNICES
ACROTELEUTIUM, *a courtesan*
MILPHIDIPPA, *her maid*
A SLAVE BOY, *belonging to* PERIPLECTOMENUS
CARIO, *the cook of* PERIPLECTOMENUS

Argument I (Acrostic)

A soldier carries off a courtesan from Athens to Ephesus. The young man in love with the girl is on an embassy abroad; his slave tries to get word of the abduction to his master, but is himself captured at sea and handed over as a gift to this same soldier. The slave summons his master from Athens and secretly digs a passage through the party wall of the two houses so that the two lovers may meet. The girl's watchman sees them embracing each other from the roof, and, by an amusing deception, he is made to believe that she is another girl. Moreover, Palaestrio persuades the soldier to give up his concubine, saying that the wife of the old man next door wants to marry him. The soldier of his own accord begs the girl to go away, and gives her many presents. He himself is caught in the home of the old man and is punished as an adulterer.

Argument II

A young man of Athens and a freeborn courtesan were madly in love with each other; he left home and went to Naupactus on an embassy. A soldier comes upon the girl and carries her off to Ephesus against her will. The slave of the Athenian sets sail to tell his master of the abduction; he is captured and is handed over as a captive to that same soldier. The slave writes to his master and tells him to come to Ephesus. The young man hurries there and puts up at the house next door with a friend of his father. The slave digs a hole in the wall between the two houses so that the lovers may meet secretly. He pretends that the girl's twin sister is next door. Then the master of the house furnishes Palaestrio with a protégée of his own to arouse the soldier's passion. The soldier is deceived, hopes for marriage, sends away his mistress, and is flogged as an adulterer.

INTRODUCTION

THE VAIN and boastful soldier, always eager to exaggerate his deeds, was a popular character in ancient comedy. Both Greeks and Romans found great delight in seeing such persons portrayed and ridiculed on the stage. The professional soldier did not yet exist at Rome, but had long been known in Greece, and many Romans had doubtless themselves seen such warriors in southern Italy or in Sicily. Plautus in several plays made an effective use of this character; Cleomachus (in *The Two Bacchides*), Therapontigonus (in the *Curculio*), the unnamed soldier of the *Epidicus*, Antamoenides (in *The Carthaginian*), Stratophanes (in the *Truculentus*) all present different aspects of the vain and stupid soldier, but these are secondary characters and pale by comparison with Pyrgopolynices, the central character of *The Braggart Warrior* (the *Miles Gloriosus*) and one of Plautus' most brilliant creations. Pyrgopolynices is not only a man-killer like the others, but a lady-killer as well. He is convinced both of his bravery and his beauty and thinks that all women are crazy about him. It is this latter trait which makes possible the action of the play.

Through a complicated series of circumstances Pyrgopolynices has at his house in Ephesus both a girl Philocomasium and a slave Palaestrio, formerly the slave of a young Athenian Pleusicles. Pleusicles and Philocomasium were in love with each other before the soldier brought her to Ephesus against her will. Palaestrio gets word to Pleusicles who comes and stays next door with a very helpful old gentleman, Periplectomenus. Since the houses have a common wall, Palaestrio digs a hole through the wall so that Philocomasium can visit her lover in the neighbour's house. Sceledrus, another of the soldier's slaves, sees from the roof the young couple kissing and embracing each other. There follows a series of amusing scenes in which Palaestrio, with the aid of Philocomasium, convinces his fellow slave that he has not seen the soldier's mistress but her twin sister. When this ruse succeeds, Palaestrio devises his main trick which is directed at the soldier. The purpose is to get the soldier to send away both Philocomasium and Palaestrio of his own free will. The deception is ingenious and involves an elaborate pretense on the part of a courtesan who poses as the neighbour's wife in love with the soldier. The soldier, being what he is, cannot help falling into the trap. The situation is filled with comic irony, for Pyrgopolynices, like Periphanes in the *Epidicus,* thinks that his slave is working in his behalf.

The comedy has been criticised for the elaborate discussion of the trickery in advance and for the lack of suspense which results. It should be noted, however, that no deception in Plautus is more elaborate; Palaestrio has five helpers who all have their parts to play, and there is far greater need for preparation than usual. The very repetition of the instructions provides an element of humour. Furthermore, the dramatist introduces excellent suspense into the parting scene (Act Four, Scene VIII), where the suspicions of the soldier are almost aroused and there is danger of the whole plan collapsing. Palaestrio himself almost overdoes his reluctance to leave the soldier, but is clever enough to avoid the trap of his own making. He is one of the best of Plautus' intriguing slaves and deserves to be ranked with Chrysalus (in *The Two Bacchides*) or with Pseudolus.

The title of the Greek original (*The Braggart*) is known, but not its author. Many scholars who believe that Plautus practiced *contaminatio,* i.e. combined parts from two or more Greek plays into one Latin play, point to *The Braggart Warrior* as one of the most certain examples of this procedure; the play has two deceptions, either one of which, they say, would be sufficient to achieve the desired goal of Philocomasium's departure with Pleusicles. The first trick—that of the twin sister and the hole in the wall—is one version of a famous story which has appeared in various forms in numerous Arabian tales and in European stories of the Middle Ages. It is suggested that this part of the play came from a different source, a Greek play or novel related in some way to the original version of the many mediaeval stories. There are several objections to this view of the structure of the play. There is no reason to assume that the passageway through the wall had any other purpose in the play except to provide a means of communication for the lovers. Furthermore, the only satisfactory solution is for the soldier himself to send away both the girl and the slave. He must be made the victim of his own lustful desires. Mere flight would be disastrous for Palaestrio, since he could be brought back and punished as a runaway slave. The two deceptions in the play supplement each other and are in no way mutually exclusive, as has often been wrongly asserted.

In spite of some structural flaws and some unnecessarily long and irrelevant scenes, *The Braggart Warrior* is one of Plautus' most amusing comedies, and is usually considered one of his best. In addition to the soldier whose stupidity and lechery motivate much of the action, there are several excellently drawn characters. Periplectomenus, the genial bachelor, discourses at great length on the blessings of celibacy and the affectations of the society of his day. Philocomasium is faithful to Pleusicles and represents the higher type of courtesan so well portrayed by Philematium in *The Haunted House*. Acroteleutium, the pseudo-wife, is a very different type, clever, impudent, and not ashamed to admit her depravity. She is often compared to Cleareta in *The Comedy of Asses* or to Phronesium in the *Truculentus*. *The Braggart Warrior* is a long play—the longest in Roman comedy—and there are many excellent scenes. Pyrgopolynices and his parasite in the opening scene, and the deception of Sceledrus in Act Two provide delightful comedy; in Act Four the second, sixth, and eighth scenes are splendid illustrations of the way the soldier is duped by the various woman characters.

The reference to Naevius, the Roman poet, in lines 211 f. dates the play about 206-204 B.C. It is thus one of Plautus' earlier plays and this is confirmed by its relatively simple metrical structure and the almost complete lack of song in changing lyric meters. C. H. Buck points out that in 205 B.C. the Plebeian Games were given eight times instead of the officially ordained single performance. He believes that *The Braggart Warrior* was produced at this time and that it was the popularity of the play which accounts for the unusually large number of repeated performances of the festival.

The character of the boastful soldier was very popular in later European comedy. Pyrgopolynices appears in various forms—as Torquato in Dolce's *Il Capitano* (1560), as Captain Taillebras in Baif's *Le Brave* (1567), as Captain Matamore in Corneille's *L'Illusion Comique* (1636), as Matamore in Mareschal's *Le Capitan Fanfaron* (1640). The influence of Plautus' play and its chief character is apparent on plays by Aretino, Cecchi, Scarron, Cyrano de Bergerac, Goldoni, Cailhava, Lenz, Holberg, and other dramatists. The boastful coward appears in English drama in *Thersites* (1537) and in Udall's famous *Ralph Roister Doister* (1553). Shakespeare's Falstaff and Pistol, Sir Tophas in Lilly's *Endimion* (c. 1585) and Captain Bobadill in Jonson's *Every Man in His Humour* (1598) are later developments of the same amusing soldier. Few characters of ancient comedy have had a more extended influence.

THE BRAGGART WARRIOR

(SCENE:—*A street in Ephesus in front of the adjoining houses of* PYRGOPOLYNICES *and* PERIPLECTOMENUS.)

Act One

(*Enter* PYRGOPOLYNICES *from his house, followed by* ARTOTROGUS *and orderlies; the latter carry an enormous shield.*)

PYRGOPOLYNICES (*to the orderlies, as he struts about*): Take pains to make my shield shine far more brilliantly than do the rays of the sun when the sky is cloudless; when the need arises and the conflict commences, I want it to dazzle the enemy's sight on the battle-site. (*Examining his sword*) Now I wish to comfort this poor blade of mine, so that it won't be miserable or downcast at heart because it's been hanging here at my side so long on a holiday; it's awfully eager to make mincemeat of the enemy. But where is Artotrogus?

ARTOTROGUS (*stepping forward*): He stands beside a man who's brave and blessed and as beautiful as a prince; and as to your fame as a fighter—Mars himself wouldn't dare mention it, or compare his achievements with yours.

PYRGOPOLYNICES: Was that the fellow I saved in the battle of Weevil Plains, where the commander in chief was Bumbomachides Clutomestoridysarchides, the grandson of Neptune?

ARTOTROGUS: Ah, I remember. You mean the one with the golden armour, whose legions you puffed away with a breath, just as the wind blows away leaves or a thatched roof.

PYRGOPOLYNICES: Heavens! That was a mere nothing.

ARTOTROGUS: A mere nothing, to be sure, compared to the other deeds I could mention—(*aside*) which you never did. (*To the audience, in a disgusted tone*) If anyone has seen a greater liar or a bigger bundle of conceit than this fellow, he can have me as his own and I'll guarantee

548

the title. (*Pauses*) There's one thing to consider, though; his olive salad is excellent eating.

PYRGOPOLYNICES (*looking around*): Where are you?

ARTOTROGUS (*coming to attention*): Right here, sir. Gad! That elephant in India, for instance! How you smashed its forearm with your fist!

PYRGOPOLYNICES: What? Forearm?

ARTOTROGUS: Foreleg, I meant to say.

PYRGOPOLYNICES: I didn't hit very hard.

ARTOTROGUS: Of course not. If you had really put your strength into it, your arm would have transpierced the elephant all the way through, hide, flesh, bone, and all.

PYRGOPOLYNICES: I'd rather not talk about this now.

ARTOTROGUS: Heavens! It really isn't worth while for you to tell me about it; I know all your achievements. (*Aside*) It's my belly that's responsible for all my sufferings. I have to 'ear him with my ears, so that my dental work can make dents in food; and I have to agree to any lie he tells.

PYRGOPOLYNICES: What was it that I was saying?

ARTOTROGUS: Ah! I know already what you want to say. Heavens! You did it. I remember that you did it.

PYRGOPOLYNICES: Did what?

ARTOTROGUS: Whatever it is you did.

PYRGOPOLYNICES: Do you have—

ARTOTROGUS (*interrupting*): You want a tablet. I have it, and a pen, too.

PYRGOPOLYNICES: Clever of you to be so attentive with your attention.

ARTOTROGUS: It's right for me to know your character through and through and to take pains that I get the first whiff of your wishes.

PYRGOPOLYNICES: Well, what do you recall?

ARTOTROGUS (*calculating*): Let me see. I recall there were one hundred and fifty in Cilicia, a hundred in Scythobrigandia, thirty Sardians, sixty Macedonians—those are the men you slaughtered in one day.

PYRGOPOLYNICES: And what's the sum total of the men?

ARTOTROGUS: Seven thousand.

PYRGOPOLYNICES: Yes, that's what it ought to be. Your calculation is quite correct.

ARTOTROGUS: I don't write any of it down, either; I just rely on my memory.

PYRGOPOLYNICES: Well, you've a damned excellent one.

ARTOTROGUS (*aside*): The thought of food helps it.

PYRGOPOLYNICES: If you behave as you have in the past, you'll have plenty to eat; I shall always share my table with you.

ARTOTROGUS (*eager for more praise*): What about the time in Cappadocia, when you would have killed five hundred men all with one stroke, if your sword hadn't been dull?

PYRGOPOLYNICES: But they were worthless infantrymen; I let them live.

ARTOTROGUS: Why should I tell you what all mortals know, that you are the one and only Pyrgopolynices on earth, unsurpassed in valour, in beauty, and in brave deeds? All the women are in love with you, and not without reason, since you're so handsome. Take, for instance, those girls yesterday who caught me by my cloak.

PYRGOPOLYNICES (*concealing his eagerness*): What did they say to you?

ARTOTROGUS: They kept asking about you. "Is this fellow Achilles?" one of them says to me. "No," says I, "but it is his brother." Then the other one says to me, "Dear me, but he's handsome, and such a gentleman, too. Just look how lovely his hair is. The women that sleep with him are certainly lucky."

PYRGOPOLYNICES: Did they really say that?

ARTOTROGUS: Why, didn't both of them beg me to lead you past there today, as if you were on parade?

PYRGOPOLYNICES (*pretending indifference*): It's such a nuisance for a man to be so handsome.

ARTOTROGUS: Absolutely right, sir. They're a bother to me; they beg, urge, beseech to be allowed to see you; they keep sending for me, so that I can't devote myself to your business.

PYRGOPOLYNICES: Well, I guess that it's time for us to go to the forum, so that I can pay the recruits I enlisted here yesterday. King Seleucus earnestly requested me to collect and enlist recruits for him. I've decided to devote this day to the king.

ARTOTROGUS: Well, then, let's do it.

PYRGOPOLYNICES (*to the orderlies*): After me, you attendants! (*All march off towards the forum.*)

Act Two.   Scene I[1]

(*Enter* PALAESTRIO *from the house of* PYRGOPOLYNICES.)

PALAESTRIO (*to the audience*): I wish to oblige you by outlining the plot of our play, if you will all be kind enough to listen. Moreover, if anyone should not desire to listen, he may arise and leave, so that there will be a seat for the person who does so desire. Now as to your reason for assembling in this festive spot, I shall tell you both the plot and the name of the comedy which we are about to present. The name of this comedy in Greek is *Alazon,* and we translate it into Latin as *Gloriosus.*[2] This is the city of Ephesus. That soldier who just went off to the forum is my master, a bragging, impudent stinker, filled with lies and lechery; he says all the women chase after him. Actually, wherever he goes, he's the laughingstock of them all. And consequently most of the harlots you see here have wry mouths from twisting their lips at him.

Now, I've not been a servant in his service very long. I want you all to know how I came into his service and ceased to serve my former master. Give me your attention, for now I shall begin the plot.

My master in Athens was an excellent young man. He was in love with a courtesan who lived in Athens in Attica, and she returned his love—which is the nicest kind of love to cherish. He was sent as state envoy to Naupactus on a matter concerning the welfare of the state. Meanwhile this soldier happens to come to Athens and works his way to an acquaintance with my master's sweetheart. He began to entice her mother with wine and jewelry and dainty delicacies, and he gets on most intimate terms with the old procuress there. Then, as soon as he had the chance, he bamboozled the procuress, the mother of the girl my master loved; for he put the daughter on board ship without the knowledge of her mother and carried the girl here to Ephesus against her will.

When I learned that my master's mistress had been carried off from Athens, I got myself a ship as quickly as I possibly could and set sail to tell the news to my master at Naupactus. When we were out on the deep, the will of the gods was done; pirates capture the ship on which I was sailing; I was lost before I could get my message to my master. The man who captured me gave me as a gift to this same soldier. When he takes me home to his dwelling, I see there the girl who had been my master's mistress at Athens. When she saw me there before her, she gave me a signal with her eyes not to let on that I knew her; later, when there was an opportunity, she complained to me of her bitter fate; she said that she was anxious to get away from the house and escape to Athens, for she loved that master of mine who lived in Athens and detested no one more thoroughly than that soldier.

When I realised how the girl really felt, I seized a tablet, sealed it, and slipped it to a certain merchant to deliver to my master, the Athenian one who loved her; I urged him to come here. He didn't disregard the message; he's arrived and is staying here next door with a friend of his father's, a lovely old gentleman, who is assisting his guest in his love affair and aiding and abetting us with his help and advice. Consequently, I've prepared a delightful device inside here, to enable the lovers to be together. The soldier gave his concubine a certain room where no one but herself was to set foot; I dug a hole through the wall of that room so that the girl could have a secret passage from the soldier's house to this one (*pointing to the house of* PERIPLECTOMENUS); I did this with the knowledge of the old gentleman; in fact, he suggested it.

Now, this fellow slave of mine that the soldier selected to keep watch over his concubine is an utterly worthless fellow. With clever contrivances and deceitful devices we'll throw dust in his eyes and make him admit that he hasn't seen what he has seen. And to keep you from being confused, this one girl today will play the part of two girls, one from each house; she'll be the same one, but will pretend to be a different one. In that way the guard of the girl will be completely fooled. But I hear the door of the old man's house next door. The man's coming out. This is the charming old gentleman I just mentioned.

Act Two. Scene II

(*Enter* PERIPLECTOMENUS *from his house.*)

PERIPLECTOMENUS (*to slaves within*): Damn it! I'll cut your sides into strips if you don't break the legs of any stranger you see on the roof after this. Already, I suppose, my neighbours know what's going on in my house; imagine, their looking in through the skylight! Here are my orders now to all of you: any person from the soldier's house that you see on our roof, with the one exception of Palaestrio, is to be hurled headlong down to the street! It doesn't make any difference whether he says he chasing a chicken, or a dove, or a monkey; you're done for if you don't batter his body to death! And to keep them from breaking the Dicing Law, be sure that they haven't any bones left when they give a party at home.

PALAESTRIO (*aside*): Something's amiss, to judge from his words, and somebody from our house is to blame; that's why the old man wants the bones of my fellow slaves to be crushed. But he made an exception of me, and I don't give a damn what happens to the rest of them. I'll approach him. (*He advances.*)

PERIPLECTOMENUS: Isn't this Palaestrio coming towards me?

PALAESTRIO: How do you do, Periplectomenus?

PERIPLECTOMENUS: There aren't many men, if I had my choice, that I'd rather see and meet right now than you.

PALAESTRIO: What's up? What trouble are you having with our household?

PERIPLECTOMENUS: We're ruined!

PALAESTRIO: What's the matter?

PERIPLECTOMENUS: It's known.

PALAESTRIO: What's known?

PERIPLECTOMENUS: Somebody from your house, on the roof just now, looked in through the skylight and saw Philocomasium and my guest kissing each other here in my house.

PALAESTRIO: Who's the person that saw it?

PERIPLECTOMENUS: A fellow slave of yours.

PALAESTRIO: Who was he?

PERIPLECTOMENUS: I don't know. He dashed off too quickly.

PALAESTRIO: I suspect that I'm done for!

PERIPLECTOMENUS: As he hurried off, I shouted after him. "Hey, you!" says I, "What are you doing on the roof?" "Chasing a monkey," says he, and off he goes.

PALAESTRIO: Damnation! To be ruined on account of a worthless beast like that! But is Philocomasium still here in your house?

PERIPLECTOMENUS: She was when I came out.

PALAESTRIO: Go, please, and tell her to come over to our house as quickly as possible, so that the slaves can see her at home—that is, unless she wants all of us slaves to be admitted to the Companionship of the Cross just on account of her love affair.

PERIPLECTOMENUS: I did tell her that. Anything else you wish?

PALAESTRIO: Yes. Tell her this too: she's not to depart a single inch from women's wiles, and she's to cherish all the cleverness and skill they have.

PERIPLECTOMENUS: In what way?

PALAESTRIO: So that she can convince the fellow who saw her here that he didn't see her. Even if she were seen here a hundred times, she's still to deny it. She's got plenty of cheek and a smooth tongue, and she's treacherous, cunning, and confident; she's full of conceitedness, resoluteness, deceitfulness. If anyone accuses her, she's to prove the opposite on her solemn oath; she's got a goodly supply of crooked talk, crooked tricks, crooked oaths; she's stocked with cunning, with captivating caresses, with crafty contraptions. As a matter of fact, sir, a woman who's wicked enough never applies to a gardener; she has her own garden stuff with plenty of seasoning for serving up every kind of corruption.

PERIPLECTOMENUS (*a little weary*): I'll tell her all this, if she's still inside. (*As* PALAESTRIO *becomes thoughtful*) What is it, Palaestrio, that you're turning over in your mind?

PALAESTRIO: Be silent a moment, please, while I call together a council in my heart and consider what to do, what device to draw up against my devilish fellow slave who saw her kissing here, so that what was seen will be unseen.

PERIPLECTOMENUS: Think carefully. In the meantime I'll step over here a bit. (*He moves away and comments to himself as he watches* PALAESTRIO's *gesticulations*) Just look at that, now, how he stands there, with frowning brow, considering and cogitating. With his fingers he's knocking at the door of his breast; he's going to invite his intelligence to come out, I imagine. There, he turns away. He rests his left hand on his left thigh, and with the fingers of his right does some calculating. Now he slaps his right thigh! A right lusty blow! He's having a difficult time deciding what to do. Now he's snapped his fingers; what a struggle! He constantly changes his position. But look at that! He's shaking his head; he doesn't like that notion. No matter what it is, he won't put forth a half-baked idea; he'll provide one well done. And now look! (*As* PALAESTRIO *rests his head on his arm*) He's doing some building; supporting his chin on a column. The devil with it! I don't like that style of building. I've heard it said that a foreign poet had a columned countenance and two guards always on watch day and night.[3] (*As* PALAESTRIO *changes his position*) Bravo! How becoming! By Jove, he stands there just like slaves in comedies. He'll never rest today until he succeeds in what he is seeking. There! He's got it, I think. (*Aloud, as* PALAESTRIO *seems to hesitate*) If you're going to do anything, do it! Wake up; don't sink into slumber, that is, unless you want to keep watch here battered with blows until you're black and blue. Yes, I'm talking to you. You didn't get drunk yesterday, did you?[4] Hey, Palaestrio! It's you I'm speaking to. Wake up, I say! Arouse yourself, I say! It's dawn, I say!

PALAESTRIO (*without enthusiasm*): I hear you.

PERIPLECTOMENUS: Don't you see that the enemy is upon you and attacking your rear? Take counsel; seize aid and assistance for this emergency. Now's the time for sweeping on, not sleeping. Steal a march in some way, lead around your army by some route; blockade the enemy, but aid our troops; shut off supplies from the foe, procure a passage so that provisions and supplies can reach you and your legions in safety. Attention! The need is urgent! Devise something, hit upon something, make haste to hatch a plot that's hot; the things that have been seen here must be unseen, or the things that have been done will be undone. The man is reaching for something big; high-reaching are the ramparts he's raising. If you say that you'll undertake it yourself, I'm confident that we can crush the foe.

PALAESTRIO: I say it and I undertake it.

PERIPLECTOMENUS: And I say that you'll gain your wish.

PALAESTRIO: May Jupiter bless you!

PERIPLECTOMENUS: Won't you inform me of your scheme?

PALAESTRIO: Hush, while I conduct you to the land of my machinations, that you may know my plots as well as I.

PERIPLECTOMENUS: You shall take back the same in safety.

PALAESTRIO: My master is covered with the hide of an elephant, instead of his own skin; he's as stupid as a stone.

PERIPLECTOMENUS: I know that.

PALAESTRIO: Now, sir, this is the plan I'll begin; this is the cunning scheme I'll set up. I'll say that Philocomasium's own true twin sister has arrived from Athens with a certain lover of hers, and that the two sisters are as much alike as two drops of milk; I'll say that they're being lodged and entertained at your house.

PERIPLECTOMENUS: Excellent! Excellent! Perfect! I praise your scheme.

PALAESTRIO (*continuing*): So if that fellow slave of mine should complain to the soldier that he saw Philocomasium here kissing a strange man, I'll assert in reply that he saw the sister here in your house embracing and kissing her own lover.

PERIPLECTOMENUS: Splendid! I'll tell the same story, if the soldier asks me about it.

PALAESTRIO: Be sure to say that they're exactly alike. And Philocomasium must be instructed so that she'll know about this and won't make a slip, if the soldier should ask her.

PERIPLECTOMENUS: A most clever contrivance! But if the soldier wants to see both of them at one time, what are we to do?

PALAESTRIO: That's easy. A thousand pretexts can be provided. "She's not at home, she's gone for a walk, she's asleep, she's dressing, she's bathing, she's dining, she's drinking; she's occupied; she's not at leisure, it's impossible." There are lots of ways of putting him off, provided we convince him at the beginning to accept our lies as the truth.

PERIPLECTOMENUS: I like what you say.

PALAESTRIO: Go in, then, and if the girl's there, tell her to return home quickly, and inform her, instruct her, advise her, so that she'll understand the scheme about the twin sister that we've started.

PERIPLECTOMENUS: I'll make her as skilled as skilled can be. Anything else?

PALAESTRIO: Just be off indoors.

PERIPLECTOMENUS: I'm off. (*He goes into his house.*)

PALAESTRIO (*to himself*): And now I'll go home and aid him secretfully by digging out the identity of that fellow slave of mine who was chasing a monkey today. He couldn't keep from informing someone in the house about his master's mistress, how he saw her kissing some strange young man here next door. I know the habit: "I just can't keep a secret all to myself." If I find the man who saw her, I'll bring up my sheds and my siege-works. Everything's prepared; I'm determined to take the fellow by force and violence. If I don't find him, I'll go sniffing about like a hunting dog until I track down the fox and overtake him. (*He pauses*) But the door of our house creaked; I'll lower my voice. Here is my fellow slave, the guard of Philocomasium, coming out.

Act Two.   Scene III

(*Enter* SCELEDRUS, *much troubled.*)

SCELEDRUS (*to himself*): Unless I was walking around on the roof in my sleep today, I know for certain that I saw Philocomasium, my master's mistress, here in the house next door bringing trouble on herself.

PALAESTRIO (*aside*): He's the one that saw her kissing, as far as I can tell from his words.

SCELEDRUS (*hearing his voice*): Who's here?

PALAESTRIO (*stepping forward*): Your fellow slave. How are you, Sceledrus?

SCELEDRUS: Awfully glad I've met you, Palaestrio.

PALAESTRIO: What is it? What's the trouble? Tell me.

SCELEDRUS: I'm afraid—

PALAESTRIO: Afraid of what?

SCELEDRUS: Damn it! That all of us slaves in the household today are going to be plunged into painful punishment.

PALAESTRIO: You plunge in alone, then; I don't care for that sort of plunging and lunging.

SCELEDRUS: Maybe you don't know about the horrible, new crime that has occurred at our house.

PALAESTRIO: What sort of crime?

SCELEDRUS: Oh, a shameless one!

PALAESTRIO: You keep it to yourself then; don't tell me. I don't want to know it.

SCELEDRUS: Well, I won't stop until you do know it. I chased our monkey today on their roof.

PALAESTRIO: By Jove, Sceledrus! A worthless beast chased by a worthless man!

SCELEDRUS: Damn you!

PALAESTRIO: You, I'd prefer— (*changing his tone*) to speak on, since you've begun.

SCELEDRUS: It just so happened that I chanced to look down through the skylight into the house next door; and there I saw Philocomasium kissing some strange young man, I don't know who.

PALAESTRIO: What's this villainy that I hear from you, Sceledrus?

SCELEDRUS: I certainly saw her.

PALAESTRIO: You yourself?

SCELEDRUS: I certainly did, with these two eyes of mine.

PALAESTRIO: Get out! What you say isn't likely. You didn't see her!

SCELEDRUS: You don't think I have sore eyes, do you?

PALAESTRIO: You'd better ask a doctor about that. But, for the love of the gods, don't be rash in fathering that fable; you're creating here a fatal disaster for your head and heels. If you don't put a stop to this stultiloquy of yours, you're destined to die a double death.

SCELEDRUS: How do you mean, double?

PALAESTRIO: I'll tell you. In the first place, if you accuse Philocomasium falsely, you're done for; in the second place, if it's true, you're done for because you're her guard.

SCELEDRUS (*worried, but stubborn*): What will happen to me I don't know; but I do know for certain that I saw this.

PALAESTRIO: Keeping right on, you poor wretch?

SCELEDRUS: What do you want me to say, except what I really saw? Why, even now she's here in the house next door.

PALAESTRIO: What! Isn't she at home?

SCELEDRUS: Go and see. Go inside, yourself. I don't expect anyone to believe me.

PALAESTRIO (*rushing towards the door*): I'm determined to do it.

SCELEDRUS: I'll wait for you here! At the same time I'll be on watch to see how soon the heifer comes back from pasture to her stall here. (*To himself, as* PALAESTRIO *goes into the house of* PYRGOPOLYNICES) What am I to do now? The soldier made me her guard; now if I reveal it, I'm ruined; I'm ruined just the same if I keep silent, if the truth leaks out. What is there more worthless or more audacious than a woman? She slipped away from her house while I was on the roof. Gad! She did a daring deed, all right. If the soldier finds out about it, damned if he won't hurl the whole house, me included, to the devil! Whatever the outcome, I'll keep still rather than come to a bad end. I just can't guard a woman that's always putting herself up for sale.

(*Re-enter* PALAESTRIO.)

PALAESTRIO: Sceledrus, Sceledrus, where on earth is there a more impudent person than you? Who was ever born when the gods were more angry and enraged?

SCELEDRUS: What's the matter?

PALAESTRIO: Why don't you order someone to gouge out your eyes, since they see things that nowhere exist?

SCELEDRUS: What? Nowhere exist?

PALAESTRIO: I wouldn't pay a rotten nut for your life.

SCELEDRUS: What's the trouble?

PALAESTRIO: You ask what's the trouble?

SCELEDRUS: Why shouldn't I ask?

PALAESTRIO: Have that talkative tongue of yours torn out, won't you?

SCELEDRUS: What for?

PALAESTRIO: Well, there Philocomasium is at home, whom you said you saw kissing and hugging some man next door.

SCELEDRUS: It seems strange that you live on darnel,[5] when wheat is so cheap.

PALAESTRIO: What do you mean?

SCELEDRUS: Because you're blear-eyed.

PALAESTRIO: You hangman's delight! You're not blear-eyed, you're blind-eyed! She's right there at home.

SCELEDRUS: What, at home?

PALAESTRIO: Damn it! She certainly is.

SCELEDRUS: Get out! You're playing with me, Palaestrio.

PALAESTRIO: Then my hands are filthy.

SCELEDRUS: How so?

PALAESTRIO: Because I'm playing with filth.

SCELEDRUS: You go to the devil!

PALAESTRIO: That'll be your fate, Sceledrus, I promise you, if you don't get yourself different eyes and ideas. (*Listening*) But our door's creaked. (*The door opens and* PHILOCOMASIUM *is visible in the doorway.*)

SCELEDRUS (*with his back to the door of* PYRGOPOLYNICES' *house and his eyes intent on* PERIPLECTOMENUS' *door*): And I'm keeping by eyes fixed on this door, for there's no way that she can get from this house to the other except right through this door.

PALAESTRIO: But look! There she is at home! Some deviltry or other possesses you, Sceledrus.

SCELEDRUS (*refusing to turn his head*): I see for myself, I think for myself, I have faith most of all in myself. No man shall keep me from believing that she is right here in this house. (*Blocking* PERIPLECTO-MENUS' *door*) I'll take my stand right here, so that she can't slip by without my knowledge.

PALAESTRIO (*aside, as* PHILOCOMASIUM *disappears and* PYRGOPOLYNICES' *door is closed*): I've got the fellow now. I'll hurl him down from his stronghold. (*To* SCELEDRUS) Want me to make you admit that you're fool-sighted?

SCELEDRUS: Go on, do it.

PALAESTRIO: And that you have neither sense in your brains nor sight in your eyes?

SCELEDRUS (*still defiant*): Yes, I want you to.

PALAESTRIO: Do you still say that master's concubine is in there?

SCELEDRUS (*watching* PERIPLECTOMENUS' *door*): Yes. And I maintain that I saw her and a strange man kissing each other inside here.

PALAESTRIO: You know, don't you, that there's no passage between our house and this one?

SCELEDRUS: I know that.

PALAESTRIO: And that there's no sun deck, no garden, no means of communication except through the skylight?

SCELEDRUS: I know that.

PALAESTRIO: Well then! If she's at home, if I have you see her come out of the house here, do you deserve a good thrashing?

SCELEDRUS: Of course.

PALAESTRIO: You watch that door, then, so that she doesn't secretly slip away from there and cross over to our house.

SCELEDRUS: Just what I'm going to do.

PALAESTRIO: I'll stand her right here in the street in front of you. (*He goes into the house of* PYRGOPOLYNICES.)

SCELEDRUS (*a little less confident*): Just go and do it, then. (*To himself*) I'd like to know whether I saw what I saw, or whether he can do what he says he'll do—prove that she's home. I certainly have eyes of my own in my head, and I don't have to go borrowing a pair from other people. (*Reflecting*) This fellow, though, is always flattering her, he's her right-hand man; he's the first to be called to dinner, he's the first to get his fodder. And yet he's been with us only about three years, and there isn't a single servant in the entire household better treated than he. But I must tend to my business here and watch this door. (*Spreading his arms before* PERIPLECTOMENUS' *door*) I'll stand like this. They'll never pull the wool over my eyes, I know that, by gad!

Act Two. Scene IV

(*Enter* PALAESTRIO *and* PHILOCOMASIUM *from the house of* PYRGO-POLYNICES.)

PALAESTRIO (*aside to* PHILOCOMASIUM): Be sure you remember my instructions.

PHILOCOMASIUM (*aside to* PALAESTRIO): I'm surprised that you warn me so often.

PALAESTRIO (*to* PHILOCOMASIUM): I'm afraid that you won't be quite cunning enough.

PHILOCOMASIUM (*to* PALAESTRIO): Why, give me ten women without a trace of deceit; I'll teach them to be full of deceit and still have an abundant supply left over for myself. Come now, push on with your trickery. I'll step aside a bit.

PALAESTRIO (*to* SCELEDRUS): Look here, Sceledrus.

SCELEDRUS (*not turning his head*): I'm tending to my job here. I have ears; say whatever you want.

PALAESTRIO (*seeing his position*): You'll soon perish outside the gate in that pose, I guess, with your arms outstretched, when you're on the cross.

SCELEDRUS: What for?

PALAESTRIO: Just look here to the left. What woman is this?

SCELEDRUS (*turning his head at last*): Immortal gods! (*Horrified*) Why, it's master's concubine!

PALAESTRIO (*dryly*): Damned if I don't think the same. But come now, when you wish—

SCELEDRUS: To do what?

PALAESTRIO: Make haste to die.

PHILOCOMASIUM (*advancing angrily*): Where is that excellent slave who falsely accused me, an innocent woman, of such shameful behaviour?

PALAESTRIO (*to* PHILOCOMASIUM): There he is. He's the one that told me what I told you.

PHILOCOMASIUM: You say that you saw me here in the house next door kissing, you rascal?

PALAESTRIO: You and some strange young man, so he told me.

SCELEDRUS: Yes, I did say it, by heaven!

PHILOCOMASIUM: It was me you saw?

SCELEDRUS: Yes, confound it! With my own eyes.

PHILOCOMASIUM: You'll soon lose them, I daresay, since they see more than they see.

SCELEDRUS: Never, by heaven, will I be frightened out of having seen what I did see.

PHILOCOMASIUM: I'm a stupid and foolish person to waste my breath on this idiot; by the powers, I'll punish him to perfection!

SCELEDRUS: Don't threaten me. I know the cross will be my tomb. That's where my ancestors lie, my father, my grandfather, my great-grandfather, my great-great-grandfather.[6] You can't dig out these eyes of mine with your threats. Palaestrio, I want a few words with you. (*He draws him aside*) In the name of heaven, where did she come from?

PALAESTRIO: Where but from home?

SCELEDRUS: From home?

PALAESTRIO: You see me, don't you?

SCELEDRUS: Yes, I see you. (*Pondering*) It's awfully strange how she got from that house to ours. For there certainly isn't any sundeck in our house nor any garden nor any window that isn't grated. (*To* PHILOCOMASIUM) And yet I certainly saw you here next door.

PALAESTRIO: Keeping right on with your accusation, you rogue?

PHILOCOMASIUM: Good gracious! The dream that I had last night has turned out to be true, then.

PALAESTRIO: What was your dream?

PHILOCOMASIUM: I'll tell you. Both of you pay attention, please. Last night in my dream my own twin sister seemed to have come from Athens to Ephesus with a certain lover of hers; they both seemed to be visiting here next door.

PALAESTRIO (*aside*): She's relating the dream of Palaestrio. (*Aloud*) Go right on.

PHILOCOMASIUM: I seemed happy that my sister had come, but on her account I seemed to incur a most outrageous suspicion. For in my dream my own servant seemed to accuse me, just as you are now doing, of having been kissing some strange young man, when actually that twin sister of mine had been kissing her own sweetheart. And thus I dreamed that I was wrongly, falsely accused.

PALAESTRIO: And doesn't the same thing happen to you when you're awake, that you say you saw in your sleep? Jupiter! How well the dream fits! Inside now, and make a prayer. I recommend that the soldier be told.

PHILOCOMASIUM: I intend to do so. I shan't permit such a false accusation of dreadful behaviour to go unpunished. (*She goes into the house of* PYRGOPOLYNICES.)

SCELEDRUS (*in alarm*): I'm afraid that I've done it now; my back itches all over.

PALAESTRIO: You realise you're done for, don't you?

SCELEDRUS: Anyway, she's certainly home now. (*Placing himself in front of* PYRGOPOLYNICES' *door*) Now I've made up my mind to watch our door, wherever she is.

PALAESTRIO: But just think, Sceledrus, how like was the dream she dreamed to reality, to your suspicion that you saw her kissing!

SCELEDRUS (*wavering*): Now, I don't know what to believe; I'm beginning to think that I didn't see what I believe I did see.

PALAESTRIO: You'll come to your senses when it's too late, by Jove! If this story gets to master first, you'll die a fine death.

SCELEDRUS: I realise now at last that there was a mist before my eyes.

PALAESTRIO: Gad! That's been obvious for some time, since she's been inside here all along.

SCELEDRUS: I don't know what to say for sure. I didn't see her, but I did see her.

PALAESTRIO: Damned if your folly didn't almost destroy us all. You just about ruined yourself, trying to be faithful to your master. But our neighbour's door creaked. I'll hush.

Act Two. Scene V

(*Enter* PHILOCOMASIUM *as the twin sister from the house of* PERIPLECTOMENUS.)

PHILOCOMASIUM (*to a slave within*): Light the fire on the altar, that I may gratefully give praises and thanks to Diana of Ephesus and offer her the pleasing odour of Arabian incense; she saved me in the realms and boisterous abodes of Neptune, where I was so tossed about by angry waves.

SCELEDRUS: Palaestrio! Oh, Palaestrio!

PALAESTRIO: Oh, Sceledrus! Sceledrus! What do you want?

SCELEDRUS: This woman that just came out here—is she master's concubine, Philocomasium, or isn't she?

PALAESTRIO (*pretending amazement*): By Jove, I think so! She seems to be. But it's an awfully strange thing how she could get from our house over here to our neighbour's, if it is she.

SCELEDRUS: Do you have any doubt that it's Philocomasium?

PALAESTRIO: She seems to be.

SCELEDRUS: Let's approach and speak to her. (*To* PHILOCOMASIUM) Hey, Philocomasium! What's going on here? What are you doing in that house? What's your business there? Why are you silent? I'm talking to you.

PALAESTRIO (*amused*): Hell, no! You're talking to yourself. She doesn't answer a single word.

SCELEDRUS (*angrily*): I'm talking to you, you vehicle of vice and corruption, you who go roaming around among our neighbours.

PHILOCOMASIUM (*coolly*): To whom are you speaking?

SCELEDRUS: To whom, indeed, except to you?

PHILOCOMASIUM: Who are you? What business have you with me?

SCELEDRUS: What? You ask me who I am?

PHILOCOMASIUM: Why not, since I don't know?

PALAESTRIO: Who am I, then, if you don't know him?

PHILOCOMASIUM: A great nuisance to me, whoever you are; you and he both.

SCELEDRUS (*incredulous*): You don't know us?

PHILOCOMASIUM: No, neither of you.

SCELEDRUS: I'm fearfully afraid—

PALAESTRIO: Afraid of what?

SCELEDRUS: That we've lost our identity somewhere or other; she says that she doesn't know either you or me.

PALAESTRIO: I want to find out here, Sceledrus, whether we're really ourselves or somebody else; maybe one of our neighbours changed us when we weren't looking.

SCELEDRUS (*examining himself*): Well, I'm certainly myself.

PALAESTRIO: Gad, and so am I! (*To* PHILOCOMASIUM) Woman, you're looking for trouble. (*As she pays no attention*) I'm talking to you, Philocomasium. Hey, there!

PHILOCOMASIUM: What sort of insanity possesses you, that you keep addressing me wrongly by an unintelligible name?

PALAESTRIO: Oho! What is your name, then?

PHILOCOMASIUM: My name is Dicea.

SCELEDRUS: You're wrong, Philocomasium; you're trying to take a false name. You're not Dicea, you're Deceit-ea, and you're playing the hypocrite with my master.

PHILOCOMASIUM: I?

SCELEDRUS: Yes, you.

PHILOCOMASIUM: Why, I arrived in Ephesus last evening from Athens, with my sweetheart, an Athenian youth.

PALAESTRIO: Tell me; what is your business here in Ephesus?

PHILOCOMASIUM: I heard that my own twin sister was here. I came to look for her.

SCELEDRUS: You're a bad one!

PHILOCOMASIUM: Mercy me! I'm certainly a very foolish one to be chattering with the two of you. (*Turning away*) I'm going.

SCELEDRUS (*seizing her arm*): I won't let you go.

PHILOCOMASIUM: Let me loose.

SCELEDRUS: You're caught in the act! I won't let you loose.

PHILOCOMASIUM: My hands will smack and your cheeks will crack, if you don't let me loose.

SCELEDRUS (*to* PALAESTRIO): What the devil are you standing still for? Grab her on the other side, won't you?

PALAESTRIO: I don't care to have my back battered with blows. How do I know that she is Philocomasium? Maybe she's another person just like her.

PHILOCOMASIUM: Will you let me loose or not?

SCELEDRUS: I will not. Unless you go along willingly, I'm going to drag you home by force, willy-nilly.

PHILOCOMASIUM (*pointing to the house of* PERIPLECTOMENUS): This is my lodging while I'm abroad. My home is in Athens and so is my master.[7] I have no interest in that home of yours and I don't know who you are.

SCELEDRUS: Go to law about it, then. I won't let you go anywhere, unless you give me your solemn promise that you'll enter our house here, if I let you loose.

PHILOCOMASIUM: You're using force, whoever you are. I'll promise that I'll go inside where you say, if you let me loose.

SCELEDRUS (*releasing her*): There, you're loose!

PHILOCOMASIUM: And now that I am, I'm going in. (*She darts into the house of* PERIPLECTOMENUS.)

SCELEDRUS: There's a woman's word for you!

PALAESTRIO: Sceledrus, you let the booty slip through your fingers. It's as sure as can be that she's master's mistress. Do you want to act like a man of spirit?

SCELEDRUS: What am I to do?

PALAESTRIO: Bring me out a sword from inside.

SCELEDRUS: What'll you do with it?

PALAESTRIO: I'll burst right into the house. And any person I see inside kissing Philocomasium I'll slaughter right on the spot!

SCELEDRUS: You think it was she, then?

PALAESTRIO: Damned right it was!

SCELEDRUS: But how she did pretend!

PALAESTRIO: Go on! Bring me the sword!

SCELEDRUS: I'll have it here in a minute. (*He goes into the house of* PYRGOPOLYNICES.)

PALAESTRIO (*to himself*): There isn't a single soldier, on horse or on foot, that can do anything as bravely and as boldly as a woman can. How cleverly she changed her speech for each part! And how my fellow slave, the wary guard, is being gulled! A very happy thought— that passage piercing the wall!

(*Re-enter* SCELEDRUS, *much confused.*)

SCELEDRUS: Hey, Palaestrio! You don't need the sword.

PALAESTRIO: What now? What's the matter?

SCELEDRUS: Master's mistress—she's inside the house.

PALAESTRIO: What? Inside?

SCELEDRUS: She's lying on the couch.

PALAESTRIO: Well! Damned if you haven't brought disaster on yourself! I can see that from your words.

SCELEDRUS: How so?

PALAESTRIO: Why, because you dared to lay your hands on the lady here next door.

SCELEDRUS: Gad! I'm getting scared!

PALAESTRIO: Now, no one shall ever make her be anything but the twin sister of the girl in our house. She's the one, obviously, that you saw kissing.

SCELEDRUS: It's clear now that she's the one, just as you say. How close I would have been to destruction, if I had mentioned it to master!

PALAESTRIO: You'll keep quiet, then, if you're wise. A slave ought to know more than he tells. I'm going to leave you, so that I won't get mixed up in this muddle of yours. I'll be here in the neighbour's house. Your troubles don't interest me. If master comes and wants me, I'll be here, and you can send for me. (*He goes into the house of* PERIPLECTOMENUS.)

Act Two. Scene VI

SCELEDRUS (*to himself*): Has he really gone? Doesn't he care any more for master's affairs than if he weren't a slave in slavery? Well, the girl is surely in our house now, I know that, for I found her there lying down just now. I'd better get on with my work of watching.

(*Enter* PERIPLECTOMENUS *from his house, in great anger.*)

PERIPLECTOMENUS (*to himself*): By gad, these fellows here, these slaves of the soldier next door, take me for a woman, not a man! The way they impose on me! Is the girl that I'm entertaining to be mauled and mocked at against her will? A lady that's free and freeborn, too, who came here yesterday from Athens with my guest!

SCELEDRUS (*overhearing*): Heavens, I'm ruined! He's striding straight towards me. I'm afraid that there's some terrible trouble in store for me, judging from the words of this old fellow.

PERIPLECTOMENUS (*aside*): I'll approach him. (*To* SCELEDRUS) Look here, Sceledrus, you fount of iniquity! Did you trifle with my guest here in front of the house just now?

SCELEDRUS: Good neighbour, listen to me, please.

PERIPLECTOMENUS: I listen to you?

SCELEDRUS: I want to clear myself.

PERIPLECTOMENUS: What? Clear yourself, when you've done so serious and dreadful a deed? Just because you people are freebooters, do you think you have the freedom to do anything you want, you gallows bird?

SCELEDRUS: May I speak, sir?

PERIPLECTOMENUS (*taking a deep breath*): Now, may all the gods and goddesses so love me, if I don't have the chance to give you a long and continuous raking with rods, from morning till night, because you broke my gutters and my tiles when you were chasing a monkey as worthless as yourself, and because you spied upon my guest embracing and kissing his sweetheart in my house, and because you dared to accuse your master's mistress, a decent girl, with dreadful conduct and likewise accused me of horrible behaviour, and because you maltreated my guest in front of my house—if I don't have permission to apply the whip-penalty to you, I say, I'll fill your master with more disgrace than the sea has waves in a heavy storm!

SCELEDRUS (*abjectly*): I'm sunk to such a state, Periplectomenus, that I don't know whether I ought to argue the matter with you; unless, if that girl isn't this one and this one isn't that one, you prefer that I apologise. In fact, even now, I don't know what I saw. That girl of yours is so like this one of ours—if she isn't the same one.

PERIPLECTOMENUS: Go in my house and look. Then you'll know.

SCELEDRUS: May I?

PERIPLECTOMENUS: Why, I order you to. Observe her at your leisure.

SCELEDRUS: I'll certainly do it. (*He goes into the house of* PERIPLEC-TOMENUS.)

PERIPLECTOMENUS (*calling at* PYRGOPOLYNICES' *door*): Hey, Philo-comasium! Quick! Speed over to our house; it's absolutely necessary! Then, when Sceledrus leaves, speed quickly back to your own house! (*To himself*) Damn it! I'm afraid that she'll make a muddle of it now. If he doesn't see the woman— (*Listening*) The door's opening.

(*Re-enter* SCELEDRUS.)

SCELEDRUS: Ye immortal gods! I don't think the gods themselves could make a woman more like another, and more the same, considering that she isn't the same.

PERIPLECTOMENUS: What now?

SCELEDRUS (*humbly*): I deserve to be punished.

PERIPLECTOMENUS: Well? Is it Philocomasium?

SCELEDRUS: It is, but it isn't.

PERIPLECTOMENUS: Did you see that one?

SCELEDRUS: I saw her and the guest, hugging and kissing.

PERIPLECTOMENUS: Is it Philocomasium?

SCELEDRUS: I don't know.

PERIPLECTOMENUS: Do you want to know for certain?

SCELEDRUS: Of course.

PERIPLECTOMENUS: Go into your house, then. Quick! See whether that girl of yours is inside.

SCELEDRUS: All right. An excellent suggestion! I'll be back with you in a minute. (*He goes into the house of* PYRGOPOLYNICES.)

PERIPLECTOMENUS (*to himself*): Heavens! I've never seen a mortal more cleverly and more marvellously bamboozled! But here he is again.

(*Re-enter* SCELEDRUS, *completely convinced.*)

SCELEDRUS (*kneeling before* PERIPLECTOMENUS): I beseech you, Periplectomenus, by immortals and mortals, by my folly and by your knees—

PERIPLECTOMENUS: Why do you beseech me?

SCELEDRUS: To pardon my ignorance and folly. I realise now at last that I've been stupid, senseless, insane. Why, Philocomasium is inside there.

PERIPLECTOMENUS: Well, now, you Knave of the Cross! Did you see them both?

SCELEDRUS: Yes, sir.

PERIPLECTOMENUS: I'd like to meet your master.

SCELEDRUS: Indeed, sir, I admit that I deserve dreadful punishment and I confess that I maltreated the girl that's visiting you. I thought, though, that she was my master's mistress, over whom my master, the soldier, made me guard. You can't draw two drops of water from the same well more like each other than are this girl of ours and that guest of yours. And I admit also that I looked down through the skylight into your house.

PERIPLECTOMENUS: Why shouldn't you admit what I saw you do? And there you saw my guests kissing each other, I suppose?

SCELEDRUS: Yes; why deny what I saw? But I believed it was Philocomasium.

PERIPLECTOMENUS: And did you think that I was so worthless a mortal that I would knowingly permit such an outstanding outrage done in my house to my neighbour, the soldier?[8]

SCELEDRUS: Now at last, since I understand the situation, I realise that I have acted foolishly; but I didn't mean to do wrong.

PERIPLECTOMENUS: It was a dishonourable deed, just the same. A slave ought to keep his eyes and his hands and his words under control.

SCELEDRUS: If after this day I so much as utter a word, even what I know for certain, just give me over to be tortured. I'll give myself up to you. Pardon me this time, I beg of you.

PERIPLECTOMENUS: I'll force my feelings to believe that you didn't mean to do it. I'll pardon you this time.

SCELEDRUS: And may the gods bless you for it!

PERIPLECTOMENUS: But damn it! If the gods are to love you, you'll hold your tongue; after this you'd better not know even what you do know, or see what you do see.

SCELEDRUS: Good advice! I'm going to follow it. (*Still worried*) Have I entreated you enough?

PERIPLECTOMENUS: Oh, get out!

SCELEDRUS: Nothing else you wish of me, is there?

PERIPLECTOMENUS (*turning away*): Yes, that you don't know me.

SCELEDRUS (*aside*): He's deceived me. How kind and considerate of him not to be angry! (*As his suspicions increase*) I know what he's going to do. As soon as the soldier comes home from the forum, I'm to be seized in the house. He and Palaestrio together have me up for sale; I sensed it some time ago and I'm sure of it. By the Lord! I'll never take a bite from the bait in that basket today; I'll dash off somewhere and hide myself for a few days, until the turmoil dies down and their anger subsides. I've deserved enough punishment for a whole wicked nation. (*Changing his mind*) Nevertheless, whatever the outcome, I'll go home just the same.[9] (*When* PERIPLECTOMENUS' *back is turned,* SCELEDRUS *slips into the soldier's house.*)

PERIPLECTOMENUS (*to himself*): He's gone away from here. By Jove! I'm certain that a stuck pig often has much more sense. The way he was hocus-pocussed out of seeing what he did see! Well, his eyes and ears and thoughts have fled to our side. So far everything has gone splendidly; and the wench played her part delightfully! I'll go back and join the senate; Palaestrio is now at my house, and Sceledrus is now away; we can have a full session of the senate now. I'll go inside; I don't want a distribution of the parts to be made while I'm absent.[4] (*He goes into his house.*)

Act Three.   Scene I

(*Enter* PALAESTRIO *from the house of* PERIPLECTOMENUS.)

PALAESTRIO (*to* PLEUSICLES *within*): You folks stay inside for a while, Pleusicles; let me make my observations first, so that the council we want to hold won't be ambushed. (*To himself*) We need a good, safe place now, where no enemy can despoil us of our plans. For a well-planned plot is ill-planned, if it aids the enemy, and if it does aid the enemy, it naturally injures you. In fact, the well-planned plot is constantly being cribbed, if the place for the conference is chosen with too little care or caution. For if the enemy learn your plans, with your own plans they tie your tongue and bind your hands, and do to you the very same things you intended to do to them. So I'll scout around and make sure that no hunter with long-eared snares will come after our counsels from the right or the left. (*Looking around*) Good! A clear view to the very end of the street. I'll call them out. (*Calling at the door*) Hey! Periplectomenus! Pleusicles! Come on out!

(*Enter* PERIPLECTOMENUS *and* PLEUSICLES.)

PERIPLECTOMENUS: Here we are, your humble servants!

PALAESTRIO (*smiling*): It's easy to give orders to good men. But I'd like to know if we're to carry on with the same plan we considered inside.

PERIPLECTOMENUS: It couldn't be more suitable to our purpose.

PALAESTRIO: No, but what do you think, Pleusicles?

PLEUSICLES: Why should I dislike what you like? What person is more after my own heart than you are?

PALAESTRIO: Pleasantly and fittingly spoken!

PERIPLECTOMENUS: Bless me! That's the way he ought to speak.

PLEUSICLES: But this wretched affair afflicts me, and bothers me, body and soul.

PERIPLECTOMENUS: What is it that bothers you? Tell me.

PLEUSICLES: That I am casting on you, a man of your age, these youthful concerns that befit neither you nor your character; that, through your regard for me, you are striving with all your might to aid me in my love affair and doing such actions as men of your age are more accustomed to avoid than to engage in. I'm ashamed that I'm causing you this anxiety in your old age, sir.

PALAESTRIO: You're a new kind of lover, if you're ashamed of anything you do! You're not in love, you're more a ghost of a lover than a live lover, Pleusicles.

PLEUSICLES: But to distress a man of his age with my love affair?

PERIPLECTOMENUS (*somewhat indignant*): What's this you say? Do I seem to you such a dreadful Death's-head? Mere coffin-stuffing? You think I've lived such a long life, eh? Really, now, I'm not over fifty-four. My eyes are keen, my feet are nimble, my hands are quick.

PALAESTRIO (*to* PLEUSICLES): He may have white hair, but as far as spirit is concerned he doesn't seem the least bit old. He has the very same disposition he was born with.

PLEUSICLES: To be sure, I find it to be as you say, Palaestrio. His kindness towards me is quite that of a young man.

PERIPLECTOMENUS (*delighted*): Well, my young friend, the more you make trial of me, the more you'll realise how well disposed I am towards your love affair.

PLEUSICLES: Why learn what is already known?

PERIPLECTOMENUS: But I want you to experience it at first hand, without going elsewhere.[4] Unless a person has himself been in love, he can hardly know the nature of a lover; as far as love is concerned, I still have a bit of use and juice in my body; I haven't yet withered away from all pleasures and delights. Likewise I'll prove to be either a merry jester or a gracious guest, nor do I contradict others at the banquet. I duly desire not to be disagreeable to the guests, and I prefer to proceed with the proper part of my speech, and likewise to be silent in my turn, when someone else is talking. In short, I'm not one of these spitting, hawking, snivelling fellows; I was born in Ephesus, not in Apulia; I'm not an Animulian.[10]

PALAESTRIO (*to* PLEUSICLES): Oh, what a gracious young-old man, if he has all the virtues he mentions! He was clearly reared amid the charms of Venus!

PERIPLECTOMENUS: And I'll prove to be even more charming than I've promised. I never meddle with another man's mistress at a party; I don't make a grab for the food or snatch up a cup out of turn; nor am I ever the one to start a quarrel over the wine; if anyone annoys me there, I go on home, I cut off the conversation.

PALAESTRIO: Surely, sir, your nature abounds in charm.[4] Find me three men of such character, and I'll pay their weight in gold.

PLEUSICLES: You won't find another man of that age more delightful in every way, and more a friend to his friend.

PERIPLECTOMENUS (*enjoying their praise*): I'll make you admit that I'm still youthful in my ways; I'll show myself so rich in kindnesses to you in every respect. Do you need a severe, fiery lawyer? Here I am!

Do you want one that's calm? You'll say that I'm calmer than the silent sea; I'll be gentler even than a western zephyr. And from this same source I'll produce for you a most jovial guest, or a peerless parasite, or the cleverest of caterers. And as for dancing, no wanton can whirl more persuasively than I. (*He tries a few dance steps.*)

PALAESTRIO (*to* PLEUSICLES): What would you wish added to these choice talents, if you had a choice?

PLEUSICLES: That I could thank him for his services as he deserves, and you too; I realise that I'm an ample annoyance to both of you. (*To* PERIPLECTOMENUS) And it grieves me that I'm the cause of so much expense.

PERIPLECTOMENUS: You're stupid! Whatever is expended on a wicked wife or an enemy, that's real expense; but what is spent on a good guest and a friend is gain, and whatever is spent on religious rites is pure profit for a wise man. Thanks to the gods, I have the money with which to entertain you in pleasant fashion. Eat, drink, enjoy yourself, indulge in gaiety; this is Liberty Hall, and I too have my liberty. I want to live as I wish. Thanks to the gods, I say, I'm wealthy, and I could have married a well-bred and well-dowered wife; but I have no wish to introduce a she-barker into my house.

PALAESTRIO: Why not? It's a pleasant business to beget children.

PERIPLECTOMENUS: By Jove, to be keeping one's freedom—that's far more pleasant! [11]

PALAESTRIO: You're a man that can give good advice to yourself, as well as to others.

PERIPLECTOMENUS (*reflecting*): Well, it's nice to marry a good wife— if there's a place on earth where you can find one. But am I to bring home a wife who'd never say this to me: "Buy me some wool, my dear husband, so that a soft, warm cloak can be made for you, and some nice heavy underwear, to keep you from being cold this winter"? You'd never hear a wife talk that way; but before the cocks crow she'd wake me out of a sound sleep and say: "Give me some money, my dear husband, for a present to my mother on the matrons' holiday; give me some money to make preserves; give me money to give to the sorceress at the Minerva-festival, and to the dream interpreter, the fortune teller, the soothsayer. It would be terrible for the woman who foretells your fate from your eyebrows to get nothing. And I can't decently avoid giving something to the laundress; and the cateress has long been grumbling at receiving nothing; and then too, the midwife has complained that she didn't receive enough. What? Won't you send something to the nurse who brings up the home-born slaves?" All these and many other similar extravagances of the women keep me from taking a wife, who would worry me with such words as these.

PALAESTRIO: The gods show you favour, by heaven! If you once lose that liberty of yours, you'll not find it easy to restore it to its rightful place.

PLEUSICLES (*unconvinced*): And yet it's praiseworthy for a man of noble birth and great wealth to rear children as a memorial to his family and himself.

PERIPLECTOMENUS: But I have many relatives; what need have I of children? Now I live well and happily, as I wish and as I please. When I die I'll bequeath my property to my relatives, I'll share it among them. They'll be at my house, they'll look after me, they'll come to see how I am, whether I want anything. They arrive before dawn, they inquire if I had a good night's sleep; I'll have them in place of children to send me presents. They offer sacrifice, and give me a larger part of it than they give themselves; they lead me to the sacrificial feast; they invite me to their houses for lunch, for dinner. The one that's rendered me the least considers himself the most wretched. They compete with each other in giving me gifts, and I mutter to myself: "They're gaping after my property; but their competition is feeding and enriching me."

PALAESTRIO: You provide for yourself and your life in a mighty good manner; if you're happy, that's as good as having twins and triplets.

PERIPLECTOMENUS: Gad! If I'd had children, I'd have suffered plenty of anxiety. I'd be tormented in mind immediately. If a fever chanced to fall upon my son, I'd expect him to die; if he got drunk and had a fall or tumbled off his horse, I'd be afraid he had broken his legs or cracked his skull.

PLEUSICLES: It's right that riches and a long life be given to this man; he preserves his property, enjoys life, and is helpful to his friends.

PALAESTRIO: Oh, a delightful person! So love me, ye gods and goddesses, 'twere right for the gods to provide that all mortals should not live according to the same principle. Just as a good market-inspector puts a price on the merchandise, marks up the price on perfect goods so they will sell as they deserve and lowers the owner's price on faulty goods in proportion to the flaws, so should the gods have allotted human life. The man of charming character should receive a long life, while the reprobates and rascals should quickly hurry off to Hades. If the gods had so provided, wicked men would be less numerous, and would do their dirty deeds with less boldness, and moreover, for all the good citizens, the cost of living would come down.

PERIPLECTOMENUS (*reprovingly*): A man is silly and stupid to criticise the gods and to find fault with their decisions. And now it's necessary to put a stop to all this. I want to do some marketing, my friend, so that I can entertain you at home in the style that suits us both, in a kind and jolly fashion, with jolly things to eat.

PLEUSICLES: I think I've already caused you quite enough expense. No guest can be entertained at the house of a friend without becoming a nuisance after a three days' visit; but when he stays for ten days in succession, he becomes an Iliad of disasters. Even if the master is willing to put up with it, the slaves grumble.

PERIPLECTOMENUS: I've trained my slaves to serve in my service, my friend, not to boss me or to give me orders. If what I like is disagreeable to them, well, they're rowing the boat at my command, and what they hate they'll have to do, whether they like it or not, to the threat of a thrashing. Now, as I planned, I'll proceed with the marketing.

PLEUSICLES: Well, if you're determined to do so, buy within reason; don't go to great expense. Anything at all is enough for me.

PERIPLECTOMENUS: Why don't you drop that old-fashioned and antiquated talk? My friend, you're indulging now in the cheap talk of the common classes. Why, they always say, when they're seated and the dinner is set before them: "What need of going to all this expense just on our account? Heavens! You were insane; this would be enough for ten people." They find fault with what's provided for them—but they gobble it down, just the same.

PALAESTRIO (*grinning*): Jove, sir, that's exactly what they do! (*To* PLEUSICLES): How shrewd and clever he is!

PERIPLECTOMENUS (*continuing*): But no matter how stupendous the servings, these same men never say: "Have that dish taken away; remove this platter; take away the ham, I don't care for it; away with that pork; this conger eel will be excellent cold; put it aside, take it away." You wouldn't hear a one of them insisting on this; but they hurl their upper halves over the table and grab for food.

PALAESTRIO: How neatly a good man has described bad manners!

PERIPLECTOMENUS: I haven't told you a hundredth part of the things I could, if I only had the time.

PALAESTRIO (*relieved*): Well, then, we ought first to turn our thoughts to the business at hand. At attention, now, both of you! I need your assistance, Periplectomenus; for I've just thought of a delightful trick that will shear our long-haired soldier friend, and give Philocomasium's lover a chance to carry her off and keep her as his own.

PERIPLECTOMENUS: I'd like to hear the plan.

PALAESTRIO: And I'd like to have that ring of yours.

PERIPLECTOMENUS: How will it be used?

PALAESTRIO: When I have it, then I'll tell you the plan I've devised.

PERIPLECTOMENUS: Use it. (*Handing him the ring*) Here, take it.

PALAESTRIO: You take from me in return the wiles that I've worked out.

PERIPLECTOMENUS: We're listening eagerly with attentive ears.

PALAESTRIO: My master is a great rascal with women, such as, I'm sure, there never has been and never will be.

PERIPLECTOMENUS: I'm sure of that, too.

PALAESTRIO: He states, too, that his beauty surpasses that of Alexander,[12] and that's why, he says, all the women in Ephesus keep chasing him.

PERIPLECTOMENUS: Heavens! There are many husbands who wish that this were the truth about him![13] But I understand perfectly that he's just as you say. And so, Palaestrio, make your words as brief as possible.

PALAESTRIO: Can you locate for me some lovely lady, with her heart and breast packed full of cunning and trickery?

PERIPLECTOMENUS: Freeborn or a freedwoman?

PALAESTRIO: It makes no difference, provided you furnish one who's out for profit, who supports her body with her bodily charms, whose wits are awake. I can't expect intelligence; no one of them has that.

PERIPLECTOMENUS: Do you want a swell girl, or one that hasn't yet swelled out?

PALAESTRIO: Oh, fairly juicy; and just as charming and youthful as possible.

PERIPLECTOMENUS (*reflecting*) Well, there's a client of mine, a lovely young courtesan; but why do you need her?

PALAESTRIO: You're to take her home to your house, and then to bring her here all dressed up like a married woman, her hair coiled up high with ribbons; and she's to pretend to be your wife. That's the way you must coach her.

PLEUSICLES: I don't see what you're driving at.

PALAESTRIO: You will. (*To* PERIPLECTOMENUS) Does the girl have a maid?

PERIPLECTOMENUS: Yes; a right cunning one.

PALAESTRIO: I need her too. You give the girl and her maid these instructions: she's to pretend she's your wife and madly in love with this soldier, and that she gave this ring to her little maid, who gave it at once to me, for me to deliver to the soldier; as if I were the go-between in this matter.

PERIPLECTOMENUS: I hear you. He's deafened me with his demands! If you please, I can use my ears . . .[4]

PALAESTRIO (*somewhat subdued*): I'll give it to him and say it's a present from your wife, given over to me to bring the two of them together. That's the sort of person he is; the poor fool will be eager for her; the rascal isn't interested in a single thing except adultery.

PERIPLECTOMENUS: If you sent old Sol himself to hunt for them, he couldn't find two more charming ladies for this business than I can. Don't worry a bit.

PALAESTRIO: See to it, then. But we need them quickly. (PERIPLECTOMENUS *departs*) And now, Pleusicles, listen to me.

PLEUSICLES: Yours to obey.

PALAESTRIO: When the soldier comes home, be sure you remember not to mention the name Philocomasium.

PLEUSICLES: What name should I mention?

PALAESTRIO: Dicea.

PLEUSICLES: Of course; the same name that was agreed upon formerly.

PALAESTRIO: Enough! Off with you!

PLEUSICLES: I'll remember. But I want to know what's the point of remembering it.

PALAESTRIO: Well, I'll tell you that when the occasion warrants it. Meanwhile, just hush. As the old gentleman acts his part now, you can play your part soon after.

PLEUSICLES: I'm going inside, then. (*He goes into the house of* PERIPLECTOMENUS.)

PALAESTRIO (*calling after him*): And be sure you carry out my instructions carefully.

Act Three. Scene II

PALAESTRIO (*to himself*): What a turmoil I'm creating, what machines I'm moving forward! I'll snatch the concubine away from the soldier this very day, provided my cohorts are properly drilled. And now I'll call out that fellow. (*Shouting at* PYRGOPOLYNICES' *door*) Hey Sceledrus! If you're not busy, come out here in front of the house! Palaestrio's calling you.

(*Enter* LURCIO, *somewhat unsteadily.*)

LURCIO: Sceledrus, he's—he's not at leisure.

PALAESTRIO: Why not?

LURCIO: He's taking a snorter in his sleep.

PALAESTRIO: What? Snorter?

LURCIO: Snoring, I meant to say. But snoring is just about the same as —as when you snort.

PALAESTRIO: Oho! And is Sceledrus asleep inside?

LURCIO: Not with his nose anyhow; he's making an awful noise with that.

PALAESTRIO: He grabbed a goblet on the sly, I guess, when he was putting some nard in the wine-flagon,[4] being the butler. But look here, you rascal! You're his under-butler, and—

LURCIO: What d'ye want?

PALAESTRIO: How did he happen to go to sleep?

LURCIO: With his eyes, I suppose.

PALAESTRIO: I didn't ask you that, you scamp. Come here! (*As* LURCIO *obeys*) You're a dead dog right now, if I don't learn the truth. Did you draw wine for him?

LURCIO: No, I didn't.

PALAESTRIO: You deny it?

LURCIO: Damn it! Of course I—I deny it, for he told me not to admit it. And I really didn't draw off eight half-pints into a pitcher, and—and he really didn't drink it off hot for lunch, either.

PALAESTRIO: And you didn't drink anything?

LURCIO: The gods damn me if I drank, if I could drink!

PALAESTRIO: How's that?

LURCIO: Why, because I guzzled it down; it was too hot, it burned my throat.

PALAESTRIO (*enviously*): Some people get gloriously drunk, while others swig vinegar and water. A nice, honest under-butler and butler the storeroom's been entrusted to!

LURCIO: By Jove, you'd be doing the same, if it had been entrusted to you. You're just envious now, because you can't follow our example.

PALAESTRIO: Look here, now! Did he ever draw wine before this? Answer, you rascal. And so you won't be in the dark, I'll tell you this: if you tell any lies, Lurcio, there'll be a cross lurking for you.

LURCIO: Is that so? Just so you can tattle what I've told, and then, when I'm ousted from my storeroom-saturation, you can get yourself another under-butler, if you get the butler's job for yourself.

PALAESTRIO: Heavens! I won't do that. Come on, tell me frankly.

LURCIO: To be sure, I never saw him draw—draw any wine. But this is how it was: he'd give me the order and then I'd draw it.

PALAESTRIO: And that's why the wine casks were constantly standing on their heads there.

LURCIO: No, indeed! That's not why the casks were tottering about. There was a little spot in the storeroom that was very slippery, and a two-pint jar stood there near the casks, and—and it kept getting itself filled up, ten times over. I saw it get full and then get empty. And when the jar went on a jag, then especially the casks began to totter.

PALAESTRIO: Off with you! Get inside now! You're the ones on a jag in the storeroom. Damned if I won't bring master back from the forum!

LURCIO (*aside*): I'm ruined! Master will torture me, when he comes home and learns what's happened, because I didn't tell him. Damn it! I'll run off somewhere and postpone this punishment to another day. (*To the audience*) Don't tell him, I beg of you. (*He turns away.*)

PALAESTRIO: Where are you going?

LURCIO: I've been sent off somewhere; I'll be back here in a minute.

PALAESTRIO: Who sent you?

LURCIO: Philocomasium.

PALAESTRIO: Go on, come back quickly.

LURCIO: And if any punishment is parceled out, you can please just take my share during my absence. (LURCIO *departs.*)

PALAESTRIO (*to himself*): Now I understand what the girl's been up to. Since Sceledrus is asleep, she's sent this under-guard of hers into banishment, so that she could cross from her house to the one next door. That's fine. (*Looking down the street*) Why, Periplectomenus is bringing the woman I commissioned him to get, and a lovely figure she has! The gods are certainly giving us their aid! What a dignified garb and gait, not at all like a courtesan! The business at hand is shaping up successfully.

Act Three.   Scene III

(*Enter* PERIPLECTOMENUS, *accompanied by* ACROTELEUTIUM *and* MILPHIDIPPA.)

PERIPLECTOMENUS: I've explained the whole matter in detail to you at your house, Acroteleutium, and to you also, Milphidippa. Now, if you don't understand clearly our devices and deceptions, I want you to learn your lesson over again. If you do understand them, then we can talk about something else.

ACROTELEUTIUM: It would be silly and stupid on my part, my dear patron, to work for another person or to promise my assistance there, if in the workshop I didn't know how to be wicked or deceitful.

PERIPLECTOMENUS: Well, it's a good thing to remind you.

ACROTELEUTIUM: Everyone realises what a good thing it is to remind a courtesan like me! Why, I had hardly heard the opening of your oration, when I told you myself how the soldier could be polished off.

PERIPLECTOMENUS: But no one is sufficiently smart, all by himself. In fact, I've often seen many people lose the road to good advice before they realised where it was.

ACROTELEUTIUM: If a woman has to do anything with wickedness and wiliness, she has an immortal memory for remembering forever; but if anything decent or honest has to be done, immediately they become forgetful and can't remember a thing.

PERIPLECTOMENUS: That's why I'm afraid you'll be forgetful; the two of you have to do both things; whatever mischief you girls do to the soldier will be a benefit to me.

ACROTELEUTIUM: As long as we do good without realising it, you needn't fear.

PERIPLECTOMENUS: You deserve a thousand punishments.

ACROTELEUTIUM: Hush! Don't fear; that's fitting for women even more worthless.

PERIPLECTOMENUS (*gruffly*): It suits you, too. (*Approaching his house*) Follow me.

PALAESTRIO (*aside*): Why delay to go and meet them? (*He approaches*) Delighted at your safe return! You come charmingly equipped (*indicating the girls*), by gad!

PERIPLECTOMENUS: You meet me at just the right time, Palaestrio. Here are the girls you wanted me to bring, and garbed as you wished.

PALAESTRIO: Fine! You're my man, all right. (*Turning to* ACROTELEUTIUM) Palaestrio pays his respects to Acroteleutium.

ACROTELEUTIUM (*to* PERIPLECTOMENUS): Who is this fellow, please, that addresses me like an acquaintance?

PERIPLECTOMENUS: This is the man that drew up our plans.

ACROTELEUTIUM: Good day to you, architect.

PALAESTRIO: And good day to you. But tell me, has this gentleman given you full instructions?

PERIPLECTOMENUS: I'm bringing them both thoroughly prepared.

PALAESTRIO: I'd like to hear how well. (*To the girls*) I fear you might falter in something.

PERIPLECTOMENUS: I haven't added anything new of my own to your instructions.

ACROTELEUTIUM: You want your master, the soldier, to be tricked, of course?

PALAESTRIO: You've said it.

ACROTELEUTIUM: Everything's arranged cleverly and skilfully, fittingly and delightfully.

PALAESTRIO: And I want you to pretend to be this gentleman's wife.

ACROTELEUTIUM: So shall I be.

PALAESTRIO: And to pretend that you've fallen in love with the soldier.

ACROTELEUTIUM: That's just what will happen.

PALAESTRIO: And that the affair is being handled by me, as go-between, and by your maid.

ACROTELEUTIUM: You could be a grand **fortuneteller,** for you keep announcing what will come true.

PALAESTRIO: And that your maid brought me this ring from you, for me to give to the soldier in your name.

ACROTELEUTIUM: You speak the truth.

PERIPLECTOMENUS: What need now of repeating all the things they remember?

ACROTELEUTIUM: It's better so. For consider this, my dear patron: when a shipbuilder is skilful and has laid down the keel properly to the very line, it's easy to build a ship, when everything is laid and set into place. Now this keel of ours has been skilfully laid and firmly placed; workmen and designers are here not untrained for the job. If we're not delayed by the timber-merchant[14] who's to furnish the necessary raw material—I have confidence in our talents for trickery—our ship will soon be ready.

PALAESTRIO: You know my master, the soldier, I suppose?

ACROTELEUTIUM: A strange question! How could I help knowing that public plague, that boastful, frizzle-headed, perfume-reeking adulterer?

PALAESTRIO: He doesn't know you, does he?

ACROTELEUTIUM: He's never seen me, so how could he know who I am?

PALAESTRIO: Very pleasing, these words of yours! What we do, then, will be all the more delightful.

ACROTELEUTIUM (*impatiently*): Can't you give me the fellow, and stop worrying about the rest? If I don't provide a delectable deception for him, just put all the blame on me.

PALAESTRIO: Come, then; inside, all of you! Apply your cunning to this matter.

ACROTELEUTIUM: Just leave it to us.

PALAESTRIO: All right, Periplectomenus; you take these girls inside now. I'll meet him in the forum and give him this ring and say it was given me by your wife who is madly in love with him. As soon as we come back from the forum, send this maid over to our house, as though she had been sent to him secretly.

PERIPLECTOMENUS: We'll do it; leave it to us.

PALAESTRIO: You tend to it, then. I'll bring him back here well burdened with lies. (PALAESTRIO *departs*.)

PERIPLECTOMENUS (*calling after him*): A pleasant walk, and success to your undertaking! (*To* ACROTELEUTIUM) Now, if I can manage this properly, so that my guest this day can gain the soldier's concubine and take her off to Athens, if we can polish off this project today, what a gift I'll send to you!

ACROTELEUTIUM: Is the girl next door helping us?

PERIPLECTOMENUS: Most delightfully and obligingly.

ACROTELEUTIUM: I trust it will turn out so. When we add together all our artifices, I have no fear of being defeated at cunning deception.

PERIPLECTOMENUS: Let's go in, then, and consider our plans carefully; what has to be done we must do neatly and skilfully, so that we won't make any mistakes when the soldier comes.

ACROTELEUTIUM: You're the one delaying us. (*They go into the house of* PERIPLECTOMENUS.)

Act Four. Scene I

(*Enter* PYRGOPOLYNICES *and* PALAESTRIO *from the forum.*)

PYRGOPOLYNICES: Well, it's a great pleasure to have your affairs progress successfully and as you wish. Today, for instance, I sent my parasite to King Seleucus to take to him the recruits I enrolled here; they can protect his kingdom while I take a vacation.

PALAESTRIO: You should attend to your own business rather than that of Seleucus. There's a splendid new proposal that I'm commissioned to offer to you.

PYRGOPOLYNICES: Well then, I'll put everything else aside and turn my attention to you. Speak forth; my ears are at your disposal.

PALAESTRIO: Look around and make sure that no one can overhear our conversation. I was ordered to handle this matter with great secrecy.

PYRGOPOLYNICES (*looking about*): There's no one here.

PALAESTRIO (*handing him* PERIPLECTOMENUS' *ring*): In the first place, I proffer you this pledge of her passion.

PYRGOPOLYNICES (*puzzled*): What's this? Where does this come from?

PALAESTRIO: From a charming and delightful lady, who loves you and wants to enjoy your beautiful beauty. And now her maid brought me this ring for me to give to you.

PYRGOPOLYNICES (*examining the ring*): What about her? Is she freeborn, or some slave that has been freed?

PALAESTRIO: Tut, tut! Would I have the nerve to be a messenger to you from a person once a slave, when you can't adequately meet the demands of all the freeborn women desirous of you.

PYRGOPOLYNICES: Married or unmarried?

PALAESTRIO: Both married and unmarried.

PYRGOPOLYNICES: How is it possible for the same woman to be both married and unmarried?

PALAESTRIO: Because she's a young woman married to an old man.

PYRGOPOLYNICES: Splendid!

PALAESTRIO: She's a most agreeable and gracious lady.

PYRGOPOLYNICES: Don't lie, now.

PALAESTRIO: Why, she's the one person worthy of being compared with you.

PYRGOPOLYNICES: God! What a beautiful creature she must be! But who is she?

PALAESTRIO: The wife of Periplectomenus, the old fellow next door. She's just dying for you, sir, and she wants to leave him; she hates the old man. And now she asked me to beg and beseech you to give her permission and opportunity to love you.

PYRGOPOLYNICES (*unable to conceal his eagerness*): Heavens! I certainly desire it, if she wants to.

PALAESTRIO: Wants to? She longs for it!

PYRGOPOLYNICES: What shall we do with this concubine of mine here in the house?

PALAESTRIO: Why not tell her to go away somewhere, wherever she pleases; I mean, her twin sister has come here to Ephesus and her mother too; they've come to take her away.

PYRGOPOLYNICES: Aha! What's that? Her mother has come to Ephesus?

PALAESTRIO: That's the story from those who know.

PYRGOPOLYNICES: Mighty Mars! What a wonderful chance to get the wench out of the house!

PALAESTRIO: Well, sir, do you want to do it in a nice way?

PYRGOPOLYNICES: Speak; give me your advice.

PALAESTRIO: Do you want to get rid of her at once, and have her go gratefully?

PYRGOPOLYNICES: I'd like it.

PALAESTRIO: Then this is what you ought to do. You have plenty of money; tell her to keep as a present the jewelry and trinkets you supplied her with, to leave your house, and go away wherever she wishes.

PYRGOPOLYNICES: I like your suggestion. But make sure that I don't let her go, and then have this new one change her mind.

PALAESTRIO: Pooh! You're silly; why, she loves you like her own eyes.

PYRGOPOLYNICES (*proudly*): Venus loves me.

PALAESTRIO: Sh-h! Hush! The door's opening! Come over here out of sight. (*They step back.*)
     (*Enter* MILPHIDIPPA *from the house of* PERIPLECTOMENUS.)
This is her packet-boat coming out here, her go-between.

PYRGOPOLYNICES: What do you mean—packet-boat?

PALAESTRIO: It's her maid coming out of the house; she's the one that brought the ring I gave to you.

PYRGOPOLYNICES: She's a damned pretty wench.

PALAESTRIO: She's only an ape and an owl in comparison to her mistress. (*As* MILPHIDIPPA *looks around*) Do you see how she's hunting with her eyes and bird-catching with her ears?

Act Four. Scene II

MILPHIDIPPA (*aside, as she comes forward*): Here's the circus now in front of the house where my tricks must be performed. I'll pretend that I don't see them and don't know they're here yet.

PYRGOPOLYNICES (*aside to* PALAESTRIO): Hush! Let's listen quietly to see if there's any mention of me.

MILPHIDIPPA (*loudly*): Is there anyone around here who prefers to mind other people's business instead of his own, who wants to pry into my doings, the sort of person that doesn't have to earn his evening meal?[15] I'm afraid now that such men will hamper and hinder me somewhere, if they come from their home while my mistress is on her way across here. Poor dear, she's so eager to embrace him, and her heart's all in a flutter with love for him; she dotes on this man who's so charming and so handsome—the soldier Pyrgopolynices!

PYRGOPOLYNICES (*aside to* PALAESTRIO): So this girl too is dying with love for me, eh? She praises my beauty. To be sure, her words need no cleanser.

PALAESTRIO (*to* PYRGOPOLYNICES): How do you mean?

PYRGOPOLYNICES: Why, her words are clean-spoken and smartly polished.

PALAESTRIO: Whenever she says anything about you, she has a smartly polished subject.

PYRGOPOLYNICES: Then too, her mistress is a very sleek and dainty wench. Gad, Palaestrio, I'm beginning to fancy her a bit already.

PALAESTRIO: Before you've even set eyes on her?

PYRGOPOLYNICES: I believe you; isn't that the same as seeing her? Then too, though she is absent, this little packet-boat drives me to thoughts of love.

PALAESTRIO (*in alarm*): Heavens, sir! Don't you fall in love with this girl; she's engaged to me. If the mistress marries you today, I'm going to marry the maid immediately.

PYRGOPOLYNICES: Why delay, then, to speak to her?

PALAESTRIO (*advancing*): Follow me this way.

PYRGOPOLYNICES: I'm at your heels.

MILPHIDIPPA: Oh, I wish I could meet the man I came out to see!

PALAESTRIO (*to* MILPHIDIPPA): You shall. Your desire will be fulfilled. Be of good courage and have no fear. A certain man knows the whereabouts of the person you seek.

MILPHIDIPPA (*pretending not to see them*): Whose voice have I heard here?

PALAESTRIO: A partner in your councils and a sharer of your counsels.

MILPHIDIPPA: Gracious! Then what I'm concealing is not concealed.

PALAESTRIO: No; it's both concealed and not concealed.

MILPHIDIPPA: How's that?

PALAESTRIO: It's concealed from faithless fellows; but I'm your faithful friend.

MILPHIDIPPA: Give me the sign, if you are one of the initiated.

PALAESTRIO: A certain woman loves a certain man.

MILPHIDIPPA: Goodness! Many women do that.

PALAESTRIO: But not many give a gift from their own finger.

MILPHIDIPPA: Well, now I know you; now you've smoothed out the slope for me. But is anyone here?

PALAESTRIO (*stepping forward*): Just as you please.

MILPHIDIPPA: Let me have you alone.

PALAESTRIO: For a short or a long talk?

MILPHIDIPPA: Just a couple of words.

PALAESTRIO (*aside to* PYRGOPOLYNICES): I'll be back to you in a minute.

PYRGOPOLYNICES: What about me? Am I to stand here a long time in this pointless fashion, charming and courageous as I am?

PALAESTRIO: Be calm and stand still; it's your affair that I'm working on.

PYRGOPOLYNICES (*with sarcasm*): It's your haste—that's killing me.

PALAESTRIO: You have to feel your way gradually with this sort of baggage; you know that.

PYRGOPOLYNICES: All right; do as you think best.

PALAESTRIO (*aside*): This man's as stupid as a stone. (*Crossing to* MILPHIDIPPA) I'm at your service; what did you wish of me? (*They withdraw beyond the soldier's hearing.*)

MILPHIDIPPA: How you want this Troy attacked, that's the plan I want to discuss with you.

PALAESTRIO: Pretend that she's dying for him—

MILPHIDIPPA: I know that.

PALAESTRIO: Refer to his beautiful face and figure and recall his courageous deeds.

MILPHIDIPPA: I'm all in readiness for that, as I showed you just now.

PALAESTRIO: You manage the rest, pay attention, and take your cue from my words.

PYRGOPOLYNICES (*calling to* PALAESTRIO): Give me some share in this business here today, won't you? (*As* PALAESTRIO *returns to him*) Now you're here at last.

PALAESTRIO (*to* PYRGOPOLYNICES): Right here, sir. Command whatever you wish.

PYRGOPOLYNICES: What's that woman telling you?

PALAESTRIO: She says that her poor mistress is suffering and in torment, and worn out with weeping, because she needs you and because she doesn't have you. That's why the maid has been sent here to you.

PYRGOPOLYNICES: Tell her to approach.

PALAESTRIO: You know how you should act, don't you? Make yourself very disdainful, as though you didn't like the idea; shout at me for making you so common.

PYRGOPOLYNICES: I remember; I'll follow your advice.

PALAESTRIO: Shall I call the woman, then, who's looking for you?

PYRGOPOLYNICES: Let her approach, if she wants anything.

PALAESTRIO (*to* MILPHIDIPPA): Approach, woman, if you want anything.

MILPHIDIPPA (*to* PYRGOPOLYNICES): Good day, handsome sir!

PYRGOPOLYNICES (*aside*): Handsome? Why, she mentioned my surname. (*Aloud*) The gods give you whatever you wish!

MILPHIDIPPA: That permission to spend a lifetime with you—

PYRGOPOLYNICES (*haughtily*): You're asking too much.

MILPHIDIPPA: I don't mean for myself; it's my mistress that's dying for you.

PYRGOPOLYNICES (*proudly*): Many other women want the same thing, but they're not given the opportunity.

MILPHIDIPPA: Gracious me! I don't wonder that you set a high value on yourself—a man so priceless and so preeminent in beauty and bravery! Was there ever a man more worthy of being a god?

PALAESTRIO: Heavens! He isn't human, in fact— (*aside*) for I'm sure there is more humanity in a vulture.

PYRGOPOLYNICES (*aside*): Now I shall make myself important, since she praises me so. (*He struts about.*)

PALAESTRIO (*aside to* MILPHIDIPPA): Just look how the jackass struts about! (*To* PYRGOPOLYNICES) But why don't you answer her? She's from the woman I mentioned to you just now.

PYRGOPOLYNICES (*with assumed indifference*): From which one of them? So many chase after me; I can't remember them all.

MILPHIDIPPA: From the woman who robs her fingers and enriches yours. (*Pointing to the ring on the soldier's finger*) For this is the ring that I brought him from a woman who is eager for you, and he at once gave it to you.

PYRGOPOLYNICES: What do you want now, woman? Tell me.

MILPHIDIPPA: That you don't scorn the lady who desires you, who now lives only in your life. Whether she is to exist or not depends on you alone.

PYRGOPOLYNICES: What does she wish, then?

MILPHIDIPPA: To talk to you and embrace you and enfold you in her arms. For unless you come to her assistance, her heart will break. Oh, my Achilles! Come, do what I ask, save a charming woman with your charm; display your generous nature, O taker of cities, O slayer of kings!

PYRGOPOLYNICES: Gad! What a nuisance this is! (*To* PALAESTRIO) How often have I told you, you rascal, not to promise my services to the common mob?

PALAESTRIO (*concealing his laughter*): Woman, do you hear that? I told you a while ago and now I tell you again: unless this boar gets his proper fee, he won't bestow his seed on every little sow.

MILPHIDIPPA: He'll receive any price he demands.

PALAESTRIO: He needs a talent of golden Philips; he won't take less from anyone.

MILPHIDIPPA: Goodness gracious! That's really very cheap!

PYRGOPOLYNICES: There's never been any greed in my nature. I have enough wealth; in fact, I have more than a thousand pecks of gold coins.

PALAESTRIO (*keeping a straight face*): That's in addition to his treasures. And then of silver—why, he has mountains of it, not merely masses! Mount Aetna isn't even as high.

MILPHIDIPPA (*aside to* PALAESTRIO): Heavenly day! What a liar!

PALAESTRIO (*aside to* MILPHIDIPPA): How am I doing?

MILPHIDIPPA: Well, how am I? Wheedling him all right?

PALAESTRIO: Elegantly!

MILPHIDIPPA (*to* PYRGOPOLYNICES): Please now, send me back at once.

PALAESTRIO: Why don't you give her your answer, either that you will or you won't?

MILPHIDIPPA: Yes, why torture the poor lady's heart, who has never done you any wrong?

PYRGOPOLYNICES (*yielding*): Tell her to come out here to us. Say to her that I'll do what she wishes.

MILPHIDIPPA: Now, sir, you're acting as you ought to act, since you want the woman who wants you—

PALAESTRIO (*aside*): Nothing half-baked about her brains!

MILPHIDIPPA: And since you did not scorn my entreaty but permitted me to gain my request. (*Aside to* PALAESTRIO) Well? How am I doing?

PALAESTRIO (*aside to* MILPHIDIPPA): Jumping Jupiter! I just can't keep from laughing. Ha, ha, ha!

MILPHIDIPPA (*to* PALAESTRIO): That's why I turned away from you.

PYRGOPOLYNICES: Woman, you don't fully realise what a great honour I am paying that mistress of yours.

MILPHIDIPPA: Oh, yes, I do, and I'll tell her.

PALAESTRIO: He could sell this favour to another woman for his weight in gold.

MILPHIDIPPA (*trying not to laugh*): Gracious! I can believe that.

PALAESTRIO: Great warriors are born of those he makes pregnant, and his sons live eight hundred years.

MILPHIDIPPA (*aside to* PALAESTRIO): Oh, you awful liar!

PYRGOPOLYNICES: Actually, they live straight on for a thousand years, from one age to the next.

MILPHIDIPPA: Bless me! How many years will this man live, when his sons live so long?

PYRGOPOLYNICES: Woman, I was born on the day after Jupiter was born to Ops.

PALAESTRIO: And if he had been born a day ahead of Jupiter, this man would now be ruler of heaven.

MILPHIDIPPA (*aside to* PALAESTRIO): Enough, enough, I beg of you! Let me leave you now, if I can, while I'm still alive.

PALAESTRIO: Why don't you go, then, since you have your answer?

MILPHIDIPPA (*to* PYRGOPOLYNICES): I'll go now and bring here the lady I'm acting for. Is there anything else you wish?

PYRGOPOLYNICES: Yes, that I be no handsomer than I am. My beauty is such a bother to me.

PALAESTRIO (*to* MILPHIDIPPA): Why do you stand here now? Why don't you go?

MILPHIDIPPA: I'm going.

PALAESTRIO (*following* MILPHIDIPPA, *as she approaches the door*): Yes, and listen, will you? Tell her with cunning and cleverness, so that her heart will leap with joy. (*In a lower tone*) Tell Philocomasium, if she's there, to cross over to our house; the soldier's here.

MILPHIDIPPA (*to* PALAESTRIO): She's here with my mistress; they've been listening to our conversation on the sly.

PALAESTRIO: Excellent! From our conversation they will steer their course all the more cleverly.

MILPHIDIPPA: You're delaying me; I'm going now.

PALAESTRIO: I'm neither delaying you nor touching you nor—I won't talk about that.

PYRGOPOLYNICES (*calling*): Tell her to hasten out here. We'll give especial attention to this matter now. (MILPHIDIPPA *goes into the house of* PERIPLECTOMENUS.)

Act Four. Scene III

PYRGOPOLYNICES: What do you advise me to do now with my concubine, Palaestrio? For I can't in any way let this new lady into my house before I get rid of her.

PALAESTRIO: Why ask me what you're to do? I told you the most decent method of handling the matter. Let her keep all the jewelry and the garments that you fitted her out with; let her have them, keep them, carry them away. You can tell her it's an excellent time for her to go home. Say that her twin sister and her mother are here, and that she can have a happy trip home in their company.

PYRGOPOLYNICES: How do you know that they're here?

PALAESTRIO: Because I saw her sister here with my own eyes.

PYRGOPOLYNICES: Did the sister meet her?

PALAESTRIO: Yes, sir.

PYRGOPOLYNICES: She seemed like a fine wench, eh?

PALAESTRIO (*in disgust*): You want to get everything.

PYRGOPOLYNICES: Where did the sister say the mother was?

PALAESTRIO: Sick abed in the ship with sore and swollen eyes; that's what the ship-captain who brought them told me; he's lodging here with the people next door. (*He indicates the house of* PERIPLECTOMENUS.)

PYRGOPOLYNICES: Well, what about him? A fine, lusty fellow, eh?

PALAESTRIO (*still more disgusted*): Oh, get out, won't you, sir! A fine stallion for the mares you are! You chase after the males as much as the females. Come, sir; down to business!

PYRGOPOLYNICES: As to that advice of yours—I'd rather you talked over the matter with her yourself; you get along so well with her in your conversations.

PALAESTRIO: How's that any better than for you to go and handle the matter yourself? You can say that it's necessary for you to marry; your relatives are begging you to, your friends are forcing you.

PYRGOPOLYNICES: You really think so?

PALAESTRIO: Of course I do.

PYRGOPOLYNICES: I'll go in, then. Meanwhile you watch here in front of the house so that you can call me when that lady comes out.

PALAESTRIO: You just tend to the business you're on.

PYRGOPOLYNICES: That's already tended to. If she won't go of her own free will, I'll drive her out forcibly.

PALAESTRIO: Oh, don't do that; it would be much nicer to have her leave you with deep gratitude. And give her the things I mentioned; let her take away the jewelry and the clothing you furnished her with.

PYRGOPOLYNICES: I certainly want her to.

PALAESTRIO: I think you'll prevail upon her without difficulty. But go on in; don't keep standing here.

PYRGOPOLYNICES: I obey your command. (*He goes into his house.*)

PALAESTRIO (*to the audience*): This wenching warrior doesn't seem to differ much, does he, from the way I described him to you a while ago? Now I need to have Acroteleutium appear, or her maid, or Pleusicles. (*As* PERIPLECTOMENUS' *door opens*) Jupiter! How old Nick-of-Time aids me in every respect! I see the very ones I wanted, all coming out of the house next door.

Act Four.   Scene IV

(*Enter* ACROTELEUTIUM, MILPHIDIPPA, *and* PLEUSICLES *from the house of* PERIPLECTOMENUS.)

ACROTELEUTIUM (*to her companions*): Follow me; at the same time make sure that there isn't anyone here to spy on us.

MILPHIDIPPA: Mercy, I don't see a soul, except the man we want to meet.

PALAESTRIO: And I you.

MILPHIDIPPA: How goes it, architect of ours?

PALAESTRIO: I the architect? Bah!

MILPHIDIPPA: What's the matter?

PALAESTRIO: Why, in comparison with you, I'm not fit to drive a spike into a wall.

MILPHIDIPPA: Oh, come now!

PALAESTRIO: Yes, you're a very fine and fluent rogue. (*To* ACROTELEU-TIUM) How very cleverly she trimmed the soldier!

MILPHIDIPPA: But not enough yet.

PALAESTRIO: Don't worry. The undertaking as a whole is shaping up nicely now. You just continue to give a helping hand, as you've done so far. The soldier has gone inside to beg his mistress to leave him and to go off to Athens with her sister and mother.

PLEUSICLES: Excellent! Superb!

PALAESTRIO: Why, he's even presenting her with the jewelry and the clothing he furnished her with, to persuade her to leave. I advised him to do it.

PLEUSICLES (*confidently*): Her departure is certainly a simple matter, if she wants to go and he's eager to have her go.

PALAESTRIO: Don't you know, sir, when you climb out of a deep well to the very top, that then the danger's greatest of falling back down again from the top? This business of ours is now at the top of the well; if the soldier gets suspicious, nothing can be carried off. That's why we have particular need of cunning now.

PLEUSICLES: We have plenty of material at home for our purpose, I see: three women, you're the fourth, I'm fifth, and the old gentleman makes a sixth. With the talents that the six of us have for trickery, I'm sure, any city whatsoever can be captured by our cunning. Just give your assistance.

ACROTELEUTIUM (*to* PALAESTRIO): That's why we've come, to learn what you wish.

PALAESTRIO: Splendidly done! Now this is the task I command of you.

ACROTELEUTIUM: Commander, you'll gain your request, so far as I am able.

PALAESTRIO: I want the soldier to be neatly, deftly, and delightfully deceived.

ACROTELEUTIUM: Gracious! What a pleasure your command is!

PALAESTRIO: And you know how, don't you?

ACROTELEUTIUM: To be sure; I'm to pretend that I'm bursting with passion for him.

PALAESTRIO: Just the thing.

ACROTELEUTIUM: And that because of this passion I've left my husband, being eager to marry him.

PALAESTRIO: All correct. But there's this one additional point: you must say that this house (*indicating the house of* PERIPLECTOMENUS) is part of your dowry, and that the old man left you after you divorced him. We don't want the soldier afraid to enter another man's house later on.

ACROTELEUTIUM: A clever bit of advice!

PALAESTRIO: But when he comes out from the house, I want you to stand over there and pretend to despise your own beauty in comparison with his, and to be amazed at his excessive wealth; and at the same time praise to the skies his handsome figure, his charming manner, his beautiful face. Enough coaching?

ACROTELEUTIUM: I've got it. Will it be enough for you if I polish off my assignment so perfectly that you can't find a single fault in it?

PALAESTRIO: Quite enough. (*Turning to* PLEUSICLES) Now, sir, here are my orders for you, in your turn. As soon as all this is finished and the lady here has gone inside, you be sure to join us here at once in the guise of a ship-captain. Have a broad-brimmed, dark-coloured hat, a woollen patch over your eyes, a dark-coloured cloak (since that's the seaman's colour) that's fastened over your left shoulder, with the right arm bared to the breast; be neat and trim. Pretend you're the master of the ship. All these things are in the old man's house, for he has fishermen among his slaves.

PLEUSICLES: Well? Why don't you tell me what I'm to do when I get dressed up?

PALAESTRIO: Come here and call for Philocomasium in her mother's name; tell her that if she's going to go to Athens she must go quickly with you to the harbour and she must have everything taken to the ship that she wants put on board; and that if she doesn't go you'll set sail, for the wind is favourable.

PLEUSICLES: The picture's very pleasing. Proceed.

PALAESTRIO: At once the soldier will urge her to go, to hurry, so as not to delay her mother.

PLEUSICLES: It's wondrous wise you are!

PALAESTRIO: I'll tell her to ask for me as an assistant to carry the luggage to the harbour. Then he'll order me to go with her to the harbour. And then—for this is my plan—immediately I'm straight off for Athens with you.

PLEUSICLES: And when you get there, I won't let you be a slave for three days with giving you your freedom.

PALAESTRIO: Go quickly now, and get on your garb.

PLEUSICLES: Anything else?

PALAESTRIO: Yes; remember the instructions.

PLEUSICLES: I'm off. (*He goes into the house of* PERIPLECTOMENUS.)

PALAESTRIO (*to the women*): You too be off inside at once; I'm quite sure that the soldier will soon be coming out.

ACROTELEUTIUM: We honour your commands.

PALAESTRIO: Come, come; off with you then. (ACROTELEUTIUM and MILPHIDIPPA *enter the house of* PERIPLECTOMENUS) And now look! The door's opening at just the right time. Out he comes in splendid spirits! He's gained his request. The poor fool, he's gaping after a phantom!

Act Four.   Scene V

(*Enter* PYRGOPOLYNICES *from his house.*)

PYRGOPOLYNICES: I've gained from Philocomasium what I wished just as I wished it, on friendly and gracious terms.

PALAESTRIO: How in the world am I to explain your long absence?

PYRGOPOLYNICES: I never realised before now how much that woman loved me.

PALAESTRIO: How do you mean?

PYRGOPOLYNICES: How many words I had to say! What stubborn material she was! But finally I got what I wanted. I granted her, I gave her everything she wanted, everything she demanded. I even gave you to her as a gift.

PALAESTRIO: What? Me too? How can I live without you?

PYRGOPOLYNICES: Come, cheer up! I'll free you from her. In fact, I tried in every way possible to persuade her to leave without taking you with her; but she wore me down.

PALAESTRIO (*pretending to resign himself*): I'll put my hopes in the gods and you. In the final analysis, however, although it is bitter to be deprived of so excellent a master as you, I can at least take pleasure in this—that, as a result of your own beauty and my efforts, there has come to you this affair with the woman next door, whom I am now winning over to you.

PYRGOPOLYNICES: Why say more? I'll give you liberty and wealth, if you finish this affair for me.

PALAESTRIO: Finish it I shall, sir.

PYRGOPOLYNICES: But I'm so eager for her.

PALAESTRIO: You must take it easy now; control your desires; don't be too anxious. Ah! There she is now! Coming out doors!

Act Four.   Scene VI

(*Enter* MILPHIDIPPA *and* ACROTELEUTIUM *from the house of* PERIPLEC-TOMENUS.)

MILPHIDIPPA (*aside to* ACROTELEUTIUM): Look, mistress! There's the soldier all ready for you.

ACROTELEUTIUM (*to* MILPHIDIPPA): Where?

MILPHIDIPPA: To the left.

ACROTELEUTIUM: I see him.

MILPHIDIPPA: Look sideways, so that he won't know we see him.

ACROTELEUTIUM: I see him. Goodness! Now is the time for us bad girls to become worse.

MILPHIDIPPA: It's your turn to begin.

ACROTELEUTIUM (*loudly, for the soldier's benefit*): Pray tell me, did you really meet him? (*In a lower tone*) Don't spare your voice; I want him to hear.

MILPHIDIPPA: Heavens! I even spoke with him, calmly too, as long as I wished, at my ease and my pleasure.

PYRGOPOLYNICES (*aside to* PALAESTRIO): Do you hear what she says?

PALAESTRIO: I do. How happy she is because she approached you!

ACROTELEUTIUM: Oh, what a lucky woman you are!

PYRGOPOLYNICES (*aside to* PALAESTRIO): How everybody seems to love me!

PALAESTRIO: You deserve it.

ACROTELEUTIUM (*to* MILPHIDIPPA): Gracious me! 'Tis a miracle you mention—that you approached him and persuaded him. Why, they say that people approach him like a king, with letters and messengers.

MILPHIDIPPA: Really, though, I had great difficulty in approaching him and winning him over.

PALAESTRIO (*aside to* PYRGOPOLYNICES): How great is your fame among women, sir!

PYRGOPOLYNICES: I must submit to it, since Venus so wishes.

ACROTELEUTIUM (*loudly to* MILPHIDIPPA): I am grateful to Venus, and I beg and beseech her that I may win the man I love and desire, and that he may be kind to me and not refuse me what I want.

MILPHIDIPPA: I hope so, in spite of the fact that many women desire him; he scorns them all, he spurns them all, except you alone.

ACROTELEUTIUM: That's why I'm tormented with terror, because he is disdainful; I'm afraid that when he sees me his eyes will make him change his mind, and that so magnificent a mortal will immediately be scornful of my poor charms.

MILPHIDIPPA: He won't do that; just be free from anxiety.

PYRGOPOLYNICES (*aside*): How she despises herself!

ACROTELEUTIUM: I fear that your praise exaggerated such beauty as I have.

MILPHIDIPPA: I saw to it that he wouldn't expect you to be as beautiful as you really are.

ACROTELEUTIUM: Ah me! If he is unwilling to marry me, I'll clasp his knees and beseech him to. If I can't prevail upon him, I'll seek some means of death; I just know that I cannot live without him.

PYRGOPOLYNICES (*aside to* PALAESTRIO): I must prevent this woman's death, I see that. Shall I approach?

PALAESTRIO (*to* PYRGOPOLYNICES): Not at all. You'll make yourself common, if you hand yourself over to her unasked. Let her come to you of her own accord; let her do the seeking and courting and wait-ing. Do you want to lose that glorious reputation that you have? Please see to it that you don't. Why, I know well that it has never happened to any mortal except to two, yourself and Phaon of Lesbos,[16] to be so passionately loved by a woman.

ACROTELEUTIUM: Shall I go in, or will you call him out, my dear Mil-phidippa?

MILPHIDIPPA: Oh, no! Let's wait until someone comes out.

ACROTELEUTIUM: I just can't restrain myself from going in.

MILPHIDIPPA: The doors are closed.

ACROTELEUTIUM: Then I'll break them open.

MILPHIDIPPA: You're out of your senses.

ACROTELEUTIUM: If he has ever been in love, or if he has understand-ing equal to his beauty, he'll be merciful and forgive me for anything that I do through love for him.

PALAESTRIO (*aside to* PYRGOPOLYNICES): Look, I beg of you! How the poor thing is perishing with passion!

PYRGOPOLYNICES (*languishing*): It's beginning to be mutual.

PALAESTRIO: Hush! Don't let her hear you.

MILPHIDIPPA: Why do you stand there stupefied? Why don't you knock?

ACROTELEUTIUM: Because the man I want is not inside.

MILPHIDIPPA: How do you know?

ACROTELEUTIUM: My sense of smell tells me; if he were inside, my nose would sense it from the odour.

PYRGOPOLYNICES (*aside to* PALAESTRIO): She's a diviner. She's in love with me, and that's why Venus has given her powers of prophecy.

ACROTELEUTIUM: The man that I want to see is around here somewhere; I can certainly smell him.

PYRGOPOLYNICES (*aside to* PALAESTRIO): Gad! This woman sees more with her nose than she does with her eyes.

PALAESTRIO (*grinning*): That's because she's blind with love, sir.

ACROTELEUTIUM (*catching sight of the soldier*): Hold me up, I implore you!

MILPHIDIPPA (*supporting her*): Why?

ACROTELEUTIUM: So that I won't fall.

MILPHIDIPPA: Why so?

ACROTELEUTIUM: Because I can't stand; My eyes make my senses falter.

MILPHIDIPPA: Heavens! Have you seen the soldier?

ACROTELEUTIUM: Yes.

MILPHIDIPPA (*pretending to look around*): I don't see him. Where is he?

ACROTELEUTIUM: If you were in love, you would certainly see him.

MILPHIDIPPA: Gracious me! You don't love him a bit more than I would, ma'am, if I had your permission.

PALAESTRIO (*aside to* PYRGOPOLYNICES): There's no doubt about it; all the women fall in love with you as soon as they see you.

PYRGOPOLYNICES: I don't know whether you've heard me mention this or not—but I'm the grandson of Venus.

ACROTELEUTIUM (*gazing at the soldier*): My dear Milphidippa, go up to him, I beg of you; speak to him.

PYRGOPOLYNICES (*aside to* PALAESTRIO): How she stands in awe of me!

PALAESTRIO: She's coming towards us.

MILPHIDIPPA (*approaching them*): I want the two of you.

PYRGOPOLYNICES: And we you.

MILPHIDIPPA: I have brought my mistress outside, as you requested.

PYRGOPOLYNICES (*coldly*): So I see.

MILPHIDIPPA: Do tell her to come near you.

PYRGOPOLYNICES (*haughtily*): Since you begged in her behalf, I have persuaded myself not to hate her, as I do other women.

MILPHIDIPPA: Heavens! She won't be able to say a word, if she comes near you. While she was looking at you, her eyes cut off her tongue.

PYRGOPOLYNICES: The woman's ailment must be remedied, I see.

MILPHIDIPPA: What a quiver she's in! And how terror-stricken she was when she saw you!

PYRGOPOLYNICES: Well, armed warriors are the very same way. So don't wonder at a woman being afraid. But what is it that she wishes me to do?

MILPHIDIPPA: To go to her house. She longs to live with you and spend her whole life with you.

PYRGOPOLYNICES: What? I go to a woman that's married? Her husband would find me there.

MILPHIDIPPA: Why, for your sake she has turned her husband out of the house.

PYRGOPOLYNICES: How could she do that?

MILPHIDIPPA: The house is part of her dowry.

PYRGOPOLYNICES: Oh, really?

MILPHIDIPPA: Yes indeed, sir.

PYRGOPOLYNICES: Tell her to go home. I'll be there soon.

MILPHIDIPPA: Please don't keep her waiting; don't torture her poor mind.

PYRGOPOLYNICES: No, of course not. Go on in.

MILPHIDIPPA: We're going. (MILPHIDIPPA *and the lovesick* ACROTELEUTIUM *go into the house of* PERIPLECTOMENUS.)

PYRGOPOLYNICES (*looking down the street*): But what do I see?

PALAESTRIO: What do you see?

PYRGOPOLYNICES: Look! Somebody or other is coming this way in a sailor's outfit.

PALAESTRIO: He's coming towards us; he obviously wants you. Why, it's the shipmaster.

PYRGOPOLYNICES: To be sure; coming to get her now.

PALAESTRIO: I believe so.

Act Four.   Scene VII

(Enter PLEUSICLES *from the direction of the harbour.)*[17]

PLEUSICLES *(to himself)*: If I didn't know that other men had in other ways done many shameful things on account of love, I'd have more scruples at going around here in this garb because of love. But since I've learned that many men have committed many disgraceful and wicked deeds as a result of their love affairs—I pass over how Achilles permitted his comrades to be slain.[18] *(Seeing* PALAESTRIO *and* PYRGO-POLYNICES*)* But there's Palaestrio, standing with the soldier! Now I have to change my tune! *(Loudly)* Woman is assuredly the daughter of Delay herself! Any other delay, for instance, even though it's just as great, seems less than that which a woman causes. I suppose they act this way just from force of habit. Well, I'll summon this Philoco-masium. *(Approaching the house of* PYRGOPOLYNICES*)* I'll knock on the door. Hey! Is there anyone here?

PALAESTRIO *(stepping up to him)*: Young man, what's the matter? What do you want? Why are you knocking?

PLEUSICLES: I'm seeking Philocomasium; I come from her mother. If she intends to go, she must go now. She's delaying us all; we're anxious to set sail.

PYRGOPOLYNICES *(stepping up)*: Everything's been ready for a long time. Go, Palaestrio, get some assistants to help you take to the ship her jewelry, trinkets, clothing, all her precious things. Everything I gave her is packed; she can take it away.

PALAESTRIO: I'm off. *(He goes into the soldier's house.)*

PLEUSICLES *(calling after him)*: And hurry, damn it!

PYRGOPOLYNICES: He won't keep you waiting. *(Looking at the bandage over* PLEUSICLES' *eyes)* But what the devil is the matter with you? What happened to your eye?

PLEUSICLES *(pointing to his right eye, which is less bandaged)*: Well, by Jove, I've got this eye.

PYRGOPOLYNICES: But I mean the left one.

PLEUSICLES: I'll tell you: it's on account of a love affair that I don't use this eye so much, confound it! If I'd kept away from love, I'd be able to use this as much as the other. But these people are delaying me too long.

PYRGOPOLYNICES: Here they come out.

Act Four.   Scene VIII

(*Enter* PALAESTRIO *and* PHILOCOMASIUM *from the house of* PYRGO-POLYNICES.)

PALAESTRIO (*to* PHILOCOMASIUM): When in the world will you stop weeping, I want to know?

PHILOCOMASIUM (*sobbing*): How can I help weeping? I've had such a happy life here, and—and now I'm going away.

PALAESTRIO (*pointing to* PLEUSICLES): See! There's the man who has come from your mother and sister.

PHILOCOMASIUM (*without interest*): I see him.

PYRGOPOLYNICES: Listen, Palaestrio, will you?

PALAESTRIO: What do you wish?

PYRGOPOLYNICES: Go and order those things I gave her to be brought out. (PALAESTRIO *goes to the door and gives the orders to the slaves*.)

PLEUSICLES: Good day, Philocomasium.

PHILOCOMASIUM: Good day to you, sir.

PLEUSICLES: Both your mother and your sister asked me to give you their greetings.

PHILOCOMASIUM: I hope they're well.

PLEUSICLES: They beg you to come so that they can set sail, while the breeze is favourable. They would have come along with me, if your mother had not been suffering from sore eyes.

PHILOCOMASIUM: I'll go. But I do it against my will; my devotion to the soldier—

PLEUSICLES: I understand; you're sensible.

PYRGOPOLYNICES: But she'd still be stupid today, if she hadn't been spending her life with me.

PHILOCOMASIUM: That's just what tortures me, that I'm being separated from such a man; why, you can make anyone at all overflow with cleverness; and I was so elated at heart when I was with you. This distinction I see I must give up. (*She sobs bitterly.*)

PYRGOPOLYNICES: Ah! Don't cry.

PHILOCOMASIUM: I—I can't help it, when I look at you.

PYRGOPOLYNICES: Be of good cheer.

PHILOCOMASIUM: No one but myself knows the anguish I feel.

PALAESTRIO: Well, I don't at all wonder that you were happy here, Philocomasium, and that his beauty, his manners, his valour touched your heart with tenderness; for, when I, a mere slave, look at him, I weep that we are being parted. (*He turns away, pretending to cry.*)

PHILOCOMASIUM: Please may I embrace you once before I go?

PYRGOPOLYNICES: You may.

PHILOCOMASIUM (*embracing him*): Oh, my darling! Oh, my life!

PALAESTRIO (*leading her to* PLEUSICLES): Hold the woman, I beg of you, or she'll dash herself to the ground. (PLEUSICLES *holds her tenderly, as she pretends to faint.*)

PYRGOPOLYNICES (*looking at them suspiciously*): Hey! What the devil does this mean?

PALAESTRIO: The poor girl has suddenly fallen into a faint at the thought of leaving you.

PYRGOPOLYNICES: Run inside and bring out some water.

PALAESTRIO: I don't want any water; I'd rather have her rest a bit. Don't interfere, please, while she's recovering.

PYRGOPOLYNICES (*watching* PLEUSICLES *and* PHILOCOMASIUM): These two have their heads too close together; I don't like it. (*As* PLEUSICLES *forgets himself and kisses her*) Sailor, get your lips away from her lips; look out for trouble!

PLEUSICLES: I was trying to find out whether she was breathing or not.

PYRGOPOLYNICES: Then you should have used your ear.

PLEUSICLES: If you prefer, I'll let her go.

PYRGOPOLYNICES (*hastily*): I don't want that. Keep holding her.

PALAESTRIO (*as a hint to the lovers*): I'm unhappy.

PYRGOPOLYNICES (*to the slaves inside*): Come out and bring out here all the things I gave her.

(*Enter the slaves with the luggage.*)

PALAESTRIO (*solemnly*): And now, Household God, before I go, I bid you farewell! And all my fellow slaves, both male and female, good-bye and a happy life to you! And in your conversations I hope that you will speak well of me, even though I am absent. (*He pretends to weep.*)

PYRGOPOLYNICES: Come, come, Palaestrio! Cheer up!

PALAESTRIO: Oh! Oh! I just can't keep from weeping at leaving you.

PYRGOPOLYNICES: Endure it calmly.

PALAESTRIO: No one but myself knows the anguish I feel.

PHILOCOMASIUM (*pretending to regain consciousness*): But what's this? What has happened? What do I see? Greetings, O light of day!

PLEUSICLES: Have you recovered now?

PHILOCOMASIUM (*looking at* PLEUSICLES *in feigned horror*): Heavens! What man have I embraced? I'm ruined! Am I in my senses? (*She sinks back again into* PLEUSICLES' *arms.*)

PLEUSICLES: Have no fear, (*in a lower tone*) my darling!

PYRGOPOLYNICES: What does this mean?

PALAESTRIO: The girl has just fainted away. (*Aside to* PLEUSICLES) I'm fearfully afraid that this business will become too public. (PHILO-COMASIUM *revives again.*)

PYRGOPOLYNICES (*overhearing*): What's that you say?

PALAESTRIO: I mean, sir, if all this stuff is carried through the city behind us; I fear that people may criticise you for it.

PYRGOPOLYNICES: I gave away my own property, not theirs; it's damned little I care for what they think. Come, go now with the blessings of the gods.

PALAESTRIO: I mention this for your sake.

PYRGOPOLYNICES: I believe you.

PALAESTRIO: And now good-bye, sir.

PYRGOPOLYNICES: Good-bye to you.

PALAESTRIO (*to the others*): You go on quickly; I'll follow you in a moment. I want a few words with my master. (PHILOCOMASIUM *and* PLEUSICLES *depart, followed by the slaves with the luggage*) I am most grateful to you for everything, sir, in spite of the fact that you have always considered other slaves more faithful than me to you. If it were your wish, I should prefer to be your slave than another person's freedman. (*Pretending to weep.*)

PYRGOPOLYNICES: Be of good courage!

PALAESTRIO: Ah me! When I consider how I must change my way of life, learn the ways of women and set aside the soldiers' ways!

PYRGOPOLYNICES: Come now, be a worthy fellow.

PALAESTRIO: I can't now; I've lost all my desire.

PYRGOPOLYNICES: Go, follow them, don't delay!

PALAESTRIO (*tearfully*): Good-bye.

PYRGOPOLYNICES: Good-bye to you.

PALAESTRIO (*stopping*): If I happen to find myself a free man, I'll send you a message; remember, I beg of you, not to desert me.

PYRGOPOLYNICES: That's not the way I do things.

PALAESTRIO (*trying to keep a straight face*): And every now and then just consider how faithful I've been to you. If you do this, you'll know finally who is a good servant and who is a bad servant.

PYRGOPOLYNICES: I do know; I've often thought about it.

PALAESTRIO: But you'll know it particularly today, even though you've realised it before this. Why, today you'll speak even more of my achievements, I'll guarantee.

PYRGOPOLYNICES (*impressed*): I can hardly refrain from bidding you to stay.

PALAESTRIO (*in alarm*): Oh, don't do that, sir. People would say that you were deceitful and untruthful and faithless; and they would say that I was the only faithful slave you had. If I thought you could do it with honour, I'd urge you to; but it just can't be. Don't do it.

PYRGOPOLYNICES: Be off, then.

PALAESTRIO (*sadly*): I'll endure whatever happens.

PYRGOPOLYNICES: Well, good-bye.

PALAESTRIO (*apparently at the point of breaking down*): It's better to go quickly. (*He hastens off towards the harbour.*)

PYRGOPOLYNICES (*calling after him*): Once more, good-bye. (*To himself*) Before this affair came up, I always thought he was the greatest rascal among the slaves; now I find that he is devoted to me. Now that I think it over, I've been very stupid to let him go. Well, I'll go in now to my beloved. (*He turns towards the door of* PERIPLECTOMENUS' *house.*) But the door has made a noise, I perceive. (*He pauses.*)

Act Four.　Scene IX

(*Enter a* SLAVE BOY *from the house of* PERIPLECTOMENUS.)

BOY (*to those within*): Don't be giving me orders; I remember my duty. I'll find him, no matter where he is. I'll track him down; I won't spare any labour.

PYRGOPOLYNICES (*aside*): He's looking for me. I'll go to meet the lad.

BOY: Oho! You're the person I'm looking for. Greetings to you, you most delightful man, abounding in opportuneness, the one mortal beloved beyond all others by the two deities.

PYRGOPOLYNICES: Which two?

BOY: Mars and Venus.

PYRGOPOLYNICES (*approvingly*): Smart boy!

BOY: She begs you to come inside, she wants you, she desires you, she anxiously awaits you. Do help the lovesick lady. Why do you stand there? Why don't you go inside?

PYRGOPOLYNICES: I'm going. (*He enters the house of* PERIPLECTO-MENUS.)

BOY (*elated*): Now he's entangled himself in the toils; the trap is all ready. The old man is at his post ready to plunge at this adulterer, who boasts of his beauty, who thinks that every woman that sees him falls in love with him. Everyone despises him, men and women both. Now I'll go in and join the uproar. I hear them shouting inside. (*He returns to the house.*)

Act Five

(*Enter* PERIPLECTOMENUS *from his house, followed by* CARIO *and other slaves who are holding the struggling* PYRGOPOLYNICES.)

PERIPLECTOMENUS: Drag him along! If he won't follow, pick him up and throw him out! Lift him up between heaven and earth! Tear him to pieces!

PYRGOPLYNICES: Oh, God! Periplectomenus, I beg you to have mercy.

PERIPLECTOMENUS: You beg in vain. (*To* CARIO) See that that knife of yours is well sharpened, Cario.

CARIO (*testing his knife*): Why, it's been anxious for a long time to rip open the abdomen of this adulterer, so that I can hang trinkets around his neck the way they hang from a baby's neck.

PYRGOPOLYNICES (*in terror*): I'm killed!

PERIPLECTOMENUS: Not yet. You speak too soon.

CARIO (*waving the knife*): Can I fly at the man now?

PERIPLECTOMENUS: No. I want him clubbed with cudgels first.

CARIO: With lots of them, I hope.[19]

PERIPLECTOMENUS: How did you dare to seduce another man's wife, you lecher?

PYRGOPOLYNICES: As the gods love me, she came to me of her own accord.

PERIPLECTOMENUS: He lies. Strike him! (*They raise their clubs.*)

PYRGOPOLYNICES: Wait, while I explain.

PERIPLECTOMENUS (*to the slaves*): Why do you hesitate?

PYRGOPOLYNICES: Won't you let me speak?

PERIPLECTOMENUS: Speak.

PYRGOPOLYNICES: I was urged to come to her.

PERIPLECTOMENUS: But how did you dare? There, take that! (*He strikes him, the slaves joining in.*)

PYRGOPOLYNICES: Ow! Ow! I've had enough. Oh, heavens!

CARIO (*eagerly*): How soon am I to begin cutting?

PERIPLECTOMENUS: As soon as you wish. Spread the fellow apart; stretch him out.

PYRGOPOLYNICES: Oh, God! I beseech you, listen to me before he starts cutting.

PERIPLECTOMENUS: Speak.

PYRGOPOLYNICES: I had some justification; damn it, I thought she was divorced! That's what her maid, the go-between, told me.

PERIPLECTOMENUS: Swear that you won't injure a living soul because of this—that you've had a thrashing here today or that you will have a thrashing—if we send you away from here alive, you darling little grandson of Venus!

PYRGOPOLYNICES: I swear by Jupiter and Mars that I won't injure a soul because I've had a thrashing here today, and I think I deserved it. If I go away from here as a man,[20] I'm being well treated for my offence.

PERIPLECTOMENUS: And if you don't keep your word?

PYRGOPOLYNICES: Then may I always live unmanned.

CARIO (*to* PERIPLECTOMENUS): Let's beat him once more; then I move we let him go.

PYRGOPOLYNICES: May the gods bless you forever, since you plead so well in my behalf.

CARIO: Well, give us (*pointing to the slaves*) a mina of gold, then.

PYRGOPOLYNICES: What for?

CARIO: So that we'll let you go away from here today with your manhood intact, you darling little grandson of Venus! Otherwise you shan't get away from here; don't deceive yourself about that.

PYRGOPOLYNICES (*in haste*): You'll get it.

CARIO: Now you show more sense. But don't count on your tunic and your cloak and your sword; you won't get them back.

A SLAVE: Shall I hit him again, or are you going to let him beat it?

PYRGOPOLYNICES: I've been beaten to a jelly already. Please have mercy.

PERIPLECTOMENUS (*to slaves*): Let him loose. (*They do so.*)

PYRGOPOLYNICES: I am grateful to you.

PERIPLECTOMENUS (*sternly*): If I ever catch you here again, you will lose your manhood.

PYRGOPOLYNICES: I accept your terms.

PERIPLECTOMENUS: Let's go inside, Cario. (PERIPLECTOMENUS *goes into his house, followed by* CARIO *and the other slaves.*)

PYRGOPOLYNICES (*looking down the street*): Well, I see my slaves! (*Enter* SCELEDRUS *and other slaves from the harbour.*) Has Philocomasium departed already? Tell me.

SCELEDRUS:[21] A long time ago.

PYRGOPOLYNICES: Oh, damn it!

SCELEDRUS: You'd damn it still more, if you knew what I know. That fellow with the woollen patch over his eye was no sailor.

PYRGOPOLYNICES: Who was he, then?

SCELEDRUS: Philocomasium's lover.

PYRGOPOLYNICES: How do you know?

SCELEDRUS: I know, all right. Why, from the time they left the city gate, they never stopped kissing and hugging each other.

PYRGOPOLYNICES: What a confounded fool I am! I've been deceived; I see that now. That rogue of a fellow, Palaestrio! He's the one that lured me into this trap. (*Reflecting*) Well, I believe I've deserved it. If the same treatment were given to other adulterers, there would be fewer adulterers about; they would have greater fear of punishment, and less desire for such pursuits. (*To the slaves*) Let's go home. (*To the audience*) Give us your applause.

1. This scene is really a prologue, but is deferred to permit the introduction of Pyrgopolynices in the opening scene, since his character is extremely important to the later action of the play. For a similarly postponed prologue, cf. *The Casket*, Act One, Scene III.

2. *Alazon* and *Gloriosus* both mean "Braggart."

3. This refers to the Roman ("foreign," i.e. non-Greek) poet Naevius, who was imprisoned for his attacks on the aristocratic family of the Metelli, probably about 206 B.C. The "two guards" are the chains on his hands and feet.

4. The text is corrupt here.

5. Darnel was said to be bad for the eyes.

6. Sceledrus' enumeration of his ancestors is particularly amusing, since a slave in Roman law had no father.

7. The text is uncertain here. Periplectomenus later speaks of the twin sister as being free.

8. Riley has an amusing note here: "The old gentleman must surely have changed colour when he said this."

9. This final statement is considered by many critics a later addition to account for Sceledrus' presence in the house in Act Three, Scene II. Periplectomenus clearly believes that Sceledrus has gone away from the house of the soldier.

10. Animula was a small town in Apulia.

11. There is a play here between *liberos,* "children," and *liberum,* "a free person."

12. Alexander was another name for Paris, son of Priam of Troy.

13. Lindsay reads *nunc,* suggested by Acidalius. *Non,* the reading of the Mss., seems preferable.

14. The "timber-merchant" is of course the soldier who will supply the raw material for the deception.

15. Such a person would have plenty of leisure to pry into the business of other people.

16. The story is told of the poetess Sappho that she committed suicide when deserted by her lover Phaon.

17. Although Plautus does not so state, it is probable that Pleusicles left the house by a rear entrance in order to come from the direction of the harbour. Palaestrio, however, told the soldier in 1110 that

the shipmaster was lodging with Periplectomenus, and it is possible that Pleusicles comes directly from the house.

18. Achilles withdrew from the battle when his captive Briseis was taken by Agamemnon; Achilles' wrath on this occasion and its results are the theme of Homer's *Iliad*.

19. One verse is lost at this point.

20. In this and the following verses, there is a play upon the two meanings of *testis*, "witness," and "genital gland"; See *Curculio*, note 1.

21. Many editors assign the speeches of Sceledrus in this scene to an unnamed slave.

XIII
THE HAUNTED HOUSE

Characters in the Play

GRUMIO, *slave of* THEOPROPIDES
TRANIO, *slave of* THEOPROPIDES
PHILOLACHES, *a young Athenian*
PHILEMATIUM, *his mistress*
SCAPHA, *maid of* PHILEMATIUM
CALLIDAMATES, *a young man*
DELPHIUM, *a courtesan*
SPHAERIO, *slave of* THEOPROPIDES
THEOPROPIDES, *father of* PHILOLACHES
MISARGYRIDES, *a moneylender*
SIMO, *an old man, neighbour of* PHILOLACHES
PHANISCUS, *slave of* CALLIDAMATES
PINACIUM, *slave of* CALLIDAMATES
Other slaves and attendants

Acrostic Argument

Philolaches purchases and sets free his sweetheart during his father's absence, and squanders all his property. Tranio deceives the old man on his return with the story that frightful apparitions have been seen in the house and that the family has been forced to leave. A money-loving moneylender comes in at this point and asks for his interest. Again the old man is tricked, for Tranio says that they have borrowed money for the purchase of a house. When he is asked whose house has been bought, Tranio says it is the house next door. The old man examines the house. Later he is distressed at being deceived, but is finally appeased by his son's friend.

INTRODUCTION

The Haunted House (the *Mostellaria*) has several features of unusual
interest. The element of the supernatural is present, for the deception
involves a fictitious ghost which is said to have driven a family from
its house. Both a dressing scene and a banquet take place on the stage,
and there is an amusing scene of drunkenness when the already tipsy
Callidamates arrives at the banquet with his sweetheart. The characters
are the usual types, the son in love, the courtesan, the father who returns unexpectedly from abroad, the wily and impertinent slave who
endeavours to save the situation, but all are portrayed with particular
care; they are less conventional and more true to life than is often the
case in Plautine comedy. The presentation of several characters in
pairs, e.g. Tranio and Grumio, Phaniscus and Pinacium, Philematium
and Scapha, gives emphasis to their individual traits. Philematium is
"a model of gratitude," one of the most faithful and devoted courtesans
to be found in Roman comedy. Philolaches is amusing as the rather
maudlin and semi-repentant lover; his song comparing a young man's
life to the building and destruction of a house is in the original one of
the most elaborate of Plautus' lyric *cantica*. Misargyrides, the moneylender, is something of an ancient Shylock as he demands his interest.
Grumio, the faithful servant who disapproves of Tranio's conduct and
yearns for the return of his master, has been likened to Eumaeus, the
loyal swineherd of Homer's *Odyssey*. Tranio is a delightful rogue who
keeps his aged master away from his house with his improvised ghost-
story. One lie leads to another until the climax of the trickery when he
deceives two old men simultaneously, his master Theopropides and
the neighbour Simo, and makes open fun of them at the same time.

The structure of the play is unusual, for almost one-third of the
dialogue is purely expository. The excellent opening scene between
Tranio and Grumio, Philolaches' monody, the somewhat lengthy dressing scene between Philematium and her maid with amusing asides by
Philolaches, the banquet scene—all serve to introduce the characters
and make clear the situation prior to the arrival of Theopropides. This
first section of the play contains some of its best scenes. When the

father returns and Tranio begins his deception of the old man, the other characters of the exposition necessarily disappear and are seen no more, with the exception of Callidamates who comes back at the end as a human *deus ex machina* to win pardon for Philolaches and Tranio after the old man has discovered the truth. Such a discovery is inevitable. Tranio's lies are clever and amusing, but, like Epidicus' trickery, can have only a temporary success. Tranio is one of the rascally slaves who delights in trickery for its own sake; his treatment of the two old men in Act Three, Scene II, is an illustration of this. Since Tranio develops the different stages of his plan on the spur of the moment, there can be no foreknowledge of the action; the reader therefore is held in suspense throughout. The final scenes of the play are reminiscent of those in the *Epidicus,* for Tranio's impudence is in no way lessened by the knowledge that his lies have been found out. "Why are you unwilling to forgive me?" he asks at the end. "As if I shouldn't be committing another offence tomorrow. Then you can take proper punishment for both together—this one and the next one."

An ancient citation from Festus quotes a passage from *The Haunted House* under the title *The Ghost* (the *Phasma*), and it is assumed that this was the title of the Greek original. Comedies of this title were written by Menander, Philemon, and Theognetus. The plot of Menander's *Phasma* is known but bears no relation to the Plautine play, and most critics agree that the original is to be assigned to Philemon. The reference to Diphilus and Philemon in lines 1149 ff. is interesting in this connection, since Plautus may be claiming to have improved on the Greek original, or the passage may have been written by Philemon himself in the original.

The Haunted House is considered by some critics to be one of Plautus' best plays. Others point to the uselessness of Tranio's lies, amusing though they are, and to the irrelevance of some of the jests and soliloquies, and consider the latter part of the play inferior to the opening act. The interest of the subject and the effective portrayal of many of the characters have nevertheless made it one of Plautus' best-known plays. Although its influence on later drama has been less than that of the *Amphitryon, The Pot of Gold, The Twin Menaechmi,* and *The Braggart Warrior,* there have been numerous translations and adaptations. Berrardo's *Mostellaria* (1501), Bentivoglio's *I Fantasmi* (1545), Montfleury's *Le Comédien Poète* (1674), Regnard's *Le Retour Imprévu* (1700), and Holberg's *Abracadabra* (a version which omits all the female characters) reveal the influence of the Latin play. One of the two plots of Heywood's *The English Traveller* (1633) is modelled closely upon the story of the Plautine comedy. Reminiscences are found also in Jonson's *The Alchemist* (1610), Addison's *The Drummer*

(1716), and Fielding's *The Intriguing Chambermaid* (1733), a play based primarily upon Regnard's adaptation. E. W. Fay and E. A. Sonnenschein point out in their editions of the *Mostellaria* several interesting likenesses between Plautus' comedy and Shakespeare's *The Taming of the Shrew;* not only is the portrayal of Tranio and Grumio somewhat similar, but Philolaches' delight at seeing his sweetheart is not unlike the raptures of Lucentio when he beholds Bianca.

THE HAUNTED HOUSE

(SCENE:—*A street in Athens in front of the houses of* THEOPROPIDES
and SIMO. *An alley-way separates the two houses. On the stage is
an altar.*)

Act One.   Scene I

(Enter GRUMIO *from the country.*)

GRUMIO (*calling at the door of* THEOPROPIDES' *house*): Come out of the
kitchen, you lout! You needn't show me how clever you are among the
platters. Get out of the house, you pest! By gad, when we're on the
farm, I'll give you the thrashing you deserve, as sure as I'm born. Come
on out, you kitchen-smell! What are you hiding for?

(Enter TRANIO, *calm and collected.*)

TRANIO: What the devil is this fuss out here in front of the house?
Think you're in the country? Get away from here! Go to the country!
Go to—perdition! Get away from that door! There! (*Striking him*)
Is this what you were looking for?

GRUMIO: Ow! What are you striking me for?

TRANIO: Oh, just because you exist.

GRUMIO: That's all right. But just you wait till the old man comes
back; just wait till he gets back in safety—the man you're eating up
while he's away!

TRANIO: If you say that anyone can eat up a man when he's gone off,
you're either talking nonsense or lying, blockhead.

GRUMIO: You dude, you fop! Who are you to accuse me of being a
farmer? But I suppose you do it, Tranio, because you know you'll be
sent off to the treadmill pretty soon. In a few days from now, Tranio,
you'll be added to our chain gang in the country. So go on drinking and

ruining the estate, now while you have the chance to do what you like. Corrupt our good young master; drink night and day, be merry as a crowd of Greeks; buy mistresses and set 'em free; feed parasites and buy expensive banquets. Is this what the old man told you to do when he went away? Is this the way he'll find his property's been managed? Is this the way you think a good slave ought to act—to spoil his master's property and his master's son at the same time? (*Turning passionately to the audience*) For spoiled he certainly is, I think, from the sort of thing he's going in for now. And before this there wasn't a person of his age in all Attica who was so thrifty and upright as he was. Now he takes the cake in the opposite direction. (*Turning savagely to* TRANIO) And it's thanks to you and your instruction that this has happened!

TRANIO: Plague take you! What concern have you with me and my affairs? Haven't you any cows to mind in the country? I *like* to drink and make love and have wenches; it's my funeral, not yours.

GRUMIO: How boldly he speaks!

TRANIO: Oh, go to perdition! (*Sniffing*) Phaugh! You smell of garlic. You thing of filth, you hick, goat, pig-sty, you mud-and-manure, you![1]

GRUMIO: Well, what do you want? Everybody can't smell of French perfumes just because you do, or sit at the head of the table, or live on the fine food you do. You can have your grouse and fancy fish and fowl. But let me go my way on a meal of garlic. You're rich and I'm poor, and that's that. But I can look for something better, and you for something worse.

TRANIO: I do believe you envy me a little, Grumio, because the world is right with me and wrong with you; but that's just as it should be. I court the ladies and you court the cows. I live on the fat of the land and you on the lean: quite proper, too.

GRUMIO: I'll bet you'll look like a sieve, if the old man comes back; the hangman'll fill you so full of holes when he drives you through the streets with pitchforks.

TRANIO: How do you know that won't happen to you before it does to me?

GRUMIO: Because I've never deserved it; but you have deserved it and still do.

TRANIO: Well, cut your talk short, unless you want to be thrashed good and proper.

GRUMIO: Are you going to give me some fodder to feed the cows? Give it to me—unless you're eating it.² (*He retreats, as* TRANIO *attacks him*) All right, go on; keep on going the way you've begun. Drink and live like Greeks, eat and stuff yourselves. Down with the victuals!

TRANIO: Shut up, and get back to the farm. I'm going to the Piraeus to get myself some fish for supper. I'll have someone bring the fodder to the farm tomorrow. (*As* GRUMIO *makes no move to go*) Well, what's the matter now? What are you staring at me for, jailbird?

GRUMIO: *You'll* be called that pretty soon, I'll bet.

TRANIO: While things are as they are, what should I care about your "pretty soon"?

GRUMIO: All right; but remember this: what you don't want comes much quicker than what you want.

TRANIO: Don't bother me. Stir your stumps, and go back to the farm. By gad, you won't keep me waiting any longer. (*He departs in the direction of the harbour.*)

GRUMIO (*to himself*): So he's gone, and what I've been saying doesn't jar him at all. Ye immortal gods, I appeal to you! Bring back our old master, who's been away for three years now, before everything goes to pot—both house and farm. If he doesn't come soon, there are only enough leavings left for a few months. (*Suddenly catching sight of* PHILOLACHES) Now I'll go back to the farm, for I see master's son coming. Ah, he was a fine lad once, but he's ruined now. (GRUMIO *departs.*)

Act One.   Scene II

(*Enter* PHILOLACHES, *slightly drunk and very moody.*)

PHILOLACHES (*to himself*): I've been wond'rin' 'n' thinkin' for a long time 'n' I've marshalled an array of arguments in my brain—if I've got a brain—'n' I've pondered 'n' discussed just this: to what can I compare a man 'n' what's he like, when he's born. And this is the example I've found. A man is like a new house, I think, when he's born, an' here's why. Perhaps this doesn't seem likely to you, but I'll soon fix it so you'll believe me.

Right off I'll convince you that I'm on the right track, 'n' when you hear my reasons, you folks'll all agree that it's just as I say. Listen to my arguments then 'cause I want you to know all about it, like me.

When a house's all built, varnish dry, 'n' everythin' shipshape, everybody says it's swell and pats the builder on the back, and wants his blueprint, so they can have one just like it; money's no object, nor labour either. But then some useless fellow moves in, careless, with a lazy-bones family, messy, shiftless; then the good house is spoiled by bad caretakers. And often a storm comes, and cracks the shingles 'n' drains. But the lazy owner won't fix it, and the rain comes along and soaks the walls, rains in, and rots the beams, and all the builder's pains go to pot. Now the house is the worse for wear. The builder's not to blame. The owner's just like most people; when they can patch up the damage for a few cents, they let it go, and then you've got to start in all over again.

That's the story on buildings; now let me tell you why you should think men are like houses.

First of all, parents build their children—lay the foundations for 'em, raise 'em, strengthen 'em; they try to make them attractive and useful to the community and to themselves, giving all they can. They spare no expense, give them their veneering, send them to college, even to law-school. All this wealth and toil is expended in the hope that others will say, "I wish my Marcus were like him." Then they send them off to army camps and ask Uncle Gaius to look out for them. And so the sons leave the builder's hands after one year in camp, and then you may see how the building will turn out.

Now when I was still under my parent's thumb, I was a good lad and well-enough behaved. But as soon as I got to be twenty-one, my upbringing went to the dogs completely. First came Laziness: that was the storm I ran into, and it brought plenty of hail down about my ears. That cracked my modesty, my moral veneer, and quite unroofed me. And I never bothered to patch up the damage. Soon along came Love, in place of rain, in great drops, trickling into my breast and soaking into my heart. And now my cash and credit, my reputation and merit, all my honour, have left me altogether. I'm surely the worse for wear! And these underpinnings of mine are quite rotted away; I don't think I can repair my house without tearing the whole thing down to the foundations. And no one can help me.

It cuts me to the quick when I think what I am now and what I was; none of my classmates was a harder worker or better known as an athlete. I used to love the discus, javelin, baseball, track, fencing, and horseback-riding; I was a model of thrift and endurance. The very best fellows used to come to me for coaching. Now I'm absolutely worthless; that's my real nature, I've now discovered. (*He retires to the alley, from which he observes the following scene.*)

Act One. Scene III

(*Enter* PHILEMATIUM *from the house of* THEOPROPIDES, *followed by* SCAPHA, *who carries a table and various articles of dress and decoration.* PHILEMATIUM *sits on a couch in front of the table and busies herself with her toilet, continuing it throughout the scene. They do not see* PHILOLACHES.)

PHILEMATIUM: My, my! I've just had the most wonderful cold shower. I haven't been cleaner in ages, Scapha darling.

SCAPHA: All things have consequences, just as this spring's sowing brought a big harvest.

PHILEMATIUM: Why, what's the connection between the harvest and my washing?

SCAPHA: No more than between your washing and the harvest.

PHILOLACHES (*aside, seeing* PHILEMATIUM): O beauteous beauty! There she is, the storm that wrecked the modesty that walled my house! Then Love and Desire streamed like rain into my heart, and now I'll never be able to make repairs. Now the ramparts of my breast are soaked, and my house is a total ruin.

PHILEMATIUM (*prinking*): Scapha dear, look—does this frock fit me well? I want to be beautiful for dear, dear Philolaches, my sweet guardian.

SCAPHA: You might just as well put on only your charming ways, you're so charming yourself. Why not? A lover doesn't love the dress itself, but what's in it.

PHILOLACHES (*aside*): Well, I'll be darned! Scapha's a charmer herself, and the old girl knows her stuff, too. She grasped right off the way we lovers act and think.

PHILEMATIUM (*trying various ornaments*): Well, how's that?

SCAPHA: What?

PHILEMATIUM: Come on! Look me over and tell me how I look in this.

SCAPHA: Anything would fit a lovely figure like yours.

PHILOLACHES (*aside*): You'll certainly be rewarded for those words, Scapha. You won't praise my one and only for nothing.

PHILEMATIUM: Now I wouldn't have you flatter me.

SCAPHA: You silly goose! See here: would you prefer to be criticised falsely or praised truly? As for me, I'd much rather get false flattery than true blame; I don't want people laughing at my looks!

PHILEMATIUM: I love the truth and I want to hear the truth; I hate liars.

SCAPHA: As you love me, and as Philolaches loves you, I swear you're completely charming.

PHILOLACHES (*aside*): What's that, you wretch? What kind of an oath was that? "As I love her?" What about "her" loving "me"? Why wasn't that tacked on? I take back my present. You're lost! You've lost that gift I promised you.

SCAPHA: You know, I'm awfully surprised that a girl as shrewd and clever and as well-trained as you are acts so foolishly.

PHILEMATIUM: Do tell me, please, if I'm doing anything wrong.

SCAPHA: Doing anything wrong, when you pay attention to one man, grant your favours to him alone, and turn up your nose at all the others? Let married women submit to one lover—that's not the business of a mistress.

PHILOLACHES (*aside*): Ye gods! What she-devil is this I'm keeping in my house? God damn me to the lowest depths of Hell if I don't kill that hag with hunger, thirst, and cold.

PHILEMATIUM: I don't want you to give me bad advice, Scapha.

SCAPHA: Well, you are a simple creature. You think Philolaches will always be loving and faithful, do you? Watch out! He'll throw you over with age and usage.

PHILEMATIUM: Oh, I hope not!

SCAPHA: More often we get what we've not hoped for than what we want. Besides, if you can't be persuaded by words to believe me, consider the facts: just look at me, and then think of what I used to be in the good old days. . . .[3] Once upon a time I too was the object of passion, and I was faithful to my one and only. But when my hair had turned to silver, he left me, forsook me. I'm afraid you're headed the same way.

PHILOLACHES (*aside*): I can hardly keep myself from tearing out her eyes, the busybody!

PHILEMATIUM: He set me free with his own money—to be his and his only; surely I ought to save myself for him.

PHILOLACHES (*aside*): Heavens, what a lovely girl! She's as pure as the snow. I'm glad I've ruined myself for her; it's well worth it.

SCAPHA: You're just plain stupid, I tell you.

PHILEMATIUM: Why?

SCAPHA: For worrying about his loving you.

PHILEMATIUM: Why shouldn't I, for mercy's sake?

SCAPHA: You're free now, aren't you? You've got what you were after. If he doesn't love you now, he'll lose all the money he paid for you.

PHILOLACHES (*aside*): Damn me if I don't kill that hag with slow torture! The old bawd is luring the girl from the straight and narrow.

PHILEMATIUM: I can never repay him for all he's done for me. Now Scapha, don't you try to persuade me not to think so much of him.

SCAPHA: But just think this over: if you let him walk all over you when you're young, you'll be sorry when you're old.

PHILOLACHES (*aside*): Oh, how I'd like to change myself into a case of diphtheria! I'd get that old witch by the throat and kill her, the wicked bawd.

PHILEMATIUM: I ought to show the same grateful spirit towards him now that I've got what I wanted, as I used to before I coaxed and wheedled this out of him.

PHILOLACHES (*aside*): May the gods have their will of me, if I don't liberate you again for that speech—and if I don't lacerate Scapha!

SCAPHA: Well, if you're quite sure that you'll always have plenty to live on, and that he will be your one and only all your life, then I agree you ought to give in to him—and put on your bridal veil at once!

PHILEMATIUM: If a person has a good reputation, he can usually get along. If I keep my good name, I'll be rich enough.

PHILOLACHES (*aside*): If it has to be done, I'd much rather sell my father than ever see you in want or going begging.

SCAPHA: But what will become of your other lovers?

PHILEMATIUM: They'll love me all the more when they see how grateful I am to my benefactor.

PHILOLACHES (*aside*): How I'd love to hear the news that my father is dead! I'd immediately disinherit myself and make her my heir.

SCAPHA: His property will soon be done for, anyway; day and night, nothing but eating and drinking, and never a thought of saving anything. Why, it's outright gorging!

PHILOLACHES (*aside*): By God, you'll be the first I'll practise saving on, of that I'm sure. You'll get nothing to eat or drink in my house for the next week.

PHILEMATIUM (*sternly*): If you've anything complimentary to say about him, go ahead. But if you continue to abuse him, I'll have you whipped.

PHILOLACHES (*aside, much delighted*): By heavens, if I'd built a church with the money I gave for her, I couldn't have made as good use of it. It's plain she loves me through and through. I've set free a lawyer to do my pleading for me.

SCAPHA: Well, since it's evident you're completely gone on Philolaches, I might as well save myself the whipping and say you're right.

PHILEMATIUM: Give me the mirror and my jewel-box, quickly, Scapha. I must look all dolled up for my sweetheart, Philolaches, when he comes.

SCAPHA (*handing over the mirror*): A woman never needs a mirror till she's not sure of her aging looks. What do you want with it? Why, you're a better mirror yourself.

PHILOLACHES (*aside*): So your words won't be in vain, Scapha, I'll give a little present today—to my darling Philematium!

PHILEMATIUM: Am I all set? My hair all right in back?

SCAPHA: Since you're so comely, you can be sure your hair's all right.

PHILOLACHES (*aside, in disgust*): Bah! Ever hear anything so disgusting? Now she's all compliments; before the devil had nothing but back-talk.

PHILEMATIUM: Bring me the powder.

SCAPHA: Powder? What for?

PHILEMATIUM: Why, to put on my cheeks.

SCAPHA: You might as well try to bleach ivory with shoe-polish!

PHILOLACHES (*aside*): Chalk up one for you, Scapha. Ivory and shoe-polish—darn good!

PHILEMATIUM: Well, let's have the rouge.

SCAPHA: I will not. You're too smart—gilding the lily, eh? A young thing like you doesn't need a jot of rouge, lipstick, mascara, or any other war-paint.

PHILEMATIUM: Oh, all right. Hold the mirror. (*Kisses it and hands it to* SCAPHA.)

PHILOLACHES (*aside*): Hang it! She kissed the mirror! Oh, what I'd give for a stone, to smash its face in.

SCAPHA: Here's a towel. Better wipe off your hands.

PHILEMATIUM: What for?

SCAPHA: You've had your hands on that mirror, and I'm afraid they smell of silver; don't ever let Philolaches think you've taken that from any man!

PHILOLACHES (*aside*): I don't think I've ever seen a wilier old hen. The way she thought up that business about the mirror, the old wretch.

PHILEMATIUM: How about a little perfume? Think so?

SCAPHA: Why, of course not!

PHILEMATIUM: Why not?

SCAPHA: Because the right way for a woman to smell is not to smell at all. Those old hags that smear themselves up and make themselves all greasy, painted, toothless old witches, who cover their faults under layers of paint—when their perspiration mixes with the perfume, it's just as if a cook had poured all his soups together. You'd never know what it is they smell like—but the stench is awful!

PHILOLACHES (*aside*): She knows all the answers, like a book. Pretty wise bird! Most of you fellows know it too, you who have old wives, who got you with their dowries.

PHILEMATIUM: Well, now! How does everything look to you, Scapha? The gown and the jewelry all on right?

SCAPHA: That's none of my business.

PHILEMATIUM: What? Whose is it, then?

SCAPHA: Oh, that's easy. It's Philolaches' business. He oughtn't to buy anything, except what he likes. But why exhibit such stuff, which he wouldn't want to own? Beauty unadorned is fairer far than silks and satins; if a woman's pretty, she's dressed more than enough.

PHILOLACHES (*starting out from the alley*): My fingers have been itching too long. (*Aloud*) What are you two up to?

PHILEMATIUM: I'm getting all fixed up to make you happy.

PHILOLACHES (*kissing her*): You're dolled up enough. (*To* SCAPHA) Get inside with all that finery. (SCAPHA *goes into the house*) But sweetheart, Philematium darling, let's have a drink together.

PHILEMATIUM: Oh, yes, let's! I like whatever you do, darling.

PHILOLACHES: That word is worth twenty minae, sweetheart!

PHILEMATIUM: I'll take ten; special bargain, just for you!

PHILOLACHES: That still doesn't square us. Count it up yourself. I paid thirty for you—

PHILEMATIUM (*drawing away*): Why reproach me with that?

PHILOLACHES: Reproach you? I, who love to have myself blamed for it? Why, I never did better with my money!

PHILEMATIUM (*mollified*): And I'm sure I've done the best I could by giving my all to you.

PHILOLACHES: Good! The budget's balanced. You love me, and I love you, and we both think that's just swell. And may those who are happy with us always have their full measure of happiness; and may those who envy us never have anything to excite the envy of others.

PHILEMATIUM: Come, sit down. Boy! Bring in some water for our hands. Where are the dice? Will you have some perfume?

PHILOLACHES: No need. I've got a rose-garden next to me. (*Looking down the street*) Say, that looks like my old friend coming along with his girl. It is! Here comes Callidamates with his girl friend. Isn't that nice, darling? The gang's getting together. They're coming to share the loot! (*He and* PHILEMATIUM *settle down on the couch to watch the approach of the new arrivals.*)

Act One. Scene IV

(*Enter* CALLIDAMATES, *very drunk, and supported by* DELPHIUM, *and by a young slave.*)

CALLIDAMATES (*to the slave*): Come 'n' call for me at Philolaches'—an' be on time. Y' hear? That's your orders! (*To the world at large, happily*) I just had to get out of that place, where I was before. I got *so* bored with the people and the conversation! Now I'm going to raise Cain over at Philolaches' place. They'll give us a merry welcome, and it'll be lots of fun. (*Capers about in anticipation, then stops short as a horrid suspicion strikes him*) Say, I don't look at all t-t-t-tight, do I?

DELPHIUM (*disgusted*): No more than usual. You're getting in your own way. (*Turning him around*) Here's where you were bound.[4]

CALLIDAMATES (*in a sudden burst of affection*): Let's you and me have a big hug, huh?

DELPHIUM (*still disgusted*): If you must, I suppose it's all right.

CALLIDAMATES (*falling on her neck*): I say, you're swell! Better help me along.

DELPHIUM: Watch out, or you'll fall. Oh, do stand up!

CALLIDAMATES: Aw—aw—aw—sweetie, I'm your baby, my honeysuckle. (*Threatens to collapse completely.*)

DELPHIUM (*struggling to keep him on his feet*): That's fine, but be careful you don't sprawl out in the gutter before we can go and lie down on the couch they've prepared for us.

CALLIDAMATES: Oh, let me—let me—fall!

DELPHIUM: All right. (*Lets go of him; he drops suddenly, dragging* DELPHIUM *down on top of him.*)

CALLIDAMATES (*seizing her, not quite understanding what it is*): But what is this in my hands?

DELPHIUM (*struggling to get up*): But as you see, if you fall down, I'll be right on top of you.

CALLIDAMATES (*settling himself for a quiet nap*): Some nice fellow will come along and pick us up.

DELPHIUM (*finally rising*): Oh, boy, is he plastered!

CALLIDAMATES (*indignantly*): What? P-p-plastered?

DELPHIUM: Hold on to my hand. It won't do to have you break your neck.

CALLIDAMATES: Here, take it. (*She drags him to his feet.*)

DELPHIUM: All right now, let's go.

CALLIDAMATES: Where'll I go?

DELPHIUM: Don't you even know?

CALLIDAMATES (*thinking for a moment*): Sure, I just thought of it. We're going home for a drink! (*Starts off home.*)

DELPHIUM (*catching him and turning him around again*): No, you're going *there*.

CALLIDAMATES: Oh, sure enough.

PHILOLACHES (*rising from couch*): Do you mind if I go welcome them, darling? I like him best of all my friends. I'll be right back.

PHILEMATIUM: Even that's a long time to me.

CALLIDAMATES (*reeling drunkenly about and finally backing into* PHILO- LACHES): Anybody home?

PHILOLACHES: Sure, we're all here.

CALLIDAMATES (*embracing him effusively*): Hello, Philolaches, old top. How's the best fellow in the world?

PHILOLACHES (*leading him to a couch*): Bless you, Callidamates! There's a couch for you. Where've you been?

CALLIDAMATES: I've been—gettin' drunk!

PHILEMATIUM (*rising and embracing* DELPHIUM): Do sit down, Delphium dear. (*To slave*) Give him a drink.

CALLIDAMATES (*takes a long drink, then sprawls out on couch*): I'm going to sleep.

PHILOLACHES (*laughing*): Nothing very remarkable or unusual about that, is there?

DELPHIUM (*almost weeping*): Oh, now what'll I do with him?

PHILEMATIUM: He'll be all right just as he is, dear. (*To slave*) Boy! Get the drinks started with Delphium.

Act Two. Scene I

(*Enter* TRANIO, *carrying a basket; he is running violently, and in his excitement he runs past the party in front of* PHILOLACHES' *house to the centre of the stage.*)

TRANIO (*to himself*): Old Nick's sure trying as hard as he can to drag me and young master Philolaches to perdition! Hope's dead, no more place for confidence, and Salvation herself couldn't redeem us, even if she wanted to. I've just had a view of the vilest vision of evil and woe down at the pier! The boss is back from abroad; poor Tranio's done for! (*To the audience*) Any of you fellows interested in making some ready cash by taking my part as the subject of a crucifixion? Where are your beating-bearing, torture-tried martyrs, or your heroes who rush into the enemy's trenches for a dollar a day, where they're sure of getting five or ten bayonets rammed into them? There's a talent for the first man who'll attack and capture my cross for himself—on condition his arms and legs are tacked on double. As soon as that's done he can claim the cash. But what a fool I am for not galloping home as fast as I can. (*He picks up his basket and starts for the house.*)

PHILOLACHES: Hurrah! Here come the eats! Tranio's back from downtown. (*He seizes the basket and pulls out the contents.* TRANIO *makes futile efforts to get his attention.*)

TRANIO: Philolaches!

PHILOLACHES (*without looking up*): What now?

TRANIO: You and I, we're both—.

PHILOLACHES: What about us?

TRANIO (*tragically*): Goners!

PHILOLACHES (*interested, but not alarmed*): How come?

TRANIO: Your father's back! (*A shocked silence, then general consternation.*)

PHILOLACHES (*wildly*): What? Did I hear right?

TRANIO: It's all over with us. I said, your father's come!

PHILOLACHES: For goodness sake, where is he?

TRANIO: He's here—at the harbour!

PHILOLACHES: Who says so? Who saw him?

TRANIO: I'm telling you, I saw him myself.

PHILOLACHES (*sinking down on the couch*): Oh, Lord! Now where am I?

TRANIO (*sneering*): Why the deuce do you ask me that? You're right there on the couch.

PHILOLACHES: You saw him yourself?

TRANIO: Myself, I'm trying to tell you!

PHILOLACHES: You're quite sure?

TRANIO: Of course—positive!

PHILOLACHES (*rushing madly about, his head in his hands*): If that's true, there's no hope left for me.

TRANIO: What would be the sense of lying?

PHILOLACHES: Oh, what'll I do now?

TRANIO: Have them take away all this junk. (*A loud snore from* CAL-LIDAMATES) Who's that sleeping over there?

PHILOLACHES: Callidamates.

TRANIO: Wake him up, Delphium. (*Busies himself with the other slaves in clearing up the banquet.*)

DELPHIUM: Callidamates, Callidamates! Wake up!

CALLIDAMATES (*starting up*): I am awake. Gimme a drink!

DELPHIUM: Oh, get up! Philolaches' father's just got home from abroad!

CALLIDAMATES (*seizing a cup*): A health to his father!

PHILOLACHES (*running over*): Oh, he's in excellent health, and I'm dead and gone!

CALLIDAMATES: Dead and gone? Then you've died twice. How can that be?

PHILOLACHES (*exasperated*): Please get up; my father's here!

CALLIDAMATES: Your father's here? Tell him to go 'way. What's the idea of his coming back here?

PHILOLACHES (*to himself, walking wildly up and down*): What will I do? Father will be here any minute, catch me tight, the house full of drunks and women. What a mess! We've waited to dig the well till we're dying of thirst! Just what's happened to me—idiot! Fine time to think up a way out, now that my father's here!

TRANIO (*pointing to* CALLIDAMATES): There he's gone and cuddled up to sleep again. Wake him up!

PHILOLACHES (*rushing over to him*): Wake up, I say! I'm trying to tell you my father will be here any minute!

CALLIDAMATES (*leaping into action*): Your father, huh? Where are my slippers? Give me my armour! I'll murder him! (*Rushes about madly, falls over a slave, and sprawls on the floor.*)

PHILOLACHES: Oh, you're gumming up the whole works!

DELPHIUM: Please hush up, won't you?

TRANIO (*to the other slaves*): Drag him off into the house!

CALLIDAMATES (*as the slaves carry him towards the house*): Better bring me a basin—before I use you for one. (*He goes into the house.*)

PHILOLACHES: Perdition!

TRANIO: Courage! I'll heal up all your fears, just fine.

PHILOLACHES: Oh, I'm lost!

TRANIO: Come now, I'm the doctor to think up the cure for all this business. Will it be good enough if I arrange it so that he not only won't want to go into the house, but actually will beat it as far away as he can? Just go on in and get rid of all this, hurry!

PHILOLACHES: Where'll I be?

TRANIO (*cool and collected*): Where you like it best: with her, and her.

DELPHIUM (*approaching, with* PHILEMATIUM): Suppose we leave?

TRANIO: Not necessary at all, Delphium. And don't drink a bit less inside on account of this.

PHILOLACHES: Oh! I'm in a cold sweat, wondering how all your lovely speeches will turn out!

TRANIO: Won't you quiet down and obey orders?

PHILOLACHES: I will.

TRANIO: First of all, Philematium, go on in, and you with her, Delphium.

DELPHIUM: We're both at your disposal. (*They go into the house.*)

TRANIO (*leering*): I wish you were! (*To* PHILOLACHES) Now listen to what I want done. First of all, have the whole place shut up tight. And not a peep out of any of you.

PHILOLACHES: I'll attend to it.

TRANIO: Just as if not a mother's son of you were in the house.

PHILOLACHES: All right.

TRANIO: And don't answer when your old man knocks.

PHILOLACHES: Is that all?

TRANIO: Send out the key. I'm going to lock up from the outside.

PHILOLACHES: I'm putting my life and hopes into your hands, Tranio. (*He goes inside.*)

TRANIO (*to himself*): It doesn't make the least bit of difference whether the patron or the client's the better man. It's easy enough for any fellow without a backbone to mix up everything in a minute. But you need a genius to arrange the outcome of a mix-up that's been planned and carried out in such a way as to keep him out of trouble and have everything come out so he won't wish he were dead. I'm going to manage to calm down all this turmoil we're in and bring us all off clear.
(*Enter* SPHAERIO *from the house.*)
But what's the idea of coming out, Sphaerio?

SPHAERIO (*extending a key*): Just—.

TRANIO: Oh, good! My orders have been obeyed.

SPHAERIO: He ordered me to beg you with all my heart to scare off his father any way you can, so long as he doesn't come inside.

TRANIO: Just tell him, I'll fix things so he won't even want to look at the house. He'll hide his head and fly off in a fright. Let's have the key. Go on in and close the door while I lock it out here. (SPHAERIO *goes inside;* TRANIO *locks the door*) Now bring him on! We'll give the old boy fireworks today while he's alive—and that's more than he'll have at his funeral. I'll just step aside from the door, and watch from a little way off. We'll see how we can pile it on when he turns up. (*He steps into the alley.*)

Act Two. Scene II

(*Enter* THEOPROPIDES, *followed by two slaves with luggage.*)

THEOPROPIDES: My heartfelt thanks to you, Neptune, for letting me off with some spark of life still left in me. But if ever again you catch me one inch off terra firma, do to me whatever you wanted to this time, and I'll admit I've had no cause for complaint. "Get thee behind me!" now and for all time. You've had all the vantage of me that I meant to give you.

TRANIO (*aside*): What a sin that was, Neptune! To let opportunity knock like that and go unheeded!

THEOPROPIDES (*advancing towards his house*): After three long years in Egypt I've come home at last. The family must be waiting with open arms.

TRANIO (*aside*): Our arms would open a good deal more easily to some-one bringing tidings of your death!

THEOPROPIDES (*trying the door*): But what's this? Latch on in the middle of the day? I'll knock. (*Knocking*) I say there! Who's at home? Will you open the door?

TRANIO (*advancing and pretending not to recognise* THEOPROPIDES): Who could that be, walking right up to our house like that?

THEOPROPIDES: Ah! If it isn't my servant Tranio.

TRANIO (*pretending to recognise him at last*): Oh, Theopropides! Dear, dear sir! Welcome! It *is* good to see you safely back again. And have you been in good health while you were away?

THEOPROPIDES (*strutting up pompously*): All along, as you see.

TRANIO: That's just fine.

THEOPROPIDES: But what's wrong with you? Have you gone out of your mind?

TRANIO: Why, what makes you say that?

THEOPROPIDES: Just this: here you are out for a walk. Not one of you is watching the house; no one's around to open the door or even to see who's knocking. Why, I've almost broken down the door by banging on it.

TRANIO (*in great horror*): What? You mean you touched the house?

THEOPROPIDES: And why wouldn't I touch it? I tell you I darn near splintered the door, pounding.

TRANIO (*in great distress*): Oh-oh! You touched it?

THEOPROPIDES (*exasperated*): Touched it, I say, and banged on it too!

TRANIO: Oh, how terrible!

THEOPROPIDES: Well, what's wrong?

TRANIO: You've done something *terrible*!

THEOPROPIDES: Why, what's the matter?

TRANIO (*groaning*): Oh, I can't tell you what an *awful, terrible* thing you've done!

THEOPROPIDES: Well, what *is* it?

TRANIO (*seizing him and pulling him away*): For heaven's sake, run— come away from the door! Quick—run—towards me! You mean to say you've really touched the door?

THEOPROPIDES: How the deuce could I bang on it without touching it?

TRANIO: Oh, you've murdered—

THEOPROPIDES: What? Whom?

TRANIO: Your whole family!

THEOPROPIDES: Oh, plague take you and your confounded superstitions!

TRANIO: I'm afraid you'll never absolve yourself and (*noticing the two slaves with the baggage*) those poor devils!

THEOPROPIDES (*bewildered*): Why? What on earth are you pulling off here?

TRANIO (*pointing to the slaves*): Oh, sir, tell those fellows to run away.

THEOPROPIDES: Off with you! (*Kicks the slaves off.*)

TRANIO: Don't touch the house! Touch wood—you too!

THEOPROPIDES (*impatiently*): Well, spit it out, will you!

TRANIO: Not a soul has been inside that house for seven months, that is, since we moved out.

THEOPROPIDES: How come? Tell me!

TRANIO (*looking about*): Look around! No one will hear what we say, will they?

THEOPROPIDES (*looking cautiously up and down*): Go on! The coast's clear.

TRANIO: Look again! Better make sure.

THEOPROPIDES: No one's in sight, I tell you. Speak up, at once! What is it?

TRANIO: It's first-degree *murder*!

THEOPROPIDES: Wh-what? I don't get you.

TRANIO: I'm telling you, a crime was committed—a long, long time ago.

THEOPROPIDES (*stupidly, echoing* TRANIO): Long ago?

TRANIO: Yes, but we've just now turned up the evidence.

THEOPROPIDES: What crime was it? Who committed it? Oh, *out* with it!

TRANIO: He—he got hold of his *guest,* and *murdered* him! It must have been the man who sold you the house.

THEOPROPIDES: Murdered him?

TRANIO: Yes, and stole all his money! His *guest's,* mind you! And buried him—the guest—right here, in your house!

THEOPROPIDES: And how come you found out all this?

TRANIO: I'll tell you; listen. (*Dropping his voice*) Your son came home from a dinner party one night, and we all went up to bed. Soon we were all asleep. By chance, I had left the light on. And all at once—he *screamed*—at the top of his lungs!

THEOPROPIDES: Who? My son?

TRANIO: Sh-h-h! Keep quiet and listen for a moment. He said that in his sleep, *he* came to him—the dead man.

THEOPROPIDES: Oh, just in his sleep?

TRANIO: Yes. But listen! He said that the dead man spoke to him.

THEOPROPIDES: In his sleep?

TRANIO (*impatiently*): You wouldn't expect a corpse, dead for sixty years, to come babbling in when he was awake, would you? You *can* be thick sometimes, Theopropides.

THEOPROPIDES: Sorry. I'm all ears.

TRANIO: Well, this is what the dead man said to him, in his sleep: (*In a sepulchral voice*)

"My name is Transatlanticus; a guest was I from across the deep. Here is my abode. To me this house has been appointed as my haunt. For Orcus has refused me admittance to Acheron, since before my time I lost my life. My misplaced faith proved my undoing. My host it was who murdered me, and secretly, without benefit of clergy, buried me here, in this same house, the despicable wretch, because he coveted my riches. Begone then! At once! This roof is doomed, these walls polluted!"

It would take me *years* to tell all the ghastly things that have happened here. (*The door of the house rattles.*)

THEOPROPIDES: Sh! Sh!

TRANIO: Oh heavens! What was that?

THEOPROPIDES (*trembling*): The door—it creaked!

TRANIO (*running over to the door, and pointing to* THEOPROPIDES): It was *he*! He knocked!

THEOPROPIDES: My heart's in my mouth! The dead are dragging me down to Acheron, alive!

TRANIO (*aside*): Oh Lord! They'll throw a monkey wrench into the works yet. I'm scared stiff he'll catch me red-handed.

THEOPROPIDES (*advancing cautiously towards the house*): What are you whispering over there?

TRANIO (*intercepting him*): Stay back from the door! Run, for heaven's sake, get going!

THEOFROPIDES (*backing off*): Where should I go? You run too!

TRANIO (*pompously*): I've no cause for alarm. There is peace between me and the dead.

A VOICE WITHIN: Hey, Tranio!

TRANIO (*pretending to answer the ghost*): You won't call me, if you know what you are doing. *I'm* not guilty! *I* didn't pound on your door.

THE VOICE: Say there, will you—[5]

TRANIO (*whispering at door*): Shut up! Not another peep out of you!

THEOPROPIDES (*approaching again*): Say, how about letting me in on all this?

TRANIO (*the same*): Oh, beat it, will you!

THEOPROPIDES: What's got your dander up, Tranio? To whom were you speaking?

TRANIO (*looking up*): Oh, was it you who called? Darned if I didn't think that dead fellow was starting an argument because you rapped on the door. But how come you're still here? Won't you listen to what I say?

THEOPROPIDES: What shall I do?

TRANIO: Be off at once! Don't look behind you! And cover your head!

THEOPROPIDES: But what about you?

TRANIO: There is peace between me and the dead.

THEOPROPIDES: Yes, yes, I heard you the first time. But then, what was it flustered you so a moment ago?

TRANIO: Don't worry about me. I tell you I can take care of myself. (*Steals back to the door, where he makes a few ghastly moans. Observing* THEOPROPIDES' *terror, he leaps up*) Off with you—as fast as your legs will carry you! And better call for God's help.

THEOPROPIDES: God help me! (*He departs on a run.*)

TRANIO: And me too—to run you ragged today, old boy! Lord, what a broth I've brewed in one day's work!

Act Three. Scene I

(*Enter* MISARGYRIDES, *checking his accounts.*)

MISARGYRIDES (*to himself*): A more depressing depression than this I've never seen. The moneylending business has gone to the dogs. I'm on the job from nine to five and never a penny can I manage to put out.

TRANIO (*aside*): Confound it! I'm ruined for good now! There's old Moneybags himself, the fellow who loaned us the dough to buy the girl and fill the pantry. The jig's up unless I get hold of him before the old man finds out. I'll go up to him. I'm scared stiff somebody'll get wind of this deal. I'll go up and call him. Boy, I'm shivering! Unlucky devil! There's nothing sicker than a guilty conscience—and I certainly have that, all right! Well, as the matter stands, I'll have to go on mixing things up—that's my racket! (*Starts over, then catches sight of* THEO-PROPIDES *returning. Goes over to keep him away from the money-lender*) Where did you come from, sir?

THEOPROPIDES: I have just met the man who sold me that house.

TRANIO: You didn't mention that little matter I told you about, did you?

THEOPROPIDES: I certainly did,—told him the whole story.

TRANIO (*aside*): Wow! Looks as if my tricks are over forever!

THEOPROPIDES: What's that you're muttering there?

TRANIO: Oh, nothing; but tell me, you really told him, you say?

THEOPROPIDES: The whole story, from beginning to end.

TRANIO: Well then, he confessed about his guest, I suppose?

THEOPROPIDES: Not for a minute. He denies it.

TRANIO (*in great surprise*): What? Denies it, the scoundrel? [5]

THEOPROPIDES: That's what I said: *De-nies* it.

TRANIO: Are you sure? Think now! Didn't he confess?

THEOPROPIDES (*impatiently*): I'd tell you if he did. Now what do you think we should do?

TRANIO: Think we should do? Why, for goodness sake, drag him before a judge—(*aside*) but be sure you get one who'll believe my story— Why, you'll win the case hands down.

MISARGYRIDES (*looking up and seeing* TRANIO): Well, well! If it isn't Philolaches' business manager, Tranio; neither interest nor principal yet from either of those two! (MISARGYRIDES *starts towards* TRANIO; TRANIO *anxiously starts over to cut him off from* THEOPROPIDES.)

THEOPROPIDES: And where do you think you're going?

TRANIO (*halting*): Oh, I wasn't going anywhere. (*Aside*) If I'm not the unluckiest cuss! Born on Friday the thirteenth, I guess. That fellow will be on my neck while the boss is here. I'm in a hot spot now! They've got me coming and going. Might as well settle with this one.

MISARGYRIDES: Aha! Here he comes at last. Hurrah! Now for my money.

TRANIO (*aside*): He's all smiles. Lot of good that'll do him. (*Approaches* MISARGYRIDES) Hello there, Misargyrides, old top!

MISARGYRIDES: Hello yourself. Where's my cash?

TRANIO: Oh, go 'way, you blood-sucker. As soon as I'm in sight, you get your teeth ready.

MISARGYRIDES: Bah! Not a cent on him!

TRANIO: You've got the scent there all right.

MISARGYRIDES: Cut out the jokes.

TRANIO: Well, what do you want now?

MISARGYRIDES: Where's Philolaches?

TRANIO: You couldn't possibly have turned up at a better time.

MISARGYRIDES: What's up now?

TRANIO (*pulling him away from* THEOPROPIDES): Come over here.

MISARGYRIDES: Why isn't my interest paid?

TRANIO: I know you've got good lungs. No need to shout.

MISARGYRIDES (*raising his voice*): By gad, I'll yell my head off!

TRANIO: Oh, give a fellow a break.

MISARGYRIDES: What kind of a break do you want?

TRANIO (*desperately*): *Please* go home!

MISARGYRIDES (*indignantly*): What? Go home?

TRANIO: You can come back around twelve o'clock.

MISARGYRIDES: Will I get my interest then?

TRANIO: Yes, yes. You'll get it. Just go home.

MISARGYRIDES (*planting himself firmly*): What's the sense of running back and forth, expending all that energy—or wasting it? Suppose I wait here till twelve instead?

TRANIO: Oh, go home. I'm telling you the truth. Go on home!

MISARGYRIDES (*shouting*): Why don't I get my interest? Stop trying to make an ass of me!

TRANIO (*sarcastically*): That's just dandy! Go away, will you? Listen to me!

MISARGYRIDES: By gad, I'll yell his name all over the street.

TRANIO (*giving up*): Go ahead—loud!

MISARGYRIDES (*bawling*): Philolaches, Phill-loll-laches!
                          Philolaches, Phill-loll-laches! [6]

TRANIO: You're really in the seventh heaven when you're making a racket.

MISARGYRIDES: I'm only asking for what's mine. For days and days now you've been putting me off. If I'm a nuisance—pay up! I'll go away. Just pay me and it'll be settled once and for all.

TRANIO (*trying another line*): Here, you can have the principal.

MISARGYRIDES: Nothing doing! I want my interest first.

TRANIO (*pretending indignation*): What's that you say, you viper? Did you come here to hog the stage? Sue him! You won't get a cent. He doesn't owe you anything.

MISARGYRIDES (*amazed*): Doesn't owe me anything?

TRANIO: Not a red nickel will you get away with. Afraid he'll skip town on account of your old interest? Especially when you can have the capital right off?

MISARGYRIDES: But I didn't ask for the capital. There's interest coming first.

TRANIO: Don't be a pest! Nobody's going to give it to you. And what can you do? You must think you're the only Shylock in the racket.

MISARGYRIDES (*shouting again*): Give me my interest, pay me my interest! Give it to me! Both of you! Are you going to pay up on the spot? Do I get my interest?

TRANIO: Interest to the right of him, interest to the left of him! He can't talk about anything else. Get out of here! I've never seen a dirtier dog than you!

MISARGYRIDES: "Sticks and stones"— You're not scaring *me* off like that.

THEOPROPIDES (*who has been watching this scene with growing interest*): Heated argument going on here. It's pretty warm even this far away. What the deuce is the interest the creature's screaming about?

TRANIO (*pointing out* THEOPROPIDES *to the moneylender*): There's his old man, just off the boat. He'll pay the whole thing—interest and principal too. Don't mix in now with your old bill. *He* won't keep you waiting.

MISARGYRIDES: Well, I'll just collect anything he pays down.

THEOPROPIDES (*calling to* TRANIO): What's going on there?

TRANIO (*running back to stop* THEOPROPIDES' *advance*): Did you call, sir?

THEOPROPIDES (*advancing gradually*): Who *is* that man? What does he want? What does he mean by bawling out my son's name and quarrelling with you? Do we owe him anything?

TRANIO: For heaven's sake, let me smear the money in his dirty face.

THEOPROPIDES: Shall I—?

TRANIO: Tell me to beat his face with it.

MISARGYRIDES (*also advancing*): I guess I could stand a gilt-edged beating.

TRANIO: Did you hear that? Isn't he a perfect wolf of a moneylender —bloodthirsty lot!

THEOPROPIDES: I'm not the least bit interested in his background. The point is—what I should like to know is: What is all this about money?

TRANIO (*hesitating*): Well—y'see—er—Philolaches—that is—he owes him a small amount.

THEOPROPIDES (*advancing with a start*): How small?

TRANIO: Oh, about forty minae. Not much, don't you agree?

THEOPROPIDES: Quite a trifle, I'd say. And there's interest on it too, I hear.

TRANIO: We owe the fellow forty-four minae all told—principal plus interest.

MISARGYRIDES (*stepping up and clapping* TRANIO *on the shoulder*): Just so! That's all I'm asking for.

TRANIO: Oh, how I wish you'd ask for just one cent more.[7] (*To* THEO-PROPIDES) Give him your I.O.U. so he'll go home.

THEOPROPIDES (*indignantly*): What? I?

TRANIO: Oh, go ahead.

THEOPROPIDES: Did you mean me?

TRANIO: Yes, you. Come on, now. Listen; promise him—go ahead. It's all right if I say so myself, isn't it?

THEOPROPIDES (*sternly*): Listen here! What's happened to all this money?

TRANIO (*thinking hard*): Oh, it's safe and sound, all right.

THEOPROPIDES: Sounds all right to me if you pay it yourself, if it's safe.

TRANIO (*thinking desperately*): Your son bought a—*house* with it!

THEOPROPIDES (*delighted*): A *house*?

TRANIO: Uh huh, a house.

THEOPROPIDES: Well, well; Philolaches is growing up to be a real shrewd businessman—just like his father. So he bought a house?

TRANIO (*with renewed confidence*): That's right, a house. And *what* a house!

THEOPROPIDES: Yes? What kind of a house?

TRANIO: Oh, boy!

THEOPROPIDES: Well, tell me about it.

TRANIO: Don't ask!

THEOPROPIDES: And why not?

TRANIO: Beyond description—a peach!

THEOPROPIDES: Good for him. And—what was the price?

TRANIO: Oh, a talent—times two. These forty minae were the first installment. We paid it from the loan from that fellow. D'you get it? Just as soon as we found out what I told you about the old place, he bought the new one.

THEOPROPIDES: Well, well! Good for him!

MISARGYRIDES (*interrupting*): Say there, you two. It's twelve o'clock.

TRANIO: Why not pay up and get rid of him before he pesters us to death with his bleating?

THEOPROPIDES (*to* MISARGYRIDES): You will get satisfaction from me, fellow.

MISARGYRIDES: Oh, I'll get money from you?

THEOPROPIDES: Just come 'round to the office tomorrow.

MISARGYRIDES: I'm off. Well off—so long as I finally get it tomorrow. (*He departs.*)

TRANIO (*aside*): Go and be hanged! Darn near ruined everything. There's no rottener bunch alive than these moneylenders, no—nor more dishonest, either.

THEOPROPIDES: And where is this house my son bought?

TRANIO (*aside, in great distress*): O-oh! Beginning all over again!

THEOPROPIDES: Come on! Answer me!

TRANIO: Right away. Only—the owner's name—it's slipped my mind.

THEOPROPIDES: Well, think of it.

TRANIO (*aside*): How'll I ever get out of this? Hm! Better leave it on our neighbour's doorstep. I'll tell him he bought Simo's house. They say a lie right off the fire's best. Whatever pops out with the devil's help is what I'll tell him.

THEOPROPIDES: How about it? Have you thought of it yet?

TRANIO: Confound him! (*Aside, pointing to* THEOPROPIDES) —or *him* rather—Your son bought this fellow's house, your neighbour's.

THEOPROPIDES (*greatly delighted*): No fooling?

TRANIO: Nobody'll be fooled if you pay up. If you don't, you'll make fools of all of us. Picked a pretty nice neighbourhood, didn't he?

THEOPROPIDES: Pretty nice! Why it's the very best. I *should* like to look it over. Go ahead. Knock at the door and see if you can call out some-one, Tranio.

TRANIO (*aside*): Oooo! Again! Now what'll I tell him this time? I'm on the rocks again. What'll I do now? Can't get round it this time. Looks as if I'm stuck.

THEOPROPIDES: Come, come! Call out someone to show us around.

TRANIO: But listen! There are women living there. We've got to find out first whether they're receiving.

THEOPROPIDES: A very good idea. Go find out. I'll be waiting out here for you.

TRANIO (*aside, as he approaches* SIMO'S *house*): Plague take you, bag and baggage! Old fool! You've aced me every time. (*Seeing* SIMO *at the door*) Well! There's the owner Simo coming out. Thank heaven for that. I'll disappear and collect my wits for a Congressional session in my head. When I get up a program I'll be back and let him have it. (*Steps back behind a column.*)

Act Three.   Scene II

(*Enter* SIMO *from his house.*)

SIMO (*to himself*): I haven't been better entertained at home this year, and I haven't had a meal I liked better. My wife gave me a fine lunch. Now she tells me to lie down. Nothing doing! I knew right off it wasn't any accident she gave me a better lunch than usual. The old woman wanted to lead me astray in the bedroom. But it isn't good to sleep on a full stomach. I sneaked out of the house; the wife's inside boiling over, I'll bet!

TRANIO (*aside*): Something terrible's been cooked up for this fellow's supper; he'll catch it good and plenty tonight—at the table and in bed.

SIMO: The more I think it over—if any one has a wife who's rich, and old too, he gets precious little sleep. In such a case a man hates to turn in. Take me, for instance: I'm quite resolved to beat it. I'm going off to town now so I shan't have to lie abed at home. (*To the audience*) So help me if I know how you fellows get on with your wives, but I know plenty about this one of mine—what a life she leads me! And it'll be still worse before I'm through.

TRANIO (*aside*): You'll be the one to suffer for going off like this, old top. It's not your luck you'll have to blame, but yourself—and rightly, too. Now it's time for me to speak to the old codger. I've got it! I've found a way to take in the geezer; I'll skin him to save my own hide. I'll go to meet him. (*Approaches*) Bless you, Simo.

SIMO: Good health, Tranio.

TRANIO: How are you?

SIMO: Not bad. What are you doing now?

TRANIO (*shaking hands with him*): I'm shaking hands with a very fine fellow.

SIMO: You're really very kind to praise me.

TRANIO: But you deserve it.

SIMO: Well, it's mutual, I assure you; I'm shaking hands with a very fine—rascal. (*Confidentially*) What now? How much more of this?

TRANIO: What?

SIMO: Oh, what usually goes on in there. (*Nodding towards* PHILOLACHES' *house*.)

TRANIO: What do you mean?

SIMO: You know what I mean. That's the way! Look out for yourself. And at the same time, remember how short life is.

TRANIO: What? Oh, I've just caught on: You're talking about our affairs.

SIMO (*enviously*): You live the life of Riley, you do! Just the right way. You fill up on good liquor and victuals, the finest and best fish.

TRANIO (*mournfully*): We did lead a life worth living once; but now everything's gone to the dogs.

SIMO: How's that?

TRANIO: We're completely ruined, Simo, every one of us.

SIMO: Oh, hush! Everything's gone splendidly up to now.

TRANIO: Yes, I don't deny it. We've lived pretty well, just as we wanted to. But now, Simo, the wind's been taken right out of our sails.

SIMO: What? In what way?

TRANIO: In the worst possible way.

SIMO: You mean, the sails that brought you safely into port?

TRANIO (*almost weeping*): O-oh!

SIMO: What's the matter?

TRANIO: Oh, poor me—I'm done for!

SIMO: How?

TRANIO: A ship's come in that'll shiver our timbers all to pieces.

SIMO: I'm sorry for you, Tranio. But what's up?

TRANIO: I'll tell you: master's back from abroad.

SIMO (*turning away*): That means for you, first a whipping, then the chain gang, and then the gallows!

TRANIO (*falling on his knees*): Oh, please, don't tell master on me!

SIMO: Don't worry, he won't learn anything from me.

TRANIO (*rising joyfully*): Greetings, my protector.

SIMO: I don't want any dealings with followers like you.

TRANIO: Now this matter the old man sent me to you about—

SIMO: You answer me this first: has your master any suspicions about these carryings-on of yours?

TRANIO: Not a one.

SIMO: Didn't he give his son a talking-to?

TRANIO: He's as serene as a sunny day. Now this is what he ordered me particularly to ask you, whether you'd let him look over your house.

SIMO: It's not for sale.

TRANIO: I know that; but the old man wants to build a lady's sitting room onto the house, and some baths and a promenade and a portico.

SIMO: What's he dreaming of?

TRANIO: I'll tell you: he wants to find his son a wife right away; so he intends to build the lady's sitting room. He says some architect or other praised this house and called it a remarkably fine piece of work. Now he wants to model his on this, if you don't mind. And he's all the more anxious to follow your model, since he's heard you have excellent shade here in the summer, all day long, even when the sun's at its hottest.

SIMO: That's where he's wrong. When it's shady everywhere else, the sun is always shining here, from morning till night. It hangs around the door like a bill collector. I haven't any shade here anywhere, unless there's some down the well.

TRANIO: Well, what about a jade from Sarsina,[8] if you haven't any shade. (*Roars with laughter at his joke.*)

SIMO: Don't be a pest! I'm telling you the truth.

TRANIO: Well, he still wants to see the house.

SIMO: Let him, if he likes. If he finds anything to his fancy, he can take it for his model.

TRANIO: Shall I go and tell him to come here?

SIMO (*turning away*): Yes, go on and call him.

TRANIO (*aside, as he goes back to* THEOPROPIDES): Alexander the Great and Agathocles, they say, were two men who did mighty deeds; now I'm the third in line, for these deathless deeds I've done all by myself. Here's one old codger with a pack-saddle on, and there's the other too. I've set up a new racket—not bad, either. Mule-drivers have mules to carry their packs, but I have men to carry mine. They've got broad backs, too; no matter how you pile it on, they bear it. (*Hesitating*) Now I don't know whether to speak to him or not. Yes, I'll go up to him. (*Approaches* THEOPROPIDES) Hey there, Theopropides.

THEOPROPIDES: Humph! Who's this calling me?

TRANIO: A servant ever faithful to his master.

THEOPROPIDES: Where are you coming from?

TRANIO: From the errand you sent me on; everything's settled.

THEOPROPIDES: Tell me. Why did you stay so long?

TRANIO: The old fellow was busy; I had to wait till he was free.

THEOPROPIDES: Up to your old tricks; late as usual.

TRANIO (*much offended*): Say, kindly remember the old proverb: you can't whistle and drink at the same time. And so I couldn't be here and there both at once.

THEOPROPIDES: Well, what's the answer?

TRANIO: Look all you like.

THEOPROPIDES: Come on, then. You lead the way.

TRANIO: Am I stopping you?

THEOPROPIDES: I'm right behind you. (*They start towards* SIMO.)

TRANIO: Look, the old man himself is waiting for you in front of the house. Boy, is he sorry he sold his house!

THEOPROPIDES: Why, what's the matter?

TRANIO: He asks me to get Philolaches to give it back.

THEOPROPIDES: Not so you'd notice it. Charity begins at home. If we'd been stung, we wouldn't have a chance to give it back. If you've got a good thing, hang on to it. Every man for himself—that's the idea!

TRANIO: Say, you're holding us up with all your talk. Come on.

THEOPROPIDES: All right. I'm all attention. (*They approach* SIMO.)

TRANIO: There's the old fellow. (*To* SIMO) See, I've brought him.

SIMO: I'm glad you've come home safely from your travels, Theopropides.

THEOPROPIDES: Bless you, Simo. (*They shake hands.*)

SIMO (*indicating* TRANIO): He was telling me you wanted to look over the house.

THEOPROPIDES: Yes, if it isn't any trouble to you.

SIMO (*graciously*): No trouble at all. Go in and look around.

THEOPROPIDES: But the women—?

SIMO: Oh, don't worry about them. Go anywhere you like, just as if the house were yours.

THEOPROPIDES (*aside, to* TRANIO): "Just as if" it were mine!

TRANIO: Oh, don't bring that up! He feels pretty sick about your buying his house. Don't you see what a long face he has?

THEOPROPIDES: Right you are.

TRANIO: So don't say a word about buying the place, and then it won't look as if you were laughing and gloating over him.

THEOPROPIDES: I understand. I think you've given good advice; you're very considerate. (*Turning back to* SIMO) Now what?

SIMO: Why don't you go inside and have a look around; take your time.

THEOPROPIDES: You're very kind; thank you.

SIMO: You're entirely welcome.

TRANIO (*running over to the doorway*): Do you see this porch and promenade here in front?

THEOPROPIDES: Yes, indeed, it's perfectly splendid.

TRANIO: Come, look at these doorposts. (*Slyly indicating the two old gentlemen*) See how solid and how thick they are!

THEOPROPIDES (*in admiration*): I don't think I've ever seen finer posts.

SIMO: By gad, you haven't. I paid a fine price for them once.

TRANIO (*aside, to* THEOPROPIDES): Did you hear him say "once"? He can hardly hold back his tears.

THEOPROPIDES (*to* SIMO): How much did they cost you?

SIMO: I paid three minae for the two of them—F.O.B.

THEOPROPIDES: Goodness, they're a lot worse than I thought.

TRANIO: How's that?

THEOPROPIDES (*bending over to examine them closely*): There's a worm hole down here.

TRANIO: I think they were cut out of season; that's what's the matter with them. And they're all right even now, if they get a coat of varnish. There's no seditious, foreign influence been at work here; it's a one hundred per cent Greek job! Do you see the joints on the doors?

THEOPROPIDES: Yes.

TRANIO (*again indicating the old men*): Notice how tight their eyes are shut?

THEOPROPIDES: Their *eyes* are shut?

TRANIO: What I meant was, "how tight the doors are shut." Do you get me?

THEOPROPIDES: The more I look at everything, the better I like it.

TRANIO (*getting between the two old men*): Look at the picture of the crow making fools of two silly, old geese.

THEOPROPIDES: I don't see it.

TRANIO: Well, I do. The crow's standing between the two. Look, he's pulling pieces out of both. Please look this way; then you'll see the crow. Now do you see it?

THEOPROPIDES: No, I don't see any crow there at all.

TRANIO: Well, look towards yourselves then, since you can't see the crow. Perhaps you'll see the geese.

THEOPROPIDES (*angry with this fooling*): I tell you, I don't see any picture of a bird here at all. Shut up!

TRANIO: All right, let it pass. I make allowances for you. You're too old to see it.

THEOPROPIDES: Everything I do see here suits me to a T.

SIMO: It'll pay you to look around here still further.

THEOPROPIDES: That's a good idea.

SIMO (*calling within*): Here, boy, show this gentleman around the rooms. (*To* THEOPROPIDES) I'd take you in myself, if I didn't have business downtown.

THEOPROPIDES: No *taking in* for me; I'd rather not be *taken in*. Whatever happens, I'll lose my own way around rather than have anyone lead me by the nose. (*Laughs immoderately at his little joke.*)

SIMO (*laughing too*): But I meant the house.

THEOPROPIDES: Well, I'll go in without a guide.

SIMO: All right.

THEOPROPIDES: Then I'll go in.

TRANIO: Wait a minute, please. Let me see about the dog.

THEOPROPIDES (*in sudden alarm*): Yes, do see about it.

TRANIO (*pretending to shoo away a dog*): Off with you! Get out of here! Get out and go to perdition! Won't you budge? Get out!

SIMO (*much amused, and joining in the jest*): She won't hurt you; she's as gentle as a lamb. You can go in without fear. Well, I'm off to town. (*He departs.*)

THEOPROPIDES: Thank you very much. Have a pleasant walk. Come here, Tranio, and have someone take this dog away from the door, even if she doesn't bite!

TRANIO: Just look at her. See how quietly she's lying there. Unless, of course, you want to look like a bothersome sissy.

THEOPROPIDES: As you please. Follow me this way then.

TRANIO: I'll certainly do so; I'll not budge from your heels. (*They go into* SIMO'S *house*.)

Act Four. Scene I

(*Enter* PHANISCUS.)

PHANISCUS (*to himself*): Slaves who're scared of a licking, even when they aren't to blame, are likely to be useful to their masters. But those who aren't scared of anything take up silly notions, when they've earned a spanking. They go in for sprinting! But if they're caught, they get more from their whipping than they ever got before. They start with a shoestring and end with a fortune.

But I intend to avoid punishment before my back is sore. My hide is still whole, and I propose to keep it so. If I can rule my itching fingers, I'll keep a good roof over me; and when blows rain on others, they won't rain on me. For a master's usually what his slaves want him to be. If they're good, he's good; if they're dishonest, then he becomes harsh.

Now there are so many rascals living at our house, who blow in their savings and get blows on their backs. When they're asked to go fetch master, they say: "No, I won't; don't bother me! I know where you're off to in such a hurry: you're itching for some old dive of yours. You're off to pasture like any jackass." This is what I get for my good services. So I left. And now I'm the only one out of the whole bunch who's going to fetch master. Tomorrow morning when he finds out, he'll set 'em right with cowhide. But I consider their backs worth much less than mine. Tanning's their future business, all right.

Act Four. Scene II

(*Enter* PINACIUM, *running*.)

PINACIUM: Wait a minute, Phaniscus; stay where you are. Won't you look back?

PHANISCUS: Don't trouble me.

PINACIUM: See how high-hat the monkey is. Won't you wait there, you dirty parasite?

PHANISCUS: Why am I a parasite?

PINACIUM: I'll tell you: you'd go anywhere for a square meal.

PHANISCUS: That's my business; I *like* to eat. Any of your business?

PINACIUM: You put on a bold front just because master likes you.

PHANISCUS: Dear me, my eyes are running.

PINACIUM: Why?

PHANISCUS: Your gassing's getting me.

PINACIUM: Shut up, you; you're always making stale jokes.

PHANISCUS: You can't make me swear at you. Master knows me.

PINACIUM (*laughing*): And well he ought to know his own mattress!

PHANISCUS (*sorrowfully*): If you were a nice boy, you wouldn't say such mean things.

PINACIUM: Should I give in to you, when you won't give in to me?

PHANISCUS: Well, come along with me then, you nasty boy. Do stop talking about those things.

PINACIUM (*running over to* PHILOLACHES' *house*): All right. I'll bang on the door. (*Knocks loudly*) Hey there! Isn't there someone here to protect the door from this mighty attack? (*Knocks again*) Won't anyone open? No one's coming out, I can tell you that. They're in just the condition you'd expect of such worthless folk. But I'll have to be careful; I don't want anyone to come out here and give me a licking.

Act Four.   Scene III⁹

(*Enter* THEOPROPIDES *and* TRANIO *from* SIMO'S *house; they do not see the two slaves at the door of the other house.*)

TRANIO: Well, how does this bargain look to you?

THEOPROPIDES: I'm completely enchanted with it.

TRANIO: You don't think it's too dear, do you?

THEOPROPIDES: Heavens, no! I don't think I ever saw a house so dirt-cheap as this.

TRANIO: Is it all right, then?

THEOPROPIDES: "Is it all right!" Man alive, it's more than just "all right."

TRANIO: What do you think of the lady's sitting rooms, and the portico?

THEOPROPIDES: Absolutely fine. I don't think I've ever seen a public portico that's a bit bigger.

TRANIO: Why, Philolaches and I measured all the public ones.

THEOPROPIDES (*eagerly*): What did you find?

TRANIO (*stretching his arms to their utmost*): It's the longest of all, by a long shot!

THEOPROPIDES: O Heavens above! What a fine bargain! Why, if anyone offered me a million in cash for it, I wouldn't take it.

TRANIO: And what's more, if you wanted to take it, I wouldn't let you.

THEOPROPIDES: Our funds are well invested in such a purchase.

TRANIO: Now be frank about it and admit that it was all done at my suggestion and persuasion. I was the one who made him go to a money-lender and borrow the money for the first installment.

THEOPROPIDES: You've saved the day! Now is it eighty minae we owe him?

TRANIO: Not a bit more!

THEOPROPIDES: He'll have it today.

TRANIO: Quite right; we don't want him to have any excuse for backing out. (*As a sudden idea strikes him*) Say, count it over to me; I'll pay him right away.

THEOPROPIDES: No monkeyshines now, if I do give it to you!

TRANIO (*much offended*): Do you think I'd dare to trick you in any way, even in fun?

THEOPROPIDES: Do you think I'd dare be off my guard in trusting anything to you?

TRANIO (*protesting*): What? Have I ever cheated you since I've been with you?

THEOPROPIDES: No; I've always been too careful! You can be grateful to me and my character for that. I'm wise enough, if I watch out for you alone.

TRANIO (*aside, in great amusement*): Agreed on that!

THEOPROPIDES (*brusquely*): Now go out to the farm and tell my son I'm back.

TRANIO (*starting off*): I'll do as you say, sir.

THEOPROPIDES (*calling after him*): Tell him to come back with you as fast as he can.

TRANIO: All right. (*Aside*) Now I'll go in to see the bunch by the back door. I'll tell 'em how quiet things are and how I got rid of him. (*Watches* THEOPROPIDES, *who is still admiring* SIMO's *house; at last, seeing his opportunity, slips in through the alley.*)

Act Four.   Scene IV¹⁰

PHANISCUS (*listening at door of* PHILOLACHES' *house*): I don't hear any noise from the party, as there used to be. There's no flute girl playing here, nor anyone else.

THEOPROPIDES (*suddenly noticing the two slaves*): What's that? What do those fellows want at my house? What are they up to? Why do they peek inside?

PHANISCUS (*knocking*): I'll keep on banging at the door. Hey, Tranio, unlock the door and open up, will you?

THEOPROPIDES: What's all this funny business?

PHANISCUS (*knocking*): Open up, won't you. We've come for our master Callidamates.

THEOPROPIDES (*advancing and raising his voice*): Hey, you fellows! What are you doing there? Why are you banging the house down?

PINACIUM: Hey, old grandpa, what are you asking questions for? Is it any of your business?

THEOPROPIDES: None of my business, eh?

PINACIUM (*approaching him*): Yes, unless you've just been made the new proctor, to snoop and sneak and look and listen to other people's affairs.

THEOPROPIDES (*threatening him*): That house where you're standing is mine.

PINACIUM: What's that? Has Philolaches sold it? (*Turning to* PHANIS- CUS) Or is this old man just trying to trick us?

THEOPROPIDES: I'm telling you the truth. But what business have you here?

PHANISCUS: I'll tell you. Our master's on a party here.

THEOPROPIDES: Your master's on a party here?

PHANISCUS: Just what I say.

THEOPROPIDES (*striking him and pushing him aside*): Boy, you're too fresh!

PHANISCUS (*wailing*): But we've come to fetch him home.

THEOPROPIDES: Whom?

PHANISCUS: Our master. (*Stamping his foot*) How many times do you have to be told?

THEOPROPIDES: No one lives here, boy. (*Hesitating*) And yet—I do think you're an honest fellow.

PHANISCUS: Doesn't young Philolaches live here?

THEOPROPIDES: He did live here, but he moved out of this house some time ago.

PINACIUM: The old codger's got bats in his belfry.[11]

PHANISCUS: You're all wrong, father. Unless he moved out today, I know for certain he does live here.

THEOPROPIDES (*angrily*): Why, no one's been living here for six months.

PINACIUM: Pipe-dreams!

THEOPROPIDES (*advancing towards him angrily*): Talking to me?

PINACIUM: Yes, you!

THEOPROPIDES (*threatening him*): Don't try to be smart. Let me talk with the young fellow here. (*Turning back to* PHANISCUS) No one lives here!

PHANISCUS: Yes, he does live here! Yesterday and the day before yes- terday and the day before that and the day before that—in fact, ever since his father went abroad, there's not been a space of three days without a brawl here.

THEOPROPIDES: What's that?

PHANISCUS: There haven't been three days here without a party— eating and drinking, bringing in strumpets and flute girls and lute girls, and fast living.

THEOPROPIDES (*now much interested*): Who was doing that?

PHANISCUS: Philolaches.

THEOPROPIDES: What Philolaches?

PHANISCUS: The son of Theopropides, I believe.

THEOPROPIDES (*aside*): I'm done for, if what he says is true. I'll keep after him. (*To* PHANISCUS) You say that this Philolaches, whoever he is, often drinks here with your master?

PHANISCUS: Yes, here in this house.

THEOPROPIDES: Boy, you're dumber than you look. Try to recollect, please, if you didn't stop off at some saloon and have a drop too much.

PHANISCUS: Why?

THEOPROPIDES: I want to make sure you haven't come to the wrong house by mistake.

PHANISCUS (*indignantly*): I know the way I ought to go, and I know the place I've come to. Philolaches lives here; his father is Theopropides. And after his father went abroad on business, he set free a flute girl.

THEOPROPIDES (*horrified*): Philolaches did?

PHANISCUS: Yes; a girl named Philematium.

THEOPROPIDES: How much did he pay?

PHANISCUS: Thirty—

THEOPROPIDES (*interrupting*): Talents!

PHANISCUS: *Donner wetter*, no! Minae.

THEOPROPIDES: He set her free?

PHANISCUS: Indeed he did, for thirty minae.

THEOPROPIDES: You mean it cost thirty minae to get a mistress for Philolaches?

PHANISCUS: That's what I mean.

THEOPROPIDES: And he set her free?

PHANISCUS: That's what I mean.

THEOPROPIDES: And that after his father went away, he's been getting drunk continually with your master?

PHANISCUS: That's what I mean.

THEOPROPIDES: What? Hasn't he bought this house next door?

PHANISCUS: Oh, no, that's what I don't mean.

THEOPROPIDES: And gave the owner forty minae down?

PHANISCUS: No, I don't mean that either.

THEOPROPIDES: Oh, you'll be my ruin!

PHANISCUS: No, he's done all the ruining; he's ruined his father.

THEOPROPIDES (*bitterly*): You speak the truth there.

PHANISCUS: I wish it weren't. You're evidently a friend of his father's.

THEOPROPIDES: Ah, his father—poor fellow!

PHANISCUS (*in mock consolation*): Oh, it's really nothing, thirty minae, in comparison with the other extravagant expenses he makes.

THEOPROPIDES (*wildly*): He'll be the death of his father!

PHANISCUS: There's one particular rascal of a slave, named Tranio. He can throw away more money than Congress.[12] I tell you, I pity his poor old father; when he finds this out, he'll have heart-failure, poor fellow.

THEOPROPIDES (*stalking up and down*): Oh, if all this is true!

PHANISCUS: What would I gain by lying?

PINACIUM (*back at the door*): Hey you, won't someone open!

PHANISCUS (*joining him*): Why are you banging on it? No one's at home. They've gone somewhere else to drink, I guess. Let's go and look for them. Follow me.

PINACIUM: Oh, all right. (*They start off.*)

THEOPROPIDES: Are you leaving, boy?

PHANISCUS: Your freedom's an overcoat for you; as for me, I've got nothing to cover my back, except obedience to my master, and minding my own business. (*They depart.*)

Act Four.   Scene V[13]

(*Enter* SIMO.)

THEOPROPIDES (*rushing about in wild rage*): Heavens above, I'm done for! Enough said! From what I hear, I haven't been on a trip to Egypt only; I've been taken for a ride—to the very ends of the earth. Now I don't know where I am. (*Seeing* SIMO *approaching*) But I'll know soon, for here comes the fellow my son bought the house from. (*To* SIMO) How goes it?

SIMO: I'm going home from town.

THEOPROPIDES: Anything new turn up at the market today?

SIMO: Yes.

THEOPROPIDES: Well, what?

SIMO: I saw a stiff carried out.

THEOPROPIDES: Humph!

SIMO: They said it had been alive a moment before.

THEOPROPIDES: Go to the deuce!

SIMO: Why do you keep loafing about here and asking for news?

THEOPROPIDES: Because I've just come home from abroad.

SIMO (*in mock alarm*): I'm already invited out; don't expect me to ask you to dinner.

THEOPROPIDES: Heavens, I'm not even thinking of it.

SIMO: But tomorrow, if no one else invites me first, I'll dine with you— at *your* house.

THEOPROPIDES (*impatiently*): I'm thinking of that still less. Look here, if you haven't any more important business, listen to me.

SIMO: All right, I'm listening.

THEOPROPIDES: You received forty minae from Philolaches, I believe.

SIMO: Never a penny— (*sarcastically*) I believe.

THEOPROPIDES: Well, from my servant Tranio, then?

SIMO (*really surprised*): Good grief! Much less from him.

THEOPROPIDES: Didn't he make a down-payment?

SIMO: What are you dreaming of?

THEOPROPIDES: What am I dreaming of? You mean yourself. You're hoping you can wreck the deal by this deceit.

SIMO (*bewildered*): What deal?

THEOPROPIDES: The one my son made with you while I was away.

SIMO: He made a deal here with me while you were away? What deal? When?

THEOPROPIDES (*trying another attack*): I owe you eighty minae.

SIMO: Heavens, no! (*After a pause, holding out his hand*) Well, if you do, give it to me. We must keep our agreements. Don't expect to get out of it!

THEOPROPIDES: I'll not deny the debt, of course I won't, and I'll pay it. But look here, you, don't say you haven't received forty minae from us.

SIMO: Kindly look at me and answer me this.[14] Why did your son owe me those forty minae, as you say?

THEOPROPIDES: Here's why. He bought your house—so Tranio told me —for two talents.

SIMO (*in amazement*): He bought my house? Why, Tranio said you wanted your son to get married, and so you wanted to build on to your house.

THEOPROPIDES (*also amazed*): I wanted to build on to my house?

SIMO: That's what he told me.

THEOPROPIDES: Oh, ruined completely! I'm tongue-tied. I'm done for, Simo; that's the last straw.

SIMO: Has Tranio upset anything?

THEOPROPIDES: He certainly has—he's upset *everything*! He made a fool of me today outrageously.

SIMO: What are you saying?

THEOPROPIDES: It's just as I tell you: he's made a fool of me for good and all. Now please be kind enough to help me, and give me your services.

SIMO: What do you want?

THEOPROPIDES: Go along with me to your house, will you, please?

SIMO: All right.

THEOPROPIDES: Give me the use of your slaves, and lend me some handcuffs.

SIMO: Take them.

THEOPROPIDES: On the way I'll tell you all about this— (*in a sudden burst of passion as he reaches* SIMO's *door*) the awful tricks he's played on me today! (*They go into* SIMO's *house.*)

Act Five.   Scene I

(*Enter* TRANIO.)

TRANIO: The man who's afraid when things are doubtful isn't worth a continental (but I haven't the slightest idea how to explain what a "continental" means!). Well, after master sent me to the farm to bring back his son, I sneaked off to our backyard by the alley (there's a gate into the yard from the alley, you see), opened the gate, and led out all my troops, both male and female. When I'd completed the evacuation and led my troops to safety, I planned to call a council of war; but when I'd summoned them, they read me out of the party. Since I see I'm stewed in my own juice, I'm going to do my best to do what everyone else does when things are alarming or in a mess: they go on messing them up still more, so they can't be settled at all. For I know very well that this can't possibly be kept from the old man any longer. . . .[15]

I'll seize the ground in advance, get the start on 'em and strike a treaty. I'm looking out for Number One! (SIMO's *door opens*) What's this? Our neighbour's door creaked. Why, it's master! (*Hides behind the further column*) I'd like to get a taste of what he says.

THEOPROPIDES (*coming out of* SIMO's *house with two slaves, carrying handcuffs, pitchforks, and various other weapons. He addresses the slaves*): Stand right there inside the threshold, so you can jump out the minute I give the signal—like this. (*Coughs loudly, and claps his hands*) Then be quick, and snap on the handcuffs. (*Slaves retire to doorway*) I'll wait for him in front of the house. He's been making game of me, and I'll make game of his hide, in proper fashion, sure as I live.

TRANIO (*aside*): The secret's out. Now you'd better see what you can do, Tranio.

THEOPROPIDES (*gloating over his coming revenge*): I'll play my fish neatly and deftly when he comes this way. I'll not show him the hook at once; I'll let out my line little by little. I'll pretend I don't know anything about the matter.

TRANIO (*aside*): Why, he's Old Harry himself on earth! There's no cleverer man than he in all Athens, I'll say. You can't pull the wool over his eyes any more than you could fool a rock. I'll go up to the fellow and speak to him.

THEOPROPIDES (*looking the other way*): Now I wish he'd come along.

TRANIO (*stepping up behind him*): If it's me you're looking for, here I am; and here you are, too.

THEOPROPIDES (*startled*): Hello, Tranio, what's up?

TRANIO: The farmers are coming back from the farm. Philolaches will be here soon.

THEOPROPIDES: Well, he'll arrive just in time, too. I think this neighbour of ours is a dirty scoundrel.

TRANIO: Why?

THEOPROPIDES: Because he says he doesn't know you at all.

TRANIO: He does?

THEOPROPIDES: And he says you never gave him any money.

TRANIO: Go on, you're teasing me! I don't believe he denies it.

THEOPROPIDES: Indeed he does deny it, and he says he never sold this house to Philolaches.

TRANIO: What, does he deny the money was given him?

THEOPROPIDES: Why, he even promised to take an oath on it, if I wanted him to, that he hadn't sold this house, and that the money hadn't been given him. (*As* TRANIO *makes a derisive noise*) That's just what I told him.

TRANIO: What did he say?

THEOPROPIDES: He promised to hand over all his slaves to me for cross-examination.

TRANIO: Nonsense! He'll never do it. (*At the mention of the slaves,* TRANIO *looks about for a convenient refuge. He makes one or two motions towards the altar, but* THEOPROPIDES *is in the way.*)

THEOPROPIDES: Oh, yes he will.

TRANIO: All right then, sue him. (*Trying to get off in the other direction*) I'll go find him.

THEOPROPIDES: I'll try the slaves, I think. I've made up my mind.

TRANIO (*still trying to brazen it out*): No, leave the fellow to me. Or tell him to attach the property.

THEOPROPIDES: No, no. First of all I want to take his slaves for examination.

TRANIO (*resigned*): Quite the thing, I think.

THEOPROPIDES: Supposing I send for them. (*Coughs significantly. Nothing happens, and a loud snore from within indicates that the slaves have gone to sleep.* THEOPROPIDES *dashes over to wake them up, and during this diversion* TRANIO *makes his escape to the safety of the altar.*)

TRANIO: You should have done that long ago; while you're about it, I'll stay by this altar.

THEOPROPIDES (*returning from his excursion*): Why?

TRANIO: Stupid ass! Why, so the slaves he'll give you to examine can't run to it. I'll keep guard for you here, so the examination won't go to pot.

THEOPROPIDES: Get up!

TRANIO: No, I won't.

THEOPROPIDES: Don't hold on to the altar, please!

TRANIO: Why?

THEOPROPIDES (*thinking rapidly*): I'll tell you. I—er—really want them to run to the altar. Let them do so. Then it'll be all the easier for me to get him condemned in court to pay damages.

TRANIO: Do what you will. But why do you want to make more bother. Don't you know what a ticklish thing the law is?

THEOPROPIDES: Get up and come to me. There's something I want to consult about with you.

TRANIO: I can give my advice from here. I'm a whole lot wiser sitting down. Besides, you get better advice from holy places.

THEOPROPIDES: Get up! No more of your fooling! (*Giving up pretences altogether*) Look me in the eye!

TRANIO: I've done so already.

THEOPROPIDES: Do you see—?

TRANIO: I see. If any third person should come between us, he'd die of starvation.

THEOPROPIDES: Why?

TRANIO: There wouldn't be anything left for him; we're both so terribly clever!

THEOPROPIDES: I'm done for. (*Claps his hands in distress. The slaves jump up with a start and rush out. General confusion.*)

TRANIO (*after quiet has been restored*): What's the matter with you?

THEOPROPIDES: You've roped me in!

TRANIO (*innocently*): How?

THEOPROPIDES: You've cleaned me out all right.

TRANIO (*still pretending not to understand*): Let me see. Did I do a good job? Is your nose clean?

THEOPROPIDES: Why, you've even cleaned the brains right out of my head. I've found out all your villainy—from roof to basement, and even to the sub-basement!

TRANIO: Well, I tell you, as sure as I'm alive, I'll never leave this place unless I want to.

THEOPROPIDES (*raging*): I'll have fire and faggots set around you, jail-bird.

TRANIO (*calmly*): Oh, don't do that; I taste better boiled than roasted.

THEOPROPIDES: I'll make an example of you, I will!

TRANIO: You mean you'll set me up as an example, because you like me?

THEOPROPIDES: Tell me, what kind of son did I leave here when I went away!

TRANIO: Oh, the usual kind—with hands, feet, fingers, ears, eyes, and lips.

THEOPROPIDES (*nearly mad with rage*): I'm asking you something different!

TRANIO (*mocking him*): Well, I'm giving you a different kind of answer! (*Pointing to* CALLIDAMATES, *who now appears*) But look! I see your son's friend Callidamates approaching. Do your business with me while he's here, if you want anything.

Act Five.   Scene II

(*Enter* CALLIDAMATES.)

CALLIDAMATES (*to himself*): When I'd buried all my drunkenness in sleep, and slept off my debauch, Philolaches told me his father had come back from abroad and his servant had made a fool of him on his arrival. He said he was afraid to see his father. Now I've been made the spokesman for the entire bunch, to try to make peace with his father. (*Catching sight of* THEOPROPIDES *by the altar*) But there he is. Hurrah! (*Approaching*) How do you do, Theopropides. I'm glad you've got back safely from your travels. Will you have dinner here with me today?

THEOPROPIDES: Bless you, Callidamates. As for the dinner—no, thank you.

CALLIDAMATES: Oh, come on!

TRANIO: Say you will; and I'll go in your place, if you don't want to.

THEOPROPIDES: Are you still mocking me, you public enemy?

TRANIO: You mean, because I promise to go to dinner in your place?

THEOPROPIDES: Well, you shan't go. I'll have you hanged, as you deserve.

CALLIDAMATES (*to* THEOPROPIDES): Leave all that, and say you'll come to dinner.

TRANIO: Why don't you answer?

CALLIDAMATES (*to* TRANIO): But you there, why have you run over to the altar?

TRANIO: A downright fool came along and frightened me. (*To* THEO-PROPIDES) Now tell my crimes; here's an umpire for us both. Come, begin your case.

THEOPROPIDES: I say you've corrupted my son.

TRANIO: Just listen. I admit he has sinned, and set his mistress free, while you were away, borrowed money at interest—and squandered it. That's all done in the best of families, isn't it?

THEOPROPIDES: By gad, I'll have to watch out for you. You're the silver-tongued orator, all right.

CALLIDAMATES: Come, let me be judge in this matter. (*Shoving* TRANIO *off the altar*) Get up. I'll sit there.

THEOPROPIDES: By all means. Take up the case yourself.

TRANIO (*uncomfortably, as* THEOPROPIDES *makes a dash for him*): There's some trap here, I know. (*To* CALLIDAMATES) Please relieve me of my fears, and take them on yourself.

THEOPROPIDES: I don't mind the rest so much; what I can't stand is the way he made a fool of me.

TRANIO: Well done, by George, and I'm glad of it! Men with white hair ought to have some sense.

THEOPROPIDES: What shall I do now?

TRANIO: If you're a friend of Diphilus or Philemon, tell them how your servant fooled you. You'll give 'em the best plot in the whole history of the comic stage.

CALLIDAMATES: Shut up a minute. Let me talk instead. (*To* THEOPRO-PIDES) Listen.

THEOPROPIDES (*relieved to have* TRANIO *shut up*): All right.

CALLIDAMATES: You know I'm your son's best friend. He came to me; he was ashamed to appear before you, because of what he's done—for he knows you know all about it. Now please forgive him his youthful foolishness. He's your own son, after all. You know that youths often play such pranks. Whatever he did, we did with him; we too went wrong. We'll come to an agreement and pay the interest and the principal, and the whole cost of buying the girl—out of our own pockets, not yours.

THEOPROPIDES (*after a moment's deliberation*): No more eloquent speaker could have come to me. I'm not angry with him any more. I don't hold any grudge against him. Why, let him love and drink and do what he pleases, and in my presence. If he's ashamed of having spent so much money, that's punishment enough.

CALLIDAMATES: Oh, he's terribly ashamed.

TRANIO: Now that he's forgiven, what about *me*?

THEOPROPIDES (*bursting out again*): I'll hang you up and have you flogged to bits.

TRANIO: Even if I'm ashamed?

THEOPROPIDES: By gad, I'll have you killed, as sure as I'm alive.

CALLIDAMATES: Oh, make your pardon complete. Forgive Tranio this offence, for my sake.

THEOPROPIDES: Ask me anything else you wish; it's yours. But I won't give up my determination to get the upper hand of this fellow for his underhand tricks.

CALLIDAMATES: Come, let him off, please!

THEOPROPIDES: Let him off? (*As* TRANIO *strikes an insulting pose*) See how the jailbird stands there!

CALLIDAMATES (*to* TRANIO): Keep still, Tranio, if you have any sense.

THEOPROPIDES: And you keep still about this request. As for him, I'll quiet him with a good beating.

TRANIO: You don't need to do that, I assure you.

CALLIDAMATES: Come now, grant this favour I ask of you.

THEOPROPIDES: Please don't ask it.

CALLIDAMATES: *Please!*

THEOPROPIDES: I don't want you to ask me.

CALLIDAMATES: It's useless not to want it. Forgive this one offence— PLEASE—for my sake.

TRANIO (*falling on his knees*): Why are you so unwilling? As if I shouldn't be committing another offence tomorrow. Then you can take proper punishment for both together—this one and the next one.

CALLIDAMATES: I beseech you.

THEOPROPIDES: All right, get off—scot-free. (*Pointing to* CALLIDAMATES) But there's the man to thank.

TRANIO (*leaping up in joy*): Spectators, the play is over; give your applause.

1. Leo's emendation has been adopted here; the Mss. read *canem capram commixtam,* "you mixture of bitch and she-goat."

2. The reading *date, si non estis* has been adopted.

3. Lindsay indicates a lacuna of one verse here.

4. Leo's emendation (*moratus tu te. ire huc debebas*) has been adopted.

5. The lacuna in these two verses has been filled in by Leo.

6. This speech does not occur in the Latin text.

7. This is a purely Roman touch. According to Roman law, to demand more than was due (*plus petitio*) invalidated a claim.

8. The play here on *umbra,* which means both "shade" and "an Umbrian woman" was introduced by Plautus to make possible an allusion to Sarsina, the town in Umbria where he was born.

9. In early editions this scene was placed at the end of Act Three. Many modern editors, e.g. Lindsay and Leo, still list the scene as Act Three, Scene III, although they have restored it to its proper position in the text.

10. This scene is listed as a continuation of Act Four, Scene II, in Lindsay's edition.

11. Lindsay assigns this speech to Phaniscus.

12. Literally, "he can squander the wealth of Hercules." The Romans dedicated a tenth of all booty or sudden gain to Hercules.

13. This is the third scene of Act Four in Lindsay's edition.

14. The lacunae in the next four verses have been filled in by Leo.

15. There is a lacuna of four verses in the text at this point.

XIV
THE GIRL FROM PERSIA

Characters in the Play

TOXILUS, *a slave, in love with* LEMNISELENIS
SAGARISTIO, *a slave, friend of* TOXILUS
SATURIO, *a parasite*
SOPHOCLIDISCA, *maid of* LEMNISELENIS
LEMNISELENIS, *a courtesan belonging to* DORDALUS
PAEGNIUM, *a young slave*
DAUGHTER *of* SATURIO
DORDALUS, *a pimp*

Acrostic Argument

In the absence of his master, Toxilus buys his ladylove and has the pimp set her free. He persuades the pimp to buy a kidnapped maiden from a brigand and dresses up the daughter of his parasite as the maiden. Thus he ensnares Dordalus, the pimp, and makes sport of him during a drinking bout.

INTRODUCTION

The Girl from Persia (the *Persa*) is an amusing comedy which deals entirely with characters from the lowest strata of ancient society. The characters are slaves, a slave-dealer, and a parasite and his daughter. The plot involves the deception of the pimp, and the man and girl needed for the purpose of the trickery must be free. The dramatist, in choosing for this purpose the parasite and his daughter, selected characters from the lowest level of free citizenship. After the conclusion of the intrigue these free citizens depart and the play ends with a carousal of slaves not unlike the celebration at the end of the *Stichus*.

Toxilus, a young slave, is deeply in love with a girl in the possession of Dordalus. The money for the girl is found by a fortuitous occurrence resembling the manner in which money is procured in *The Comedy of Asses* and the *Truculentus*. The sale to Dordalus of a second girl, supposed to be a Persian captive, provides the means of regaining the money paid out. It is perhaps somewhat improbable that a rogue like Dordalus would purchase a girl without guarantee of title, but the description of the circumstances and the cleverness with which the so-called captive acts her part make this basic weakness less noticeable. Dordalus' greed is an added factor; he rushes into a bargain which, he realises, has elements of danger, but he does not of course suspect the truth. The intrigue is successful, as always in Plautus when a pimp is the object of the trickery; this is true of Cappadox in the *Curculio*, Lycus in *The Carthaginian*, Ballio in the *Pseudolus*, and Labrax in *The Rope*. In none of these other plays, however, is the pimp made so ridiculous as in *The Girl from Persia*. While the celebration of the slaves in Act Five has been called an afterpiece, it serves in reality to bring about the culmination of Dordalus' discomfiture.

The action of play is rapid and the dialogue is witty. There is considerable invective and abuse, as we should expect from persons of low life. The conversation in Act Two, Scene II, between Sophoclidisca, the maid of Toxilus' sweetheart, and Paegnium, the pert and wanton slave boy, illustrates the sharp repartee and racy abuse often found in Plautus' slave dialogues. The errands of the two characters were unnecessary and served merely as an excuse to bring the two persons together

677

on the stage for the amusement of the spectators. Saturio as a parasite deserves to rank with Ergasilus in *The Captives* and Gelasimus in the *Stichus*. But he plays a more active part than the parasite usually does, and in this respect he more closely resembles Curculio and Terence's Phormio. By far the most interesting character in the play is Saturio's daughter. In spite of her low status she is an admirable person; she is a girl of spirit with high ideals and she hates the pretence which her father forces on her (Act Three, Scene I). As H. W. Prescott says, "her modesty and idealism are in amusing contrast with the coarse practical wisdom of her father." When she appears as the captive (Act Four, Scene IV) she plays her part with amazing cleverness. Her moralising on the ten deadly sins shows her serious-mindedness and she frames her answers to the questions with great ingenuity; her words are ambiguous, and in practically every instance she speaks the literal truth, although Dordalus does not realise it. She is forced to be her father's accomplice but she still is able to retain her honesty. Saturio's daughter is in many ways one of the most interesting characters in Roman comedy.

The reference in line 506 to the Persians is thought by many to date the Greek original in the period of the Middle Comedy, before the overthrow of Persia. The argument is not convincing, for the statement occurs in a purely fictitious letter which mentions the capture of a fabulous "Goldtown." To find a definite allusion here to contemporary history seems unwise. The structure and technique of the comedy is similar to that of many other plays of Plautus, and the original in all probability belonged to the later period of the Greek New Comedy.

THE GIRL FROM PERSIA[1]

(SCENE:—*A street in Athens before the house of* TOXILUS' *master and the house of the pimp* DORDALUS.)

Act One. Scene I

(Enter TOXILUS *from the forum.)*

TOXILUS (*to himself, gloomily*): When a needy lover first starts out on the path of Love, he outdoes the toils of Hercules with his toils. Why, I'd rather wrestle with the lion, the Hydra, the Aetolian boar, the Stymphalian birds, with the hind, and with Antaeus than wrestle with Love. I'm so upset with looking for a loan, and the fellows I ask can't say anything but "Nothing doing."

(Enter SAGARISTIO *from the opposite direction.)*

SAGARISTIO (*to himself, without seeing* TOXILUS): The slave who wants to serve his master well must find lodgings in his mind for many things which he thinks will please his master, whether he's here or away from home. Now I'm no willing slave, nor am I quite to my master's liking; but I'm just like a sore eye—he can't keep his hands off me, or refrain from giving me all his orders and making me the mainstay of his business.

TOXILUS: Who's that standing over there?

SAGARISTIO: Who's this standing over there?

TOXILUS: Looks like Sagaristio.

SAGARISTIO: It's my friend Toxilus.

TOXILUS: It's he, for certain.

SAGARISTIO: It's he, I think.

TOXILUS: I'll go to meet him.

SAGARISTIO: I'll up to him.

TOXILUS: O Sagaristio, God bless you.

SAGARISTIO: O Toxilus, God will answer your prayers. How do you do?

TOXILUS: The best I can.

SAGARISTIO: What are you doing?

TOXILUS: I'm getting along.

SAGARISTIO: Quite to your liking, eh?

TOXILUS: Quite, if my wishes come true.

SAGARISTIO: You're very stupid in the way you use your friends.

TOXILUS: Why?

SAGARISTIO: You ought to command them.

TOXILUS: As far as I was concerned, you were dead; I haven't seen you for some time.

SAGARISTIO: A business matter, you see—

TOXILUS: Something to do with chains, perhaps?

SAGARISTIO: For a little more than a year I've been captain of the chain-gang at the mill, and commander of the first beat-talion.

TOXILUS: An old campaigning-ground of yours.

SAGARISTIO: Have you kept pretty well?

TOXILUS: No, not very.

SAGARISTIO: Oh, that's why you're pale.

TOXILUS (*sighing*): I've been wounded in a battle with Venus; Cupid's dart has pierced my heart.

SAGARISTIO: What? Are slaves lovers here?

TOXILUS: What am I to do? Oppose the gods? Should I act like the Titans and make war on them, when I'm no match for them?

SAGARISTIO: Just take care no artillery of birch-rods makes a breach in your flanks!

TOXILUS: I'm keeping the Festival of Freedom in right royal style.

SAGARISTIO: How so?

TOXILUS: Master's abroad.

SAGARISTIO: He's abroad, you say?

TOXILUS: If you can put up with a fine time, come along: you'll live with me and be entertained with fare fit for a king.

SAGARISTIO: Oh, boy! My shoulders smart already, just to hear you talk!

TOXILUS: But there's one thing that's killing me.

SAGARISTIO: What's that?

TOXILUS: Today is the very last day, the day that tells whether my mistress shall be free or shall be a slave forever.

SAGARISTIO: Whatever you want, that's what I want too.

TOXILUS: You can buy me as your friend for life.

SAGARISTIO: How?

TOXILUS: By giving me six hundred nummi to pay for her freedom; I'll pay them back in the next three or four days. Come now: be a good fellow; help me out.

SAGARISTIO: What a nerve to dare to ask for that much money from me! Such cheek! Why, if I put myself up for sale, I could hardly raise the sum you ask. You can't expect to get blood out of a stone, you know.

TOXILUS (*reproachfully*): Is that the way you treat me?

SAGARISTIO: What can I do?

TOXILUS: You're asking me? Beg a loan from someone.

SAGARISTIO: Do that yourself!

TOXILUS: I've looked, but I can't find a cent anywhere.

SAGARISTIO (*dubiously*): Well then, I'll look for it—if anyone will trust me.

TOXILUS (*sarcastically*): Fine! I've all but got the cash in my hands, no doubt.

SAGARISTIO: If I had it at home, I'd promise it. All I can do is to try my best.

TOXILUS: Well, whatever comes, do pay me a visit. And look around for the cash, and I'll do the same.

SAGARISTIO: If anything turns up, I'll let you know.

TOXILUS (*earnestly*): I beg you—

SAGARISTIO (*mockingly*): And I in turn beg you—

TOXILUS: Give me your loyal aid.

SAGARISTIO: Bah! You're killing me.

TOXILUS: Blame it on my love; it's not my fault that I'm babbling to you so.

SAGARISTIO: Well I'll just leave you. (*He departs towards the forum.*)

TOXILUS: Leaving so soon? Enjoy your walk. But come back as soon as you can; see you're not among the missing when I want you. (*To himself*) I'll stay at home here, until I cook up some mischief for the pimp. (*He goes into his master's house.*)

Act One. Scene II

(*Enter* SATURIO *from the forum.*)

SATURIO (*to the audience*): The ancient and honourable profession of my ancestors I follow, practice, and pursue with greatest care. For there never was any ancestor of mine who didn't nourish his belly by the art of dining out. My father, grandfather, great-grandfather, great-great-grandfather, great-great-great-grandfather, great-great-great-great-grandfather—all of them, like mice, lived on other people's food; no one could beat 'em at gluttonacity, and they never had the name of Hard-Heads.[2] From them I got this trade and the station of my sires. I don't want to be an informer; for it isn't decent to go and seize another's goods without any risk of my own; and I don't like those who do so. Do I make myself clear? Well then, if anyone does this for the sake of the state rather than for his own profit, I can be persuaded that he is a good and loyal citizen. . . .[3] If anyone shall procure the conviction of a malefactor, let him give half to the public treasury. And let this be enacted in that law: when an informer summons anyone to court, let the defendant also summon him for just the same damages; thus both will go before the magistrates on equal terms. If this were done, those fellows who attack their neighbours' property with their nets of foolscap would soon disappear, I'll bet. But ain't I a fool to worry about the state when there are magistrates whose duty it is to take care of it? Now I'll go in here. (*Pointing to house of* TOXILUS) I'll pay a call on yesterday's left-overs, to see if they had a good night's rest or not and whether they have a fever, or if they were well covered so no one could creep up on them. But the door is opening; I'd better go slow. (*He retires to the alley.*)

Act One.   Scene III

(*Enter* TOXILUS *from his house.*)

TOXILUS (*to himself*): I've found just the way to make the pimp set her free today at his own expense. (*Seeing* SATURIO) But there's the parasite; I need his help. I'll pretend not to see him, and lure the fellow on. (*Shouting to the slaves inside the house*) You there inside, take care of things, and hurry up! I don't want any delay when I come in. Mix up the mead; get the quinces and the fruit ready; see that everything is well warmed in the platters—put plenty of kindling-reeds on the fire. My friend and bosom pal will soon be here, I'm sure.

SATURIO (*aside*): Oh, goody! He means me!

TOXILUS (*without noticing* SATURIO): He'll soon be here, all washed from the baths, I suppose.

SATURIO (*aside*): He's certainly got the whole story in full detail!

TOXILUS (*still calling into the house*): See that the ravioli and the meat-sauce is well done: don't serve them up to me uncooked.

SATURIO (*aside*): How well he puts it! These undercooked foods are good for nothing; you don't want to gulp them down unless they're nice and juicy. And unless the ravioli-sauce has a good, thick body to it, it's no good at all—that thin, transparent stuff, sheer as a chiffon dress! Why, ravioli-sauce has to be as solid as an overcoat.[4] I don't want food that fills the bladder; I want something for my belly!

TOXILUS (*looking around*): Someone's talking nearby.

SATURIO (*approaching him*): O Jupiter that walks the earth, your dining-companion greets you!

TOXILUS: Oh, you've come just in time, Saturio.

SATURIO: That's a lie, by God, and it's mean of you. I come Hungurio, not Sate-urio.

TOXILUS: Well, you'll eat; the stoves are smoking hot for your belly within. I ordered them to heat up the left-overs.

SATURIO: But how about the ham? It's the rule to serve up ham cold on the second day.

TOXILUS: That's the way I've ordered it.

SATURIO: Any relish?

TOXILUS: Oh, hush! What a question!

SATURIO: Ah, what excellent taste you show!

TOXILUS: But do you remember there was something I mentioned to you yesterday?

SATURIO: I remember: a lamprey or an eel must not be warmed over. They're much better to pick at cold. But why this delay in beginning our attack? While it's morning, all mankind should eat.

TOXILUS: It's too early in the morning.

SATURIO: "Thou shalt begin thy business early in the morning"—and keep it up all day!

TOXILUS (*impatiently*): Please pay attention to me. Yesterday I talked with you and begged you to lend me six hundred nummi.

SATURIO: I remember, and I am well aware that you begged me—and that I had none to lend. A parasite would be worthless if he were a Moneylendson. If he had anything at home, he'd be too eager to begin a feast and gobble up his own possessions. A good parasite must be like a needy Cynic: he should have a flask, a strigil, a cup, slippers, a cloak, and a wallet with a very little in it, just to entertain his own household.

TOXILUS: Well, I don't want money; just give me your daughter to use.

SATURIO (*indignantly*): Heavens, no! I never gave her to anyone to use.

TOXILUS: I don't mean for what you suspect.

SATURIO: What do you want of her?

TOXILUS: I'll tell you. Because she's pretty and quite ladylike.

SATURIO: That's so.

TOXILUS: The pimp here doesn't know you or your daughter.

SATURIO: How could anyone know me unless he entertains me at dinner?

TOXILUS: Quite so. In this way you can find the money for me.

SATURIO: Indeed, I'd like to.

TOXILUS: Then let me sell her.

SATURIO: What? You sell her?

TOXILUS: Oh, no; I'll commission someone else to sell her; he'll say he's a foreigner. For the pimp moved here from Megara not six months ago.

SATURIO (*impatiently*): The left-overs are spoiling! Your business can wait.

TOXILUS: You think so, do you? Well, you'll never eat a bite today, don't fool yourself, until you promise to do what I ask! And unless you bring your daughter here just as fast as you can, I'll expel you from this fraternity of mine. Now what? What is it? Why don't you tell me what you're going to do?

SATURIO (*with resignation*): Why, please sell me too, if you like— provided you sell me with a full belly.

TOXILUS: Well, if you're going to do it, do it.

SATURIO: I'll do just what you wish.

TOXILUS: Thank you. Now hurry, go home. Coach your daughter shrewdly, teach her carefully what she's to say: where she's to say she was born, who her parents were, where she was kidnapped. She's to claim that she was born far away from Athens; and she's to weep when she tells the story.

SATURIO: Keep still, won't you? She's three times as naughty as you want her to be.

TOXILUS: Very pretty, that! But do you know what to do? You must get a tunic and a girdle, and bring a travelling-cloak and a hat for the fellow to wear who's going to sell her to the pimp.

SATURIO: Bravo! Very good.

TOXILUS: He'll pretend to be a foreigner.

SATURIO: My compliments on your scheme.

TOXILUS: And bring your daughter here nicely decked out in some foreign style.

SATURIO: Whence these trappings?

TOXILUS: Get them from the stage-manager; he has to give them: the aediles have contracted to furnish them.

SATURIO: They'll be here directly. But I don't understand any of this business.

TOXILUS: Not a bit of it, of course. Well then, when I get the money, you'll claim her at once from the pimp, as a freeborn girl.

SATURIO: Let him keep her if I don't get her away from him in a jiffy. (*He departs towards the forum.*)

TOXILUS: Go on, and take care of your end of the job. (*To himself*) Meanwhile I want to send a boy to my mistress to cheer her up and tell her that I'll accomplish the affair today. But I talk too much. (*He goes into his house.*)

Act Two. Scene I

(*Enter* SOPHOCLIDISCA *from the house of* DORDALUS; *she is followed by* LEMNISELENIS, *who stands in the doorway.*)

SOPHOCLIDISCA (*to* LEMNISELENIS): Why, it would be enough for a stupid, forgetful, silly girl—you've told me so many times! I'm sure you must take me for a country bumpkin. Though I may guzzle away the wine, I'm not in the habit of guzzling away your orders too. I thought myself and my habits were sufficiently well known to you; for this is the fifth year I've been attending you, and in that time, I imagine,
⸱ the stupidest sheep, if it went to school, could learn its A-B-C's; but you, in all this time, have not yet learned my talents, waking and sleeping. Can't you keep quiet? Can't you stop your suggestions? I remember, I know, I understand, I've got it all in my mind. You're in love, poor thing! Your heart is overflowing with it. I'll calm everything down for you. A lover's so unhappy, you say? Surely; but a loveless person is a worthless person; what use in life for such a fellow? (LEMNISELENIS *retires into the house.*)
    But I'd better get along, to oblige my mistress, so she'll get her freedom all the sooner. I'll meet this Toxilus and unload this message of mine into his ears. (*She starts towards the house of* TOXILUS.)

Act Two. Scene II

(TOXILUS *comes out of his house, with the young slave,* PAEGNIUM. *They stand in the doorway during the following dialogue.*)

TOXILUS: Is it all quite clear and plain to you? Do you remember, and have you got it pat?

PAEGNIUM (*insolently*): Better than you, who taught me.

TOXILUS: Is that so, you young limb of Satan?

PAEGNIUM: Yes, that's so.

TOXILUS: Well then, what did I say?

PAEGNIUM: I'll tell it all to *her*. (*Pointing to house of* DORDALUS.)

TOXILUS: By God, you don't know it at all!

PAEGNIUM: What'll you bet I don't know and remember everything— and that you even know how many fingers you have on your hand?

TOXILUS: What, bet with you?

PAEGNIUM: Go right ahead, if you yearn to lose.

TOXILUS: Let's call it off instead.

PAEGNIUM: Then just let me go.

TOXILUS: I let you, and indeed I order you to go. But this is the way I want it: run so fast that you'll be home while I think you're still over there.

PAEGNIUM (*starting back into the house*): I'll do so.

TOXILUS: Where are you going now?

PAEGNIUM: Home—so I'll be at home while you think I'm over there.

TOXILUS: You're a young rascal: I'll give you something for this, something for your very own!

PAEGNIUM: Indeed, I know how people usually reproach a master's promises with faithlessness, and you can't ever force them to face a jury for their promises.

TOXILUS: Get along now, will you?

PAEGNIUM: You'll be pleased with me, I'm sure.

TOXILUS: Now Paegnium, see you give this letter to Lemniselenis herself, and give her my message.

SOPHOCLIDISCA (*to herself*): I'm too slow; I'd better get going on my errand. (*Starts again for* TOXILUS's *house.*)

PAEGNIUM: I'm going.

TOXILUS: Yes, yes, go on. I'll go home; carry out my errand carefully. Run along, fly! (*He goes back into the house.*)

PAEGNIUM: That's what the ostrich does at the circus. He's gone off inside. (*Seeing* SOPHOCLIDISCA) But who's this who's coming towards me?

SOPHOCLIDISCA (*noticing* PAEGNIUM): Why, here's Paegnium.

PAEGNIUM: Here's Sophoclidisca, the private maid of the girl I'm going to see.

SOPHOCLIDISCA (*aside*): They say there's no naughtier knave alive today than this lad.

PAEGNIUM: I'll accost her.

SOPHOCLIDISCA: I'll have to slow up.

PAEGNIUM (*deliberately bumping into* SOPHOCLIDISCA): I'll have to stop at this obstacle.

SOPHOCLIDISCA: Paegnium, you sweet boy, good day. How goes it? How are you?

PAEGNIUM: Sophoclidisca, God bless—me!

SOPHOCLIDISCA: What about me?

PAEGNIUM: Whatever He pleases: but if He treats you as you deserve, He'll hate you and make trouble for you.

SOPHOCLIDISCA: Stop your nasty talk!

PAEGNIUM: Since that's the kind of talk you deserve, it's good talk, not nasty talk.

SOPHOCLIDISCA: What are you doing?

PAEGNIUM: I'm standing in front of a naughty jade and looking at you.

SOPHOCLIDISCA: Well, I've certainly never known a worse boy than you!

PAEGNIUM: Why, what harm do I do, or whom do I abuse?

SOPHOCLIDISCA: Everyone you get the chance to.

PAEGNIUM: No one ever thought so.

SOPHOCLIDISCA: But plenty of people know it's so.

PAEGNIUM: Bah!

SOPHOCLIDISCA: Pah!

PAEGNIUM: Don't judge others by yourself!

SOPHOCLIDISCA: I admit, of course, that I'm just the sort of person that's proper in a pimp's household.

PAEGNIUM: Enough said!

SOPHOCLIDISCA: But how about you? Do you admit you're what I say?

PAEGNIUM: I'd admit it, if I were.

SOPHOCLIDISCA: Oh, get out! You're too much for me.

PAEGNIUM: Well, get along yourself, then.

SOPHOCLIDISCA: But tell me this: where are you bound?

PAEGNIUM: Where are *you* bound?

SOPHOCLIDISCA: Do tell me.

PAEGNIUM: Do tell *me*.

SOPHOCLIDISCA: I asked first.

PAEGNIUM: But you'll find out last.

SOPHOCLIDISCA: I'm not going very far from here.

PAEGNIUM: And I'm not going very far.

SOPHOCLIDISCA: Where are you going, you wretch?

PAEGNIUM: You'll never get an answer from me, unless I learn from you first.

SOPHOCLIDISCA: Well, mercy me! You'll never learn until you tell me.

PAEGNIUM: Is that so?

SOPHOCLIDISCA: Yes, that's so!

PAEGNIUM: You vixen!

SOPHOCLIDISCA: You rogue!

PAEGNIUM: Just what I should be.

SOPHOCLIDISCA: Well, it's not what I should be.

PAEGNIUM: I say there! Are you determined to hide where you're going, you vile jade?

SOPHOCLIDISCA: Are you going to be stubborn and conceal where you're bound, you vile knave?

PAEGNIUM: You're pretty good at tit for tat, aren't you? Well then, get along, since that's what you've decided. I don't care a hang whether I find out. Farewell. (*He starts to leave.*)

SOPHOCLIDISCA: Stop!

PAEGNIUM: But I'm in a hurry.

SOPHOCLIDISCA: Well, so am I.

PAEGNIUM: Have you got anything?

SOPHOCLIDISCA: What about you?

PAEGNIUM: Not a thing.

SOPHOCLIDISCA: Show me your hand, then.

PAEGNIUM (*holding out his right hand*): How about this hand?

SOPHOCLIDISCA: Where's the other one—that thievish left hand?

PAEGNIUM: I left it home. I didn't bring it here.

SOPHOCLIDISCA (*pulling at his left hand, which is hidden behind him*): You've got something or other there.

PAEGNIUM (*pushing her away*): Hands off there, you vamp!

SOPHOCLIDISCA: But if I love you?

PAEGNIUM: You're wasting your time.

SOPHOCLIDISCA: Why?

PAEGNIUM: Because it's no love at all when love is not returned.

SOPHOCLIDISCA (*trying to pet him*): Better wake up in time, while you have those pretty looks and your youth, or when you become a Silverlocks, you'll be a dirty slave forever. Why, you're scarcely eighty pounds!

PAEGNIUM: But that sort of campaign is waged more by shamelessness than by weight. And yet I'm wasting my time.

SOPHOCLIDISCA: Why?

PAEGNIUM: Because I'm telling this to an expert. But I'm delaying.

SOPHOCLIDISCA: Wait.

PAEGNIUM: You're a nuisance.

SOPHOCLIDISCA: Then I'll keep on being one, unless I learn where you're off to.

PAEGNIUM: To your house.

SOPHOCLIDISCA: Mercy me! I'm on my way to yours.

PAEGNIUM: Why there?

SOPHOCLIDISCA: What business is that of yours?

PAEGNIUM: Well, you won't go, unless I know it too.

SOPHOCLIDISCA: You're mean!

PAEGNIUM: I like to be mean. By heavens, you'll never dig it out of me; you won't be any more mischievous than I am.

SOPHOCLIDISCA: Competing with you in mischief is very painful.

PAEGNIUM: You're no bargain, yourself! But what are you afraid of?

SOPHOCLIDISCA: The same thing you are: loitering.

PAEGNIUM: Tell me, then.

SOPHOCLIDISCA: But I was forbidden to tell this to a soul; all the mutes were to speak before I should.

PAEGNIUM: Well, it was solemnly proclaimed to me not to tell this to a living soul; and all the mutes were to speak before *I* should.

SOPHOCLIDISCA: Oh, come on and do it. Let's make a promise and trust each other.

PAEGNIUM: I know; all these bawds are light of faith; the promise of a bawd is lighter than a water-spider.

SOPHOCLIDISCA: Be a good boy and tell me.

PAEGNIUM (*mocking*): Be a good girl and tell me.

SOPHOCLIDISCA: I don't want to be a good girl.

PAEGNIUM: You'll get your wish quite easily.

SOPHOCLIDISCA: Keep this to yourself.

PAEGNIUM: Keep this quiet.

SOPHOCLIDISCA: I'll keep it quiet.

PAEGNIUM: I'll keep it dark.

SOPHCLIDISCA: I'm taking this letter to your master, Toxilus.

PAEGNIUM: Go on: there he is at home. And I'm carrying this sealed tablet of ashwood to your mistress Lemniselenis.

SOPHOCLIDISCA: What's written in it?

PAEGNIUM: I know no more than you—probably some soupy words.

SOPHOCLIDISCA: I'm off.

PAEGNIUM: I'm going, too. (*He goes into* DORDALUS' *house.*)

SOPHOCLIDISCA: March on! (*She goes into* TOXILUS' *house.*)

Act Two.　Scene III

(*Enter* SAGARISTIO *from the forum, with a wallet on his back.*)

SAGARISTIO (*singing jubilantly*): "O Jupiter, thou rich and far-renowned,
　　　　O son of Wealth, Almighty, God of power,
　　　　Who giveth riches, hope, and all good cheer,
　　　　On thee my heart-felt thanks I gladly shower"—
since the friendly gods give my friend such abundance of good luck, so I can bring him aid when he's in need of a loan. Why, I never dreamed of this; I hadn't the slightest idea I'd get a chance to help, and now this opportunity has dropped right out of the sky. For my master has sent me off to Eretria to buy some oxen trained to the plough; he gave me the money and said there was a fair there a week from now. The fool! To give me that money, when he knows what I'm like. For I'll find some other use for this money. "There were no oxen that I could buy, sir." Now I'll do my friend a favour and give my inner man a treat as well; I'll have a fine time for a long while and pay the piper for it in one short day. There'll be thwacks upon my back. But I don't care. Now I'll present my friend with plenty of plough-broken fellows from this wallet of mine. It's just swell to get your teeth into those pinch-penny, doddering, greedy, dried-up old chaps, who lock away their saltcellars, salt and all, from their slaves. (*Thoughtfully*) And

yet, it's only right to take a look around when you have the chance. What will he do to me? He'll have me flogged to bits and fastened up in chains. (*Shrugging his shoulders*) He can go chase himself! He needn't think I'm going to get down and beg. The devil with him! There's nothing new he can offer me now; I'm an expert. But here comes Paegnium, Toxilus' lad.

Act Two. Scene IV

(*Enter* PAEGNIUM *from the house of* DORDALUS.)

PAEGNIUM (*to himself*): I've completed my assignment; now I'm hurrying home.

SAGARISTIO: Wait, even though you're in a hurry. O Paegnium, listen here!

PAEGNIUM (*without stopping*): You ought to buy a slave, if you want someone to obey you.

SAGARISTIO: Stop!

PAEGNIUM: You'd make lots of trouble, I suppose, if I owed you anything, since even now you're such a nuisance.

SAGARISTIO: You scoundrel, won't you even look at me?

PAEGNIUM (*stopping and looking at him*): I know how young I am; that's why you get away with that abuse.

SAGARISTIO: Where's Toxilus, your master?

PAEGNIUM: Where he pleases; he doesn't ask your opinion about it.

SAGARISTIO: Won't you even tell me where he is, you imp?

PAEGNIUM: I don't know, I tell you, you whipping post.

SAGARISTIO: Such impudence, and to your elder, too.

PAEGNIUM: You started it, so take it! I work as a slave, but master told me my tongue is free.

SAGARISTIO: Will you tell me where Toxilus is?

PAEGNIUM: I tell you—to go to the devil once and for all!

SAGARISTIO: You'll catch it today from a rope's end.

PAEGNIUM: For your sake, you cuckoo? Why, I wouldn't be afraid of that if I'd smashed your face in, you carrion.

SAGARISTIO: I see: you're master's bedfellow.

PAEGNIUM: So I am. What business is that of yours? At any rate, I don't do it for nothing, like you.

SAGARISTIO: Pretty sure of yourself, aren't you?

PAEGNIUM: Indeed I am; for I'm sure that I'll be free someday—something you can't hope for.

SAGARISTIO: Can't you stop making a nuisance of yourself?

PAEGNIUM: That's something you can't do yourself.

SAGARISTIO: Go to the devil!

PAEGNIUM: No, you go—home! You'll find him ready and waiting for you there.

SAGARISTIO: I suppose I've given you bail for my appearance.

PAEGNIUM: I only hope you can't get bail, so you'll stay in jail.

SAGARISTIO: What's that?

PAEGNIUM: What's what?

SAGARISTIO: Are you still abusing me, you rascal?

PAEGNIUM: Since you're a slave yourself, surely you'll permit a slave to abuse you.

SAGARISTIO (*with a threatening gesture*): Is that so? Just watch what I'll give you.

PAEGNIUM: Just nothing; for you have nothing.

SAGARISTIO (*approaching* PAEGNIUM): May God damn me—

PAEGNIUM: You're a good friend of mine: I hope you get your wish.

SAGARISTIO: —if I don't nail you to the ground today with my fists, if I ever catch you. (*He swings at* PAEGNIUM, *who retreats.*)

PAEGNIUM: You nail me? Why, they'll soon nail you to a cross.

SAGARISTIO: May all the devils in Hell—you know what I was going to say, if I hadn't checked my tongue. Can't you get out?

PAEGNIUM: You'll easily drive me away. For my shadow's already getting a thrashing inside the house here. (*He goes into the house of* TOXILUS.)

SAGARISTIO: May God damn him! He's a snake, the rascal, with his double-forked tongue! I'm certainly glad he's gone. But the door's opening, and here comes the man I was so eager to meet.

Act Two. Scene V

(TOXILUS *and* SOPHOCLIDISCA *come out of the house.*)

TOXILUS (*to* SOPHOCLIDISCA, *without seeing* SAGARISTIO): Tell her that I've arranged to get the money, bid her be brave, and tell her I love her dearly. She helps me by helping herself. Have you got the message, so you can deliver it properly?

SOPHOCLIDISCA: I've got it more thoroughly than a thoroughbred.

TOXILUS: Hurry up, then; go on home. (SOPHOCLIDISCA *crosses the stage and enters the house of* DORDALUS.)

SAGARISTIO (*to himself*): Now's the time to play the perfect fool for him; I'll approach him with arms akimbo, and drape my cloak in a fancy style.

TOXILUS (*seeing* SAGARISTIO *approaching*): Who's this two-handled demijohn walking around here?

SAGARISTIO (*clearing his throat loudly*): I'll hawk and spit like a professional.

TOXILUS: Why, it's Sagaristio. What's up, Sagaristio? How goes it? What about my commission? Have you a wee bit of hope for me?

SAGARISTIO (*impressively*): Approach. We shall see. I want to help. Come here. Advise me of your needs.

TOXILUS (*noticing the wallet*): What's this swelling on your neck?

SAGARISTIO: It's a goiter; don't squeeze it. When anyone touches it roughly, it begins to hurt.

TOXILUS: When did you get that?

SAGARISTIO: Today.

TOXILUS: You ought to have it lanced.

SAGARISTIO: I'm afraid I might lance it too soon, and it would cause me a lot more trouble.

TOXILUS: I'd like to examine your complaint.

SAGARISTIO (*backing away*): Ah! Get away and watch out for the horns!

TOXILUS: Why?

SAGARISTIO: There's a team of oxen in this purse.

TOXILUS: Oh, let them out, please! You'll starve them to death. Let them out to pasture.

SAGARISTIO: But I'm afraid I won't be able to get them back to the stall; they might wander off.

TOXILUS: I'll send them back. Don't worry.

SAGARISTIO: I'll trust you; I'll oblige you. Come over here, please. I've got the money here you begged me for.

TOXILUS: What's that you say?

SAGARISTIO: My master sent me to Eretria to buy oxen. Now your house will be my Eretria.

TOXILUS: A very witty remark! And I'll give you all this money back, without losing a cent, in a jiffy. For I've drawn up and prepared all my tricks to get this money away from the pimp.

SAGARISTIO: So much the better.

TOXILUS: And to set my girl free, and make him give the money himself. But follow me; I need your assistance in this matter.

SAGARISTIO: I'm at your service. (*They go into the house of* TOXILUS.)

Act Three.   Scene I

(*Enter* SATURIO *and his* DAUGHTER, *dressed up as a Persian, from the forum.*)

SATURIO: Heaven grant that this affair may turn out well for me and you—and for my belly. Grant, O Lord, thy eternal—food, now and forever, for me and my descendants. (*To his* DAUGHTER) Follow me, my child, with the grace of God. You know and understand what your task is; I've informed you of all our plans. That's why I've dressed you up like this. You're going to be sold today, my girl.

DAUGHTER: Please, father dear; I know you like to eat other people's food, but are you really going to sell your daughter for the sake of your stomach?

SATURIO: It's a wonder I don't sell you for the sake of King Philip or Attalus, rather than for my own sake, seeing that you're mine.

DAUGHTER: Do you take me for a servant-girl, or for your daughter?

SATURIO: Whichever seems more useful to my belly. I have the right to command you, I think; you don't have the right over me.

DAUGHTER: Yes, father; you have that power. But nevertheless, even though our fortunes are quite small, father, it's better to live modestly and within our means. For if disgrace be added to poverty, poverty becomes heavier and reputation suffers.

SATURIO: Look here, girl, you're disagreeable.

DAUGHTER: No I'm not; I don't think I am, when I give my father good advice, despite my years. You see, enemies misrepresent things when they spread a rumour.

SATURIO: Well, let them spread it, and go to the devil. I don't fear all the enemies in the world nearly so much as having an empty table set before me.

DAUGHTER: But, father, disgrace and scandal never die; they keep on living even after you think they're dead.

SATURIO: What? Are you afraid I'll really sell you?

DAUGHTER: No, father; but I don't want you to pretend to.

SATURIO: It's no use your not wanting it. This is going to be done my way, not yours.

DAUGHTER: All right.

SATURIO: What's the matter with this, anyway?

DAUGHTER: Just think this over, father: when a master threatens a slave with a beating, even though that beating isn't going to take place, when master picks up the whip and the slave takes off his tunic, how do you suppose the poor wretch feels? So I'm now terribly afraid of what's not going to happen.

SATURIO: There never was a girl or woman who wasn't good for nothing, if she was smarter than her parents liked.

DAUGHTER: There never was a girl or woman who wasn't good for nothing if she kept quiet when she saw things done wrongfully.

SATURIO (*angrily*): You'd better look out for trouble!

DAUGHTER: But if you won't allow me to look out for it, what am I to do? You see, I want to look out for *you*.

SATURIO: Am I a trouble?

DAUGHTER: No, and it's not proper for me to say so; but I'm doing my best to keep others from having the chance to say so.

SATURIO: Let them say what they like; I'll not be moved from this decision.

DAUGHTER: But if you'd let me have my way, you'd act wisely instead of foolishly.

SATURIO: It's my pleasure.

DAUGHTER: Your pleasure is your privilege, I know, as far as I'm concerned; but this pleasure wouldn't be your privilege, if I had my pleasure.

SATURIO: Are you going to heed your father's order or not?

DAUGHTER: I will.

SATURIO: Do you remember your instructions?

DAUGHTER: All of them.

SATURIO: How you were kidnapped?

DAUGHTER: I know it well.

SATURIO: And who your parents were?

DAUGHTER: I remember. You're forcing me to be naughty. But take care that when you wish to marry me to someone this scandal doesn't spoil the match.

SATURIO: Hush, you silly goose! Don't you see our modern standards? Even with a scandalous reputation it's easy to get married here; provided there's a dowry, nothing is considered a dishonour.

DAUGHTER: Then just call to mind the fact that I'm without a dowry.

SATURIO: Don't say that. Thanks to the gods and my ancestors, I tell you, don't say you have no dowry, when you've got one at home. See here! I've got a hope chest full of books. If you do this task that we're engaged on nicely, you'll get a dowry of a thousand *bon mots,* and all of them Attic; you won't get a single Sicilian one.[5] With such a dowry you could marry even a pauper.

DAUGHTER: Why then, father, lead me where you're going to take me. Sell me, or do whatever pleases you.

SATURIO: A fair and just request. Follow me, this way.

DAUGHTER: I obey. (*They go into the house of* TOXILUS.)

Act Three.   Scene II

(*Enter* DORDALUS *from his house.*)

DORDALUS (*to himself*): I wonder what this neighbour of mine is going to do; he swore he'd give me the money today. If this day passes without his paying me, I'll forfeit the money and he his oath. But the door's creaking over there. Who's coming out?

Act Three.   Scene III

(*Enter* TOXILUS *from his house, with a wallet.*)

TOXILUS (*to the slaves within the house*): Take care of things inside; I'll be back home directly.

DORDALUS: Toxilus, what's up?

TOXILUS: Oh, you greasy, grimy pimp, you filthy public dunghill, you dirty, dishonest miscreant, you lawless public menace, you greedy, spiteful money-hawk, mendacious, rapacious, grabbacious—in three hundred verses no one could recount your villainies—will you take this money? Come, take the money, you shameless rascal. Come get your money; what, have you got your money? Can't I make you take the money, you mucker? You didn't think I could get any money, did you, when you wouldn't trust me except on oath?

DORDALUS (*taken aback*): Let me catch my breath, to answer you. (*Shouting at the top of his voice*) You public hero number one, you hangout of dirty slaves, liberator of whores, you whipping-ground, fetter-wearing citizen of Milltown, slave forever, you glutton, greedy, thievish, runawayish! Come, hand over the money; give me my money, you shameless rascal! Can't I force the money out of you? Money, I say! Gimme! Why don't you give me the money? Have you no shame? A pimp demands money of you, you incarnation of slavery, to set your mistress free, for all the town to hear.

TOXILUS (*nervously*): For heaven's sake, keep quiet! What a powerful voice you've got!

DORDALUS: I've got my tongue trained to repay favours. I get my salt at the same price as you, and if my tongue doesn't defend me, it'll never get a lick of salt.

TOXILUS: Don't be angry. I was just mad at you because you said you wouldn't trust me for the money.

DORDALUS: It's remarkable I wouldn't trust you, so you could do the same as some of the bankers do: when you trust them with anything, they abscond from the forum faster than the rabbit when it's let out from the barrier at the races.

TOXILUS (*holding out the wallet*): Take this, if you please.

DORDALUS (*eagerly*): Why, just give it to me!

TOXILUS: There are six hundred good pieces here, all counted. Now set the girl free and bring her to my house right away.

DORDALUS: She'll be here at once, I promise you. But I don't know whom I can give this money to for testing.

TOXILUS: Perhaps you're afraid to trust it in anyone's hands.

DORDALUS: And no wonder, since bankers disappear from the forum nowadays faster than a chariot-wheel turns around in the races.

TOXILUS: Go off there, through the back alley, to the forum; and have the girl come over to me by the same path, through the garden.

DORDALUS: She'll be here soon; I'll see to it.

TOXILUS (*nervously*): But not too openly.

DORDALUS: Oh, of course; very smart of you.

TOXILUS: Tomorrow she'll go to make her thank-offering.

DORDALUS: Quite right.

TOXILUS: You could have been there and back in the time you've been standing around here. (DORDALUS *goes out to the forum.*)

Act Four.   Scene I

TOXILUS (*to himself*): If you manage any affair carefully and decently, you can usually handle matters so it turns out well. And indeed, everyone's affairs turn out just about as they manage them; if a fellow's no good and useless, the things he does usually turn out to be no good; but if he's a decent sort of chap, his affairs come out decently. Now I've made a shrewd and witty beginning of this affair, and so I am sure that it will turn out well for me. I'll get this pimp so tangled up today, he won't know how to get himself out of it. (*Calling into the house*) Hello, Sagaristio! Come on out, and bring the maiden, and that letter I sealed for you—the one you brought me from my master, all the way from Persia.

Act Four.   Scene II

(*Enter* SAGARISTIO, *dressed as a Persian, with* SATURIO'S DAUGHTER, *also in Persian dress.*)

SAGARISTIO: I'm not keeping you waiting, am I?

TOXILUS: Bravo! Bravo! What a princely dress! That's a charming turban you have to go with your get-up. (*Looking over the* DAUGHTER) And those sandals are awfully becoming to this little stranger. But have you rehearsed your parts well?

SAGARISTIO: No tragic or comic actor ever rehearsed so well.

TOXILUS: By heavens, you're just too helpful! Come now, go over there, way out of sight, and keep quiet. When you see me talking with the pimp, that will be the time to come up. Now, get along with you. (SAGARISTIO *and the* DAUGHTER *go out towards the harbour.*)

Act Four.　Scene III

(*Enter* DORDALUS *from the forum.*)

DORDALUS (*to himself*): When the gods favour a man, they put him in the way of a little profit. Now I've just made a saving of two whole loaves of bread a day. For that slave-girl I owned is now her own owner; Toxilus' cash won him the victory. So now she'll dine today at someone else's expense and won't taste a morsel of mine. What a patriotic, lovely citizen I am! I've made the state of Athens greater today and increased the population by one female citizen. But how generous I've been today! How many people I trusted! I didn't demand collateral from anyone; that's how liberal I've been to all. And I'm not afraid that anyone I trusted today will deny his debt on oath before a court. From this day on I want to be an honest man—something that never will happen and never did!

TOXILUS (*aside*): Now I'll lead this fellow into the snare with my artful dodges; the trap is neatly set to catch him. I'll go up to him. (*Approaching* DORDALUS) How are you?

DORDALUS (*benignly*): In a mood to trust you.

TOXILUS: Where've you been, Dordalus?

DORDALUS: Trusting you. May God grant your every wish.

TOXILUS: I say, have you set the girl free yet?

DORDALUS: I trust you, by God! I trust you, I say.

TOXILUS (*impatiently*): Have you one more freedwoman by now?

DORDALUS: You're the death of me. Why, I'm telling you I trust you.

TOXILUS: Tell me on your honour: is she really free?

DORDALUS: Indeed she is; go to the forum; ask the praetor, if you don't want to believe me. She's free, I tell you; can't you hear?

TOXILUS: Well, may God in heaven bless you! I'll never again wish anything unpleasant for you or any of your household.

DORDALUS: Get out! Don't swear it; I believe you.

TOXILUS: Where is your freedwoman now?

DORDALUS: At your house.

TOXILUS: What? At my house, you say?

DORDALUS: Yes; at your house, I say.

TOXILUS: So help me God, you're going to get a generous reward from me for that! For there's a certain matter which I've kept from telling you; now I'll tell you about it, so you can make a huge profit. I'll guarantee that you'll remember me as long as you live.

DORDALUS: My ears require some kind deeds to back up these kind words of yours.

TOXILUS: You certainly have earned my services. And I want you to know what I'm going to do for you: take this letter and read it.

DORDALUS: What has it got to do with me?

TOXILUS: Why, it has a lot to do with you, and it's to your interest; for it's just now been brought to me from Persia, from my master.

DORDALUS: When?

TOXILUS: Not long ago.

DORDALUS: What does it say?

TOXILUS: Ask the letter itself; it will tell you.

DORDALUS (*taking the letter*): Well then, give it here.

TOXILUS: Read it aloud.

DORDALUS: Keep quiet while I read through it.

TOXILUS: Read it; I won't say a word.

DORDALUS (*reading*): "Greetings from Timarchides to Toxilus and all the household. I hope this finds you all well. I am the same, and I'm very busy making money; I won't be able to return to you for eight months, there's so much business here to keep me. The Persians have taken Chrysopolis in Arabia, an ancient town filled with riches; so much booty was taken that there was a public auction; that's what keeps me away from home. I want you to assist and entertain the bearer of this letter. Take care of all his desires; for he honoured me most hospitably at his own home." What's all this got to do with me? What does it matter to me what the Persians or your master are doing?

TOXILUS: Hush, you silly babbler! You don't know what an opportunity is knocking at your door, or how Our Lady of the Profits is smiling on you.

DORDALUS: Who's that "Our Lady of the Profits" of yours?

TOXILUS: Ask the letter; it knows. I know as little as you, except that I read the letter first. Just find out about the matter from the letter, as you started out to.

DORDALUS: That's good advice. Keep quiet.

TOXILUS: Now you're coming to the part that concerns you.

DORDALUS (*reading*): "The bearer of this letter has brought with him a highborn maiden of a tempting appearance, who was stolen and kidnapped from the depths of Arabia. I want you to arrange to sell her in Athens. But let the purchaser buy her at his own risk; no one will promise or sell her with legal title. See that he gets honest money and isn't short-changed. Take care of this, and see that my friend is well cared for. Farewell."

TOXILUS: Well now! Now that you've read what is written on the tablet, do you believe me?

DORDALUS: Where is the foreigner who brought this letter here?

TOXILUS: He'll soon be here, I think; he went to fetch the girl from the ship.

DORDALUS (*doubtfully*): I have no use for lawsuits or red tape. Why should I pay out my cash for outsiders? Unless I get her with legal title, what do I want with these wares?

TOXILUS: Won't you keep quiet? I never would have thought you were such a numbskull. What? Are you afraid?

DORDALUS: Indeed I am afraid. I've had much experience, and it wouldn't be anything new for me to get stuck in such a mudhole.

TOXILUS: It doesn't seem at all dangerous to me.

DORDALUS: I know that, but I'm afraid it's dangerous for me.

TOXILUS: Well, it makes no difference as far as I'm concerned. I'm only doing this for your sake, to give you the first chance to get her at a bargain.

DORDALUS: No, thank you. It's much nicer to learn from someone else's experience than to have others learn from yours.

TOXILUS: But surely no one would follow her all the way from the depths of Arabia. You really intend to buy her, don't you?

DORDALUS: Well, just let me see the goods.

TOXILUS: That's fair enough. (*Signaling to* SAGARISTIO *off-stage*) Ah, fine! Look, here comes the foreigner who brought the letter.

DORDALUS: Is that he?

TOXILUS: It is.

DORDALUS: Is that the stolen maiden?

TOXILUS: I don't know any more than you—except that she looks very ladylike, whoever she is.

DORDALUS: By God, she *is* pretty well put together.

TOXILUS (*aside*): How he slights her, the scoundrel! (*Aloud*) Let's look her over in silence.

DORDALUS: A very good plan. (*They withdraw.*)

Act Four.   Scene IV

(*Enter* SAGARISTIO *and* SATURIO'S DAUGHTER, *still in Persian dress.*)

SAGARISTIO: Does Athens seem rich and prosperous enough for you?

DAUGHTER: I've only seen the city's appearance; I haven't studied the characters of the citizens very thoroughly.

TOXILUS (*aside, to* DORDALUS): She's not slow to speak up wisely from the very first, is she?

DORDALUS (*to* TOXILUS): I couldn't discern her wisdom from her very first words.

SAGARISTIO: Well, what about what you have seen? Does the city seem well fortified with its wall?

DAUGHTER: If the inhabitants are people of good character, I think that's the finest sort of fortification. If treachery, graft, and greed are exiled from the city, and fourthly, envy; fifth, political corruption; sixth, gossip; seventh, perjury—

TOXILUS (*aside, poking* DORDALUS): Aha!

DAUGHTER: —eighth, laziness; ninth, fraud; and tenth and worst of all, crime—a city which lacks these faults will be well fortified with a single wall; but where they are present, a hundred-fold wall will not suffice to save the state.

TOXILUS (*to* DORDALUS): I say, there!

DORDALUS: What do you want?

TOXILUS: You're in one of those ten fraternities: you ought to go off into exile.

DORDALUS: Why?

TOXILUS: Because you're a perjurer.

DORDALUS: There's sense in what she says, I admit.

TOXILUS: She'll be useful to you, I tell you. Buy her.

DORDALUS: By God, the more I look her over, the more I like her.

TOXILUS: Ye gods! If you buy her, no pimp in the world will be richer than you. You'll turn men out of their farms and possessions, just as you please. You'll have dealings with men of quality; they'll court your favour; they'll come to your house to carouse.

DORDALUS (*ironically*): But I won't let them in, of course!

TOXILUS: Well then, they'll serenade your door by night, and burn down the doors. Then you must have your house shut up with iron doors, change the house itself to iron, put in iron thresholds, iron bolts and iron rings. Oh, please don't be sparing of iron: have some iron made up into good, stout fetters for yourself!

DORDALUS: Go to the devil, if you please!

TOXILUS: Why, go yourself—to buy the girl. Mind what I say!

DORDALUS: I'd just like to know what price he sets.

TOXILUS: Do you want me to call him over here?

DORDALUS: I'll go to meet him. (*They approach* SAGARISTIO.)

TOXILUS (*to* SAGARISTIO): How are you, my friend?

SAGARISTIO: I've come. I've brought the girl, as you told me. For the ship came into port last night. I want the girl sold, if possible. If not, I want to get away as soon as possible.

DORDALUS: Good health to you, young man.

SAGARISTIO: Oh, I'll be well enough, if I can sell this girl for what she's worth.

TOXILUS: Why, if this fellow buys her, you'll sell her at a fine price; you couldn't do better with anyone else.

SAGARISTIO: Are you a friend of his?

TOXILUS: As friendly as all the gods in heaven.

DORDALUS: Then you're no friend of mine. No god was ever generous enough to favour the profession of pimps.

SAGARISTIO: Come to the point. Do you want to buy this girl?

DORDALUS: If you want to sell her, I want to buy. If you're in no hurry, then neither am I.

SAGARISTIO: Name a price; make me an offer.

DORDALUS: You own the merchandise; it's your business to set a price.

TOXILUS: That's a fair request.

SAGARISTIO: Do you want to buy her for a nice sum?

DORDALUS: Do you want to sell her for a tidy sum?

TOXILUS: By heaven, I'm sure that's what you both want.

DORDALUS: Come, come! Set a definite price.

SAGARISTIO: I tell you in advance: no one will sell her to you with a legal title. Do you understand?

DORDALUS: I understand. Name your rock-bottom price—the lowest price I can take her home for.

TOXILUS: Hush, hush! Goodness, you're a childish, stupid fellow!

DORDALUS: Why?

TOXILUS: Because I want you to ask the girl a few important questions first.

DORDALUS: By God, that's not a bad piece of advice. Just look, will you! Here I, the clever pimp, had almost fallen into a pit, if you hadn't been here. How important it is to have a friend at hand when you do business!

TOXILUS: I want you to ask her who her family is, where she was born, who her parents are, so you won't say you bought her too hastily at my advice or because I urged you on.

DORDALUS: Why, I like your plan very much, I tell you.

TOXILUS (*to* SAGARISTIO): If it's no trouble, he'd like to ask her a few questions.

SAGARISTIO: Certainly; just as you like.

TOXILUS (*to* DORDALUS): Why are you standing here? Go up and ask her yourself, so you can ask her whatever you wish. Even though he said he gave me permission, I prefer to have you approach her; I don't want him to slight you.

DORDALUS: That's pretty good advice. (*To* SAGARISTIO) Young man, I'd like to ask her some questions.

SAGARISTIO: Anything you like, from A to Izzard.

DORDALUS: Just tell her to come over here to me.

SAGARISTIO (*to the girl*): Go on, and do his bidding. (*To* DORDALUS) Ask your questions; cross-examine her if you like.

TOXILUS (*aside to* SATURIO'S DAUGHTER): Come on, now! See that you enter the battle with good omens.

DAUGHTER (*aside to* TOXILUS): The omens are favourable; keep still! I'll see that you return to camp fairly staggering under the booty.

TOXILUS (*to* DORDALUS): Move back there a bit; I'll bring her to you.

DORDALUS: Do so—whatever you think is to my advantage.

TOXILUS: Come over here, my girl. (*To the girl, in a low voice*) Now mind your p's and q's.

DAUGHTER (*aside to* TOXILUS): Oh, hush! I'll fix everything to suit you.

TOXILUS (*aloud*): Follow me. (*To* DORDALUS) Here she is, if you want to ask her any questions. (*Starts to leave.*)

DORDALUS: But I want you to stay here too.

TOXILUS: I can't. I have to devote my attention to this foreigner, as master ordered. Supposing he doesn't want me to stay with you?

SAGARISTIO: Oh, that's all right. Go ahead.

TOXILUS (*to* DORDALUS): I'll give you my assistance.

DORDALUS: You give it to yourself, when you help your friend.

SAGARISTIO: Examine her.

TOXILUS (*to the girl*): Say there, wake up!

DAUGHTER: Say no more. Although I'm a slave, I know my duty; I'll answer all questions truthfully, just as I've been taught.

TOXILUS: Young lady, this is a very honest gentleman.

DAUGHTER: I believe it.

TOXILUS: You won't be his slave for very long.

DAUGHTER: Indeed, I hope not—if my parents do their duty.

DORDALUS: Don't think it strange if we ask you some questions about your country and your parents.

DAUGHTER: Why should I think it strange, sir? The fact that I'm a slave prevents me from thinking any trouble strange.

DORDALUS (*sympathetically*): Don't cry.

TOXILUS (*aside*): What a shrewd and crafty wench she is, confound her! She's got a smart head on her shoulders, all right. She says just what's needed.

DORDALUS: What's your name?

TOXILUS (*aside*): Now I'm afraid she'll make a slip.

DAUGHTER: In my own country my name was Lucratis.

TOXILUS (*to* DORDALUS): The name's an omen; it's worth any price. Why don't you buy her? (*Aside*) I was so afraid she'd blunder. But she got out of it.

DORDALUS: If I buy you, I trust that you'll be Lucrative for me too.

TOXILUS: Why, if you buy her, I swear she won't stay your slave for one whole month.

DORDALUS: By God, that's just what I wish.

TOXILUS: Then do your best to make that wish come true. (*Aside*) She hasn't made a mistake yet.

DORDALUS: Where were you born?

DAUGHTER: As my mother told me, in the kitchen, in the left-hand corner.

TOXILUS: She'll be a lucky courtesan for you; she was born in a hot spot, where there's always plenty of good cheer. (*Aside*) That's a good one on the pimp! When he asked her to tell him where she was born, she fooled him nicely.

DORDALUS: But I'm asking what your native country is.

DAUGHTER: What country is there for me except the one I'm now in?

DORDALUS: I mean, what *was* your country in the past?

DAUGHTER: I count everything that was as nothing, since it's past. Just as with a man: when he's breathed his life away, why ask who he was?

TOXILUS: Heaven help me, what wisdom! And yet I pity her. Nevertheless, young lady, what is your native land? Come, speak out! Why this silence?

DAUGHTER: I'll tell you: since I'm a slave here, this is my native land.

TOXILUS (*to* DORDALUS): Well, stop asking about that. Don't you see she doesn't want to tell? You don't want to remind her of her sufferings.

DORDALUS: Well then: was your father captured?

DAUGHTER: Not captured, but he lost all he had.

TOXILUS: She must be of a noble family: she doesn't know how to tell anything but the truth.

DORDALUS: Who was he? Tell me his name.

DAUGHTER: Why should I tell who my wretched father was? Now it's only right to call both him and me Wretched.

DORDALUS: What was his standing with his fellow-citizens?

DAUGHTER: No one was so well treated; all loved him, slaves and free men alike.

TOXILUS: He's a wretched man indeed, just as you say, since he himself is ruined and has ruined those that love him.

DORDALUS: I'll buy her, I think.

TOXILUS: Is it still "I think"? Why, I'm sure she's of royal blood. You'll make a fortune from her.

DORDALUS: Heaven grant it!

TOXILUS: Just buy her.

DAUGHTER: Let me tell you this: my father will soon be here, when he learns that I've been sold, and he'll ransom me from you.

TOXILUS: What now?

DORDALUS: What is it?

TOXILUS: Do you hear what she says?

DAUGHTER: For even though his fortunes are shattered, he still has friends.

DORDALUS: There, there! Don't cry. You'll be free very soon, if you're laid often enough. Do you want to belong to me?

DAUGHTER: Provided that I don't belong to you too long, I'm willing.

TOXILUS: See how she keeps her freedom in mind? She'll bring you a huge haul. Act now, if you're going to do anything. I'll go back to him. Come along. (*Approaching* SAGARISTIO) I've brought her back to you.

DORDALUS: Young man, do you want to sell her?

SAGARISTIO: I'd rather sell her than lose her.

DORDALUS: Well then, cut it short. Set the price you'll sell her for.

SAGARISTIO: Since I see you want her, I'll let you buy her. Take her for a hundred minae.

DORDALUS: Too much.

SAGARISTIO: Eighty.

DORDALUS: Still too much.

SAGARISTIO: I can't knock a single penny off the price I'm going to mention.

DORDALUS: What is it, then? Speak up and name the price.

SAGARISTIO: Take her at your own risk for sixty minae.

DORDALUS: Toxilus, what shall I do?

TOXILUS: Have the gods driven you mad, you scoundrel, that you don't rush to close the deal?

DORDALUS: It's a bargain.

TOXILUS: Go in and bring out the money. By God, she's cheap at three hundred minae. You've got a bargain.

DORDALUS: . . . .[3]

TOXILUS: Bravo! You've made a beautiful haul.

SAGARISTIO: See here! There will be ten minae more for her clothes.

DORDALUS: Ten less, you mean, not more.

TOXILUS: Oh, hush! Don't you see he's looking for an opening to call the deal off? Go in and get the money . . .³ (*aside*) and go to the devil, as you deserve!

DORDALUS: Mind you keep an eye on him.

TOXILUS: Why don't you go in?

DORDALUS: I'm going, and I'll bring the money. (*He goes into his house.*)

Act Four.   Scene V

TOXILUS: By God, my girl, you've accomplished a laudable feat—a noble, skilful, clever job.

DAUGHTER: If you do a favour to good people, it's usually taken seriously and with gratitude.

TOXILUS: Listen here, my Persian friend. When you get the money from him, pretend that you're going directly to your ship.

SAGARISTIO: You needn't coach me.

TOXILUS: Then come back to my house by the alley, through the garden there.

SAGARISTIO: You're telling just what's going to happen.

TOXILUS: But don't set sail for home the minute you get the money, I'm warning you.

SAGARISTIO: Do you think I'm the sort of fellow who'd do what you deserve?

TOXILUS: Quiet! Lower your voice. Our loot is coming out.

Act Four.   Scene VI

(*Enter* DORDALUS *from his house, carrying a sack of money.*)

DORDALUS: Here are sixty minae in honest money, less two nummi.

SAGARISTIO: What are those two nummi for?

DORDALUS: To pay for this sack—or make it return home.

SAGARISTIO: You want to be the complete pimp, eh? Are you afraid of losing that little purse, you greedy, dirty wretch?

TOXILUS: Oh, let him be, please. Since he's a pimp, it's not surprising.

DORDALUS: All the signs point to a profitable day for me; no sum is so small but that I'd hate to lose it. Come on, take this, if you please.

SAGARISTIO: Put it on my shoulder, if you don't mind.

DORDALUS (*doing so*): Well, all right.

SAGARISTIO: Anything else you want of me?

TOXILUS: Why are you in such a hurry?

SAGARISTIO: I'm very busy: I want to deliver some letters that were entrusted to me. And I've heard that my twin brother is a slave here; I want to hunt for him and ransom him.

TOXILUS: Good heavens, that reminds me: I think I've seen someone here just like you in appearance, and just your size.

SAGARISTIO: Of course. That must be my brother.

DORDALUS: What's your name?

TOXILUS: What difference does it make to you?

DORDALUS (*suspiciously*): What difference does it make if I don't know?

SAGARISTIO: Listen then, that you may know it: Blabberodorus Maidvendorovich Lightchatterson Cashscreweroutstein Ibn Saidwhatyoudeserve MacTrifle McBlarney Whatonceyougetyourhandson Neverpartwithitski. There you are!

DORDALUS: Wow! Your name must be hard to write out.

SAGARISTIO: That's the Persian custom; we have long, contortuplicated names. (*Starts to leave*) Anything else you want?

DORDALUS: Farewell.

SAGARISTIO: Farewell to you; my mind's already on board ship.

TOXILUS: You could go tomorrow instead and dine here today.

SAGARISTIO: Farewell. (*He goes out towards the harbour.*)

Act Four.   Scene VII

TOXILUS: Since he's gone away, I can speak out frankly; by heaven, what a profitable day has dawned for you today! Why, you haven't bought the girl: you've made your fortune!

DORDALUS (*thoughtfully*): That fellow knows what sort of business he's done; why, he sold me stolen goods at my risk, took the money and went off. How do I know if the girl won't be claimed? Where shall I go to find him then? To Persia? Nonsense!

TOXILUS: I thought you'd be grateful for my kindness.

DORDALUS: Why, I am grateful to you, Toxilus, indeed I am; for I felt that you were doing me a favour very diligently.

TOXILUS (*momentarily startled*): I did you a favour? (*Recovering himself*) Oh, yes, very diligently.

DORDALUS: Blast it! I forgot some orders I wanted to give them in the house. Keep an eye on the girl. (*He goes into his house.*)

TOXILUS: Oh, she'll be safe.

DAUGHTER: Father's awfully slow.

TOXILUS: Suppose I warn him.

DAUGHTER: It's high time.

TOXILUS (*calling into his house*): Hey, Saturio, come out! Now's the chance to get even with our enemy.

(*Enter* SATURIO *from* TOXILUS' *house.*)

SATURIO: Here I am. I'm not keeping you waiting, am I?

TOXILUS: Come on! Get over there, out of sight, and keep quiet. When you see me talking with the pimp, start a row.

SATURIO: *Verbum sap,* as they say.

TOXILUS: But wait till I get away.

SATURIO: Keep quiet, won't you? I know what you want. (*He retires into hiding.*)

Act Four.   Scene VIII

(*Enter* DORDALUS *from his house.*)

DORDALUS: I cut 'em all to pieces with my whip when I came home; the furnishings and all the house were so dirty.

TOXILUS: Have you come back at last?

DORDALUS: I have.

TOXILUS: Indeed, I've done you many favours today.

DORDALUS: I admit it, and I'm grateful.

TOXILUS (*starting to leave*): Anything else you want of me?

DORDALUS: Have a good time.

TOXILUS: By George, that's a suggestion I'm going to follow up at home; for I'm going to lie down with your freedwoman. (*He goes into his house.*)

Act Four.   Scene IX

SATURIO (*rushing out of his hiding-place*): The devil take me if I don't destroy the fellow! Good! There he is before the house.

DAUGHTER: All hail, father dear!

SATURIO: Hail, my daughter.

DORDALUS: Ow! That Persian's made me perish.

DAUGHTER: This is my father.

DORDALUS: What? Your father? I'm completely ruined! Ah, why then do I delay to go into mourning for my sixty minae, unhappy man?

SATURIO: By God, I'll make you go into mourning for yourself too, you scoundrel.

DORDALUS: I'm done for!

SATURIO: Come, let's go to law, pimp.

DORDALUS: Why do you summon me to court?

SATURIO: I'll tell that to the judge. I'm summoning you to court.

DORDALUS: You're going to call a witness, aren't you?

SATURIO: What, you hangdog? Shall I touch the ear of any free man,[6] when you traffic in freeborn citizens in the city?

DORDALUS: Let me explain.

SATURIO: I won't.

DORDALUS: Listen!

SATURIO: I'm deaf. Come to court. Follow me, you villainous maiden-snatcher. Follow me, my child, right to the magistrate.

DAUGHTER: I'm coming. (*They go out towards the forum.*)

Act Five.   Scene I

(*Enter* TOXILUS *from his house.*)

TOXILUS (*singing triumphantly*): The battle o'er, the foe subdued,
    The citizens saved, the state secure,
       Peace firmly ratified,
    The fires of war are quenched at last,
    Success today our effort crowns,
       No losses in our ranks:
For this, O Lord and all ye heavenly powers above,
And for your aid, receive my gratitude and thanks,
Since I have well avenged myself upon my foe.
And now I'm going to divide and share the booty with my partners. (*Calling into the house*) Come on out! I want to entertain my mates here before the door.
(*Enter* LEMNISELENIS, SAGARISTIO, PAEGNIUM, *and several other slaves from the house.*)
Set up the couches here, arrange here all that's customary. I want to hold court here and make everybody happy, joyful, and sportive—everybody whose assistance made it easy for me to accomplish what I wanted. For a man's a knave who knows how to receive a favour but not how to return it.

LEMNISELENIS: Toxilus dear, why am I alone? Why aren't you with me?

TOXILUS: Come then: approach and give me a hug.

LEMNISELENIS (*embracing him*): There you are.

TOXILUS: Oh, there's nothing sweeter than this. Please, my darling, let's stretch out on this couch right now.

LEMNISELENIS: All your wishes are mine.

TOXILUS: That goes for me, too. Come on then! Come, come! Sagaristio, you take the place at the head of the table.

SAGARISTIO: I don't care about that. Just give me the partner I bargained for.

TOXILUS: All in good time.

SAGARISTIO: That "all in good time" is too late for me.

TOXILUS: To business! Take your place. Let's spend this day in pleasant revelry; it's my birthday. Here slaves! Pour water on our hands and set the table. (*To* LEMNISELENIS) Here's a garland of flowers for you, my little flower. You'll be our toastmistress.

LEMNISELENIS (*to* PAEGNIUM): Come, boy! Begin the game at the head of the table there with two-quart mugs all around. Get moving there! Hurry up!

TOXILUS: Paegnium, you're too slow with the drinks. Give me one. (*Taking a drink*) Good health to me, good health to you, good health to my mistress! The gods have granted me this day I longed for; now, my dearest, I can embrace you as a free woman.

LEMNISELENIS: Thanks to you, dear.

TOXILUS (*raising his cup again*): Here's to all of us. My hand presents your hand with this cup, as is proper for lovers.

LEMNISELENIS: Give it to me.

TOXILUS: Take it.

LEMNISELENIS: Here's to the man who envies me, and here's to one who rejoices with me.

Act Five. Scene II

(Enter DORDALUS *from the forum.)*

DORDALUS *(mournfully)*: Of all men who are, who ever were, and who ever shall be, I, I alone, certainly head the procession in misery. Alas! I'm ruined! What a villainous, ruinous day this has been for me! The way that Toxilus put it over on me and tore my fortune to pieces! I've thrown away a carload of money; I've lost it, and I don't have what I threw it away for. May all the gods damn that Persian, and all Persians, and all persons too! Toxilus stirred up this trouble for me, curse him! Because I didn't trust him for the money he turned his guns on me. By God, if I don't get him shackled and crucified, as sure as I live, if only his master comes back here, as I hope, I'll—but what's this I see? Just look at that! What an act this is! Why, they're drinking right here. I'll go up to them. *(Approaching* TOXILUS*)* Greetings, my honourable friend—and greetings to you, my honourable freedwoman.

TOXILUS: Why, here's Dordalus.

SAGARISTIO: Why not ask him over?

TOXILUS: Come on over, if you like.

SAGARISTIO: Come on, let's all applaud him!

TOXILUS: Oh, Dordalus, my charming fellow, greetings. Here's a place for you; lie down here. Bring water for his feet. Come, boy, will you serve him?

DORDALUS *(to* PAEGNIUM*)*: If you lay one finger on me, sir, I'll smite you to the ground, you rascal!

PAEGNIUM: And I'll knock your eye out with this cup.

DORDALUS *(to* TOXILUS*)*: I say, you worn-out whipping post! How have you plagued me today? How did you trip me up and manage this Persian trick on me?

TOXILUS: You'll stop that brawling, if you're smart.

DORDALUS *(turning on* LEMNISELENIS*)*: And you, you fine freedwoman! You knew all this and hid it from me?

LEMNISELENIS: It's silly to start a quarrel when you can have a good time. You can take up that matter later.

DORDALUS: It burns me up!

TOXILUS: Quick! Give him a pitcher; put out the fire, if he's burning up, so that his head doesn't catch fire.

DORDALUS: You're making game of me, I know.

TOXILUS: Want me to give you a new playmate, Paegnium? Go on and play with him, in your usual style; this is Liberty Hall here. (*As* PAEGNIUM *minces up to* DORDALUS) Whee! Baby! What a pretty, high-class swagger you've got!

PAEGNIUM: It's very becoming to me. I just love to make fun of this pimp, since he deserves it.

TOXILUS: Keep right on in the same way.

PAEGNIUM (*striking* DORDALUS): Here, pimp, that's for you!

DORDALUS: Ouch! He hit me!

PAEGNIUM (*striking again*): There! Watch out for this one too!

DORDALUS: Make sport of me as you like, while your master's away.

PAEGNIUM: See how I obey you? (*Strikes again*) But why don't you obey my orders in your turn and follow my suggestion?

DORDALUS: What's that?

PAEGNIUM: Take a good stout rope and hang yourself.

DORDALUS: Don't you touch me, or I'll give you a good thrashing with my cane.

PAEGNIUM: Go on and use it. I give you leave. (*Dodges briskly as* DORDALUS *lays about him with his stick.*)

TOXILUS: Now, now, Paegnium, that's enough.

DORDALUS: By God, I'll wipe you out, all of you!

PAEGNIUM: And you'll be wiped out by Him who dwells above us, since He hates you and will make you suffer. They're not telling you this, but I do.

TOXILUS: Come, pass around the honey-wine; fill up the cups and give us a drink. It's an age since we had a drink; we're dry as dust.

DORDALUS: God grant you drink something that won't pass through you!

SAGARISTIO (*getting up from his couch*): I can't help dancing for you, pimp; here's the *pas-seul* that Hegea used to do. See if you like it. (*Dances.*)

TOXILUS (*getting up*): I want to dance too; I'll perform the dance that Diodorus used to do in Ionia. (*Dances.*)

DORDALUS: I'll give you both a thrashing if you don't get away!

SAGARISTIO: Are you still grumbling, you brazen rascal? If you provoke me, I'll bring back that Persian.

DORDALUS: That shuts me up, by God! (*Looking at* SAGARISTIO *curiously*) Why, you're the Persian who completely skinned me!

TOXILUS: Hush, you fool! This is his twin brother.

DORDALUS: Is this he?

SAGARISTIO: Yes, the twinniest twin there is.

DORDALUS: May all the gods confound you and your twin brother too!

SAGARISTIO: You mean the fellow who ruined you. For I didn't do anything.

DORDALUS: But I'd like to see you catch it for what he did.

TOXILUS: Come on, if you please: let's make fun of him some more.

LEMNISELENIS: Unless he deserves it, there's no need; and it isn't right for me to do it.

TOXILUS: I suppose he didn't make any trouble when I tried to buy you.

LEMNISELENIS: But still—

TOXILUS: Just you look out for trouble, and follow me. It's only fair for you to obey me now; for were it not for me and my protection, he'd have soon made a common prostitute of you. But that's the way of freedmen: unless they oppose their patron, they don't think they're really free; they don't think they've become good, honourable gentlemen unless they do this and revile their benefactor and prove ungrateful.

LEMNISELENIS: Mercy me! Your kindness urges me to obey your orders.

TOXILUS: Well, I'm clearly your patron, since I paid my money to him for you. Now I want you to make a perfect fool of him.

LEMNISELENIS: I'll do my very best.

DORDALUS (*aside*): These fellows are certainly cooking up some trouble for me.

SAGARISTIO (*to* TOXILUS): Hey you!

TOXILUS: What is it?

SAGARISTIO: Is this Dordalus the pimp, who traffics in freeborn maidens here? Is this he, who was once so bold?

DORDALUS: What's all this? (*As* SAGARISTIO *strikes him*) Ouch! He hit me in the face! I'll make trouble for you for this!

TOXILUS: But we've already made trouble for you, and we'll keep on making it.

DORDALUS (*as* PAEGNIUM *pinches him*): Ouch! He's pinching my rear!

PAEGNIUM: That's all right; it's often been plucked before.

DORDALUS: Are you still talking, you half-pint?

LEMNISELENIS: My dear patron, do come in to dinner, please.

DORDALUS: My dear Good-for-nothing, are you making fun of me now?

LEMNISELENIS: Because I invite you to dinner, so you can have a good time?

DORDALUS: I don't want to have a good time.

LEMNISELENIS: All right, don't.

TOXILUS: What now? What about those six hundred nummi? Do they upset you?

DORDALUS: Oh God! Undone, undone! How well they know how to pay back an enemy!

SAGARISTIO: We've punished him enough.

DORDALUS: I admit it; I surrender to you.

TOXILUS: And we'll soon surrender you to the gallows.

SAGARISTIO: Go on in—and hang yourself!

DORDALUS (*to the audience*): These fellows haven't been too easy on me, have they? (*He goes into his house.*)

TOXILUS: You'll not soon forget that you met Toxilus. And now, spectators, fare you well. The pimp is ruined.

ALL: Give us your applause.

1. Literally, *The Persian* (*Persa*), referring to the slave who comes dressed as a Persian to sell the girl to the pimp.

2. Parasites were often called "Hard-heads" because of the blows and buffets they had to endure to entertain their patrons. Cf. the remarks of the parasite in *The Captives*, lines 88-90.

3. There is a lacuna in the text here.

4. The text is corrupt here; *sisuram,* the emendation of Ritschl, has been adopted.

5. Although the Sicilians were noted for their ready wit, Athenian jests were considered the choicest of ancient witticisms.

6. If a Roman litigant summoned his opponent to court, he could ask a bystander to witness the summons, and the bystander's ear was touched as a sign that he was a witness to the proceedings.

XV
THE CARTHAGINIAN

Characters in the Play

AGORASTOCLES, *a young Carthaginian, living in Calydon*
MILPHIO, *his slave*
ADELPHASIUM, *a girl, bought by* LYCUS
ANTERASTILIS, *her sister, also bought by* LYCUS
LYCUS, *a pimp*
ANTAMOENIDES, *a soldier*
COUNSELLORS, *acquaintances of* AGORASTOCLES
COLLYBISCUS, *overseer of* AGORASTOCLES
SYNCERASTUS, *slave of* LYCUS
HANNO, *a Carthaginian*
GIDDENIS, *nurse of the two sisters*
A SLAVE BOY, *belonging to* HANNO

Acrostic Argument

A boy, seven years old, is stolen at Carthage. An old man, a hater of women, buys him, adopts him as his son, and makes him his heir. His two kinswomen and their nurse are also stolen. Lycus buys them, and torments the youth who is in love. But he palms off his overseer with some gold upon the pimp, and in this way makes him guilty of theft. Hanno, the Carthaginian, arrives, discovers the youth to be his nephew, and recognises his daughters whom he had lost.

INTRODUCTION

THE prologue of *The Carthaginian* (the *Poenulus*) gives the reader the impression that the play is essentially a comedy of mistaken identity and recognition. This is misleading; although the motive of recognition is prominent at the end, the greater part of the play deals with Milphio's attempt to trick the pimp Lycus. His purpose is to aid his master Agorastocles who is in love with the elder of two sisters now in the power of Lycus. The plot thus combines trickery and recognition as do those of the *Curculio* and the *Epidicus*. Milphio's deception is elaborate and involves impersonation; Collybiscus, Agorastocles' overseer, comes to Lycus' establishment as a stranger from abroad who is anxious for a good time. Lycus by taking in the supposed newcomer is accused of theft and harbouring a slave. The trick itself is brought to a successful conclusion, but the case has not yet been brought to court when Milphio learns that the two sisters are freeborn Carthaginians. He devises a second plan in which a newly arrived Carthaginian will pose as the father of the girls and claim them as his daughters. Milphio's second trick collapses when the motives of deception and recognition are combined, for it so happens that Hanno the Carthaginian actually is the father of the two maidens.

The play is long and, in spite of several excellent scenes, is usually considered as a whole somewhat dull. The two sisters who are on the verge of becoming courtesans are amusingly portrayed. Antamoenides is a good example of the braggart soldier; he and Lycus provide considerable humour. Agorastocles is ridiculous as a lover, and Milphio is a good intriguing slave, though hardly the equal of an Epidicus or a Pseudolus. He is at his best when he pleads with Adelphasium in his master's behalf and when he attempts to translate Hanno's Punic which he professes to understand. Hanno the Carthaginian is pious and dignified, and the passages which he speaks in his native tongue provide a feature of unusual interest in the play.

The Carthaginian, like *The Braggart Warrior* which also contains two different deceptions, has been considered one of the plays which Plautus constructed from two Greek originals; i.e. the trick which Milphio and Collybiscus play on Lycus did not come from the same

Greek comedy as the story of the Carthaginian girls and their final recognition by their father. Although there are several structural flaws in the play, many scholars now reject the double source theory. It has recently been suggested that the entire Collybiscus episode was Plautus' own invention to enrich the plot of the original play.

It is not certain when *The Carthaginian* was produced at Rome, but it was clearly produced more than once; not only does the comedy have two titles (like the *Casina*), but there are two different versions of the ending of the play. There seems little doubt that *The Carthaginian* is one of the plays which was revived after Plautus' death, as we know was done in the case of the *Casina*.

THE CARTHAGINIAN

(SCENE:—*A street in Calydon in front of the houses of* AGORASTOCLES *and* LYCUS.)

Prologue

I wish to imitate the *Achilles* of Aristarchus; from that tragedy I shall take my opening: "Hush and be silent and pay attention; that you listen is the order of the general"—manager, that both those who have come hungry and those who have come well-filled may cheerfully be seated on the benches; those of you who have eaten have done much more wisely, but you who haven't eaten can have your fill of the play. For it's very stupid for a person who has something to eat to come here for our sake to sit with an empty stomach. "Arise, herald, order the people to be silent." I've been waiting for a long time to see if you know your duty; exercise your voice by which you live and support yourself; for if you don't shout out, starvation will creep upon you in your silence. (*The herald tries to quiet the house*) Well now, sit down again, that you may get your wages doubled. (*To the audience*) You've done well to obey my commands. Let no worn-out harlot sit in front of the stage, nor the lictor or his rods make a sound, nor the usher roam about in front of people or show anyone to a seat while the actor is on the stage. Those who have had a long leisurely nap at home should now cheerfully stand, or at least refrain from sleeping. Keep slaves from occupying the seats, that there will be room for free men, or let them pay money for their freedom; if they can't do that, let them go home and avoid a double misfortune—being raked with rods here, and with whips at home, if their masters return and find they haven't done their work. And let the nurses keep tiny children at home and not bring them to see the play, lest the nurses themselves get thirsty and the children die of hunger or cry for food like young goats. Let matrons view the play in silence, laugh in silence, refrain from tinkling tones of chatter; they should take home their gossip, so as not to annoy their husbands both here and at home. And now, as to what concerns the directors of the games, no actor should receive the prize unjustly, nor should any be driven out through favouritism so that inferior actors are preferred to the good ones. And there's this point, too, which I had almost forgotten: while the show is going on, lackeys, make an attack on the bakery; rush in now while there is an opportunity, while the tarts are hot. These orders have been given at the command of the manager, and it's a good thing for each man to remember them for himself.

Now I wish to return to the plot of the play that you may know it as well as I do. I shall now determine its sites, limits, and boundaries; I've been selected surveyor for that purpose. I wish to give you the name of this comedy, if you have no objection; if you have, I'll give it just the same, since I have permission from the management. The comedy is called the *Carchedonian;* Plautus named it in Latin *The Porridge-eating Uncle.*[1] You have the name, then; now hear the rest of the story; for the plot will be judged here by you. Its own stage is the court where the plot will be tried; you are the jury. Pay attention, please. There were two Carthaginian cousins of high birth and wealth piled high; one is alive, the other dead. I can tell you this with more assurance, since the undertaker who put him under told me about it. But the old man who died had an only son who was stolen away from his father in Carthage when he was a mere child, seven years old; this happened six years before the death of the father. When the father learns that his only son is lost, he falls sick from grief; he makes his cousin his heir and goes off to Acheron without travelling expenses. The person who stole the child carried him off to Calydon and sold him here to a certain rich old man who wanted children but hated women. The old man without realising it bought the son of a friend, adopted him as his own son, and made him his heir when he himself departed this life. (*Pointing to the house of* AGORASTOCLES) The young man lives here in this house.

Now I return again to Carthage; if anyone wishes some business transacted for him there, he will be a fool if he doesn't give me the money; but if he does give me the money, he'll be a much greater fool. But to resume: the old uncle of this young man is still alive at Carthage; he had two daughters who disappeared with their nurse from Magara[2] when one was five years old, the other four. The fellow who kidnapped them carried them off to Anactorium, and sold them all, both nurse and girls, for cash to a man (if a pimp is a man), who is the greatest rascal on the whole earth. But figure out for yourselves what sort of man he is, when he has the name of Lycus.[3] This fellow moved not long ago from Anactorium, where he had been living, to Calydon for the sake of his business. He dwells in this house (*pointing to the house of* LYCUS). This young man is madly in love with one of the girls, his own relative, but he doesn't know that; he doesn't know who she is, nor has he ever touched her, the pimp so keeps him in torment. He has never had any intercourse with her, nor has he ever taken her home, for the pimp wasn't willing to send her; he sees that the youth is in love, and he wants to touch him for a good haul. The younger girl is beloved by a certain soldier, who wants to buy her as his mistress.

The father of the girls, the Carthaginian, has been searching for them constantly on land and sea, ever since he lost them. Whenever he enters a city, he straightway hunts out the homes of all the harlots; he pays the money, spends the night, then asks where she comes from, what country, whether she has been captured or kidnapped, who her family and her parents were. So cleverly and shrewdly he seeks for his daughters. He knows all languages, too; but though he knows them he pretends not to; he's a true Carthaginian; why say more? He arrived here at the harbour last night on board ship; he's the father of these girls and likewise the uncle of the young man here. You've got it, haven't you? If so, pull; but don't break the thread, please; let me finish. I had almost forgotten to tell you the rest. The man who adopted this youth as his son was a friend of the young man's Carthaginian uncle. [The Carthaginian will arrive here today and will discover his daughters and his nephew, as I have learned. I shall go now and dress for my part; pay cheerful attention.][4] The man who will arrive today will discover his daughters and his nephew. As to the rest, fare well and give us your support. I shall go, for I wish to become another person; as for what follows, others will follow to make it clear. Fare well and give us your support, that Safety may keep you safe.

Act One. Scene I

(Enter AGORASTOCLES *from his house, followed by* MILPHIO.*)*

AGORASTOCLES: Often I have entrusted to you, Milphio, many matters that were doubtful and troublesome and in need of advice, and you with your aid smoothed everything out for me wisely, cleverly, and prudently, and shrewdly. I admit that in return for these good services I owe you both your liberty and many kind thanks.

MILPHIO: An old saying is clever, if it fits the occasion. For your compliments to me are, as they say, stuff and nonsense; *c'est de la bêtise.* Now you're full of smooth talk; yesterday, without any trouble at all, you wore out three bulls' hides on my back.

AGORASTOCLES: If, being in love, I did anything on account of my love affair, Milphio, you ought to forgive me.

MILPHIO (*with sarcasm*): Naturally! Now I too am dying with love. Let me beat you up, just as you did to me, for no good reason at all; and then you pardon me, being in love.

AGORASTOCLES: If you wish it or find pleasure in it, go ahead; hang me up, bind me up, beat me up; I'll take the responsibility, go ahead.

MILPHIO: But if you withdraw your responsibility later, when you're released, I'll hang.

AGORASTOCLES: Would I dare to do a thing like that, especially to you? Why, if I see you get a beating, it hurts at once.

MILPHIO: Yes, by heaven, me.

AGORASTOCLES: No, me.

MILPHIO: That's what I'd prefer. But what now do you wish?

AGORASTOCLES: Why should I lie to you? I'm shamelessly in love.

MILPHIO: My shoulder blades realise that.

AGORASTOCLES (*pointing to the house of* LYCUS): I mean with the girl here next door, Adelphasium, the pimp's older courtesan.

MILPHIO: I heard that from you a long time ago.

AGORASTOCLES: I'm distracted with my desire for her. But there's no filth any filthier than the pimp Lycus, her master.

MILPHIO: Do you want to give him some trouble?

AGORASTOCLES: I'd like to.

MILPHIO: Well then, give him me.

AGORASTOCLES (*annoyed*): Go to the devil!

MILPHIO: But tell me seriously; do you want to give him some misfortune?

AGORASTOCLES: I'd like to.

MILPHIO: Well then, give him this selfsame me; he'll have both trouble and misfortune, I guarantee.

AGORASTOCLES (*disgusted*): You're full of jokes.

MILPHIO: Do you wish to free that girl of yours today without any expense on your part?

AGORASTOCLES (*despairingly*): Oh, Milphio, I'd like to.

MILPHIO: I'll see that you do it. Have you three hundred gold pieces in the house?

AGORASTOCLES: Yes, even six hundred.

MILPHIO: Three hundred are sufficient.

AGORASTOCLES: What will you do with them?

MILPHIO: Hush! I'll make you a gift today of the pimp and his whole household.

AGORASTOCLES: How will you do it?

MILPHIO: You'll soon know. Your overseer Collybiscus is now in the city; the pimp doesn't know him. Now do you understand?

AGORASTOCLES: I understand that, but I don't know what you're driving at.

MILPHIO: You don't know?

AGORASTOCLES: No, damn it!

MILPHIO: Well, you'll soon know, I'll see to that. The money will be given to him to take to the pimp; he's to say that he's a stranger from another town; that he wants to do some loving and have himself a gay time; and that he wants a quiet place provided for him where he can enjoy himself secretly without anyone knowing about it. The pimp is eager for gold and will immediately take him in. He'll conceal the man and his gold.

AGORASTOCLES: The plan sounds all right.

MILPHIO: Then you ask whether your slave has come to his house; he'll think you're asking about me; he'll deny it at once. You don't doubt, do you, that immediately the pimp will be guilty of theft and liable to twice the value of the gold and the slave? And he doesn't have any means of raising the money; when he comes to trial, the praetor will award the entire household to you. Thus we'll catch the pimp Lycus in our snare.

AGORASTOCLES (*still not enthusiastic*): The plan sounds all right.

MILPHIO: You'll say so all the more when I've polished it up; now it's still crude.

AGORASTOCLES: Unless you want me for anything, Milphio, I'm going now to the temple of Venus; today's the Aphrodisia.[5]

MILPHIO: I know.

AGORASTOCLES: I want to feast my eyes on the charms of the courtesans.

MILPHIO: Let's tend to this plan of ours first. Let's go inside to instruct Collybiscus to tend to the trickery.

AGORASTOCLES: Although Cupid has made his home in my heart, still I'll obey you.

MILPHIO: You won't regret it, I'll see to that. (AGORASTOCLES *goes into his house;* MILPHIO *soliloquises*) There's a speck of love in this fellow's heart that can't be washed out without great expense. And this pimp Lycus is such a rogue; but my heavy artillery is aimed right at him, and before long I'll let him have it full-blast. But look, there come Adelphasium and Anterastilis. It's the first one that's driving my master crazy. I'll call him out. Hey, come out, Agorastocles, if you want to see a lovely show!

AGORASTOCLES (*hurrying from the house*): What's this uproar, Milphio?

MILPHIO: Well, there's your love affair, if you want to see her.

AGORASTOCLES: All the blessings of the gods upon you for presenting me with such a charming spectacle!

Act One. Scene II

(ADELPHASIUM *and* ANTERASTILIS *enter from the house of* LYCUS, *accompanied by a maid; they do not see* AGORASTOCLES *and* MILPHIO.)

ADELPHASIUM: A man who wants to win trouble for himself should get these two things, a ship and a woman; for no two things cause more trouble if you begin to fit them out; nor are these two things ever sufficiently fitted out, nor is there any fitting end to the fitting out. And I say this, having learned my lessons at home. And from dawn until this very hour [from the break of day we never cease],[6] the two of us never cease washing or rubbing or scrubbing or dressing, smoothing, polishing, painting, trimming, with all our might. Two maids, assigned to each of us, have assisted us in our washing and bathing, and two men were worn out carrying water for us. How much trouble one woman causes! But two of them, I'm sure, can furnish more than enough trouble to a whole nation, since day and night, all their life, they're being dressed, bathed, scrubbed, decked out. There's no golden mean to a woman, and we never know how to end our washing and rubbing. And in my opinion, being clean is just like being dirty, if a girl isn't beautifully dressed.

ANTERASTILIS: Sister, I'm really surprised that you can say such things, when you're so clever and sharp and shrewd. For in spite of the way we make ourselves attractive, we have great difficulty in finding lovers.

ADELPHASIUM: That's the truth. But just the same, consider this one thing: it's best to have moderation in everything, sister. Everything in excess brings excessive trouble to mortals.

ANTERASTILIS: Just realise, sister, that we're said to be like pickled fish that are considered salty and lacking in taste and sweetness; unless they're soaked in a lot of water a long time, they're so strong and salty that you don't want to touch them. That's the way we are; women are from the same stock, lacking in taste and charm, unless they add elegance and expense.

MILPHIO (*aside to* AGORASTOCLES): This woman's a cook, Agorastocles, in my opinion; she knows how to soak pickled fish.

AGORASTOCLES (*to* MILPHIO): Why bother me?

ADELPHASIUM: Stop, sister, please; it's enough for others to say this to us; we shouldn't talk about our own faults.

ANTERASTILIS: I'll cease.

ADELPHASIUM: Thanks. But now tell me this: is everything here that we need for winning the favour of the gods? (*She points to the offerings which the maid is carrying.*)

ANTERASTILIS: I've taken care of everything.

AGORASTOCLES (*aside*): O beautiful, festive, delightful day, well worthy of Venus, whose festival today is the Aphrodisia!

MILPHIO (*aside to* AGORASTOCLES): Any thanks to me for calling you out of doors? Don't you think I ought to get a cask of old wine? Say that you'll give it. No answer, eh? He's lost his tongue, I guess. Why the devil do you stand here stupefied?

AGORASTOCLES (*to* MILPHIO): Let me love on; don't disturb me; be quiet.

MILPHIO: I am quiet.

AGORASTOCLES: If you had been quiet, that "I'm quiet" would never have come forth.

ANTERASTILIS: Let's go now, sister.

ADELPHASIUM: My dear, why are you hurrying there now?

ANTERASTILIS: You ask? Because our master is waiting for us at the temple of Venus.

ADELPHASIUM: Let him wait. Stop, there's a crowd just now at the altar. Or do you want to associate with these cheap harlots, bakers' wenches, millers' leavings, wretched women reeking with rank odours, sordid servants of slaves, stinking of stable and stool, of seat and shed, women that no free man ever touched or took home, two-penny sluts sold to shameless slaves?

MILPHIO (*aside*): You go to the devil! Do you dare to scorn slaves, you filthy hag? Just as if she were a beauty, just as if kings desired her, the worm of a woman, such big words she utters! I wouldn't pay a cup of smoke for seven whole nights with her.

AGORASTOCLES (*aside*): O gods immortal and omnipotent, what do you have more beautiful? Why should I believe that you are more immortal than I, who behold such blessings as these? Venus is no longer Venus; this is the Venus I'll worship, that she may favour me with her love. Milphio, hey, Milphio, where are you?

MILPHIO: Here.

AGORASTOCLES: I'd rather not hear you.[7]

MILPHIO: Master, now you're really joking.

AGORASTOCLES: I learned it all from you.

MILPHIO: Even to love a girl whom you've never touched?

AGORASTOCLES: By heaven, I love and respect the gods, but I keep my hands off them, just the same.

ANTERASTILIS: Really, my dear, when I look at our dresses, I'm grieved that we're dressed this way.

ADELPHASIUM: But it's quite becoming; we're dressed quite well enough, according to master's income and our own. There can't be any income without expense, I realise, but there's no income at all, if the expense exceed it, sister. It's better to have what's enough to have, than to have what's more than enough.

AGORASTOCLES (*to* MILPHIO): By the love of the gods, Milphio, I'd rather have her love than the love of the gods. That woman has the power to inflame flint with love for her.

MILPHIO (*to* AGORASTOCLES): That's certainly no lie, for you're more foolish than flint to love her.

AGORASTOCLES: But just think, I've never soiled her beauty.

MILPHIO: Then I'll run somewhere to a fish-pond or a lake, to get some muddy soil.

AGORASTOCLES: What for?

MILPHIO: I'll tell you: to soil the two of you.

AGORASTOCLES: Go and be hanged!

MILPHIO: I am hanging around.

AGORASTOCLES: You're killing me.

MILPHIO: I'll be quiet.

AGORASTOCLES: Forever, I hope.

MILPHIO: Now look here, master, you're getting me at my own game and cracking my jokes.

ANTERASTILIS: I suppose, sister, that you think you're nicely enough dressed; but when you compare yourself with the other courtesans, you'll have a heartache if you happen to see anyone else better dressed.

ADELPHASIUM: Envy and malice have never been a part of my nature, my dear sister. I'd much rather be adorned with a good disposition than with gold; gold comes from luck, a good disposition from one's own nature; I'd rather be considered good than lucky. A courtesan should cloak herself with modesty rather than with purple; it's better for a girl to have modesty than gold. A dirty character soils a lovely dress worse than mud.

AGORASTOCLES (*to* MILPHIO): Hey, you, do you want to do a dainty and darling deed?

MILPHIO: Of course.

AGORASTOCLES: Can you obey me?

MILPHIO: I can.

AGORASTOCLES: Then go home and hang yourself.

MILPHIO: What for?

AGORASTOCLES: Because you'll never again hear so many words as sweet as these. What need have you to live now? Just obey me and hang yourself.

MILPHIO: If you'll hang with me, like a bunch of dried grapes.

AGORASTOCLES: But I love the girl.

MILPHIO: And I love to eat and drink.

ADELPHASIUM: Look here, my dear.

ANTERASTILIS: What is it?

ADELPHASIUM: Look, please. My eyes were full of dirt; are they clean now?

ANTERASTILIS: There's still a speck of dirt in the middle of this eye. (*To the maid*) Give me your right hand.

AGORASTOCLES (*aside*): Would you touch or rub her eyes with your dirty hands?

ANTERASTILIS: We're much too lazy today.

ADELPHASIUM: In what way?

ANTERASTILIS: Because we didn't go before dawn to the temple of Venus, to be the first to put fire on her altar.

ADELPHASIUM: Oh, there's no need of that. Girls with dark and ugly faces hurry to make their sacrifices in the dark. They're in a rush to sacrifice before Venus wakes up; for if they come when Venus is awake, they're so ugly that I swear they would drive Venus herself from the temple.

AGORASTOCLES (*to* MILPHIO): Hey, Milphio.

MILPHIO: Oh, damn! Poor Milphio. What do you want now?

AGORASTOCLES: Just listen to her honeyed words.

MILPHIO (*disgusted*): Nothing but pure pastry; sesame and poppy seeds, wheat flour and roasted nuts!

AGORASTOCLES: Do I seem to be in love?

MILPHIO: To your financial loss, a thing that Mercury doesn't love.[8]

AGORASTOCLES: Well, my dear man, no lover ought to be in love with gain.

ANTERASTILIS: Let's go, sister.

ADELPHASIUM: Very well, as you wish.

ANTERASTILIS: Follow this way.

ADELPHASIUM: I'm coming. (*The women prepare to leave the stage.*)

MILPHIO (*to* AGORASTOCLES): They're going.

AGORASTOCLES: What if we accost them?

MILPHIO: You do it.

AGORASTOCLES (*approaching the women*): First to you (*to* ADELPHASIUM) my first greetings; and to you second (*to* ANTERASTILIS) my secondary greetings; and third to you (*to the maid*) my worthless greetings.

NURSE: In that case, I've wasted both oil and effort.

AGORASTOCLES: Whither bound?

ADELPHASIUM: I? To the temple of Venus.

AGORASTOCLES: Why go there?

ADELPHASIUM: To propitiate Venus.

AGORASTOCLES: Oho! Is she angry?

ADELPHASIUM: Heavens, no! Quite propitious.

AGORASTOCLES: Well, I'll vouch for her. (*Holding her by the arm*) Look here!

ADELPHASIUM: Why do you bother me, pray?

AGORASTOCLES: Ah, so cruel!

ADELPHASIUM: Let me go, please.

AGORASTOCLES: Why do you hurry? There's a crowd there now.

ADELPHASIUM: I know that. There are others there that I want to look at, and I want to be looked at.

AGORASTOCLES: Why do you want to look at ugly women, and let them look at a beauty?

ADELPHASIUM: Because it's the courtesan market today at the Aphrodisia; dealers are meeting there and I want to be on display.

AGORASTOCLES: It's necessary to entice a buyer for unsalable goods; good merchandise easily finds a purchaser, even if it's concealed. But tell me! When will you let me cuddle and fondle you at my house?

ADELPHASIUM: On the day that Orcus sends the dead from Acheron.

AGORASTOCLES: I have some gold coins at home that are getting restless.

ADELPHASIUM: Bring them to me; I'll put them to rest quick enough.

MILPHIO (*aside*): Jove! What a beautiful little wench! Go straight to everlasting perdition! The more I look at her, the more worthless a bit of trash she seems.

ADELPHASIUM: Stop speaking. I'm weary.

AGORASTOCLES (*more amorous*): Come now, lift your skirt a little.

ADELPHASIUM: I'm purified; please don't touch me, Agorastocles.

AGORASTOCLES: What am I to do now?

ADELPHASIUM: If you're wise, you can put an end to your worry.

AGORASTOCLES: Why should I worry you? Look here, Milphio!

MILPHIO: There's my pest again! What do you want of me?

AGORASTOCLES: Why is she angry at me?

MILPHIO: Why is she angry at you? Why should I worry about that? That's more your worry than mine, isn't it?

AGORASTOCLES: By heaven, you're a dead man if you don't make her as calm for me as is the sea, when the halcyon hatches its young.

MILPHIO: What am I to do?

AGORASTOCLES: Entreat her, soothe her, flatter her.

MILPHIO: I'll do it with energy; but just see to it that you don't fasten any fists on your ambassador afterward.

AGORASTOCLES: I won't do that.

ADELPHASIUM (*to* AGORASTOCLES): You're not nice to me, but you delay me and wrong me. Promise after promise you make; all to no avail. Not once but a hundred times you swore that you would free me; while waiting for you, I've neglected to make any other provision for myself, nor does any appear; and now I'm as much a slave as ever. Come, sister. (*To* AGORASTOCLES) You get away from me.

AGORASTOCLES: I'm done for. Say something, Milphio, won't you?

MILPHIO (*to* ADELPHASIUM): My darling, my delight, my life, my pleasure, apple of my eye, my little Cupid's bow, my health, my kiss, my honey, my heart, my milk, my soft little cheese—

AGORASTOCLES (*aside in anger*): Am I to allow these things to be said in my presence? I'm a poor distracted fool, if I don't have him dragged off in a chariot to the hangman at once.

MILPHIO (*to* ADELPHASIUM): Please, for my sake, don't be angry at my master. If you're not angry, I'll see that he pays a ninny[9] for you, and makes you a free Attic citizen. Why don't you let him approach? Why aren't you well disposed to those who wish you well? Even if he told you lies before, from now on he'll be truthful. Let me prevail upon you, let me touch your ears, let me give you a kiss.

ADELPHASIUM: Please get away from me; you're a trickster like your master.

MILPHIO: And do you know what? Unless I can persuade you to be help-ful, I'll certainly make him tearful, and I very much fear that he will make it painful for me, unless I win your favour. I know the cranky character of this crabbed fellow. Therefore, please, my darling, let me persuade you.

AGORASTOCLES: I'm not worth three cents if I don't tear out the eyes and teeth of that rascal. (*He beats* MILPHIO *angrily*) There's your darling! There's your honey! There's your heart! There's your little Cupid's bow! There's your health! There's your kiss!

MILPHIO: Master, you're committing a sin; you're beating an ambassa-dor.

AGORASTOCLES: And even more. (*Beats him again*) I'll add apple of your eye, little Cupid's bow, and tongue, too.

MILPHIO: When will you stop?

AGORASTOCLES: Was that the way I asked you to persuade her?

MILPHIO: How then was I to persuade her?

AGORASTOCLES: You ask? You should have spoken this way, you rogue: his darling, I beseech you, his honey, his heart, his little Cupid's bow, his tongue, his kiss, his delight, his charming health, his gayety, his milk, his sweet little cheese, you rascal; his heart, his desire, his kiss, you rascal. Everything that you said was yours should be called mine.

MILPHIO (*obediently, to* ADELPHASIUM): I do beseech you, his delight (*aside*) and my disgust; his well-breasted friend (*aside*) and my ill-disposed foe; apple of his eye, (*aside*) sore of my eye; honey to him, (*aside*) poison to me; please don't be angry at him, (*aside*) or, if that's impossible, get a rope and go hang yourself with your master and the household. For I see that I'll have to go on a liquid diet because of you, and my back is as rough from blows as an oyster-shell, all on ac-count of your love affair.

ADELPHASIUM: Pray tell me, do you expect me to prevent him from beating you, when I can't keep him from being deceitful to me?

ANTERASTILIS (*to* ADELPHASIUM): Say something kind to him (*nodding to* AGORASTOCLES), please, so that he won't be unkind to us. For he's keeping us from our business.

ADELPHASIUM: True. Agorastocles, I'll overlook this one fault again. I'm not angry.

AGORASTOCLES: You're not?

ADELPHASIUM: No.

AGORASTOCLES: Then give me a kiss to prove it.

ADELPHASIUM: I'll give you one later, when I return from the sacrifice.

AGORASTOCLES: Be off, then, in haste.

ADELPHASIUM: Follow me, sister.

AGORASTOCLES: And listen, will you?

ADELPHASIUM: Yes.

AGORASTOCLES: Give my very best greetings to Venus.

ADELPHASIUM: I'll give them.

AGORASTOCLES: Listen to this, too.

ADELPHASIUM: What is it?

AGORASTOCLES: Make the offering in a few words. And listen, will you? Give me a smile. (ADELPHASIUM *looks back with a smile*) She gave it! I trust that Venus will do the same for you. (ADELPHASIUM, ANTERASTILIS, *and the maid depart to the temple of Venus.*)

Act One.   Scene III

AGORASTOCLES: What do you suggest now, Milphio?

MILPHIO: That you keep on beating me and hold an auction. For you can sell this house of yours without the least disadvantage.

AGORASTOCLES: How so?

MILPHIO: You keep hanging around my jaw most of the time.

AGORASTOCLES: Stop this talk.

MILPHIO: Well, what do you want?

AGORASTOCLES: I gave the three hundred gold pieces to the overseer Collybiscus just now, before you called me outside. Now I beg you, Milphio, by this right hand, and by this left hand its sister, and by your eyes, and by my passion, and by my Adelphasium, and by your liberty—

MILPHIO: Which means, by nothing at all.

AGORASTOCLES: My darling Milphio, my Benefit, my Safety, do what you promised to do, that I may destroy this pimp.

MILPHIO: That's very easy. Go and bring back with you some witnesses; meanwhile I'll go in and deck out the overseer with disguise and trickery. Hurry and be off!

AGORASTOCLES: I'll run off.

MILPHIO: That's more my job than yours.

AGORASTOCLES (*distracted and maudlin*): I—I, if you cleverly carry out this plan—

MILPHIO: Hurry off now.

AGORASTOCLES: So that I don't today—

MILPHIO: Hurry off now.

AGORASTOCLES: Give freedom—

MILPHIO: Hurry now.

AGORASTOCLES: By heaven, I wouldn't deserve—

MILPHIO: Oh!

AGORASTOCLES: Ah!

MILPHIO: Hurry off now.

AGORASTOCLES: By all the dead in Acheron—

MILPHIO: Aren't you going to hurry?

AGORASTOCLES: Nor by all the water in the sea—

MILPHIO: Will you hurry off?

AGORASTOCLES: Nor by all the clouds—

MILPHIO: Still keeping on?

AGORASTOCLES: Nor by the stars in the sky—

MILPHIO: Still dinning my ears?

AGORASTOCLES (*completely incomprehensible*): Neither this nor that nor—but yet seriously—nor truly by heaven—why use many words? Why not? But in a word—you can say what you wish here—And yet not really seriously—do you know how it is? By the love of the gods— do you want me to speak sincerely? What can between ourselves—may Jupiter—do you know how it seems? Do you believe what I say?

MILPHIO: If I can't make you hurry off, I'll hurry myself off; to get the meaning of that speech, I'd need the help of Oedipus, who interpreted the riddle of the Sphinx. (*He goes into the house of* AGORASTOCLES.)

AGORASTOCLES (*laughing*): He's hurried away from here in anger. Now I must be careful not to delay my love affair through my own fault. I'll go and get the witnesses, since Love compels me, a free man, to obey my slave. (*Exit* AGORASTOCLES *to the forum.*)

Act Two

(*Enter* LYCUS *in anger.*)

LYCUS (*to himself*): May the gods damn any pimp who after this day offers a single victim to Venus or presents her with a single grain of incense. Today, like a fool, with the gods angry at me, I sacrificed six lambs, and still I couldn't make Venus propitious. Since I couldn't appease her, I immediately left in anger; I refused to have the sacrificial meat cut off; [I didn't want to offer it, since the soothsayer said it wasn't good; I didn't think the goddess deserved it.][4] In this way I cleverly got the better of that greedy Venus. Since she wasn't willing enough to have what was enough, I put a stop to it. That's the way I act, that's the way I ought to act. I'll guarantee that all the other gods and goddesses will be more contented and less greedy after this, when they know how a pimp outsmarted Venus. That soothsayer is a fine fellow, not worth three cents! He said that all the entrails foretold for me misfortune and loss and the anger of the gods. Ought I to entrust anything divine or human to that fellow? Afterwards I received a silver mina as a gift. But where in the world did that soldier stop, who gave me the money? I've invited him to lunch. Ah, there he comes.

(*Enter* ANTAMOENIDES.)

ANTAMOENIDES: As I was saying, my pretty pimp, about that Pente-tronic battle, when with my own hands I killed sixty thousand flying men in one day—

LYCUS: What? Flying—men?

ANTAMOENIDES (*pompously*): That's what I say.

LYCUS: Tell me, are there flying men anywhere?

ANTAMOENIDES: There were; but I killed them all.

LYCUS: How could you do that?

ANTAMOENIDES: I'll tell you. I gave birdlime and slings to my troops; beneath they laid leaves of coltsfoot.

LYCUS: What for?

ANTAMOENIDES: So that the birdlime wouldn't stick to the slings.

LYCUS: Keep on. (*Aside*) You're a damned good liar, anyway. (*To the soldier*) What next?

ANTAMOENIDES: They put large balls of birdlime in their slings; I ordered them to open fire at the flying men. Why say more? All that they hit with the birdlime fell to the ground as thick as pears. As each one dropped, I straightway pierced him through the brain with one of his own feathers, just like a turtledove.

LYCUS: By heaven, if that ever happened, may I always have to sacri-fice to Jupiter without ever appeasing him.

ANTAMOENIDES (*indignant*): You don't believe me?

LYCUS: I believe you—as I expect to be believed. Come, let's go inside.

ANTAMOENIDES: While the sacrificial meat is being brought, I want to tell you about still another battle.

LYCUS: I don't care about it.

ANTAMOENIDES: Listen.

LYCUS: Damn it! I won't listen.

ANTAMOENIDES: What's that? I'll smash your head with my fists this instant, if you don't listen or—else go to the devil.

LYCUS: I'll choose the devil.

ANTAMOENIDES: You're determined, then?

LYCUS: Determined.

ANTAMOENIDES (*changing his manner*): Well, then, on this lucky day, the Aphrodisia, make over to me the younger of your courtesans.

LYCUS: I've had tough luck today with sacred matters; I'm postponing serious business until another day. I've decided not to distinguish between holy days and ordinary days. Let's go in now; follow me this way.

ANTAMOENIDES: I follow. For this day I'm your hireling. (*They enter the house of* LYCUS.)

Act III.   Scene I

(*Enter from the forum* AGORASTOCLES, *followed at a distance by several* COUNSELLORS.)

AGORASTOCLES: The gods love me, there's nothing worse than a slow-moving friend, especially for a man in love, who's in a hurry about everything. For example, I'm bringing these counsellors, most crawling-footed loafers, slower than freighters on a calm sea. And I purposely avoided my aged friends; I knew they would be slow on account of their years; I presumed they would postpone my passion. I selected these bandy-legged beaus, but to no avail; pure slow-pokes! (*Turning to the* COUNSELLORS) If you intend to come today, come along, or else go to the devil! Is this the way for friends to help a man in love? That step of yours was sifted through a flour-sieve, unless it's a prison-pace that you've learned.

COUNSELLORS: Look here, you! Though you, being rich and noble, look upon us as poor and common, don't start abusing us; we're usually bold enough to bestow some misfortune upon the rich. We're under no obligation to your loves or your hates; when we bought our freedom, we paid our own money, not yours. It's right for us to be free men. You don't count with us; don't think that we're slaves to serve your love affair. It's much better for free men to make their way through the streets at a moderate pace; to hustle along in a hurry is the habit of slaves. Especially when the city is calm and our enemies are slain, it isn't decent to make haste. If you were in such a rush, you should have brought us here as your counsellors yesterday. Don't think that anyone of us will go running through the streets today and have people pelt us with stones as if we were madmen.

AGORASTOCLES: But if I had told you to come to the temple for lunch, you'd have surpassed a stag in speed, or out-stepped a stilt-walker. But now that I said that I wanted you as counsellors and witnesses, you're full of gout and you've outdone the snail in slowness.

COUNSELLORS: Well, isn't it a good reason to race rapidly to a place where you can drink and eat at another's expense as much as you wish until you're full, which you need never return to your host, whose food you've been eating? But, nevertheless, in one way or another, we have food at home to eat, even though we are poor; so you needn't contemplate us with such contempt. It may be a very little, but it's all ours at home; we don't dun anyone and no one duns us. Not a one of us is going to burst a blood-vessel for your sake.

AGORASTOCLES: You're too hotheaded; I merely said that in fun.

COUNSELLORS: Then consider our response to you likewise said in fun.

AGORASTOCLES: I beg of you, supply me with a fast cutter, not a freighter; hobble along, at least, for I hardly expect you to hurry.

COUNSELLORS: If you want to do anything calmly and leisurely, we'll assist you; if you're in a hurry, you'd better get runners to be your counsellors.

AGORASTOCLES: You know the plan; I told you what need I had of your assistance, about this pimp who has been making a fool of me and my love affair for so long, and how a trick has been planned against him with my gold and my slave.

COUNSELLORS: We know all this already, if the spectators know it; it's for the benefit of these spectators that this play is now being acted here; you'd better instruct them, so that they will know what you're doing when you do it. Don't bother about us; we know the whole plan, since we all learned it along with you, so as to be able to make our responses.

AGORASTOCLES: That's quite true. But quickly now, tell me what I just told you, so that I'll be sure that you know it.

COUNSELLORS: So? Trying to find out if we know? Do you think we don't remember how you gave your overseer Collybiscus three hundred gold pieces, which he was to take to your enemy the pimp and pretend that he was a stranger from some other town somewhere? When he has taken him in, you'll come there to seek the slave and the money.

AGORASTOCLES: A remarkable memory! You've saved me.

COUNSELLORS: He'll deny it; he'll think you're looking for your slave Milphio; this will double the entire theft. The pimp will be assigned to you. You wish us to witness the affair.

AGORASTOCLES: You've got it.

COUNSELLORS: Well, barely by the finger-tips; it's such a trifling matter.

AGORASTOCLES: We must act with hurry and haste. Speed it up as much as possible.

COUNSELLORS (*again showing annoyance*): Good-bye then. You had better get some speedy counsellors; we're slow-moving.

AGORASTOCLES: You show enough hurry, but your words cause some worry. I wish your thighs would fall down to your heels.

COUNSELLORS: And we'd be damned glad to have your tongue fall down to your loins and your eyes to the sole of your foot.

AGORASTOCLES: Hey! Don't be angry at what I said in jest.

COUNSELLORS: And don't you speak unkindly to your friends in jest.

AGORASTOCLES: Drop this now. You know what I wish.

COUNSELLORS: We're very clever; you want to ruin that perjured pimp.

AGORASTOCLES: You've got it. Excellent! Here comes Milphio and the overseer along with him, at just the right moment. He's decked out royally and skilfully for our scheme.

Act Three.   Scene II

(*Enter* MILPHIO *and* COLLYBISCUS *from the house of* AGORASTOCLES.)

MILPHIO: You've got your instructions by heart?

COLLYBISCUS: Perfect.

MILPHIO: See that you make it tough for him.

COLLYBISCUS (*grinning*): Why speak? I'll be tougher than a wild boar's hide.

MILPHIO: Be sure that you're trained in your speeches for this trick.

COLLYBISCUS: Jove! I'm better trained than actors in tragedy or comedy.

MILPHIO: He's an excellent fellow.

AGORASTOCLES (*to* COUNSELLORS): Let's go nearer. (*To* MILPHIO *and* COLLYBISCUS) Here are the witnesses.

MILPHIO: You couldn't have brought so many men better suited for this plan. Not one of them is a holiday-man; they're genuine assembly-men; that's where they live, you can see them there more frequently than the praetor. The men who stir up litigation can't cook up a lawsuit today any quicker than these fellows; if there isn't any lawsuit to litigate about, they buy one.

COUNSELLORS: You be damned!

MILPHIO: You, however—are acting both kindly and generously in one way and another, when you assist my lovelorn master. (*To* AGORASTOCLES) But do these fellows know what the situation is?

AGORASTOCLES: In complete detail.

MILPHIO (*to* COUNSELLORS): Then give me your attention. Do you know this pimp Lycus?

COUNSELLORS: Readily.

COLLYBISCUS: Damn it! I don't know what he looks like. I wish you'd point out the fellow to me.

COUNSELLORS: We'll tend to that. There's been enough instruction.

AGORASTOCLES: The three hundred pieces have been paid to him.

COUNSELLORS: Then we ought to examine that gold, Agorastocles, so that we'll know what to say later on by way of testimony.

COLLYBISCUS: Come on, examine it.

COUNSELLORS (*to the audience*): This is surely comic stage money,[10] spectators; in foreign lands cattle get fat on this money when it's soaked; but for carrying out this trick it's good gold coin; so we'll make believe.

COLLYBISCUS: And make believe that I'm a foreigner.

COUNSELLORS: Of course, as if you arrived today and asked us to point out to you a delightful private place, where you could make love, drink, and dissipate.

COLLYBISCUS: Gad! What crafty fellows!

AGORASTOCLES: Naturally, since I instructed them.

MILPHIO: And who instructed you?

COLLYBISCUS: Come, you two go inside, Agorastocles, so that the pimp won't see you here with me. We don't want anything to spoil our deception.

COUNSELLORS: This chap is painfully prudent. Do what he suggests.

AGORASTOCLES (*to* MILPHIO): Let's be off. (*To* COUNSELLORS) But you—

COUNSELLORS: Enough said. Off with you.

AGORASTOCLES: I'm off.

COUNSELLORS: Immortal gods! Why don't you go, then?

AGORASTOCLES: I'm going.

COUNSELLORS: That's wise. (AGORASTOCLES *and* MILPHIO *go into the house.*)

COLLYBISCUS: Hush! Be quiet!

COUNSELLORS: What's the matter?

COLLYBISCUS: This door (*pointing to the house of* LYCUS) just did a terrible thing.

COUNSELLORS: What terrible thing?

COLLYBISCUS: It let out a loud crack.

COUNSELLORS: The gods damn you! Get behind us.

COLLYBISCUS: All right.

COUNSELLORS: We'll stay in front.

COLLYBISCUS (*aside*): That's what city-boys usually do; they put the men in the rear.

COUNSELLORS: That fellow that's coming out is the pimp.

COLLYBISCUS: Then he's a good one, for he looks bad enough. Even now, as he comes out, I'll suck his blood at a distance.

Act Three.   Scene III

(Enter LYCUS *from his house.)*

LYCUS *(speaking to* ANTAMOENIDES *within)*: I'll return there in a moment, soldier. I want to find some agreeable guests to join us. Meanwhile the servants will bring the sacrificial meat; at the same time, I suppose, the women will arrive home from the sacrifice. *(To himself, as he looks down the street)* But why is such a crowd of men coming this way? I wonder what they're bringing. And who in the world is that becloaked fellow who's following them at a distance?

COUNSELLORS: We citizens of Aetolia greet you, Lycus, although we give you this greeting against our will and although we're sparing in our good wishes to pimps.

LYCUS: The best of luck to all of you, which I certainly know you won't have, and which Fortune won't permit you to have.

COUNSELLORS: Fools have a treasure hoarded in their tongues, since they consider it profitable to abuse their betters.

LYCUS: The man who doesn't know the way to the sea ought to seek a river as his companion. I didn't know the proper way to abuse you; therefore you are my rivers; I'm determined to follow you. If you're polite, I'll follow along your bank; if you're abusive, along your track I'll go.

COUNSELLORS: There's just as much danger in doing good to a bad man as there is in doing bad to a good man.

LYCUS: How so?

COUNSELLORS: You'll find out. If you do good to a bad man, the favour is wasted; if you do bad to a good man, it lasts all your life.

LYCUS: Cleverly spoken! But how does that concern me?

COUNSELLORS: Because we have come to do you a good turn, although we're sparing in our good wishes to pimps.

LYCUS: If you bring something good, I'm grateful to you.

COUNSELLORS: We don't bring you anything good of our own, nor give it, nor promise it, nor, in fact, want you to get it.

LYCUS *(dryly)*: By heaven, I believe you; you have such a generous disposition. But what do you want now?

COUNSELLORS: This fellow that you see here in a cloak, well, Mars is angry at him.

COLLYBISCUS (*aside*): At your own heads, I hope!

COUNSELLORS: Now we bring this fellow for you, Lycus, to be plundered.

COLLYBISCUS (*aside*): This hunter will go home today with game; the dogs are driving the wolf neatly into the nets.

LYCUS: Who is this fellow?

COUNSELLORS: We really don't know who he is. When we went down to the harbour this morning, we saw him landing from a freighter. As soon as he landed, he made a beeline for us; he greeted us and we replied.

COLLYBISCUS (*aside*): Clever chaps! How trained they are for trickery!

LYCUS: What then?

COUNSELLORS: He joined us in conversation. He said he was a stranger, didn't know the town, and wanted a private place furnished him where he could have some fun. We've brought the fellow to you. If the gods love you, you have a chance to ply your trade.

LYCUS: Is he so anxious?

COUNSELLORS: He's got money.

LYCUS (*aside*): This plunder is mine.

COUNSELLORS: He wants to drink and do some loving.

LYCUS: I'll find him a pleasant place for it.

COUNSELLORS: But he wants it to be private and secret, so that no one will know about it or eavesdrop. He has been a mercenary in Sparta, as he told us, with King Attalus; he fled from there when the city was captured.

COLLYBISCUS (*aside*): That's neat, about the mercenary; and about Sparta, fine stuff!

LYCUS: The gods and goddesses give you many blessings, since you have instructed me so kindly and have reserved for me this excellent plunder.

COUNSELLORS: Why, as he himself told us, he's bringing a reserve of three hundred gold pieces, so that you'll welcome him all the more.

LYCUS: I'm a king, if I can entice this fellow to my house today.

COUNSELLORS: Well, he's certainly all yours.

LYCUS (*eagerly*): I beg you, by heaven, do persuade him to put up at my house, where he will have excellent entertainment.

COUNSELLORS: It's not our business either to persuade or dissuade a stranger; you'll transact your own business, if you're wise. We've brought the dove for you all the way to the fowling-door. Now it's up to you to catch him, if you want him caught. (*They move away.*)

COLLYBISCUS: Are you going now? What about that business of mine, friends?

COUNSELLORS: You'd better talk over your business with this fellow, young man; he's an excellent person for the matters that you're interested in.

COLLYBISCUS (*aside to* COUNSELLORS): I want you to watch when I give him the money.

COUNSELLORS (*aside to* COLLYBISCUS): We'll view that from a distance.

COLLYBISCUS (*aloud to* COUNSELLORS): It's been kind of you to help me.

LYCUS (*aside*): Profit is coming my way!

COLLYBISCUS (*aside*): Yes, coming the way an ass kicks with his heels.

LYCUS (*aside*): I'll give the fellow a persuasive greeting. (*To* COLLYBISCUS) The host greets the guest. I'm delighted that you have arrived safely.

COLLYBISCUS: The blessings of the gods upon you, since you desire my safety.

LYCUS: They say that you're looking for a lodging.

COLLYBISCUS: That's right.

LYCUS: And a lodging free from flies, as those persons said who left just now.

COLLYBISCUS: Not for the world.

LYCUS: What do you mean?

COLLYBISCUS: Because if I were looking for a lodging free from flies, I'd go straight to prison on my arrival. I'm looking for the kind of lodging where I'll be treated more delicately than the eyes of King Antiochus.

LYCUS: By Jove, I can certainly furnish you with a delightful one, that is, if you can endure being in a charming corner on a cozy couch, where you can cuddle and caress a lovely lady.

COLLYBISCUS: Pimp, you're on the right track.

LYCUS: And where you can soak yourself with toothless and timeless wine, Leucadian, Lesbian, Thasian, Chian. And I'll drench you there with a profusion of perfumes; in a word, when you bathe, I'll have the bathkeeper set up a regular perfumery for you. But all these things that I've mentioned are mercenary.

COLLYBISCUS: How so?

LYCUS: Because they want cash down for their services.

COLLYBISCUS: Gad, you're no more eager to receive than I am to give.

COUNSELLORS (*aside*): What if we call Agorastocles to come out here, so that he can see this for himself? (*They call at the door of* AGORAS-TOCLES) Hey, you thief-catcher, come out quickly, so that you can watch him give the money to the pimp.

Act Three.   Scene IV

(*Enter* AGORASTOCLES *in haste from his house.*)

AGORASTOCLES: What's the matter? What do you want, witnesses?

COUNSELLORS: Look to the right.

COLLYBISCUS (*to* LYCUS): Come, take this, please; here in cash are three hundred gold coins, called Philippi. (*He gives him the purse*) You provide for me with these; I wish them spent with all speed.

LYCUS: Jove, you've found yourself a lavish provider. Come, let's go in now.

COLLYBISCUS: Right after you.

LYCUS: Come now, step along; we'll talk about the rest of the matters inside.

COLLYBISCUS: I'll tell you at the same time how things are in Sparta.

LYCUS: Well then, follow me.

COLLYBISCUS: Lead the way. I'm in your hands. (*They go into the house of* LYCUS.)

AGORASTOCLES: What do you advise me to do now?

COUNSELLORS: Be discreet.

AGORASTOCLES: What if my feelings won't permit?

COUNSELLORS: Then act as they do permit.

AGORASTOCLES: Did you see the pimp receive the money?

COUNSELLORS: We saw it.

AGORASTOCLES: You know that he's my slave?

COUNSELLORS: We know it.

AGORASTOCLES: And that it's against the law of the land?

COUNSELLORS: We know it.

AGORASTOCLES: Well, I want you to remember all this later before the praetor when the occasion arises.

COUNSELLORS: We remember it.

AGORASTOCLES: What if I pound on his door while the matter is fresh?

COUNSELLORS: I advise it.

AGORASTOCLES: What if I pound and he doesn't open?

COUNSELLORS (*annoyed at his questions*): Then cut the pound-cake.

AGORASTOCLES: If the pimp comes out, do you think I should ask him if my slave has come to his house?

COUNSELLORS: Why not?

AGORASTOCLES: With two hundred gold pieces?

COUNSELLORS: Why not?

AGORASTOCLES: Then the pimp will at once be mistaken.

COUNSELLORS: In what way?

AGORASTOCLES: You ask? Because the sum mentioned will be a hundred pieces less.

COUNSELLORS: A good suggestion.

AGORASTOCLES: He'll think I'm looking for another person.

COUNSELLORS: Of course.

AGORASTOCLES: He'll deny it at once.

COUNSELLORS: And on oath, to be sure.

AGORASTOCLES: He'll involve himself in theft.

COUNSELLORS: No doubt about that.

AGORASTOCLES: For the whole sum that was brought to him.

COUNSELLORS: Why not?

AGORASTOCLES (*annoyed at their attitude*): Jupiter damn you!

COUNSELLORS: Why not—you?

AGORASTOCLES: I'll go and pound his door.

COUNSELLORS: Of course, why not?

AGORASTOCLES: It's time to hush, for his door's creaked. I see pimp Lycus coming outside. Assist me, please.

COUNSELLORS: Why not? Cover our heads, if you wish, so that the pimp won't know that we're the men who lured him to his destruction.

Act Three.   Scene V

(*Enter* LYCUS *with the purse.*)

LYCUS (*to himself*): Now all the soothsayers can go hang themselves before I'll believe anything they say after this; just now at the sacrifice they said that great misfortune and loss were in store for me; and right after that I make a nice profit.

AGORASTOCLES: How are you, pimp?

LYCUS: God bless you, Agorastocles.

AGORASTOCLES: Now you give me a much kinder greeting than a little while ago.

LYCUS: Like a ship, I've reached calm waters; where the wind is, there the sail is shifted.

AGORASTOCLES: The best of health—I wish for those in your house; I don't wish it for you.

LYCUS: They're in the best of health, as requested—but not for you.

AGORASTOCLES: Please send your Adelphasium to my house today, on this joyful, festive, splendid Aphrodisia.

LYCUS: Did you have a hot lunch today? Tell me.

AGORASTOCLES: What do you mean?

LYCUS: Because you're merely cooling your mouth, when you ask that.

AGORASTOCLES: Now look here, pimp. I've heard that my slave is at your house.

LYCUS: At my house? You'll never find that to be the case.

AGORASTOCLES: You lie. He came to you and brought you money. I have it on the authority of men whom I fully believe. (*He points to the* COUNSELLORS.)

LYCUS: Scoundrel, you're trying to trip me up with witnesses. There's neither any man nor any thing of yours at my house.

AGORASTOCLES: Remember that, counsellors.

COUNSELLORS: We remember.

LYCUS (*aside, recognising* COUNSELLORS): Ha, ha, ha! Now I know what's up; I've just now seen through it. These are the men who just now introduced the Spartan stranger to me; now they're hot and bothered at the fact that I'm going to make a profit of three hundred gold pieces. Since they know that this young fellow is an enemy of mine, they've persuaded him to say that his slave is at my house with gold; they've devised a trick to deprive me of it and divide it among themselves. They expect to snatch a lamb from a wolf. They're wasting their time.

AGORASTOCLES: Do you deny that my gold and my slave are at your house?

LYCUS: I deny it; and I'll shout myself hoarse with denial, if it makes any difference.

COUNSELLORS: Pimp, you're done for. That fellow we told you was a Spartan, who just now brought you the three hundred gold pieces, happens to be this man's overseer. And you've got the gold right there in your purse.

LYCUS (*in anger, as he realises the truth*): You all be damned!

COUNSELLORS: The very thing in store for you.

AGORASTOCLES: Come, you rascal, give up that purse at once; you're a thief caught in the act. (*He takes the purse and addresses* COUNSELLORS) Now, please give me your attention and watch me take my slave away from him. (*He goes into the house of* LYCUS.)

LYCUS (*aside*): God! I'm completely ruined! No doubt about it! This was done purposely to lay a trap for me. But why don't I flee from here to utter perdition, before I'm dragged off to the praetor by the neck? Damnation! When I had diviners and soothsayers! Anything good that they prophesy comes like a snail; but if they prophesy anything bad, it's right on your heels. Now I'll go and consult my friends as to how they think I ought to—hang myself. (LYCUS *departs to the forum.*)

Act Three.   Scene VI

(*Enter* AGORASTOCLES *from the house of* LYCUS, *driving out* COLLYBISCUS.)

AGORASTOCLES: Come along, get out, that they may see you coming out of there. (*To* COUNSELLORS) Isn't this my slave?

COLLYBISCUS: I certainly am, Agorastocles.

AGORASTOCLES: What do you say now, you rascally pimp?

COUNSELLORS: The man you're quarreling with has departed.

AGORASTOCLES: I hope he's gone to hang himself.

COUNSELLORS: We share your wish.

AGORASTOCLES: I'll bring my action against the fellow tomorrow.

COLLYBISCUS: Want anything else of me?

AGORASTOCLES: You can go; put on your own clothes.

COLLYBISCUS: It wasn't for nothing that I turned soldier; I got a little booty indoors; while the pimp's household was sleeping, I had my fill of sacrificial meat. I'll go inside.

AGORASTOCLES (*to* COUNSELLORS): You've done kindly, Counsellors, and rendered me excellent assistance. Please meet me at the Courthouse early tomorrow morning. (*To* COLLYBISCUS) Follow me inside, you. (*To* COUNSELLORS) Farewell. (AGORASTOCLES *goes into his house, followed by* COLLYBISCUS.)

COUNSELLORS (*annoyed at receiving no money*): Farewell to you. (*To themselves*) The fellow is damned unfair; he thinks we're serving him at our own expense. But that's the way with these rich people of ours. If you do them a favour, their thanks are lighter than a feather; but if you make a mistake, their wrath is as heavy as lead. Come now, let's go home, since we have achieved our purpose of ruining this corruptor of citizens. (*The* COUNSELLORS *depart.*)

Act Four.   Scene I

(*Enter* MILPHIO *from the house of* LYCUS.)

MILPHIO (*to himself*): I wonder how my tricks are turning out. I'm eager to ruin this pimp that's wrecking my wretched master; and he in turn beats me and strikes me with fist and heel. It's tough to be the slave of a man in love, especially when he's deprived of the object of his love. Aha! I see the pimp's slave, Syncerastus, coming back from the temple. I'll listen to what he has to say.

Act Four.   Scene II

(*Enter* SYNCERASTUS *with sacrificial utensils.*)

SYNCERASTUS (*to himself*): It's pretty clear that both gods and men have no consideration for a person who has a master like this one of mine. There isn't a greater perjurer or worse rascal anywhere on earth than my master, nor one so filthy or so defiled with dirt. The gods so love me, I'd rather live my life in a stone quarry or a mill, chained to a great iron brick, than to stay in servitude at the house of this pimp. What a race this is! What seduction of men goes on there! The gods protect us! You can see any kind of man there you wish, just as if you went to Acheron: rich man, poor man, freedman, thief, runaway slave, whipped, fettered, or bonded. All kinds are welcomed; it makes no difference who he is, provided he has the money to pay. All over the house there are dark hiding places, and there's constant drinking and eating, just as in a cookshop, not a bit different. And you can see there epistles written in clay, sealed with pitch, and the names have letters a cubit long; we have a whole levy of wine-merchants at our house.

MILPHIO (*aside*): By heaven, it's a wonder if his master doesn't make him his heir; judging from his words, he's making a funeral oration for the pimp. I'd like to speak to the fellow, and yet I'm listening to him with great pleasure.

SYNCERASTUS (*to himself*): I'm in anguish when I see these things go on here; slaves that cost a high price stripped of their savings at our house! And at the end, not a cent left; easy come, easy go.

MILPHIO (*aside*): This fellow keeps on with his speech as though he were a decent citizen, when he's more shifty than Shiftlessness herself.

SYNCERASTUS (*to himself*): Now I'm bringing home these utensils from the temple of Venus, where my master couldn't win over Venus on her own holiday with his sacrifices.

MILPHIO (*aside*): Charming Venus!

SYNCERASTUS (*to himself*): But our courtesans with their very first sacrifice straightway won Venus' favour.

MILPHIO (*aside*): O doubly charming Venus!

SYNCERASTUS (*moving towards the house*): Now I'll go home.

MILPHIO (*approaching*): Hey, Syncerastus!

SYNCERASTUS: Who calls Syncerastus?

MILPHIO: Your friend.

SYNCERASTUS: You don't act like a friend, to delay me with this load.

MILPHIO: But in return for this delay, I'll give you my services when you wish, when you order. Consider the matter settled.

SYNCERASTUS: If that's the case, I'll do you this service.

MILPHIO: In what way?

SYNCERASTUS: That you can offer your hide, when I have to have a beating. Get away; I don't know what sort of man you are.

MILPHIO: Mischievous.

SYNCERASTUS: Do yourself some mischief, then.

MILPHIO: I want you.

SYNCERASTUS: But this load is heavy.

MILPHIO: But set it down and look back at me.

SYNCERASTUS: I'll do it, although I hardly have time.

MILPHIO: How are you, Syncerastus?

SYNCERASTUS (*finally turning and recognising* MILPHIO): Oh, Milphio, the blessings of all the gods and goddesses—

MILPHIO: On whom?

SYNCERASTUS: Neither you nor me, Milphio; nor, to be sure, my master.

MILPHIO: Whom then are they to bless?

SYNCERASTUS: Some person that deserves it. For no one of us does.

MILPHIO: Witty words!

SYNCERASTUS: That's my way.

MILPHIO: What are you doing?

SYNCERASTUS: What adulterers hardly ever do, when they're caught in the act.

MILPHIO: What's that?

SYNCERASTUS: I'm bringing home my tools in safety.

MILPHIO: The gods ruin you and your master!

SYNCERASTUS: They won't ruin me; but I can make them ruin him, if I wish; I could make them ruin my master, if I weren't afraid for myself, Milphio.

MILPHIO: What's this? Tell me.

SYNCERASTUS: Are you a bad one?

MILPHIO: I'm a bad one.

SYNCERASTUS: Well, things are bad with me

MILPHIO: Tell me, isn't that the way it ought to be? But why are things bad with you, when you have plenty in the house for eating and loving, and you don't give a single nickel to a courtesan, but take her for nothing?

SYNCERASTUS: Jupiter so love me—

MILPHIO: As you deserve, by Jove.

SYNCERASTUS: How I desire the destruction of this household!

MILPHIO: If you desire it, apply some effort.

SYNCERASTUS: It isn't easy to fly without feathers; my wings have no feathers.

MILPHIO: Heavens, don't pluck out any hairs. (*Pointing to his armpits*) In two months' time you'll fly on wings as strong as a goat.

SYNCERASTUS: You go to the devil!

MILPHIO: No, you and your master.

SYNCERASTUS: True. For the man who knows him knows. The fellow can be ruined with ease.

MILPHIO (*still more interested*): How so?

SYNCERASTUS: Just as if you could keep anything quiet.

MILPHIO: I'll keep the story in stricter secrecy than what's told to a dumb woman.

SYNCERASTUS: I could easily persuade myself to believe you, if I didn't know you.

MILPHIO: Trust me boldly, at my risk.

SYNCERASTUS: I'll be a fool to trust you, but I'll do it just the same.

MILPHIO: Don't you know that your master is the mortal enemy of my master?

SYNCERASTUS: I know.

MILPHIO: On account of his love—

SYNCERASTUS: You're wasting all your time.

MILPHIO: How so?

SYNCERASTUS: Because you're teaching one already taught.

MILPHIO: Why then do you doubt that my master would do all possible harm to your master, just as he deserves? Then, if you render some assistance, he'll be able to do it all the more easily.

SYNCERASTUS: But I'm afraid of this, Milphio.

MILPHIO: What are you afraid of?

SYNCERASTUS: Having this trick against my master backfire and destroy me. If my master finds out that I have spoken to a single person, he'll change me at once from Syncerastus to Hipawreck.

MILPHIO: Not a person will ever find it out from me, with the one exception that I'll inform my master, and him on the condition that he doesn't tell that the information came from you.

SYNCERASTUS: I'll be a fool to trust you, but I'll do it just the same. But keep it buried in your breast.

MILPHIO: Faith herself won't keep it safer. Speak freely; it's the time and place; we're alone.

SYNCERASTUS: If your master wants to do a grand deed, he'll ruin my master.

MILPHIO: How can it be done?

SYNCERASTUS: Easily.

MILPHIO: Help me to understand this "easily" so that he'll understand it.

SYNCERASTUS: Because that Adelphasium your master dotes on is free by birth.

MILPHIO (*excited*): How's that?

SYNCERASTUS: In the same way that the other one is, her sister Anterastilis.

MILPHIO: Tell me how I can believe it.

SYNCERASTUS: He bought them as tiny girls in Anactorium from a Sicilian pirate.

MILPHIO: For how much?

SYNCERASTUS: For eighteen minae, the two of them, and their nurse Giddenis as a third. And the man who sold them admitted that he was selling stolen goods; he said that they were freeborn from Carthage.

MILPHIO: The gods help us! What a delightful bit of news! For my own master Agorastocles was born there, and was stolen from there when he was about six years old; afterwards the man who kidnapped him brought him here and sold him to my old master; he adopted him as his heir when he died.

SYNCERASTUS: Everything you say makes it easier to do; he can bring suit to claim them as freeborn, since they're his own fellow-citizens. Are you silent?

MILPHIO (*planning the deception*): Quiet a minute!

SYNCERASTUS (*helpful*): He'll certainly put a stop to the pimp's game, if he gets the girls away from him.

MILPHIO: Why, I'll guarantee that he'll be finished before he moves a single piece. I'm all ready for him.

SYNCERASTUS: I hope to heaven that I don't have to keep on slaving for this pimp.

MILPHIO: The gods willing, I'll make you my fellow freedman.

SYNCERASTUS: I hope to Heaven you will! No need of any more delay, is there, Milphio?

MILPHIO: Farewell and blessings on you.

SYNCERASTUS (*still troubled*): This matter is now in your hands and your master's. Good-bye, and see that you keep the secret safe.

MILPHIO: It wasn't even said. Good-bye!

SYNCERASTUS: And the matter's no good, unless you strike while it's hot.

MILPHIO: Nice of you to advise me. That's the way it will be done.

SYNCERASTUS: You've received excellent material, if you provide an excellent workman.

MILPHIO (*annoyed*): Can't you keep still?

SYNCERASTUS: I'm still, and off.

MILPHIO (*as* SYNCERASTUS *enters the house of* LYCUS): You've been a great benefit to me. (*To himself*) The immortal gods want my master saved and the pimp completely plundered; such destruction awaits him. Is another gun really aimed at him before the first one's been fired? Now I'll go in and inform my master of this. (*To the audience*) For it would be sheer stupidity for me to call him out in front of the house and repeat here again the same things that you've just heard. I'd rather be a nuisance to one man inside than to all of you out here. [Immortal gods, what disaster, what destruction is coming today upon this pimp. But now I'm delaying myself. With such a business under way, no pause is permitted. For the news that's just been handed out must be handled with discretion, and this homemade plan must be properly hatched. Now I'll go in and wait in the house until my master returns from the forum.]⁴

Act Five. Scene I

(Enter HANNO *from the harbour, followed by slaves with luggage.)*

HANNO *(to himself)*:¹¹ Gods and goddesses who cherish this city, I pray that I may succeed in the undertaking wherefore I have come hither, and that you grant me to find here my own daughters and the son of my brother, [my brother's son, and the girls that were stolen from me,]⁶ O gods, I beg of you! Formerly my friend Antidamas lived here; they say that he has gone where everyone has to go. They tell me that his son Agorastocles lives here. I'm bringing with me to take to him this token of hospitality. He's been pointed out as living in this neighbourhood; I'll ask these people who are coming out of the house.

Act Five. Scene II

(Enter AGORASTOCLES *from his house, followed by* MILPHIO.)*

AGORASTOCLES *(to* MILPHIO): Do you say, Milphio, that Syncerastus told you that those two girls were freeborn Carthaginians and were kidnapped?

MILPHIO: I say so, and, if you want to do what's right, you should bring suit to claim them as free. For it's a disgraceful thing to permit your fellow-citizens, who were free at home, to be in slavery before your very eyes.

HANNO *(aside)*: Immortal gods, help me! This speech is sweet music to my ears. The words of these men are certainly composed of chalk. How they've cleansed away all the blackness of my misery!

AGORASTOCLES: If I had witnesses for this matter, I'd do as you say.

MILPHIO: Why speak to me of witnesses? Why don't you go after him boldly? Fortune will favour you in some way.

AGORASTOCLES: It's much easier to begin a job than to finish it.

MILPHIO (*spying* HANNO): But who's this bird that comes here with flying tunic? I wonder if he was robbed of his cloak at the baths.

AGORASTOCLES: Jove! His appearance is certainly Carthaginian. The man's a gug.[9]

MILPHIO: He's certainly got old and antiquated fellows for slaves.

AGORASTOCLES: How do you know?

MILPHIO: Don't you see those be-luggaged fellows following him? In my opinion, they haven't any fingers on their hands.

AGORASTOCLES: Why so?

MILPHIO: Because they're coming with rings in their ears.

HANNO (*aside*): I'll approach and speak to them in Punic. If they reply, I'll continue to speak in Punic; if not, then I'll change my language to suit them.

MILPHIO (*to* AGORASTOCLES): But look here! Do you remember any Punic?

AGORASTOCLES: Not a damned word of it! How could I know it, tell me, when I was stolen from Carthage at the age of six?

HANNO (*aside*): Immortal gods! Many freeborn children have been stolen from Carthage in this fashion.

MILPHIO: I say!

AGORASTOCLES: What do you wish?

MILPHIO: Do you want me to speak to him in Punic?

AGORASTOCLES: Why, do you know it?

MILPHIO: There isn't a more Punic Punic alive today.

AGORASTOCLES: Go up to him then, and ask him what he wants, why he's come, who he is, what's his country and his city; don't spare your questions.

MILPHIO (*addressing* HANNO): *Avo!* (*His Punic fails him*) What country are you fellows from, or what city?

HANNO: *Annobynmytthymballebechaedreanech.*

AGORASTOCLES: What does he say?

MILPHIO: He says that he is Hanno from Carthage, the son of a Carthaginian named Mytthumbal.

HANNO: *Avo!*

MILPHIO: He says, "How are you?"

HANNO: *Donni.*

MILPHIO (*to* AGORASTOCLES): He wants to give you some sort of donation. Don't you hear him promise it?

AGORASTOCLES: Say "How are you?" to him in Punic for me.

MILPHIO (*to* HANNO): *Avo donni,* he says to you for himself.

HANNO: *Meharbocca.*

MILPHIO: I hope that happens to you rather than to me.

AGORASTOCLES: What does he say?

MILPHIO: He says he has a pain in his back jaw. Maybe he thinks we're doctors.

AGORASTOCLES: If that's the case, tell him we aren't; I don't want the stranger to get a wrong idea.

MILPHIO (*to* HANNO): Are you listening?

HANNO: *Rufeenycchoissam.*

AGORASTOCLES: I certainly want everything explained to him clearly. Ask him if he's in need of anything.

MILPHIO (*to* HANNO): Hey, you fellow there without a belt, why have you all come to this city, and what are you looking for?

HANNO: *Muphursa.*

AGORASTOCLES: What does he say?

HANNO: *Miuulechianna.*

AGORASTOCLES: What's he here for?

MILPHIO: Don't you understand? He says that he wants to give African mice to the aediles to display at the games.

HANNO: *Lechlachananilimniichot.*

AGORASTOCLES: What does he say now?

MILPHIO: He says he has brought latchets, channels, and nuts; he wants you to help him have them sold.

AGORASTOCLES: He's a merchant, I presume.

HANNO: *Assam.*

MILPHIO: And certainly fat.

HANNO: *Palumergadetha.*

AGORASTOCLES: Milphio, what does he say now?

MILPHIO: He says that he's got pails and garden tools for sale, for harvest time, I suppose, unless you've a better idea; probably for digging a garden and reaping grain.

AGORASTOCLES: What's that to me?

MILPHIO: He wants you to know it, so you won't think he has stolen anything on the sly.

HANNO: *Muphonnimsycorathim.*

MILPHIO (*to* AGORASTOCLES): Oh! Oh! Don't you do what he's asking of you.

AGORASTOCLES: What's he saying? What's he asking? Tell me.

MILPHIO: He wants you to have him put under a crate, and have a lot of stones put on it, so as to kill him.

HANNO: *Gunebelbalsameniyrasa.*

AGORASTOCLES: Tell me, what's that? What's he saying?

MILPHIO: Damn it! Now I don't understand anything at all.

HANNO: Well, so that you can understand it, I'll speak in Latin from now on. (*To* MILPHIO) Jove! You must be a rascally, good-for-nothing slave, to make fun of a foreigner and a stranger.

MILPHIO: Jove! And you must be a swindler and a sharper, to have come here to take us in with a double tongue like a snake, you migdilix.[9]

AGORASTOCLES (*to* MILPHIO): Stop your abuse and keep a civil tongue. You'll keep from abusing him, if you're wise. I don't want you to speak harshly to my fellow-countrymen. (*To* HANNO) I'd like to inform you that I was born in Carthage.

HANNO: Greetings, man of my people.

AGORASTOCLES: And the same to you, whoever you are. And if you have need of anything, please mention it and command me for the sake of our common country.

HANNO: I thank you. [But I have a lodging-place here; I'm looking for the son of Antidamas, Agorastocles; point him out to me if you know him.]⁴ Do you know any young man here named Agorastocles?

AGORASTOCLES: If you're looking for the adopted son of Antidamas, I'm the very man you're looking for.

HANNO: Ah! What's this I hear?

AGORASTOCLES: That I'm the son of Antidamas.

HANNO: If that's so, if you want to compare the tokens of hospitality, here is the one I brought.

AGORASTOCLES: Come, show it to me. (*He examines the token*) It's an exact match; for I have one at home.

HANNO: The best of greetings, my host! For your father Antidamas was a family friend of ours; this was my token of hospitality with him.

AGORASTOCLES: Then you will be entertained here at my house. I reject neither the entertainment nor Carthage; I was born there.

HANNO: The gods give you every blessing you desire! But what's this you say? How could you have been born in Carthage? You had an Aetolian father here.

AGORASTOCLES: I was stolen from there. Your friend Antidamas bought me and adopted me as his son.

HANNO: And he himself was the adopted son of Demarchus. But no matter about him; to return to you: tell me, do you remember the names of your parents, your father's and mother's names?

AGORASTOCLES: I remember them.

HANNO: Tell me then; perhaps I know them, or maybe they're relatives of mine.

AGORASTOCLES: My mother was Ampsigura, my father Iahon.

HANNO (*sadly*): I wish your father and mother were still alive.

AGORASTOCLES: Are they dead?

HANNO: Yes, and I grieved bitterly. For your mother Ampsigura was my cousin; your father was my uncle's son, and he made me his heir when he died. I suffer deeply at his loss. But if it's true that you are the son of Iahon, you ought to have a mark on your left hand, where a monkey that you were playing with as a child bit you. Show me your hand, let me look. Open it up. (*Excitedly*) Listen! There it is!

AGORASTOCLES: My uncle, welcome!

HANNO: And welcome to you, Agorastocles! (*They embrace*) I seem to be born again, since I have found you.

MILPHIO: I'm certainly delighted that this matter has turned out well for the two of you. But you wouldn't mind a bit of advice, would you?

HANNO: I'd welcome it.

MILPHIO: The father's property ought to be restored to the son. It's right that he should have the property his father owned.

HANNO: I do not wish differently; everything will be restored. I'll put him in safe possession of his property, when he comes there.

MILPHIO: And please see that you return it just the same, even if he continues to live here.

HANNO: Why, he'll have mine too, if anything should happen to me.

MILPHIO: A pleasant project has just now occurred to me.

HANNO: What is it?

MILPHIO: It needs your assistance.

HANNO: Tell me what you wish. You can certainly have as much help as you want. What's the plan?

MILPHIO: Can you play the part of a trickster?

HANNO: Yes, towards an enemy; towards a friend it's foolish.

MILPHIO: It's an enemy of master's.

HANNO: I'd be glad to do him dirt.

MILPHIO: Master's in love with a girl at the pimp's house.

HANNO: I'm sure that he's acting wisely.

MILPHIO: The pimp lives here next door.

HANNO: I'd be glad to do him dirt.

MILPHIO: The pimp has two slave girls, courtesans, sisters; master is madly in love with one of them, but has never taken any liberties with her.

HANNO: That's a painful kind of passion!

MILPHIO: The pimp keeps playing with him.

HANNO: That builds up his own profits.

MILPHIO: My master want to get the better of him.

HANNO: He's a fine fellow, if he does it.

MILPHIO: Now this is the plan I'm preparing, the trick I have in mind—
to get you to say that these girls are your daughters, kidnapped from
Carthage when very young, and you're to bring suit to claim them as
freeborn, just as if they were both your own daughters. Understand?

HANNO: I assuredly do understand. For my two daughters *were* kidnapped from Carthage when very young in just this way, along with
their nurse.

MILPHIO (*thinking* HANNO *is pretending*): By Jove, that's a clever
pretence! I like the way you're starting out.

HANNO (*sadly*): Yes, much more than I could wish.

MILPHIO (*to* AGORASTOCLES): Gad, what a clever mortal! He's a tough
rascal, and crafty and tricky! How he weeps, in order to act his part
more perfectly! He even outdoes me, the architect, with his deception.

HANNO: But describe the appearance of the girls' nurse.

MILPHIO: Rather short, and she has a dark complexion.

HANNO: She's the very one.

MILPHIO: Nice-looking, and very dark eyes.

HANNO: Your words have pictured her perfectly.

MILPHIO: Do you wish to see her?

HANNO: I'd rather see my daughters. But go and call her out; if they
are my daughters, if she is their nurse, she'll know me at once.

MILPHIO (*knocking at* LYCUS' *door*): Hey, is there anyone here? Tell
Giddenis to come outside. There's someone here who wants to meet her.

Act Five.   Scene III

(*Enter* GIDDENIS *from the house.*)

GIDDENIS: Who knocks?

MILPHIO: One who's close to you.

GIDDENIS: What do you wish?

MILPHIO: Well, do you know that fellow in the tunic? (*Points to* HANNO.)

GIDDENIS (*in amazement*): Who's this I see? Mighty Jupiter! It is my master, the father of my darlings, Hanno of Carthage.

MILPHIO: Look now, she's a cunning one! That Punic person is a perfect prestidigitator; he's persuaded everyone to agree with him.

GIDDENIS: Welcome, master! Welcome, Hanno, whom neither your daughters nor I hoped to—oh, don't marvel at me and gaze so at me! Don't you recognise Giddenis, your own servant?

HANNO (*dazed*): Of course. But where are my daughters? I'm eager to know that.

GIDDENIS: At the temple of Venus.

HANNO: What are they doing there? Tell me.

GIDDENIS: Today is the Aphrodisia, the festive day of Venus. They've gone to entreat the goddess to be propitious to them.

MILPHIO (*now convinced*): Well, they've gained their desire, I'm sure of that, since this man's here.

AGORASTOCLES (*to* GIDDENIS): What, are they his daughters?

GIDDENIS: It's true, sir. (*To* HANNO) Your devotion has certainly saved us, and you've arrived today in the nick of time. For today they were to change their names and make a shameful living by prostitution. (*One of* HANNO's *slaves approaches.*)

SLAVE BOY (*to* GIDDENIS): *Avonesilli.*

GIDDENIS: *Havonbanesilliimustine. Mepsietenestedumetalannacestimim.*

AGORASTOCLES: What are they saying to each other? Tell me.

HANNO: He's greeting his mother, and she her son. (*To* GIDDENIS) Hush now, and do away with all that female stuff.

AGORASTOCLES: What stuff is that?

HANNO: This endless loud talking.

AGORASTOCLES: Oh, let them be.

HANNO (*to* MILPHIO): Take these servants of mine inside, and order the nurse to go along to your house.

AGORASTOCLES: Do as he orders.

MILPHIO (*to* HANNO): But who will point out the girls to you?

AGORASTOCLES (*dryly*): I have sufficient skill for that.

MILPHIO: I'm going, then.

AGORASTOCLES: *I* wish you'd do it instead of talking about it. I want a dinner prepared for my uncle to celebrate his arrival.

MILPHIO (*to* GIDDENIS *and the servants*): *Lachanna,* you! (*To the servants*) I'll pack you off to the mill, and then off to the dungeon and a stout block of wood. You'll prefer not to praise your reception here, I'll see to that.[12]

AGORASTOCLES (*to* HANNO): Listen, please, uncle; and don't say I haven't said this: promise me your older daughter.

HANNO: Consider the matter arranged.

AGORASTOCLES: You promise her, then?

HANNO: I promise.

AGORASTOCLES (*delighted*): Thank you, my dear uncle! Now you are really mine. Now at last I'll be able to talk with her freely. Now, uncle, if you wish to see your daughters, follow me.

HANNO: Naturally! I've long been anxious to see them.

AGORASTOCLES: What if we go to meet them?

HANNO: But I'm afraid that we'll pass them on the street. Mighty Jupiter, turn this uncertainty into certainty for me.

AGORASTOCLES: And I hope that my sweetheart will soon be with me. But there! I see them coming.

HANNO: Are these my daughters? How they've grown from such tiny children!

AGORASTOCLES: Don't you know how it is? They're tragic actors; it's a usual thing for them to be up on buskins.[13]

MILPHIO: Gad, I guess that what I said in jest will turn out today to be serious and sober fact, and they'll be found to be his daughters.

AGORASTOCLES: There's certainly no doubt about it. You lead these others inside, Milphio. We'll wait for the girls here. (MILPHIO *and the servants go into the house of* AGORASTOCLES.)

Act Five. Scene IV

(*Enter* ADELPHASIUM *and* ANTERASTILIS.)

ADELPHASIUM: It was well worth while today for anyone who had leisure for loveliness to give his eyes a feast by going to see how the temple was decked out. I was truly delighted today by the lovely gifts of the courtesans; the gifts were worthy of the charming goddess, and I didn't scorn her power today either. Such an abundance of charming gifts was there, each nicely arranged in its proper place. Arabian myrrh and every sort of scent filled the temple. Venus, there seemed nothing cheap about your holy day or your shrine. And such a crowd of girls had come to worship Venus of Calydon!

ANTERASTILIS: Certainly, as far as the two of us were concerned, we were pretty powerful in our prayers, sister, and we weren't ridiculed by the young men there, as were all the other women.

ADELPHASIUM: I'd rather have others think that, sister, than have you praise yourself.

ANTERASTILIS: I hope they do.

ADELPHASIUM: I too, when I think of the difference between our nature and that of the others. Our birth is such that we ought to be free from reproach.

HANNO (*aside*): Jupiter, who dost nourish and cherish the human race, through whom we live our mortal life, in whose hands are the hopes and lives of all mankind, I pray that thou dost grant this day to be prosperous for my fortunes. Restore to liberty those of whom I have been deprived these many years, those whom I lost from their native land when little, that I may know that enduring devotion gets its due reward.

AGORASTOCLES (*to* HANNO): Jupiter will do it all, I'll see to that. (*Joking*) He's under my power and quite afraid of me.

HANNO (*weeping*): Hush, please!

AGORASTOCLES: Don't weep, uncle.

ANTERASTILIS (*to* ADELPHASIUM): Sister, just as a man is delighted to be victorious in anything he undertakes, so we today outstripped all the others in beauty.

ADELPHASIUM: Sister, you're much too silly. Do you think you're a beauty just because no one's smeared your face with soot?

AGORASTOCLES (*to* HANNO): Oh, uncle, dear uncle!

HANNO: What is it, nephew, what do you wish? Tell me.

AGORASTOCLES: I want you to pay attention to this.

HANNO: I am.

AGORASTOCLES: Oh, uncliest uncle!

HANNO: What is it?

AGORASTOCLES (*indicating* ADELPHASIUM): How neat and nice she is! Such wisdom!

HANNO: She gets that from her father.

AGORASTOCLES: How's that? Heavens! She's used up that wisdom of yours long since. Now she gets her wisdom from me; whatever wisdom she wants comes from my love.

ADELPHASIUM (*to* ANTERASTILIS): Although we are slaves, sister, we are not born of such a stock that we ought to do anything that anyone can laugh at. Women have many faults, but this is the greatest of all: they're too pleased with themselves and don't try hard enough to please men.

ANTERASTILIS: It's very delightful what was foretold from our sacrifice, sister, and what the soothsayer said about the two of us—

AGORASTOCLES (*aside*): I wish he had said something about me.

ANTERASTILIS: That we should be free within a few days, in spite of our master. But I don't know how I can hope for it, unless the gods or our own parents do something about it.

AGORASTOCLES (*aside to* HANNO): It was through confidence in me, uncle, that the soothsayer promised them their liberty, I'm sure. He knows that I love her.

ADELPHASIUM: Sister, follow me this way. (*She moves towards the house of* LYCUS.)

ANTERASTILIS: I'm coming.

HANNO (*approaching them*): Before you depart, I'd like a word with the two of you. Stop a minute, if you don't mind.

ADELPHASIUM: Who's calling us back?

AGORASTOCLES: A man who wants to do you a favour.

ADELPHASIUM: We have need of it. But who is this person?

AGORASTOCLES: A friend of yours.

ADELPHASIUM: I certainly hope he is.

AGORASTOCLES: He's a good man, my dear.

ADELPHASIUM: I'd prefer him to a bad man.

AGORASTOCLES: If you're going to be friendly to anyone, you ought to be to this person.

ADELPHASIUM: I don't ask for that.

AGORASTOCLES: He wants to do you a lot of good.

ADELPHASIUM (*to* HANNO): It's good of you to do good to the good.

HANNO: I'll bring you joy—

ADELPHASIUM: Heavens! We'll provide you with pleasure.

HANNO: And freedom.

ADELPHASIUM: On those terms you'll easily make us your own.

AGORASTOCLES (*aside to* HANNO): May the gods love me, dear uncle, if I were Jupiter, damned if I wouldn't marry her at once and drive out Juno. How chaste and considerate and becoming were her words! How modestly she spoke!

HANNO (*to* AGORASTOCLES): She's undoubtedly my daughter. How cleverly I accosted them!

AGORASTOCLES: Very neat and fitting. Keep on teasing them; but make it brief; the audience is getting thirsty.

HANNO: Well, then, why don't we get down to business? (*To the girls*) I summon you to court.

AGORASTOCLES: That's the right way to act, uncle. Do you want me to grab this one? (*He seizes* ADELPHASIUM.)

ADELPHASIUM: Is this person really your uncle, Agorastocles?

AGORASTOCLES: You'll soon know, I'll see to that! Now I'm going to get a fine revenge on you, for I'll make—you my wife.

HANNO: Go to court! No delay! (*To* AGORASTOCLES) Take her along, and call me as your witness.

AGORASTOCLES: I'll make you my witness, and then I'll love and caress her. But I meant to say—why, damn it, I did say what I meant to.

HANNO (*to the girls*): You're lingering. I summon you to court, unless you prefer to be seized.

ADELPHASIUM: Why summon us to court? What do we owe you?

AGORASTOCLES: He'll tell it there.

ADELPHASIUM (*angrily*): So even my own dogs are barking at me.

AGORASTOCLES: Well, just pet them a bit; give me a kiss instead of meat, and I'd like your tongue instead of a bone. In that way this dog will be smoother than oil.

HANNO (*to the girls*): Go on, if you're going!

ADELPHASIUM: What have we done to you?

HANNO: You're a pair of thieves.

ADELPHASIUM: We're thieves?

HANNO: Yes, both of you!

AGORASTOCLES: And I know it, too.

ADELPHASIUM: What theft is it?

AGORASTOCLES: Ask him.

HANNO (*to the girls*): For many years you've concealed my daughters from me, girls who were freeborn and free and from a fine family.

ADELPHASIUM: Heavens, you'll never prove that we committed such a crime.

AGORASTOCLES: Bet me a kiss that you're not lying, the loser to pay the other.

ADELPHASIUM: I've no business with you; get away from me, please.

AGORASTOCLES: Gad! I've got plenty of business with you. This man is my uncle, and it's right for me to take his part. I'll tell him how you girls are guilty of theft, and how you keep his daughters enslaved at your house, although you know they are freeborn girls stolen from their native land.

ADELPHASIUM: Where are they? Who are they?

AGORASTOCLES (*aside to* HANNO): They've been teased enough, now.

HANNO (*to* AGORASTOCLES): What if we tell them the truth?

AGORASTOCLES (*to* HANNO): I think you should, uncle.

ADELPHASIUM (*to* ANTERASTILIS): Sister, I'm terribly worried about the meaning of all this; I just stand here stupefied and senseless.

HANNO: Give me your attention, young women! I would first of all wish, if it were at all possible, that the gods would give nothing undeserved to those who don't deserve it; for the good that the gods now bring to me, to you, and to your mother, we must give them our everlasting thanks, since the immortal gods approve and reward our devotion. You are both my daughters, and Agorastocles here is your relative, since he is the son of my cousin.

ADELPHASIUM (*to* ANTERASTILIS): My dear, they're not comforting us with imaginary joys, are they?

AGORASTOCLES: The gods save me, he really is your father! Give him your hands.

ADELPHASIUM (*embracing* HANNO): Welcome, unhoped-for father! Let us hug you. Welcome, father, for whom I've longed and waited!

HANNO: They are both my daughters.

ANTERASTILIS (*also embracing him*): Then we should both hug you.

AGORASTOCLES: Who's going to hug me next?

HANNO: Now I am a happy man! With this joy I bring to an end my sufferings of many years.

ADELPHASIUM: We can hardly believe it's true.

HANNO: I'll tell you how you can believe it; your nurse first recognised me.

ADELPHASIUM: Where is she now, please?

HANNO: At his house. (*Nodding towards* AGORASTOCLES.)

AGORASTOCLES (*to the girls*): Tell me, why do you want to hang on his neck so long? (*To* ADELPHASIUM) One of you at least let him go. I don't want him killed before he can promise you to me.

ADELPHASIUM: I'll let him go.

ANTERASTILIS: Welcome, my hoped-for parent!

HANNO: Let's throw each other into the prison of our arms; who now on earth can be happier?

AGORASTOCLES: The deserving get what they deserve.

HANNO: At last I've gained my desire.

AGORASTOCLES: Oh, Apelles! Oh, painter Zeuxis! Why did you die too soon to paint this picture? I don't want other painters to handle subjects of this sort.

HANNO (*reverently*): All ye gods and goddesses, I duly render to you great thanks for blessing me with such joy and such delight, that my daughters are safe again in my possession.

ADELPHASIUM: Father dear, your piety has saved us.

AGORASTOCLES: Uncle, don't forget that you have promised me your older daughter.

HANNO: I won't forget.

AGORASTOCLES: And the dowry that you promised.

Act Five.   Scene V

(*Enter* ANTAMOENIDES *from the house of* LYCUS.)

ANTAMOENIDES (*to himself*): If I don't get a proper revenge for that mina I gave the pimp, then all the wits in the city can make a butt of me. The worthless old loafer invited me to his house for lunch; then he went away and left me standing there in the house like a doorkeeper. Neither the pimp nor the girls came back, and not a single thing was given me to eat! But I seized some security for the greater part of the lunch, and left the house. That's the way I'll pay him back! I'll touch that rascally pimp for his military tax! He got hold of a proper person to cheat of a mina of silver! And I'd like to have that girl of mine meet me now while I'm angry! By gad, I'll blacken her with my fists until she looks like a blackbird; I'll make her darker than the Aethiopians who carry the water-buckets at the Circus games!

ADELPHASIUM (*embracing* AGORASTOCLES): Please hold me close, my darling! I'm terribly afraid of vultures; he's a wicked creature, and I fear he might carry off this little chick of yours.

ANTERASTILIS (*clasping* HANNO): Oh, I can't embrace you enough, dear father!

ANTAMOENIDES (*to himself*): I'm wasting time. With this plunder I can pretty well produce a lunch for myself. (*Seeing the others*) But what's this? What *is* it? What is *this?* What do I see? How now? What means this doubling? What means this coupling? Who's this fellow with the long tunics, just like a tavern boy? Do I really see this? Is it my sweetheart, Anterastilis? It certainly is. I've known for a long time that she had no regard for me. Isn't the girl ashamed to be hugging a porter in the middle of the street? Damned if I don't give him over to the hangman to be tortured all over! A tunic-dragging race of woman-chasers, that's what they are! Now I'm going up to that amorous African. (*To* HANNO) Hey, there! You, I mean, you she-male! Don't you have any shame? What business have you with that girl? Tell me that!

HANNO (*politely*): Good day, young sir.

ANTAMOENIDES: It isn't a good day, and this doesn't concern you. What right do you have to touch her with your finger?

HANNO: I so choose.

ANTAMOENIDES: You so choose?

HANNO: That's what I say.

ANTAMOENIDES (*thundering*): Go to the devil, you shoe-strap! Do you dare to make love here, you toe of a man? Or to touch what real he-men love? You skinned sardine! You Sarrapian[9] seedling! You piece of pelt, you pinch of salt, you olive-pulp, you stink worse of onions and garlic than a row of Roman oarsmen!

AGORASTOCLES: Young man, your jaws or teeth don't itch, do they, as you insult this gentleman? Or are you looking for trouble?

ANTAMOENIDES: Why didn't you accompany your words with a tambourine? You look to me more like a dancer than a man.

AGORASTOCLES (*in anger*): You know what kind of dancer I am? (*Calling inside*) Come out here, slaves, and bring some clubs.

ANTAMOENIDES (*frightened*): Look here, you, don't you take seriously anything that I said in jest.

ANTERASTILIS: Tell me, Antamoenides, why do you want to speak rudely to our relative and our father? For he is our father; he just now found us, and discovered that Agorastocles here is his nephew.

ANTAMOENIDES: Jupiter love me, that's wonderful! I'm happy and delighted if any misfortune has come to the pimp and good fortune to you, as you deserve.

ANTERASTILIS: We ought to believe what he says. Do believe him, father dear.

HANNO: I believe him.

AGORASTOCLES: And I, too. But look, there's the pimp just in time, I believe.

ANTAMOENIDES: And I, too.

AGORASTOCLES: Gad, a fine fellow is coming! Look, I see the worthy gentleman, betaking himself homeward.

[HANNO: Who is he?

AGORASTOCLES: A pimp or a Lycus, whichever you wish. He kept your daughters in slavery, and stole some gold from me.

HANNO: A nice person for you to know!][14]

AGORASTOCLES: Let's bring him to justice.

HANNO: Not at all!

AGORASTOCLES: Why not?

HANNO: Because it's much better to punish him for injustice.

Act Five.   Scene VI

(*Enter* LYCUS *from the forum, much depressed.*)

LYCUS (*to himself*): In my own opinion, no one is deceived when he sets forth his situation to his friends; for all my friends agreed upon one and the same thing—that I should hang myself to escape being awarded to Agorastocles.

AGORASTOCLES (*stepping forward*): Pimp, let's go to court!

LYCUS: Please, Agorastocles, do let me hang myself.

HANNO: And I summon you to court!

LYCUS (*in surprise*): What business do you have with me?

HANNO: I declare that these two girls are my daughters; they were born free and are now free. They were kidnapped with their nurse when they were young.

LYCUS: In fact, I've known that for a long time, and I wondered why no one came to claim them. They're certainly not mine.

ANTAMOENIDES: Pimp, go to court!

LYCUS: You're talking about the lunch. I owe it, I'll give it.

AGORASTOCLES: I want twofold compensation for the theft.

LYCUS (*pointing to his neck*): Take what you want from here.

HANNO: And I want plenty of punishment.

LYCUS (*as before*): Take what you want from here.

ANTAMOENIDES: And I want a mina of silver.

LYCUS (*as before*): Take what you want from here. I'll use my neck for all of you, like a porter.

AGORASTOCLES: You have no objections of any sort?

LYCUS: Not a single word.

AGORASTOCLES: Girls, you go inside. (*They enter the house of* AGORASTO-CLES.) Uncle, you give me your daughter, as you promised.

HANNO: I couldn't do otherwise.

ANTAMOENIDES: Farewell!

AGORASTOCLES: Farewell to you!

ANTAMOENIDES (*revealing his plunder as he departs*): Pimp, I'm taking this along as security for the mina.

LYCUS: By heaven, I'm ruined!

AGORASTOCLES: You mean you soon will be, when you go to court.

LYCUS: I award myself to you; why bother about the praetor? But let me settle for the original sum—three hundred gold pieces; I suspect that can be scraped together. Tomorrow I'll hold an auction.

AGORASTOCLES: On the condition that you stay in the stocks at my house.

LYCUS: Agreed.

AGORASTOCLES: Follow me inside, uncle, that we may have a happy festal day, celebrating his misfortune and our good fortune. (*To the spectators*) Fare you well! We've spoken at great length, but finally all possible woe has come upon the pimp. Now, for the final seasoning of the play—if it has given you pleasure, it asks your applause.

Act Five.   Scene VII[15]

(*On the stage are* AGORASTOCLES, ANTAMOENIDES, HANNO, ADELPHASIUM, *and* ANTERASTILIS; LYCUS *enters from the forum.*)

AGORASTOCLES: What are you up to, soldier? Why do you want to speak rudely to my uncle? Don't be surprised that the girls are following him about; he's just found out that the two of them are his own daughters.

LYCUS (*aside*): Ha, what's that I hear? Now I am done for!

ANTAMOENIDES: From what place were they lost?

AGORASTOCLES: They're Carthaginians.

LYCUS (*aside*): But I'm the one that's lost. I was always afraid that someone would recognise them; now it's happened!

ANTAMOENIDES: Poor me!

LYCUS: The eighteen minae that I paid for them are gone, I suppose.

AGORASTOCLES: You're the one that's a goner, Lycus.

HANNO: Who is this fellow?

AGORASTOCLES: A pimp or a Lycus, whichever you wish. He kept your daughters in slavery, and stole some gold from me.

HANNO: A nice person for you to know!

ANTAMOENIDES: Pimp, I've always considered you to be avaricious, but the people who know you better say that you're robber-icious also.

LYCUS (*aside*): I'll approach him. (*He kneels before* AGORASTOCLES) By your knees, sir, I beseech you, and by this man whom I understand to be your relative; since you are worthy gentlemen, act as worthy gentlemen should, and come to the aid of your suppliant. For a long time I've known that these girls were free, and I was waiting for someone to claim them. They're not my girls at all. And I'll restore that gold of yours that's in my house, and swear an oath, Agorastocles, that I didn't do any wrong intentionally.

AGORASTOCLES: I'll consider carefully what I ought to do. Let go of my knees.

LYCUS: All right, if that's your decision. (*He rises from the ground.*)

ANTAMOENIDES: Hey, there, you pimp!

LYCUS: What do you want of a pimp who's busy?

ANTAMOENIDES: I want that mina of silver back before you're led off to jail.

LYCUS: The gods save me from that!

ANTAMOENIDES: That's what will happen; you'll be dining away from home. Pimp, you owe three things now at once—gold, silver, and your neck.

HANNO: I wonder what I ought to do about this matter. If I want to punish this fellow, I'll be going to law in a strange city, from what I've heard about the nature and customs of this place.

ADELPHASIUM: Father dear, please don't have anything to do with this man.

ANTERASTILIS: Listen to my sister. Come, put an end to your quarrel with the rascal.

HANNO: Look here, pimp. Although I know that you have deserved utter ruin, I won't go to law with you.

AGORASTOCLES: Neither will I; if you return my gold, when you're let out of jail, you can be plunged into prison.

LYCUS: Up to your old tricks, eh?

ANTAMOENIDES (*to* HANNO): Carthaginian, I wish to clear myself. If I said anything in anger that you didn't like, please forgive me. And as the gods may love me, I'm delighted that you have found your daughters.

HANNO: I forgive you, and believe your words.

ANTAMOENIDES: Pimp, see that you either give me a sweetheart or return my mina.

LYCUS: Would you like to have my flute girl?

ANTAMOENIDES: I don't want a flute girl. You can't tell which are bigger, her cheeks or her breasts.

LYCUS: I'll find one to please you.

ANTAMOENIDES: Be sure you do.

LYCUS (*to* AGORASTOCLES): I'll return your gold to you tomorrow.

AGORASTOCLES: Be sure to remember it.

LYCUS: Soldier, follow me.

ANTAMOENIDES: Gladly. (LYCUS *goes into his house, followed by the soldier.*)

AGORASTOCLES: Well, uncle, when do you plan to go to Carthage? For I've decided to accompany you.

HANNO: As soon as I possibly can.

AGORASTOCLES: You'll have to wait a few days, while I hold an auction.

HANNO: I'll do as you wish.

AGORASTOCLES: Come, please, let's go and enjoy ourselves. (*To the spectators*) Give us your applause.

NOTES

1. The title is perhaps merely "The Uncle"; in this case, "porridge-eating" refers to Plautus. The term "uncle" in this comedy means not merely a father's brother, but also a father's cousin.
2. This was a suburb or a park in Carthage.
3. *Lycus* means "Wolf."
4. Lindsay brackets this passage as a later addition.
5. This was a festival in honour of Venus.
6. Lindsay brackets this verse as spurious.
7. A play upon the word *assum,* which means both "here I am" and "roasted." Agorastocles takes the second meaning and replies: "I'd prefer to have you boiled."
8. Mercury was the god of trading and profit.
9. A word of uncertain meaning.
10. Lupines were used to represent money on the stage.
11. The following speech is preceded by a Punic passage, the sense of which the Latin apparently reproduces.
12. Milphio and the others perhaps go into Agorastocles' house at this point; if so, the two speeches at the end of the scene must be considered a later addition. But it is not impossible that Milphio loiters on the stage until the end of the scene.
13. The text is corrupt here; Leo's reading has been adopted.
14. Lindsay brackets this passage as spurious; the lines are repeated in Scene VII.
15. This scene is apparently a substitute for the end of Scene V and all of Scene VI; the double ending of the play is doubtless the result of changes introduced into the text at some production after Plautus' death. Earlier editors considered one or the other of the two endings genuine; many now believe that both endings contain a mixture of the Plautine text and the spurious text of the later period.

XVI
PSEUDOLUS

CHARACTERS IN THE PLAY

PSEUDOLUS, *slave of* SIMO, *confidential attendant of* CALIDORUS
CALIDORUS, *son of* SIMO, *in love with* PHOENICIUM
BALLIO, *a pimp*
SIMO, *father of* CALIDORUS
CALLIPHO, *neighbour of* SIMO
HARPAX, *slave of an officer in the Macedonian army*
CHARINUS, *a friend of* CALIDORUS
SLAVE *of* BALLIO
COOK
SIMIA, *slave of* CHARINUS' *father*
House slaves and courtesans belonging to BALLIO

ARGUMENT I (ACROSTIC)

A soldier pays fifteen minae down in cash, and at the same time arranges for a token, with the understanding that the pimp is to give Phoenicium to the man who brings that token with the balance. The soldier's servant, when he comes with the token, is intercepted by Pseudolus, who says he's Syrus, the slave of Ballio; thus he aids his master. For the pimp hands over the girl to Simmia, whom Pseudolus sends as a substitute. Then the real Harpax comes; the trick comes to light and the old man pays the money which he'd wagered.

ARGUMENT II

Calidorus, a young man, is madly in love with a courtesan, Phoenicium, but he has no cash; a soldier, who bought the same girl for twenty minae, paid fifteen down and went away. He left the harlot with the pimp and gave him a token; anyone who should bring a seal like that token and the balance of the price was to take the girl away with him. Then the servant of the soldier comes to take the harlot away. He is deceived by Pseudolus, the slave of the young man, who pretends to be the steward of the pimp; he takes away the token, borrows five minae, and gives them both to a false servant. This sharper deceives the pimp; Calidorus gets the girl and Pseudolus gets drunk.

INTRODUCTION

CICERO in his essay *On Old Age* refers to the delight which Plautus as an old man found in his *Pseudolus* and in his *Truculentus*. It is not surprising that Plautus enjoyed the *Pseudolus,* for, in spite of certain structural difficulties, it is one of Plautus' best comedies of intrigue. It is remarkable for its dramatic vigour, its originality of treatment and thoroughly Roman tone. The *Pseudolus* is a long play with much jesting and coarse invective, and the pimp Ballio is the most elaborately portrayed and the most distasteful and villainous specimen of this class to be found in Plautus. It is probable that the part of Ballio was in antiquity considered the main role, since Cicero's friend Roscius, the famous comic actor, played the part of Ballio in the first century B.C.

It is the shrewd and resourceful Pseudolus rather than Ballio, however, who is the centre of attention from beginning to end. He is on the stage during three-quarters of the action and is amusing from his first cynical comments on Calidorus' love affair in Act One, Scene I, until his final appearance in an intoxicated condition in Act Five. During the course of the action he engineers the trickery of Ballio with the aid of the false Harpax. The deception is all the more amusing since Ballio has been warned against Pseudolus; although he falls into the trap and gives the girl to the false Harpax, he is convinced that the real Harpax is an imposter sent by Pseudolus. The comic irony resulting from Ballio's confusion and self-deception here anticipates Terence's procedure, especially in *The Woman of Andros* where Simo is constantly on his guard against trickery and deceives himself by refusing to accept the truth.

The greatest difficulty in the structure of the play occurs in Act One, Scene V, where Pseudolus assures Simo, Calidorus' father, that he will get the twenty minae needed by Calidorus from Simo himself. "But," he adds, "first I'll swindle the pimp Ballio out of that flute girl your son loves." Then he asks, "If I do this, will you give me of your own free will the money for the pimp?" Simo agrees. The passage implies that Simo is to pay twenty minae to Pseudolus if the slave (1) tricks Ballio and (2) gets money from Simo himself. The difficulty is that the

787

play contains no tricking of Simo, but in Act Five Simo pays Pseudolus the promised sum just as if both terms of the agreement had been fulfilled. This and other difficulties, e.g. the disappearance from the action of Simo's friend Callipho, have led some scholars to believe that two Greek originals have been awkwardly combined by Plautus; one original would thus contain the deception of the father, the other that of the pimp. There is another possibility, even if we assume that the wager necessarily involves the tricking of Simo; both deceptions may have been in one Greek comedy and Plautus in order to make room for his own jests and Roman allusions may have used only one of the two intrigues. On the other hand, Simo's promise to pay may be the very means which Pseudolus has in mind when he makes the wager with Simo. Logically there are two conditions to be fulfilled, but Simo apparently does not so understand it, and Pseudolus says when he receives the money from Simo, "You said that you wouldn't give it to me, but you are paying it just the same." Pseudolus speaks here as if he has made good his earlier threat to get money from Simo. However great the logical inconsistency which the careful reader finds between Act One, Scene V, and the later action of the play, it is extremely doubtful if the Roman spectators would have noticed any flaw here, especially in a play so full of fun and so rapid in its treatment as the *Pseudolus*.

The Ambrosian Ms. preserves a fragment of the *didascalia*, or official notice, of the production of the *Pseudolus*. This dates the Roman play in the praetorship of Marcus Junius Brutus, or 191 B.C. The only other didascalic notice preserved for Plautus is that of the *Stichus*, produced in 200 B.C.

The influence of the *Pseudolus* on later comedy was not great. A few comedies are indebted to it, e.g. Della Porta's *La Trappolaria*, Regnard's *La Sérénade*, Holberg's *Diderich Menschen-Skräk*, and Lessing's *Justin*. Pseudolus himself, as one of the most knavish slaves in Roman comedy, was the inspiration of numerous rogues of a later date; Mascarille, Scapin, and other amusing servants of French comedy recall many of his traits.

PSEUDOLUS

(SCENE:—*a side street in Athens, before the houses of* CALLIPHO, SIMO, *and* BALLIO; *there are alleyways between the houses.*)

Prologue

You'd better stand up and stretch your legs: a long play by Plautus is going to be staged.

Act One. Scene I

(*Enter* CALIDORUS *and* PSEUDOLUS *from the house of* SIMO.)

PSEUDOLUS: If I could learn from your silence, master, what terrible troubles disturb you so, I'd gladly spare two men some trouble—myself the trouble of asking you, and you that of answering. Now since that isn't possible, I'm compelled to ask you. Tell me this: why have you been walking around in a daze these past few days, carrying those writing-tablets with you and bathing them with your tears, without letting anyone share in your plans? Speak up: let me enlighten my ignorance.

CALIDORUS (*gloomily*): Alas! How wretched I am, Pseudolus!

PSEUDOLUS: Jupiter forbid!

CALIDORUS: This has nothing to do with Jupiter's jurisdiction; it's under Venus' rule that I'm taking a beating, not under Jupiter's.

PSEUDOLUS: May I learn what the matter is, sir? For you used to consider me an excellent fellow-conspirator.

CALIDORUS: I'm still of the same opinion.

PSEUDOLUS: Please do inform me what's the matter with you; I'll assist you with my cash, my services, or—with good advice!

CALIDORUS (*handing over the writing-tablets which he is holding*): Take these tablets and see for yourself the cares and troubles that are gnawing at my heart.

PSEUDOLUS: Your orders will be obeyed, sir. (*Taking the tablets and looking them over curiously*) But I say, what's this?

CALIDORUS: What?

PSEUDOLUS: These letters must want to raise a family, I guess; they're mounting on each other!

CALIDORUS: Up to your usual jokes, are you?

PSEUDOLUS (*squinting closely at the tablet*): Unless you can find a Sibyl to read this, no one in the world will be able to understand it.

CALIDORUS: Why do you insult such *lovely* letters, such *lovely* tablets, written by such a *lovely* hand?

PSEUDOLUS: Oh, for heaven's sake, do chickens have hands? Surely a chicken made these hen-tracks.

CALIDORUS: You're a pest! Either read it or give it back to me.

PSEUDOLUS: No, I'll read through it. Mind what I say, now!

CALIDORUS: Mind? I haven't any.

PSEUDOLUS: Well then, send for one.

CALIDORUS: Oh no; I'll keep quiet and you send for one from that tablet there; for my mind is there, not in my head.

PSEUDOLUS (*looking at the letter*): I see your mistress, Calidorus.

CALIDORUS (*eagerly*): Where is she, for heaven's sake?

PSEUDOLUS: Here she is stretched out on the tablet: she's taking a nap on the wax here!

CALIDORUS: May all the gods and goddesses—

PSEUDOLUS (*interrupting*): —preserve me, you mean!

CALIDORUS (*relapsing into his sullen gloom*): I'm just like the grass in June: quickly I sprang up, and quickly faded away.

PSEUDOLUS: Quiet, while I read the letter.

CALIDORUS: Well, why don't you?

PSEUDOLUS (*reading*): "Phoenicium to her lover Calidorus: through this wax and seal, through these letters I send you salutations, and beg you for salvation,[1] in tears, with trembling heart and breast."

CALIDORUS: Alas! I can't find that salvation anywhere, Pseudolus.

PSEUDOLUS: What kind of salvation?

CALIDORUS: In cash.

PSEUDOLUS: What? (*Showing the tablet*) For wooden salutations you want to send her salvation in cash? Just think what you're doing!

CALIDORUS: Read on: you'll soon learn from the letter how urgently I need to find some money.

PSEUDOLUS (*reading*): "O darling, the pimp has sold me abroad, to a Macedonian soldier for twenty minae. Before leaving, the soldier paid fifteen minae; now only five minae are left to pay. The soldier left here a token, his picture stamped in wax by his seal-ring; when a messenger comes with a similar token, the pimp is to send me away with him. The day set for this transaction is the coming festival of Dionysus."

CALIDORUS: That's tomorrow. The end is near, unless you can help me.

PSEUDOLUS: Let me finish the letter.

CALIDORUS: All right; for when you read I seem to hear her talking. Read on: it's bittersweet you're mixing for me now.

PSEUDOLUS (*reading*): "Now farewell to all our love, our familiar intercourse, our jests and games and talk and kissings sweet, the close embrace of ardent bodies, the gentle nibblings of tender lips, the playful squeezing of pouting breasts; all these pleasures are snatched and torn away from me and you, unless I can find salvation in you or you in me. I've taken care to inform you of what I know; now I'll see how much you love me and how much you're just pretending. Farewell."

CALIDORUS (*with a deep sigh*): O Pseudolus, it's a pitiful letter.

PSEUDOLUS (*dryly, looking at the writing*): Oh! Pitiful's no word for it!

CALIDORUS: Why don't you weep?

PSEUDOLUS: I've got eyes of stone; I can't prevail upon them to shed a single tear.

CALIDORUS: Why?

PSEUDOLUS: I come from a long line of dry-eyes.

CALIDORUS: Don't you want to help me at all?

PSEUDOLUS: What can I do for you?

CALIDORUS (*sighing*): Dear me!

PSEUDOLUS: "Dear me"? Well, I certainly don't begrudge you that; I'll give you plenty.

CALIDORUS: I'm so wretched! I can't borrow any money anywhere—

PSEUDOLUS: Dear me!

CALIDORUS: —and I haven't a penny of my own.

PSEUDOLUS: Dear me!

CALIDORUS: He'll take away my girl tomorrow.

PSEUDOLUS: Dear me!

CALIDORUS: Is that the way you help me?

PSEUDOLUS: I'm giving you what I've got; I've got an unlimited store of them at home.

CALIDORUS: It's all up with me now. Can you lend me a drachma? I'll pay you back tomorrow.

PSEUDOLUS: I doubt it, even if I mortgaged myself. But what do you want to do with that drachma?

CALIDORUS: I want to buy myself a rope.

PSEUDOLUS: What for?

CALIDORUS: To hang myself. I'm resolved to join the shades before the shadows fall.

PSEUDOLUS: Who'll pay me back that drachma then, if I lend it to you? Or do you want to hang yourself on purpose, just to cheat me, if I lend you a drachma?

CALIDORUS: It's just completely impossible for me to keep on living if she is sold and taken away from me.

PSEUDOLUS: What are you crying for, my little chickadee? You'll live.

CALIDORUS: Why shouldn't I weep, when I haven't a dime in cash and no hope of getting a penny anywhere in the world?

PSEUDOLUS: If I understand the meaning of this letter, you'd better shed some silver-dollars; for showing off with those tears of yours does no more good than carrying water in a sieve. But don't worry: I won't desert you in your love affair. I hope that in some honest way—or in my usual way—I can find you some aid—in cash. I don't know where it's coming from; I only know it will come: my eyebrow twitches so.

CALIDORUS: If only your deeds live up to your promises!

PSEUDOLUS: Surely you know how things are and what nice commotions I can stir up once I start my act.

CALIDORUS: All the hope of my life now rests on you alone.

PSEUDOLUS: Will you be satisfied if I either make you the owner of the girl today or give you twenty minae?

CALIDORUS: I'll be satisfied—if it happens.

PSEUDOLUS: Ask me for twenty minae, so you'll know I'll accomplish what I promised. Go on; ask me, for heaven's sake! I'm itching to promise you.

CALIDORUS (*in a formal tone*): Will you give me twenty minae today?

PSEUDOLUS (*also formally*): I will.[2] Now don't bother me. And in case you'll say I didn't tell you, I'll tell you now: if I can't find anyone else, I'll touch your father for the money.

CALIDORUS: God bless you and keep you! But out of regard for family loyalty, if it's possible—try mother too.

PSEUDOLUS: As far as that goes, you can rest easy, on either—eye.

CALIDORUS: What? On either ear, you mean.

PSEUDOLUS: My version's less banal. (*Turning to the audience*) Now, lest anyone should say he wasn't warned, I make proclamation to all people, in the presence of all the adults and all the populace, in full assembly: I bid all my friends and acquaintances be on their guard today and not to trust me.

CALIDORUS: Sh-h! Keep quiet, please.

PSEUDOLUS: What's the matter?

CALIDORUS: The pimp's door cracked.

PSEUDOLUS: I wish it were his legs!

CALIDORUS: The pimp himself is coming out, the dirty double-crosser! (*They retire to one of the alleys.*)

Act One.   Scene II

(BALLIO *comes out of his house with a huge whip; he is followed by a group of slaves and courtesans.*)

BALLIO (*cracking his whip*): Out with you! Get a move on! Out with you, you bunch of bad bargains who don't earn your keep! Not one of you ever thinks of behaving; I can't get a bit of use out of you unless I treat you like this. (*Beats the nearest slave*) I've never seen men more like mules; their sides are calloused with blows. Why, when you beat them, it hurts you more than them. That's the way with these whip-breaking rascals: they have just one idea: whenever there's a chance, grab, steal, loot, swipe, drink, eat, and run! That's the way they function; you'd sooner leave wolves to guard the sheep than these fellows to watch your home. And yet they don't seem so bad when you look at them; but they'll fool you when you put 'em to work.

Now then, all of you! Unless you pay attention to this proclamation and shake the sleep and slothfulness out of your eyes and hearts, I'll beat your backs so bloody black and blue no Campanian carpet or Alexandrian tapestry can match them for embroidery. And yet, yesterday I gave you all your official duties; but you are all such natural lazy rascals,[3] you force me to remind you of your tasks with whippings. So that's the way you feel about it, eh? You're tough enough to wear out me and *this*! (*Shakes the whip; the slaves scatter*) Look at that, will you? Wool-gathering again! Watch *this*! (*Shakes the whip again*) Pay attention to *this*, and listen closely to what I say, you bunch of stumble-bums! By God! Your hides are no tougher than this rawhide of mine. (*Beating another slave*) Now what? Does it hurt? There, take that! That's what an impudent slave gets. Now all of you stand over there and pay attention to my words.

You there with the pail, fetch some water and fill the pots for the cook. (*The slave leaves*)

You with the axe! I put you in charge of the Department of Wood-splitting.

THE SLAVE (*showing his axe*): But it's dull.

BALLIO: All right! And you're all dull from beatings; but I use you all just the same. (*To another slave*) You're to make the house spick and span. You've got your orders; hurry up, go in! (*The slave goes into the house*) (*To another slave*) You're to be Bed-Maker-in-Chief. (*To another slave*) You there! Go polish up the silver and set the table.

See that when I return from the market I find everything ready, swept, polished, sprinkled, washed up, and cooked. For today is my birthday, and you all must help me celebrate. (*Calling in to the house*) Ham, bacon-rind, sweetbreads, tripe: put 'em in to soak. Do you hear? I want to give a real stylish dinner for some swells, so they'll think I'm in the money. Go on in the house and get busy right away; I don't want any delay when the cook comes. I'm going to the meat market to buy up all the fish in sight. (*To his attendant*) Go ahead, boy. Take care no one cuts a hole in that purse. (*As the boy starts*) No, wait a minute; there's something I almost forgot to say. (*Calling to the courtesans, who have started into the house*) Listen here, you women! I've got a proclamation for you, too.

You spend your tender years in primping, in ease and luxury; you consort with swells, like famous courtesans; today I'm putting you on trial and I'll find out which of you cares for her freedom, or only for her belly; who is concerned for her own interests, and who for sleep. I'll just find out who is likely to be set free and who's to be sold. You'd better make sure I get plenty of gifts from your lovers today. For if I don't get enough to live on for a whole year, tomorrow I'll send you out as common whores among the lower classes. You know this is my birthday: where are those lovers who call you "apple of my eye," and "my life, my darling, my soul-kiss, my little tit, my honey-lamb"? See that you bring a whole squadron of gift-convoyers here before the house. Why do I give you clothes and gold and everything you need? What do you bring in to the House by your efforts except trouble? You bitches, you're only interested in wine. You wash yourselves and your bellies down with wine, while I go dry. Now then, I'd best address you each by name, so none of you can say she wasn't warned. Pay attention, all of you!

Hedylium, I'll begin with you: you're the mistress of the grain-dealers, those fellows who all have mountainous heaps of grain at home. You take care that they bring me enough grain for a year—enough for me and all the household, so that I'm overflowing with grain and the townsfolk change my name and call me, instead of Ballio the Pimp, Jason the Tyrant.[4]

CALIDORUS (*aside to* PSEUDOLUS): Do you hear him, the gallows bird? Isn't he just too pompous?

PSEUDOLUS: Indeed he is, and criminous too! But keep quiet and pay attention.

BALLIO (*to another courtesan*): Aeschrodora, your lovers are the butchers who rival us pimps: they make their money by dealing in such adulterated meats. Now listen here! Unless I get three meat-racks today laden with fat sides of pork, I'll treat you like Dirca: you remember, the two sons of Jupiter tied her to a bull, they say; well, I'll hang you up on a meat-rack. That's the kind of bull you'll get!

CALIDORUS (*to* PSEUDOLUS): It just burns me up to listen to his talk!

PSEUDOLUS (*to* CALIDORUS): To think of our young men allowing such a fellow to live here! Where are these vigorous young chaps, where are they hiding, those fellows who buy their loving from this pimp? Why don't they rally around and all together free the city from this plague? Oh, bah! I'm just too silly and stupid: would they dare to do it, when their love makes them his slaves? Besides, they're prevented from action by their very unwillingness.

CALIDORUS (*to* PSEUDOLUS): Hush! Quiet!

PSEUDOLUS: What is it?

CALIDORUS: You're very unobliging and annoying to chime in on him with your prattle.

PSEUDOLUS: I'll keep quiet.

CALIDORUS: I'd rather have you *keep* quiet than have you *say* you're quiet.

BALLIO (*to another courtesan*): You there! Xytilis, pay attention: your lovers keep at home huge private stocks of olives. Unless they bring me olive-oil by the sackful, tomorrow I'll put you in a sack and carry you to the common brothel; and you'll be given a bed there, where you won't get any sleep, but you'll get all worn out with—do you get my drift? (*As Xytilis tries to speak*) What's that, you viper? When you have so many friends just overburdened with oil, has any one of your fellow-slaves got his hair slicked down today through your efforts? Is *my* food any the oilier? But you don't care much for oil, I know; wine is your weakness. All right, then: I'll take care of all your faults at once, unless you accomplish what I say. (*Turning to* PHOENICIUM)

Now for you, you who are always just about to pay me for your freedom; you know how to arrange things, but you don't know how to pay up. Phoenicium, I'm talking to you, you darling of the upper-classes: unless you bring me every sort of provision from your lovers' farms today, tomorrow you'll go to the common brothel with a hide that's dyed Phoenician purple, Phoenicium. (*The courtesans go into the house.*)

Act One. Scene III

CALIDORUS (*to* PSEUDOLUS): Pseudolus, do you hear what he says?

PSEUDOLUS: I hear, sir, and I'm paying strict attention.

CALIDORUS: What would you suggest I give him not to make my mistress a common prostitute?

PSEUDOLUS: Don't worry! Keep cool! I'll do all the worrying for you—and for myself. Ballio and I have been on good terms for a long time; we've been friendly for ages. So I'll send him a fine birthday present today: a mighty and speedy disaster.

CALIDORUS: What's the use of that?

PSEUDOLUS: Can't you find something else to worry about?

CALIDORUS: But—

PSEUDOLUS: Tut!

CALIDORUS: I'm in agony!

PSEUDOLUS: Be brave!

CALIDORUS: I'm not able.

PSEUDOLUS: Make yourself able.

CALIDORUS: How can I overcome my emotions?

PSEUDOLUS: Turn your attention to something useful, and don't give in to your emotions when things are bad.

CALIDORUS: You're talking nonsense; a lover can't have any fun unless he's playing the fool!

PSEUDOLUS: Are you still at it?

CALIDORUS: O my dear Pseudolus, let me be good for nothing; please leave me alone!

PSEUDOLUS (*starting to leave*): Oh, all right. I'll just be leaving, then.

CALIDORUS (*running after him*): Wait! Wait! I'll be just the way you want.

PSEUDOLUS (*stopping*): Now you're being sensible.

BALLIO (*to his slave*): The day's a-wasting; I'm delaying myself. Go on ahead, boy. (*He starts to leave for the forum.*)

CALIDORUS (*to* PSEUDOLUS): Hey! He's going! Call him back.

PSEUDOLUS: What's your hurry? Take it easy.

CALIDORUS: Please, before he gets away.

BALLIO (*to the slave*): What the hell is this? What are you loitering for, boy?

PSEUDOLUS (*calling after* BALLIO): Hey there, Birthday Boy! Birthday Boy! Hey, I'm talking to you, Birthday Boy! Turn around, look at us! Even if you're busy, we'll stop you. Look! Here are some people who want to talk with you.

BALLIO (*without looking around*): What's this? Who's causing me this damned delay when I'm busy?

PSEUDOLUS: A former saviour of yours.

BALLIO: A former one is a dead one; I need one who still is.

PSEUDOLUS: How haughty you are!

BALLIO: What a nuisance you are!

CALIDORUS: Seize the fellow; run after him.

BALLIO: Go on, boy. (*He again starts off the stage.* PSEUDOLUS *runs around and intercepts him.*)

PSEUDOLUS: Let's head him off on this side.

BALLIO: I'd like to see you in hell, whoever you are!

PSEUDOLUS: It's *you* (*sweetly*) I wish to see.

BALLIO: I mean both of you! (*To the slave*) Boy, go over in that direction.

PSEUDOLUS (*intercepting them as they try to leave by the alley*): Isn't it permitted to talk with you?

BALLIO (*haughtily*): It doesn't please me.

PSEUDOLUS: But if there's a little profit in it?

BALLIO: For God's sake, will you let me go or not?

PSEUDOLUS (*seizing him*): Bah! Wait a minute!

BALLIO: Let go!

CALIDORUS: Listen, Ballio!

BALLIO: I'm stone deaf for you empty-handed windbags.

CALIDORUS: But I gave when I had something.

BALLIO: I'm not looking for what you *gave*.

CALIDORUS: And I'll give again whenever I get anything.

BALLIO: Well, you can have *her* when you have something to give.

CALIDORUS: Oh, dear! I've completely wasted everything I ever brought and gave you.

BALLIO: Now your cash is dead, you babble on with speeches. You're a fool! What's done is done.

PSEUDOLUS: At least learn who this is.

BALLIO (*contemptuously, still without looking*): I've known for a long time who he *was*; let him learn for himself who he is now. (*To the slave*) Walk along, there!

PSEUDOLUS: Can't you take just one look, Ballio; there's money in it for you.

BALLIO (*stopping suddenly*): On those terms I will take a look. For even if I were making an offering to God Almighty and were holding the offerings in my hands, in order to lay them on the altar, and then something with money in it turned up—well, I'd just walk out on the ceremony. Money-making's a religion you can't withstand, no matter what other things may be.

PSEUDOLUS (*aside, disgusted*): He hasn't the slightest regard even for God, though all men ought to fear Him.

BALLIO: I'll address him. (*Approaching* PSEUDOLUS) Good day, you big rascal.

PSEUDOLUS: God bless you, Ballio, just the way master and I wish; or if you are worthy of blessings in any other way, God bless and keep you—not at all!

BALLIO: How are you, Calidorus?

CALIDORUS (*mournfully*): I'm terribly in love and terribly in need.

BALLIO: I'd pity you, if I could feed my household on pity.

PSEUDOLUS: Bah! *We* know what you're like; don't bother to tell us. But do you know what we'd like?

BALLIO: Yes, pretty nearly: you'd like to see me in trouble.

PSEUDOLUS: Yes, that and another matter for which we called you back. Please give this matter your attention.

BALLIO: I'm listening. And cut it short: I'm very busy.

PSEUDOLUS: Master's ashamed because he promised you twenty minae for his mistress by a certain date and he's not yet paid you.

BALLIO: Shame's a feeling that's much easier to bear than annoyance. He's ashamed at not paying; I'm annoyed at not getting paid.

PSEUDOLUS: But he will pay you; he'll find the means. Just wait a few days. He's afraid you may sell her to spite him.

BALLIO: He's had plenty of opportunity to pay me if he wished.

CALIDORUS: But what if I didn't have anything?

BALLIO: If you were in love, you could have borrowed it, gone to a moneylender, compounded a little interest, or stolen it from your father.

PSEUDOLUS (*outraged*): Stolen from his father, you villain? There's no danger of your giving any decent advice.

BALLIO: That's not a pimp's business.

CALIDORUS: Could I steal anything from my father, when he's so shrewd? (*Piously*) And besides, even if I could, my respect for my father would prevent it.

BALLIO: I understand. So just cuddle up to that respect at night instead of Phoenicium. But since I see you prefer your respect for your father to your ladylove, is everybody your father? Isn't there anyone you can borrow from?

CALIDORUS: Why, the very word "borrow" has perished from the earth.

PSEUDOLUS: See here! You know what these fellows are like, who get up from their counters when they've had their fill: they call in all their loans, but never pay a single one of their creditors. Now they're awfully careful not to trust a soul.[5]

CALIDORUS: I'm so upset! I can't find a penny in cash anywhere. Oh, dear! I'm dying of love and lack of money.

BALLIO: Well then, buy oil on ninety-day terms and sell for spot cash: you'll soon make two hundred minae, cash on hand.

CALIDORUS: Alas! That law about minors ruins me;[6] everyone's afraid to trust me.

BALLIO: Well, I have the same law: I'm afraid to trust you.

PSEUDOLUS: Trust indeed! See here, aren't you satisfied with all the profit you've had from him?

BALLIO: No one's a real lover unless he keeps up his gifts; he must give and keep on giving. When he runs out of funds, let him stop loving.

CALIDORUS: Have you no mercy?

BALLIO: You come empty-handed: money talks, not mere words. And yet I could wish to see you alive and in good health.

PSEUDOLUS: Oh! Do you think he's already dead?

BALLIO: Whatever he is, as far as I'm concerned he's dead and buried when he begins to talk like that. A lover's life is all over when he begins to plead with a pimp. You can always reach me if you bring a few complaints in solid silver. As for your present whinings over your lack of money, you're complaining to a stepmother.

PSEUDOLUS: Oho! When did you marry his father?

BALLIO: God forbid!

PSEUDOLUS: Do what we ask, Ballio; take my word, if you're afraid to trust him. In three days, in some way or other, from earth or sea, I'll raise this money for you.

BALLIO: What? Trust *you*?

PSEUDOLUS: Why not?

BALLIO: My God! Trusting you would be just as good as tying up a runaway dog with sheep-guts.

CALIDORUS (*sorrowfully*): Is this the return I get from you for all my services?

BALLIO: Well, what do you want?

CALIDORUS: Just wait a week or so without selling her and ruining her lover.

BALLIO: Cheer up! I'll even wait six months.

CALIDORUS: Hurrah! That's a good fellow!

BALLIO: That's nothing; would you like me to overwhelm you with joy?

CALIDORUS: How?

BALLIO: I have decided that Phoenicium is not for sale.

CALIDORUS: Not for sale?

BALLIO: No, on my word.

CALIDORUS (*overjoyed*): Pseudolus, run fetch some sacrificial victims and the sacrificial butchers; I want to sacrifice to Jupiter Almighty. Ballio is now my Jupiter—a hundred times more than Jupiter himself.

BALLIO (*ironically*): No large victims, please; I only want a few lambs' entrails to make me propitious.[7]

CALIDORUS (*to* PSEUDOLUS): Hurry up! What are you standing there for? Go fetch some lambs. Don't you hear what our Jupiter says?

PSEUDOLUS: I'll be back directly; but first I've got to run all the way beyond the city gate.

CALIDORUS: Why so?

PSEUDOLUS: That's where I'll get your two "sacrificial butchers" with their clanking chains, and I'll drive up two "herds" of birch-rods too; I'll "propitiate" this Jupiter today until he's had enough of "sacrifices."[8]

BALLIO: Go to Hell!

PSEUDOLUS: That's where you'll go, you pimpish Jupiter!

BALLIO: [It's to your advantage to have me dead.

PSEUDOLUS: Why?

BALLIO: Because while I'm alive you'll never be good for anything.][9] It's not to your advantage that I die.

PSEUDOLUS: Why?

BALLIO: Because if I am dead, there won't be any greater rascal than you in Athens.

CALIDORUS: For mercy's sake, tell me, please; in all seriousness, answer this question: you're not going to sell my mistress Phoenicium?

BALLIO: No, I'm certainly not going to, because—I've already sold her!

CALIDORUS (*shocked*): How's that?

BALLIO: Without her trinkets, but with all her in'ards in place.

CALIDORUS: *What?* You've sold my mistress?

BALLIO: Exactly. For twenty minae.

CALIDORUS: For twenty minae?

BALLIO: Twenty, or four times five—call it what you like; I sold her to a Macedonian soldier, and I've already received fifteen minae.

CALIDORUS: What's this I hear?

BALLIO: I've cashed in on your mistress.

CALIDORUS (*indignantly*): How could you dare to do it?

BALLIO: I just felt like it; she was my property.

CALIDORUS: Ho there, Pseudolus! Go get me my sword!

PSEUDOLUS: What do you want with a sword?

CALIDORUS: To kill him—and me.

PSEUDOLUS: Why, just kill yourself instead; then starvation will soon do for him.

CALIDORUS (*turning furiously on* BALLIO): See here, you most perjured villain that ever took an oath! Didn't you swear an oath that you'd never sell her except to me?

BALLIO (*calmly*): I admit it.

CALIDORUS: An oath in well-chosen terms?

BALLIO: Yes, and well-concocted, too.

CALIDORUS: You broke your oath, you scoundrel!

BALLIO: Yes, but I've pocketed the money. I'm a scoundrel but I can dig up plenty of the wherewithal; you, with all your scruples, with your noble birth, haven't a penny to your name.

CALIDORUS: Pseudolus, stand over there on the other side and dress him down for me.

PSEUDOLUS: Right, sir! I'll do it faster than I'd run to the magistrates to be set free.

CALIDORUS: Give him the works!

PSEUDOLUS (*to* BALLIO): I'll give you a tongue-lashing that will cut you into mincemeat. You shameless villain!

BALLIO (*with a calm smile*): That's right.

PSEUDOLUS: Scoundrel!

BALLIO: Quite true.

PSEUDOLUS: Whipping-boy!

BALLIO: Why not?

CALIDORUS: Grave-robber!

BALLIO: Sure.

PSEUDOLUS: Jailbird!

BALLIO: Excellent.

CALIDORUS: Double-crosser!

BALLIO: That's me all over.

PSEUDOLUS: Murderer!

BALLIO: Do go on.

CALIDORUS: Church-robber!

BALLIO: Granted.

PSEUDOLUS: Perjurer!

BALLIO: Old stuff; try a new tune.

CALIDORUS: Gangster!

BALLIO: Very good.

PSEUDOLUS: Seducer of the youth!

BALLIO: Pretty bitter!

CALIDORUS: Robber!

BALLIO: Bravo!

PSEUDOLUS: Runaway!

BALLIO: Bravissimo!

CALIDORUS: You confidence man!

BALLIO: Certainly.

PSEUDOLUS: Cheat!

CALIDORUS: Dirty dog!

PSEUDOLUS: Pimp!

CALIDORUS: Dung!

BALLIO: What charming voices!

CALIDORUS: You beat your own father and mother!

BALLIO: Yes, and murdered them rather than feed them. Nothing wrong with that, was there?

PSEUDOLUS (*to* CALIDORUS): It's like pouring water into a cracked pitcher; we're wasting our strength.

BALLIO (*starting to leave*): Anything else you wanted to say?

CALIDORUS: Have you no shame?

BALLIO: Yes; I'm ashamed to discover that as a lover you're as empty-handed as a hollow nut. But despite your many insulting remarks, unless the soldier pays me today the five minae which he owes—this is the last day for the payment, you see—well, if he doesn't bring it today, I imagine I can find out what I ought to do.

CALIDORUS: What's that?

BALLIO: If you bring me the money, I'll break my bargain with him. That's what I ought to do. If I were at leisure, I'd continue this conversation. But except for cash down, you're a fool to expect me to pity you. (*With a majestic air*) This is my considered opinion; continue your deliberations about your course from this point. (*He starts to leave.*)

CALIDORUS (*weakly*): Are you going?

BALLIO: I have much to attend to. (*He goes out with the slave.*)

PSEUDOLUS (*threateningly*): You'll have a lot more to attend to pretty soon. (*To* CALIDORUS, *exultantly*) He's my meat, unless all the gods and men abandon me. I'll skin him just like a cook with an eel. Now Calidorus, I want you to assist me.

CALIDORUS: What are your orders?

PSEUDOLUS: I want to storm this town today; I need a man for the job —a clever, shrewd, cunning fellow who can carry out my orders and doesn't go to sleep standing up.

CALIDORUS: Tell me, what are you going to do?

PSEUDOLUS: You'll learn in good time. I don't want to tell it twice; these comedies are long enough as it is.

CALIDORUS: A very fair and just remark.

PSEUDOLUS: Hurry, then; bring me the fellow right away.

CALIDORUS: I have hosts of friends, but very few are reliable.

PSEUDOLUS: I know. So there are two things to do: make a selection from that host, and then out of the few bring me the one reliable fellow.

CALIDORUS: I'll see that he's here directly.

PSEUDOLUS: Can't you get a move on? All this talk just holds you up. (CALIDORUS *goes out to the forum.*)

Act One.   Scene IV

PSEUDOLUS (*to himself*): Now that he's gone, you stand alone, Pseudolus. What are you going to do now, since you've been so generous with your promises? Where are your plans? You haven't the ghost of an idea ready, and certainly no money, and not a notion what to do. You don't know even where to begin to start, or what's to be the end of weaving your web. Oh, well! It's just like a poet: when he takes up his writing-tablets, and hunts for something that doesn't exist anywhere in the world, he discovers it all the same. So I've got to be a poet: those twenty minae don't exist anywhere, but I'll find them just the same. I promised long ago to give him the money, and I wanted to set a snare for old master. But somehow or other he always got an inkling of it beforehand. (*Sees* SIMO *and* CALLIPHO *approaching from the forum*) But I'd better lower my voice and stop this talk; here comes old master Simo with his neighbour, Callipho. I'll dig twenty minae out of this old tomb today, to give to young master. I'll step over here and listen to what they say. (*He retires to the alley.*)

Act One.   Scene V

(*Enter* SIMO *and* CALLIPHO *from the forum.*)

SIMO (*in a disgusted tone*): If the Athenians were going to elect a dictator from the ranks of the prodigals and debauchees, no one would beat my son, I'm sure. He's the only topic of conversation through all the town—that he wants to free his mistress and is looking for the wherewithal. Others tell me this, and I myself have long suspected it; I got wind of it, but said nothing.

PSEUDOLUS (*aside*): His son's in bad odour already! It's all up with my plans; this scheme has broken down. I wanted to set out on the highroad to cash, but this road's completely blocked now. He's divined the matter; there's no loot here for looters.

CALLIPHO: If I were allowed to deal with them, these fellows who carry malicious gossip and those who listen to it would all be hung—the bearers by the tongues and the listeners by the ears. For this tale you've been hearing, that your son is in love and wants to swindle you of your money, may very well be false. But even if it's completely true, considering our modern standards what's so strange about it? Is it any novelty for a young man to be in love and set free his mistress?

PSEUDOLUS (*aside*): What a nice old fellow!

SIMO (*angrily*): Well, I'm an old man, and I don't want him to do it!

CALLIPHO: It's no use your not wanting it. Or else, you shouldn't have done the same when you were young. A father has to be awfully good, if he expects his son to be better than he himself was. As for you, you sowed enough wild oats to distribute to the population without omitting anyone! Do you wonder if your son's a chip off the old block?

PSEUDOLUS (*aside*): *Lieber Gott!* How scarce such decent fellows are! Now there's a father who is just what a father ought to be.

SIMO (*looking around*): Who's that talking? Oh! It's my slave, Pseudolus. (*Furiously*) Here's the fellow who ruins my son, the source of all evil! He's the ringleader, he's his teacher, he's the man I'd like to hang!

CALLIPHO: Now, that's very foolish, to flaunt your rage so. It's much better to go up to him with agreeable words and try to find out whether this story you've been hearing is true or not. (*Sententiously*) A good spirit is half the battle, you know.

SIMO: I'll follow your suggestion.

PSEUDOLUS (*aside, as they approach*): Here it comes, Pseudolus! Get your speeches ready for the old man. (*Aloud*) First of all, my greetings to my master, as is right; then, if I have any left over, I'll bestow some on our neighbour.

SIMO (*making an effort to be agreeable*): Greetings. What's up?

PSEUDOLUS (*flippantly, striking an attitude*): I'm standing up here, as you see.

SIMO: Just look at the fellow, Callipho. What a royal pose!

CALLIPHO: He has the air of a good and self-confident fellow, I'm sure.

PSEUDOLUS: It's quite proper for a guiltless and harmless slave to keep his head up, especially before his master.

CALLIPHO: There are a few things we want to ask you—some things we've learned and heard of in a foggy sort of way.

SIMO: He'll soon wear you out with his talk; why, you won't believe this is Pseudolus; it will be just like a Socratic Dialogue.

PSEUDOLUS (*reproachfully*): Yes, you've always had it in for me, I know. I realise how little confidence you have in me. You will have it that I'm worthless; but still I'm good for something.

SIMO (*dryly*): Kindly vacate those apartments in your ears, Pseudolus, so these remarks of mine can move in.

PSEUDOLUS: Come, say what you will, even though I'm angry at you.

SIMO: What? You, my slave, are angry at me, your master!

PSEUDOLUS: Do you think that's so surprising?

SIMO (*sarcastically*): By God, to hear you talk, I'd better look out for your anger! I suppose you've got a beating in mind for me—a different kind of beating than I usually give you. (*To* CALLIPHO) What do you think?

CALLIPHO: Why, I think he's got a right to be angry, since you have so little confidence in him.

SIMO: I don't care; let him be angry. I'll take good care he doesn't hurt me. (*To* PSEUDOLUS) I say, there: what about this question of mine?

PSEUDOLUS: Ask what you like. If I know the answer, you can call me the Delphic Oracle.

SIMO: Pay attention and see that you remember your promise. Tell me: do you know that my son is in love with a flute girl?

PSEUDOLUS: *Mais oui.*

SIMO: And he wants to set her free?

PSEUDOLUS: *Mais oui, aussi.*

SIMO: And you are getting ready to pilfer a matter of twenty minae from me by some swindling sharper's trick?

PSEUDOLUS (*with an air of injured innocence*): I pilfer from you, sir?

SIMO: Yes, twenty minae to give my son, so he can free his mistress? Confess, say, "*Mais oui, aussi*" again.

PSEUDOLUS: *Mais oui, aussi.*

CALLIPHO (*surprised*): He admits it!

SIMO: Didn't I tell you, Callipho?

CALLIPHO: I remember.

SIMO (*to* PSEUDOLUS): Why was this kept from me, when you found it out? Why wasn't I told?

PSEUDOLUS: I'll tell you: I didn't want to set any bad precedents for a slave to accuse one master before another.

SIMO (*to* CALLIPHO): Wouldn't you have him dragged headlong to the treadmill?

CALLIPHO: Why, he hasn't done anything wrong, has he?

SIMO: Yes, indeed he has!

PSEUDOLUS: Enough, Callipho; I know my own business. Yes, I did do wrong. Now learn why I didn't inform you of your son's affair: I knew the treadmill was ready and waiting for me, if I did that.

SIMO: Didn't you know the mill was also ready and waiting when you kept it quiet?

PSEUDOLUS: Yes.

SIMO: Then why wasn't I told?

PSEUDOLUS: Because the one punishment was right there before me; the other was a little further off.

SIMO: Well, now what will you do? You can't get any money out of me, especially when I've learned all about it. And I'll warn everyone not to trust you for a penny.

PSEUDOLUS (*cool and confident*): I won't go begging to anyone as long as you're alive. You yourself will give me the money, I swear; I'll get it out of you.

SIMO (*in amazement*): You'll get it out of *me*?

PSEUDOLUS: In a jiffy!

SIMO: By God! Knock my eye right out, if I give it!

PSEUDOLUS: You'll give it. I'm giving you fair warning: be on your guard.

CALLIPHO: I'm quite sure of this: it will be a magnificent and remarkable achievement if you get it.

PSEUDOLUS: I'll do it, all right.

SIMO: And if you don't get it?

PSEUDOLUS: Whip me to shreds. But what if I do get it?

SIMO: So help me God, I swear you can keep it forever and will go unpunished.

PSEUDOLUS: See that you remember.

SIMO: The very idea of my not being able to look out for myself now I've been warned!

PSEUDOLUS: I'm warning you to look out. I'm telling you, look out! Look out! Why, with those very hands you'll give me the money this very day.

CALLIPHO: Heavens! He's a real Old Master, if he keeps his word.

PSEUDOLUS (*to* CALLIPHO): Make me your slave, if I don't do it.

SIMO (*ironically*): You're too kind and obliging! You no longer belong to me, I suppose.

PSEUDOLUS: Do you want me to tell you something which will surprise you still more?

CALLIPHO: Indeed, I'm eager to hear it; I just love to listen to you talk.

PSEUDOLUS: Before I fight my battle with you, there will be another battle that will be famous and historic.

SIMO: What battle?

PSEUDOLUS: You see this pimp who lives next door? Well, by some sharper's trick or shrewd device I'll swindle him out of that flute girl your son loves so desperately.

SIMO: What's that?

PSEUDOLUS: And I'll complete both these jobs by evening today.

SIMO: If you really accomplish these tricks as you promise, you'll outdo King Agathocles. But if you don't, do you see any good reason why I shouldn't bury you in the treadmill?

PSEUDOLUS: None—and for all the rest of my days, too. But if I accomplish it, will you give me the money to give the pimp on the spot, of your own free will?

CALLIPHO: That's a just and fair request; give him your word.

SIMO (*hesitating*): But do you know what just occurred to me? Supposing these two fellows are in cahoots and have concocted some prearranged trick to defraud me of my money?

PSEUDOLUS: Who would be more rash than I, if I dared such a trick? Oh, no, Simo; it's this way: if he and I have made any bargain or arranged any plan, or if we've even met together on this matter, you can make your mark all over me with a pen of birch-rods, just as if you were writing in a book.

SIMO (*giving in, grudgingly*): Well then, start your games whenever you like.

PSEUDOLUS: Callipho, please give me your aid for this one day and don't engage in any other business.

CALLIPHO: Why, yesterday I'd arranged to go to the country today.

PSEUDOLUS: Well, just disarrange those arrangements you've made up.

CALLIPHO: All right; I've decided not to go, for your sake. I want to see these games of yours, Pseudolus. And if I see that Simo here fails to give you the money he promised, rather than see the bargain broken I'll give it myself.

SIMO: I won't back down.

PSEUDOLUS: Indeed you won't; for if you don't give it, I'll dun you at the top of my lungs. Now then, out of the way with you! Go inside and make room for my tricks.

CALLIPHO: All right; we'll give in to you.

PSEUDOLUS: But I want you to stay at home.

CALLIPHO: Certainly; I'm at your service. (*He goes into his house.*)

SIMO: I'm going to the market. I'll be back directly. (*He goes out towards the forum.*)

PSEUDOLUS: Come back soon. (*To the audience*) I have a suspicion that you are suspecting that I've promised all these amazing feats just to amuse you while this play is going on, and that I'm not going to do what I said I'd do. But I won't back out of it. And yet I don't know for certain how I'm going to do it—only that it shall be done. When an actor appears on the stage, he's got to bring on some novel device with a novel angle to it. If he can't do that, let him make way for one who can. Now I want to retire to the house for a few minutes, while I marshall my regiment of come-on games. I'll soon come out again; I won't delay you long. In the meantime, the flute player here will entertain you. (*He goes into the house of* SIMO. *There is a short interval of flute music before the next Act.*)

Act Two. Scene I

(*Enter* PSEUDOLUS *from the house of* SIMO.)

PSEUDOLUS (*joyfully*): Ye gods! How nicely and successfully all my enterprises turn out! It's no dubious or faint-hearted plan I've got stored away in my head. It's outright foolishness, you see, to trust a mighty feat to a fearful heart; for everything's just what you make it, everything has the importance that you give it. Well then, I've already disposed all my forces in my head, and arranged a double and a triple line of tricks and double-dealing; wherever I meet the enemy—thanks to the valour of my ancestors, and my own efforts and unscrupulous trickery—I'll win an easy victory and easily despoil my enemies by my treachery. Now as for this public enemy, this enemy of mine and all of you, I'll mow down this Ballio with cannon balls. Just pay attention: I want to besiege and capture this town (*pointing to* BALLIO's *house*) today; I'll lead my legions up here. If I storm this town, I'll see there's easy pickings for my fellow-citizens; then I'll lead my army right away against this ancient city. (*Pointing to* SIMO's *house*) With booty from this town I'll load and stuff myself and all my accomplices, that all may know that I was born to spread fear and panic amongst my foes. That's the stuff I'm made of; I've got to perform great deeds to make my name famous and renowned in history. (*Sees* HARPAX *approaching down the street*) But who's this I see? Who is this stranger who strikes my eye? I'd like to know why he's coming here with that sword. What's he up to? I'll lay an ambush for him over here. (*He withdraws to the alley.*)

Act Two.   Scene II

(*Enter* HARPAX *in military dress, wearing a short sword and carrying a knapsack.*)

HARPAX (*to himself, counting on his fingers*): Yes, this is the place and the district that master told me, as far as I can reckon with my eyes. The Captain said it was the seventh block from the city gate, where the pimp lives; he ordered me to give him this token and the money. I'd like awfully much to have someone tell me what house Ballio the pimp lives in.

PSEUDOLUS (*aside*): Sh-h! Quiet! Quiet! This fellow's my meat, unless all the gods abandon me. Now I need a new plan for this new opportunity that's popped up. I'll turn to this to begin with; I abandon all those other plans I'd started to carry out. Now for this letter-carrying warrior that's just come; I'll stick him good and proper.

HARPAX (*approaching the door of* BALLIO'S *house*): I'll knock at this door and call someone out.

PSEUDOLUS (*running over to stop him*): You there, whoever you are, kindly refrain from knocking, if you please. I've come out to intercede for the door; it's under my protection.

HARPAX: Are you Ballio?

PSEUDOLUS: Why no, I'm his Under-Ballio.

HARPAX: What do you mean by that?

PSEUDOLUS: I'm his layer-in and layer-out; I'm in charge of supplies.

HARPAX: You mean you're his steward?

PSEUDOLUS: Oh, no; the steward takes orders from me.

HARPAX: What are you, slave or freeman?

PSEUDOLUS: For the moment, I'm a slave.

HARPAX: So I thought; you don't seem to deserve your freedom.

PSEUDOLUS: Don't you ever look at yourself when you make such dirty cracks at others?

HARPAX (*aside*): This fellow must be a rascal.

PSEUDOLUS (*aside*): God loves me, all right! Here's an anvil ready for me; I'll forge plenty of frauds on him today!

HARPAX (*aside*): What's he muttering about there?

PSEUDOLUS (*aloud*): I say there, young fellow.

HARPAX: What is it?

PSEUDOLUS: Are you from that Macedonian soldier or not? Are you the slave of the fellow who bought a woman from us and paid fifteen minae to my master the pimp? And he still owes five.

HARPAX: Yes, I am. But where in the world did you ever know me or see me or meet me? You see, I've never been to Athens before and I never set eyes on you before today.

PSEUDOLUS: I guessed from your appearance that you come from him. For at his departure this day was set for payment, and he's not yet paid us.

HARPAX (*pointing to his knapsack*): Well, here it is.

PSEUDOLUS: Have you brought it?

HARPAX: I have indeed.

PSEUDOLUS (*holding out his hand*): Why hesitate to hand it over?

HARPAX: Give it to *you*?

PSEUDOLUS: Yes, to me, of course. Why, I handle all of Ballio's cash and accounts, and I take in the money and pay it out.

HARPAX: By God! Even if you're the treasurer of God Almighty, I won't trust you with a penny.

PSEUDOLUS (*impatiently, still holding out his hand*): We can complete the transaction in a second.

HARPAX (*clutching his knapsack suspiciously*): I'll just keep it all complete in here, thank you.

PSEUDOLUS: The devil with you! You're the first to try to undermine my credit. As if I didn't handle a thousand times such sums all by myself!

HARPAX: It's quite possible that others think this of you without my trusting you.

PSEUDOLUS: You're as much as saying that I want to swindle you of your money.

HARPAX: Oh no! *You're* as much as saying it and I'm as much as suspecting it. But what's your name?

PSEUDOLUS (*aside*): The pimp here has a slave named Surus; I'll say that's my name. (*Aloud*) I'm Surus.

HARPAX: Surus?

PSEUDOLUS: That's my name.

HARPAX: We're talking too much. If your master's at home, just call him out, so I can do the business I was sent on.

PSEUDOLUS: Whatever your name is—if he were at home I'd call him. But if you're willing to give me the money, it will be paid better than if you put it right in his hands.

HARPAX: D'you know something? Master sent me to pay this money, not to lose it. I'm certain of one thing: you're in a sweat because you can't get your hooks on this. I won't trust a penny to anyone but Ballio himself.

PSEUDOLUS: But he's busy right now; he's got a lawsuit.

HARPAX: Good luck to him! When I know he's at home I'll come back. As for you, just take this letter and give it to him. There's a token there that our masters agreed upon.

PSEUDOLUS: I know: he said he wanted the girl sent with the man who brought us the money and his picture stamped in wax. He left a copy of it here.

HARPAX: You've got the whole story.

PSEUDOLUS: Of course; why shouldn't I?

HARPAX (*handing over the letter*): Well then, just give him that seal.

PSEUDOLUS: All right. But what's your name?

HARPAX: Harpax.[10]

PSEUDOLUS: Get out of here, Harpax! You please me not! You'll not get inside here, by God! We want no snatching Harpies here.

HARPAX: I'm in the habit of snatching prisoners alive on the battle-field; that's how I got the name.

PSEUDOLUS: You're much more likely to snatch the silver service from the house, I think.

HARPAX (*indignantly*): That's not true. But do you know what I want of you, Surus?

PSEUDOLUS: I'll know, if you tell me.

HARPAX: I'm going to put up at the third inn outside the gate, with a tubby, limping, fat old hag—Chrysis.

PSEUDOLUS: What then?

HARPAX: Send for me there, when your master comes.

PSEUDOLUS: Certainly; just as you like.

HARPAX: I'm tired from my trip; I want to refresh myself.

PSEUDOLUS: A very wise plan; I like it. But mind I don't need a searching-party when I send for you.

HARPAX: Oh, no; I'm going to eat, and then take a nap.

PSEUDOLUS: Of course—my idea, exactly.

HARPAX (*starting to leave*): Anything else you want?

PSEUDOLUS: Go have a good nap.

HARPAX: I'm off. (*He goes out towards the harbour.*)

PSEUDOLUS (*calling after him*): And listen here, Harpax: tell 'em to cover you up well; you'll feel swell if you get up a good sweat.

Act Two. Scene III

PSEUDOLUS (*to himself*): Ye gods! This fellow has saved my life with his arrival. He's set me back on the road when I was wandering off and has paid my fare out of his own pocket. Why, Opportunity herself couldn't have turned up at a more opportune moment than the opportune way this letter has arrived. (*Waving the letter joyfully*) Here's my Horn of Plenty; everything I want is right in here: my tricks, my traps, my come-on games! Here's the money, here's a mistress for my lovesick master. And to be boastful and chesty about it, I might add that I already knew what I was going to do and how to do it, to filch the girl from the pimp. I already had my plans drawn up in full-dress parade in my mind, just as I wished; everything was in fine shape. But this is the way things are: the plans of a thousand wise men can be beaten by this one goddess, Fortune. And this too is true: when a man makes good use of his Fortune, he reaches the top of the ladder and we all call him a wise man. And when we know that he's used good counsel

too, we say he's a smart fellow; but we call a man a fool when his
affairs turn out badly. Fools that we are! We don't know how mistaken
we are when we yearn to get something; as if we could know what's
good for us. "We take the credit and let the cash go." And meanwhile,
amidst our toil and trouble, death catches up with us. But enough of
this lecture on philosophy. I talk too long. Good God! That lie I made
up on the spur of the moment was worth its weight in solid gold—I
mean when I said I belonged to the pimp. And now, with this letter I'll
dupe three people: my master, the pimp, and the man who gave me
the letter. Hurrah! I never even prayed for a stroke of luck equal
to this. (*Looking down the street*) Look! Here comes Calidorus; he's
got someone or other with him.

Act Two.   Scene IV

(*Enter* CALIDORUS *and* CHARINUS *from the forum.*)

CALIDORUS (*to* CHARINUS, *without seeing* PSEUDOLUS): I've told you all
my pleasures and pains; you know about my love, my toils, my need.

CHARINUS: I've got it all in mind; just let me know what you want me
to do.

[CALIDORUS: I've told you everything else; are you sure you understand
about the token?

CHARINUS: Everything, I say. Just tell me what you want me to do.][9]

CALIDORUS: Pseudolus told me to bring him a vigorous fellow who was
well disposed towards me.

CHARINUS: You carry out his orders excellently; for in me you're bringing a friend who is well disposed towards you. But that Pseudolus you
mention—I don't know him.

CALIDORUS: He's an Old Master; my inventor-in-chief. He said he'd accomplish what I told you.

PSEUDOLUS: I'll greet the fellow in a flowery style.

CALIDORUS: Whose is that voice I hear?

PSEUDOLUS: Hi-yo! Hi-yo! Thee, thee I seek, my prince, who givest
thy commands to Pseudolus. To thee I'll give blessings thrice three
times three, thrice earned with triple arts in triple ways, three joys thrice
swindled from three dupes through mischief, snares, and fraud. I've
brought it all to you in this little sealed letter.

CALIDORUS (*to* CHARINUS): That's the fellow.

CHARINUS: How he rants, the rascal!

PSEUDOLUS: Step up and meet me! Be brave, stretch out your hand in greeting.

CALIDORUS: Tell me, Pseudolus: am I to greet you as Expectation or Fulfilment?

PSEUDOLUS: As both.

CALIDORUS: Greetings, Both. But what's happened?

PSEUDOLUS: What are you afraid of?

CALIDORUS (*indicating* CHARINUS): Here's the fellow I've lifted for you.

PSEUDOLUS: Lifted?

CALIDORUS: "Brought," I meant to say.

PSEUDOLUS: Who is he?

CALIDORUS: Charinus.

PSEUDOLUS: Bravo! Now don't be chary with your Charinus.

CHARINUS: If you need anything, why, don't be afraid to give me orders.

PSEUDOLUS: Thanks just the same; I wish you luck, Charinus. But I don't want to bother you with our troubles.

CHARINUS: Bother me? Why, it's no bother at all.

PSEUDOLUS: Then wait a minute. (*He holds up the letter.*)

CALIDORUS: What's that?

PSEUDOLUS: A letter I've just intercepted—and a token.

CALIDORUS (*startled*): A token? What token?

PSEUDOLUS: The one the soldier sent. His slave brought this, with five minae; he was going to fetch your mistress, but I put one over on him.

CALIDORUS: How?

PSEUDOLUS: We're acting this play for the benefit of the spectators here; they know, since they were here. I'll tell you later.

CALIDORUS: What are we up to now?

PSEUDOLUS: This very day your mistress will be free, and in your arms.

CALIDORUS: In mine?

PSEUDOLUS: Yes, in yours, I say, if your humble servant stays alive. Now, if you'll just find me some fellow promptly.

CALIDORUS: What kind?

PSEUDOLUS: A shrewd and cunning knave who can grasp of his own accord what he has to do as soon as he's been given a hint. And his face mustn't be too familiar around here.

CHARINUS: Does it matter if he's a slave?

PSEUDOLUS: Why, no; I much prefer a slave to a freeman.

CHARINUS: I think I can lend you one: a clever rascal who's just come from my father in Carystus; he hasn't been out of the house yet and has never been to Athens before yesterday evening.

PSEUDOLUS: That's a great help. But I also need a loan of five minae; I can pay you back tomorrow; for Calidorus' father owes it to me.

CHARINUS: I'll lend it; look no further.

PSEUDOLUS: What a godsend you are! But I also need a soldier's cloak, a sword, and a hat.

CHARINUS: I can lend you those too.

PSEUDOLUS: Ye gods! Nothing Chary about you, Charinus; you're Abundance herself. But about that slave who's just come from Carystus: is he pretty sharp?

CHARINUS (*holding his nose, with a meaning wink*): Well, he's pretty sharp under the armpits.

PSEUDOLUS: The fellow ought to wear long sleeves. How's his wit: pretty pungent?

CHARINUS: Oh, yes, sharp as vinegar.

PSEUDOLUS: Well, if he has to ladle out something sweet, has he any of that on tap?

CHARINUS: What a question! He's got spiced wine, raisin wine, cherry brandy, honey syrup, honey of every sort. Why, he once thought of setting up a bazaar in his head.

PSEUDOLUS: Bravo! Very nice, Charinus; you beat me to shreds at my own game. What's the name of this slave?

CHARINUS: Simia.

PSEUDOLUS: When things go badly can he shift for himself?

CHARINUS: Shift? Like a breeze.

PSEUDOLUS: A man of convictions, is he?

CHARINUS: Convictions? Why, he's been convicted of every crime in the book.

PSEUDOLUS: What if he's caught in the act?

CHARINUS: He's an eel: he wiggles out of it.

PSEUDOLUS: Plenty of ability?

CHARINUS: More ability than a Bill of Rights.

PSEUDOLUS: He's a fine fellow, according to your account.

CHARINUS: Why, if you only knew! As soon as he takes a look at you, he'll tell you what you want of him. But what are you going to do?

PSEUDOLUS: I'll tell you. When I've dressed up the fellow, I want him to substitute for the soldier's slave. He's to carry this token and the five minae to the pimp and take away the girl. There's the whole story. As for the rest, I'll tell him in person how he's to do everything.

CALIDORUS (*impatiently*): What are we standing here for?

PSEUDOLUS: Bring me the fellow all decked out in his costume to the bank of Aeschinus. And hurry up!

CALIDORUS: We'll be there before you. (CALIDORUS *and* CHARINUS *depart towards the forum.*)

PSEUDOLUS: Step on it! (*To himself*) Now all the uncertainties and doubts in my mind have cleared up; my mind's easy now; I see my way clear. I'll lead forth the legions under my standard in good order, and with favourable omens; the auspices are good and everything is to my liking. I'm confident I can beat my enemies. Now I'll go to the market and give Simia a cargo of instructions; I'll tell him just what to do, so there won't be any slips and he'll carry out this trick like a professional. I'll soon make a shambles of this town of Pimpton. (*He departs to the forum.*)

Act Three.   Scene I

(Enter a young SLAVE *from the house of* BALLIO.*)*

SLAVE *(to himself)*: When the gods make a lad the slave of a pimp, and in addition to that make him ugly too, as far as I can tell, they give him many a heavy sorrow and trouble. For example, take this slavery of mine: all sorts of cares, both great and small, lean their weight on me. And I can't find any *galant* to love me and make my treatment a little more pleasant. And now, today's the pimp's birthday, and he threatens every one of us, the highest and the lowest: whoever gives him no birthday present today shall die tomorrow on the rack! In my present state, I don't know what to do. *(Looking at himself mournfully)* I haven't the gift of doing what those who have the gift usually do. Now, unless I give this pimp a present today, tomorrow it's a bitter brew I've got to drink. Alas! How small I am for such pursuits! And yet, by God! Such is the fearful fright I feel, that if someone would only put a little something in my hand to make it heavier, (although they say that doing it makes you groan) I think I could grit my teeth and bear it somehow. *(Looking down the street)* But I'd better cut short my talk: here's master coming back home with the cook.

Act Three.   Scene II

(Enter BALLIO *and* COOK *from the forum, with attendants and provisions.)*

BALLIO: They're fools to call it the Cooks' Market; why, it's not a Cooks' Market, it's a Thieves' Market. If I'd taken my oath to find a worse fellow, I couldn't have found one to beat this cook I'm bringing, the babbling, boastful, witless, useless fool! Why, Old Nick himself wouldn't take him in Hell: he wants us to have someone here to cook for funerals; he's the only fellow that can cook to please a corpse!

COOK: If you think I'm as bad as you say, why did you hire me?

BALLIO: No choice. There wasn't anyone else. But why were you still sitting in the market-place, if you're a cook—you alone, and no one else?

COOK: I'll tell you: it's stinginess that makes me an unpopular cook, not my own talents.

BALLIO: Why's that?

COOK: I'll speak up and tell you: when people come to engage a cook, no one looks for the one who's best and most expensive; they hire the one who charges least. Today I was the only cook who sat in the market. Those other wretched fellows are one-drachma-men; no one can make me get up off my seat for less than two drachmas. For I don't season my dinners like other cooks; they season and serve up whole pastures on their platters; they treat the guests like cattle and give them grass to eat and then season that grass with other grasses. They stick in coriander, fennel, garlic, parsley; they set out sorrel, cabbage, beets, and spinach and pour in a pint of silphium; they grate in some vile mustard that makes the eyes of the graters stream with tears before they've even grated it. Why, when these fellows cook and season a dinner, they don't season it with condiments but with condors, that tear the living guts out of the guests. That's why men's lives are so short, since they stuff herbage like that in their bellies, stuff that makes you shudder to mention, let alone eat it. Men eat fodder that cattle wouldn't touch.

BALLIO: What about you? Do you use celestial seasonings, which can prolong men's lives, since you find fault with those other condiments?

COOK: You can say that without hesitation. Why, men could live two hundred years if they'd eat the foods I prepare. When I slip a little cinnamoprika in my dishes, or some gingeria, thymemeg, and savoranise, the dishes come to a boil of their own accord. Such are the spices I use for Neptune's cattle; for terrestrial animals I use chicorchevril, tabasclovia, or chilimarjoram.

BALLIO: May all the devils in Hell damn you with your sauces and all your lies!

COOK: Allow me to continue, if you please.

BALLIO: Talk on—and go to the devil!

COOK: Then when all the pots are boiling, I take the lids off, and the odour goes flying to the sky with downcast feet. Jupiter dines on that odour every day.

BALLIO: An odour with downcast feet?

COOK: A mere slip of the tongue.

BALLIO: Why?

COOK: I meant to say, "with downcast—hands."[11]

BALLIO: What if you don't go out to cook, what does Jupiter dine on then?

COOK: He goes to bed without his supper.

BALLIO: Go to the devil! Am I going to pay you two drachmas today for that sort of stuff?

COOK: I admit I'm a very expensive cook. But I see that people get something for their money wherever I go to cook.

BALLIO: To steal, you mean.

COOK: Well, do you expect to find any cook who hasn't claws like a kite or an eagle?

BALLIO: Well, do you expect to go anywhere to cook without having to cook dinner with your claws tied up? (*To the* SLAVE) Hey there, you! You belong to me; now I'm giving you your orders: hurry and get all our stuff out of sight, and then keep your eye on this fellow's eyes. Wherever he looks, you're to look there too. If he goes anywhere, you're to go along. If he stretches out his hand, hold yours out too; if he takes anything of his own, let him have it; but if he takes anything of ours, grab it on the other side. If he moves, you move; if he stands still, stand still; if he squats down, you squat down. And I'll appoint special guards for each of his disciples. (*He glares at the* COOK's *attendants.*)

COOK: Oh, don't worry.

BALLIO: How can I help it—kindly tell me that—when I've brought you to my house?

COOK: I'll fix you up today with my stews; just like Medea, who cooked up old Pelias and turned him from an old man into a youth, they say, by her drugs and poisons. I'll do just the same with you.

BALLIO: What? A poisoner too?

COOK: Oh no; I'm rather the Preserver of Mankind.

BALLIO: Aha! What will you take for teaching me just one of your recipes?

COOK: Which one?

BALLIO: The one that will preserve me from your thievish ways.

COOK (*unruffled*): If you trust me, for two drachmas; otherwise, not for a mina. But are you entertaining friends or enemies today?

BALLIO: Good Lord! Friends, of course.

COOK: Better invite your enemies instead: I'm going to serve up such a dinner and season it with such sweet sauces that every guest, when he tastes the sauce, will gnaw his fingers to the bone.

BALLIO: If you please, before serving to the guests, just taste the dish yourself and give some to your pupils, so you'll gnaw off your own light-fingered hands!

COOK: Perhaps you don't believe my words?

BALLIO: Don't make a nuisance of yourself! You gabble too much. Shut up! (*Pointing to his house*) Look; there's where I live. Go in and cook the dinner. Hurry up.

SLAVE: Why, go and take your place at the table; bring on your guests. Dinner's a-spoiling now. (*The* COOK *and attendants go into* BALLIO'S *house.*)

BALLIO: Well, well! Just look at that sprout, will you! Here's a fine, dirty under-licker! I haven't the slightest idea what to watch out for first: there are so many thieves in my house, and a bandit next door. You see, just a little while ago at the market my neighbour here, the father of Calidorus, carefully warned me to look out for his slave Pseudolus and not to trust him. He said he was going to get around me today and swindle me of the woman, if he could; he made a bold promise, he said, to steal my girl Phoenicium from me by some trick. Well then, I'm going in to tell my household not to trust Pseudolus one single inch. (*He goes into his house.*)

Act Four. Scene I

(*Enter* PSEUDOLUS *from the forum.*)

PSEUDOLUS (*speaking to* SIMIA, *who has not yet appeared*): If ever the gods above wanted to aid any man, it's Calidorus and me; yes, they certainly want to save us and blot out this pimp, since they produced in you such a shrewd and crafty accomplice for me. (*Looking around*) But where is he? What a fool I am, talking to myself here! By God! He's pulled a fast one on me, I'm afraid. I'm one bad egg dealing with another, and I didn't keep my eyes peeled! Damn it! I'm done for, if the fellow's got away; I'll never finish the job I want to do. Ah! There he comes, the picture of a whipping post. What a walk, what a pompous swagger! Hey there, I was just looking for you; I was terribly afraid you'd run away.

(Enter SIMIA *in military dress.)*

SIMIA: That would have been my usual practice, I admit.

PSEUDOLUS: Where did you stop?

SIMIA *(calmly)*: Where I pleased.

PSEUDOLUS: I'm well aware of that.

SIMIA: Well then, why ask me what you're well aware of?

PSEUDOLUS: I want to give you a bit of advice.

SIMIA: Be advised not to give me any advice.

PSEUDOLUS: Say, you're pretty insolent to me.

SIMIA: Why shouldn't I be insolent to you, when I'm a far-renowned military man?

PSEUDOLUS: I want to carry out the plan we've started on.

SIMIA: You don't see me doing anything else, do you?

PSEUDOLUS: Walk a little faster, then.

SIMIA: No; I like this leisurely gait.

PSEUDOLUS: This is our chance; I want you to get in first, while that other fellow's asleep.

SIMIA: What's your hurry? Take it easy; don't worry. I hope and pray that he'll turn up too and meet me on the spot—that fellow who's come from the soldier. By God! He won't be Harpax nearly so much as I. Cheer up; I'll fix this matter up for you beautifully. My tricks and lies will terrify that stranger from the army so badly that he'll deny he's the man he is and say that I'm himself.

PSEUDOLUS: How's that possible?

SIMIA: You wear me out with those questions.

PSEUDOLUS: Oh, what a swell fellow!

SIMIA: For your information, I can beat you with my tricks and dodges, though you're my tutor.

PSEUDOLUS: God keep you safe for me!

SIMIA: For myself, rather. (*Pulling at his clothes*) Look here: does this getup suit me?

PSEUDOLUS: It's perfect.

SIMIA: All right.

PSEUDOLUS: God be good to you and give you as much as you desire; for if I prayed him to give you as much as you deserve, you'd get less than nothing. You're a perfect rogue and rascal, if ever I saw one.

SIMIA: *You* say this to me?

PSEUDOLUS: I'll say no more. But what a reward I'll give you, if you take care of this matter decently.

SIMIA: Can't you keep still? To remind a man who's mindful and who remembers, often makes that mindful man unmindful. I've stored up everything in my mind; I've mulled over my tricks very shrewdly.

PSEUDOLUS: Here's a good fellow!

SIMIA: Neither here nor (*pointing to* PSEUDOLUS) there either!

PSEUDOLUS: But see you don't make any slips.

SIMIA: Can't you hush up?

PSEUDOLUS: As God loves me—

SIMIA (*interrupting*): But he doesn't! Now you'll pour out some undiluted lies.

PSEUDOLUS: —I love and fear and honour you, Simia, you're such a tricky rascal.

SIMIA: I'm an expert at dishing out that sort of stuff to others; you can't make me swallow such flattery.

PSEUDOLUS: What a lovely party I'll give you today, when you finish this job—

SIMIA: Ha, ha, ha!

PSEUDOLUS: Good food, wine, perfume, and titbits with the drinks. And there'll be a charming girl too, to give you kiss after kiss.

SIMIA: A lovely party, indeed!

PSEUDOLUS: Why, if you do the job, I'll see that you say even more.

SIMIA: If I don't succeed, let the executioner stretch me on the rack. But hurry up and show me the opening of this pimp's house.

PSEUDOLUS: It's the third one.

SIMIA: Sh-h! Quiet! The house is gaping open.

PSEUDOLUS: The house is sick, I imagine.

SIMIA: Why?

PSEUDOLUS: It's belching out the pimp himself.

SIMIA: Is that he?

PSEUDOLUS: It's he.

SIMIA: He's bad baggage, all right. Just look, will you, how he comes out sideways, not forward, like a crab! (PSEUDOLUS *and* SIMIA *retire to the alley.*)

Act Four.   Scene II

(BALLIO *comes out from his house, looking back to see the activity of the cooks in the kitchen.*)

BALLIO: This cook isn't as bad as I thought; so far he hasn't filched anything but a cup and a pitcher.

PSEUDOLUS (*in a low voice, to* SIMIA): Hey, you! Now's your chance.

SIMIA (*to* PSEUDOLUS): I agree with you.

PSEUDOLUS: On your way, then, and be sharp. I'll stay here in ambush.

SIMIA (*aloud, stepping out into the street*): I've counted very carefully: this is the sixth side-street from the gate, and he told me to turn in at that street. But how many houses did he say? I don't know about that at all.

BALLIO (*noticing him*): Who's this fellow in the soldier's coat? Where's he from and what's he looking for? A foreigner, by the looks of him, and a stranger here.

SIMIA (*pretending to see* BALLIO *for the first time*): But here's someone to give me some information about my search.

BALLIO (*as* SIMIA *approaches*): He's coming right up to me. Where in the world can he be coming from?

SIMIA: Say there, you with the goatee, answer a question for me.

BALLIO: Oho! Aren't you going to say hello first?

SIMIA: I've no hellos available.

BALLIO: Well, you'll get just the same from me.

PSEUDOLUS (*aside*): He's off to a good start!

SIMIA: Do you know a certain fellow in this street? Tell me.

BALLIO: I know myself.

SIMIA: Very few men do; in the market-place scarcely one man in ten knows who he is.

PSEUDOLUS (*aside*): I'm saved; he's a philosopher!

SIMIA: I'm looking for a rascal here, a law-breaking, godless, perjured villain.

BALLIO (*aside*): He's looking for me. Those are my surnames. Now if he'd just mention my real name. (*Aloud*) What's the name of this man?

SIMIA: Ballio the Pimp.

BALLIO: Do I know him? My boy, I'm the very man you're seeking.

SIMIA: Are you Ballio?

BALLIO: Yes indeed, that's me.

SIMIA: Judging by your clothes, you're a burglar.

BALLIO: I presume that if you saw me in a dark alley you wouldn't touch me.

SIMIA: My master wanted me to give you his best greetings. Take this letter; he told me to give it to you.

BALLIO: Who's this man who told you?

PSEUDOLUS (*aside*): Damn it! Now the fellow's stuck in the mud. He doesn't know the name. That stops our game.

BALLIO: Who did you say sent me this letter?

SIMIA (*unperturbed*): See if you recognise this picture. (*Showing* BALLIO *the seal*) Tell me his name yourself, so I'll know you're really Ballio.

BALLIO: Give me the letter.

SIMIA: Here it is; now identify the seal.

BALLIO (*to himself*): Oh, it's MacSaberswipes,[12] it's his spitting image. (*To* SIMIA) I recognise it. Say there, his name is MacSaberswipes.

SIMIA: I see now that I've given the letter to the right person, since you mention the name MacSaberswipes.

BALLIO: And how goes it with him?

SIMIA: As befits a brave and far-famed warrior. But hurry up and read this letter, please—that's my business here—take the money and give me the girl. I've got to be in Sicyon today, or meet my fate tomorrow; master's so bossy.

BALLIO: I know; you're talking to a man who's met him.

SIMIA: Hurry up and read the letter then.

BALLIO: I'm doing so; just keep quiet. (*Reading*) "Captain MacSaberswipes to Ballio the Pimp: I'm sending you a letter sealed with the likeness we agreed upon some time ago."

SIMIA: That's the token on the letter.

BALLIO: I see and recognise the seal. But doesn't he usually send any word of good cheer in his letters?

SIMIA: It's his military training, Ballio: soldiers bring good cheer by their actions to those who are friendly, and bring trouble to those who aren't. But continue; go on and find out what the letter tells you.

BALLIO: Just listen. (*Reading*) "This is my orderly, Harpax, who comes to you—" Are you Harpax?

SIMIA: I am—and I live up to my name.[10]

BALLIO (*reading*): "—and brings this letter to you. Take the money from him and send the woman away with him. It's proper to send greetings in a letter to those who deserve them; if I'd thought you deserved them, I would have sent them."

SIMIA: Well then?

BALLIO: Give me the money and take away the woman.

SIMIA: Which of us is holding up the business?

BALLIO: Just come inside with me.

SIMIA: I'm coming. (*They go into the house of* BALLIO.)

Act Four. Scene III

PSEUDOLUS (*to himself*): By God! I've never seen a worse scoundrel or a more polished rascal than this Simia! And I'm terribly afraid of the fellow: I fear he may be as tricky towards me as he was towards the pimp and in the midst of our success turn his horns towards me, if he gets the chance; he's such a scoundrel. And I don't want that; for I like him well. So now I'm in an awful fret for three reasons: I'm afraid this colleague of mine will leave me in the lurch and desert to the enemy. Then I'm afraid my master may return from the market and the freebooters may be captured when the booty's captured. And with this fear I also have a fear that the other Harpax may come before this Harpax of ours gets away with the girl. Oh, damn it! They're much too slow in coming out. My heart has packed up its baggage and moved up to my throat; if he doesn't bring the girl out with him, it will jump out of my mouth and go into exile. (*Seeing* SIMIA *appear in the doorway*) I win! In spite of their precautions, I've conquered my watchmen.

Act Four. Scene IV

(*Enter* SIMIA *with* PHOENICIUM *from* BALLIO'S *house.*)

SIMIA: Don't cry, Phoenicium; you don't know how things are, but you'll soon find out when you go to dinner. I'm not taking you to that bucktoothed Macedonian who makes you weep; you're on your way to the man you most want to belong to: it's Calidorus you'll soon be hugging, I promise you.

PSEUDOLUS (*coming out from the alley*): Why did you loaf in there so long, if you please? My heart's numb from pounding against my chest.

SIMIA: You've found a fine time to ask me, you jailbird! There are ambushes all about. Let's just step out of here on the double quick.

PSEUDOLUS: By God! You're good for nothing, but that's good advice. Forward to the victory parade! This way, straight to the drinks! (*They go out towards the forum with* PHOENICIUM.)

Act Four. Scene V

(Enter BALLIO *from his house.)*

BALLIO *(to himself)*: Aha! At last my mind's at rest, since this chap
has gone away with the woman. Now tell Pseudolus, that ringleader of
criminals, to come and take away the woman with his wiles. I'm quite
sure of this: I'd rather take a solemn oath and then perjure myself a
thousand times than let that fellow bamboozle me and make me a
laughingstock. Now, by God! I'll have the laugh on him, if I meet him;
but I guess he'll be in the treadmill, according to their agreement. But
now I'd like to run across Simo, so he can share my joy.

Act Four. Scene VI

(Enter SIMO *from the forum.)*

SIMO: I'm going to see what my Ulysses has accomplished, and whether
he's got the Palladium from the citadel of Ballonia.[13]

BALLIO *(rushing up to* SIMO): O Simo, you lucky fellow, give me your
lucky hand!

SIMO: What is it?

BALLIO: Just now—

SIMO: What "just now"?

BALLIO: There's nothing to be afraid of.

SIMO: What is it? Has the fellow come to you?

BALLIO: No.

SIMO: What's this good news, then?

BALLIO: Your twenty minae are safe and sound—and your bet with
Pseudolus today.

SIMO *(doubtfully)*: I only wish they were.

BALLIO *(with great confidence)*: Demand that I pay you twenty minae,
if he gets his hands on that girl today or gives her to your son, as he
promised. Go on! Do ask me, for heaven's sake. I'm so anxious to make

the promise: then you'll know that everything is completely safe. (*As* SIMO *still hesitates*) And you can have the girl as a gift, too.

SIMO (*thoughtfully*): There's no danger in the bet, as far as I can see, in view of your terms. (*Formally*) Will you give me twenty minae?

BALLIO: I shall give them.[2]

SIMO: Well, this is a good job, at any rate. But did you meet him?

BALLIO: Why, I met both of them.

SIMO: What did he say? What did he tell you? Come on, tell me: what did he say to you?

BALLIO: The usual theatrical nonsense; the sort of thing they always say to a pimp in a comedy; every child knows it. They called me a villain and a rogue and a perjurer.

SIMO: By gosh, he didn't tell any lies there!

BALLIO: And so I wasn't angry. For what's the use of calling a man names when he doesn't care and doesn't deny them?

SIMO: What is it? Why am I not to be afraid of him? I'm curious to learn this.

BALLIO: Because he'll never take the girl away from me now; he can't. You remember I told you I'd sold her to a Macedonian soldier?

SIMO: I remember.

BALLIO: Well, his slave brought the money here to me and the seal, as the token—

SIMO: What then?

BALLIO: —which had been agreed upon between us. He took the girl away with him a little while ago.

SIMO: On your honour, is that so?

BALLIO: Honour? Where would I get any of that?

SIMO: Just think a minute: are you sure our friend hasn't framed up something?

BALLIO: The letter and the soldier's likeness make me certain. Why, he's just taken her out of town to Sicyon.

SIMO: Well done, by God! Why should I hesitate to make Pseudolus sign up as an emigrant for the treadmill? (*Seeing* HARPAX *approaching*) But who's this fellow in the military cloak?

BALLIO: I'm sure I don't know; let's watch where he goes and what he does. (*They retire to the alley.*)

Act Four.   Scene VII

(*Enter* HARPAX *from the harbour.*)

HARPAX (*without seeing* BALLIO *and* SIMO): It's a worthless and a useless slave who disregards his master's orders; and he's also no account who can't remember to do his duty unless he's warned. For slaves who think themselves free the minute they get out of their master's sight, and go in for high-living and harlots, eating up all they possess, will long bear the name of slaves. There's nothing good in their characters, except that they keep on being bad. With such slaves I have no truck: I don't meet or talk with them, I'm not acquainted with them. When I've got my orders, I think my master's with me, even though he's not. I fear him when he's not here, lest I should have to fear him when he is here. I'll pay attention to my task. For I've been waiting in the inn, to see if that Syrus to whom I gave the token would come; he told me to wait and said he'd send for me when the pimp was at home. But since he didn't come or send for me, I've come here myself to see what the matter is; I don't want the fellow to make game of me. I'd better knock at this door and call someone out. I want the pimp to take this money (*holding up his purse*) and give me the girl to take away.

BALLIO (*aside to* SIMO, *looking at the purse*): Hey, you!

SIMO: What do you want?

BALLIO: This fellow is mine.

SIMO: Why?

BALLIO: Because there's booty here for me: he wants a wench, he's got money! I'd like to get my teeth in him.

SIMO: Are you going to eat him up?

BALLIO: Yes, while he's fresh and hot; you should gulp these fellows down while they're in a giving mood. Decent men cause my ruin, rakes make me rich. Hard-working citizens are useful to the state, but wastrels are useful to me.

SIMO: The gods will punish you, you scoundrel!

HARPAX (*approaching* BALLIO'S *door*): I'm delaying myself by not knocking at this door; I'll find out if Ballio's at home.

BALLIO (*to* SIMO): It's Venus that gives me these blessings; she sends me these profit-shunning, loss-loving fellows, who spend their lives in self-indulgence, eating, drinking, wenching. They're quite different from you: you won't allow yourself to have a good time and you envy those who do.

HARPAX (*knocking at the door*): Hello! Where are you?

BALLIO: He's making a beeline straight for me.

[HARPAX (*knocking*): Hello there! Where are you?

BALLIO: Say there, young fellow: what debt are you collecting there?][9] (*To* SIMO) I'll get plenty of loot from him. I know it; the omens are good.

HARPAX (*knocking*): Open up, someone!

BALLIO (*calling to* HARPAX): Hey there, you in the cloak! What debt are you collecting there?

HARPAX: I'm looking for the owner of the house, Ballio the pimp.

BALLIO: Whoever you are, young man, spare yourself the trouble of searching.

HARPAX: Why?

BALLIO: Because you're looking at him, face to face.

HARPAX (*pointing at* SIMO): Is it you?

SIMO (*angrily shaking his stick*): See here, my well-cloaked friend! Just look out for trouble from this stick, and point your finger at him. (*Indicating* BALLIO) He's the pimp; I'm an honourable man.

BALLIO: But you, the honourable man, are often dunned in the forum, and can't get a penny anywhere, unless this pimp comes to your rescue.

HARPAX (*to* BALLIO): Why don't you talk to me?

BALLIO: All right, I'm talking. What do you want?

HARPAX: I want you to take this money.

BALLIO (*holding out his hand*): I've had my hand out for hours, waiting for you to give it.

HARPAX (*handing him the purse*): Take it; there are five minae here, carefully counted out in good money. My master, MacSaberswipes, ordered me to bring it to you to pay his debt; and you're to send off Phoenicium with me.

BALLIO (*in surprise*): Your master—

HARPAX: That's what I said.

BALLIO: —the soldier—

HARPAX: That's it.

BALLIO: —from Macedon—

HARPAX: Exactly.

BALLIO: —MacSaberswipes, sent you to me?

HARPAX: Quite correct.

BALLIO: To give me this money?

HARPAX: Yes, if you're really Ballio the pimp.

BALLIO: And you're to take the woman away with you?

HARPAX: Yes.

BALLIO: He said it was Phoenicium?

HARPAX: Your memory's quite accurate.

BALLIO: Wait a minute; I'll come back to you directly.

HARPAX: Well, make it snappy; I'm in a hurry. It's already late in the day, as you see.

BALLIO: I see. But I want to consult my friend here. Just wait there; I'll return at once. (*Drawing* SIMO *to one side*) Now what, Simo? What shall we do? I've caught the fellow in the act—this fellow who brought the money.

SIMO: How so?

BALLIO: Don't you see what this game is?

SIMO: I'm completely in the dark.

BALLIO: Your Pseudolus has delegated this chap to play the part of the soldier's messenger.

SIMO: Do you have his money?

BALLIO (*showing the purse*): Can you ask, when you see this?

SIMO: See here! Don't forget to go halves with me; share and share alike with this loot.

BALLIO: What the devil! It all comes from you, anyway.

HARPAX (*impatiently*): How soon are you going to pay any attention to me?

BALLIO: I am paying attention to you. (*To* SIMO) What do you suggest now, Simo?

SIMO: Let's have some sport with this fake lookout-man, until he realises that we're making game of him.

BALLIO: Come on then. (*Approaching* HARPAX) I say, there! Are you really the slave of the soldier?

HARPAX: Certainly.

BALLIO: How much did he pay for you?

HARPAX: He got me as a prize of valour, for his victory on the field. For I was commander-in-chief in my native country.

BALLIO: What? Did he ever storm your native jail?

HARPAX: If you insult me, you'll hear a few insults yourself.

BALLIO: How long did it take you to come from Sicyon?

HARPAX: From yesterday morning till this noon.

BALLIO: Pretty fast travelling, by George!

SIMO: Oh, he's as nimble as you like. You can tell by looking at his legs that he's used to—heavy chains!

BALLIO: I say: when you were a baby, did you sleep in a cradle?

SIMO: Of course he did.

BALLIO: And did you use to—you know what I mean?

SIMO: Of course he used to.

HARPAX (*bewildered*): Are you both crazy?

BALLIO: How about this? At night, when you and the soldier stood watch together, did his sabre fit your sheath?

HARPAX: Go to hell!

BALLIO: Certainly—that's where you can go, and in good time, too.

HARPAX: Why don't you give me the woman? Or give me back my money.

BALLIO: Wait.

HARPAX: Why should I?

BALLIO: Tell me: how much did you pay to rent this cloak?

HARPAX: What's that?

SIMO: What did the sword cost?

HARPAX: These chaps certainly need a dose of hellebore.[14]

BALLIO (*reaching for* HARPAX's *hat*): I say—

HARPAX: Let go!

BALLIO: How much rental does this hat earn for its owner today?

HARPAX: What do you mean, "its owner"? What are you dreaming about? These things are all mine, paid for with my own private property.

BALLIO (*leering*): Something private right above your thighs, no doubt.

HARPAX (*with a threatening gesture*): These old fellows are well-oiled; now they want the usual rub-down.

BALLIO: Seriously now, answer me this question: what's your salary? How much did Pseudolus hire you for?

HARPAX: What Pseudolus are you talking about?

BALLIO: Your tutor; the man who taught you this trick, to steal my girl away from me with your dodges.

HARPAX: What Pseudolus? What dodges do you mean? I don't know the man from Adam.

BALLIO: Get out! There's no profit here today for sharpers. Go tell Pseudolus that someone else has taken the booty off, the Harpax who got here first.

HARPAX: But I'm Harpax myself, I tell you.

BALLIO: You mean, you're pretending to be Harpax. (*To* SIMO) He's an impostor pure and simple.

HARPAX: I gave you the money, and when I was here before I gave the token to your slave, a letter sealed with the image of my master, right here before the door.

BALLIO: You gave a letter to my slave? What slave?

HARPAX: Surus.

BALLIO: This swindler hasn't much confidence in his flimflam; he's got his story twisted. But by God! That rascal Pseudolus! How cleverly he's made up this ruse. He's given this chap just the sum the soldier owed and dressed him up to take away the girl. (*To* HARPAX) The real Harpax brought me that letter.

HARPAX (*with increasing indignation*): I'm called Harpax; I'm the slave of that Macedonian soldier; I have nothing to do with swindling and wickedness; and as for your Pseudolus, I don't know who the fellow is.

SIMO (*impressed*): Well, pimp, I'll be much surprised if you haven't lost the girl completely.

BALLIO (*worried*): By God! I'm more and more afraid of that myself, as I listen to him. That Surus gave me cold shivers just a moment ago —the chap who took the token from him. I'll be surprised if it isn't Pseudolus. (*To* HARPAX) See here: what did the fellow look like you gave the token to?

HARPAX: A redheaded chap, with a pot belly, thick legs, dark complexion, large head, bright eyes, red face, and very big feet.

BALLIO: You ruined me, when you mentioned those big feet. It was Pseudolus himself! It's all up with me! Oh, Simo, I'm dying!

HARPAX: By God! I won't let you die until you pay me back the money —the twenty minae.

SIMO (*to* BALLIO): And there's another twenty minae coming to me.

BALLIO: What? Will you take away my cash, which I promised in jest?

SIMO: When you deal with rascals, the cash and carry plan is quite proper.

BALLIO: At least, hand Pseudolus over to me.

SIMO: Hand Pseudolus over to you? What's he done? Didn't I tell you a thousand times to look out for him?

BALLIO: He's ruined me.

SIMO: Well, he's cost me a mere twenty minae.

BALLIO: What to do now?

HARPAX: When you've given me my money, go hang yourself!

BALLIO: God damn you! Well then, come along with me to the forum;
I'll pay you.

HARPAX: I'm coming.

SIMO: What about me?

BALLIO: I'm paying off aliens today; I'll deal with citizens tomorrow.
Pseudolus certainly called a Grand Jury to sentence me to death today,
the way he sent that fellow to take the girl away. (*To* HARPAX) Come
along, there. (*To the audience*) Don't wait for me to come home by the
street here; the way things have gone I've decided to take to the alleys.

HARPAX: If you'd walk as hard as you talk, you'd be at the forum by
now.

BALLIO: I've made up my mind to turn my birthday into my deathday.
(BALLIO *and* HARPAX *go out to the forum.*)

Act Four.   Scene VIII

SIMO (*to the audience*): I certainly did a swell job on him, and it's a
swell job my slave did on his enemy. Now I've decided to set an ambush for Pseudolus—a different kind than they set in other comedies,
where they lie in wait for their slaves with whips and goads. I'm going
in to get the twenty minae I promised him, if he succeeded; I'll actually
bring it to him. The fellow's just too clever, too shrewd, and too sly.
Pseudolus has surpassed Ulysses and that trick at Troy. Now I'm going
in; I'll get the money, and lie in wait for Pseudolus. (*He goes into his
house.*)

Act Five. Scene I

(*Enter* PSEUDOLUS *very drunk, with a garland on his head.*)

PSEUDOLUS (*singing tipsily*): O feet, feet, wha's a matter now? Is this
any way to behave? Stand up, stand up, won't you? Ya' want me to
fall, and have someone pick me up here? If I fall down, it'll be all your
fault. (*Staggering wildly*) Still at it, eh? Ha! Wanna make me lose my
temper? (*To the audience, confidentially*) Tha's the trouble with
drinking: goes right to your—feet; trips you up, like a tricky wrestler.
Oh boy, oh boy! What a swell bender I'm having: choice food, everything so nice—fit for the gods; such a jolly place—and such a jolly
party. I'd better come right out with it, and tell you: this is what makes
a fellow in love with life. Here's every pleasure—everything charming.
It's just next to being a god, I think. When a chap's in love—and is
hugging his sweetie—when he presses lip to lip—when they snatch each
other's tongues with kisses—and don't hide it—when tender breasts are
pressed, and when the fancy takes you—bodies joined together—and a
fair white hand with a sweet tankard—drinking healths to love;[3] and
no one there to annoy you or pester you—no silly twaddle; perfumed
oil, incense, ribbons, lots of flowers, no expense spared—as for the rest
of the banquet, don't ask me! That's the way young master and I
have merrily spent the day, after I put across my job, just as I wished,
and put the enemy to flight. I left 'em lying there, still drinking and
petting with their wenches—left my own wench there too—all of 'em
giving themselves a swell time. But when I got up to go, they all begged
me to dance. I showed off for 'em with a few fancy steps—like this.
(*Staggers drunkenly around the stage*) I've had pretty good teaching,
you see—I'm an honour graduate of the Ionic School of the Dance.
Then I draped myself in my cloak—like this—strutted around like this
(*with a few suggestive movements*) —all in fun, ya' understand. Got a
big hand; they yelled "Encore!" so I'd come back again. I started up
again—with this step. (*Illustrating*) Didn't like it—still, I wanted to
show off to my sweetie, so she'd love me. I was whirling around when—
down I went! That killed the show! And while I was trying to get up—
whoops!—I all but ruined my cloak. Oh boy! The fun they got out of
my fall! They gave me the cup—I took a drink—changed my cloak—
took off that other one. Then I came out here, to walk off my jag. Now
I'm coming from master to my older master, to remind him of his bargain. (*Knocking at the door of* SIMO'S *house*) Open up! Open up! Hello!
Someone tell Simo I'm here!

Act Five. Scene II

(Enter simo *from his house, carrying a large sack of money.)*

simo: The voice of a complete rascal brings me out of the house. *(Looking at* pseudolus*)* But what's this? How now? What's this I see?

pseudolus: Your slave Pseudolus, be-garlanded and—be-drunken!

simo: Pretty free, upon my word! *(As* pseudolus *strikes a flippant pose)* Just look at that pose! Not the slightest bit of respect for me, has he? *(Aside)* I wonder if I should speak to him severely, or treat him gently. *(Looking at the sack)* But this burden of mine forbids me to use violence, if I can still hope for anything from him.

pseudolus *(staggering up to* simo*)*: This rascal comes to greet this honourable gentleman.

simo: God bless you, Pseudolus.

pseudolus *(belching violently)*: Ur-rp!

simo *(pushing him away)*: Go to the devil!

pseudolus: Why do you shove me?

simo: What the devil do you mean by belching in my face, you drunken sot?

pseudolus *(wrapping his arms around* simo*)*: Gently—please—hold me up; don't let me fall. Don't you see—how soused I am?

simo: What insolence! What do you mean by going around drunk, in the middle of the day, with garlands on?

pseudolus *(belching again)*: I—urp!—like to.

simo *(trying to push him away again)*: You like to, eh? You're going to keep on belching in my face, are you?

pseudolus: I've got a very pleasant belch. Just let me be, Simo.

simo: You scoundrel, I believe you could drink up four vintages of Massic wine in one hour.

pseudolus: Slight correction: "in a winter hour."[15]

SIMO: Not a bad suggestion. But tell me this: at what port did you fill up this tanker you're navigating?

PSEUDOLUS: I've been guzzling with your son. But, Simo—what a beauty of a job we did on Ballio! I've completed everything I said I would.

SIMO: You're a villain.

PSEUDOLUS: The girl's the cause of this; she's a free woman now, dining with your son.

SIMO: I know everything you've done, in full detail.

PSEUDOLUS: Why then so slow in giving me the money?

SIMO: Your claim is just, I admit. Here, take it. (*He holds out the sack.*)

PSEUDOLUS: You said you wouldn't give it to me, and still you are giving it. (*Turning his shoulder towards* SIMO) Just load me up and follow along.

SIMO (*indignantly*): I load you?

PSEUDOLUS: Oh, you'll load me up, I know it.

SIMO: What can you do with a fellow like that? Will he take away my money and laugh at me into the bargain?

PSEUDOLUS (*dramatically*): "Woe to the vanquished."[16]

SIMO (*reluctantly*): Well, turn around then.

PSEUDOLUS (*turning*): There. (SIMO *slings the sack over his shoulder.*)

SIMO (*falling on his knees*): I never thought I'd come to this, and play the suppliant to my own slave. (*Weeping*) Ow! Ow! Ow!

PSEUDOLUS: Stop it.

SIMO: I'm in pain.

PSEUDOLUS: If you weren't in pain, I'd be the one to be in pain.

SIMO: What? Will you take this from me, Pseudolus, from your own master?

PSEUDOLUS: Cheerfully, and with the greatest of pleasure.

SIMO: Won't you be kind enough, please, to let me off of some part of this money?

PSEUDOLUS: You won't call me greedy, will you? Because you'll never be a penny the richer from this money; you'd have had no mercy on my back if I'd not accomplished this trick today.

SIMO: A time will come when I'll get even with you, as sure as I'm alive!

PSEUDOLUS: Why threaten? I've got a back.

SIMO (*starting towards the house*): All right, go on!

PSEUDOLUS: Come back!

SIMO: Why should I?

PSEUDOLUS: Just come. I won't cheat you.

SIMO: I'm coming.

PSEUDOLUS (*magnanimously*): Come have a drink with me.

SIMO: I—with you?

PSEUDOLUS: Do as I say. If you come, you can have half or even more of this, (*patting the sack*) on my word.

SIMO: I'll go. Take me where you like.

PSEUDOLUS: What now? You're not angry, are you, at me or your son on account of all this?

SIMO: Not at all.

PSEUDOLUS: This way, then; I'll follow you.

SIMO: Why don't you invite the audience too?

PSEUDOLUS: Good heavens! They're not in the habit of inviting me, nor I them. (*To the audience*) But if you want to applaud and show your approval of the cast and the play, I'll invite you for tomorrow. (*They go out to the forum.*)

1. In the original there is a play on two meanings of *salus*, "greetings" and "safety."

2. It should be noted that the words in these two lines represent the formal stipulatio or verbal contract used by Roman business men.

3. The text is corrupt in this line.

4. Probably not the leader of the Argonauts, but a tyrant of Pherae in Thessaly, a district rich in grain.

5. These lines seem to refer to a recent financial crisis in Rome.

6. The *lex Plaetoria* made all men under twenty-five minors and hence contracts made by them were not binding.

7. Ballio complacently accepts the comparison with Jupiter, who was regularly appeased with the entrails of a lamb.

8. Pseudolus means that he'll go get two public executioners, who live outside the city gate, and have Ballio flogged to death with birch-rods.

9. These lines are possibly an interpolation.

10. Harpax means in Greek, "robber, snatcher."

11. The text is corrupt in these lines. Some editors read *dimissis pedibus*, "with outstretched feet," instead of *demissis pedibus*, "with downcast feet." Whatever the joke was, it now seems lost beyond recovery.

12. Polymachaeroplagides, "son of many a sabre blow," in the original.

13. The Palladium, an image of Pallas Athena (Minerva), was stolen from the citadel of Troy by Ulysses and Diomedes.

14. Hellebore was the ancient specific for insanity.

15. The Romans counted twelve hours from sunrise to sunset; the winter hours were shorter than the summer hours.

16. The famous remark of Brennus the Gaul at the ransoming of Rome in 390 B.C.

XVII
THE ROPE

Characters in the Play

ARCTURUS, *the speaker of the prologue*
SCEPARNIO, *slave of* DAEMONES
PLESIDIPPUS, *a young man in love with* PALAESTRA
DAEMONES, *an old man from Athens, now living near Cyrene, in Africa*
PALAESTRA, *daughter of* DAEMONES, *now owned by* LABRAX
AMPELISCA, *a young woman in the possession of* LABRAX
PTOLEMOCRATIA, *priestess of Venus*
FISHERMEN, *poor men from Cyrene*
TRACHALIO, *slave of* PLESIDIPPUS
LABRAX, *a procurer*
CHARMIDES, *an old man, friend of* LABRAX
SLAVE OVERSEERS, *belonging to* DAEMONES
GRIPUS, *fisherman, and slave of* DAEMONES

Acrostic Argument

R ight from the sea a fisherman a hamper drew;
U nlocked, it showed the tokens of his master's child;
D aughter she was, though servant to procurer vile,
E stablished, after shipwreck, as her father's ward—
N ow safe, though still unknown. At last, his daughter proved,
S he weds her erstwhile love, Plesidippus true.

INTRODUCTION

The Rope (the *Rudens*) is based on a Greek comedy by Diphilus. If not Plautus' masterpiece, as many claim, it deservedly ranks among the very best of his comedies. It is rich in both character and action, and its unusual setting gives it an atmosphere of romance and poetry utterly unlike any other Roman comedy. The play has often been likened in this respect to Shakespeare's *The Tempest*. Instead of the street scene in front of one or more houses, the action takes place on a lonely stretch of seacoast near Cyrene in Africa. In the background are a temple of Venus and the cottage of the aged Daemones. The play opens on the morning after a storm. There has been a shipwreck and one by one the survivors reach shore, first Palaestra, then Ampelisca, finally the pimp Labrax and his friend Charmides. By a curious coincidence this is the very spot where Labrax had agreed to meet Plesidippus, a young man in love with Palaestra. Labrax had broken his promise and had set out for Sicily with the girls and all his earthly possessions. The element of chance or coincidence should not be stressed here, however, for it is the god Arcturus (the speaker of the prologue) who is responsible for the storm; it is his will that evildoers like Labrax be punished.

The Rope is an excellent example of the recognition play. There is no intrigue and the interest resides primarily in the characters themselves and the difficulties which they must face. The desire of the unhappy maidens to escape from Labrax, their flight to the temple, the attempt of Labrax to tear them away, the assistance brought by Daemones—all this provides a serious basis on which are built many humorous scenes. A few of the scenes are perhaps superfluous or unnecessarily prolonged and there is occasionally inadequate motivation of the entrances and exits of the characters. But the action, as W. Y. Sellar states, "entirely enlists both the moral and the humane sympathies. There is imaginative as well as humorous originality in the soliloquies of Gripus, and in his altercation with Trachalio; and a sense of sardonic satisfaction is experienced in contemplating the plight of Labrax (a weaker and meaner villain than Ballio) and his confederate chattering with cold and bewailing the loss of their illgotten gains." A sentiment of natural piety pervades the drama. The helplessness and innocence of the two girls, the

847

compassion of the priestess, Daemones' honesty, and the faithfulness of Trachalio are all on the same moral plane as Arcturus' speech in the prologue.

Gripus' amusing efforts to keep for himself the profits from his "hamper-fish" are thwarted by the desire of Trachalio and Daemones that Palaestra receive her lost property which will enable her to establish her real identity. Gripus is one of the most outstanding characters in Roman comedy. Plautus has portrayed with an expert hand his sudden hopes, and his despair and bad humour. The final scenes between Gripus and Labrax may be structurally unnecessary, as has often been noted, but they serve to pull together the loose threads of the play and to bring to an amusing conclusion one of Plautus' best works.

Modern adaptations of *The Rope* are Dolce's *Il Ruffiano* (1560) and Echard's *Rudens* (1694). One of the two plots of Heywood's *The Captives* (1624) is a close imitation of the Plautine comedy.

THE ROPE

(SCENE:—*A wild part of the African coast near Cyrene. In the background are two buildings, a small temple of Venus with an altar in front, and the cottage of* DAEMONES. *Cyrene lies off stage towards the left; on the right is the seashore.*)

Prologue

ARCTURUS: Compatriot am I, from the realms of the immortals, of him who shakes all lands and seas. I am, as you may see, a gleaming constellation bright; and ever in due season I rise. Arcturus am I called, both here and in heaven, and fair I shine at night among the gods; by day I pass the time with mortals, I and other signs that make their way to earth. Our supreme commander, Jove, doth station us about the world, to note the ways and deeds of men, their faith, their reverence, to give them aid. Whoso falsely swears, to win his suit, or forswears his obligations, his name is entered forthwith in Jove's book of accounts. And however great his perjured gains, the judge on high reopens the case, and reverses the decision; and now he loses more than in the courts of men he falsely made. And Jove knows each day whose heart desires the evil course. But virtue finds its name in another column entered. And the evil wretch who hopes by gift and victim to appease the god has his toil for his pains. For Jove cares naught for the perjured offering; while he who keeps faith will ever find leniency from him. One word of advice then, to those who know yourselves good, who keep faith with men and show reverence to the gods: stand steadfast, that hereafter you may reap due reward.

Now hear the reason why I've come. It was the poet's will that the town here be Cyrene; and here too, in a house on a farm hard by the sea, dwells Daemones, an old man far from his native Athens, whose exile here was through no fault of his, for his life was blameless. Rather does he suffer the penalty of a kindly heart, his property lost in the service of his friends. He had a daughter once, but the wretch who stole her, a mere child, sold her to a vile pander, who hither brought her. And now a youth from Athens, sojourning here, seeing her as she returned home from her music school, fell in love with her, approached her master, and for thirty minas bought her. And straightway he made ample deposit upon the purchase and bound the pander by an oath to complete the transfer. But that vile wretch, as one might know, cared no whit for plighted word or oath.

It chanced a friend of his from Sicily, old, vicious, a man who well his own country might betray, was visiting him. He praised the girl's beauty, and likewise that of the other women in the pander's train, and urged him to take them all to Sicily, where, thus he declared, men were so given to pleasure that such trade as his would reap great profit. He gained his point. A ship was chartered and all the pander had was secretly placed by night upon it. To the youth who had bought the girl, he told of a vow to Venus (note here her shrine) and bid him to a breakfast here; then clapped sail upon his ship, and cleared the harbour with his women, leaving it to others to let the youth know what had befallen. The young man, seeking him at the port, found the ship far out at sea.

Now I, when I saw the maiden's plight, thus stolen, brought aid to her, but ruin to the pander. With wintry blast I raged, and roughened all the surface of the sea. For know that I am Arcturus, of all the constellations none more fierce, whether at the rising, or when, at my course's end, in storm I hide my light. Look you now, both pander and his Sicilian friend cast forth upon the rocks, shipwrecked. But see, the young girl and a little maid, her friend, all trembling have leaped from the waves into a tiny boat, and the flood bears them landward from the rocks, towards this very cottage, where dwells the old man from Athens; his cottage too, and roof have suffered from the storm. The slave who now comes out is his slave, and soon you shall see with your own eyes the youth who bought the girl. Farewell now, and may your enemies give way before you.

Act One. Scene I

(*Enter* SCEPARNIO *from the cottage of* DAEMONES.)

SCEPARNIO (*to himself*): Ye gods! What a storm on the sea last night! And how the winds raised the roof! In fact, it was no mere wind, but what Euripides sent to Alcmena;[1] for see how all the tiles are loose or gone; and the storm has made new windows to let in light.

Act One. Scene II

(Enter PLESIDIPPUS *with three friends.)*

PLESIDIPPUS: I have brought you from your affairs, and yet have failed in what I sought; and the procurer we couldn't catch at the harbour. But I could not bear to lose my hopes through lack of effort, and so have kept you with me all this while. But I want now to visit this shrine of Venus, where he said he had a vow to pay.

SCEPARNIO *(to himself)*: If I'm wise, I'll be getting this confounded clay dug.

PLESIDIPPUS: Somebody's talking here.

(Enter DAEMONES, *from cottage.)*

DAEMONES: Hello, Sceparnio!

SCEPARNIO: Who's calling?

DAEMONES: The man who paid for you.

SCEPARNIO: Hm! You'll be calling me your slave next, Daemones.

DAEMONES: Well, we shall need a lot of clay, so dig the earth up thoroughly. I see the whole house will have to be patched over—hm! "whole" is good; it's all holes.

PLESIDIPPUS *(advancing)*: Good morning, good father—and to both of you.

DAEMONES: Good morning, sir.

SCEPARNIO: I say, are you a man or a woman, to be calling him father?

PLESIDIPPUS: Why, I am a man.

SCEPARNIO: Then go look for another father.

DAEMONES: I did have a daughter once, you see, but I lost her when she was young; I never had a son.

PLESIDIPPUS: But the gods will surely give you—

SCEPARNIO *(interrupting, to* PLESIDIPPUS): Well, if you ask me, they'll surely give *you* the devil for coming here, whoever you are, to trouble those who've got troubles of their own.

PLESIDIPPUS: Do you live here?

SCEPARNIO: What do you want to know for? Looking up places to rob?

PLESIDIPPUS: That slave of yours must be a privileged character, to talk so much in the presence of his master, and to address a gentleman so uncivilly.

SCEPARNIO: And you must be a bold, nervy fellow, to be butting into other people's houses, where no one owes you anything.

DAEMONES: Keep quiet, Sceparnio. (*To* PLESIDIPPUS) What is it you wish, young man?

PLESIDIPPUS: Well first, a curse on this fellow for not letting his master get in a word first. But, if it is not too much trouble, I should like to ask you a few questions.

DAEMONES: Certainly, although you find me in the midst of work.

SCEPARNIO: Say, why don't you go down to the marsh instead, while the weather's clear, and cut reeds to thatch the house?

DAEMONES: Be quiet. (*To* PLESIDIPPUS) If I can be of assistance, let me know.

PLESIDIPPUS: Please tell me whether you have seen a rascally looking chap, with curly, grey hair, a false, fawning sort of a scoundrel.

DAEMONES (*bitterly*): I've seen many of that breed, and it's thanks to such that I lead an unhappy life.

PLESIDIPPUS: I mean *here*—a man who was bringing two women with him to the shrine of Venus, to offer a sacrifice either yesterday or today.

DAEMONES: Emphatically not. I've seen no one sacrificing here for several days, and it would be impossible to do so without my knowledge. For they are always asking at the house for water, or coals, or a knife, or a spit, or a dish, or something—in fact one would think my utensils and well belonged to Venus and not to me.

PLESIDIPPUS: You pronounce death sentence upon me by those words.

DAEMONES: Not I, sir; you may live as long and happily as you wish, as far as I am concerned.

SCEPARNIO: I say, you, who make the rounds of the temples to get your belly full, why don't you have your meals served at home?

DAEMONES: Perhaps you've been invited here to a breakfast, and he who invited you hasn't come?

PLESIDIPPUS: Exactly.

SCEPARNIO: There's no harm, then, in your going home without break-fast. You ought to pray to Ceres rather than to Venus; for she gives you grub, and Venus only love.

PLESIDIPPUS (*to his friends*): That scoundrel, Labrax, has fooled me shamefully.

DAEMONES: By the gods! Sceparnio, what's that crowd down by the shore?

SCEPARNIO: That's a party invited to a farewell breakfast, I should say.

DAEMONES: How so?

SCEPARNIO: Because they took their bath after dinner yesterday, a sea-bath that is, and so are ready for lunch today.

DAEMONES: Their ship has been wrecked on the sea.

SCEPARNIO: That's true; but so has our house been wrecked on land, by Jove, and the roof too.

DAEMONES: Ah, poor creatures! See how they swim from the wreck!

PLESIDIPPUS: Where are they, pray?

DAEMONES: Off here to the right, along the shore.

PLESIDIPPUS: I see. (*To his friends*) Come on. I hope the man we're looking for is there, curse him. (*To the others*) And you, farewell. (PLESIDIPPUS *and friends hurry off towards the shore.*)

SCEPARNIO: We can fare well without any help from you. But holy Palaemon, partner of Neptune and Hercules, what a sight!

DAEMONES: What do you see?

SCEPARNIO: Two women sitting alone in a little skiff. How the poor things are tossed about! Good! Good for you! That's fine! The waves have driven the boat off the rocks towards the shore; a pilot couldn't have done better. I never saw the sea so high; but they're safe, if they escape the breakers. Now, now's the danger. One of them is overboard, but she's in shallow water, and will easily get out. Oh, great! Did you see how the waves washed her out? But she's up and coming this way. It's all right now. But the other has jumped from the boat. She's so frightened, she's down on her knees in the waves. No, she's safe now, and out of the water. There, she is safe on the shore. But she's turning now towards the right, to sure death. Oh, she'll be lost there.

DAEMONES: Well, that's no concern of yours.

SCEPARNIO: If she falls down on those rocks where she's headed, it will be the last of her wanderings.

DAEMONES: See her, Sceparnio, if you're going to have your dinner at their expense this evening, it's all right to worry about them; but if you eat here, I want you to get to work.

SCEPARNIO: All right; that's a fair demand.

DAEMONES: Follow me then.

SCEPARNIO: I'm coming. (DAEMONES *and* SCEPARNIO *go into the cottage.*)

Act One.   Scene III

(*Enter* PALAESTRA, *wet and exhausted.*)

PALAESTRA (*to herself*): Ah, how much more bitter is life than the tales men weave about it. And here am I, left like this (*looks at her dress*), in terror, cast upon an unknown shore, at the will of heaven. Was it for this I was born? Is this the reward of a life without offence? If in piety to parents or to gods I have been lacking, this would be no injustice. But if exactly in this I have been most careful, then you are wrong, immortals, and most unfair. For how will you repay hereafter the impious, if so you honour the innocent? I should not feel so sorry for myself, if either my parents or I were to blame. But it's my vile master, and his impiety, that have got me into this trouble. Well, he has lost everything, his ship included; I am the last remains of his fortune. She who was with me on the boat is gone; I am alone. If only she were left, it would not be so hard. Where shall I turn for help? Alone, by lonely sea and rocks, meeting no one, what I wear my only fortune; no roof, no food, why should I hope to live? Will there be no one who lives nearby to show me a road or pathway out, to relieve me from my uncertainties? Cold, and fear, and all distractions overwhelm me. My poor parents, you know not how wretched is your daughter—in vain born free; for how am I other than slave, or of what help have I ever been to you? (*She sinks down exhausted.*)

Act One. Scene IV

(*Enter* AMPELISCA, *in the same state of exhaustion, from another part of the shore. She does not see* PALAESTRA.)

AMPELISCA (*to herself*): What better can I do than end it all with death? So wretched I am, so consumed by anxiety! I care no longer to live; I have no hope. All the shore along I have searched, and the undergrowth; calling, looking, listening; but no trace of her. And there is none to ask, and I know not where to turn. There never was desert so deserted as this spot. And yet, if she lives, while I live, I shall never stop until I find her.

PALAESTRA (*rising*): Whose voice is that so near? I am afraid.

AMPELISCA: Who's speaking there?

PALAESTRA: Oh, dear hope, do not forsake me.

AMPELISCA: Away from me, fear!

PALAESTRA: It's surely a woman's voice.

AMPELISCA: It's a woman; it's a woman speaking.

PALAESTRA: Can it be Ampelisca?

AMPELISCA: Oh, is it you, Palaestra?

PALAESTRA: Why don't I call out her name? (*She calls*) Ampelisca!

AMPELISCA: Who is it?

PALAESTRA: It's I, Palaestra.

AMPELISCA: Oh, where are you?

PALAESTRA: Alas, I am in deep trouble.

AMPELISCA: In that I am with you, but I long to see you.

PALAESTRA: That is my one wish too.

AMPELISCA: Then let our voices lead our steps. (*Calling*) Now where are you?

PALAESTRA: Here; come over to me.

AMPELISCA: How eagerly I come. (*Crosses quickly over to* PALAESTRA.)

PALAESTRA (*almost too overcome to stand*): Your hand!

AMPELISCA: Take it.

PALAESTRA: Tell me; is it you, and alive?

AMPELISCA: At last I have the will to live, now that I can hold you—or do I hold you? Take me to your arms. My only hope for life is the comfort you give me.

PALAESTRA: How quick you are to outstrip me; your words speak all my thought. Now we have only to leave this place.

AMPELISCA: But how? By what path?

PALAESTRA: We'll follow the shore.

AMELISCA: I'll follow you anywhere. Shall we go as we are, with our clothing drenched?

PALAESTRA: We shall endure what we must. (*Stopping suddenly*) But do see there, my dear Ampelisca!

AMPELISCA: What?

PALAESTRA: Don't you see the shrine?

AMPELISCA: Where?

PALAESTRA: Back, to the right.

AMPELISCA: I see—a place worthy of the gods.

PALAESTRA: Some one must live near by; it's such a charming spot. (*They advance supplicatingly to the altar, by which they kneel*) To this divinity, whoever he be, I pray for help from their troubles, for two poor women in want and despair.

Act One. Scene V

(*Enter* PTOLEMOCRATIA, *aged priestess of Venus, from the temple.*)

PTOLEMOCRATIA: Who asks a boon here of my patron goddess? I heard the voice of supplication. They entreat a patron kind and indulgent, who does not grudge her favours.

PALAESTRA: We give you greetings, mother.

PTOLEMOCRATIA: My greetings to you, maidens; and whence come ye in your dripping weeds, so dismally clad?

PALAESTRA: From the sea nearby; but far away is the port from which we sailed.

PTOLEMOCRATIA: You journeyed then over the darkling paths of ocean on the sea-swung wooden steed?

PALAESTRA: Yes, mother.

PTOLEMOCRATIA: It is scarce seemly to approach the shrine as you are, without white garments or victims.

PALAESTRA: I pray you, where should we, but lately cast up from the sea, find victims? (*They embrace the priestess' knees*) Behold, we who clasp your knees are strangers in an unknown land, hopeless, and in want; we pray for protection and shelter. Take pity on those who need it; we have lost our all, our goods, our homes, our hope even.

PTOLEMOCRATIA: Do not kneel; give me your hands. No one ever had a heart more compassionate than mine. But you will find me poor. My service of Venus here gives me barely enough to support life.

AMPELISCA: This is a shrine of Venus, then?

PTOLEMOCRATIA: It is, and I am her priestess. But all I have is at your service. Come with me.

PALAESTRA: You honour us most generously, mother.

PTOLEMOCRATIA: It is my duty. (*All go into the temple.*)

Act Two.   Scene I

(*Enter three* FISHERMEN, *roughly clad, carrying rod and line. They chant their chorus in unison.*)

FISHERMEN: In all ways poor folk have a sorry lot,
　　　　　　Especially they who lack both trade and skill.
　　　　　　The little that they have must them content.
　　　　　　Take us—from our equipment you can tell
　　　　　　How poor we are—these hooks and lines our all.
　　　　　　For wrestling and gymnastics we have this:
　　　　　　To exercise the while we fish the sea.
　　　　　　Sea-urchins, limpets, star-fish, mussels, shells,
　　　　　　Sea-nettles, fluted scallops, with our hands
　　　　　　We catch, and from the rocks, too, cast our lines.

Our larder is the sea, but when unkind
He gives no catch, ourselves, well cleaned and salt,
Are all the fish we carry sadly home,
While tired and supperless to bed we go.
Small hope for us today; the sea's too rough;
We've dined already, should we find no clams.
Our Lady Venus we'll now beg for aid.
(*They approach the shrine and pray.*)

Act Two.   Scene II

(*Enter* TRACHALIO *from Cyrene.*)

TRACHALIO (*to himself*): I've been careful not to pass my master on the way, for when he left a little ago, he said he would stop at the harbour, and that I should meet him here at the temple of Venus. (*Sees the* FISHERMEN) But good luck! Here's a chance to ask; I'll speak to these fellows. Good day to you, thieves of the sea, Messrs. Hooker and Shelly! How fare you, or, since you have no fare, how starve you, comrades of the empty gut?

FISHERMEN: We fare as our calling allows—hunger, thirst, and false hopes, fisherman's luck.

TRACHALIO: Have you seen, while standing about here, a bold, determined young chap, with a ruddy countenance? There were three men with him, wearing cloaks and swords.

FISHERMEN: There's been no one here like that, I know.

TRACHALIO: Well then, have you seen a frowning, big-bellied old Silenus, hobbling about on a stick; with a bald forehead and twisted eyebrows? A cheating, scoundrelly, vicious-looking devil, a plague of gods and men; with a couple of pretty girls with him?

FISHERMEN: A man of such character would better go to the gallows than to a temple of Venus.

TRACHALIO: But have you seen him?

FISHERMEN: He's not been here. (*Going*) Well, good day to you.

TRACHALIO: Good-bye. (*To himself as the* FISHERMEN *depart*) That's what I thought. I always suspected him. The rascally procurer has fooled us, and cleared out. He's sailed away with his women. I'm a wizard, I am. Didn't I say so all along? And then invited us here to breakfast, the cheat! I might as well wait now until the master comes. But perhaps the priestess will know something more. I'll go in and find out.

Act Two.   Scene III

(Enter AMPELISCA *from the temple.)*

AMPELISCA *(to those within)*: Yes, I understand—to knock at the cot· tage next door and ask for water.

TRACHALIO *(aside)*: Now whose voice is that?

AMPELISCA *(aside)*: Who's that man talking there?

TRACHALIO: Is that Ampelisca coming out of the temple?

AMPELISCA: Why, that's surely Plesidippus' man, Trachalio.

TRACHALIO: It is.

AMPELISCA: Of course it is. *(Aloud)* Welcome, Trachalio.

TRACHALIO: Well, well, Ampelisca, what are you doing here?

AMPELISCA: I'm passing most unhappily what should be my time of happiness.

TRACHALIO: Don't say that; it will bring bad luck.

AMPELISCA: If we are wise, we admit the truth. But tell me please, where is your master, Plesidippus?

TRACHALIO: As if he were not there with you!

AMPELISCA: Faith, he is not; he hasn't been here.

TRACHALIO: He hasn't?

AMPELISCA: It's the truth you're speaking.

TRACHALIO: That wouldn't be like me, would it, Ampelisca? But I say, when will the breakfast be ready?

AMPELISCA: What breakfast, pray?

TRACHALIO: Aren't you sacrificing here?

AMPELISCA: You're dreaming.

TRACHALIO: Your master, Labrax, certainly invited my master, Plesidippus, to a sacrificial breakfast.

AMPELISCA: Now, isn't that like him? To cheat both gods and men is in his line of business.

TRACHALIO: Neither you nor your master is sacrificing here?

AMPELISCA: Right you are!

TRACHALIO: Then what are you doing here?

AMPELISCA: We have suffered many misfortunes and have been in great danger and fear of our lives, and in our need we were welcomed by the priestess, Palaestra and I.

TRACHALIO: Is Palaestra here, the girl my master loves?

AMPELISCA: Certainly.

TRACHALIO: Oh, that's good news; my dear Ampelisca, that's splendid. But tell me about your hard luck.

AMPELISCA: Our ship was wrecked by the storm last night, Trachalio.

TRACHALIO: What ship? What are you talking about?

AMPELISCA: Haven't you heard how Labrax tried to carry us off secretly to Sicily, along with all his property? And now he's lost everything.

TRACHALIO: Good boy, Neptune! I always said you were a fine dicer; that was a master throw; you've dished the procurer. But where is the pimp?

AMPELISCA: Dead drunk, I think. Too many drinks of sea water last night.

TRACHALIO: Well, he didn't choose the drink, if there was water in it. Ampelisca, your words are a real treat; what a dear you are! But how did you and Palaestra escape?

AMPELISCA: I'll tell you. Although we were terribly afraid, we jumped into the little lifeboat, when we saw the ship making for the rocks, and quickly untied the rope; the men were too frightened to do anything. The storm drove our boat off here to the right. We pitched about in a rough sea all night, in the greatest distress, until the wind at last drove us ashore; we were nearly dead, I can tell you.

TRACHALIO: I know; that's the way of the old sea-dog; Neptune is some market-inspector, when he gets started—he throws out any goods he doesn't like.

AMPELISCA: Get out now; don't be impudent.

TRACHALIO: Apply that to yourself, please. I told you so! I knew the pimp would be acting that way. I think I'll let my hair grow, and set up for a prophet.

AMPELISCA: Well, if you knew so much, why didn't you and your master prevent his getting away?

TRACHALIO: What should he have done?

AMPELISCA: What should he have done? He should have been on the watch day and night. But on my word, I think his care was the exact measure of his regard for her.

TRACHALIO: What do you mean?

AMPELISCA: It's clear enough.

TRACHALIO: See here, Ampelisca; when a man goes to the bathhouse, no matter how sharply he watches out, he sometimes loses his clothing. It's hard to catch the thief when you don't know whom to suspect. But take me to her.

AMPELISCA: Just go into the temple; you'll find her sitting by the statue of Venus, in tears.

TRACHALIO: Oh, that's too bad; what is she crying for?

AMPELISCA: I'll tell you. She had a little casket containing the tokens of identification by which she hoped sometime to find her father. The procurer had taken this from her, and now she's afraid it's lost; that's why she is so distressed.

TRACHALIO: Where was the casket?

AMPELISCA: On the ship with him; he had locked it away in his luggage, just to make sure she shouldn't find her father.

TRACHALIO: What a scurvy trick, to try to keep in slavery a girl who by rights should be free.

AMPELISCA: And now it's gone to the bottom, along with all his gold and silver.

TRACHALIO: Some one has probably gone in by this time and got it.

AMPELISCA: That's why she's so sad; it's the loss of her tokens.

TRACHALIO: All the more reason for my consoling her. She shouldn't distress herself so; things are always happening to people beyond their expectations.

AMPELISCA: And on the other hand, so many people indulge in false hopes.

TRACHALIO: The more need then of keeping up your spirits in the face of troubles. I'll go in, unless you've something else in mind.

AMPELISCA: Go; meanwhile I'll get the water from the house here, as the priestess wished. (*To herself as* TRACHALIO *goes into the temple*) She said they would give it, if I asked in her name. There never was a woman who deserved better of gods and men. How sweetly and kindly and generously she received us, like daughters; and we were so destitute, wet, dejected, and frightened. And then the way she tucked up her dress and warmed the water for our bath! I must not keep her waiting; it's high time to get the water. (*Knocks at door of cottage*) Hello, is there any one at home? Won't some one come to the door? Is anyone coming out?

Act Two. Scene IV

(Enter SCEPARNIO *from the cottage.*)

SCEPARNIO: Who's battering in the door?

AMPELISCA: It is I.

SCEPARNIO: I say! Here's luck. On my word, a likely wench!

AMPELISCA: Good day to you, young man.

SCEPARNIO: A very good day to you, young lady.

AMPELISCA: I was coming to your house.

SCEPARNIO: I'd treat you royally, if you'd only come a little later; I'm busy this morning. But what a pretty baggage it is! (*Chucking her under the chin*) There's a dear!

AMPELISCA: Not so familiar, *if* you please.

SCEPARNIO: By gad, she's a love—a twinkle in the eye, too. A sweet confection—complexion, I mean! And some figure! And a classy little mouth, to top it off!

AMPELISCA: I'm no dish for the village, young man; kindly keep your hands off.

SCEPARNIO: But a sweet kiss for a sweet girl is surely not amiss.

AMPELISCA: None of your merry pranks now, if you please; there will be time for that later, perhaps. Will you give me what I'm sent for? Say yes or no.

SCEPARNIO: What do you want?

AMPELISCA: You can tell by looking at me what I want. (*Holds out her pitcher.*)

SCEPARNIO: Yes, and you can tell by looking at me what I want.

AMPELISCA: The priestess has asked me to get water from your house.

SCEPARNIO: But I'm the king around here, and if you don't beg very prettily, not a drop will you get. I had to work hard on that well, at some risk, and the water will not come without rare coaxing.

AMPELISCA: Why do you refuse to give what any enemy would give to another?

SCEPARNIO: And why do you refuse to give what any friend would give to another—a bit of encouragement?

AMPELISCA: Very well, my dear; anything you want.

SCEPARNIO (*aside*): Oh, joy! She calls me her dear. (*Aloud*) You shall have your water; it shall never be said a lady loved me in vain. Give me the pitcher.

AMPELISCA: Here; hurry now; there's a love.

SCEPARNIO: Wait here, my dear; I'll be back directly. (*He goes into the house.*)

AMPELISCA (*to herself*): What shall I say to the priestess for staying so long? (*Looks towards the sea*) Ah me, how I shudder every time I look at the sea. But what's that on the shore? Alas, my master, Labrax, and his Sicilian friend, whom I thought at the bottom of the sea, both of them! There's more trouble in store for us now than we thought. I'll fly to the shrine to let Palaestra know, that we may take refuge at the altar before the villain comes and carries us off. Run, Ampelisca; the crisis is at hand. (*She goes into the temple.*)

Act Two.   Scene V

(*Enter* SCEPARNIO *from the cottage.*)

SCEPARNIO (*to himself*): Gad, I never knew there was so much pleasure in mere water. How I enjoyed filling the pitcher! The well didn't seem deep at all today; it came up easy. What a devil of a fellow I am, to start this love affair today! (*Aloud*) Here's your water, dearie; I want you to take it prettily, as I give it to you, so that I'll be pleased with you— Where is the jade? Come now, take the water, please. Where are you? By Jove, she must be in love with me! The little witch wants to play peek-a-boo. I say, where are you? Won't you be taking the water now? You're pretending very nicely to be afraid of me; but seriously, will you please take the pitcher? Where in the world is she? By Jove, I can't see her anywhere; she's making fun of me. I'll just set this pitcher down in the middle of the road. But what if it should be stolen? It's sacred to Venus. That would get me into a pretty pickle. I'm afraid it's a frame-up to get me caught with stolen goods. I'd get a proper jail sentence, if I were seen with it. The inscription on it would give me away. I'll just go up to the door and call the priestess out, and let her take it. (*Calls aloud*) If you please, Ptolemocratia! Will you take your pitcher, left with me by some woman from the temple? Oh, I'll have to go in with it. I've found a job with a vengeance, if I've got to carry their water for them. (*He goes into the temple.*)

Act Two.   Scene VI

(*Enter* LABRAX, *followed by* CHARMIDES, *wet and shivering.*)

LABRAX (*to himself*): If you want to be a beggar and down on your luck, just trust yourself to Neptune; after a mixup with him you will look like this. (*Looks at his clothing*) By Jove, Liberty, you were a bright lass, never to set foot on ship with your pal, Hercules.[2] But where's that friend of mine who played the devil with me so? (*Looking back*) Here he comes.

CHARMIDES: Where in the deuce are you going in such a hurry, Labrax? This pace is too swift for me.

LABRAX: I wish you'd been hanged in Sicily before I ever set eyes on you. All this trouble comes from you.

CHARMIDES: I wish the day you were bringing me to your house, I had slept in jail instead. I hope to heaven that after this, all your guests will be like yourself; it's no place for an honest man.

LABRAX: It was bad luck I had for a guest, when you came. I was a cursed fool when I listened to you. Why did we go away, or get on the ship, where I lost all I had—and more, too?

CHARMIDES: Any ship would sink that carried a rogue like you, and your rogue's fortune.

LABRAX: You got me in bad with your flatteries.

CHARMIDES: That last dinner I had with you was worse than the one served up to Thyestes.[3]

LABRAX (*coughing*): I feel sick myself; hold my head, will you?

CHARMIDES: I hope you'll cough your lungs up.

LABRAX: O Palaestra, Ampelisca, where are you?

CHARMIDES: They're food for the fishes at the present moment.

LABRAX: It's your fault I'm a beggar; it's all from listening to you and your big lies.

CHARMIDES: On the contrary, it's due entirely to me that a man as flat as you has had a little salt put in him.

LABRAX: Will you get to hell out of here?

CHARMIDES: I'll just return that advice; go to the devil yourself.

LABRAX: Was there ever a man had worse luck than I?

CHARMIDES: I have; much worse.

LABRAX: How do you make that out?

CHARMIDES: Because you deserve it, and I do not.

LABRAX (*going up to bulrushes growing near*): O enviable, water-shedding bulrush, I would I were as dry as thou!

CHARMIDES (*his teeth chattering*): Brr! I'm trembling for a skirmish; even my words are jumping about.

LABRAX: Yes, confound it, Neptune does run a cold bathhouse. With all my clothes on I'm cold.

CHARMIDES: He doesn't even serve hot drinks when you go out; nothing but ice-water.

LABRAX: Lucky fellows, these blacksmiths; they've always got a fire.

CHARMIDES: Well, I'd like to be a duck myself, so as to be dry after coming out of the water.

LABRAX: I think I'll go to the country fairs and hire out as an ogre.[4]

CHARMIDES: Why so?

LABRAX: Because I'd need no hinge to work my jaws; my chattering teeth would do it.

CHARMIDES: Do you know, I deserved to be cleaned out in this deal.

LABRAX: Why?

CHARMIDES: For daring to get into a boat with a Jonah like you; you're enough to stir up any sea.

LABRAX: It all came from listening to you. Didn't you promise me that a man could pile up wealth there in my business?

CHARMIDES: Did you expect, like a greedy shark, to swallow up the whole island of Sicily?

LABRAX: Well, I'd like to know what shark swallowed up my hamper, with all my gold and silver stored away in it.

CHARMIDES: Probably the same one that got mine, with a purse full of money.

LABRAX: All I've got left is this one shirt and cloak. Oh, dear, dear, dear!

CHARMIDES: Well, I'm your partner in that, on even shares.

LABRAX: If I could at least have saved my girls, there'd be some hope. If I ever meet that chap Plesidippus, who gave me part payment for Palaestra, I'll catch it. Oh-h-h!

CHARMIDES: What are you crying about? As long as you've a tongue in your head, you'll never get caught.

Act Two. Scene VII

(Enter SCEPARNIO *from the temple.)*

SCEPARNIO *(to himself)*: What a to-do is this? With two young women in the temple weeping, and clasping the statue of the goddess, frightened out of their wits at somebody or other; shipwrecked last night, and cast up on the shore today, they say.

LABRAX: Look here, young man, where are those two young women you are talking about?

SCEPARNIO: In the temple.

LABRAX: How many are there?

SCEPARNIO: As many as you and I together would make.

LABRAX: They surely are mine.

SCEPARNIO: I surely don't know anything about that.

LABRAX: What do they look like?

SCEPARNIO: Not half bad; I could love either one of them, if I were drunk.

LABRAX: They're certainly the girls, aren't they?

SCEPARNIO: I know you're certainly a bore. Go and see them, if you wish.

LABRAX: My dear Charmides, those women of mine must be here.

CHARMIDES: A plague on you, whether they are or not.

LABRAX: I'll break into the temple. *(He goes into the temple.)*

CHARMIDES: I wish you would break into jail instead. *(To* SCEPARNIO*)* I say, friend, could you give me a place to sleep?

SCEPARNIO: Sure! Sleep anywhere here; it's a public road.

CHARMIDES: But see how wet my clothes are; can't you take me into the house, and give me others, while mine are drying out?

SCEPARNIO: Take this covering of mine; that's all I need to keep dry. If you want, I'll give you this. When I've got it on, the rain can't touch me. Just give me your clothes and I'll have them dried out.

CHARMIDES: See here, because I've been cleaned out by the sea, do you want to clean me out again on land?

SCEPARNIO (*angrily*): I don't care a fig whether you are cleaned out or steamed out. I wouldn't trust you with a penny, unless I had good security. Freeze or sweat, be sick or well; I don't care. I haven't any use for foreigners anyway. 'Nough said. (*He goes into the cottage.*)

CHARMIDES: Wait a moment! (*To himself*) He has no more sense of pity than a slave-driver. But why do I stand around in these cursed wet clothes? I'll go into the temple and sleep off the drinks I took so unwillingly last night. Like some of the Greek wines, we've had salt water poured into us, enough in fact to get us well diluted. If Neptune had treated us to one more drink, we'd be dead drunk now; it was with difficulty we got home from that spree at all. Now I'll go and see what my friend the procurer is up to. (*He goes into the temple.*)

Act Three. Scene I

(*Enter* DAEMONES *from his cottage.*)

DAEMONES: What a plaything of the gods we men are! What strange dreams they send us! Not even in our sleep will they give us peace. That was an uncanny dream I had last night—a she-ape trying to climb up to a swallow's nest; and when she was unable to reach the birds, coming to me and demanding a ladder. Then I remember my reply: that the swallows are descended from Philomela and Procne, and I begged her not to harm one of my compatriots. How fierce she became and seemed to threaten me, and called me to court. Whereupon, becoming suddenly angry, I seemed to seize her about the middle and thrust the vile beast into chains. But I can't get any inkling of what the dream may mean. But what's the racket, I wonder, in the temple?

Act Three. Scene II

(*Enter* TRACHALIO, *hastily, from the temple.*)

TRACHALIO: Men of Cyrene, farmers hereabout, neighbours, I beg you to bring aid to virtue and utterly confound villainy. Show that the power of the notoriously wicked shall not be greater than that of the innocent. Make an example of impudence, and put a premium on modesty. Prove that law is of more value here than mere force. All you who are within the sound of my voice, hasten to the shrine of Venus, I implore you, and help those who have entrusted their lives, as is their right, to Venus and her servant. Choke to death wrong and aggression before they lay hold upon you.

DAEMONES: What's the trouble here?

TRACHALIO (*running up to him*): By your knees, which I embrace, I implore you, good father, whoever you are—

DAEMONES: Let go my knees, and tell me what this uproar means.

TRACHALIO: —and entreat you, and beg you, as you hope this year for a good crop of assafoetida and silph, and for the safe arrival of your exports at Capua, and for freedom from sore eyes—

DAEMONES: Are you crazy?

TRACHALIO: —and for plenty of silph seed, be willing, aged sir, to grant my request.

DAEMONES: And I beg of you, by your legs and ankles, and by this back of yours, as you hope for a large harvest of rods upon it, and for a generous crop of punishments this year, tell me the meaning of all this commotion you are raising.

TRACHALIO: Why do you speak so harshly, when I hoped for fair words only from you?

DAEMONES: On the contrary, I speak you fair, since I wish for you what you deserve.

TRACHALIO: Then please attend to this matter.

DAEMONES: What is it?

TRACHALIO: There are two women inside who are innocent of all wrong and need your help. Contrary to law and justice, they are being infamously handled in the temple of Venus; and the priestess is no less shamefully mistreated.

DAEMONES: Who would dare offer violence to her? But tell me who the women are, and the wrong done them.

TRACHALIO: Just listen: they were clasping the very statue of the goddess, and this man has the audacity to take them away forcibly; and they both really should be free women.

DAEMONES: Who is it, who so defies the gods?

TRACHALIO: A cheat, a rogue, a murderer, a law-breaker without sense of shame or honour, a perjured scoundrel—in short, to describe him in one word, a procurer.

DAEMONES: A man like that deserves the severest punishment.

TRACHALIO: Yes, and he choked the priestess too.

DAEMONES: Well, by Jove, he'll pay for it. (*Calls his* SLAVE OVERSEERS *out of the cottage*) Come out there, Turbalio, Sparax! Where are you?

TRACHALIO: Now go in and help them.

DAEMONES (*shouting*): Don't let me have to call you again. (*Enter the* OVERSEERS *from the cottage.*) Follow me.

TRACHALIO: Have them smash his eyes in as the cooks do a cuttlefish.

DAEMONES: Drag him out by the legs like a butchered hog. (DAEMONES *and the* OVERSEERS *go into the temple.*)

TRACHALIO: I hear a racket; they're landing with their fists. I hope they knock the scoundrel's teeth out. But here are the women running out, scared to death.

Act Three.   Scene III

(*Enter* PALAESTRA *and* AMPELISCA, *in great fear, from the temple.*)

PALAESTRA: Now we are utterly lost; there is no help for us. All hope of safety has disappeared, and in our fright we know not where to turn. What outrage we have suffered from this vile master of ours, who has shamefully maltreated the priestess and dragged us from the very statue of the goddess. We can endure no more; death is the only resort from such misery.

TRACHALIO (*aside*): This is sad language; I must try to console them. Palaestra!

PALAESTRA: Who calls? Who is it?

TRACHALIO: Ampelisca!

AMPELISCA: Who's that? Who's calling me?

TRACHALIO: Look and see.

PALAESTRA: O Trachalio, you are our only hope.

TRACHALIO: Keep calm and don't make a noise; just leave it to me.

PALAESTRA: If only we can escape his violence! I should lay violent hands upon myself, rather than submit to that.

TRACHALIO: Don't be foolish.

PALAESTRA: There is no use in trying to comfort us with mere words. Unless you can give us real help, we're done for.

AMPELISCA: For my part, I'd rather die than submit to the procurer's anger. But my heart fails me when I think of death, and a chill fear creeps over my body at the very mention of it; I am only a woman. Ah, bitter, bitter day!

TRACHALIO: Keep up your courage.

PALAESTRA: Courage? Where shall we find it?

TRACHALIO: There, there; don't be afraid; sit down by the altar.

AMPELISCA: How shall the altar help us more than the statue of Venus, from which he tore us violently?

TRACHALIO: Just the same, sit down. I'll protect you from here. This altar will be your walled camp, your fortifications; and I'll be your defender. With the help of Venus, I'll resist the cunning of your master. (*Both girls kneel at the altar.*)

PALAESTRA: Kind Venus, to thee we hearken; and on our knees, embracing this altar, we beseech thee with our tears, that thou vouchsafe to help us. Punish the wicked who have set at naught thy sanctuary, and suffer us in peace to remain at thy altar. We were stripped of all we had by the storm last night. Hold it not against us, if thus unkempt we approach thy holy shrine.

TRACHALIO: I think that is a fair request, Venus, and that you should grant it. Their fears have driven them to it. If you came yourself from a sea-shell, as they say, you should not object to the soiled shell of their garments. But good! Here comes that excellent old man, your patron and mine.

Act Three.   Scene IV

(*Enter* DAEMONES *and the* SLAVE OVERSEERS *who drag* LABRAX *from the temple.*)

DAEMONES: Come out of the temple, most sacrilegious of men. And you (*addressing the women*), sit down by the altar. But where are they?

TRACHALIO: See! Here!

DAEMONES: That's good; that's what I wanted. (*To his* OVERSEERS) Tell him to come nearer. (*To* LABRAX) Do you think you can thus defy the gods in our presence? (*As* LABRAX *fails to move*) Give him a punch.

LABRAX: You'll pay for what I'm suffering.

DAEMONES: He dares to threaten us!

LABRAX: You are robbing me of my rights, and taking my servants against my will.

TRACHALIO: Choose as arbitrator any respectable man from the senate of Cyrene, and let him decide whether they should belong to you, or whether they ought not rather to be free women, and you oughtn't to be clapped into jail, to spend the rest of your life there, until you have worn the pavement through.

LABRAX: I don't propose to talk with a gallows bird; I'm talking to you, sir.

DAEMONES: Talk first with the man who knows you.

LABRAX: My business is with you.

TRACHALIO: It will have to be with me. You say these are your maid-servants?

LABRAX: They are.

TRACHALIO: Well then, just touch either one of them with the tip of your little finger.

LABRAX: What then?

TRACHALIO: Then I'll at once make a punching-bag of you, you per-jured scoundrel.

LABRAX (*to* DAEMONES): Can't I take my own girls away from the altar of Venus?

DAEMONES: You may not; that's the law here.

LABRAX: What have I to do with your laws? I'll take them both away at once. But, I say, old man, if you're in love with them, you may have them, for spot cash; or if they've found favour with Venus, she may have them, if she will pay the price.

DAEMONES: The gods pay money to you? Now understand me clearly; just start, even in joke, to offer them violence, and I'll send you away with such a dressing-down that you won't know yourself. And if you (*to* OVERSEERS), when I give you the signal, don't gouge his eyes out, I'll wrap the whip around your legs, as tightly as they wrap a bundle of sticks into a faggot.

LABRAX: This is forcing me.

TRACHALIO: And you reproach us with that, you sink of iniquity?

LABRAX: Do you dare, you double-dyed scoundrel, to speak uncivilly to me?

TRACHALIO: I'm a double-dyed scoundrel all right, and you are a highly moral party; but just the same oughtn't these women to be free?

LABRAX: Free?

TRACHALIO: Yes; and instead of your being master, they should be; for they come from the mother country, and one of them was born at Athens of free parents.

DAEMONES: What's that?

TRACHALIO: She (*pointing to* PALAESTRA) was born free and at Athens.

DAEMONES: Is she a compatriot of mine?

TRACHALIO: Aren't you from Cyrene?

DAEMONES: I was born and bred at Athens, and brought up there.

TRACHALIO: Then defend your fellow citizens, worthy sir.

DAEMONES: O my daughter, when I look upon this young girl, how I am reminded of what your loss makes me suffer! She who was taken from me when only three years old, if she now lives, would be like this girl, I know.

LABRAX: I paid their former owner for them, and it makes no difference to me whether they were born at Athens or Thebes, so long as they obey me.

TRACHALIO: Is it so, impudence? Are you, like a cat, to be pouncing on young girls stolen from their parents, to ruin them in your disgraceful profession? I don't know about the birthplace of this other girl, but I do know that she is far above you, you vile scoundrel.

LABRAX: Apply your abuse to yourself.

TRACHALIO: Shall we prove by the trial of backs which of us is the cleaner? If your back isn't cut into as many ribbons as a man-of-war has nails, I'm the worst of liars. Then, after I've looked at your back, you look at mine; and if it isn't clean and whole, so that any flask-maker would say it was a perfect hide for his business, what reason is there why I shouldn't baste you until I'm tired of it? What are you looking at them for? I'll gouge your eyes out if you touch them.

LABRAX: And just because you forbid me, I'll take them both off with me directly.

DAEMONES: What are you going to do?

LABRAX (*starting towards the cottage*): I'm going to fetch Vulcan; he's opposed to Venus.

TRACHALIO: Where's he going?

LABRAX: Hello there, any one here?

DAEMONES: By Jove, if you touch that door, I'll harvest a crop of hay on your face, with my fists as pitchforks.

OVERSEER: We don't use fire here; we live on dried figs.

TRACHALIO: I'll give you fire, if you'll let me apply it to your head.

LABRAX: I'll get fire somewhere else.

DAEMONES: What will you do when you have found it?

LABRAX: I'll make a big blaze.

DAEMONES: With which to burn the meanness out of yourself?

LABRAX: No; I'll burn these two alive at the altar.

TRACHALIO: And, by gad, I'll throw you by the beard into the fire, and when you're half-done give you to the vultures for food.[5]

DAEMONES (*aside*): When I come to think of it, this is the ape that in my dream tried to steal the swallows from their nest, against my will.

TRACHALIO: Do you know what I should like you to do, worthy sir? Guard these girls until I fetch my master.

DAEMONES: Go and get him.

TRACHALIO: But don't let this fellow—

DAEMONES: It will be at his peril, if he touches them.

TRACHALIO: Be on your watch.

DAEMONES: I will see to that; be off.

TRACHALIO: And don't let this fellow get away, for we are engaged to deliver him to the hangman today, or forfeit a talent of silver.

DAEMONES: Be off now; I'll take care of him until you return.

TRACHALIO: I'll be back shortly. (TRACHALIO *departs towards the shore.*)

Act Three.   Scene V

DAEMONES: See here, pander; would you rather keep quiet with a beating or without one, if you could choose?

LABRAX: I don't care a fig for what you say, old man. I'm going to take them away from the altar, in spite of you, or Venus, or Jove himself.

DAEMONES: Just touch them.

LABRAX: Sure, I'll touch them.

DAEMONES: Very well; try it.

LABRAX: Tell these fellows to retreat a bit.

DAEMONES: On the contrary, they will advance.

LABRAX: I don't think so.

DAEMONES: If they advance, what will you do?

LABRAX: Oh, I'll—retreat. But see here, old chap, if I ever catch you in town, if I don't have sport with you before you get away, never call me pimp again.

DAEMONES: Threaten away, but meanwhile, if you so much as touch them, I'll give you the devil of a punishment.

LABRAX: How much will that be?

DAEMONES: Enough for even a procurer.

LABRAX: A fig for your threats; watch me take them both in spite of you.

DAEMONES: Again I say, just try it.

LABRAX: I will, by Jove.

DAEMONES: Yes, you will; but do you know at what cost? (*To one of the* OVERSEERS) Turbalio, go into the house and get two clubs; run.

TURBALIO: Clubs?[6]

DAEMONES: Yes, and big ones; hurry now. (*To* LABRAX, *as* TURBALIO *goes into the cottage*) I'm going to give you the reception you deserve.

LABRAX: And I unluckily left my helmet on the ship; it would come in handy now. May I at least speak to them?

DAEMONES: You may not. Ah, here comes the cudgel-bearer.

(*Re-enter* TURBALIO *with two large clubs.*)

LABRAX: This means a tingling for my ears.

DAEMONES: Here, Sparax, take the other club. (SPARAX *obeys*) You stand here, and you there, one on either side; so. Now listen to me. If he lays a finger on them, against their will, and you don't give him such a reception that he won't know where he's at, it will be the end of you both. If he addresses either one, you reply for them; and if he tries to get at them, wrap your cudgels about his legs.

LABRAX: Won't they even let me go away?

DAEMONES: I've said enough to you. (*To the* OVERSEERS) And when that slave returns with his master, come into the house at once. I want you to show the greatest vigilance. (*He goes into his cottage.*)

LABRAX: I say, this temple's changing hands; it formerly belonged to Venus, and now Hercules is in charge. The old man has set up two statues of Hercules and his club! Now in very truth, I don't know which way to turn; everything's against me, on land, as well as on sea. Palaestra!

SPARAX (*gruffly*): What do you want?

LABRAX: Get out now; I protest. That was not my Palaestra who answered. Ampelisca!

TURBALIO: Look out for trouble.

LABRAX (*aside*): As well as they can, these cowardly fellows give me good advice. See here, you, will it cause any trouble if I go a bit nearer to them?

OVERSEERS: No—not to us.

LABRAX: To me?

OVERSEERS: Not if you take care.

LABRAX: Take care for what?

OVERSEERS: A sound beating.

LABRAX: But I entreat you to let me go closer to them.

OVERSEERS: Very well, if you wish.

LABRAX: Oh, that's good; I am much obliged to you. (*As he starts forward, they threaten with clubs*) No, no, I won't go; stay where you are. Oh, how wretchedly everything turns out! But I'll get them yet, if I have to lay siege to them.

Act Three.   Scene VI

(*Enter* PLESIDIPPUS *with* TRACHALIO, *from the shore.*)

PLESIDIPPUS: And the pimp tried to take my mistress away by force from the altar of Venus?

TRACHALIO: Exactly.

PLESIDIPPUS: Why didn't you kill him?

TRACHALIO: I had no sword.

PLESIDIPPUS: Why didn't you take a club or a rock?

TRACHALIO: Should I have stoned him to death like a mad dog?

LABRAX: The jig's up; here's Plesidippus. He'll mop up the earth with me.

PLESIDIPPUS: And were they still by the altar when you left?

TRACHALIO: They're there now.

PLESIDIPPUS: Who is guarding them?

TRACHALIO: An old man who lives next to the temple, and his slaves; I told him what to do.

PLESIDIPPUS (*advancing*): Take me to the pimp; where is he?

LABRAX: Good morning.

PLESIDIPPUS: I don't want any of your "good mornings". Make your choice quickly. Would you rather be taken away with a rope around your neck; or be dragged off by the heels? Decide while you can.

LABRAX: Neither.

PLESIDIPPUS: Run to the shore, Trachalio, and tell those men whom I brought that they're to meet me at the harbour, so we can take this fellow to the hangman. Then return and keep guard here. I'm going to take this rascal to court. (TRACHALIO *departs*) Come along with you.

LABRAX: What have I done that's wrong?

PLESIDIPPUS: Do you ask me that? Didn't you accept part payment from me for this girl, and then take her away?

LABRAX: I didn't take her away.

PLESIDIPPUS: Why do you deny it?

LABRAX: Because I only tried, but couldn't get her away, unfortunately. And besides, didn't I tell you I would be here at the shrine of Venus? Did I break my word? Aren't I here?

PLESIDIPPUS: Tell that to the judge; we've had talking enough. (*Throws rope over his head*) Come on here.

LABRAX: Help, dear Charmides; they're dragging me off with a rope.

(*Enter* CHARMIDES *from the temple.*)

CHARMIDES: Who's calling?

LABRAX: Don't you see how they're taking me away?

CHARMIDES: Yes, and glad to see it too.

LABRAX: Won't you please help me?

CHARMIDES: Who's taking you?

LABRAX: The young man, Plesidippus.

CHARMIDES: Make the best of a bad business, and go to jail cheerfully. In this way you will attain what many desire.

LABRAX: What's that?

CHARMIDES: The goal you've always headed for.

LABRAX: Do please follow me.

CHARMIDES: Your advice is as bad as you are; they are taking you to jail and you ask me to follow you.

PLESIDIPPUS (*to* LABRAX): Are you still holding back?

LABRAX: I'm lost.

CHARMIDES: I hope you are.

PLESIDIPPUS (*turning to the two women*): And you, Palaestra dear, and Ampelisca, remain where you are until I return.

OVERSEER: I suggest that they go to our house until you return.

PLESIDIPPUS: I like that; that's an excellent offer.

LABRAX: Oh, you thieves!

OVERSEER: "Thieves," is it? Jerk him along.

LABRAX: I beg of you, Palaestra!

OVERSEER: Come along, jail bird.

LABRAX: My friend!

CHARMIDES: I'm no friend of yours; I repudiate your friendship.

LABRAX: Do you so spurn me?

CHARMIDES: I do; I've had one drink with you already.

LABRAX: A curse on you then.

CHARMIDES: On your own head, rather. (PLESIDIPPUS *and* LABRAX *depart in the direction of* CYRENE. *The girls and the* OVERSEERS *go into* DAEMONES' *cottage*) I suppose men are changed into all sorts of animals, as the philosophers say. This procurer, for instance, will be turned into a stock-dove; his neck will shortly be in the stocks; and the jail will be his dove-cote. But just the same I'll go and act as his counsel, so that, if possible, he'll be the more quickly—sentenced. (CHARMIDES *departs.*)

Act Four. Scene I

(*Enter* DAEMONES *from his cottage.*)

DAEMONES: It's a pleasure to have done a good turn to these young women, and to have them as my wards, both young and pretty, too. But my wife, confound her, is always on the watch for fear I'll have some understanding with them. But I wonder what in the world that slave of mine, Gripus, is doing. He left last night to fish in the sea. He would have been wiser to sleep at home; the rough weather, last night and this morning, must have played the deuce with his fishing, and his nets, too. I can fry on my fingers all he'll catch, with a sea running like this. But there's my wife calling luncheon; I'll go and have my ears filled with her idle talk. (*He returns to the cottage.*)

Act Four. Scene II

(*Enter* GRIPUS. *From his shoulder he drags a net, in which is secured a traveling hamper. The hamper is tied about with a rope, one end of which goes, with the net, over his shoulder, while the other trails lengthily behind him.*)

GRIPUS: To Neptune, patron of fishermen, who dwells in the salt domain of the finny tribe, all thanks for this, in that he hath sent me back from his realms so well supplied, with so rich a booty, and my fishing-boat safe. In spite of rough seas, in strange and marvellous way, he has prettily enriched me with a haul the like of which none other has ever seen. And not a pound weight of fish have I caught this day, except what is here in this net. By rising in the middle of the night, I preferred gain to peaceful sleep, tried in the face of storm to relieve my poor master and my own slave's lot. I spared not myself. A lazy man is a man of nought, and I despise the tribe. He who would do his tasks in good season, should be awake, nor wait till his master stir him up. He who prefers sleep, takes his rest, to be sure, but without gain, and he suffers for it.

Now I, who have always worked hard, have found the means to be idle, if I will. For this, whatever it is, I have found in the sea; and whatever it is, it's heavy. There's gold without doubt; and no one knows about it but me. The time has come to be free, Gripus. I have a plan: I'll approach my master cunningly and shrewdly. I'll offer little by little small sums for my freedom. And when I am free, I'll have me an estate and house to match, my own property. I'll do merchandising in great ships, and be the mightiest of the mighty. And then for my own pleasure I'll build me a ship, and like Stratonicus[7] sail from port to port. When my fame is complete, I'll build a great city, and call it Gripus, a monument to my fame and fortunes. I shall then become king of the country. I have in mind to do mighty things. But first I'll hide this hamper. (*Starts towards the cottage and then stops*) To think that I, this great king, must go without dainties for my breakfast, and be content with sour wine, and salt for relish. (*Moves towards the cottage.*)

Act Four.   Scene III

(*Enter* TRACHALIO, *observing the hamper with interest.*)

TRACHALIO: Wait there.

GRIPUS: What for?

TRACHALIO: While I coil up this rope you're dragging. (*He begins to coil it up.*)

GRIPUS: Just let that go.

TRACHALIO: But I'm helping you; bread cast upon the waters, you know, always comes back—and that kind of stuff.

GRIPUS: The weather was stormy yesterday, and I haven't a fish; so don't expect anything. Don't you see I'm bringing back only a wet net, with no haul?

TRACHALIO: It isn't fish I want; but only a little talk with you.

GRIPUS: You bore me to death. (*Starts to go.*)

TRACHALIO (*grasping the rope*): You shall not go; hold on.

GRIPUS: You look out for trouble. What the devil are you holding me back for?

TRACHALIO: Listen.

GRIPUS: I won't.

TRACHALIO: By George, you will.

GRIPUS: Well, later.

TRACHALIO: No, now.

GRIPUS: What do you wish, then?

TRACHALIO: It will pay you to hear what I have to say.

GRIPUS: Then why don't you talk?

TRACHALIO: See if anyone's following us.

GRIPUS: Does that interest me at all?

TRACHALIO: Certainly it does. Could you give me a little good advice?

GRIPUS: Speak up; what is it?

TRACHALIO: Be quiet now—I'll tell you, if you'll pledge your word to keep faith with me.

GRIPUS: I will, whoever you are.

TRACHALIO (*impressively*): Listen.
   I saw a man steal something.
   I knew the man from whom he stole it.
   I went to the thief and made him an offer, like this:
   "I know the man from whom you have stolen;
   Divide the loot with me, and I'll not peach."
   But he wouldn't give me any answer.
   How much do you think I should get out of him?
   I hope you'll say "a half."

GRIPUS: On the contrary, more than half; and if he doesn't give it to you, I advise you to inform the original owner.

TRACHALIO: I'll follow your advice. Now pay attention, for this concerns you.

GRIPUS: Why so?

TRACHALIO: I've known for a long time the man to whom that hamper belongs.

GRIPUS: What do you mean?

TRACHALIO: And how it was lost.

GRIPUS: You do, do you? Well, I know how it was found, and I know the man who found it, and who now owns it. How does this fact concern you, any more than the other concerns me? I know whose it is now; you know whose it was before. No one shall ever get it from me; don't you hope to.

TRACHALIO: If the owner should turn up, wouldn't he get it?

GRIPUS: Don't fool yourself; there's no man alive that will ever own it except me, who took it in my catch.

TRACHALIO: Is that so?

GRIPUS: You'll have to admit, won't you, that the fish I catch are mine? I treat them as mine, and no one else ever claims them or any part of them. I sell them openly in the market as mine. The sea is surely common to all.

TRACHALIO: I admit that; but why then should this hamper not be common to me, as well as to you? It was found in the common sea.

GRIPUS: Of all the impudence! If what you say is true, it's the end of all fishermen. For as soon as they offered fish in the market, no one would buy. They would say they were caught in the common sea, and each demand his share.

TRACHALIO: Talk about impudence! Have you the nerve to compare a hamper with a fish? Do they seem the same thing to you?

GRIPUS: I'm not responsible for the catch; I drop in my net and hooks, and draw in whatever's caught. And all that comes in in that way is most decidedly mine.

TRACHALIO: Quite the contrary, by Jove, if what you've caught is a hamper.

GRIPUS: You're some sophist, you cutthroat!

TRACHALIO: But have you ever seen a fisherman catch and bring a hamper into market? You can't follow all the trades at once; you can't be a maker of hampers, and a fisherman at the same time. You'll have either to prove to me that a hamper's a fish, or else give up your claim to what's not raised in the sea, and has no scales.

GRIPUS: What! Have you never seen a hamper-fish?

TRACHALIO: There's no such thing, wretch.

GRIPUS: Sure, there is. I'm a fisherman, and ought to know. But they're rare, and you don't often land them.

TRACHALIO: Get out, thief. Do you think you can fool me? What colour is it?

GRIPUS: The smaller ones are of this colour. (*Points to hamper*) The big ones are red; and then there are some that are black.

TRACHALIO: I know; and you'll be turning into one yourself, if you don't look out; first your hide will be red, and then black.

GRIPUS (*aside*): What a rascal it is!

TRACHALIO: We're wasting time; the day's going. See here, at whose arbitration do you want this settled?

GRIPUS: At the arbitration of the hamper.

TRACHALIO: So?

GRIPUS: Yes, so!

TRACHALIO: You're a fool.

GRIPUS: My compliments, Philosopher!

TRACHALIO: You'll not get away with this today, without either a trustee or an arbitrator, at whose decision the matter will be settled.

GRIPUS: You must be crazy.

TRACHALIO: I do need hellebore.[8]

GRIPUS: I'm cracked, myself; but nevertheless I'll not let this go.

TRACHALIO: Say another word, and I'll beat your head in with my fists; I'll squeeze the juice out of you like a new sponge.

GRIPUS: Just touch me; I'll smash you to the ground like a jellyfish. You want to fight?

TRACHALIO: Oh, what's the use? Why don't we divide up instead?

GRIPUS: The only thing you can get here is trouble. I'm going.

TRACHALIO (*jerking him around by the rope*): I'll put the ship about, so that you can't go. Heave to, now.

GRIPUS: If you man the prow, I'll take the tiller. Avast on that rope, lubber!

TRACHALIO: Avast yourself; let go the hamper, and I'll let go the rope.

GRIPUS: You'll not be a penny the richer from coming here.

TRACHALIO: Well, you can't satisfy me by refusals; either give me a share, or else agree to an arbitrator or trustee.

GRIPUS: Even though I caught it in the sea?

TRACHALIO: But I saw it from the shore.

GRIPUS: It was my boat and net and work.

TRACHALIO: But if the true owner should appear, would I, who saw the act, be any less a thief than you?

GRIPUS: Not at all.

TRACHALIO: Wait then, you crook; how do you prove that I share in the theft and yet not in the booty?

GRIPUS: I can't say, and I don't know about your city laws; but I do know that this is mine.

TRACHALIO: And just as emphatically I say it's mine.

GRIPUS: Wait a minute; I've found a way for you not to share in the theft.

TRACHALIO: How?

GRIPUS: Let me go away; then you go away quietly. Don't you tell on me, and I'll not tell on you. You keep quiet, and I'll be mum.

TRACHALIO: Come, won't you make me an offer?

GRIPUS: I've made one: be off; drop that rope, and cease bothering me.

TRACHALIO: Wait until I make *you* an offer.

GRIPUS: Clear out instead.

TRACHALIO: Do you know anyone in these parts?

GRIPUS: I should know my neighbours.

TRACHALIO: Where do you live hereabouts?

GRIPUS: Off over there, by that further farm.

TRACHALIO: Are you willing that the man who lives here (*pointing to the cottage*) be arbitrator?

GRIPUS: Ease off on that rope a bit, while I step aside and consider.

TRACHALIO: All right.

GRIPUS (*aside*): By George, it's all safe now; this haul is mine for ever. He offers me my master as judge and my own home as the court; and *he* will never award a penny of that away from me. I'll accept him. This fellow doesn't know what he's offering.

TRACHALIO: Well, what do you say?

GRIPUS: While I know I'm absolutely in the right, yet rather than fight, I'll give in.

TRACHALIO: I'm glad to hear it.

GRIPUS: Although you are offering me an unknown arbiter, if he's an honourable man, a stranger is as good as one who is known; but even one's friend, if not honest, is utterly unsatisfactory.

Act Four. Scene IV

(*Enter* DAEMONES, *with* PALAESTRA *and* AMPELISCA, *from the cottage. The* OVERSEERS *follow.*)

DAEMONES: Seriously now, although I wish you very well, I fear my wife will drive me out of the house on your account; she will say I brought rivals in under her eyes. You must take refuge again at the altar, or I must.

GIRLS: Alas! We are lost. (*They go to the altar.*)

DAEMONES: I'll place you here in safety; don't fear. But (*to the* OVERSEERS) what are you following for? No one will harm them, while I am here. Go home, both of you; you're no longer on guard. (*The* OVERSEERS *go inside.*)

GRIPUS: Good morning, master.

DAEMONES: Good morning, Gripus; how are things?

TRACHALIO (*to* DAEMONES): Is he your slave?

GRIPUS: Yes, and not ashamed to admit it.

TRACHALIO (*to* GRIPUS): I've nothing to do with you.

GRIPUS: Then please leave.

TRACHALIO: Tell me, worthy sir, is he your slave?

DAEMONES: He is.

TRACHALIO: Well, I'm very glad he is. For the second time, I give you good day.

DAEMONES: Good day to you. Wasn't it you who left here, a little while ago, to fetch your master?

TRACHALIO: Yes.

DAEMONES: What do you want now?

TRACHALIO: But is he (*pointing to* GRIPUS) really yours?

DAEMONES: He is.

TRACHALIO: Well, I'm very glad.

DAEMONES: What's the trouble?

TRACHALIO: He's a rascal.

DAEMONES: What's the rascal done to you?

TRACHALIO: I want you to crack his shins for him.

DAEMONES: What is it you two are quarrelling about?

TRACHALIO: I'll tell you.

GRIPUS: Let me tell.

TRACHALIO: I'm doing this, I believe.

GRIPUS: If you had any shame, you'd get out of here.

DAEMONES (*to* GRIPUS): Pay attention, and keep quiet.

GRIPUS: Shall he speak first?

DAEMONES: Hear him. (*To* TRACHALIO) Speak on.

GRIPUS: Will you let an outsider speak first?

TRACHALIO: Can nothing shut him up? As I was about to say: this slave of yours has the hamper which belongs to the procurer you drove away from the temple.

GRIPUS: I don't have it.

TRACHALIO: Do you deny what I see with my own eyes?

GRIPUS: But I wish you couldn't see. What difference does it make to you whether I have it or don't have it?

TRACHALIO: It makes a great deal of difference whether you have it rightly or wrongly.

GRIPUS: You may hang me, if I didn't catch it in the sea, with my own net; how is it then yours rather than mine?

TRACHALIO: He's only bluffing; it's just as I tell you.

GRIPUS: What's that?

TRACHALIO: Can't you shut him up, until his betters have spoken?

DAEMONES: See here, what do you want?

TRACHALIO: I don't ask for any share in the hamper, and I haven't said it was mine. But there is in it a little casket, belonging to the woman I told you was freeborn.

DAEMONES: The one you said was a compatriot of mine?

TRACHALIO: Yes; and the trinkets which she had as a little child are in that casket inside the hamper. This is of no use to him (*pointing to* GRIPUS), but, if given to her, would help the poor girl identify her parents.

DAEMONES: I'll see that he gives it to her. (*To* GRIPUS) Be silent.

GRIPUS: By Jove, I'll not do it.

TRACHALIO: I ask for nothing but the casket and trinkets.

GRIPUS: What if they are gold?

TRACHALIO: That would not affect you. You will receive your equivalent, gold for gold.

GRIPUS: Let me see the gold first; then you may take the casket.

DAEMONES: Take care now; and keep quiet. (*To* TRACHALIO) Go on with what you were saying.

TRACHALIO: I entreat you to have pity on the poor girl, if the hamper does belong to the procurer, as I suspect; of course I don't speak from certainty.

GRIPUS: You see? He's setting a trap for us.

TRACHALIO: Let me continue. If it does belong to the pander, as I suggest, these two will be able to tell. Let him show it to them.

GRIPUS: Show it?

DAEMONES: That's not unfair, Gripus—to show them the hamper.

GRIPUS: On the contrary, it's most unfair.

DAEMONES: How?

GRIPUS: Because, if I show it to them, they'll of course say, at once, it's theirs.

TRACHALIO: You scurvy knave! Do you think everybody's like your-self?

GRIPUS (*to* TRACHALIO): I don't mind all this, so long as he's on my side.

TRACHALIO: He may be on your side now, but he's going to hear the evidence.

DAEMONES: Gripus, pay attention. (*To* TRACHALIO) State briefly your demand.

TRACHALIO: I've told you, but I'll tell you again, if you didn't under-stand. Both of these women, as I've just said, ought to be free. This one was stolen from Athens, when a child.

GRIPUS: What's it got to do with the hamper, whether they're slaves or free?

TRACHALIO: Are you trying to kill time, you piker, by having every-thing told twice?

DAEMONES: Stop your abuse, and answer my question.

TRACHALIO: There should be a willow casket in that hamper, in which are the tokens by which she can identify her parents; she had them when she disappeared from Athens, as I have told you.

GRIPUS: Oh, you be damned! Look here, you body-snatcher, what's the matter with these women? Are they dumb? Can't they speak for themselves?

TRACHALIO: They're silent because a woman is good when she's quiet, not when she's talking.

GRIPUS: Then you are neither man nor woman.

TRACHALIO: Why is that?

GRIPUS: Because, whether talking or quiet, you're never good. But (*to* DAEMONES) when will you give me a chance to say something?

DAEMONES: If you add another word, I'll break your head.

TRACHALIO: As I was about to say, sir, I wish you'd tell him to return the casket to them; and if he wants a reward, he shall have it. And let him keep the rest for himself.

GRIPUS: You're saying that at last, because you recognise my rights; a while ago you demanded a half share.

TRACHALIO: And so I do now.

GRIPUS: I've seen a hawk before this swoop down, and yet, like you, get nothing.

DAEMONES: Can't I shut you up except by a beating?

GRIPUS: I'll be quiet, if he will; if he talks, then let me.

DAEMONES: Give me that hamper, Gripus.

GRIPUS: I'll give it to you, but on the condition that it be returned to me, if these things are not in it.

DAEMONES: Very well.

GRIPUS: Here it is.

DAEMONES (*calling to the girls*): Palaestra, you and Ampelisca, listen carefully. Is this the hamper, in which you say your casket was?

PALAESTRA (*approaching*): It is.

GRIPUS: I lost out there; almost before she saw it, she said it was.

PALAESTRA: I will tell you all about it. There should be a wicker casket in the hamper; and I will name everything in it without looking. If I make a mistake, it will be my loss, and you may keep everything. If I am right, then please give it to me.

DAEMONES: Very well; that's mere justice.

GRIPUS: Mere injustice, by Jove. What if she's a witch, or fortuneteller, and knows everything in it? Will she get it just the same?

DAEMONES: She'll not get it without telling the truth; there's nothing in this fortunetelling business. Untie it, that we may know the facts as soon as possible.

TRACHALIO (*aside, exultingly*): That does for him!

GRIPUS: It's untied.

DAEMONES: Open it. (GRIPUS *does so*) I see the casket. (*Lifting it out*) Is this it?

PALAESTRA: It is. O my father and my mother! In this little box I hold you; here is my one hope of finding you.

GRIPUS: The gods must be angry with you for getting your parents into such a tight box.

DAEMONES: Step here, Gripus; your interests are at stake. And you, girl, keep back, and describe every article here; everything, remember. If you should make the slightest mistake, something you'd like later to correct, it will be in vain.

GRIPUS (*emphatically*): That's right.

TRACHALIO: Then it's nothing to do with you; for you're all wrong.

DAEMONES: Speak now, girl. Gripus, keep quiet, and pay attention.

PALAESTRA: There are tokens.

DAEMONES: Yes, here they are.

GRIPUS: Down and out in the first round! (*As* DAEMONES *begins to lift out tokens*) Stop! Don't show them to her.

DAEMONES: Describe them one after another.

PALAESTRA: First, there is a little sword of gold, with an inscription on it.

DAEMONES: What does the inscription say?

PALAESTRA: It gives my father's name. Next, there is a little double-headed battle-axe, also of gold, with my mother's name on it.

DAEMONES: Stop! What's the name of your father, on the sword?

PALAESTRA: Daemones.

DAEMONES (*in a low voice*): Good heavens! Where are my hopes now?

GRIPUS: Rather, where are mine?

TRACHALIO: Go on; don't stop.

GRIPUS: On the contrary, go slow—or go to the deuce.

DAEMONES: What's the name of your mother here?

PALAESTRA: Daedalis.

DAEMONES: The gods wish me saved.

GRIPUS: And me, ruined.

DAEMONES: This must be my daughter, Gripus.

GRIPUS: She may be, for all of me. But (*shaking his fist at* TRACHALIO) curses on you for seeing me, and on myself, for not looking around a thousand times before drawing the net out of the water.

PALAESTRA: Then there's a little silver sickle, with two hands clasped about it; and then a crane—

GRIPUS: The devil take you and your cranes—I think you're a cormorant, yourself.

PALAESTRA: And a gold amulet, that my father gave me the day I was born.

DAEMONES: Without doubt it is she; I can wait no longer. (*Holds out his arms*) Come to me, my daughter! I am Daemones, your own father; and your mother Daedalis is within the house.

PALAESTRA: O my father unexpected!

DAEMONES (*embracing her*): Find welcome in your father's arms.

TRACHALIO: It's a pleasure to see a daughter's piety so rewarded.

DAEMONES: Come, Trachalio, take this hamper, if you can, and carry it inside.

TRACHALIO (*to* GRIPUS): Here's a blow for you, Gripus; congratulations on your luck.

DAEMONES: Let us go, my dear, to your mother. She had more to do with you, and is acquainted with the tokens; and she will know the proofs better than I.

PALAESTRA: Let us all go in, as we have a common interest. Come, Ampelisca.

AMPELISCA: I am so pleased that fortune favours you at last.

(*All but* GRIPUS *go into the cottage.*)

GRIPUS (*to himself*): Am I not a blockhead to have fished up this hamper, or, having caught it, to fail to hide it? A troubled sea was certain to bring a troublesome catch; and it was sure full of gold and silver. I might as well go in and hang myself—for a little while, at least, until I stop feeling so bad. (GRIPUS *goes into the cottage.*)

Act Four. Scene V

(Enter DAEMONES *from cottage, much pleased with himself.)*

DAEMONES *(to himself)*: By the gods, was ever man more fortunate? I, who had neither hopes nor expectations, have suddenly found a daughter. When the gods wish us well, in some way our piety is rewarded by the granting of our hopes. And she shall marry this young man, of a good family, an Athenian gentleman, and, as it turns out, even a connection of ours. And I want his slave to summon him from town immediately. But I wonder where he is. I'll go to the door and see. Now look here—my wife with her arms still about her daughter's neck! There is almost too much of this affection; it's a bit boring.

Act Four. Scene VI

DAEMONES *(calling into the cottage)*: It's time to put a stop to the kissing now, and prepare for the sacrifices which I shall offer, as soon as I return, to the gods of this house for their aid to us; we have sacrificial lambs and pigs all ready. But why do you women keep Trachalio so long? *(A moment later)* Good; here he comes.

(Enter TRACHALIO.*)*

TRACHALIO: I'll find Plesidippus and bring him back with me, wherever he is.

DAEMONES: Tell him about my daughter; ask him to drop everything and come.

TRACHALIO: Sure.

DAEMONES: Tell him he's to marry her.

TRACHALIO: Sure.

DAEMONES: And that I know his father, and find him a connection of mine.

TRACHALIO: Sure.

DAEMONES: But hasten.

TRACHALIO: Sure.

DAEMONES: So that we may have dinner ready for him soon.

TRACHALIO: Sure.

DAEMONES: Are you so *sure* of everything?

TRACHALIO: Sure. But do you know what I want of you? To remember your promise, so that I may get my freedom today.

DAEMONES: Sure.

TRACHALIO: Persuade Plesidippus to free me.

DAEMONES: Sure.

TRACHALIO: And get your daughter to urge him; she'll easily have her way with him.

DAEMONES: Sure.

TRACHALIO: And have Ampelisca marry me, when I'm free.

DAEMONES: Sure.

TRACHALIO: And let me find you grateful.

DAEMONES: Sure.

TRACHALIO: Are *you* so sure of everything?

DAEMONES: Sure; I'm just returning in kind. But go quickly to the city, and be back again.

TRACHALIO: Sure; I'll be back immediately. You, meanwhile, attend to the rest.

DAEMONES: Sure. (TRACHALIO *departs toward the town*) The curse of Hercules be on him and his sureness. He has split my ears with his continual "sure" to everything I said.

Act Four.   Scene VII

(*Enter* GRIPUS *from the cottage.*)

GRIPUS: How soon may I speak to you, Daemones?

DAEMONES: What's the matter, Gripus?

GRIPUS: About that hamper—a word to the wise! Keep what the gods have given you.

DAEMONES: Shall I claim what belongs to another?

GRIPUS: But I found it in the sea!

DAEMONES: All the better for the man who lost it; it doesn't make it any more yours on that account.

GRIPUS: This is why you're poor, Daemones; you're too good.

DAEMONES: O Gripus, Gripus, we find many pitfalls in this life, and traps to ensnare us; and the bait is so cunningly placed, that while in our greed we reach for it, we are caught. When a man is very careful, and clever, he may enjoy for a long time that which is honestly his. But this appears to be plunder that will soon be plundered from you again, wherein you lose more than you get. Shall I conceal what you have brought here, when I know it belongs to another? Your master will never do that. The wise man will always find it best to have no part in another's wrong. I don't care for wealth gained by deception.

GRIPUS: I've often gone to the play and heard talk like that, with the audience applauding the words of wisdom. But when we went back home, no one acted on the advice he had heard.

DAEMONES: Hold your tongue, and don't be troublesome; you may go inside. I'll not give it to you; don't deceive yourself.

GRIPUS: I hope to heaven everything in that hamper, whether gold or silver, turns to ashes. (*He departs.*)

DAEMONES (*to himself*): That's the reason we have such dishonest slaves. If he had applied to one of his fellows, he would have implicated both himself and the other in theft. While he would think to gull some one else, he would himself be gulled; one act would bring on the other. But I will go in and sacrifice, and then order dinner. (*He goes into his cottage.*)

Act Four.   Scene VIII

(*Enter* PLESIDIPPUS *and* TRACHALIO.)

PLESIDIPPUS: Tell me that again, my dear Trachalio, my freedman, nay rather my patron, my father. Has Palaestra really found her parents?

TRACHALIO: She has.

PLESIDIPPUS: And is an Athenian?

TRACHALIO: I understand so.

PLESIDIPPUS: And will marry me?

TRACHALIO: I suspect as much.

PLESIDIPPUS: Do you think he will betroth her today?

TRACHALIO: I reckon.

PLESIDIPPUS: Shall I congratulate her father on finding her?

TRACHALIO: I reckon.

PLESIDIPPUS: And her mother?

TRACHALIO: I reckon.

PLESIDIPPUS: What is it then you reckon?

TRACHALIO: I reckon on what you ask.

PLESIDIPPUS: Do you reckon up the amount then?

TRACHALIO: Oh, I reckon.

PLESIDIPPUS: But I am here in person; so will you not close your reckoning?

TRACHALIO: I reckon.

PLESIDIPPUS: Would you say the same, if I ran?

TRACHALIO: I reckon.

PLESIDIPPUS: If I walked slowly, like this?

TRACHALIO: I reckon.

PLESIDIPPUS: Shall I salute her when I see her?

TRACHALIO: I reckon.

PLESIDIPPUS: And her father?

TRACHALIO: I reckon.

PLESIDIPPUS: And her mother, too?

TRACHALIO: I reckon. What next?

PLESIDIPPUS: Well then, shall I embrace her father when I see him?

TRACHALIO: I reckon not.

PLESIDIPPUS: Her mother?

TRACHALIO: I reckon not.

PLESIDIPPUS: But the girl herself?

TRACHALIO: I reckon not.

PLESIDIPPUS: The devil! He has stopped the review; just when I want him to go on, he puts an end to his reckonings.

TRACHALIO (*laughing*): What a fool you are! Come on.

PLESIDIPPUS: My dear patron, take me where you will.
(*They go into the cottage.*)

Act Five.   Scene I

(*Enter* LABRAX, *very disconsolate.*)

LABRAX (*to himself*): I am certainly the unluckiest man alive; I'm ruined, with the court deciding in favour of Plesidippus, and awarding Palaestra to him. Your procurer is the only real son of joy; he gives such joy to others, when he gets into trouble. I'll try at least to get the other girl away from the temple of Venus; she's all that's left of my property.

Act Five.   Scene II

(*Enter* GRIPUS, *carrying a spit; he talks to those within the cottage.*)

GRIPUS: You'll not see Gripus alive by evening, unless you return me the hamper.

LABRAX (*aside*): The devil! Every time I hear the word "hamper", it's like driving a stake through my heart.

GRIPUS: That scoundrel is free, while I, who fished the hamper out of the sea with my net, get nothing.

LABRAX (*aside*): That puts a flea in my ear, by Jove.

GRIPUS: I'll put up a sign, I will, with letters a yard high, telling anyone who has lost a hamper full of gold and silver to see Gripus. You'll not get away with that as you think.

LABRAX (*aside*): This fellow apparently knows who has my hamper; I'll speak to him. (*Approaching* GRIPUS) Help me, ye gods.

GRIPUS (*to those within*): What are you calling for now? I want to clean this, outside. (*To himself*) Jove! There's no iron left; it's all rust. The more I rub, the thinner and rustier it gets; it's bewitched, and dissolves in my hand.

LABRAX: Good day, young man.

GRIPUS: Lord bless you, you of the bald forehead.

LABRAX: How do you find yourself?

GRIPUS: Busy cleaning this spit.

LABRAX: How are you, I mean?

GRIPUS: Are you a doctor?

LABRAX: No, but I'm what comes from having one.[9]

GRIPUS: A beggar?

LABRAX: That strikes the nail on the head.

GRIPUS: Well, you look the part. What's happened to you?

LABRAX: Shipwrecked last night, and lost all I had.

GRIPUS: What did you lose?

LABRAX: A hamper full of gold and silver.

GRIPUS (*jumping up in great excitement*): Do you remember what was in the lost hamper?

LABRAX: What's the difference, now that it's lost?

GRIPUS: And yet—

LABRAX: Excuse me; let's talk of something else.

GRIPUS: Perhaps I know who found it. How can it be identified?

LABRAX: There were eight hundred gold pieces in it, in a purse, and a hundred Philippic pieces, in addition, in a leather bag.

GRIPUS (*aside*): Here's plunder for you; there will be a large reward. I'm a favourite of the gods, and will just annex this plunder. It's his hamper, all right. (*To* LABRAX) Go on with the rest.

LABRAX: Then you'll find a full-weight talent of silver, in a money-bag, and besides that, a drinking-bowl, a tankard, a pitcher, a jug, and a ladle.

GRIPUS: My, but you had a rich pile!

LABRAX: That's a miserable and cursed word, to say I "had."

GRIPUS: What would you care to give to the man who discovered this and showed it to you? Tell me quickly.

LABRAX: Three hundred drachmas.

GRIPUS: Stuff and nonsense!

LABRAX: Four hundred then.

GRIPUS: A dirty bagatelle!

LABRAX: Five hundred.

GRIPUS: An empty nut!

LABRAX: Six hundred.

GRIPUS: That's weevil talk.

LABRAX: I'll give eight hundred.

GRIPUS: Your mouth's hot, and you're trying to cool it off.

LABRAX: Make it a thousand, then.

GRIPUS: You're dreaming.

LABRAX: I'll not add another penny.

GRIPUS: Good-bye, then.

LABRAX: Hold on; if I go away from here, I'll be gone. Do you want eleven hundred?

GRIPUS: You're asleep.

LABRAX: Tell me how much you do want.

GRIPUS: A talent of silver; and you needn't add to that unless you wish to—but not a cent less. Say yes or no.

LABRAX: Well, as I see it's necessary, I'll give the talent.

GRIPUS (*going to the altar*): Come here; I want Venus to hear your oath.

LABRAX: Anything you wish; give me your orders.

GRIPUS: Touch the altar.

LABRAX: I'm touching it.

GRIPUS: Swear before Venus, here.

LABRAX: Swear what?

GRIPUS: What I tell you.

LABRAX: Dictate any oaths you want; but, as I am never at a loss for them, I don't need help.

GRIPUS: Now touch the altar.

LABRAX: I'm touching it.

GRIPUS: Swear that you will give me the money, as soon as you get your hamper.

LABRAX: Very well.

GRIPUS: Repeat after me: Venus of Cyrene, I call thee to witness—¹⁰

LABRAX: Venus of Cyrene, I call thee to witness—

GRIPUS: —if I find the hamper full of gold and silver, which I lost in the sea—

LABRAX: —if I find the hamper full of gold and silver, which I lost in the sea—

GRIPUS: —then I to this Gripus—(When you say that, touch me.)—

LABRAX: —then I to this Gripus—(I say this that thou mayest hear, O Venus.)—

GRIPUS: —will at once give to him an Attic talent.

LABRAX: —will at once give to him an Attic talent.

GRIPUS: Pray also that if you cheat me, Venus shall curse you and your profession, root and branch. (*Aside*) And I pray that she does this, exactly as you swear it.

LABRAX: If, O Venus, I fail in my oath in any respect, I pray that all procurers may suffer.

GRIPUS (*aside*): They will, even if you keep your oath. (*To* LABRAX) Wait here; I'll bring the old man out. Then you ask at once for the hamper. (*He goes into the cottage.*)

LABRAX: Even if he does return, he'll never get a penny out of me. It's for me to decide what I shall swear to. But soft, here he comes with the old man.

Act Five.   Scene III

(*Enter* GRIPUS *with* DAEMONES, GRIPUS *carrying the hamper.*)

GRIPUS: This way.

DAEMONES: Where's the procurer?

GRIPUS (*to* LABRAX): Here's your man; he has the hamper.

DAEMONES (*to* LABRAX): I acknowledge that I have; if it is yours, you may have it. You will find the contents untouched. Take it, if it is yours.

LABRAX: Immortal gods, it's mine. (*Kissing and embracing it*) Welcome back, my hamper.

DAEMONES: It's yours then?

LABRAX: Even if it were Jove's, it's mine just the same.

DAEMONES: Everything is there safe, with the exception of the little casket containing tokens by which I have discovered my daughter.

LABRAX: Your daughter?

DAEMONES: The girl whom you knew as Palaestra has proved to be my daughter.

LABRAX: That's good, by Jove; I'm glad things have turned out so well for you.

DAEMONES: I can't readily believe that.

LABRAX: Well, by Jove, to make you believe it, don't give me a penny for her; she's yours, free.

DAEMONES: That's certainly very generous.

LABRAX: On the contrary, you are the generous one.

GRIPUS: I say, you've got your hamper now.

LABRAX: I have.

GRIPUS: Then hurry up.

LABRAX: Hurry up about what?

GRIPUS: To hand over the money.

LABRAX: I'll give you nothing, nor do I owe you anything.

GRIPUS: What does this mean? You don't owe me anything?

LABRAX: No, by Jove.

GRIPUS: Didn't you just swear to me?

LABRAX: Yes, and I'll swear again, if I please. Oaths were invented to save property, not to lose it.

GRIPUS: Come, hand that Attic talent over, oath-breaker.

DAEMONES: What's this talent you're demanding, Gripus?

GRIPUS: The one he swore he would give me.

LABRAX: I make an oath when I please; are you my father confessor?

DAEMONES (*to* GRIPUS): For what did he promise you the money?

GRIPUS: He swore to give me a full silver talent, if I returned his hamper.

LABRAX: Come, name me some patron with whom I may go to court, to prove that you made the bargain under false pretences, and that I am not yet twenty-five years old.

GRIPUS (*pointing to* DAEMONES): Take him.

LABRAX: I'd rather have some one else.

DAEMONES: Did you promise him this money?

LABRAX: I confess I did.

DAEMONES: What you promised my slave, you owe me. Don't think you can be using a procurer's honour with me; you can't do it.

GRIPUS (*to* LABRAX): Did you think you had found a man you could cheat? You'll have to pay this in full; then I'll give it to him for my freedom.

DAEMONES: Since this was saved for you by my kindness and assistance—

GRIPUS: By mine; don't say by yours.

DAEMONES (*to* GRIPUS): If you're wise, you'll keep quiet— (*To* LABRAX) You will do well to repay my kindness by kindness on your part.

LABRAX: You recognise my rights then by your request?

DAEMONES: It would be strange if I should risk trying to take your own rights from you.

GRIPUS (*aside, as* LABRAX *hesitates*): It's all safe; the procurer is wavering; freedom is at hand.

DAEMONES: He found the hamper, and he is my property. I've saved this for you, with all the money in it.

LABRAX (*after further hesitation*): I'm obliged to you, and as to the talent I swore to give him, you may have it.

GRIPUS: Here, give that to me, please.

DAEMONES: Will you keep quiet?

GRIPUS (*to* DAEMONES): While pretending to look after my interests, you're looking after your own. You'll not beat me out of this, by Jove, if I did lose the other.

DAEMONES: You'll get a thrashing, if you say another word.

GRIPUS: Beat me to death, but you'll never shut me up except with a talent.

LABRAX (*to* GRIPUS): Keep quiet; he's doing this in your interest.

DAEMONES: Step over this way, Labrax.

LABRAX: Very well.

GRIPUS: No, do it openly; I don't like this secret diplomacy.

DAEMONES: Shall I make you a first-rate offer?

LABRAX: By all means.

DAEMONES: I'll divide that talent with you.

LABRAX: That's very kind.

DAEMONES: Take one half of the talent yourself for the freedom of that other girl, and give the other half to me.

LABRAX: By all means.

DAEMONES: With this half, I'll free Gripus, through whom you found your hamper, and I my daughter.

LABRAX: That's all right, and I'm very much obliged. (*They now turn towards* GRIPUS.)

GRIPUS: How soon will the money be paid me?

DAEMONES: It's all paid, Gripus; I have it.

GRIPUS: Yes, by Jove, but I prefer to have it myself.

DAEMONES: There's nothing here for you; don't expect it. I want you to acquit him of his oath.

GRIPUS: Curse the luck; I'm damned if I don't hang myself. You'll never cheat me again after today.

DAEMONES: Labrax, dine with me.

LABRAX: Very well; I should be pleased.

DAEMONES: Follow me in. (*To the audience*) I should invite you in the audience also, except that we're going to have nothing worth eating, and I think you all have dinner invitations anyway. But if you are willing to applaud the play heartily, come and make a night of it with me— sixteen years from now. (*To* LABRAX *and* GRIPUS) You two will dine here.

LABRAX *and* GRIPUS: Very well.

DAEMONES: Now, your applause.

1. This is an allusion to a lost play of Euripides.

2. Labrax refers here to a myth concerning Hercules, but the meaning of the allusion is not clear.

3. Atreus murdered the sons of Thyestes and served their bodies to their father at a banquet. This gruesome story of revenge is the theme of Seneca's tragedy, *Thyestes*.

4. Literally, "as a Manducus." Manducus is believed by many to have been a fixed character in the Atellan farces; it seems doubtful if he was a separate character, and he is probably to be identified with the character Dossennus.

5. Lindsay assigns this speech to Daemones.

6. Lindsay assigns this speech to Labrax.

7. Gripus probably refers to the celebrated musician of the time of Alexander the Great, who travelled from place to place displaying his skill.

8. Hellebore was an ancient remedy for mental diseases.

9. Literally, "I'm one letter more than a doctor" (*medicus*); i.e. a beggar (*mendicus*).

10. The first part of the oath (lines 1338-1341) is assigned to Gripus by Leo and Lindsay, to Labrax by other editors. The passage has been somewhat expanded by the translator.